Law, Governance and Technology Series

Volume 80

The *Law, Governance and Technology Series* is intended to attract manuscripts arising from an interdisciplinary approach in law, artificial intelligence and information technologies. The idea is to bridge the gap between research in IT law and IT-applications for lawyers developing a unifying techno-legal perspective. The series will welcome proposals that have a fairly specific focus on problems or projects that will lead to innovative research charting the course for new interdisciplinary developments in law, legal theory, and law and society research as well as in computer technologies, artificial intelligence and cognitive sciences. In broad strokes, manuscripts for this series may be mainly located in the fields of the Internet law (data protection, intellectual property, Internet rights, etc.), Computational models of the legal contents and legal reasoning, Legal Information Retrieval, Electronic Data Discovery, Collaborative Tools (e.g. Online Dispute Resolution platforms), Metadata and XML Technologies (for Semantic Web Services), Technologies in Courtrooms and Judicial Offices (E-Court), Technologies for Governments and Administrations (E-Government), Legal Multimedia, and Legal Electronic Institutions (Multi-Agent Systems and Artificial Societies).

Carmen Pastor Sempere ·
David Amable Morán Bovio
Editors

UNIDROIT Principles on Digital Assets and Private Law

Context, Content, Perspectives

Springer

Editors
Carmen Pastor Sempere
Faculty of Law
University of Alicante
San Vicente del Raspeig, Alicante, Spain

David Amable Morán Bovio
Jerez de la Frontera, Spain

University of Cádiz
Cádiz, Spain

ISSN 2352-1902 ISSN 2352-1910 (electronic)
Law, Governance and Technology Series
ISBN 978-3-032-11000-8 ISBN 978-3-032-11001-5 (eBook)
https://doi.org/10.1007/978-3-032-11001-5

This work was financed within the framework of the Prometeo 2023 project of the Regional Ministry of Innovation, Universities, Science and Digital Society (CIPROM/2022/26) "Present and future of the regulation of cryptoassets in the EU [LegalCripto]", whose principal investigator is Carmen Pastor Sempere. The basic ideas contained herein were presented in the author's paper with the same title, given on November 13, 2024 at the IV International Congress on "UNIDROIT Principles on Digital Assets and Private Law: Context, Content, Perspectives", organized also by BAES Research Group of the University of Alicante on November 13 and 14, 2024.

This Springer imprint is published by the registered company Springer Nature Switzerland AG
The registered company address is: Gewerbestrasse 11, 6330 Cham, Switzerland

Preface

This collective volume has been written within the framework of the ongoing evolution of contemporary private law in response to the emergence of a new category of assets: digital assets. In the absence of a universally accepted definition, these assets—understood as electronic records capable of being subject to exclusive control and capable of being uniquely identified—have been the subject of thorough analysis by leading international legal institutions, including the International Institute for the Unification of Private Law (UNIDROIT) and the UK Law Commission, in an effort to provide legal systems with the requisite tools to address the transactions of an increasingly digitised present and future with legal certainty.

In this context, the UNIDROIT Governing Council formally adopted the *UNIDROIT Principles on Digital Assets and Private Law* (hereinafter, the "Principles") in May 2023, thereby concluding a comprehensive and collaborative drafting process which formally commenced in November 2020. This undertaking involved eight formal sessions of the Working Group and the consideration of over 300 suggestions from legal scholars and practitioners worldwide. As a contribution to this effort, and with the objective of equipping the Spanish-speaking legal community with the interpretative tools necessary to engage with this novel legal framework, the LEGALCRIPTO research group—recognised as a Group of Excellence by the Generalitat Valenciana (Valencian Regional Government),"*Presente y futuro de la regulación de los Criptoactivos en la UE [Legalcripto].Proyecto Prometeo CIPROM/2022/26*" (Present and Future of Cryptoasset Regulation in the EU [Legalcripto]. Prometeo Project CIPROM/2022/26)—in conjunction with investigators at the University of Cádiz, undertook the official Spanish translation of the Principles, accompanied by a series of doctrinal reflections intended to support their understanding, dissemination, and practical application.

This volume represents the culmination of a unique academic collaboration on digital asset law, brought to fruition through multiple scientific meetings, international conferences—including the IV International Conference "UNIDROIT Principles on Digital Assets and Private Law: context, content, perspectives", held in November 2024—and a sustained research effort conducted in close cooperation with the principal drafters of the Principles, namely Professor Hideki Kanda (Chair of the Working

Group), Professors Neil Cohen, Steven Weise, and Edwin Smith, as well as the Secretary-General of UNIDROIT, Professor Ignacio Tirado.

The volume is structured as follows:

- **Part I** contains expert contributions that contextualise the development and scope of the Principles, highlighting their key milestones and influence on national legal reforms, particularly the recent amendments to the United States *Uniform Commercial Code* (UCC). This section further includes two analytical essays on the concept of "control" as a functional equivalent to possession, and a pioneering case study on verified carbon credits as digital assets.
- **Parts II–IX** present the *UNIDROIT Principles on Digital Assets and Private Law*, accompanied by interpretative guidelines aimed at clarifying their scope and application, in adherence to the principle of technological neutrality that underpins the entire regulatory framework.

The methodology employed in this work is grounded in a systematic analysis of UNIDROIT's preparatory materials, explanatory reports, and official Commentaries, complemented by ongoing engagement with the original drafters of the Principles. This approach ensures interpretative coherence and the faithful transmission of the legal and conceptual foundations of the Principles.

Ultimately, this volume aspires to serve as a comprehensive tool for jurists, legislators, judges, notaries, registrars, legal scholars, and practitioners operating within the sphere of digital assets. It seeks to clarify not only *why* the Principles were drafted and *how* they are structured but also *what* their broader implications there are for the future of private law in an age increasingly defined by dematerialised assets and digital markets. In doing so, the work aligns with the principles of open science and legal innovation that characterise the scientific and normative challenges of the 21st century.

Alicante, Spain
Jerez de la Frontera
Cádiz, Spain

Carmen Pastor Sempere
Full Professor of Commercial Law

David Amable Morán Bovio
Full Professor of Commercial Law

Contents

Contributors

Ignacio Alamillo-Domingo University of Murcia, Murcia, Spain

Manuel Alba Fernández Carlos III University of Madrid, Madrid, Spain

Ángel María Ballesteros Barros University Pablo de Olavide, Sevilla, Spain

Pablo Sanz Bayón UNED National University of Distance Education, Madrid, Spain

David Amable Morán Bovio University of Cádiz, Cádiz, Spain

José Caro Catalán University of Cádiz, Cádiz, Spain

Rafael del Castillo Ionov CEU San Pablo University, Madrid, Spain

Luis Arnáez Fernández Tamarite de Litera, Aragon, Spain

Ester Becerril Fernández University of Valladolid, Valladolid, Spain

Jorge Feliu Rey Universidad Carlos III de Madrid, Madrid, Spain

Rafael Illescas Carlos III University of Madrid, Madrid, Spain

Hideki Kanda University of Tokyo, Tokyo, Japan

Agustín Madrid-Parra Pablo de Olavide University, Sevilla, Spain

Maria del Mar Bustillo Saiz University of Valladolid, Valladolid, Spain

Alfonso Martínez-Echevarría y García de Dueñas Universidad San Pablo-CEU, CEU Universities, Madrid, Spain

María Teresa Touriñán Morandeira Vilalba, Galicia, Spain

Apol·lònia Martínez Nadal University of the Balearic Islands, Palma, Spain

Carmen Pastor Sempere University of Alicante, Alicante, Spain

Miguel Ángel Pendón Meléndez Departamento de Derecho Mercantil, Facultad de Derecho, University of Cádiz, Jerez de la Frontera (Cádiz), Spain

Eduardo Miranda Ribera CEGEA, Universitat Politècnica de València, Valencia, Spain

Teresa Rodríguez de las Heras Ballell Universidad Carlos III de Madrid, Madrid, Spain

Marina Echebarría Sáenz Valladolid University, Valladolid, Spain

Edwin E. Smith Morgan, Lewis & Bockius, New York, NY, USA

María Cristina Timón-López University of Murcia, Murcia, Spain

Julián Valero-Torrijos University of Murcia, Murcia, Spain

María José Vañó Vañó Department of Commercial Law, Manuel Broseta Pont, University of Valencia, Valencia, Spain

Isabel Villar Fuentes University of Cádiz, Cádiz, Spain

Steven O. Weise Proskauer Rose LLP, Los Angeles, CA, USA

Nicolás Augoustatos Zarco Pablo de Olavide University, Seville, Spain

Introductory Chapters

Brief Overview of UNIDROIT Principles on Digital Assets and Private Law

Hideki Kanda

1 Introduction

The International Institute for the Unification of Private Law (known as UNIDROIT) is an independent intergovernmental organisation with its seat in Rome. Its purpose is to study needs and methods for modernising, harmonising, and coordinating private law, particularly commercial law, as between States and groups of States.[1]

UNIDROIT launched its project on digital assets and private law in 2020. Its Working Group ("WG") met nine times, and the UNIDROIT Principles and Commentary on Digital Assets and Private Law were adopted by the UNIDROIT Governing Council on May 10, 2023.[2]

In this chapter, I offer a brief overview of the Principles on Digital Assets and Private Law (the "UNIDROIT Principles" or the "Principles"). The views in this chapter are those of the author only and do not reflect those of UNIDROIT or its WG.

UNIDROIT usually seeks to harmonise private laws around the world in areas where different laws exist in various jurisdictions. In contrast, at the time when this

[1] See https://www.unidroit.org/about-unidroit/overview/.

[2] See https://www.unidroit.org/work-in-progress/digital-assets-and-private-law/. The UNIDROIT Principles are available at https://www.unidroit.org/instruments/digital-assets-and-private-law/.

This work was financed within the framework of the Prometeo 2023 project of the Regional Ministry of Innovation, Universities, Science and Digital Society (CIPROM/2022/26) "Present and future of the regulation of cryptoassets in the EU [LegalCripto]", whose principal investigator is Carmen Pastor Sempere. The basic ideas contained herein were presented in the author's paper with the same title, given on November 13, 2024 at the IV International Congress on "UNIDROIT Principles on Digital Assets and Private Law: Context, Content, Perspectives", organized also by BAES Research Group of the University of Alicante on November 13 and 14, 2024.

H. Kanda (✉)
University of Tokyo, Tokyo, Japan
e-mail: kanda@j.u-tokyo.ac.jp

C. Pastor Sempere and D. A. Morán Bovio (eds.), UNIDROIT *Principles on Digital Assets and Private Law*, Law, Governance and Technology Series 80,
https://doi.org/10.1007/978-3-032-11001-5_1

project was launched, no established private law rules on digital assets existed in any jurisdiction, as they were under development at that time. Thus, the UNIDROIT project sought a new set of principles almost from scratch.[3]

Indeed, in most jurisdictions, private law rules on digital assets are often vague and on many occasions have led to legal uncertainty, preventing efficient commercial and financing transactions. The UNIDROIT Principles focus on core issues of private law and propose a set of principles that States are encouraged to implement by legislation, case law, or a combination of both. By focusing on core issues, the Principles permit States flexibility in developing private law rules in this area.

Also, it must be noted that public regulation is quite important in this area. However, I believe that certainty of private law rules is vital for the stability of financial systems and markets. Thus, an optimal combination of private law rules and public regulations should be explored.

2 Basic Concepts and General Principles

Figure 1 shows the entire landscape of the UNIDROIT Principles.

Principle 1 states that the Principles deal with private law issues regarding digital assets. The Principles do not deal with public regulations.

Principle 2 is an important provision in two respects. First, Principle 2 defines the scope of the subject matter of the Principles; that is, Principle 2 defines "digital asset" under the Principles. This concept will be discussed further below.

Second, Principle 2 implies that the UNIDROIT Principles are not intended to cover all private law issues in a comprehensive manner; rather, the Principles are intended to cover core issues only. The reason for this is that the WG believes these core issues are those most often disputed, litigated, and brought to court. UNIDROIT intends to enhance legal certainty while giving States flexibility in preparing their own rules in this area.

Principle 2(3) uses the notion of "principles law" to mean the part of a State's law which implements the Principles, while the remaining part is called "other law" by Principle 2(4).

As mentioned above, the Principles address core issues only. States are encouraged to implement the Principles and may do so in any form: by legislation, case law, or a combination of both.

Going back to the definition of "digital asset," Principle 2(1) and Principle 2(2) should be read together. In short, "digital asset" is defined as "an electronic record which is capable of being subject to control" (see Fig. 2). The two key words here are "electronic record" and "control."

---

[3] In the USA, new Article 12 was added and related revisions were made to the Uniform Commercial Code in 2022. In the UK, Property (Digital Assets etc.) Bill was introduced into Parliament in September 2024. These reforms are consistent with the UNIDROIT Principles.

INTRODUCTION

SECTION I: SCOPE AND DEFINITIONS

Principle 1: Scope

Principle 2: Definitions

Principle 3: General principles

Principle 4: Linked assets

SECTION II: PRIVATE INTERNATIONAL LAW

Principle 5: Applicable law

SECTION III: CONTROL AND TRANSFER

Principle 6: Control

Principle 7: Identification of a person in control of a digital asset

Principle 8: Innocent acquisition

Principle 9: Rights of a transferee

SECTION IV: CUSTODY

Principle 10: Custody

Principle 11: Duties owed by a custodian to its client

Principle 12: Innocent client

Principle 13: Insolvency of a custodian and creditor claims

SECTION V: SECURED TRANSACTIONS

Principle 14: Secured transactions: general

Principle 15: Control as a method of achieving third-party effectiveness

Principle 16: Priority of security rights

Principle 17: Enforcement of security rights

SECTION VI: PROCEDURAL LAW INCLUDING ENFORCEMENT

Principle 18: Procedural law including enforcement

SECTION VII: INSOLVENCY

Principle 19: Effect of insolvency on proprietary rights in digital assets

Fig. 1 UNIDROIT Principles on Digital Assets and Private Law (2023)

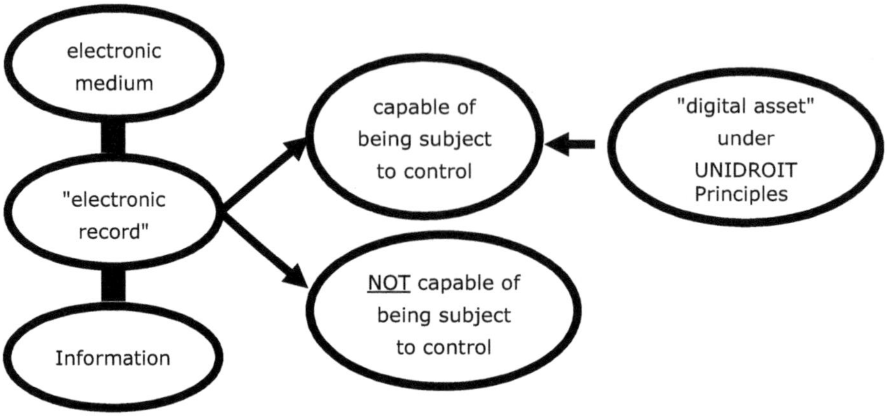

Fig. 2 Definition of Digital Asset

In reverse order, "control" is defined in Principle 6. It can be said to roughly be a functional equivalent to possession of tangible property. In most cases, it can be called "exclusive control." Typically, if someone has a private key to access a blockchain, that person has "control" as defined in the Principles.

I must emphasise that the notion of "control" in the Principles is in the factual sense, not the legal sense. This is because UNIDROIT takes a functional approach, which it believes is the best way to address this area and offer useful principles.

With respect to Principle 2(1), the notion of "electronic record" is used. Two points are important here. First, the scope of "electronic record" is not limited to cryptoassets or systems using blockchain, as UNIDROIT does not believe that limiting its focus to such technology is the most appropriate approach. In that sense, this is an attempt to maintain technological neutrality. Indeed, new technology may emerge in future years, and therefore UNIDROIT Principles must recognise that fact and prepare accordingly.

Second, although technological neutrality should be emphasised, it may be difficult for readers of the UNIDROIT Principles to imagine the specific situations they are dealing with. In this sense, examples or use cases are important. UNIDROIT tries to provide as many examples as possible in the Commentary. As such, the Commentary is highly relevant.

Figure 3 is a one-page summary of the Principles.

Principle 3 provides for a fundamental private law rule. Principle 3(1) states that digital assets can be the subject of proprietary rights. Importantly, this means that proprietary rights in digital assets survive insolvency (see Principles 19 and 13).

"Proprietary rights" in the Principles include "security rights," in addition to what many jurisdictions refer to as "ownership rights" (see Principle 14(1) for security rights).

The UNIDROIT Principles use the notion of "proprietary right," not "property right." This is because the notion of "property right" varies from jurisdiction to

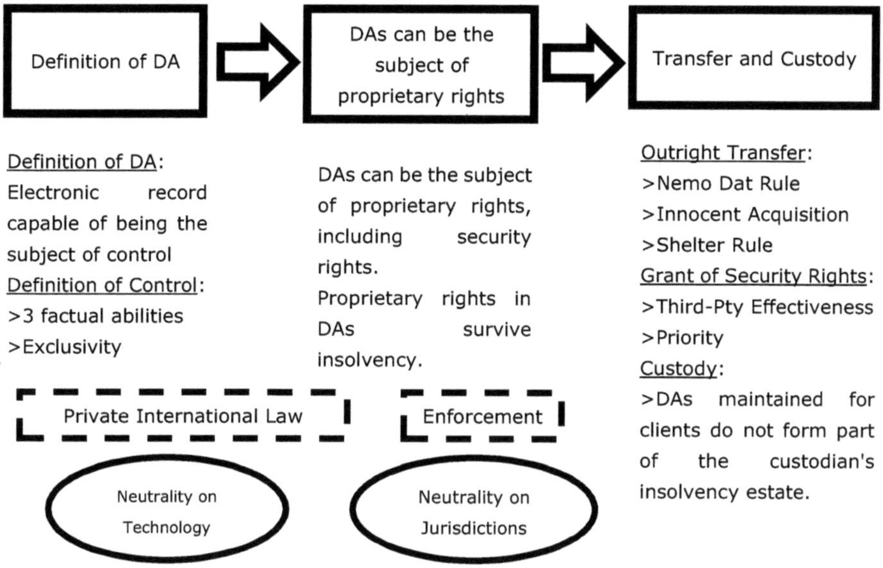

Fig. 3 UNIDROIT Principles

jurisdiction, so using the notion of "proprietary right" is preferable. "Proprietary right" is broader than "property right." For example, suppose that a client has a claim against a service provider (often called an exchange) to deliver Bitcoin to the client. If Bitcoin is subject to control under Principle 6, then the UNIDROIT Principles are expected to apply, no matter what legal doctrine applies. In this sense, UNIDROIT tries to maintain neutrality on legal doctrines and neutrality on jurisdictions.

3 How the Principles Work

The core part of the UNIDROIT Principles is based on the notion of control, and they cover three prototypical situations: outright transfers, custody, and secured transactions.

Outright Transfers

Figure 4 shows an outright transfer of a digital asset. If Person A has control of a digital asset and transfers that digital asset to Person B by means of moving control, Person A loses control, Person B obtains control, and no one else has control of such digital asset. Legally, this means that if Person A has a proprietary right, in usual cases, Person A then transfers its proprietary right to Person B. This applies "if Person A has a proprietary right" and "in usual cases." This means that a hacker, for example, does not have a proprietary right even if it obtains control. Therefore, a change of control of a digital asset from a hacker to a transferee does not transfer

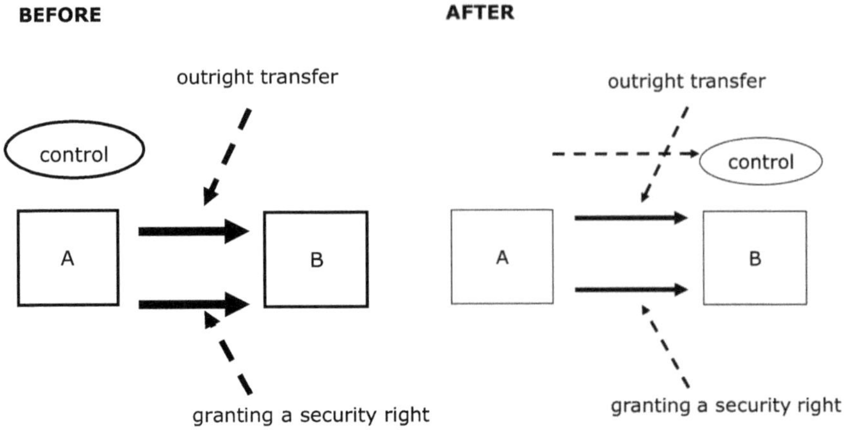

Fig. 4 Transfer

the proprietary right in the digital asset, except that the transferee may benefit from the provisions of Principle 8, Innocent Acquisition. Indeed, except for Principles 8 and 9, the UNIDROIT Principles do not offer rules in relation to outright transfers, and many issues are delegated to national law or "other law." In contrast, the UNIDROIT Principles do offer some important rules for security rights (see Principles 14 to 17).

Secured Transactions

In Fig. 4, Person A, as a debtor, can grant a security right in its digital asset to Person B, the creditor. How? Person A moves control of the digital asset to Person B. Person A loses control, and Person B obtains control. As a general matter, this is enough for Person B's security right to be effective against third parties (see Principle 15).

Custody

Principles 10 to 13 set out private law principles relevant to custody of digital assets. Other law, including regulatory law, may also apply to the provision of custody services.

Explaining the details of the UNIDROIT Principles regarding custody situations is beyond the scope of this chapter (for details, see Principles 10 to 13 and their Commentaries). Suffice it to say that "custody" is a functional term under the Principles.

As Fig. 5 shows, custody is where a person maintains a digital asset on behalf of and for the benefit of another, a client (which may be another custodian), in a manner that gives the client special protection against unauthorised dispositions of the asset, and also against the insolvency of the custodian who maintains the digital asset. It only applies where the person providing the custody services does so in the ordinary course of its business.

Whether the services provided by a provider are custody services will depend on whether the agreement between the service provider and its client is a custody

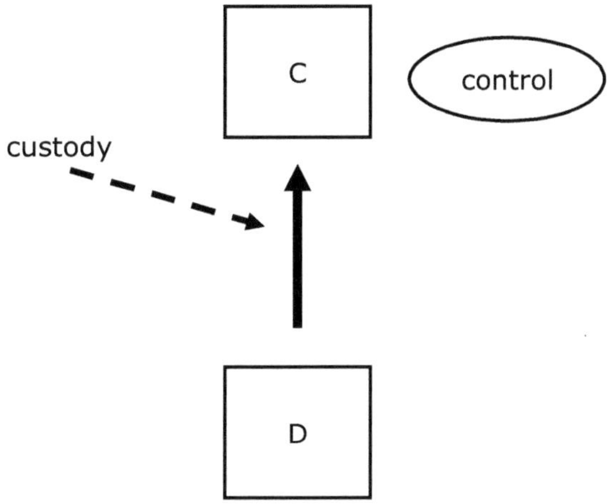

Fig. 5 Custody

agreement. Principle 10(3) defines "custody agreement." Principle 10(1) sets forth the important parties in relation to custody. The person who has control of the asset is either a "custodian" (in which case it has control of the assets for a "client" who is not a custodian) or a "sub-custodian" (in which case it has control of the asset for a client who is a custodian and who has entered into a custody agreement with a client in relation to that asset). A sub-custodian is also a custodian as per the definition in Principle 10(1).

Most importantly, Principles 13(2) to 13(8) apply if a custodian enters into an insolvency-related proceeding. "Insolvency-related proceeding" is defined in Principle 2(6).

On a different front, Fig. 6 shows how the innocent acquisition rule applies in a custody situation.

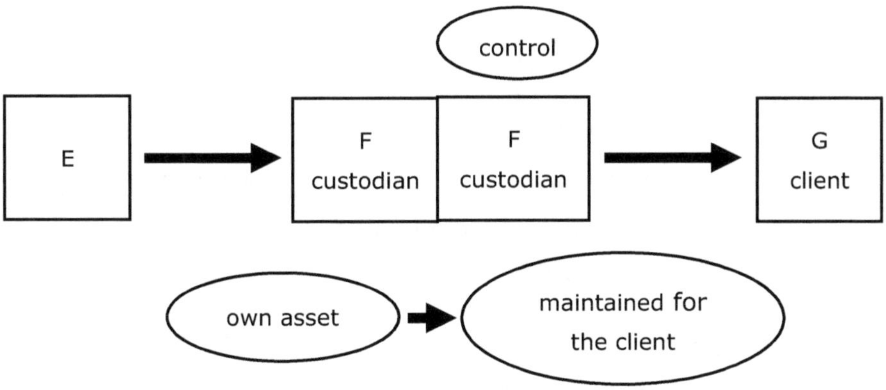

Fig. 6 Innocent Client

If Person C holds a digital asset on behalf of Person D, then C is a custodian and D is its client. In this situation, C has control of the digital asset, and D does not have control. But if C becomes insolvent, the digital asset does not, and should not, belong to C's insolvency estate (see Principle 13 and its Commentary). Note that Principle 13(1) covers situations outside the custodian's insolvency.

In the example, F buys a digital asset from E and holds it for its client. If F is not an innocent acquirer, G would be an innocent acquirer if G satisfies the innocent acquirer requirements. If F is an innocent acquirer, G would be protected by the shelter rule under Principle 9(2) even where G does not satisfy the innocent acquirer requirements.

4 Linked Assets

In the UNIDROIT Principles, Principle 4 deals with "linked assets" (see Fig. 7). In general, there are two types of digital assets: native digital assets and non-native digital assets. For example, Bitcoin and Ether are native digital assets. There are also non-native digital assets. For the latter, their value is linked to the value of one or more other assets. Examples are stablecoins, non-fungible tokens, security tokens, and so forth. The basic legal rule, I think, should be that a transfer of a non-native digital asset does not automatically lead to the transfer of the target asset (or the linked asset), unless certain exceptions apply—exceptions are where special legislation or a contract by the parties under existing law legally creates such link. Similarly, custody of a non-native digital asset does not automatically lead to custody of the target asset, unless certain exceptions apply.

The UNIDROIT Principles do not offer principles concerning the legal nature of links themselves (if they are legal issues). They do not offer principles concerning

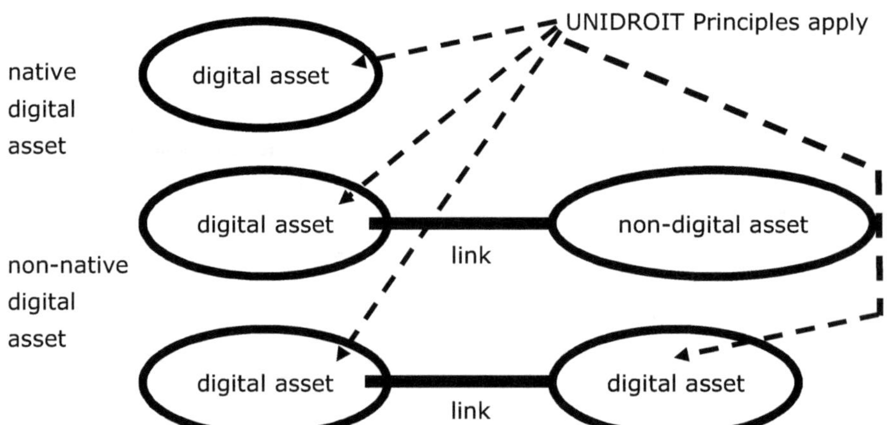

Fig. 7 Linked Asset

the legal effect on linked assets (when digital assets are transferred, for example) either. Those issues are delegated to the law of each State, or in the jargon in the Principes, "other law." The Commentary on Principle 4 explains the details by setting out various examples.

States should develop laws and public regulations concerning links and target assets. To do so, an examination of current laws and regulations in each relevant jurisdiction would be very important.

Electronic Documents

The following is a discussion on how written documents that have been "dematerialised" should be viewed. Examples are cheques, promissory notes, investment securities such as shares and bonds, transport documents such as bills of lading, and warehouse documents. In many jurisdictions, over the past years, these documents became paperless, and it was often (though not always) done through special legislation.

An interesting question might be what the relationship should be between electronic documents and the UNIDROIT Principles.

The UNIDROIT Principles do not exclude electronic documents from the definition of "digital asset," but in most situations, States provide detailed rules on electronic documents, so in those situations, those special rules apply (see Commentary 3.7).

Generally, there are two possible types of legal regimes for electronic documents: the two-step approach and one-step approach. Take shares of companies, for example. Shares used to be in the form of paper (or certificates). Today, in many jurisdictions, usually by means of legislation, shares can be (or must be) paperless (often referred to as dematerialisation). In this context, electronic records represent shareholder rights. Usually though, those electronic records are not "controllable" in the sense of the UNIDROIT Principles because they do not satisfy the definition of "control" under Principle 6. For those records, the second part of the two-step approach might be applied; that is, to convert those non-controllable electronic records into controllable electronic records, typically by deploying blockchain technology. We then have two types of electronic records: controllable electronic records and non-controllable electronic records. This is often called "tokenisation" of shares. In this situation, controllable electronic records are digital assets under the UNIDROIT Principles, but the link between the controllable electronic records and non-controllable electronic records must be addressed by "other law" or national law, in order for the entire regime to work legally.

On the other hand, when dealing with trade documents, such as bills of lading and warehouse receipts, generally speaking, as a historical development, dematerialisation has only started taking place more recently, so one-step dematerialisation might take place more commonly.[4] This means that controllable electronic records are usually recognised by national legislation, and those electronic records represent

[4] See UNCITRAL Model Law on Electronic Transferable Records (2017) available at https://uncitral.un.org/en/texts/ecommerce/modellaw/electronic_transferable_records; UNCITRAL-UNIDROIT Model Law on Warehouse Receipts (2024) available at https://www.unidroit.org/instruments/warehouse-receipts/.

rights in goods in a warehouse, for example. In this situation, while the electronic records are within the definition of "electronic record" in the UNIDROIT Principles, national law usually provides comprehensive rules, and if that is the case, those rules shall apply.

5 Security Rights

The UNIDROIT Principles provide that a security right created by control is effective against third parties. Specifically, Principle 15 provides that, in addition to any other methods of third-party effectiveness that apply to a security right in a digital asset under other law, a State should recognise that a security right in a digital asset may be made effective against third parties by control. This would apply not only in a situation where a secured creditor has control of a digital asset but also where a custodian maintains a digital asset for a secured creditor, including through a sub-custodian.

As to priority, a security right by control prevails over a security right created by registration or another method. Principle 16 specifically addresses the situation where one secured creditor has made its security right in a digital asset effective against third parties by registration or another method recognised by applicable law, but has not obtained control of the digital asset, and another secured creditor has made its security right in the same digital asset effective by control (pursuant to Principle 15). In this situation, Principle 16 provides that the latter would have priority even if it took the steps to obtain control after the former made its registration or otherwise made its security right effective against third parties. For the justifications of this rule, see the Commentary to Principle 16.

6 Private International Law

Principle 5 provides for a private international law rule. It adopts a waterfall structure of connecting factors and offers a somewhat novel approach. In other words, UNIDROIT tries to incentivise relevant parties to specify the law applicable to a digital asset itself or to its system or platform (see Principles 5(1)(a) and 5(1)(b)). That is to say, Principles 5(1)(a) and 5(1)(b) state that provisions of the Principles, in addition to the domestic law of a State, can be specified by the relevant parties as being applicable to a digital asset or its system. Today, this is not the case in existing practice, which is why UNIDROIT tries to give incentives to the relevant parties. The intention is to ensure legal certainly. One important point is that the UNIDROIT Principles take a functional approach. Here, this implies the idea that it should be easy for parties who enter into transactions involving digital assets to know the applicable law. It should be noted that Principles 5(2)(a) to 5(2)(e) are all important in the operation of Principles 5(1)(a) and 5(1)(b).

Under Principle 5, if the applicable law is not specified by the digital asset itself or by its system, then Principle 5(1)(c) applies if there is an issuer of the digital asset. "Issuer" is defined in Principle 5(2)(f).

If none of Principles 5(1)(a) to 5(1)(c) applies, then Principle 5(1)(d) states that, in short, the applicable law is the Principles. More accurately, the forum State can specify provisions of the law of that State and provisions of the Principles as the applicable law. Principle 5(1)(d) offers two options, which I believe are self-explanatory.

One important point is that the applicable law determined by Principle 5(1) would govern all proprietary issues in relation to digital assets, not limited to the proprietary issues covered by the UNIDROIT Principles, as clearly stated by the chapeau of Principle 5(1).

Principle 5(2)(d) is also important. It states that the applicable law determined by Principle 5(1) applies to all digital assets of the same description. Commentary 11.6 states that "same description" means digital assets being treated by market participants as fungible.

Finally, two carveouts must be mentioned. One is found in Principles 5(3) and 5(4). With respect to determining the law applicable to the custody issues that are addressed in Principles 10 to 13, neither Principle 5(1) nor Principle 5(2) applies; instead, the rule of private international law described in Principle 5(3) applies.

The other carveout is found in Principle 5(5). The private international law rule of Principle 5(1) or 5(2) does not apply to the issues of third-party effectiveness and priority in relation to security rights where security rights operate under systems other than control; typically registration systems. For those issues, the applicable law is determined by other law. "Other law" here means the private international law rule in the forum State. Many existing international instruments provide that the location of a transferor or grantor is the connecting factor.

7 Insolvency and Enforcement in General

Insolvency in General

The UNIDROIT Principles provide for rules on insolvency that are typical in most international instruments. As such, Principle 19 deals with the effect of insolvency on a proprietary right in a digital asset. Principle 19 confirms that a proprietary right in a digital asset which is effective against third parties is also effective against relevant parties in an insolvency-related proceeding. Specifically, Principle 19(1) provides for pre-insolvency effectiveness to continue in an insolvency-related proceeding. Note that the insolvency of custodians is dealt with by Principle 13.

Enforcement in General

Two typical enforcement situations involving digital assets are (i) where a general (or non-secured) creditor obtains a court judgment against the debtor and attempts to seize the debtor's assets, which happen to include digital assets, and (ii) where a creditor who took the debtor's digital assets as collateral attempts to realise its security right by selling the digital assets so as to satisfy its claim.

The UNIDROIT Principles do not provide specific rules on this issue and instead delegate it to each jurisdiction's national law or "other law" (see Principle 18). Note that an exception to this general rule is provided for enforcement of security rights, which is dealt with by Principle 17.

However, another UNIDROIT project, called the "Project on Best Practices for Effective Enforcement," is expected to propose basic rules on this issue.[5] At the time of writing this chapter, these rules have not yet been finalised.

Currently, among others, two basic rules are under consideration. The first rule to be expected is the duty of debtors (or third parties where they have control) to cooperate in seizures and transfers.

Cooperation by a debtor (or third party) may be required in order to effectively and efficiently seize digital assets. Seizure of digital assets for purposes of enforcement may require cooperation by the debtor (or third party) in disclosing or making relevant information available to enforcement agents or authorities for obtaining control over the digital assets. Such information includes private keys, recovery phrases, or access data to the devices or systems where they are stored, and/or to convey control over the digital assets.

The second rule concerns sanctions. The expected rule is that the law is to provide for effective, proportionate, and adequate sanctions in the event that a debtor (or third party) refuses to cooperate, without legitimate reasons, or provides inaccurate, false, or partial information.

8 Conclusion

There are many interesting, and sometimes difficult, legal issues that are likely to arise in relation to digital assets in the coming years in many jurisdictions.

Legal certainty will be achieved by new legislation, court decisions, or a combination of both.

I believe that the UNIDROIT Principles on Digital Assets and Private Law are helpful for all jurisdictions to examine this area and consider the proper interpretations of their existing private laws and the need for new legislation.

[5] See https://www.unidroit.org/work-in-progress/enforcement-best-practices/.

UNIDROIT Principles on Digital Assets and Private Law—A Comparison to the Uniform Commercial Code, with an Emphasis on Control, Transfer, Custody, Innocent Acquirers, and Secured Transactions

Edwin E. Smith and Steven O. Weise

1 Introduction

This chapter will discuss the core provisions of the UNIDROIT Principles on Digital Assets and Private Law ("DAPL") and how they relate to the Uniform Commercial Code enacted in the different units (which we call "States") of the United States. The chapter will review the underlying reasons for the provisions of DAPL and the Uniform Commercial Code for digital assets. The chapter also reviews United States common law rules in this area. The chapter includes a series of tables comparing these laws.

Important goals of DAPL and the Uniform Commercial Code are:

- To have sensible rules that encourage and facilitate commercial transactions,
- To have certainty in transactions, and
- To have uniformity across borders.

This work was financed within the framework of the Prometeo 2023 project of the Regional Ministry of Innovation, Universities, Science and Digital Society (CIPROM/2022/26) "Present and future of the regulation of cryptoassets in the EU [LegalCripto]", whose principal investigator is Carmen Pastor Sempere. The basic ideas contained herein were presented in the author's paper with the same title, given on November 13, 2024 at the IV International Congress on "UNIDROIT Principles on Digital Assets and Private Law: Context, Content, Perspectives", organized also by BAES Research Group of the University of Alicante on November 13 and 14, 2024.

E. E. Smith
Morgan, Lewis & Bockius, New York, NY, USA
e-mail: edwin.smith@morganlewis.com

S. O. Weise (✉)
Proskauer Rose LLP, Los Angeles, CA, USA
e-mail: sweise@proskauer.com

C. Pastor Sempere and D. A. Morán Bovio (eds.), UNIDROIT *Principles on Digital Assets and Private Law*, Law, Governance and Technology Series 80,
https://doi.org/10.1007/978-3-032-11001-5_2

Digital assets, of course, have no location. When one engages in transactions involving digital assets, it should not matter whether that person is located in Spain, Massachusetts, or California. Transactions will be relevant, more efficient and predictable if many States have a uniformity of approach.

As this chapter reviews these matters, we will identify the relevant principle, relate it to some of the concerns that have been raised, discuss how the principle relates to DAPL, United States common law outside of the Uniform Commercial Code, and the Uniform Commercial Code. As will be evident, there is a lot of consistency between DAPL and the Uniform Commercial Code. We think that this consistency will promote efficiency and predictability in the markets that are trading in these kinds of assets.

2 Sources of United States Law

Common Law. Our tables refer to United States common law. There are many references to what we call *Restatements*. The American Law Institute has been in existence only for 100 years, not quite the 104 years that UNIDROIT has existed. The American Law Institute was founded by a former President of the United States, William H. Taft, and other prominent professors, practicing lawyers, and judges. One of the principal projects of the American Law Institute, similar to the European Law Institute, is to prepare what is referred to as a *Restatement*. Our units of the United States have common law courts that develop rules for contracts, torts or property law (and other law). It is difficult sometimes for transactions to work predictably across unit borders if a court in one unit develops a common law rule different from that of another unit.

What the American Law Institute started doing 100 years ago is to compile all of the court decisions in all of the units, look for common rules and common threads, identify the better rules, and then restate them in a synthesised manner. That process promotes better law, because each *Restatement* provides a good analysis of the relevant issue. The analysis helps the judges and the lawyers doing transactions to follow common and more predictable approaches to these transactions. Many States give a high level of deference to these *Restatements*. There is no official status for the *Restatements* except doing a good job. Especially relevant here are the American Law Institute *Restatements* on property, contracts, torts, and a new one on consumer contracts. All these *Restatements* receive great deference from the courts and are cited thousands of times in court decisions. Our tables refer to *Restatements* in the column for the United States common law to try to develop unified and predictable approaches through the common law in the United States, and happily that works pretty well.

Uniform Commercial Code. The Uniform Commercial Code has been adopted in every unit of the United States. When the Uniform Commercial Code applies to a transaction, cross-unit predictability is much easier to achieve. The recent amendments to the Uniform Commercial Code addressing some aspects of digital assets have been adopted in about half of the units in the United States. Additional units are expected to adopt the amendments in 2025 and 2026. Our discussion assumes that the amendments are in effect in all relevant units.

3 Scope

The scope of DAPL, the Uniform Commercial Code, and the common law is critical (Table 1).

DAPL. The entire scope of DAPL flows from the definition of "digital assets" at the very beginning. Any digital asset that does not fit the definition of digital asset as used in DAPL is outside of the scope of DAPL. Thus, the various principles do not affect directly other kinds of digital (or electronic) assets that do not come within the definition of digital assets. The most important criteria for determining whether a particular digital asset is within the scope of DAPL is whether it is subject to "control".

Common Law. In the United States common law there are general rules of property law that apply to digital assets. We will discuss these shortly.

Uniform Commercial Code. The scope of the Uniform Commercial Code for digital assets is very close to the scope of DAPL. The DAPL and the Uniform Commercial Code projects worked in parallel, and the participants communicated with each other quite a lot and learned quite a lot from each other:

- We started off in our draft of the Uniform Commercial Code amendments referring to a digital asset. Everyone was confused by that term, because it means different things to different people. Some would ask "Well, when I send you an email, is that a digital asset?" What we wanted to do was to capture those digital assets to which the marketplace attributes a value and not to other digital assets.

Table 1 Scope

Issue	Principles on Digital Assets and Private Law	United States Common Law	Uniform Commercial Code (UCC)
What digital assets (DAs) are covered?	Principle 2(2): '"Digital asset" means an electronic record which is capable of being subject to control.'	No specific definition	§ 12-102(a)(1): '"Controllable electronic record" means a record stored in an electronic medium that can be subjected to control under Section 12-105.' (CER)

- We also wanted to be, like DAPL, technologically neutral. We came up with a new term, "controllable electronic record." A "record" can be a writing or in electronic form, but the record is a "controllable electronic record" if it is in electronic form and is subject to "control". We discuss below what constitutes "control". But the easiest way to think about control is to consider the elements that one would normally attribute to possessing a physical object but instead for an intangible object. DAPL, of course, took the same approach.

4 Proprietary and Property Rights

The next item in our comparison is the question of proprietary or property rights (Table 2).

DAPL. DAPL has an express statement that "digital assets" as defined in DAPL can be the subject of proprietary rights.

Common Law. In the United States, the law of property generally is all common law; it is rarely set forth in statutes. As one case, which is cited in the chart, notes: intangible things can certainly be "property" for these purposes, and there is little question about that. There is some debate in the United States about whether one can injure an intangible thing giving rise to a tort claim for injury (conversion) to it, but that is a separate question. That under DAPL digital assets can be property is not unusual or inconsistent with United States common law.

We are probably lucky in that respect. We do not have the case law that exists in the United Kingdom, which required a new legislation. As we understand the United

Table 2 Proprietary and property rights

Issue	Principles on Digital Assets and Private Law	United States Common Law	Uniform Commercial Code (UCC)
Is a DA 'property' or a 'proprietary right'?	Principle 3(1): 'A digital asset can be the subject of proprietary rights.'	*Kremen v. Cohen*, 337 F.3d 1024 (9th Cir. 2003): Conversion 'To establish that tort, a plaintiff must show "ownership or right to possession of property, wrongful disposition of the property right and damages."... The preliminary question, then, is whether registrants have property rights in their domain names. ... Property is a broad concept that includes "every intangible benefit and prerogative susceptible of possession or disposition." ... *Kremen* therefore had an intangible property right in his domain name'	Implicit in coverage of CERs in UCC Articles 9 and 12

Kingdom law, the English law, is that you can have a tangible object and you can have a "chose in action", but there was no place for a digital asset. So, there had to be new legislation to recognise a digital asset as what was referred to as a new item of property.

Uniform Commercial Code. In the United States we did not have that issue; we accepted as a premise that any sort of right in any tangible or intangible was "property."

Once again, there is consistency here through different approaches. We end up at the exact same place under DPAL, United States common law, and the Uniform Commercial Code.

5 Linked Assets

The tokenisation or other linkage to digital assets to securities or other property and whether DAPL applies or does not apply or how DAPL might apply raise important questions (Table 3).

Common Law. In the United States common law there is nothing that addresses tokenisation or other linkage as such. Tokenisation implies a linked asset, which we discuss further below. When one thinks about what a token is, it should not be surprising that the token is just the electronic record. It is just the data. To give the person who has the token the right to exercise the attributes of securities, for example, one needs to link the securities to the token itself so that whoever deals in the token is dealing with the securities. We are currently exploring that step in the United States, but it is possible that further legislation will be required.

And again, in the common law of the United States, the law relating to tokenisation is not at all clear. There are some who claim that a token can be linked to real property so that, if I obtain the token, I obtain the real property. The common law would not recognise that linkage.

DAPL. DAPL addresses the question of linked assets. As a general matter, DAPL does not address the effect a transfer of a security right on what DAPL calls a "target asset" when there is a transfer or a security right in the primary asset. Instead that effect is addressed by other law. If other law provides that some effect, particularly of a proprietary effect on the primary asset, has a comparable effect on the target asset, then the rules under DAPL can have an effect on the target asset. And if other law *does not* provide for the effect, then one must go look to other law for the effect on the target asset of a transaction to address such issues as whether the transaction is a transfer of or creates a security right in the target asset and the rights of a transferee or secured creditor in that asset.

Uniform Commercial Code. The Uniform Commercial Code takes a narrow approach to linked assets. We should emphasise that the concept of a linked asset

Table 3 Linked Assets

Issue	Principles on Digital Assets and Private Law	United States Common Law	Uniform Commercial Code (UCC)
Linked assets	Principle 4: 'The digital assets to which these Principles apply include a digital asset linked to another asset. The other asset may be tangible or intangible (including another digital asset). Other law applies to determine the existence of, requirements for, and legal effect of any link between the digital asset and the other asset, including the effect of a transfer of the digital asset on the other asset.'	*Restatement of the Law Fourth Property Tentative Draft No. 3* (April 2022), Vol. 4, Div. I, Chapter 1, § 1.2, Comment *b*: 'b. Intangible property. … Where intangibles are concerned, one cannot draw upon the existence of physical separateness or physical boundaries to help identify things; consequently, economic and social practice and social norms and customs play a larger role in delineating things.'	Except for controllable accounts and controllable payment intangibles, other law determines whether a person who acquires rights in a controllable record acquires rights in an asset linked to the controllable electronic record. Article 12, Prefatory Note 4.a and 4.b: § 12-104(a): 'This section applies to the acquisition and purchase of rights in a controllable account or controllable payment intangible, …in the same manner this section applies to a controllable electronic record.' § 12-104(f): 'Except as provided in subsections (a) and (e) for a controllable account and a controllable payment intangible or law other than this article, a qualifying purchaser takes a right to payment, right to performance, or other interest in property evidenced by the controllable electronic record subject to a claim of a property right in the right to payment, right to performance, or other interest in property.' For an account or payment intangible to be a controllable account or controllable payment intangible, the account debtor must agree to pay the person in control. § 9-102(a)(27A), (27B)

is not unusual; it is a concept with which we are all familiar. For example, a paper promissory note embodies a right to payment. The promissory note is just a piece of paper, but the law gives that piece of paper meaning by saying with that piece of paper one obtains that right to payment. The same applies to documents of title. One may have a document of title which gives that person rights in the underlying goods, but the document of title itself is just a record, such as information on a piece of paper or data on an electronic record. So, we already have linked assets in our legal systems. We just were not referring to them as "linked assets."

When we came up with our definition in the Uniform Commercial Code of "controllable electronic record", we did not want to interfere with those electronic systems that already exist and work well. Accordingly, we excluded them from the definition of "controllable electronic record". These exclusions include electronic documents of title, so-called "transferable records" under our Uniform Electronic Transactions Act, and dematerialised securities. Then that left us with the pure definition of controllable electronic record.

But when one has control of a controllable electronic record, normally one just has the control of the data on that record. That works for Bitcoin and other crypto currencies which are just data on a record. But the question remains as to how to address rights or assets purported to be linked to the record. What we did was very similar to what DAPL did. We said that area is too vast; we could not in our project practically create legal rules for real estate, for non-fungible tokens, for intellectual property, or for securities that link those assets to the controllable electronic record.

However, there was one area where there was great demand that we establish a link. That was where the controllable electronic record evidences payment rights. To have a negotiable promissory note under Article 3 of the Uniform Commercial Code the note would have to be in a writing, i.e., a paper note. There is a small exception under our Uniform Electronic Transactions Act for a "transferable record" to be an an electronic record equivalent to a negotiable promissory note under Article 3 and a similar provision, where the note is secured by an interest in real estate, under the federal Electronic Signatures in Global and National Commerce Act. But the United States does not otherwise have specific statutory law for an electronic promissory note. An electronic promissory note is just a contract that has been created electronically.

There was a demand in trade finance for there to be legal rules for electronic promissory notes and electronic bills of exchange. This was especially the case during the COVID pandemic, where there was the desire to trade with electronic promissory notes and electronic bills of exchange, and no real law in the United States to create the same attributes that would apply if those instruments were in written form instead of electronic form.

So, we said in the Uniform Commercial Code that if one has a right to payment that arises from providing goods of services or a loan, and if the controllable electronic record evidences that right to payment, then the transfer of the controllable electronic record carries with it those rights to payment as a matter of statute. We will discuss in more detail what that means. But think about the fact that a controllable electronic record that evidences a right to payment can result in an electronic promissory note or an electronic bill of exchange that is recognised under the amendments.

6 Private International Law

This subject often brings some controversy (Table 4).

Common Law. United States common law in this area is similar to the traditional connecting factors rule. There is little predictability with four, five or six factors,

Table 4 Private international law

Issue	Principles on Digital Assets and Private Law	United States Common Law	Uniform Commercial Code (UCC)
Private International Law (Applicable Law)	Principle 5: 'Waterfall' based on: • Express statement in DA • Express statement in system • Statutory seat of issuer, if there is one • Other specifications in law of forum State	*Restatement (Second) of Conflict of Laws* § 208: 'Whether, and under what conditions, a contractual right, which is not embodied in a document, can be effectively assigned is determined by the local law of the State which has the most significant relationship to the contract and the parties with respect to the issue of assignability.' *Restatement (Second) of Conflict of Laws* § 188: '(1) The rights and duties of the parties with respect to an issue in contract are determined by the local law of the State which, with respect to that issue, has the most significant relationship to the transaction and the parties under the principles stated in § 6.'	§ 12-107: Based on 'CER's jurisdiction', based on 'waterfall': • Express statement of 'CER's jurisdiction' in DA • Express statement of 'CER's jurisdiction' in system where CER is maintained • General PIL provision in CER • General PIL CER provision in system where CER is maintained • District of Columbia • However, the rights and duties of an account debtor are determined by the law of an effective agreement between the debtor and the account debtor

each of which has different weight depending on the transaction. As a result, one often does not know which State's law is going to apply to a transaction, So it is important to have as a much precision and predictability as possible in these rules and not to have to devise a balancing test or a many factors test each time in order to try to figure out which law is going to apply. Any uncertainty reduces efficiency and raises costs to a transaction.

The policy goal here, coming back to the initial comments that we have made about DAPL, is to have predictability. Under United States common law, there was little or no predictability on third party rights as against these kinds of assets or proprietary rights that might exist.

DAPL. In designing a private international law rule in DAPL, instead of using traditional connecting factors, the goal was to develop a very clear, or as clear as possible, set of factors. Clear factors permit persons engaging in these transactions to have some reasonable chance of predicting which State's law would apply and therefore predicting what the results would be in the case of a dispute relating to the transaction, whether the transaction is an outright transfer or the creation of a security right.

Uniform Commercial Code. Once again, the Uniform Commercial Code has a lot of symmetry with DAPL. The Uniform Commercial Code starts off with a very similar waterfall. One looks to the law that is stated in the controllable electronic record as the "location" of the controllable electronic record, and then one applies that law. If the controllable electronic record itself does not provide for that law, then one looks to the system in which the controllable electronic record is recorded. And if that system provides for a governing law or the location of the controllable electronic record, one applies that law.

If one looks at Bitcoin, there is no governing law and there is no system that provides for a governing law. The Uniform Commercial Code had to have a residual rule. We do not have the residual rule that you find in DAPL, where one looks to the location of the issuer. It is probably the case that many of these controllable electronic records do not have an issuer, or if they do, they relate to securities which we address in other law. But then the idea was to try to have a residual rule that points to the application of the substantive rules of our Uniform Commercial Code amendments. So, how did we do that? We said, look to the law of Washington, D.C. If Washington, D.C. has enacted the amendments, then one looks to the Washington, D.C. law. If it has not adopted the amendments, then one just applies the uniform substantive law of the amendments. Washington, D.C., we are happy to report, did enact the amendments. As a result, one does not need to think about whether to apply the uniform substantive law.

But the most important point here is that the more that the substantive law of each State is uniform, the more we do not need to worry about the private international law rules, because they get you to substantially the same result no matter which jurisdiction's law is applicable.

Through this process, we tried to work very carefully with UNIDROIT, with the United Kingdom Law Commission, and with other law reform organisations, with the hope that our applicable private international law rules will be as uniform as possible, but, even more importantly, that our substantive law rules will also be as uniform as possible.

Anything "covered" by our new Uniform Commercial Code Article 12, which we will address below, is subject to the private international law rules.

7 Transfers and Rights of Transferees

Transfers and the rights of transferee are at the core of these projects (Table 5).

Uniform Commercial Code. For predictability, we want the exact same substantive law to apply for a non-secured transaction and for a secured transaction, because somebody involved in one or both of those transactions or either transaction should achieve the same result. The same set of rules should apply, and again, all of that comes back to predictability.

"Transfer" is a very broad term. The Uniform Commercial Code has the same issue of when one refers to transfer whether one is talking about a transfer of full ownership or the creation of a security right. We had in our Uniform Commercial Code a phrase "assignment." Some courts interpreted "assignment" to be a full transfer of ownership and others interpreted it to be the creation of a security right. We had different lines of decision interpreting the same statute. Thus, we had to

Table 5 Transfer and rights of transferees

Issue	Principles on Digital Assets and Private Law	United States Common Law	Uniform Commercial Code (UCC)
Transfer	Principle 2(5)(a): '"transfer" of a digital asset means the change of a proprietary right in the digital asset from one person to another person;'	*Restatement (Second) of Contracts* § 317: '(1) An assignment of a right is a manifestation of the assignor's intention to transfer it by virtue of which the assignor's right to performance by the obligor is extinguished in whole or in part and the assignee acquires a right to such performance.'	§ 12-104(c): 'Except as provided in this section, law other than this article determines whether a person acquires a right in a controllable electronic record and the right the person acquires.' § 9-102, Comment 2(b)(1): 'Several provisions of this Article and its official comments also refer to the "transfer" of property interests. Although that term and its cognates are not defined, depending on the context it may include an "assignment." Moreover, a transfer of property is not limited to transactions of "purchase" and may include the transfer of a limited interest.'

provide in the amendments a statement that made it absolutely clear that, when the Uniform Commercial Code uses the term "transfer" or "assignment", the Uniform Commercial Code is referring to either a transfer of outright ownership or the creation of the security right. It could be either.

Let us make a brief comment on the word "resulting." That word addresses the possible circumstance where, if one wants to transfer a digital asset, what the transferee receives is not exactly what the transferor sent. This is because the system on which the digital asset is created or maintained may cancel the transferor's digital asset and create a new one. The new one is placed in the transferee's wallet and the old one in the transferor's wallet no longer exists. Without having to get metaphysical about whether the asset transferred and the asset received was the "same asset" or whether it could be traced or not, DAPL takes a very direct view that, if there is a resulting asset, the same set of rules are going to apply without having to spend a lot of time worrying about whether the asset transferred and the asset received was the same asset.

Common Law. In the United States in particular under our common law, it was not always clear whether a transaction creates a security right or constitutes an outright transfer of ownership. We call this a "true sale" question. Rather than having to solve that question every time, as we will address below, the same rules under our secured transactions law (Article 9) apply to sales of payment rights or to a security right in a payment right to secure an obligation. And the other thing to note here is that our definition of controllable electronic record, similar to digital assets as defined in DAPL, is much broader than cryptocurrencies.

Although one often thinks about this in terms of examples of controllable electronic records as Bitcoin or other cryptocurrencies, electronic rights to payment evidenced by a controllable electronic record are also inside of these new rules. While we think of the amendments as applying to cryptocurrencies, the amendments are just as likely to apply to actual transactions involving payment rights.

DAPL. So let us go on to the question of transfer, which leads into question of control. DAPL generally looks to other law as to how to accomplish a transfer. And DAPL is modest in what DAPL attempts to do. DAPL does not try to answer every question. Other law has sufficient rules for how one accomplishes or agrees to accomplish a transfer of a digital asset. And, importantly, because, as was noted before and we will come to this a little bit later, a transfer includes any kind of movement, we will avoid the word "transfer" of a proprietary right of being confined to either full ownership or something less, such as a security right in a digital asset. This approach permits the consolidation of rules so that a single body of rules applies to a set of related transactions.

Uniform Commercial Code. The result of a resulting asset is the same under the Uniform Commercial Code. We avoid United States common law under which we would have had a lengthy analysis and debate over whether the asset can be traced or not under what we call "equitable principles."

8 Control

The idea of control has received a lot of attention in these transactions (Table 6).

DAPL. There has been a concern about how one proves that one has an exclusive right when there could be anybody out there in the universe that might have one of these rights. DAPL Principle 7 anticipates that problem and addresses it. It provides that if a person can demonstrate that person's identification as it is required in Principle 6 for purposes of control, then that person is *presumed* to have the exclusive rights. The presumption shifts the burden to the person challenging control to show that somebody else, maybe the challenger, actually has the control there. One does not have to prove the negative, which would be an impossible task given that anyone might have some sort of claim or ability.

Uniform Commercial Code. The Uniform Commercial Code has a similar, almost identical, rule. So again, uniformity, consistency, and efficiency in the markets are served.

As we were preparing the Uniform Commercial Code provisions, because we knew that we did know everything about cryptocurrencies, technology, or electronics, we invited into the process business people and lawyers who knew nothing or little about commercial law but knew more than we did about cryptocurrencies and other digital assets.

We said to the digital asset experts: here is what we would like to do as a matter of commercial law. Does that make any sense as a matter of digital transactions and similar transactions? Most of the time they said fine, but some of the time they said we were crazy, and we need to deal with this. One of the comments related to

Table 6 Control

Issue	Principles on Digital Assets and Private Law	United States Common Law	Uniform Commercial Code (UCC)
Control	Principle 6: • 'exclusive ability to prevent others from obtaining substantially all of the benefit from the digital asset;' • 'ability to obtain substantially all of the benefit from the digital asset' • 'the exclusive ability to transfer the [preceding] abilities … to another person' • 'that person [allowed] to identify itself as having the [preceding] abilities'	Not applicable	§ 12–105(a)(1) and (2): • 'power to avail itself of substantially all the benefit from the electronic record' • 'exclusive power … to: (i) prevent others from availing themselves of substantially all the benefit from the electronic record' • 'exclusive power … to: … (ii) transfer control of the electronic record to another person' (2) enables the person readily to identify itself in any way… as having the [preceding] powers'

the sharing of control. The digital experts said that it was a common transaction to have what is often referred to as "multi-sig," multi-signature requirements. DAPL addresses this directly in Principle 6.3(d). The fact that one has the abilities we just referred to in the definition of control but that somebody else *also* may have those abilities does not detract from one's status of having control, as long as one has not given up control. That there may be two persons that have control is not fatal. In these transactions as a matter of United States common law we have similar concepts in property law, such as joint tenants and tenants-in-common.

We did something very similar in our Uniform Commercial Code amendments.

If one has the power to transfer the asset and the other powers and another person has them, and either one of them can exercise those powers without the consent or involvement of the other, then *each* has control.

But if one can exercise those powers but the other cannot without the consent or involvement of the first person, then only the first person has control and the second person does not.

And there are other ways even to structure control. For example, a person could have control and that person can agree that if either of the two other persons tell him to transfer the asset, the first person will do so. Then *each* of those other persons has control through the first person.

Similarly, if only one of the other persons can give the person with direct control instructions but the second other person has to consent to those instructions, the first other person does not have control.

We found some of these control mechanisms to be very prevalent in the marketplace. We were told unless we had multi-sig provisions that the marketplace would not support what we were doing. As a result, we had to create those counter-intuitive provisions which say, yes, one has exclusive control but no, we do not really mean it when we are talking about multi-signature.

And similar to DAPL, the Uniform Commercial Code has many examples in its comments. When we give lectures on this in the United States, we tell people before you read the statute, read the comments because they will tell you how to read the statute. The statute itself is perfect in the sense that, if you read the words, they say what the comments tell you they mean. But it is very hard on a first or second or third or fourth reading to get there without the help of the comments. We have been known to say that one should read the comments and only if one sees an ambiguity should one read the statute.

9 Shelter

So let us go on to one of the core substantive provisions (putting aside secured transactions). That is the question of what we sometimes refer to as the shelter rule and in DAPL, the rights of a transferee rule (Table 7).

Table 7 Shelter

Issue	Principles on Digital Assets and Private Law	United States Common Law	Uniform Commercial Code (UCC)
Shelter rule	Principle 9: 'A transferee of proprietary rights in a digital asset acquires all of the proprietary rights that its transferor had or had the power to transfer, except that the transferee acquires rights only to the extent of the rights that were transferred.')	*Restatement (Second) of Contracts* § 336: '(1) By an assignment the assignee acquires a right against the obligor only to the extent that the obligor is under a duty to the assignor; and if the right of the assignor would be voidable by the obligor or unenforceable against him if no assignment had been made, the right of the assignee is subject to the infirmity '(2) The right of an assignee is subject to any defense or claim of the obligor which accrues before the obligor receives notification of the assignment, but not to defenses or claims which accrue thereafter except as stated in this Section or as provided by statute.'	§ 12-104(d): 'A purchaser of a controllable electronic record acquires all rights in the controllable electronic record that the transferor had or had power to transfer, except that a purchaser of a limited interest in a controllable electronic record acquires rights only to the extent of the interest purchased.'

Here is the important part. Often people get caught up in trying to figure out whether there is an electronic record, whether it is subject to control, and whether one can meet all of the requirements for obtaining control. Sometimes one forgets that the reason for having control of a controllable electronic record is to be able to apply the substantive law rules relating to the rights of a transferee of a controllable electronic record. We discuss why we have these definitions and what their impact is.

DAPL. DAPL starts with the underlying concept of *nemo dat*. One cannot transfer more than one has except when one can under another legal rule. Part of *nemo dat* in DAPL is the shelter rule. What one does have one can transfer to somebody else, even if that somebody else, had they been a direct transferee of the original transferor, might have been subject to other proprietary claims to the digital asset of one form or another. The shelter principle in DAPL Principle 9 gives the transferee whatever rights the transferor has (but no more). We will come back in a moment to what rights the transferor may have. This rule does not depend on the transferee's lack of knowledge or notice, or value, or the like. It just says, whatever one has one can give to someone else.

Uniform Commercial Code. The Uniform Commercial Code deals with shelter in exactly the same way. Whatever rights the transferor had go to the transferee. Now let us say that we thought we had a controllable electronic record but someone hacked into our computer and the hacker was able to obtain control of this controllable electronic record and transfer it to a third party. So the hacker is a thief. The hacker has no right to our controllable electronic record. When the hacker transfers the controllable electronic record to a third person, the third person takes subject to our ownership rights. We can claim the controllable electronic record. But whatever rights the hacker had the third person receives from the transferee.

10 Innocent Acquirer Rights

We are now going to discuss the innocent acquirer rule, which again is a core concept of these projects. The innocent acquirer rule is going to tell us that the innocent acquirer can "take free" of the property rights of another. We first address how this rule works (Table 8).

Table 8 Innocent acquirer rights

Issue	Principles on Digital Assets and Private Law	United States Common Law	Uniform Commercial Code (UCC)
Innocent acquirer defined	Principle 8(1): • 'obtain control of a digital asset' 'comply with requirements equivalent to those found in the relevant good faith acquisition and take-free rules as specified by the relevant State.'	*Enrichment Restatement (Third) of Restitution and Unjust Enrichment,* § 66: 'A purchaser for value and without notice …'	§ 12-102(2): '"Qualifying purchaser" means a purchaser of a controllable electronic record or an interest in a controllable electronic record that obtains control of the controllable electronic record for value, in good faith, and without notice of a claim of a property right in the controllable electronic record.'
Innocent acquirer rights	Principle 8(2): 'An innocent acquirer takes a digital asset free of conflicting proprietary rights ('proprietary claims').'	*Restatement (Third) of Restitution and Unjust Enrichment Restatement (Third) of Restitution and Unjust Enrichment,* § 66: '… acquires the legal interest that the grantor holds and purports to convey, free of equitable interests that a restitution claimant might have asserted against the property in the hands of the grantor.'	§ 12-104(e): 'A qualifying purchaser acquires its rights in the controllable electronic record free of a claim of a property right in the controllable electronic record.'

DAPL. The key is the word "control" as used in establishing control of the digital asset. It is important to keep in mind that a "digital asset" is only the kind of digital asset defined in DAPL, not other kinds of digital assets.

Here is where the modesty of DAPL comes into play. DAPL could have gone on and established a set of additional components that said there has to be value, there has to be good faith, and there has to be the absence of notice of the other party's or person's proprietary claims. At UNIDROIT one State may have a particular requirement to achieve innocent acquirer status and another State may have a different requirement. UNIDROIT stepped back and did not try to establish rules for this part of innocent acquirer status. Instead DAPL understands that States have similar rules but they are not identical. The goal of "taking free" of another person's proprietary rights creates certainty in the market for trading this type of asset. DAPL provides that to be an innocent acquirer, the person must have control. Then one looks to *bona fide* purchaser, innocent acquirer, or similar rules, however phrased in a particular State. Those requirements are added on, creating the definition of the innocent acquirer for this purpose.

Again, DAPL does not answer every question; in some cases there was a specific rule and in other places a more general rule. So if one manages to be an innocent acquirer what does one get? Under DAPL an innocent acquirer acquires the asset free of or not subject to the proprietary rights of other persons. And keep in mind that in order to achieve this status one has to have control *plus* the elements of good faith, value, and lack of notice, however those requirements are expressed in a particular State for these purposes.

Common Law. The common law of the United States has very little to say on this subject. The *Restatement (Third) of Restitution and Unjust Enrichment* provides that an innocent acquirer cuts off equitable rights but not legal rights. In the United States legal rights are more important in property law. So this is a very narrow rule.

Uniform Commercial Code. The amendments to the Uniform Commercial Code do provide the full set of attributes that an innocent acquirer must have. The term that is used is "qualifying purchaser". A purchaser is any voluntary transferee. Because we start off with a purchaser that acquires control of the controllable electronic record for value, a transferee who receives a gift would not be a qualifying purchaser.

We wanted to make sure that "value" really meant monetary or other consideration. The person seeking to be a qualifying purchaser also has to act in good faith, which we defined as honesty in fact and the observance of reasonable commercial standards of fair dealing. And then finally the person who acquires control, in order to be a qualifying purchaser, must obtain control without notice of an adverse property claim to the controllable electronic record. Because we wanted to make sure that notice did not require the acquirer to do a search in a registry, we say specifically that there is no requirement for the acquirer to do the search. However, if otherwise, the acquirer is on notice of the adverse claim, the acquirer cannot be a qualifying purchaser. The Uniform Commercial Code lands substantially in the same place as DAPL for what the attributes are of an innocent acquirer.

Let us consider the innocent acquirer rule together with the shelter principle. Assume that an innocent acquirer acquires a digital asset free of other proprietary rights, then the innocent acquirer transfers the asset to a third person, and the third person knows about the prior proprietary claims to the digital asset. Because of the shelter principle the person in the middle, the first acquirer as an innocent acquirer, acquired the digital asset free of other proprietary claims. That person can then pass that status along to the second acquirer under the shelter rule, even though that person standing alone would not be an innocent acquirer.

This is in effect how how the markets work. If someone buys a digital asset and does not know of any claims to it, then the buyer is in good shape. The buyer does not have to worry about any potential property claims to the digital asset.

Again, the common law in the United States has very little to say on the subject.

The result is the same under the Uniform Commercial Code amendments as it is under DAPL. If one is a qualifying purchaser, the purchaser cuts off adverse property claims to the controllable electronic record. Now, think about what this means in the context of buying Bitcoin. Before the amendments, there was no rule that cut off adverse property claims to the Bitcoin.

Without the amendments, if the Bitcoin was stolen and transferred to A and A sold it to B and B sold it to C, the original person could come after C even though everyone in the chain was innocent. But that was not how people dealt with Bitcoin in the marketplace. They dealt with Bitcoin as if it were money and similar to a medium of exchange. So what the qualifying purchaser rule and the innocent acquirer rule do is really to codify what the market expects for the transfer of these assets.

11 Custody

We are going to move now from the innocent acquirer and shelter rules to various matters involving custody of a digital asset. It is widely expected that a lot of people one way or the other will have their digital assets in custody somehow with somebody else, whether a traditional custodian or a cryptocurrency exchange (Table 9).

DAPL. A large business may know how to acquire, hold or sell a digital asset but an individual may not. It is not usual for an individual or even a business to enter into a contract with an exchange, a service provider, or someone like that to manage the transactions in the digital assets. Accordingly, there are elaborate provisions in DAPL on custody.

If there is a customer and a custodian and the custodian holds the assets in a way where the expectations are that the assets remain those of the customer, then the assets are those of the customer. The custodian may use a sub-custodian or another custodian to hold the assets for the first custodian and there are further elaborate rules in DAPL on how one has control of a digital asset where there are two, three, four, or five custodians in a chain, each maintaining a digital asset for its customer. Then

Table 9 Custody

Issue	Principles on Digital Assets and Private Law	United States Common Law	Uniform Commercial Code (UCC)
Custodian defined	Principle 10(1): '"custodian" means a person who provides services to a client pursuant to a custody agreement as defined in paragraphs (3) and (4), and is acting in that capacity;' Principle 10(4): 'An agreement to which paragraph (3) applies is not a custody agreement if it is clear from the agreement that, if the service provider enters into an insolvency-related proceeding, the digital asset would be part of the service provider's assets available for distribution to its creditors.'	*Restatement of the Law Fourth Property Tentative Draft No. 3* (April 2022), Vol. 3, Div. III, § 1 (analogy to bailments): '(a) Bailment is any rightful possession of an item of personal property by someone other than its owner '(b) A person who assumes such possession is a bailee.'	§ 12-105(e): For purposes of Article 9 and Article 12, 'A person has control of a controllable electronic record if another person …: '(1) has control of the electronic record and acknowledges that it has control on behalf of the person;' § 12-105(e): Provided that the other person may not be: 'the transferor to the person of an interest in the controllable electronic record or a controllable account or controllable payment intangible evidenced by the controllable electronic record' Alternatively, UCC Article 8 may apply

(continued)

Table 9 (continued)

Issue	Principles on Digital Assets and Private Law	United States Common Law	Uniform Commercial Code (UCC)
Rights of client	Principle 12: '(1) Subject to paragraph (2), where a custodian maintains a digital asset pursuant to a custody agreement …, no rights based on a proprietary claim to that asset may be successfully asserted against the client '(2) Paragraph (1) does not apply if the client, at the time from which the custodian maintains the digital asset for that client, actually knows or ought to know that another person has an interest in the digital asset and that the acquisition violates the rights of that other person in relation to its interest.'	*Restatement of the Law Fourth Property Tentative Draft No. 3* (April 2022), Vol. 3, Div. III, § 9 (analogy to bailments): 'Bailors have the following rights against their bailees and third parties: '… '(b) Upon termination of the bailment … to recover possession of the item from a bailee '… '(c) To recover possession of the item from an unauthorised third party who has come into possession of it.'	§ 12-105(e): Control established through another person creates the same rights as control directly established Alternatively, UCC Article 8 may apply
Rights of creditors of custodian	Principle 13(1): 'A digital asset that a custodian maintains for a client under a custody agreement is not available for the satisfaction of claims of creditors of the custodian.'	*Restatement of the Law Fourth Property Tentative Draft No. 3* (April 2022), Vol. 3, Div. III, § 1 (analogy to bailments): *Sturm v. Boker,* 150 U.S. 312, 329, 14 S.Ct. 99, 37 L.Ed. 1093 (1893) ('The recognised distinction between bailment and sale is that, when the identical article is to be returned in the same or in some altered form, the contract is one of bailment, and the title to the property is not changed. On the other hand, when there is no obligation to return the specific article, and the receiver is at liberty to return another thing of value, he becomes a debtor to make the return, and the title to the property is changed. The transaction is a sale.')	Determined by other law. UCC Article 8 may apply

its customer is a custodian for another customer and so forth. If all those rights are maintained all the way up the chain, then we see there is a series of custodians. We discuss shortly how the various rights of control flow up that chain.

We raise one more point on custodians. What happens if the custodian is holding a digital asset for the customer and the custodian becomes subject to an insolvency proceeding? Does the customer's interest in the digital asset controlled by the custodian protect the customer from the claims of the creditors of the custodian or is the customer just another creditor of the custodian? DAPL defines "custody" as including an anticipation that the digital asset is not subject to the claims of the creditors of the custodian. DAPL's rules confirm that expectation. Accordingly, if we have a true custody relationship, then digital asset is not part of the custodian's insolvency estate and is not subject to the claims of the custodian's creditors.

Common Law. We have a property *Restatement* underway that has extensive provisions on bailments. The reporters are considering drafting some comparable—not identical—provisions to deal with custody of digital assets similar to bailments, without disrupting the law of bailments.

Uniform Commercial Code. In the United States, we have an extensive law of bailments. But the law on bailments is often limited to goods or tangible objects generally, and it may or may not be relevant to intangible objects, such as digital assets. If one looks at contracts that people use in the United States today for custody—they use the word "custody"—of digital assets, they look like bailment agreements. Someone took a form off the computer and just changed the word "goods" to "digital assets" and used the same basic form.

Putting aside the law of bailments, there are different ways that parties could structure a digital assets custodial arrangement. Under the amendments, if one has control of a controllable electronic record, that person could acknowledge to another person that the person with control has control for the second person. The arrangement makes the first person somewhat like a custodian at that point.

There is another way to do this and that is under Article 8 of the Uniform Commercial Code. Article 8 deals with the transfer of investment securities, but we also have in Article 8 provisions relating to what we call the "indirect holding system". In that context securities are accounted for by a broker for its customer, but the broker holds the securities through a clearing corporation. What the customer has is what is called a "security entitlement", a contractual and statutory relationship with the broker and a statutory property interest in the securities that the broker holds for its customer. We refer to the account with the broker as a "securities account" and the customer having a security entitlement against the broker.

However, the definition in Article 8 of what constitutes a financial asset that a broker can hold for a customer is broader than just securities. The broker can also hold for its customer any other asset that the broker and the customer agree to treat as a financial asset. If the broker and the customer agree that the broker will hold a digital asset as a financial asset credited to the customer's securities account at the broker, then the Article 8 provisions apply. The broker is the custodian for the digital asset and in the amendments we made it clear that a controllable electronic record can be a financial asset subject to Article 8.

We also made it clear in the amendments that the broker, which we call a "securities intermediary", does not even need to deal in securities; it can deal just in controllable electronic records. The large crypto exchanges that one reads about could qualify as securities intermediaries holding financial assets consisting of controllable electronic records.

So there are two ways to establish custody for a digital asset. The first way is very skeletal; it just refers to the fact that the intermediary is holding the controllable electronic record for the customer. In the second way, we bring in all of Article 8 where there is a whole statutory framework.

Under the Uniform Commercial Code, if a person has control of a controllable electronic record for a customer, that person is a custodian for the customer. If that person is subject to an insolvency proceeding, the insolvency tribunal should ideally find that the digital asset is not the custodian's asset but rather it is the customer's asset. This result is even clearer, though, under the Article 8 approach. As a matter of the Article 8 statute, the assets are not part of the insolvency estate of the custodian and are not subject to the claims of the custodian's creditors; they are assets of the customer.

12 Secured Transactions

Provisions on creating security rights in digital assets must be coordinated with transfer rights generally (Table 10).

DAPL. Under DAPL, we start off with the basic notion that there can be a proprietary right (extensive or narrow) in a digital asset. DAPL expressly states that a propriety right includes a security right in a digital asset. So under DAPL, there is no obstacle to creating a security right in a digital asset—we will discuss effectiveness against third parties and priority rules below—but there is no problem under DAPL in creating a security right.

When it comes to linked assets, which we have already discussed, there is the question of whether a security right in a principal asset extends to any target asset that is supposed to be linked to the principal asset. DAPL directs us to look to other law. DAPL will not answer that question, just as DAPL does not answer questions about linked assets generally. If other law provides that the link works for all these purposes, great; if it says that it does not, too bad.

There was a concern raised that there is no specific definition in DAPL of what a "security right" is or a secured transaction system is. Comment 14.3 it says that DAPL defers to whatever the relevant State itself characterises as a security right. It can be very broad. Some States apply their security rights law to outright transfers of payment rights, for example, and if that is so, the security right rules in DAPL will apply.

Table 10 Secured transactions

Issue	Principles on Digital Assets and Private Law	United States Common Law	Uniform Commercial Code (UCC)
Creation of security right	Principle 14(1): 'Digital assets can be the subject of security rights.'	General rules for creation of security right under UCC Article 9	§ 9-203 General rules for creation of security right under UCC Article 9
Effect of creation of security right on linked asset	Principle 14(2) and 3): (2) If a digital asset is linked to another asset, other law applies to determine the legal effect on that other asset of the creation of a security right in that digital asset (3) If a digital asset is linked to another asset, other law applies to determine the legal effect on that other asset of a security right in that digital asset being made effective against third parties	General law of property	Article 12, Prefatory Note 4.a and 4.b: 'a. … Except to the extent provided by Article 12, that Article leaves to other law the question whether P's acquisition of rights in the controllable electronic record gives P the right to receive delivery of the goods. Section 12-104(f). We would typically expect that under other law P would not acquire the right to receive the goods merely by acquiring rights in the controllable electronic record, any more than P would have acquired the right to receive the goods if the record were in paper form, the paper were physically delivered to P, and P acquired rights in the paper '… 'b. Article 12 provides an important exception to this general rule. … A qualifying purchaser of a controllable account or controllable payment intangible takes free of property claims and is protected from certain actions. See Section 12-104(a) through (e), (g), and (h), and Comments 6 through 10. As to the feasibility and rationale for this exception for controllable accounts and controllable payment intangibles, see Section 12-104, Comments 9 and 10.'

(continued)

Table 10 (continued)

Issue	Principles on Digital Assets and Private Law	United States Common Law	Uniform Commercial Code (UCC)
Effectiveness of security right against third parties	Principle 15(a): 'A security right in a digital asset can be made effective against third parties by control of the digital asset if one of the following requirements is fulfilled: '(a) the secured creditor has control of the digital asset'	General rules	§ 9-314(a): 'A security interest in … controllable accounts, controllable electronic records, controllable payment intangibles, … may be perfected by control.'
Effectiveness of security right against third parties where custodian maintains the DA	Principle 15(b): A security right in a digital asset can be made effective against third parties by control of the digital asset if one of the following requirements is fulfilled: '… '(b) a custodian maintains the digital asset for the secured creditor….'		Article 12 rule applies, § 12-105(e): For purposes of Article 9 and Article 12, 'A person has control of a controllable electronic record if another person …: '(1) has control of the electronic record and acknowledges that it has control on behalf of the person;' § 12-105(e): *Provided* that the other person may not be: 'the transferor to the person of an interest in the controllable electronic record or a controllable account or controllable payment intangible evidenced by the controllable electronic record' Alternatively, UCC Article 8 may apply

(continued)

Table 10 (continued)

Issue	Principles on Digital Assets and Private Law	United States Common Law	Uniform Commercial Code (UCC)
Priority of security right	Principle 16: 'A security right in a digital asset that is made effective against third parties by control in accordance with Principle 15 has priority over a security right in the digital asset that is made effective against third parties only by a method other than control.'	*Restatement (Second) of Contracts* § 342: 'Except as otherwise provided by statute, the right of an assignee is superior to that of a subsequent assignee of the same right from the same assignor, unless '… '(b) the subsequent assignee in good faith and without knowledge or reason to know of the prior assignment gives value and obtains '(i) payment or satisfaction of the obligation, '(ii) judgment against the obligor, '(iii) a new contract with the obligor by novation, or '(iv) possession of a writing of a type customarily accepted as a symbol or as evidence of the right assigned.'	§ 9-326A: 'A security interest in a controllable account, controllable electronic record, or controllable payment intangible held by a secured party having control of the account, electronic record, or payment intangible has priority over a conflicting security interest held by a secured party that does not have control.'

(continued)

Table 10 (continued)

Issue	Principles on Digital Assets and Private Law	United States Common Law	Uniform Commercial Code (UCC)
Enforcement of security right	Principle 17(1): 'Enforcement of a security right in a digital asset is subject to other law, including any requirement to proceed in good faith or in a commercially reasonable manner, or both.'	General rules	General application of enforcement rules of UCC, except for protections of person obligated on a controllable account or controllable payment intangible. § 12–106
Applicable law			For perfection and priority, the same rules as under Article 12 apply, except, solely for perfection by the filing of a financing statement, the law of the debtor's location, as determined by § 9-307, applies. § 9-306B

Under DAPL, the security right can be made effective against third parties by control or registration. Registration is available if the State has a system of registration of security rights. The advantage for making the security right effective against third parties by control is that the security right has priority as against another secured creditor who has made its security right effective by a method other than control.

DAPL, again being modest, did not attempt to define all of secured transactions law. There are numerous references to the Model Law of Secured Transactions from UNCITRAL. The UNCITRAL Model Law and the UNCITRAL Legislative Guide both permit two competing secured creditors to agree between themselves which will be senior and which will be junior. So the provision in DAPL that says that a secured creditor that has control has priority over another secured creditor that does not have control is a default rule. The two parties are free between themselves to enter into an agreement reversing the priorities.

Common Law. There is little common law in the United States in this area, because the Uniform Commercial Code has been in effect for sixty, sixty-five years depending on the unit of the United States. The common law has been supplanted by the Uniform Commercial Code for transactions within its scope. Because until 1999 the Uniform Commercial Code did not cover deposit accounts as collateral within its scope, there is some common law on security interests in deposit accounts. However, given today's scope of the Uniform Commercial Code, we tend to ignore it.

Uniform Commercial Code. If one looks to our Uniform Commercial Code in Article 9, we have perfection (effectiveness against third parties) and priority rules. Many countries combine the two and just refer to priority. But in the Uniform Commercial Code, we have this idea that perfection means that you can prevail over a creditor who obtains a judgment lien on the asset and priority deals with competing secured parties, buyers, lessees, and the like. So one can perfect a security right by control of a controllable electronic record and perfection by control has priority over perfection by some other method, such as registration.

If a secured creditor obtains control of a controllable electronic record, the secured creditor does not need to look at the registry to determine whether someone is claiming a security right in the same asset even if that person has notice of the security right. And that priority is only against another secured creditor but not against others who claim proprietary rights and the digital asset. If the secured person wants to be a qualifying purchaser, it cannot have notice of the security right, but to achieve priority all it needs to do is to obtain control.

What we call controllable accounts and controllable payment intangibles are these embedded payment rights in the controllable electronic record. Those transfer with the controllable electronic record. If a person obtains control of a controllable electronic record that evidences one of these payment rights, the person obtains control of the payment right as well.

The key to a payment right qualifying as a controllable account or a controllable payment intangible is that the person who is obligated on that payment right has to agree to pay the person in control of the controllable electronic record. Absent that agreement, the right to payment does not travel with the controllable electronic record.

We already have rules in our Article 9 of the Uniform Commercial Code dealing with the creation of security rights and those rules apply to controllable electronic records or one of these embedded payment rights just like they normally would.

And, as under DAPL, under the Uniform Commercial Code, a senior secured creditor can always agree to subordinate by contract its security right to that of a junior secured creditor.

13 Insolvency

It is important in commercial transactions that security rights are respected in insolvency proceedings (Table 11).

DAPL. The rights of someone under DAPL should survive the insolvency of the transferor or the person who granted or created the security right.

Table 11 Insolvency

Issue	Principles on Digital Assets and Private Law	United States Common Law	Uniform Commercial Code (UCC)
Insolvency	Principle 19(1): 'A proprietary right in a digital asset that has become effective against third parties under Principles law or other law is effective against the insolvency representative, creditors, and any other third party in an insolvency-related proceeding.'	General rules	§ 9-317(a): 'A security interest or agricultural lien is subordinate to the rights of: '… '(2) … a person that becomes a lien creditor before the earlier of the time: '(A) the security interest … is perfected' § 9-102(a)(52): '(52) "Lien creditor" means: '… '(C) a trustee in bankruptcy from the date of the filing of the petition;'

There has been concern expressed that there was no clear definition in DAPL of insolvency. There is a general definition, and the intent is clear from the comments that the term is intended to be very broad. If there is a common law system, or a judicial, administrative system, that addresses the rights generally of creditors of a person in financial trouble, that would be an "insolvency" issue.

Uniform Commercial Code. Under our insolvency law in the United States, if a security right has been perfected (made effective against third parties) by registration or by control, the security right in the controllable electronic record would be recognised in the insolvency proceeding subject to the same sort of special rules that one finds mentioned in DAPL, such as fraudulent transfers, preferences, and other general rules of the insolvency proceeding.

14 Conclusion

Overall the goal of DAPL has been to have clear, precise rules—not to try to answer every question. Where DAPL does provide an answer, the goal is to give direction to recognise market transactions and provide a legal infrastructure around the reasonable expectations of market participants. In doing so, DAPL provides certainty and predictability.

The Uniform Commercial Code does much the same and also provides uniformity among the United States units. As we have discussed, there is also a great level of consistency between DAPL and the Uniform Commercial Code, once again with a view of achieving certainty and predictability.

The Right of Control over Electronic Negotiable Documents and Electronically Documented Rights and Goods

Rafael Illescas

1 Conceptual Innovation Framework

The following is a brief reference to a newly emerged individual right that has been steadily gaining ground over the past few decades in the field of electronic commercial contracting and which is on its way to legislative and contractual generalization.[1] I am referring to the so-called Right of Control—or simply Control—which the applicable norm or normative principle typically attributes to the holder of any electronically documented negotiable right, that is, established in or by a transferable electronic document or record.

[1] Preliminary Note: From the doubtful and interrogative nature with which the referenced law and its very existence have been presented in my previous contributions to the topic, I now intend to move towards a more affirmative construction of the actual existence of right of control in the field of electronic contracting. The reader will be able to verify whether my intention has been realized.

This work was financed within the framework of the Prometeo 2023 project of the Regional Ministry of Innovation, Universities, Science and Digital Society (CIPROM/2022/26) "Present and future of the regulation of cryptoassets in the EU [LegalCripto]", whose principal investigator is Carmen Pastor Sempere. The basic ideas contained herein were presented in the author's paper with the same title, given on November 13, 2024 at the IV International Congress on "UNIDROIT Principles on Digital Assets and Private Law: Context, Content, Perspectives", organized also by BAES Research Group of the University of Alicante on November 13 and 14, 2024.

The chapter has been written within the Ministry of Science and Innovation's research project PDI2023-149583-C21, "Adaptación del Derecho Español para la adquisición, transmisión, gravamen y ejecución de los activos digitales en los negocios" (P.I. Teresa Rodriguez de las Heras Ballell/Manuel Alba Fernández).

R. Illescas (✉)
Carlos III University of Madrid, Madrid, Spain
e-mail: rafael.illescas@gmail.com

C. Pastor Sempere and D. A. Morán Bovio (eds.), UNIDROIT *Principles on Digital Assets and Private Law*, Law, Governance and Technology Series 80,
https://doi.org/10.1007/978-3-032-11001-5_3

Such a right, with this explicit designation, formally emerged in 2008 through UNCITRAL[2] within the framework of a global legal text: the "Rotterdam Rules"—the United Nations Convention on Contracts for the International Carriage of Goods Wholly or Partly by Sea,[3] hereinafter RR—which is still pending entry into force[4] but has, in practice, been considerably utilised with contractual support in international maritime traffic of goods. The right of control and the controlling party are subject to detailed, though limited, regulation in Chapter 10 of the Rotterdam Rules (RR)—Articles 50 to 56.

Following this initial regulation, UNCITRAL again mentions the Right of Control, expanding its scope to the fullest and extending the concept to the realm of international commercial obligation law in general, through its 2017 Model Law on Electronic Transferable Documents,[5] thus taking it beyond Maritime Law. Article 11 thereof is succinctly devoted to what it calls the "Control" of the issued electronic

---

[2] Prior to the date of approval of the Treaty by the United Nations General Assembly, the aforementioned expression had been consistently used in its preparatory works. The first draft text of the Treaty, formulated by UNCITRAL itself on January 8, 2002, document A/CN.9/WG.III/WP.21, already included among its various articles Article 11.1 with the following literal wording:

> 11.1 The right of control of the goods means the right under the contract of carriage to give the carrier instructions in respect of these goods during the period of its responsibility as stated in article 4.1.1. Such right to give the carrier instructions comprises rights to:
>
> (i) give or modify instructions in respect of the goods that do not constitute a variation of the contract of carriage;
>
> (ii) demand delivery of the goods before their arrival at the place of destination;
>
> (iii) replace the consignee by any other person including the controlling party;
>
> (iv) agree with the carrier to a variation of the contract of carriage.

[3] United Nations Convention on Contracts for the International Carriage of Goods Wholly or Partly by Sea, done at New York, this eleventh day of December two thousand and eight, in a single original, of which the Arabic, Chinese, English, French, Russian and Spanish texts are equally authentic.

[4] As of today, 25 states have signed the Rotterdam Rules (RR), of which 5, including Spain, have ratified the Convention. The entry into force of the Convention requires, according to its own text, 20 contracting states.

[5] UNCITRAL Model Law on Electronic Transferable Records enforced through Resolution adopted by the General Assembly on 7 December 2017 [on the report of the Sixth Committee (A/72/458)].

document,[6] provided that the creditor's right to the delivery of the contractual object is documented and negotiable.

In the different sections, the cited harmonising standard precisely applies the principle of functional equivalence between the electronic document and the paper document, both with regard to its possession and the circulation of the documented right through the transfer of the electronic document via its control. This is where the right of control appears: it is the right that allows the controlling party of the negotiable document to transfer indirect possession of the documented goods to the person to whom the right of control derived from in the original contract—the transport contract in the case of the Rotterdam Rules—is transferrred. This will involve a new party acquiring indirect possession and ownership of the contractual rights that pertain to them by virtue of their newly acquired status as the controlling party. Primarily, this includes the right to the delivery of the goods as well as the right to transfer them to a new third party, thereby creating a chain of successive ownerships until the final moment of the material delivery of the contractual object.

Thus, this application of the previously mentioned principle of functional equivalence means that the electronic contractual document fully functions as an equivalent to the centuries-old paper document issued under regimes prior to the digitalisation of the contract in question.[7] It also signifies an evolution of the equally classic principle of the circulation of movable goods, according to which possession is equivalent to

[6] Article 11. Control

> 1. Where the law requires or permits the possession of a transferable document or instrument, that requirement is met with respect to an electronic transferable record if a reliable method is used:
>
> (a) To establish exclusive control of that electronic transferable record by a person; and (b) To identify that person as the person in control.
>
> 2. Where the law requires or permits transfer of possession of a transferable document or instrument, that requirement is met with respect to an electronic transferable record through the transfer of control over the electronic transferable record.

[7] This is inferred from Article 11.1, among others, of the UNCITRAL Model Law on Electronic Commerce—UNCITRAL Model Law on Electronic Commerce 1996 with the additional Article 5 bis as adopted in 1998. The literal wording of this provision is as follows:

> Article 11. Formation and validity of contracts
>
> (1) In the context of contract formation, unless otherwise agreed by the parties, an offer and the acceptance of an offer may be expressed by means of data messages. Where a data message is used in the formation of a contract, that contract shall not be denied validity or enforceability on the sole ground that a data message was used for that purpose.

title[8]: The new right of control makes the old principle equivalent to its new formulation, according to which control is equivalent to indirect possession and, therefore, to title. Thus, the transfer of the electronic document control is equivalent to the transfer of the effective possession of the paper document, replaced in this case by the electronic document or record.

2 The Normative Emergence of the New Concept

From the moment of the publication of the two texts mentioned above—the Rotterdam Rules (RR) and the Model Law on Electronic Transferable Documents (LMDTE)—it seems as though there was a surge of the new right of control, with its existence being recognised and replicated by various norm-formulating agencies of the Uniform Law of International Trade (ULIT, hereinafter). Likewise, the right in question has even been enshrined in some national legal systems—primarily those of the United States and the United Kingdom.[9]

First and foremost, following the chronological order of events, the now not-so-new Article 12 of the Uniform Commercial Code (UCC) of the United States, approved in 2022, should be noted. Secondly, the "Electronic Trade Documents Act 2023" of the United Kingdom should be mentioned. Both contribute to granting the new right of control, or simply the control of the electronic document, a markedly global standing by providing a regulatory framework that could potentially achieve such an international dimension.

Some of the numerous provisions contained in the aforementioned Article 12 of the UCC deserve to be reproduced, as they particularly concern the right of control established therein.

The UCC provides in Article 12.105:

[8] In Spanish law, the principle is enshrined in Articles 464.1 of the Civil Code and 85.1 of the Commercial Code, although it could have been stated more directly and explicitly. The first of these provisions states that "the possession of movable goods, acquired in good faith, is equivalent to the title..." (literal translation).

Meanwhile, the provision of the aforementioned Commercial Code stipulates somewhat indirectly that "the purchase of goods in warehouses or stores open to the public will result in the prescription of rights in favour of the buyer regarding the goods acquired, reserving, where applicable, the rights of the owner of the sold objects to exercise civil or criminal actions that may correspond to them against the person who sold them improperly" (literal translation).

[9] Article 12 of the Uniform Commercial Code (UCC) of the United States was approved by the National Conference of Commissioners on Uniform State Laws and the American Law Institute (ALI) for the drafting and reform of the UCC on June 1, 2023. Similarly, the British Electronic Trade Documents Act 2023 received royal assent on July 20, 2023.

Section 12-105. Control of Controllable Electronic Record.
(a) [General rule: control of controllable electronic record.]

A person has control of a controllable electronic record if the electronic record, a record attached to or logically associated with the electronic record, or a system in which the electronic record is recorded:

(1) gives the person:

(A) power to avail itself of substantially all the benefit from the electronic record; and

(B) exclusive power, subject to subsection (b), to:

(i) prevent others from availing themselves of substantially all the benefit from the electronic record; and

(ii) transfer control of the electronic record to another person or cause another person to obtain control of another controllable electronic record as a result of the transfer of the electronic record; and

(2) enables the person readily to identify itself in any way, including by name, identifying number, cryptographic key, office, or account number, as having the powers specified in paragraph (1) ....

With regard to the British text, some of its provisions are of particular interest, and in particular, attention should be drawn to paragraphs 2 and following, where the definition of "electronic trade document," its legal regime, and its "control" are established (paragraphs 2.2.(e) and 2.3.(a)).

The literal wording of these last provisions is outlined below:

- Paragraph 2.2.(e): "… secure that a transfer of the document has effect to deprive any person who was able to exercise control of the document immediately before the transfer of the ability to do so (unless the person is able to exercise control by virtue of being a transferee)".
- Paragraph 2.3.(a): "a person exercises control of a document when the person uses, transfers or otherwise disposes of the document (whether or not the person has a legal right to do so)",

In turn, during 2023, the right of control was formulated and regulated in no fewer than four legal or pre-legal texts of the ULIT. However, these emerging uniform norms currently lack both an official or unofficial version in Spanish and the validity that corresponds to their inherent nature in each case.

I should briefly point out that the texts are as follows:

(i) The UNIDROIT Principles on Digital Assets and Private Law, 2023,[10] particularly Principle 6;
(ii) The "Principles ALI/ELI (American Law Institute/European Law Institute) for a Data Economy, Data Transaction and Data Rights, 2023",[11] especially Principle 3. (e)(f)(p) and Principle 7, with numerous references throughout its entire text.
(iii) The ELI Principles on the Use of Digital Assets as Collateral, 2023[12]; in particular, Principles 3.5 and 4.6, which specifically address control and the effective and sufficient control of the collateral by the secured creditor.[13]

From the wording of the new norms and the regulatory models introduced less than two years ago we are able to glean certain firm rules and common features across the five provisions mentioned, some of which had already been anticipated

---

[10] The UNIDROIT Principles on Digital Assets and Private Law were approved by the Governing Council of the agency during a meeting held at its headquarters in Rome on May 10, 2023, and published on October 4, 2023.

Particularly relevant to the subject is Section III: CONTROL AND TRANSFER. Within this section, there is Principle 6 - Control.

According to this principle, (1) A person has 'control' of a digital asset if:

> (a) subject to paragraphs (2) and (3), the digital asset, or the relevant protocol or system, confers on that person:
>
> (i) the exclusive ability to prevent others from obtaining substantially all of the benefit from the digital asset; (ii) the ability to obtain substantially all of the benefit from the digital asset; and
>
> (iii) the exclusive ability to transfer the abilities in sub-paragraphs (a)(i), (a)(ii) and (a)(iii) to another person; and (b) the digital asset, or the relevant protocols or system, allows that person to identify itself as having the abilities set out in sub-paragraph (a).
>
> (2) A 'change of control' means a transfer of the abilities in sub-paragraph (1)(a) to another person, and includes the replacement, modification, destruction, cancellation, or elimination of a digital asset, and the resulting and corresponding derivative creation of a new digital asset (a 'resulting digital asset') which is subject to the control of another person….

[11] The ELI Final Council Draft was approved by ALI on May 18, 2021 and by ELI Council on September 1, 2021.

It can be found in https://www.europeanlawinstitute.eu/fileadmin/user_upload/p_eli/Publications/ALI-ELI_Principles_for_a_Data_Economy.pdf.

[12] "ELI Principles on the Use of Digital Assets" as Security, s/d but from 2023, https://www.europeanlawinstitute.eu/fileadmin/user_upload/p_eli/Publications/ELI_Principles_on_the_Use_of_Digital_Assets_as_Security.pdf.

[13] Principle 3.5:

> If the applicable law makes the creation of a security interest in assets conditional on their physical delivery to the secured creditor, then that condition is deemed to be fulfilled in the case of a security interest created in a digital asset where the security provider has put the secured creditor in a position where the latter can exercise control over the digital asset concerned, even if short of the actual physical delivery of the real-world asset to the secured creditor.
>
> Principle 4.6:

in UNCITRAL'S two preceding instruments from 2008 and 2017, as previously referenced.

3 Substantive Aspects of Control Law

Among the anticipated provisions that were generalised a decade later, it is worth mentioning the following:

- Functional equivalence means that the electronic document is functionally and legally equivalent to the centuries-old paper document, granting the electronic document the same functions, attributes, and transactions as the paper document. This means that both, in terms of its possession and the circulation of the documented right through delivery, transfer the right of control over the electronic document and this implies consequently the cession of the documented right. Therefore, this transfer of the right of control produces the equivalent of a mode of transmission in movable property, although in the electronic world, the mode of transmission can obviously not consist of a piece of paper material delivery, but rather the cession of an electronically documented right, which enables the holder of the transferred and instrumented right to become the owner or possessor of the documented item—depending on the cases: that is what happens with the right of control. In the electronic world in fact, this is impossible to accomplish via endorsement or simple docummental delivery, due to the lack of any material support to endorse or deliver to the transferee. These circumstances therefore require an electronic equivalent of endorsement or document delivery.
- Functional equivalence also signifies an evolution of the equally classic principle of the circulation of corporeal movable goods, according to which possession is equivalent to title. In contrast, for electronic or digitised rights, what is equivalent to title is the ownership of the right of control over them. Furthermore, all the operations of the new electronic right of control are equivalent to the classic principle of legitimisation through possession. Therefore, the transmission of electronic document control is equivalent to the transmission of possession in the world of paper documents and, consequently, of the ownership of the documented rights.
- Is the transmission of the right of control, or must it always be, an electronic operation? It is well known that the norms of ULIT—and generally national laws as well—contemplate the possibility of changing or even alternating the support

For jurisdictions where neither a statutory transaction filing or notice filing system for security interests in respect of intangible assets nor any other system establishing third-party effectiveness and priority exists, a security interest in a digital asset becomes effective against third parties once the secured creditor has gained effective control of the digital asset, that is a degree of control sufficient to prevent the security provider from independently disposing of the digital asset.

of documented rights: one can shift from a paper medium to an electronic medium and vice versa. In my opinion, if the transmission of the documented rights takes place during an electronic phase of the documentation of the right in question, the transmission must occur through the electronic exercise of the right of control, due to the pure material impossibility of making an endorsement on a paper document, as paper is non-existent in the electronic phase under consideration. A different issue arises when the transmission occurs during a phase on paper. In this case, the law of circulation of the title must be followed, and since this is a paper document in the concerned phase, the law of circulation will be that of movable goods and not the right of control.

- The recent regulations in the field establish up to three requirements for electronic documents to acquire this legal status, therefore generating the right of control for their holder and their electronic negotiability through the exercise of that right: (i) Exclusive nature—individual, joint, or several[14]—of the ability or legitimacy, one might say in functionally equivalent terms, of the controlling party regarding the exercise of their right of control over the electronically documented rights; (ii) Certainty that the holder of the right of control can prove their status as the controlling party; and (iii) Provision that the disposal of the documented rights through the exercise of the right of control extinguishes that right for the previous holder and generates it for the acquirer, the new holder of the documented right.

Obviously, what has been stated refers to the case of full and definitive disposal of the documented rights. If this is not the case, the expressed requirements will be subject to the relevant adaptations. Indeed, the blockchain, and more prosaically, cases such as the chattel mortgage or non-possessory pledge would be sufficient examples of this.

These requirements, more or less detailed depending on the relevant regulation, are generalised, and it should be understood that their establishment, without imposing any specific technology for this purpose in the instruments analysed, is a straightforward application of the principle of technological neutrality. However, in the current state of legal electronification in Europe and Spain, the fulfilment of such legal requirements implies the use of two electronic legal instruments applied throughout the European Union under its uniform regulation: the qualified electronic signature and an electronic data registry from those available in the market, whether private or public. Through the first instrument, as is well known, the will of the signatory—in this case, the controlling party wishing to exercise their right of control—is electronically manifested and acquires legal protection practically equivalent to that which would be granted by a notarial intervention, in accordance with Articles 326.3 and 4, and 319 of the Spanish Civil Procedure Act of 2000[15] (hereinafter

[14] This is a matter of crucial importance when it comes to the enabling and negotiation of documents based on blockchain technology and its peripherals. The consent of all holders within a chain of ownership will be essential to transfer the electronically documented right, divided through various ownership links. It is a different matter when the documented right is not divided into various links, which frequently occurs despite the use of the mentioned technology.

[15] Article 326.3 and 4 of the Spanish Civil Procedure Act (LEC) stipulates:

LEC). By resorting to an electronic registry, whether private or public, the requirements for mutual recognition between the controlling party and the custodian of the electronic record documenting the controlled right are satisfied, as long as the registration technology complies with EU Regulation 910/2014[16] and its subsequent amendments.

---

3. When the party interested in the effectiveness of an electronic document requests it, or its authenticity, integrity, accuracy of date and time, or other characteristics of the electronic document that a non-qualified trust service, as outlined in Regulation (EU) 910/2014 of the European Parliament and the Council, of July 23, 2014, on electronic identification and trust services for electronic transactions in the internal market, can attest, the procedure will be carried out according to the provisions of paragraph 2 of this article and Regulation (EU) No. 910/2014. 4. If a qualified trust service, as provided in the aforementioned regulation, has been used, it will be presumed that the document meets the questioned characteristic, and that the trust service has been correctly provided if, at the relevant time for the discrepancy, it appeared on the list of trusted qualified service providers. If the electronic document is still contested, the burden of proof will fall on the party challenging it. If such verifications result in a negative outcome, the costs, expenses, and fees arising from the verification will be borne exclusively by the party that made the challenge. If, in the judgment of the court, the challenge was made recklessly, a fine of 300 to 1,200 euros may be imposed. (literal translation)

[16] This refers to the previously mentioned Regulation (EU) 910/2014 of the European Parliament and the Council, of July 23, 2014, on electronic identification and trust services for electronic transactions in the internal market (DOUE L 257 of 28.8.2014). This Regulation has undergone extensive modification through Regulation (EU) 2024/1183 of the European Parliament and the Council of April 11, 2024 (DOUE L of 30.4.2024).

Definition and Holdership of Digital Assets after Two and a Half Decades of Evolution of the Notion of Control

Manuel Alba Fernández

1 Introduction: The Ascent of Digitally Created Rival Assets

Over the last decade or so, the world has witnessed the emergence and the ascent of new forms or objects of property of a digital nature. Different technologies currently enable the creation of digital assets and their use as movable or personal property, as private (as opposed to public) goods (the term "goods" used here in a broad economic sense). Transactions for the exchange of such digital assets or goods, in several senses, follow the same logic as relations for the exchange of tangible movables, as, among other things, they are based on the assumption that digital assets can actually be treated as objects of property (other than by the common perception of such assets as valuable, in one way or another). Digital goods or assets, however, do essentially consist of digital records or structured pieces of information in digital form. Rather than on their nature and their resulting defining features, societal perceptions of digital assets as items of property significantly rely also on the ability of the technology used to shape them as rival assets and to render them capable of being held and transferred or spent as such.

Solutions for the creation, holdership and transfer of rival digital assets or records have existed in the market for quite some time. The first manifestations of this

This work was financed within the framework of the Prometeo 2023 project of the Regional Ministry of Innovation, Universities, Science and Digital Society (CIPROM/2022/26) "Present and future of the regulation of cryptoassets in the EU [LegalCripto]", whose principal investigator is Carmen Pastor Sempere. The basic ideas contained herein were presented in the author's paper with the same title, given on November 13, 2024 at the IV International Congress on "UNIDROIT Principles on Digital Assets and Private Law: Context, Content, Perspectives", organized also by BAES Research Group of the University of Alicante on November 13 and 14, 2024.

This chapter has been written in the framework of the research project "*Adaptación del Derecho español para la adquisición, transmisión, gravamen y ejecución de activos digitales en los negocios*", funded by the Spanish Ministry of Science, Innovation and Universities (ref. PID2023-149583OB-C21).

M. Alba Fernández (✉)
Carlos III University of Madrid, Madrid, Spain

C. Pastor Sempere and D. A. Morán Bovio (eds.), UNIDROIT *Principles on Digital Assets and Private Law*, Law, Governance and Technology Series 80,
https://doi.org/10.1007/978-3-032-11001-5_4

phenomenon appeared in the 90's in the form of digital records issued as transferable or negotiable instruments or documents, aimed to serve as the digital replica of paper-based equivalents. Namely, and digitally annotated securities aside, practice in some sectors (occasionally also guided by specific legislation) started to show interest in the possibility of issuing payment instruments (such as promissory notes) or documents of title (such as warehouse receipts or bills of lading) in digital form. The attractiveness of this possibility was due to the potential advantages that electronic communications clearly had when compared to paper in terms of time, cost and security. Thus, the main ambition at that time was to migrate paper-based processes to the digital space, to more or less replicate the same transactional structures but under enhanced conditions.

The advent of DLT and blockchain-based technologies, along with other subsequent factors, precipitated the expansion and massive spread of digital assets issued as crypto-tokens. Because of their greater versatility and interoperability, alleged fewer vulnerabilities, easier access and increased network dynamics,[1] DLT-based solutions for the creation of digital tokens after a certain moment in time, rapidly surpassed preexisting technologies that, for these and other purposes, were based on centralized platforms, registries and environments. As a matter of fact, DLT and blockchain were originally created to hold and transfer bitcoins.

Among other things, this technological shift entailed a remarkable change in how digital assets or records used and traded as digital objects of property started to be created. Since their emergence, far from only following any previous typification found in practice or in the law, most digital tokens have been issued as pure representations of value, like (crypto-coins or the crypto-currencies), as creations, or as the purported representation (the "tokenization") of some specified underlying asset (whether a personal right, a property right on another tangible or intangible asset, or maybe both).[2] Most of these assets, in any case, are endemic of the digital space, without known precedents in previous reality.

Solutions based on DLT and blockchain technology allow the rapid creation of different types of crypto-assets that, while sharing the same digital nature and much of their technological basis, do otherwise have important differences. Many of them are defined, and in several aspects profiled, by the business model they aim to serve, as well as by the resulting technological and transactional context in which they are used; which explains their particularities in terms of content and negotiation. The increasing spontaneous diversity of digital assets that DLT solutions sparked has completely overwhelmed the capacity of the law to fully accommodate all these new categories of digitally created property (or to somehow establish the rules for their creation and use, as it largely did in the initial phase involving negotiable documents or instruments).

---

[1] Reyes (2016), p. 197–199.

[2] Hughes (2020), p. 35

The significant and worrying gap between reality and the law, as well as the problems that in dribs and drabs began to reach the courts, triggered some reactions both in courts and in academic and institutional fora. In our view, one of the most interesting developments is the UNIDROIT Principles on Private Law and Digital Assets.[3]

2 Digital Assets as Property

The most important issue, and the first to be aired, in the context above was whether digital assets can be considered property, or if they can be the subject of property rights under existing law. Of course, by the time this matter started to be litigated or discussed, it was clear, as previously stated, that practice did indeed treat crypto-assets as property (whether wisely and realistically or not). Part of the debate centred on whether the law is in a situation to be able to address expectations in the relevant markets and the parties concerned. This question needs to be answered under each national law, particularly looking at the different categories or types of property acknowledged and conceptualized in legal rules, and the resulting property rights and legal remedies recognized for each of them.[4] Several courts have had no qualms about recognizing crypto-coins as property for varying purposes. Solutions along these lines show varying scenarios and goals. Some of them may have been conditioned by the limited scope and instrumentality of decisions to be made.[5] Several of them, however, reach quite fundamental conclusions to fit tokens into the notion of property,[6] or to exclude them therefrom.[7] In academic literature, and far from the urgency that to some extent may push court proceedings, there have been proposals to create a new legal category or form of property for digital assets,[8] and possibly build some specific rules on property rights upon that idea to adapt to digital assets.

[3] UNIDROIT Principles on Digital Assets and Private Law (available at https://www.unidroit.org/wp-content/uploads/2024/01/Principles-on-Digital-Assets-and-Private-Law-linked-1.pdf, las visited on January 2025; hereinafter, Principles or UNIDROIT Principles.

[4] See, *e.g.*, Stevens (2023), p. 9–11, 18–19; in a comparative approach and discussion, see Low and Hara (2022), p. 3–10.

[5] *AA v Persons Unknown* [2019] EWHC 3556, pars. [59]–[63] Comm.; *Ion Science Ltd v Persons Unknown* EWHC, 21 December 2020, par. [11]; *Fetch.AI Ltd v Persons Unknown Category A* [2021] EWHC 2254 Comm, Par. [9], [14]; *Wang v Darby* [2021] EWHC 3054 Comm, pars. 55–56; *CLM v CLN* [2022] SGHC 46. These decisions were prompted by requests to obtain property injunctions and/or freezing orders.

[6] Besides some of the decisions referred to in the previous note, see Ruscoe v Cryptopia Ltd. (in liq) [2020] NZHC 728.

[7] Tokyo District Court Judgement of 5 August 2015, *Z1 v MTGox/Dobayashi Nobuaki* (English translation accessed in https://www.law.ox.ac.uk/sites/default/files/migrated/mtgox_judgment_final.pdf, last visit in January 2025), sect. III (Decision).

[8] Low and Hara (2022), p. 8–10.

This is the policy that the Principles and other instruments, such as Article 12 of the US Uniform Commercial Code,[9] seem to respond to. As we will restate in this chapter, and as explained in greater detail in other chapters of this book, the UNIDROIT Principles make, in our view, two potentially important contributions in order to build a framework for property rights on rival or private digital assets. First, they create and define digital assets as a specific category or form of property.[10] And second, rather than providing for substantive or material rules on ownership of other rights (which they do on a very exceptional basis), they build a holdership system for digital assets that is meant to serve as the scaffold for their legal framework as incorporeal personal or movable property, and particularly for the allocation of rights *in rem* upon them.[11]

In the Principles, the notion that capitalizes practically all the prominence in these two objectives is the notion of control. The idea of control of digital records or tokens as a condition to consider them property has been loosely used in some court decisions. The same notion, or at least notions designated with this same term, have been used in the past in other instruments, and for other specific types of assets or records, but with the same functions and purposes. Namely, and even with their largely paper-based mentality, the rules that addressed electronic transferable or negotiable documents also made a relevant contribution to conceptualize how digital records, as documentary intangibles now based on digitally recorded information, could be used as rival assets, much like paper (tangible) documents did thanks to possession.

In its different formulations, the notion of control has been repeatedly devised as the digital replica or equivalent of possession in the digital space; that is, to provide for the same functions and effects as possession. Its definition in legal rules, possibly for this very reason, has always been annoyingly elusive, always burdened by the question of how control should mimic possession. Despite such difficulties and after years of slow evolution, control has become not just the basic condition for their holdership, but the main element that defines digital assets and records as rival digital goods susceptible to being subject to property rights. The Principles are not the first instrument to reflect this approach, however, like other later initiatives and unlike previous rules based on control, the scheme is based on an express statement that digital assets are such because, and only if, they can be subject to control. In the Principles, like in other rules, control consequently somehow accumulates all the attributes or characteristics, as gradually achieved and revealed by technology, that allow digital assets or records to become objects of property rights: their capability to be identified as singular objects or singular structured pieces of information, the

---

[9] As of the 2022 of the amendments to the Uniform Commercial Code (hereinafter UCC), available at https://www.uniformlaws.org/committees/community-home/librarydocuments?communitykey=1457c422-ddb7-40b0-8c76-39a1991651ac&LibraryFolderKey=&DefaultView=&5a583082-7c67-452b-9777-e4bdf7e1c729=eyJsaWJyYXJ5ZW50cnkiOm51bGx9 (last visit on January 2025).

[10] UNIDROIT Principles Comments 0.13, 2.20; Principle 3, par. (1) and Comments 3.1 and 3.2

[11] UNIDROIT Principles Comment 0.10 to the Introduction, Comments 1.1 and 1.2 to Principle 1, Comment 2.26 to Principle 2, Principle 3, par. (3) and Comment 3.9.

possibility they provide (also for third parties) to identify their holder to the exclusion of others, and their ability to be spent or transferred as rival or private intangible goods or assets.

The process that the definition of control has undergone to reach this status, as part of the essence of digital rival property (at least in these rules), can be better perceived, in our view, by looking to the instruments that, over time and within their specific scope, have relied on this notion to try to identify how they combine the different elements that define digital assets. This will be the focus of the rest of this chapter.

3 Early Legislation on Electronic Negotiable Instruments or Documents in the US

Uniform rules, as well as federal and State law in the US pioneered the efforts to enable the issuance of negotiable payment instruments or documents of title in electronic form, thereby facing the need to reformulate a framework to transfer rights for digital records that had been originally built on the basis of possession as a condition for holdership of paper documents. Several rules were gradually drafted to address the needs or desires of different industries that relied, for instance, on the use of promissory notes as collateralized debt backing mortgages, on chattel paper, or on warehouse receipts used as collateral in secured trade finance.[12] For payment instruments, these rules included the Electronic Signatures in National and Global Commerce Act[13] and the Uniform Electronic Transactions Act of 1999.[14] Article 9 of the UCC[15] likewise enabled chattel paper issued in electronic form, while Article 7[16] addressed the use of electronic documents of title.

The approach taken in all these rules was largely the same, specifically in two aspects that concern us here. First, seemingly following the principle of functional equivalence as also applied in international uniform law instruments, media neutrality was ensured by explicitly allowing the issuance of the written documents above,

[12] Newell and Gordon (1994–1995), p. 821 ff.; Fry and Newell (2006–2007), p. 308 ff.

[13] 15 U.S. Code §§ 7001–7031.

[14] Hereinafter UETA (which however did also refer to documents of title)–available at https://www.uniformlaws.org/viewdocument/final-act-21?CommunityKey=2c04b76c-2b7d-4399-977e-d5876ba7e034&tab=librarydocuments (last visit in January 2025).

[15] Article 9 (Secured Transactions) UCC Rev. 1998, 2010 and 2022, https://www.uniformlaws.org/committees/community-home/librarydocuments?communitykey=6317f73b-badb-47b2-8a5a-58ee62032ba1&LibraryFolderKey=&DefaultView=&5a583082-7c67-452b-9777-e4bdf7e1c729=eyJsaWJyYXJ5ZW50cnkiOm51bGx9 (last visit in December 2024).

[16] Article 7 (Documents of Title) UCC Rev. 2004 and 2022, available at https://www.uniformlaws.org/committees/community-home/librarydocuments?communitykey=9893636e-0046-498a-8ed9-3d57c192489a&LibraryFolderKey=&DefaultView=&5a583082-7c67-452b-9777-e4bdf7e1c729=eyJsaWJyYXJ5ZW50cnkiOm51bGx9 (last visit on December 2024).

not only in paper, but also in electronic form (i.e., as electronic records).[17] And second, holdership of, and title or rights to such documents (with the ensuing effects), was made dependent on possession (and endorsement, where applicable), for paper documents, and on control for electronic documents or records.[18]

Control was and is defined in these provisions so as to require that any technology used for the issuance and negotiation of negotiable records, in order to gain legal effect, should actually perform the same relevant functions that possession of a written document does; to reliably identify a person as the holder or, additionally, as the person with rights or title to the record.[19] For instance, § 16(b) UETA states that "(a) person has control of a transferable record if a system employed for evidencing the transfer of interests in the transferable record reliably establishes that person as the person to which the transferable record was issued or transferred".[20] This general principle is meant to be technologically neutral; as long as the required result is achieved, any technology may meet the test.[21]

Specifically bearing in mind that transactions in the digital space essentially depend on information (not benefiting from the concept of possession), the key element of the rule is whether the relevant information, on the basis of the technology used, can be deemed to reliably identify a person as the holder. In the text of these instruments, the threshold of reliability remains open and largely left to the market. Rather than providing further guidance as to its particular meaning, since their inception US legal rules included a safe harbour test, setting certain specific conditions, which, when met, are deemed sufficient to prove control of an electronic record. Some of those conditions do somehow recreate a situation akin to the one created through possession of a written paper identifiable as an original negotiable document. For instance, going back to § 16 UETA, its par (c) requires that a "single authoritative copy" of the record (that is "unique") can be identified and readily distinguishable from any copies, and that such authoritative copy, first, identifies the person in control as the holder, second, "is communicated to and maintained by" the identified holder or its designated custodian and, third, can only be changed in its contents (particularly those that identify a new transferee) with the consent of the person identified as the holder.[22]

---

[17] 15 U.S. Code §§ 7006 and 7021(a); § 2(5), (7), (13) UETA; § 9–102(11), (31), (70) Article 9 UCC.

[18] 15 U.S. Code § 7021(d) to (f); § 16(a) and (d) to (f) UETA; § 1–201(21); § 9–203(a) and (b) (3) (D) Article 9 UCC (on attachment and enforceability of a security interest on electronic chattel paper).

[19] See remarks in Rogers (1985), p. 202–204; Green (2008), p. 116; Gabriel (2024), p. 257–258.

[20] See, e.g., official Comment to § 16 UETA, par. 3, 8. Provisions with substantially the same contents are found in 15 U.S. Code § 7021(b); § 7–106(a) Article 7 UCC, § 9–105(a) Article 9 UCC.

[21] Gabriel (2024), p. 260; Dubovec, M. (2022), p. 274.

[22] The full wording of this section reads:

"(c) A system satisfies subsection (b), and a person is deemed to have control of a transferable record, if the transferable record is created, stored, and assigned in such a manner that:

When these provisions were drafted, issuance and transfer of negotiable documents or transferable records relied on third-party services, based on centralized platforms for multilateral communications in a closed digital environment (i.e., with access restricted to previously identified users). On the basis of this architecture, the information in these systems was structured or presented as a "title registry", where the records could be identified and verified as original writings (as the "single authoritative" copies) and holders could be likewise identified, or alternatively as "e-vault" systems, where the record was stored in a secure digital repository, thereby allowing identification of the record as a single or "unique" original that identified a person as the holder (these being frequently described at that time as the so-called "token systems").[23] These two technologically different alternatives did support the provision of the same service. In these cases therefore, issuance, holdership and user to user transfer of a transferable or negotiable record (which was essentially achieved through the identification of a new person as the transferee and new holder) was intermediated by a service provider. The main value of the service precisely focused on providing users with reliable technological means to ensure the proper verification of all relevant information, including the identification of the person in control. The provisions in the US Uniform Commercial Code were subsequently amended and once again more recently with the basic purpose to better embrace DLT technologies. Namely, a second safe harbour test was included in the 2022 amendments. We shall discuss this development further in another section later on, as it has to be framed in the rationale inspired by tokenization.

---

1. a single authoritative copy of the transferable record exists which is unique, identifiable, and, except as otherwise provided in paragraphs (4), (5), and (6), unalterable;
2. the authoritative copy identifies the person asserting control as:

(A) the person to which the transferable record was issued; or
(B) if the authoritative copy indicates that the transferable record has been transferred, the person to which the transferable record was most recently transferred;

3. the authoritative copy is communicated to and maintained by the person asserting control or its designated custodian;
4. copies or revisions that add or change an identified assignee of the authoritative copy can be made only with the consent of the person asserting control;
5. each copy of the authoritative copy and any copy of a copy is readily identifiable as a copy that is not the authoritative copy; and
6. any revision of the authoritative copy is readily identifiable as authorized or unauthorized."

Along the same lines, see 15 U.S. Code § 7021(c); § 7–106(b) Article 7 UCC, § 9–105(b) Article 9 UCC (this latter provision refers to a "single authoritative copy" of the record evidencing chattel paper).

[23] See ABA Cyberspace Committee Working Group on Transferable Records (2003–2004), 385 ff.

4 Uniform Law Instruments on Transferable Records and Negotiable Transport Documents

The notion of control reflected in US legal rules subsequently proved to have a notable influence on several instruments also addressing transferable or negotiable documents produced by the United Nations Commission on International Trade law.[24] There are currently four UNCITRAL instruments[25] that include provisions based on control, either as a condition for holdership of an electronic transferable or negotiable record, or as an equivalent to possession for the same purposes (this depending on the specific scope and formulation of each of them).

This trend in UNCITRAL instruments was inaugurated by the 2008 UN Convention on Contracts for the International Carriage of Goods Wholly or Partly by Sea; known as the Rotterdam Rules.[26] One of the priorities of this Convention is to achieve media neutrality in the context of contracts for the carriage of goods, among other things, by addressing and recognizing effects of electronic transport records, including the ones issued in negotiable form. This possibility had also long been demanded in the shipping sector in the years prior to their negotiation. Soon after the Rotterdam Rules were approved and opened to signature by States, UNCITRAL started the work that resulted in the adoption of the 2017 Model Law on Electronic Transferable Records.[27] The scope and purpose of the MLETR is partly the same as the that of the Rotterdam Rules with regard to negotiable electronic documents, but its wording and contents are very much conditioned, firstly, by its formulation as a model law and, second, by its specific aim to complement and update preexisting paper-based law on transferable documents. Like other UNCITRAL instruments on electronic commerce, although more visibly, the MLETR is guided by media and technology neutrality, as well as by functional equivalence (i.e., the aim to give legal recognition and effects to digital means and records to the same extent as paper ones, provided they achieve or perform the same relevant functions).[28] More recently, UNCITRAL also adopted a Model Law on Warehouse Receipts that does address

---

[24] Hereinafter UNCITRAL.

[25] The most recent one is the Convention on Negotiable Cargo Documents, approved by the UN General Assembly on December 2025 (see UN A/RES/80/162, available at https://uncitral.un.org/en/ncdconvention, last visited on December 2025).

[26] See General Assembly Resolution 63/122, 2 February 2009 (Doc. UN A/RES/63/122, available at https://uncitral.un.org/en/texts/transportgoods/conventions/rotterdam_rules, last visited on January 2025), hereinafter Rotterdam Rules or RR.

[27] General Assembly Resolution 72/114, 18 December 2017 (Doc. UN A/RES/72/114); available at https://uncitral.un.org/en/texts/ecommerce/modellaw/electronic_transferable_records (last visit on January 2025); hereinafter MLETR.

[28] The Rotterdam Rules provide for a legal scheme that addresses the issuance of negotiable transport documents and of negotiable electronic transport records with the same effects. In so doing, as stated above, they apply, among others, the idea of functional equivalence, but they lay down specific rules for each medium (for paper documents and for electronic records) in parallel. Negotiable documents and records are defined on the basis of the evidentiary functions and effects that these types of documents perform in practice as written documents or records (also reflected in many national laws). The Convention thereby captures in the definitions maritime bills of lading issued to order

paper and electronic warehouse receipts, likewise in a media and technology neutral way, also based on functional equivalence.[29]

These three instruments show a clearly parallel approach to electronic transferable or negotiable records or documents. Firstly, for instance, just as was implied in the US provisions, their rules are based on the assumption that the parties involved in the issuance, use and transfer of negotiable or transferable records (as is the case with digital assets in general) need to reach a minimum agreement on the technology, the procedures or the method that will be used to perform all the actions that define their lifecycle: issuance, holdership, transfer and redemption or extinction of the record as a negotiable instrument.[30] In different ways, therefore, conditions for the validity or effect of the record are laid down as functions that the method or technology agreed upon and used must (reliably) perform.

One important idea that the Rotterdam Rules expressly formulated (which, we think, was also implied in the US approach to control) is that, to qualify and have effect as a negotiable electronic transport document, the technology and procedures used for its creation and issuance must ensure that the record remains subject to control "from its creation until it ceases to have any effect or validity".[31] In the Convention, and subsequently in the Model Laws above, besides being a condition for holdership of such records, control is rendered an element that also forms part

or to bearer (although the bearer clause has become quite rare in practice)–see Art. 1, definitions in pars. 14, 15, 18 and 19 RR (Sturley, Fujita, Van der Ziel (2010), pars. 7.002 ff). Provisions based on the same rationale can be found in Arts. 2, 8, 9 and 10, par. 1(a) MLETR.

[29] The text finally approved has not been officially released yet, but the draft submitted to the Commission's plenary (Doc. UN A/CN.9/1182) is available at https://uncitral.un.org/en/commis sion (last visit in December 2024). References will be done to this text, hereinafter MLWR; see Arts. 2, 6 and 32 MLWR

[30] The Rotterdam Rules expressly require in Art. 9 that the use of a negotiable electronic transport record is subject to "procedures" that provide for the method or the manner in which different actions are performed. These include, first, its issuance in the conditions required by the Convention (including the signature by the carrier), second, its holdership (i.e., the manner in which the holder can prove that it has control of the record) as well as, third, how the record is redeemed and extinguished as a negotiable record (all steps that are based on transfer of possession or surrender of the document when issued in paper) –Arts. 9 and 38 RR. The MLETR and the MLWR reflect this approach by requiring that a "reliable method" is used to satisfy each of the conditions laid down for the validity and effects of an electronic transferable record (Arts. 9 to 11, 13, and 16 MLETR, Art. 6 MLWR).

[31] When it comes to negotiable electronic transport records, the Convention defines in the first place "electronic communication" as "information generated, sent, received or stored by electronic, optical, digital or similar means with the result that the information communicated is accessible so as to be usable for subsequent reference" (Art. 1, pars. 17 and 18 RR). Electronic transport records, as writings, are therefore also defined as "information (…) issued by electronic communication (…)". However, Art. 1, par. 21 defines "issuance" of a negotiable electronic transport record as "the issuance of the record in accordance with procedures that ensure that the record is subject to exclusive control from its creation until it ceases to have any effect of validity". Control of the record, therefore, is also a condition for the valid issuance of a record as a negotiable one.

of the definition of transferable or negotiable records, and a condition for their legal effects as such.[32]

The MLETR also expressly formulates another important principle that has occasionally been applied to recognise digital assets as property under national laws. Art. 10, par. 1(b)(i) MLETR requires that, in order to have effects as a transferable electronic record, the method or technology used for its issuance must reliably "identify *that* electronic record as *the* electronic transferable record" (emphasis added). The formulation of this principle proved to be somehow controversial. Namely, it was initially, and to some extent, guided by the rule that for paper documents it requires that a single original document is issued, as a way to ensure that only one holder can be identified through possession and, consequently, the issuer or the obligor is obliged only to perform the underlying obligation once; it being released if proper performance is fulfilled with regard to the (one) holder.[33] This principle, so essentially linked to the tangible nature of paper documents and to possession of a single original, at a fairly early stage proved to be at odds with how information and records in digital or electronic form serve transactions and contractual relations.

By the time negotiating and drafting of the MLETR began, DLT and blockchain were already around, where multiple copies of structured pieces of (otherwise) original information are equally relevant in the consensus mechanisms that are applied, precisely to verify the integrity and authenticity of the information (that is, its original character), including the identification of cypto-tokens and their holders.[34] Furthermore, previously existing registry systems also relied on the use of multiple copies of the record for security reasons (that is, to ensure reliability of the system and the solutions employed), and via those means they were able to provide for an electronic record identified as original at each point in time when needed, with the legally relevant information.[35] As finally reflected in the aforementioned rule, and also closely linked to the notion of control, the principle essentially requires that an electronic record can be identified as a singular structured piece of information that can be reliably distinguished or recognized as the transferable record. There are different ways to do this in practice. In DLT based solutions as part of a blockchain, for instance, this is achieved by designating a unique identifier to every record comprising a token (e.g., each coin or fraction thereof).[36] A key condition, for this and other requirements, is that the technology ensures and allows verifying the integrity and authenticity of

---

[32] Arts. 2 and 10, par. 1(b) (ii) MLETR, the latter of which requires that, to qualify and have effect as an electronic transferable record, the method used for its issuance and transfer must "render that electronic record capable of being subject to control from its creation until it ceases to have any effect or validity". See Art. 6, par. 1(b) MLWR.

[33] Rogers (1985), p. 205.

[34] See Fairfield (2015), p. 821–822; Reyes (2016), p. 197–198.

[35] What in the US provisions is referred to as the "authoritative copy"-ABA Cyberspace Committee Wording Group on Transferable Records (2003–2004), p. 386 ff.

[36] See UNECE–UN/CEFACT, *White Paper Transfer of Model Law on Electronic Transferable Records Compliant Titles*, September 2023, 10–11-available at https://unece.org/sites/default/files/2023-09/WhitePaper_Transfer-MLETR.pdf, last visit on January 2025).

all information recorded in the transferable record, as such information is the basic element that enables, among other things, individualization.

The Rotterdam Rules refrained from defining control. The idea that to some extent underlies their contents and the use they make of this notion is that a person proves control when the procedures agreed upon by the parties reliably identify such person as the holder of a negotiable electronic transport record; reflecting the approach in previous US rules. The difficulties found when trying to find a sufficiently clear definition were the main obstacle to reach a consensus on this issue. On the other hand, it was felt that practice would clarify how control would be achieved (as it did for these and other types of records).[37] In this Convention, for a person to qualify as the holder, he must be able to provide proof of control of the record. On these grounds, the transfer of a negotiable electronic transport record requires the transfer of control by the transferor to the transferee, as the equivalent to endorsement and delivery of a paper document[38] (given that in digital records both are done by identifying the transferee as the new holder).

The role and relevance of control is essentially the same in the schemes of the MLETR and the MLWR; i.e., it is a condition for a person to become the holder, and transfer of control is required to transfer the record or receipt.[39] In terms of the precise contents and implications, the MLETR subtly reduces the scope of the notion to strictly shape it as the equivalent to possession, thereby also expressly requiring an endorsement for the transfer of records issued to order.[40] We believe that the result of this approach in its practical application is no different from the one under US rules or the Rotterdam Rules. The MLETR and the MLWR, however, do make an attempt to define what control is. Art. 11 MLETR, for instance, states that for control to be achieved, the method and technology used must reliably establish exclusive control of the record by a person, as well as reliably identify that person as the person in control.[41] The circularity of this definition, subsequently taken by the MLWR also, is a good reflection of how difficult conceptualizing the notion of control becomes if we remain too attached to the idea of possession. The room for manoeuvre of the wording in the MLETR was also limited in this sense by the aim to draft it as a pure enabler based on functional equivalence. This provision essentially says that a person has control when it is reliably identified as the person in control because the drafters preferred to avoid the use of the term holder in order

[37] See again Art. 9, par. 1(b) RR.

[38] Arts. 47, par. 1(a) (ii), and 57, par. 2 RR. See also along these lines Art. 15, par. 2 MLWR.

[39] Art. 11, par. 1, in its chapeau and par. 2 MLETR.

[40] Art. 15 MLETR.

[41] Par. 1 of this provision reads:

"Where the law requires or permits the possession of a transferable document or instrument, that requirement is met with respect to an electronic transferable record if a reliable method is used:

(a) To establish exclusive control of that electronic transferable record by a person; and
(b) To identify that person as the person in control."

A parallel wording is used in Art. 6, par. 3 MLWR.

to eliminate the risk of moving into substantive law issues.[42] That being said, in our view, these instruments, as well as the definitions they include, have the virtue to be loyal to, and consistent with existing technologies and solutions in practice, which focus on reliably identifying a person as the holder to allow users to achieve and prove control of an electronic transferable record. Likewise, one of the key salient features of these instruments is that, for all purposes addressed (i.e., identification of a record as the transferable record, signature and identification of an issuer or obligor, identification of a person with exclusive control), the method and technology used must be sufficiently reliable and (likewise reliably) ensure the integrity of all relevant information. The precise threshold of reliability is also left partly open in this case and remains in the hands of the market, and must therefore be assessed in light of the concurring circumstances, unless the information at issue is proven in fact to be authentic or the required conditions are proven in fact to have been met. The text of these instruments provides an open list of relevant factors for the assessment of reliability.[43]

5 Control in the Principles and in Article 12 of the Uniform Commercial Code

Article 12 of the United States UCC and the Principles account for a significant breakthrough with regard to the scope of legal rules addressing digital records or assets as objects of property rights. Rather than on a specific type of records (whether present in preexisting law or not), their focus and principal aim is to create a holdership system applicable to digital rival assets, as the basis for a framework on ownership and other rights *in rem* upon them. As previously stated, digital assets in this specific context are widely defined as electronic records that can be subject to control. Along with their digital form, control is therefore the defining element of digital assets as a new type of property.[44]

[42] Like possession, the term holder and such condition in some legal systems have purely formal meaning and contents, even though holdership of a negotiable document may have substantial or material legal effects and implications (e.g., being entitled to claim performance, or qualifying as a due course, good faith or innocent purchaser, or entitling the obligor to properly perform its obligations and be released thereof). In other legal systems, possession or holdership may be characterized and treated as a right *in rem* (see Goode (2010), p. 28–29, 45–47; see also comments in Goldby (2023), p. 7–8).

[43] Art. 12 MLETR (entitled "General reliability standard"); Art. 7 MLWR.

[44] See definitions in Principle 2(1) and (2); as well as §12–102(a) (1) Article 12, UCC, which defines a "controllable electronic record" as "a record stored in an electronic medium that can be subjected to control (…)". Article 12 includes also provisions on "controllable accounts" and "controllable payment intangibles", which are generally defined as rights to payment (accounts and payment intangibles) evidenced by a controllable electronic record (§ 9–102(a) (27A) and (27B), Article 9 UCC). Holdership of all such records is also based on the notion of control (§ 12–105, Article 12). Both Article 12 and the Principles conceive digital assets or controllable electronic records, as respectively defined by each of them, as a subset, both, of digital or electronic records and of

The notion of control in these two instruments is built in a rather more sophisticated way as compared to the definitions found in the previous instruments. Control is also envisaged as a notion and a question of fact (and evidence) to serve as the basis of holdership of digital assets.[45] The Principles and Article 12, however, require two different conditions to meet the test of control. The Principles, in particular for instance, on the one hand require that the digital asset or record or the system used gives a person, first, the exclusive ability to prevent others from obtaining substantially all the benefit from the digital asset; second, the ability to obtain all of the benefit from the record or asset; and third, the exclusive ability to transfer these abilities, as well as the exclusive ability to transfer them, to another person. The second element or condition is that the digital asset or the system used allows such person to identify itself as having all three abilities.[46]

---

digital assets, which are precisely distinguishable by reason of their being capable to be subject to control (see Comment 0.11 to the Introduction, Principle 2, pars. (1) and (2), and Comments 2.1 and 2.3, Principle 3, par. (1), and Principle 14, par. (1); Prefatory Note to Article 12, comment 2, *Uniform Commercial Code Amendments (2022)*, Uniform Law Commission & American Law Institute (June 1, 2023), 230 ff.).

[45] Like the MLETR, both instruments also avoid the use of the term "holder", and refer to the person with control instead, to use a more neutral term with regard to digital assets in general–see Principle 2(5), Principle 3(3) and Principle 9, and compare with Principle 6(1), Principle 8(1) to (3) and Principle 15. The commentary to the Principles does occasionally refer to the holder of a digital asset or token, apparently referring to the person in control thereof –see Comments 4.2, 4.6 or 4.13 to 4.32 and illustrations therein–, and the working or *preparatoire* documents show that the meaning and appropriateness of the term holder in this context –as the person in control of a digital asset– was considered and discussed–*Digital Assets and Private Law Working Group*, Study LXXXII–W.G.2–Doc. 2 (rev. 1), par. 95; Study LXXXII–W.G.2–Doc. 3, par. 17.

[46] Principle 6(1). With a parallel structure and contents, but using the term "power" instead of "ability", the wording of §12–105 Article 12, UCC, reads:

"A person has control of a controllable electronic record if the electronic record, a record attached to or logically associated with the electronic record, or a system in which the electronic record is recorded:

1. gives the person:

(A) power to avail itself of substantially all the benefit from the electronic record; and
(B) exclusive power, subject to subsection (b), to:

(i) prevent others from availing themselves of substantially all the benefit from the electronic record; and
(ii) transfer control of the electronic record to another person or cause another person to obtain control of another controllable electronic record as a result of the transfer of the electronic record; and

2. enables the person readily to identify itself in any way, including by name, identifying number, cryptographic key, office, or account number, as having the powers specified in paragraph (1)."

Rules based on this wording have been also introduced in Article 7 (§ 7–105, par. (c)) for documents of title, and Article 9 (§ 9–105, par. (c)) for electronic chattel paper. However, there is an important difference between the provisions in Articles 7 and 9 as compared to Article 12 UCC. Namely, pars. (c) of the provisions in Articles 7 and 9, relating respectively to documents of title and electronic chattel paper, do provide for a second and alternative safe harbor test (besides the one referred to

With few exceptions, the Principles, as is the case of Article 12, do not provide for material or substantive rules addressing the creation, transfer or acquisition of rights on digital assets, which they are meant to complement, but instead refer to the rules on ownership or other property rights.[47] They do, however, expressly proclaim that such rules can apply to digital assets.[48] Further, they also conceive control, and a "change of control" or a transfer of control of the electronic record,[49] as a condition or possible way to acquire, confer or transfer ownership or other proprietary rights,[50] including perfection, third party effectiveness, and priority of a security interest.[51]

---

supra note 22 and accompanying text) to comply with the general standard relating to the reliable identification of the person in control in pars. (a) of § 7–105 and § 9–105. The test in letters (c) is laid down as an apparently stricter threshold, as the Official Comment clarifies that the preexisting test is kept to continue providing certainty to systems developed thereunder, and that systems complying with the new test are likely to comply with the old one (it is not clear whether this would work the other way around - par. 6 of the Official Comment to § 7–106, Article 7, and par. 4 of the Official Comment to § 9–105, Article 9 UCC). Also, letters (c) in § 7–105 and § 9–105 do expressly refer to systems based on the use and identification of "one or more authoritative copies", whereas letters (b) focus on systems based on a "single authoritative copy" of the document or record, thereby revealing to some extent how the new safe harbor test has been introduced in an attempt to embrace DLTs (intended to be however formulated in a technology neutral way).

[47] See Principle 2(4), Principle 3(3), Principle (4), as well as Comments 0.10, 1.1, 1.2, 2.26, 3.3, 3.8, 3.9, 4.1.

[48] Principle 3(1); see also Principle 1 and Comments 0.13, 2.20, 3.1.

[49] Both instruments expressly qualify as a transfer or change of control, from a person to another, the actions resulting from systems and protocols whereby such transfer is done by "burning" o cancelling a record and creating an equivalent ("derivative") new record to give control upon it to the transferee (Principle 6(2), Comment 6.8; see also Comment 4 to § 12–104 and Comment 6 to § 12–105 Article 12, UCC). This being said, there is a noticeable difference between the Principles and Article 12. Principle 6(2) defines a change of control as "a transfer of the abilities in sub-paragraph (1) (a)" -the abilities listed above-, without expressly requiring also a change in the identification of the person having those abilities under paragraph 1(b) of this Principle. Article 12, and particularly § 12–105 and related provisions, seem to conceive a transfer of control as the transfer of all powers needed, as well as the change of the person identified as having such powers (the person identified as the one with control). It is not clear what is the precise intention of the wording used to define a change of control may be in the Principles, but we wonder whether it will make a difference in their practical application; control will require for any transferee to also meet the condition laid down in paragraph 1(b) of Principle 6.

[50] For instance, the rules in § 12–104(d) and (e), Article 12, UCC, address the substantive effects of the transfer of a controllable electronic record to a "qualifying purchaser" (on the basis of which the comments do also refer to controllable electronic records as "negotiable" property –Official Comment 3 of the Prefatory Note to Article 12, Comment 10 to § 12–104, Comment 1 to § 12–105). Likewise, the Principles include in Principle 8 rules for the acquisition of rights by an innocent purchaser or acquirer, which (other than the additional conditions that the law may foresee) require the change and obtention of control by the acquirer for their application –see also Principle 2(5), Comments 2.23, 6.5.

[51] Principles 15 and 16, see also Comments 0.16 and 6.4; § 9–326A, Article 9, UCC ("(a) security interest in a controllable account, controllable electronic record, or controllable payment intangible held by a secured party having control of the account, electronic record, or payment intangible has priority over a conflicting security interest held by a secured party that does not have control")–see also Comment 1 to § 12–105. These rules parallel those that grant security interests perfected by the transfer of possession priority over any other interests based on other actions or means

The most noticeable difference between previous notions or conceptions of control and the ones devised for digital assets or controllable records is how the latter strongly rely on the abilities or powers that a person must have and be able to prove in order to achieve and prove control. As a question of fact (rather than of law),[52] and without prejudice to its possible legal consequences or effects, this aspect of control seems to outline a situation to some extent akin to possession (as it is also perceived in technologies used to create and trade with digital assets) to precisely give it the same role.[53] Strict dependence on these abilities may actually create difficulties to establish control upon digital records, given that their creation, holdership and transfer is by definition intermediated. In some cases, and at the very least, by services to simply access a network (and their providers), and by technology (even if possibly non-proprietary and publicly accessible). In other cases, this could also be through other services or solutions and their providers (including those solutions or services built upon permissioned or non-permissioned DLT networks). Some digital assets (crypto-tokens) are used with different layers of service and technological intermediation and with varying degrees of abilities and/or rights linked to holdership or control,[54] and yet the identification of the holder or person in control may be nevertheless established and accepted, for instance, upon the link created between an asset and such person's personal address or other identification means. Both the Principles and Article 12 seem to be very much aware of this fact, which is why they also include elements apparently aimed to set the precise perimeter of control in light of existing realities. First, for instance, they refer to the ability or the power of the person in control to "substantially" obtain all the benefit from the asset or record (and prevent others from so doing). Second, they also aim to include within control some situations where the abilities required depend on certain technology (are possibly achieved in an intermediated way) and where the abilities of the person in control may be consequently limited by the system or protocol used.[55] Finally, such abilities must also be combined with the identification of the person in control. To overcome evidentiary difficulties, as well as perhaps to protect market expectations, the Principles also rely on the identification of the person in control as such, i.e., as having

(e.g., registration or notice filling)–which is deemed consistent with practice followed in markets for some tokens, Tu (2018–I), p. 553, 563, 568–569; *Id.* (2018–II), p. 231; Johnson et al. (2018), p. 138, 149–150.

[52] In the Principles, see Comments 0.15, 6.7, 15.11. Article 12 seems not to be totally aligned with this approach; the Commentary suggests that control, besides maybe a question of fact, is also a question of law. Namely, when depicting the nature of the powers required for a person to have and establish control, particularly those powers to avail itself of the benefit from the electronic record and prevent others from doing so, the commentary includes within the term "benefit" the rights "afforded by the controllable electronic record" and the "uses to which" the record can be put, such as for instance to hold and dispose of the record by sale or, in case of a controllable account or payment intangible, the right to collect payment from the debtor (Comment 3 to § 12–105).

[53] Comments 6.2.

[54] See examples in Fairfield (2022), p. 1287–1288. This one fact that led to the court in *Z1 v MTGox/ Dobayashi Nobuaki* to conclude that DLT and the blockchain protocols do not confer exclusive control to its holder (see sect. III-Decision-, par. 1.iii. b).iv).

[55] Principle 6(3) (a), and Comment 6.11; see also Comment 5 to § 12–105.

the required abilities, to presume their existence and their exclusive character (where applicable).[56] Although the application of this rule in the Principles is limited to "any proceeding in which a person's control of a digital asset is at issue", it should also be relevant in other situations in the market beyond a controversial or litigation context; e.g., to assess good faith or reasonable reliance of third parties, such as *bona fide* transferees, on the (reliable) identification of a person as the person in control (possibly, also literally qualified as the holder or the owner of a digital asset in its content or by the protocol, system or solution used).

6 Distinctive Features of Control as the Basis of Holdership of Digital Records or Assets

Contemplated in perspective and with the benefit of hindsight, it is interesting to see how control has not only evolved to play a central role in the construction of a holdership system for digital assets or records as personal or movable (intangible) property, but also, despite having the same role, it has proved to be different from possession by reason of its digital context and nature. In our view, to understand how control actually performs its functions, and how it is defined and can be applied, it is crucial to take into account the fact that all transactions where it may be relevant are strictly based and dependent on information in digital form (including the records or assets themselves). Control was originally designed as a condition for holdership of digital records, to require that, regardless of the technology, method and/or solutions used to achieve it, it performs one of the most important functions that possession has with regard to tangible movables but in the digital space; to provide reliable identification of a person as the holder of a record. In different ways, however, the idea of holdership and control of a digital record has been gradually used to address the most fundamental conditions that technology has to ensure in order to enable the creation and use of digital assets as such. These include, as previously seen, the identification of the record as a distinguishable or singular asset (whatever its specific type),[57] which can be held through control or exclusive control, thereby allowing a person to prove control against third parties as a basis for appropriation (and claim holdership, and possibly ownership, title, an interest or other rights),[58] as well as to

[56] Principle 7, Comments 6.12 *in fine* and Comment 7.1 UNIDROIT Principles. § 12–105(d) sets a more limited presumption that requires in any case that a person claiming to have control proves that it has the needed powers, but spares the need to prove that they are exclusive (i.e., to prove a negative): "(i) f a person has the powers specified in subsection (a) (1) (B) (i) and (ii), the powers are presumed to be exclusive" -see also (again) Comment 5.

[57] *Ruscoe v Cryptopia Ltd*, pars. [69, 80], [104]; *AA v Persons Unknown*, par. 59; see also reasoning in *CLM v CLN*, par. 42.

[58] *Ruscoe v Cryptopia Ltd*, pars. [97]–[98], [105], [109]–[111]; *CLM v CLN* [2022] SGHC 46, par. 45

dispose of the asset or record so that third parties may likewise acquire control[59] (with the intended legal purposes and expected effects). When considering digital assets, these three conditions are fairly interrelated, which has therefore placed control at the core of their very nature as a new type of property.

In view of the foregoing, control has already been shown to entail important differences if we try to compare it with possession, as a factual phenomenon or situation. Such differences, besides the different functions and conditions for control, also relate to how control may work in practice, and how legal rules have acknowledged its greater versatility and the wider possibilities it offers to serve some of its functions. A particular feature worth highlighting is that control, while being exclusive (of third parties), can be shared or jointly established by two or more persons, to possibly provide for different rights for each of them on the same asset.

Although not the only one, probably the most popular example of shared or joint control in practice, for the time being, is multisignature DLT solutions, which provide each of the persons sharing control with a private identification key. Persons sharing control of a digital token can only transfer control of it through the joint consent and instruction of two or more (or all) of them (so that neither of them can individually dispose of the token).[60] Solutions for shared or joint control have become most popular in secured financial services relying on tokens (coins) as collateral (such as decentralized finance), under which acceleration of the debt after default and disposition of tokens for payment to the secured creditor (or, alternatively, restitution to the grantor after satisfactory payment) may be based on one or more smart contracts.[61]

Shared or joint control has been implicitly acknowledged in previous instruments,[62] but its express recognition and implications thereof are another important contribution of the Principles, as well as of Article 12 UCC. Both instruments, although drafted differently, but seemingly under a common conception, state that some of the abilities or powers required to be exclusive to establish control may be shared by two or more specific persons, and nevertheless meet the requirements of control, as long as none of the persons involved can unilaterally dispose of the asset or record.[63] Information asymmetries may be significantly mitigated or reduced with

---

[59] *AA v Persons Unknown*, par. 59; *CLM v CLN* [2022] SGHC 46, par. 45. Some of these decisions support their reasoning in the *Legal statement on cryptoassets and smart contracts*, The LawTech Delivery Panel –UK Jurisdiction Taskforce, 2019 (see, with regard to all these three aspects, pars. 29, 30, 42, 43).

[60] See remarks in Mann (2018), p. 169.

[61] For instance, in some cases the debtor, the secured lender and a third party (e.g., a service provider) share control through a multi-signature smart contract after the collateral is transferred to the wallet of such third party. Transfer of control (and disposition of the token) requires at least two keys out of the three that share control (debtor, creditor and third party). The collateralized token is either released to the grantor or disposed of in the market for payment to the creditor, also upon a smart contract and depending on the fate of the secured debt –see examples in Nguyen (2018), p. 192, 198, 203–2044.

[62] Pars. 111 and 114 of the Explanatory Note MLETR.

[63] § 12–105(b)(2), (c)(1) and (2)(A), Article 12, UCC (equivalent provisions can be found in § 7–106 (d)(2), (e)(1) and (2)(A), Article 7, § 9–105(d)(2), (e)(1) and (2)(A), Article 9, UCC)–see also Comment 5 to § 12–105 and illustrations therein. Article 12 excludes from shared exclusive

the use of digital means in many business transactions, but those based on holdership and disposal of an asset are among the ones that can potentially most benefit from this. For instance, shared (exclusive) control may enable the identification of different persons with shared control, each of them in a different capacity (e.g., owner or grantor and secured creditor or creditors), thereby giving visibility against third partis to the status of a digital asset and the underlying interests and rights of the people involved; something far from easy by merely relying on possession.[64] Similar or equivalent results may actually likewise be achieved under the provisions that in both the Principles and Article 12 address custody of digital assets[65] or control on behalf of another person.[66]

On a different but related aspect, control, in almost all the instruments briefly reviewed in the previous pages, has somehow shaped digital records and assets as negotiable property. In some of those instruments of course this has to do with the fact that control was coined to precisely serve negotiability as recognized in preexisting (paper-based) law. The Principles and Article 12 UCC, however, seem to consciously choose to conceive digital assets and controllable electronic records in general as (actually or potentially) negotiable property,[67] thereby reflecting the expectations that control and holdership create in many of their markets, and to some extent prioritizing their protection.

7 Concluding Remarks

It is not our aim in this last section to set definite conclusions after this brief review of control in the provisions discussed so far. Rather than that, it is probably more useful just to conclude by raising the question of how all notions of control, as gradually reflected in time by legal rules, may relate to each other. Even though each of the

---

control or powers those situations that involve a transferee of an interest in the record, and where the transferor retains a blocking power (being its authorization needed for the exercise of a shared power), as this prevents treating the transferee as such on the basis of control (see Comment 9 to § 12–105). For its part, Principle 6, par. (3)(b) clarifies that "an ability" required to be exclusive under this principle's wording "need not be exclusive if and to the extent that (...) the person in control has agreed, consented to, or acquiesced in sharing that ability with one or more other persons" (see also see Comment 6.13 to Principle 6, Comment 17.9 to Principle 17). This is meant to allow establishing shared control, for instance, in situations where a person retains the exclusive ability to prevent others from benefitting from the digital asset, as well as the ability to obtain substantially all of the benefit from it, while sharing with another person the ability to transfer all abilities required by control, so that none of them can unilaterally change control to a third party (Comment 6.13 to Principle 6).

64 See remarks in Rogers (1985), p. 208–209, in the context of negotiable instruments.

65 Principles 10 to 13 (although their focus is custody as a service).

66 § 12–105(e) to (g) Article 12, UCC.

67 See again § 12–104(d) and (e), Article 12, UCC, as well as Official Comment 3 of the Prefatory Note to Article 12, Comment 10 to § 12–104, Comment 1 to § 12–105 (where controllable electronic records are depicted as "highly negotiable"). Principle 8 UNIDROIT Principles.

instruments visited in previous pages has its own and specific scope, in all of them control aims to substantially serve the same purpose and applies or relates to the same thing; digital records. Despite their different genesis and context, each subsequent notion feeds from the previous ones to a varying extent, and the law-making processes involved, particularly those focusing on international uniform law, have developed, among several other things, on the basis of the memory of discussions in previous fora. It is difficult to forecast how control may evolve in practice, as new technologies will certainly arise in the future with this goal, and even new types of digital assets may come into existence, revealing new aspects of digital property. In any event, in the interpretation of all notions of control it would be worth avoiding inconsistencies, and we believe there are sufficient grounds to do so.

In practice control has consistently been based on the reliable identification of a person (through a private key, a signature or otherwise) as the holder in possibly different capacities (endorsee, bearer, owner, pledgee, bailee), depending on the context and the transactions involved. Identification is the pivotal element upon which technology defines the abilities such person can have and the sorts of uses it can make of the record.[68] This is the element that was the original focus of initial formulations of control. The more elaborated notions laid down in the Principles and in Article 12 UCC include other elements whose contents introduce more detail and probably reflect perceptions in the market as to how digital assets behave as property. It is clear that, should technology not ensure that they can be both held and transferred, and that only the person in control has the ability to do so, there would be no market for them. That being said, expectations and decisions of market participants are necessarily based on the information they can verify and recognize as being original, as keeping its integrity and, thus, as authentic; sometimes without necessarily understanding or even having complete knowledge of the technology used for that purpose. One virtue of the Principles, we believe, is how, despite being more nuanced and to that extent rendering the notion apparently stricter, they also sufficiently stress the importance to be given to the identification of the person in control when applying its conditions, through the presumptions included in Principle 6. That should probably be the common starting point to ensure uniformity in the interpretation and application of this notion across the different instruments that rely upon it.

References

ABA Cyberspace Committee Working Group on Transferable Records. (2003). Emulating documentary tokens in an electronic environment: Practical models for control and priority of interests in transferable records and electronic chattel paper. *Business Law, 59*, 379–389.

Dubovec, M. (2022). Toward decentralized commercial law for digital assets. *Northwestern Journal of Technology and Intellectual Property, 19*(3), 239–287.

Fairfield J.A.T. (2015), Bitproperty, *Santa Clara L. Rev. 88*: 805–874.

[68] See along these lines, e.g., Ruscoe v Cryptopia Ltd., par. [112]–[113]; *Fetch.AI Ltd v Persons Unknown Category A*, par. [10].

Fairfield, J. A. T. (2022). Tokenized: The law of non-fungible tokens and unique digital property. *Indiana Law Journal, 97*, 1261–1313.
Fry P.B., Newell J.A., Gordon M.R. (2006–2007), Coming to a screen near you–eMortgages–starring good Laws and Prudent standards–rated XML, Business Law. 62: 295–315.
Gabriel, H. D. (2023). The concept and necessity of "control" in the use of emerging technologies in commercial transactions. *Uniform Law Review, 28*, 257–268.
Goldby, M. (2023), The Electronic Trade Documents Act 2023 and the 2003 amendments to Article 7 of the Uniform Commercial Code: Do they do the same thing?, paper presented for the American Maritime Law Association Carriage of Goods Committee Meeting of 4th May 2023 (Retrieved January 2025 from) at https://papers.ssrn.com/sol3/papers.cfm?abstract_id=4517265
Goode R. (2010), Goode on commercial law, Mckendrik E. (Ed., Rev.), 4th Ed. Penguin Books.
Green S. (2008), To Have and to Hold? Conversion and Intangible Property, *The Modern Law Review 71*(1): 114–131.
Hughes, H. (2020). Blockchain and the future of secured transactions law. *Stanford Journal of Blockchain Law & Policy, 3*(1), 21–61.
Johnson K.N., Hsu Wilbur S.E., Sater S. (2018), (Im) Perfect Regulation: Virtual Currency and Other Digital Assets as Collateral, *SMU Science & Technology Law Review. 21*(2): 115–158.
Low K.F.K, Hara M. (2024), Cryptoassets as Property. In: van Erp S., & Zimmermann K. (eds), Edward Elgar Research Handbook on EU Property Law (2024), 146, SSRN: https://ssrn.com/abstract=4103870 or doi:https://doi.org/10.2139/ssrn.4103870
Mann, R. J. (2018). Reliable perfection of security interests in crypto-currency. *SMU Science & Technology Law Review, 21*, 159–180.
Newell J.A., Gordon, M.R. (1994–1995), Electronic commerce and negotiable instruments (electronic promissory notes), Idaho Law Review. 31: 819–834.
Nguyen, X.-T. (2018). Lessons from case study of secured transactions with bitcoin. *SMU Science & Technology Law Review, 21*, 181–204.
Reyes, C. L. (2016). Moving beyond bitcoin to an endogenous theory of decentralized ledger technology regulation: An initial proposal. *Villanova Law Review, 61*, 191–234.
Rogers, J. S. (1987). Negotiability as a system of title recognition. *Ohio State Law Journal, 48*, 197–224.
Stevens, R. (2023). *Crypto is not property*. https://doi.org/10.2139/ssrn.4416200
Sturley, M., Fujita, T., & Van der Ziel, G. (2010). *The Rotterdam rules*. Sweet & Maxwell.
Tu K.V. (2018a–I), Perfecting bitcoin, Georgia Law review. 52(2): 505–580.
Tu K.V. (2018b–II), Crypto-collateral. SMU Science & Technology Law Review. 21(2): 205–258.

Verified Carbon Credits as Digital Assets

Eduardo Miranda Ribera

1 Introduction

The concept of carbon credits was introduced in the Kyoto Protocol to the United Nations Convention on Climate Change in 1997 for reducing greenhouse gas emissions (GHG) into the atmosphere.[1] The Protocol established an international regime for trading and reducing greenhouse gas emissions (Articles 6, 12 and 17 of the Kyoto Protocol). Since then, regulations related to global warming have been issued, such as the Paris Agreement in 2015, which provides a carbon trading system to reduce carbon emissions. This has undoubtedly contributed to the development of an international market for the creation and trading of carbon certificates.

In this context, it should be noted that not all carbon credits are the same, as they may be created by different processes or allow their holders to use them for different purposes. Hence, it is difficult to provide a definition of carbon credits and this expression should be understood as a generic expression referring to the different units traded in carbon markets.[2]

Of the different credits that can be issued in this area, it is worth focusing on Verified Carbon Credits (VCC). VCC certifies that the holder, either directly or indirectly, has reduced or eliminated one ton of CO_2 from the atmosphere, as verified by an independent third party. These credits are qualified as verified, because they are issued after undergoing a certification and verification process in which a third

[1] UNCITRAL/UNIDROIT Study On The Legal Nature Of Verified Carbon Credits Issued By Independent Carbon Standard Setters (https://www.unidroit.org/wp-content/uploads/2024/04/C.D.-103-11-Legal-nature-of-Voluntary-Carbon-Credits-with-Annexe-1.pdf).

[2] Vid. ult. loc.

This work was financed within the framework of the Prometeo 2023 project of the Regional Ministry of Innovation, Universities, Science and Digital Society (CIPROM/2022/26) "Present and future of the regulation of cryptoassets in the EU [LegalCripto]", whose principal investigator is Carmen Pastor Sempere. The basic ideas contained herein were presented in the author's paper with the same title, given on November 13, 2024 at the IV International Congress on "UNIDROIT Principles on Digital Assets and Private Law: Context, Content, Perspectives", organized also by BAES Research Group of the University of Alicante on November 13 and 14, 2024.

E. Miranda Ribera (✉)
CEGEA, Universitat Politècnica de València, Valencia, Spain
e-mail: edmiri@upv.es

C. Pastor Sempere and D. A. Morán Bovio (eds.), UNIDROIT *Principles on Digital Assets and Private Law*, Law, Governance and Technology Series 80,
https://doi.org/10.1007/978-3-032-11001-5_5

party verifies that a certain amount of CO_2 has been effectively reduced or eliminated. They can be issued by public authorities and independent issuers (e.g. private entities that certify that climate mitigation projects have generated reductions in greenhouse gas emissions). The importance of these securities is because they can be used to mitigate the carbon footprint of a given entity to meet self-imposed net zero emission commitments; or they can simply be purchased as an investment [as they can be traded both on the stock market and over-the-counter markets]. As we can see, the relevance of these securities is notorious; over 500 million VCC have been issued in the last decade.[3]

However, there is legal uncertainty underlying the investments and transactions made with these credits. Therefore, UNIDROIT, with its Project on the legal nature of Verified Carbon Credits, aims to increase confidence in VCC transactions and support the development of this market as it can play a central role in the fight against climate change, achieving the objectives of the Paris Agreement and facilitating the fulfilment of the United Nations Sustainable Development Goals.[4]

In the analysis of the legal nature of Verified Carbon Credits carried out in the UNIDROIT VCC Project, the possibility of considering these securities as digital assets is assessed. The report considers that, according to the UNIDROIT principles on digital assets and private law,[5] it is unlikely that the VCC holder can control them, so it does not qualify them as digital assets.[6] However, there are different initiatives to tokenize VCC, such as Klima DAO, which aims to streamline GHG emissions offsetting processes.[7] These platforms based on blockchain technology seek to facilitate the trading of VCC, improve market transparency, reduce transaction costs by eliminating intermediaries and facilitate access to these markets for small entities interested in integrating into these sectors.

However, the purpose of this chapter is to analyse the possibilities of these securities as digital assets, in accordance with the UNIDROIT Project on the legal nature of Verified Carbon Credits, specifically, the main issues related to the tokenization of VCC through a DAO, in view of the development of new platforms created for this purpose. In doing so it is necessary to study the definition of blockchain technology, token and DAO.

[3] Vid. ult. loc.

[4] Vid. ult. loc.

[5] Vid https://www.unidroit.org/wp-content/uploads/2024/01/Principles-on-Digital-Assets-and-Private-Law-linked.pdf.

[6] Vid. ult. loc.

[7] Vid https://www.klimadao.finance.

2 Blockchain Technology

In order to explain what a token is or what asset tokenization consists of, it is necessary to mention the main characteristics of blockchain technology. This technology is a single transaction register, managed and controlled in a decentralized manner by users interacting in a system, equivalent to the general accounting ledger. The Internet plays a fundamental role in this system, allowing the connection of all users in real time (peer-to-peer or P2P). Blockchain technology is based on complex digitization processes, grouped in asymmetric encryption algorithms or double key and hash algorithms.[8]

Dual-key algorithms are essentially verification systems. Each user holds two linked encryption keys, one of which consists of a public key for user identification whereas the other is a private key for electronic signature. When a user accesses the system, a 256-bit number is randomly generated, which will be the user's private encryption key. Subsequently, a public key is generated from the private key. To request the keys, no identification is required, and therefore they can be regenerated as many times as desired.[9]

The hash algorithm is a mathematical algorithm that generates a 30-character alphanumeric code when applied to a given digital file. When this algorithm is used on a digital file, it generates a code that is repeated each time it is applied to that file; meaning that if a file is slightly modified, a new hash will be generated. This algorithm is irreversible, so that an original file cannot be constructed from a hash (no reverse engineering is possible). In this way the hash ensures the integrity of the information because its contents cannot have been modified. Consequently, the blockchain is defined as a chain of hashes.[10] Each transaction is recorded in a message in computer language (script), which contains an input on the one hand, identifying who is transferring, what is being transferred, their available balance and their signature, and, on the other hand, an output, which records what has been transmitted and its beneficiary.[11]

The unique recording of all transactions is performed by nodes or miners, which are qualified users that verify the chronology of transactions to avoid duplications in the blockchain. Each node is responsible for collecting all transactions received during a given time, with each collection or group of transactions forming a block on the blockchain. Each block, except the first one, contains the hash of the previous

---

[8] Vid. González-Meneses, M., *Entender Blockchain. Una introducción a la tecnología de registro distribuido,* Thomson Reuters Aranzadi, 2017, pp. 40 y 63; Varmaz, A., Varmaz, N., Günther, S., Poddig, T., "Rechtliche…", *ob. cit.,* p. 13.

[9] Vid. González-Meneses, M., *Entender…, ob. cit.,* pp. 65 y 70; Siegel, D., "Technische Grundlagen", en Omlor, S., Link, M., *Kryptowährungen und Token,* Fachmedien Recht und Wirtschaft, Frankfurt, 2021, p. 76.

[10] Vid. Herrero Morant, T., en Guerrero Lebrón, M. J., Alvarado Herrera, L., (Dirs.), Blanco Sánchez, M. J., *El Derecho Mercantil y la pandemia: algunos problemas del pasado, la crisis conyuntural y las perspectivas futuras,* Colex, 2023, p. 934.

[11] Vid. González-Meneses, M., *Entender…, ob. cit.,* pp. 75–81; Varmaz, A., Varmaz, N., Günther, S., Poddig, T., en Omlor, S., Link, M., *Kryptowährungen…, ob. cit.*, pp. 14–15.

block, so that, when a block is generated, a hash is automatically generated that will be incorporated into the next block, avoiding any possible manipulation and allowing the immediate identification of possible forgeries in the blockchain. The fact that the blockchain is not managed in one place, but in the network of different nodes, provides greater security to the system because of decentralization. Decentralization per se is not an advantage but acts as a differentiating factor to ensure transparency in transaction history and access to information in real-time.[12]

However, not all blocks can be incorporated into the chain, only those whose hash begins with a certain number of zeros will be introduced. This is possible by adding a nonce to the hash,[13] however, there is no algorithm that allows the desired sequence of zeros to be obtained directly, so the nodes must keep trying until they obtain the hash that can close the block. At this point, the figure of the miner is highlighted, differentiating it from the node, since all the users who oversee collecting transactions will be nodes, but only those capable of obtaining the desired hash will be miners. This process continues as many times as desired if the requirements are met. When a miner obtains a nonce capable of closing a block, it incorporates it into the network so that the other nodes can verify the concurrence of the necessary requirements for its registration. However, it may happen that at the same time two miners close two blocks on the same hash, causing the generation of two different lines of blocks known as a fork. When this happens, the miners will add blocks to the longer line, abandoning the shorter one.[14]

By means of this brief explanation, we can extract that blockchain technology is characterized by being a transparent, impartial and mathematically impassable system. In particular, our attention should be brought to the decentralization of users, as there is no central body or entity and all users of the system are authorized to process transactions and have the possibility of access to all system information in real time.[15]

[12] Vid. Verhoeven, P., Sinn, F., Herden, T. T., "Examples from Blockchain Implementations in Logistics and Supply Chain Management: Exploring the Mindful Use of a New Technology", *Logistics* 2, N. ° 3, 2018, p. 2; González-Meneses, M., *Entender…, ob. cit.,* pp. 83–85; Varmaz, A., Varmaz, N., Günther, S., Poddig, T., en Omlor, S., Link, M., *Kryptowährungen…, ob. cit.*, p. 15; Siegel, D., en Omlor, S., Link, M., *Kryptowährungen…*, ob. cit., pp. 75–76.

[13] Vid. González-Meneses, M., *Entender…, ob. cit.,* p. 88.

[14] Vid. González-Meneses, M., *Entender…, ob. cit.,* pp. 89–96; Varmaz, A., Varmaz, N., Günther, S., Poddig, T., en Omlor, S., Link, M., *Kryptowährungen…, ob. cit*, pp. 14–16.

[15] Vid. Varmaz, A., Varmaz, N., Günther, S., Poddig, T., en Omlor, S., Link, M., *Kryptowährungen…, ob. cit*, pp. 14–17.

3 Tokens

3.1 Definition and Main Characteristics

The expression token, jeton or symbolic element[16] is not new in our vocabulary as it has been recurrently used in economic traffic to acquire a product or service within a certain context, as if taking a garment off the peg (being used as a title of legitimacy).[17] However, since the emergence of blockchain technology, the term token is also used to refer to a digital asset that is assigned to a specific value and has a specific function; that is, it could be defined as a digitized promissory note of an underlying right registered in a database.[18] The main characteristics of these securities are their capacity to be traded and the attribution of a specific right to their holder.[19] Within the token concept, as applied to the financial sector, different modalities converge, which can be grouped into the following "taxonomic tripartite"[20]: security tokens or value tokens (investment tokens), utility tokens (service tokens) and currency tokens or payment tokens.[21]

Security tokens or value tokens (investment tokens) have characteristics similar to shares or stocks in a company.[22] The owner of these securities receives a share in the future profits of the issuing entity, in the form of interest or dividends. In this way, the holder of the security token acquires co-ownership of the issuer's blockchain and thus participates in its growth.[23] Utility tokens (service tokens) allow their holder to access a specific network, usually with the issuer's products or services.[24] Currency tokens or payment tokens represent means of payment, i.e. digital currencies in the context of a blockchain intended to be used as a means of payment substituting money. The thing that tokens of this kind have in common with conventional means of payment

---

[16] Vid. Jiménez Serranía, V., "Tokenización, propiedad fraccionada y mercado de valores: algunos aspectos para la reflexión", *Revista de Derecho del Mercado de Valores,* n.º 34, 2024, p. 2.

[17] Vid. Madrid Parra, A., "Del valor anotado al tokenizado", *Revista de Derecho del Sistema Financiero,* 2022, p. 69 donde se hace referencia al trabajo Floz Giralt, X., "Implicaciones jurídicas de la tokenización de activos financieros", *Alastria Lega 1,* n.º 01, 2020, *passim.*

[18] Vid. Tato Plaza, A., "Régimen jurídico de la publicidad de criptoactivos presentados como objeto de inversión", *Revista de Derecho Mercantil,* Núm. 324, 2022, p. 7; Bednarz, Z., "La representación de acciones en forma de *tokens* en la *blockchain", Revista de Derecho del Mercado de Valores,* N.º 26, 2020, pp. 2–3; Navarro LÉRIDA, M.ª S., "Tokenización de la economía: la regulación francesa de las ICOS. *Loi Pacte* y régimen de los jetons", *Revista de Derecho del Mercado de Valores,* N.º 24, 2019, pp. 3–4.

[19] Vid. Ibáñez Jiménez, J., "Criptoactivos negociables y fichas de servicio (tokens no monetarios) en la propuesta de reglamento europeo de mercados distribuidos o blockchain". *Revista de Derecho del Mercado de Valores,* n.º 28, 2021, pp. 4–5.

[20] Vid. Ibáñez Jiménez, J., *Revista de Derecho del Mercado de Valores,* n.º 28, 2021, p. 7.

[21] Vid. Tato Plaza, A., *Revista de Derecho Mercantil,* Núm. 324, 2022, p. 7; Ibáñez Jiménez, J., *Revista de Derecho del Mercado de Valores,* n.º 28, 2021, p. 7.

[22] Vid. Ibáñez Jiménez, J., *Revista de Derecho del Mercado de Valores,* n.º 28, 2021, p. 8.

[23] Vid. ult. loc.

[24] Ibid., p. 10.

is that their values are obtained through interaction between supply and demand. However, their distinguishing feature is that they reflect a value that is not created by a central bank or an authority, so they have no intrinsic value, since their value arises from the trust placed in them by users.[25] However, there is a final classification characterized by bringing together properties of different token modalities, i.e., the provider of a utility token may also allow the token to be used as a means of payment; these securities are known as hybrid tokens.[26]

These considerations have been outlined with the recent publication of Regulation 2023/1114 on crypto-asset markets. This Regulation classifies as a cryptoasset any "digital representation of a security or a right that can be transferred and stored electronically, by means of distributed registration technology or similar technology" [art. 3.1.4 RMiCA; this is also defined in art. 2.e) CNMV Circular 1/2022 on cryptoasset advertising[27]].[28] The Regulation also regulates the issuance of three types of cryptoassets: asset-referenced tokens (hereinafter ART), electronic money tokens (hereinafter EMT) and those cryptoassets that are different from ART and EMT, such as, for example, the utility tokens.[29] Asset-backed tokens are defined as "a type of cryptoasset that is not an electronic money token and that is intended to hold a stable value referenced to another security or right, or a combination of both, including one or more official currencies" (art. 3.1.6 RMiCA).[30] Electronic money tokens are "a type of cryptoasset which, in order to maintain a stable value, is referenced to the

[25] Varmaz, A., Varmaz, N., Günther, Poddig, "Rechtliche… ", *ob. cit.*, p. 25.

[26] Vid. Gaberle, O., Kühn, T., "Bewertungsfragen", en Omlor, S., Link, M., *Kryptowährungen und Token*, Fachmedien Recht und Wirtschaft, Frankfurt, 2021, pp. 131–141. Véase, igualmente, Martí Miravalls, J., "Fintech: aproximación jurídica a los retos que plantea", *Revista Española de Capital Riesgo*, N. º 2/2018, p. 36.

[27] Vid. Llopis Blanque, A., "Algunas cuestiones de interés en la nueva circular 1/2022 de publicidad sobre criptoactivos", *Revista de Derecho del Sistema Financiero*, 2022, pp. 219–240; Palá Laguna, R., "La nueva Ley de los Mercados de Valores y de los Servicios de Inversión", *Gómez-Acebo & Pombo*, marzo 2023, p. 4.

[28] Vid. Tapia Hermida, A. J., "Desafíos en la regulación y supervisión de los criptoactivos en la Unión Europea y en España", *Revista de Derecho del Mercado de Valores*, N.º 28, 2021, pp. 7–8; Muñoz García, A., "Una aproximación a la propuesta de reglamento europeo sobre mercados de criptoactivos", en AA.VV. *Derecho de Sociedades, Concursal y de los Mercados Financieros. Libro Homenaje al profesor Adolfo Sequeira Martín*, Sepín, Madrid, 2022, p. 801.

[29] Vid. Anguren, R., García Alcorta, J., García Calvo, L., Hernández García, D., Valdeolivas, E., "La regulación de los criptoactivos en el marco internacional y europeo en curso", *Revista de estabilidad financiera*, N.º 44, Banco de España, 2023, pp. 124–125; Tapia Hermida, A. J., *Revista de Derecho del Mercado de Valores*, N.º 28, 2021, p. 8; Ibáñez Jiménez, J., "Mecanismos europeos postpandemia para el control del fraude en criptoactivos. Referencia especial al caso de los tokens de servicio", en Guerrero Lebrón, M. J., Alvarado Herrera, L., (Dirs.), Blanco Sánchez, M. J., *El Derecho Mercantil y la pandemia: algunos problemas del pasado, la crisis conyuntural y las perspectivas futuras*, Colex, 2023, pp. 952–953.

[30] Vid. Madrid Parra, A., *Revista de Derecho del Sistema Financiero*, 2023, pp. 87–88.

value of an official currency" (art. 3.1.7 RMiCA); official currency being understood as that issued by a central bank or other monetary authority (art. 3.1.8 RMiCA).[31]

3.2 Legal Qualification of Tokens as Marketable Securities

Analysing the legal qualification of tokens as securities is not a simple task, as many controversial issues arise when attempting to do so.

In Germany, for example, there are two opposing trends. On the one hand, some authors understand that it is impossible to consider tokens as negotiable securities, and therefore as financial instruments, due to the lack of physical substantiation of the security. This means that they cannot be admitted to trading on the capital market because they cannot be acquired in good faith in accordance with the requirements of the German Civil Code, given the need for a physical element to qualify the security as an object of ownership and thus ensure its proper negotiability on the market (all in accordance with the requirements of the concept of a "thing" in Sect. 90 of the German Civil Code).[32]

However, the rest of the German authors are in favour of granting the qualification as a marketable security if the requirements of its securities trading regulations are met, specifically those set forth in §2.1 (Gesetz über den Wertpapierhandel or Wertpapierhandelsgesetz, hereinafter WpHG), coinciding with those configured in Art. 4. 1.44 of Directive 2014/65/EU of the European Parliament and of the Council of 15 May 2014 on markets in financial instruments and amending Directive 2002/92/EC and Directive 2011/61/EU (also known as MiFID II). Specifically, the security is required to be standardized, eligible for trading on a capital market and transferable.[33] Standardization will be presumed when a given group of tokens has the same characteristics and grants the same rights to its holder.[34] Regarding the ability to be traded and transferred, it shall be understood, on the one hand, that cryptoassets may be traded on the capital market or on an organized secondary market; and, on the other hand, that their legal and technical conditions shall remain unchanged when transferred to a third party.[35]

This latter interpretation is the one that the German Federal Financial Supervisory Authority (Bundesanstalt für Finanzdienstleistungsaufsicht, hereinafter BaFin) considers should be followed, and consequently, consider those securities represented by means of distributed ledger technology as negotiable securities. Moreover,

---

[31] Vid. Tapia Frade, A., "Las ofertas públicas de criptoactivos distintos de fichas referenciadas a activos o fichas de dinero electrónico como medio alternativo de financiación en la propuesta de Reglamento MiCA", *La LEY mercantil,* N.º 99, 2023, pp. 7–8.

[32] Vid. Varmaz, A., Varmaz, N., Günther, Poddig, "Rechtliche… ", *ob. cit.,* p. 23.

[33] Ibid., pp. 24–25.

[34] Vid. Ibáñez Jiménez, J., *Revista de Derecho del Mercado de Valores,* n.º 28, 2021, p. 5.

[35] Vid. Varmaz, A., Varmaz, N., Günther, Poddig, "Rechtliche… ", *ob. cit.,* p. 23.

the German authority is in favour of recognizing these securities as negotiable securities, especially since transactions carried out through blockchain technology offer greater security in trading by being able to identify the owners through the traceability and transparency that characterizes the cryptographic representation of the tokens. This is in line with the opinion of part of our doctrine that understands that tokenization will contribute to the improvement of trading processes of financial instruments.[36] However, BaFin also warns of the complexities that this system presents and the need to apply supervisory and consumer protection regulations to assess the profitability and risks associated with these securities.[37]

However, despite this favourable outlook on tokens being considered negotiable securities, a distinction must be made according to the modality used. In the case of security tokens, it is observed that, due to their characteristics, the securities should be standardized. However, the configuration granted by their issuer must be considered to assess their legal qualification. In this sense, it is estimated that this type of tokens is traded mainly in the so-called "cryptographic exchanges", which probably represent organized markets. As a result, these tokens would be classified as tradable securities if they meet the requirements.[38] Consequently, utility tokens and currency tokens cannot be considered as tradable securities because they do not meet the above requirements.[39]

The situation in France was different, as it was one of the first countries to recognize securities that were registered in a securities account or in a shared electronic register *-dispositif d'enregistrement électronique partagé-* (article L 211-3 of the Monetary and Financial Code) as financial instruments, in its Monetary and Financial Code (Code monétaire et financier, hereinafter CMF),.[40] Moreover, the French legislator establishes a list of digital assets, distinguishing between: tokens, excluding those meeting the characteristics of the financial instruments mentioned in Article L 211-1 of the Monetary and Financial Code itself (these requirements configured by the French legislator coincide with those cited above from the German regulations which, in turn, are identical to those of the Spanish regulations and evidently to the provisions of the MiFID II Directive); any digital representation of a security which is neither issued nor guaranteed by a central bank or public authority, which is not necessarily linked to a legal tender and which does not have the legal status of a currency, but which is accepted by natural or legal persons as a medium of exchange and which can be transferred, stored or exchanged electronically (art. L

---

[36] Vid. Madrid Parra, A., *Revista de Derecho del Sistema Financiero,* 2023, p. 98.

[37] Ibid., pp. 23–24.

[38] Vid. Varmaz, A., Varmaz, N., Günther, Poddig, "Rechtliche… ", *ob. cit.,* p. 24.

[39] Vid. Madrid Parra, A., *Revista de Derecho del Sistema Financiero,* 2023, p. 81. Sobre esta cuestión, en Ibáñez Jiménez, J., *Revista de Derecho del Mercado de Valores,* n.º 28, 2021, p. 8.

[40] Vid. Palá Laguna, R., "Los criptoactivos valores negociables como nueva categoría de los derechos-valor", en Guerrero Lebrón, M. J., Alvarado Herrera, L., (Dirs.), Blanco Sánchez, M. J., *El Derecho Mercantil y la pandemia: algunos problemas del pasado, la crisis conyuntural y las perspectivas futuras,* Colex, 2023, pp. 966–967.

54-10-1 Monetary and Financial Code). The distinction between cryptocurrencies and tokens can be inferred from this.[41]

If we look at our legislation, Law 6/2023, of March 17, on Securities Markets and Investment Services (hereinafter LMVSI[42]) and Royal Decree 814/2023, of November 8, on financial instruments, admission to trading, registration of negotiable securities and market infrastructures (hereinafter Royal Decree 814/2023[43]), they establish that securities are a type of financial instrument defined as any property right, susceptible to impersonal trading in a financial market (art. 2.1 LMVSI and art. 3.1 Royal Decree 814/2023).[44] Likewise, the above will be qualified as financial instruments even when they are issued, registered, transferred or stored using distributed registry technology or other similar technologies to support these actions, such as, for example, blockchain technology (art. 2.2 LMVSI).[45]

In this context marked by the diversity of crypto-assets and with the aim of harmonizing the criteria to qualify them as financial instruments, the European Securities and Markets Authority (hereinafter ESMA) published Draft Guidelines on January 29, 2024, on the conditions and criteria for the qualification of crypto-assets as financial instruments (hereinafter Draft Guidelines[46]). The Draft Guidelines establish certain criteria for qualifying crypto-assets as marketable securities. As a fundamental premise, it is emphasized that distributed registry technology should not alter the legal nature of crypto-assets and the fact that these systems are used to represent securities is not an impediment to their qualification as negotiable securities; especially when the principle of technological neutrality, recognized in the MiCA Regulation, guarantees their validity regardless of the format used. However, the Draft Guidelines establish that cryptoassets will be considered as negotiable securities when: they are part of a class of securities that grant their holder rights equivalent to those granted by a share or a bond; they are negotiable on the capital market; and they are not an instrument or means of payment [art. 4.1.44 MiFID II].

Firstly, the reference to certain securities is not defined either in the MiFID II Directive or in the national regulations of the Member States. However, the Draft Guidelines consider that for a certain group of cryptoassets to form part of a specific class of securities, they must grant their holders similar rights, ensuring that they can be traded on the markets. Here the ESMA authority is referring to securities that are

[41] Vid. Mekki, M., "Actifs numériques", en AA.VV., *Répertoire de droit commercial* Dalloz, 2024, sección 1, artículo 1, párrafo 17; Julienne, M., "Les actifs numériques, entre droit et technologie, *BJB,* N.° 118, 2020, p. 64.

[42] Vid. Herrero Morant, R., "Análisis de las novedades de la Ley de los mercados de valores y de los servicios de inversión", *Revista de Derecho del Sistema Financiero,* 2023, pp. 284–285.

[43] Vid. Tapia Hermida, A. J., "La arquitectura reglamentaria del mercado de valores español: la Ley 6/2023 y sus reglamentos de desarrollo", *Revista de Derecho del Mercado de Valores,* n.° 34, 2024, *passim.*

[44] Vid. Madrid Parra, A., *Revista de Derecho del Sistema Financiero,* 2023, p. 76.

[45] Ibid., p. 82; Palá Laguna, R., *Revista de derecho del mercado de valores,* N.° 31, 2022, pp. 4–5.

[46] https://www.esma.europa.eu/sites/default/files/2024-01/ESMA75-453128700-52_MiCA_Consultation_Paper_-_Guidelines_on_the_qualification_of_crypto-assets_as_financial_instruments.pdf.

standardized such as the case with government bonds or other forms of securitized debt. Therefore, cryptoassets that are interchangeable, are issued by the same issuer, are similar and grant the same rights to their holders will be integrated into the same class of securities (paragraph 32 Draft Guidelines).

According to the wording of the provision, the provisions of the MiFID II Directive require a direct investment in the underlying asset to which the cryptoasset is referenced. This premise could be interpreted as an exclusion from those cryptoasset derivatives that imply participation in the evolution of other cryptoassets or stock market indexes without granting their holder a participation in the underlying asset, and consequently they would only be made sharers of a part of the profitability derived from their progress. However, this is not the case, even more so when they could be classified as financial instruments by representing other securities or securitized debt recognized in Directive 2014/65 itself, in that they grant their holder a cash settlement, determined by reference to marketable securities, currencies, interest rates, commodities or other indices [art. 4.1.44 MiFID II] (paragraph 36 Draft Guidelines).

Secondly, the reference to the cryptoasset being tradable implies the possibility of being able to transfer it to the capital market (paragraph 33 Draft Guidelines). The reference to the capital market should be made in a broad sense and allow for the possibility of trading the securities on any market including over the counter (OTC) through, for example, a Multilateral Trading Facility (paragraph 34 Draft Guidelines).

Thirdly, payment instruments or means of payment will be explicitly excluded from the definition of transferable securities in MiFID II. In order to understand the concept of payment instruments or means of payment, it is useful to refer to the definition set out in Directive (EU) 2015/2366 of the European Parliament and of the Council of 25 November 2015 on payment services in the internal market and amending Directives 2002/65/EC, 2009/110/EC and 2013/36/EU and Regulation (EU) No 1093/2010 and repealing Directive 2007/64/EC (hereinafter PSD2[47]), as it differs from that set out in MiFID II. Directive 2014/65 defines them in line with the concept of funds set out in Directive 2015/2366 by considering banknotes, coins or electronic money as such. Furthermore, Directive 2015/2366 defines payment instruments or means of payment as any personalized device and/or set of procedures agreed between the payment service user and the payment service provider used to initiate a payment order. In both cases, the notion of payment instrument or means of payment should be understood in a broad sense, i.e. covering liquid payment methods and non-cash payment tools (paragraph 31 Draft Guidelines).

The Draft Guidelines also state that cryptoassets that are classified as financial instruments in accordance with the considerations of Directive 2014/65 (art. 2 RMiCA) will remain outside the scope of application of the MiCA Regulation. These MiFID II criteria coincide with those established in our securities market regulations because of their transposition into our legal system (art. 2.1 LMVSI and art. 3.1 Royal

[47] Vid. Bueso Guillén, P. J., "Dictamen de la autoridad bancaria europea en respuesta a la solicitud de asesoramiento sobre la revisión de la Directiva (UE) 2015/2366 sobre servicios de pago en el mercado interior (DSP2)", *Revista de Derecho del Sistema Financiero,* 2023, pp. 403–410.

Decree 814/2023); as well as those set out in the comparative regulations. Therefore, those cryptoassets that meet the characteristics of MiFID II (specifically, that they can be traded on a capital market, are transferable and grant rights to their holder) will be classified as negotiable securities and, therefore, as financial instruments.[48]

However, the Draft Guidelines point out that MiFID II does not define the concept of financial instrument, but that this is delineated by means of a list of examples rather than a set of conditions. The lack of harmonization of the term because of the different transpositions made by the Member States into their domestic legal systems further complicates the issue. This situation makes it difficult to adopt a holistic approach to the Guidelines and to set a standard applicable to all financial instruments. ESMA therefore aims to establish criteria that can be used to promote convergent practices at national level regarding the classification of cryptoassets as financial instruments. Thus, even though the qualification criteria are clear, their assessment must necessarily be carried out on a case-by-case basis.

3.3 Respect for the Guiding Principles on Securities

Asset tokenisation is nothing more than the conversion of an asset into a token; it could be said to be the digital equivalent of securitisation. To address the general considerations regarding asset tokenisation, it is interesting to look at the provisions of French law, as a pioneer in the field. The French legislator, based on the UNCITRAL Model Law on electronic transferable documents of 2017[49] and the UNIDROIT principles on digital assets and private law,[50] adopted the very interesting Law no. 2024-537 of 13 June 2024. That law aims to increase the number of tokens that can be used in the creation of a tokenised asset. Law 2024-537 of 13 June 2024 aimed at increasing corporate financing and the attractiveness of France (LOI No 2024-537 du 13 juin 2024 visant à accroître le financement des entreprises et l'attractivité de la France, hereinafter Law No 2024-537).

That law aims to legally reinforce the tokenisation of securities in order to facilitate corporate financing. Among its provisions, Title II aims to facilitate the international growth of French companies through the dematerialisation of securities (Articles 14 to 17 of Law No. 2024-537). In this sense, a transferable security is one that represents an asset or a right and gives its holder the possibility of demanding the performance of a specific obligation or enables him to transfer it (Art. 14.I Law No. 2024-537). The following are included as negotiable instruments that may be dematerialised: bills of exchange, promissory notes, guarantees, damage insurance

---

48 Vid. Varmaz, A., Varmaz, N., Günther, Poddig, "Rechtliche… ", *ob. cit.*, pp. 22–23.

49 https://uncitral.un.org/sites/uncitral.un.org/files/media-documents/uncitral/es/mletr_ebook_s.pdf.

50 https://www.unidroit.org/wp-content/uploads/2024/01/Principles-on-Digital-Assets-and-Private-Law-linked.pdf; Castillo Iborra, F., "Principios UNIDROIT sobre activos digitales y derecho privado", *Revista de Derecho del Sistema Financiero,* 2023, pp. 365–380.

policies, insurance policies on transported goods and civil liability insurance policies (Art. 14.I Law No 2024-537).

With these premises, the French legislator intends to equalise the effects of the transmission of physical and electronic certificates when it is possible to: guarantee the uniqueness of the certificate; identify the holder; establish exclusive control over the certificate; identify the contracting parties, from the moment it is created through to the moment it ceases to be valid; preserve its integrity and certify all its modifications. The integrity of the title shall be assessed by determining whether the information contained therein, including possible modifications, has remained complete and unchanged (Art. 16.I Law No. 2024-537). In laying down these provisions, the French legislator is inescapably thinking of tokenisation by blockchain technology, as this system allows all the above-mentioned requirements to be met. Furthermore, the modification of the medium of the instrument may be carried out without hindrance, maintaining the agreed rights and obligations; and the alteration of the medium does not entail a novation of its characteristics (art. 16.II Law no. 2024-537).

However, in assessing this novel measure of the French legislator, in accordance with our doctrine it is important not to neglect respect for the guiding principles of securities.[51] The dematerialisation or disincorporation of the right embodied in the paper must in any case respect the principles of literality, autonomy and legitimation by possession.[52] Disincorporation requires the registry representation of the right embodied in the security.[53] This would be overcome by incorporating the information of the security in the blockchain and registering the right.[54] Maintaining the principles of literalness and autonomy would also be guaranteed given that the registration of the right in the block would be carried out respecting the literalness of the security title, and its holder would acquire an autonomous right, to which personal defences of other parties intervening in the traffic other than those arising between whoever claims the right and whoever it is claimed from; in other words, only *inter partes* personal defences will be opposable.[55]

Regarding the principle of literality, it is important to remark that this would be a case of indirect literality, as the information on the security is necessarily contained

---

[51] Vid. Martínez-Echevarría Y García de Dueñas, A., *Sobre el concepto, naturaleza y régimen jurídico de los valores mobiliarios anotados en cuenta,* Tesis doctoral dirigida por F. Sánchez Calero, disponible en https://eprints.ucm.es/id/eprint/2198, Universidad Complutense de Madrid, 1996, pp. 132–141; Garrigues, J., "Los títulos-valores", *Revista de derecho mercantil,* N.º 36, 1951, pp. 312–361; Paz-Ares Rodríguez, J. C., "La desincorporación de los títulos-valor (el marco conceptual de las anotaciones en cuenta)", en AA.VV., *El nuevo mercado de valores: seminario sobre el nuevo Derecho español y europeo del Mercado de Valores,* Consejo General del Notariado, Madrid, 1995, pp. 87–97; Recalde Castells, A., "El conocimiento de embarque y otros documentos del transporte marítimo", *Cuadernos de Derecho y Comercio,* N. º 15, 1994, pp. 138–145; Takahashi, K., "Blockchain technology and electronic bills of lading", *Journal of International Maritime Law,* N. º 22, 2016, pp. 204–209.

[52] Vid. Palá Laguna, R., *Revista de derecho del mercado de valores,* N.º 31, 2022, p. 8; Ibáñez Jiménez, J., *Tokens valor…, ob. cit.,* pp. 172–175.

[53] Vid. Madrid Parra, A., *Revista de Derecho del Sistema Financiero,* 2023, p. 74.

[54] Vid. Palá Laguna, R., *Revista de derecho del mercado de valores,* N.º 31, 2022, p. 8.

[55] Vid. ult. loc.

in the documentation drawn up for its issue (specifically, in the issue prospectus or in the cryptoasset white paper).[56] Regarding the legitimacy and transfer of the rights, it will be necessary to consider the particularities of each token.[57] However, our doctrine warns of the need to register who holds the ownership in the distributed register, as required by our securities market regulations.[58]

4 Dao Tokenisation

VCC tokenisation consists of the creation of tokens representing these carbon credits (also called carbon tokens or VCC tokens). These tokens can be used to represent and track the carbon footprint generated by a given entity, product or service. The aim of VCC tokenisation is to use blockchain technology to measure, offset and trade greenhouse gas emissions in a more efficient, transparent and accessible way (e.g. entities that purchase VCC tokens can use them to offset their own emissions and invest in projects that reduce GHGs).

It is believed that DAOs can speed up the tokenisation of these carbon credits. The term DAO stands for Decentralized Autonomous Organisations, they are also called Decentralized Autonomous Corporations -DAC- when they are set up to carry out a specific business activity.[59] The fundamental characteristic of these organisations is that decision-making is automatic if certain pre-established milestones in a smart contract are met.[60] This facilitates decision-making without the need for human intervention. All this is possible thanks to the blockchain technology and the fact that its members oversee configuring decision-making through the aforementioned smart contracts.[61] Furthermore, all information related to DAOs (transactions and decisions) will be public and accessible to all members of the blockchain. Roughly speaking, these organisations could also be defined as a combined complex where blockchain technology, tokens and smart contracts converge.[62]

Of all the elements of DAOs, it is worth focusing on treasury and governance tokens.[63] The treasury is the fund that is constituted with the assets and resources held by the organisation; similar to the share capital of a company.[64] On the other

---

56 Vid. ult. loc.

57 Vid. Madrid Parra, A., "La legitimación en los criptovalores", *Revista de derecho del mercado de valores,* N.º 33, 2023, p. 12.

58 Ibid., p. 12.

59 Martínez Canellas, A., "Sociedades mercantiles administradas por inteligencia artificial: DAOS y entidades algorítmicas autónomas en Derecho español", *La Ley mercantil,* N.º 112, 2024, p. 2.

60 Ibid., p. 2.

61 Navarro Lérida, M.ª S., "El papel de la gobernanza en los criterios ESG: hacia modelos empresariales más sostenibles de la mano de *blockchain,* la tokenización y las DAOS", *Revista de Derecho del Mercado de Valores,* N.º 33, 2023, pp. 7–8.

62 Navarro Lérida, M.ª S., *Revista de Derecho del Mercado de Valores,* N.º 33, 2023, p. 8.

63 Vid. ult. Loc.

64 Ibid., p. 9.

hand, governance tokens give their holders control of the organisation, enabling them to manage and make decisions through smart contracts without the need to set up an administrative body to carry out this task, thus avoiding the appointment of unnecessary intermediaries from the point of view of the corporate governance requirements of the ESG criteria or principles.[65] In regard to the different modalities mentioned above, governance tokens would fall into the category of utility tokens.[66]

Depending on their characteristics, these entities could contribute to the tokenisation of VCCs or the generation of carbon tokens, as in the case of Klima DAO, which uses blockchain technology to acquire and tokenise carbon credits and thus offset the GHG emissions of the purchaser of the certificate.[67] The interest in promoting carbon tokens lies in the desire to configure a more dynamic market, which allows for the establishment of emissions traceability systems and avoids greenwashing.[68] Likewise, the use of these entities could contribute, among other things, to compliance with letter G, relating to corporate governance, of the ESG (Environmental, Social, Corporate Governance) criteria or principles, by reducing the number of intermediaries involved in the decision-making and promoting transparency in decision-making.

However, there are still many questions associated with the figure of DAOs as it is not clear how they fit into our legal system.[69] If they were to be considered as companies, it would seem logical to think that they could be irregular commercial companies as they cannot yet be incorporated in a public deed or registered in the Commercial Register, which would mean that they would be subject to the rules governing general partnerships.[70] Something similar happens with the tokenisation of VCCs, as it is necessary to set up a system that allows for accurate verification of the entities' emissions, otherwise the carbon tokens will not be able to accurately reflect the amount of GHGs offset. Furthermore, asset tokenisation in general, and VCC tokenisation in particular, lacks harmonised regulation to ensure the validity, traceability and transparency of these carbon credits in all countries.

Furthermore, it should not be forgotten that many of the presented approaches aim to reduce greenhouse gases and harmful environmental emissions. The use of blockchain technology could lead to considerable cost savings in the transmission of information,[71] while facilitating the achievement of the Sustainable Development

---

[65] Ibid., pp. 9–10.

[66] Navarro Lérida, M.ª S., *Revista de Derecho del Mercado de Valores,* N.º 33, 2023, pp. 11–13.

[67] https://www.klimadao.finance.

[68] Bataller Grau, J., "Desmontando tópicos sobre la responsabilidad social de la empresa", *Revista de Derecho Mercantil*, núm. 323, 2022, pp. 20–21.

[69] Martínez Canellas, A., *La Ley mercantil,* N.º 112, 2024, pp. 2–3.

[70] Ibid., p. 9.

[71] Vid. Pérez Rodríguez, Á. Mª., "El consentimiento en el ejercicio de los derechos del socio mediante medios de comunicación electrónicos en el Derecho español e inglés". *Derecho de sociedades. Revisando el derecho de sociedades de capital*, González Fernández, Mª. B., y Cohen Benchetrit, A. (Dirs.), Olmedo Peralta, E. y Galacho Abolafio, A. (Coords.), Tirant lo Blanch, Valencia, 2018,

Goals.[72] However, the use of blockchain technology entails a clear energy cost that could have negative implications for the environment.[73] Therefore, all these advantages proposed by the DAOs could contribute to the fulfilment of letter G, but letter E of the ESG criteria or principles would be neglected, contributing to possible environmental damage.

References

Anguren, R., García Alcorta, J., García Calvo, L., Hernández García, D., & Valdeolivas, E. (2023). La regulación de los criptoactivos en el marco internacional y europeo en curso. *Revista De Estabilidad Financiera, 44*, 119–147.

Bednarz, Z. (2020). La representación de acciones en forma de *tokens* en la *blockchain*. *Revista De Derecho Del Mercado De Valores, 26*, 1.

Blanco Sánchez, M.ª. J. (2019). Convocatoria de junta general y medios de comunicación electrónicos. Exigencia de denuncia previa de los defectos de forma para la impugnación de acuerdos. In González Fernández, M.ª. B., y Cohen Benchetrit, A. (Dirs.), Olmedo Peralta, E., y Galacho Abolafio, A. (Coords.) *Derecho de sociedades. Cuestiones sobre órganos sociales* (pp. 99–116). Tirant lo Blanch, Valencia.

Bueso Guillén, P. J. (2023). Dictamen de la autoridad bancaria europea en respuesta a la solicitud de asesoramiento sobre la revisión de la Directiva (UE) 2015/2366 sobre servicios de pago en el mercado interior (DSP2). *Revista De Derecho Del Sistema Financiero, 1*, 403–410.

Castillo Iborra, F. (2023). Principios UNIDROIT sobre activos digitales y derecho privado. *Revista De Derecho Del Sistema Financiero, 1*, 365–380.

Canalejas, J. F. (2020). Algunas cuestiones en torno a la propuesta de la Comisión europea sobre los mercados de criptoactivos (MiCA). *Revista De Derecho Del Mercado De Valores, 27*, 1.

Floz Giralt, X. (2020). Implicaciones jurídicas de la tokenización de activos financieros. *Alastria Lega, 1*, 20–26.

Gaberle, O., Kühn, T. (2021)."Bewertungsfragen". en Omlor, S., Link, M. (Eds.) *Kryptowährungen und Token* (pp. 110–172). Fachmedien Recht und Wirtschaft.

Garrigues, J. (1951). Los títulos-valores. *Revista De Derecho Mercantil, 36*, 312–361.

González-Meneses, M. (2017). *Entender Blockchain: Una introducción a la tecnología de registro distribuido*. Thomson Reuters Aranzadi.

Herrero Morant, R. (2023). Análisis de las novedades de la Ley de los mercados de valores y de los servicios de inversión. *Revista De Derecho Del Sistema Financiero, 1*, 281–310.

Herrero Morant, T. (2023). Evolución y normativa de los criptoactivos durante la pandemia de la COVID-19. El régimen jurídico de la publicidad sobre criptoactivos. en Guerrero Lebrón, M. J., Alvarado Herrera, L., (Dirs.), Blanco Sánchez, M. J. *El Derecho Mercantil y la pandemia: algunos problemas del pasado, la crisis conyuntural y las perspectivas futuras* (pp. 929–946). Colex.

pp. 171 y 172; BLANCO Sánchez, Mª. J., "Convocatoria de junta general y medios de comunicación electrónicos. Exigencia de denuncia previa de los defectos de forma para la impugnación de acuerdos". *Derecho de sociedades,* ob. cit., p. 100.

[72] Vid. Muñoz Pérez, A. F., "Blockchain, criterios ESG y objetivos ODS. Consideraciones sobre las DAOS sostenibles", *Revista de derecho del mercado de valores,* N.º 31, 2022, *passim.*

[73] Vid. Herrero Morant, T., "Evolución y normativa de los criptoactivos durante la pandemia de la COVID-19. El régimen jurídico de la publicidad sobre criptoactivos", en Guerrero Lebrón, M. J., Alvarado Herrera, L., (Dirs.), Blanco Sánchez, M. J., *El Derecho Mercantil y la pandemia: algunos problemas del pasado, la crisis conyuntural y las perspectivas futuras,* Colex, 2023, pp. 934–395.

Ibáñez Jiménez, J. (2023). Mecanismos europeos postpandemia para el control del fraude en criptoactivos. Referencia especial al caso de los tokens de servicio. en Guerrero Lebrón, M. J., Alvarado Herrera, L., (Dirs.), Blanco Sánchez, M. J., *El Derecho Mercantil y la pandemia: algunos problemas del pasado, la crisis conyuntural y las perspectivas futuras* (pp. 947–960). Colex.

Ibáñez Jiménez, J. (2021a). Criptoactivos negociables y fichas de servicio (tokens no monetarios) en la propuesta de reglamento europeo de mercados distribuidos o blockchain. *Revista De Derecho Del Mercado De Valores, 28*, 1.

Ibáñez Jiménez, J. (2021). *Tokens valor (security tokens). Régimen y técnica de los criptoactivos negociables y sus mercados (MICAs).* Reus editorial.

Jiménez Serranía, V. (2024). Tokenización, propiedad fraccionada y mercado de valores: algunos aspectos para la reflexión. *Revista De Derecho Del Mercado De Valores, 34*, 1.

Julienne, M. (2020). Les actifs numériques, entre droit et technologie. *BJB, 118*, 1.

Llopis Blanque, A. (2022). Algunas cuestiones de interés en la nueva circular 1/2022 de publicidad sobre criptoactivos. *Revista De Derecho Del Sistema Financiero, 1*, 219–240.

Madrid Parra, A. (2023a). La legitimación en los criptovalores. *Revista De Derecho Del Mercado De Valores, 33*, 1.

Madrid Parra, A. (2023b). Regulación inicial de los criptovalores. *Revista De Derecho Del Sistema Financiero, 1*, 71–104.

Madrid Parra, A. (2022). Del valor anotado al tokenizado. *Revista De Derecho Del Sistema Financiero, 1*, 65–98.

Martínez Canellas, A. (2024). Sociedades mercantiles administradas por inteligencia artificial: DAOS y entidades algorítmicas autónomas en Derecho español. *La Ley Mercantil, 112*, 1.

Martí Miravalls, J. (2018). Fintech: aproximación jurídica a los retos que plantea. *Revista Española De Capital Riesgo, 2*, 27–39.

Martínez-Echevarría y García de Dueñas, A. (1996). *Sobre el concepto, naturaleza y régimen jurídico de los valores mobiliarios anotados en cuenta.* Tesis doctoral dirigida por F. Sánchez Calero, disponible en https://eprints.ucm.es/id/eprint/2198, Universidad Complutense de Madrid.

Mekki, M. (2024). Actifs numériques. en AA.VV., *Répertoire de droit commercial* Dalloz.

Muñoz García, A. (2022). Una aproximación a la propuesta de reglamento europeo sobre mercados de criptoactivos. en AA.VV. *Derecho de Sociedades, Concursal y de los Mercados Financieros. Libro Homenaje al profesor Adolfo Sequeira Martín* (pp. 797–813). Sepín.

Muñoz Pérez, A. F. (2023). Finanzas des-intermediadas y políticas de control de los supervisores (SEC, CFTC) en Estados Unidos. En particular, la supervisión de la SEC sobre la actividad del mercado de stake. *Revista de derecho del mercado de valores, 32.*

Muñoz Pérez, A. F. (2022). Blockchain, criterios ESG y objetivos ODS. Consideraciones sobre las DAOS sostenibles. *Revista de derecho del mercado de valores, 31.*

Navarro Lérida, M.ª S. (2023). El papel de la gobernanza en los criterios ESG: hacia modelos empresariales más sostenibles de la mano de *blockchain,* la tokenización y las DAOS. *Revista de Derecho del Mercado de Valores, 33.*

Navarro Lérida, M.ª S. (2019). Tokenización de la economía: la regulación francesa de las ICOS. *Loi Pacte* y régimen de los jetons. *Revista de Derecho del Mercado de Valores, 24.*

Navarro Lérida, M.ª S. (2018). Gobierno corporativo, *blockchain* y *smart contracts.* Digitalización de las empresas y nuevos modelos descentralizados (DAOs). *Revista de Derecho del Mercado de Valores, 23.*

Paz-Ares Rodríguez, J. C. (1995). La desincorporación de los títulos-valor (el marco conceptual de las anotaciones en cuenta). en AA.VV., *El nuevo mercado de valores: seminario sobre el nuevo Derecho español y europeo del Mercado de Valores* (pp. 81–106). Consejo General del Notariado.

Palá Laguna, R. (2024). Diez años de la MiFID II: hacia un régimen único de los mercados de valores y de quienes en ellos participan. *La Ley Mercantil, 116*, 1.

Palá Laguna, R. (2023). La nueva Ley de los Mercados de Valores y de los Servicios de Inversión. *Gómez-Acebo & Pombo,* marzo.

Palá Laguna, R. (2023). Los criptoactivos valores negociables como nueva categoría de los derechos-valor. en Guerrero Lebrón, M. J., Alvarado Herrera, L., (Dirs.), Blanco Sánchez, M. J., *El Derecho Mercantil y la pandemia: algunos problemas del pasado, la crisis conyuntural y las perspectivas futuras* (pp. 961–975). Colex.

Palá Laguna, R. (2022). Los criptoactivos valores negociables como nueva categoría de los derechos-valor. *Revista De Derecho Del Mercado De Valores, 31*, 1.

Palá Laguna, R. (2021). Criptoactivos: primeras regulaciones en el Derecho español (RDL 7/2021). *Gómez-Acebo & Pombo,* Análisis, 4 mayo.

Pérez Rodríguez, Á. Mª. (2018). El consentimiento en el ejercicio de los derechos del socio mediante medios de comunicación electrónicos en el Derecho español e inglés. In González Fernández, Mª. B., y Cohen Benchetrit, A. (Dirs.), Olmedo Peralta, E. y Galacho Abolafio, A. (Coords.), *Derecho de sociedades. Revisando el derecho de sociedades de capital* (pp. 171–192). Tirant lo Blanch.

Recalde Castells, A. J. (2024). Tokens financieros: ¿Cuándo importa el "soporte"? *Revista De Derecho Del Sistema Financiero: Mercados, Operadores y Contratos, 7*, 11–44.

Recalde Castells, A. (1994). El conocimiento de embarque y otros documentos del transporte marítimo. *Cuadernos De Derecho y Comercio, 15*, 107–145.

Siegel, D. (2021). Technische Grundlagen. en OMLOR, S., LINK, M., *Kryptowährungen und Token* (pp. 72–109). Fachmedien Recht und Wirtschaft.

Takahashi, K. (2016). Blockchain technology and electronic bills of lading. *Journal of International Maritime Law, 22*, 202–211.

Tapia Frade, A. (2023). Las ofertas públicas de criptoactivos distintos de fichas referenciadas a activos o fichas de dinero electrónico como medio alternativo de financiación en la propuesta de Reglamento MiCA. *La LEY Mercantil, 99*, 1.

Tapia Hermida, A. J. (2024). La arquitectura reglamentaria del mercado de valores español: la Ley 6/2023 y sus reglamentos de desarrollo. *Revista De Derecho Del Mercado De Valores, 34*, 1.

Tapia Hermida, A. J. (2021). Desafíos en la regulación y supervisión de los criptoactivos en la Unión Europea y en España. *Revista De Derecho Del Mercado De Valores, 28*, 1.

Tato Plaza, A. (2022). Régimen jurídico de la publicidad de criptoactivos presentados como objeto de inversión. *Revista De Derecho Mercantil, 324*, 1.

Varmaz, A., Varmaz, N., Günther, S., Poddig, T. (2021). Rechtliche und finanzökonomische Grundlagen. en Omlor, S., Link, M. *Kryptowährungen und Token* (pp. 1–71). Fachmedien Recht und Wirtschaft.

Verhoeven, P., Sinn, F., & Herden, T. T. (2018). Examples from Blockchain Implementations in Logistics and Supply Chain Management: Exploring the Mindful Use of a New Technology. *Logistics, 2*(3), 1–19.

Reflections on the Introduction to the UNIDROIT Principles

Commentary on the "*Introduction to the* UNIDROIT *Principles on Digital Assets and Private Law*"

Miguel Ángel Pendón Meléndez

1 Preliminary—On the UNIDROIT *Principles on Digital Assets*

In May 2023, at the 102nd session of the UNIDROIT Governing Council, the *Principles on Digital Assets and Private Law* were approved and were subsequently published in October 2023. The very name of the work already anticipates the complexity of the task undertaken, combining in the same title the legal tradition (the concept of *Private Law*, which is the basis for the organisation of legal systems, as opposed to *Public Law*) with the technical novelty of a "new form of property" comprising the object of transactions (*digital assets*). The choice of the form of the instrument chosen (*Principles*) is also indicative of the purpose pursued by UNIDROIT in drawing up this instrument. All these issues will be dealt with in the following pages.

This work was financed within the framework of the Prometeo 2023 project of the Regional Ministry of Innovation, Universities, Science and Digital Society (CIPROM/2022/26) "Present and future of the regulation of cryptoassets in the EU [LegalCripto]", whose principal investigator is Carmen Pastor Sempere. The basic ideas contained herein were presented in the author's paper with the same title, given on November 13, 2024 at the IV International Congress on "UNIDROIT Principles on Digital Assets and Private Law: Context, Content, Perspectives", organized also by BAES Research Group of the University of Alicante on November 13 and 14, 2024.

M. Á. Pendón Meléndez (✉)
Facultad de Derecho, Departamento de Derecho mercantil, University of Cádiz, Jerez de la Frontera (Cádiz), Spain
e-mail: miguel.pendon@uca.es

C. Pastor Sempere and D. A. Morán Bovio (eds.), UNIDROIT *Principles on Digital Assets and Private Law*, Law, Governance and Technology Series 80,
https://doi.org/10.1007/978-3-032-11001-5_6

The decision on the naming of the work is primarily a result of the deliberations, and the subsequent proposal, made by the Exploratory Working Group (at the Workshop held on 17–18 September 2020). The results of that work were taken up by the UNIDROIT Governing Council at its 99th session in September [C.D. (99) B.4 rev.[1]. In this context, the project was already provisionally named "Digital Assets and Private Law". As is known, this name was eventually retained, with the addition of the form of the text, "*Principles*". Likewise, the Governing Council of UNIDROIT took up the proposal of the Exploratory Working Group on the structure and composition of the new Working Group to be created for this purpose, which would be assisted by a Steering Committee comprising experts in various fields, both technical and legal. The composition of the Working Group was also to be representative of the legal (legal systems) and geographical diversity (and, although it does not seem to have been expressly mentioned, of the level of technical and economic development of the States) that would ensure the usefulness and projection of the resulting texts. This option was for the Principles to serve as a basis for what would later be called "jurisdictional neutrality" (to which we will return later).

From the outset, one of the most significant decisions taken within UNIDROIT was to prepare an *instrument*, still in an "undefined" format, characterised by its broad terms. It did not envisage the elaboration of a convention or a model law, for example, which requires a more concrete text that States could adopt in the terms in which it was drafted. The model instrument was called *Principles*, and would consist of basic *rules* (*principles,* presented in the form of *blackletters*) accompanied by *Commentaries*. Three criteria were to govern the work to be undertaken: the development of a "taxonomy" (ordering and classification) of the digital assets present in the market and their legal regime; the work would be carried out from a functional perspective that would allow it to be useful to all States, over and above the conceptual and institutional specialities of the different jurisdictions; finally, the work was to be carried out taking into account the "best practices" that were being developed in the international markets, which would allow the States to offer regulatory proposals referring to the most common transactions involving digital assets.[2]

---

[1] "(b) Work on Artificial Intelligence, Smart Contracts and DLT (C.D. (99) B.4 rev.) [...] 8. The Governing Council approved the temporary change of name of the project to "Digital Assets and Private Law" and decided in favour of an "enhanced" structure for the project which would entail setting up a Steering Committee composed of additional experts from different technical and legal fields and reflecting a diversity in terms of legal systems background and geography; cfr. UNIDROIT 2020 - C.D. (99) B Misc. 2, p. 2.

[2] "Format of the Guidance Document It is anticipated that the Working Group will prepare a set of Principles with commentary (not - at this stage - a model law or convention) which would include a legal taxonomy relating to digital assets, plus consideration of legal issues arising in particular contexts.

A functional approach to legal concepts was deemed to be most appropriate in order to produce a set of Principles which would not be jurisdiction specific, but which could be applied and reflected in any given legal system or culture.

The Principles would embody best practice and international standards and would enable jurisdictions to take a common approach to legal issues arising out of the holding, transfer and use of

In this way, the initial aspects of an ambitious work project were sketched out, largely due to the novelty of the subject matter to be dealt with. Some of these aspects would be discarded or corrected, totally or partially, over the course of the sessions: either because in reality they were unattainable (perhaps inadequate) for the proposed objectives, due to their extraordinary length and complexity, or because it became clear that it was not necessary to deal with all of them in order to achieve the desired useful instrument.

Thus, it initially seemed advisable (perhaps, due to the technological circumstances, it was inevitable) to make constant reference to "tokens" (in fact, the first objective of the work was to draw up "principles relating to the legal nature, transfer and use of tokens"). This name is merely a functional concept of a technical reality, with legal relevance, which in reality is neither sufficiently defined (the areas in which *tokens* are used are very diverse, which implies different perspectives in their treatment) nor "exhausted" (in its manifestations, i.e. the *token* models that are appearing) in international practice. Rightly therefore, the UNIDROIT draft soon abandoned the *token* as the essential reference, and moved towards the concept of the "digital asset", which would include, among others, the different types of *tokens* that are currently generally defined. Thus, the final version of the text [and its publication: UNIDROIT Digital Assets and Private Law Principle 2(2)][3] contains no reference to *tokens* in the *Principles*, which shows that the reflection and work carried out led to the conclusion that *tokens* are not the "model" of the digital asset, but only one of the instruments that comprise such assets. In the *Commentaries* accompanying the *Principles*, however, some references to *tokens* are retained, but only as mere examples of professional practices (for illustrative purposes) and are limited exclusively to explaining the scope of *Principle 4. Linked assets*.

In fact, it was already noted in the initial texts (*ibid.*) that *tokens* are only one example (*species*) of the broader concept (for the purposes of the UNIDROIT work, *genus*) of *digital asset*. The *functional approach* that was to drive the activity of the working group required attention to be paid to the possible models of digital assets that could be identified, strictly speaking (expressly conceived as such). At the same time though, it was also necessary to reflect on the possibility that other rights and *assets* could, at any time and in any form, be represented in the form of a digital asset susceptible of commercial activity. This "duality", the new and the old, of rights born under technological premises and prior rights susceptible to digital representation, meant that the working group should not only bear in mind the need to develop new, ad hoc rules for digital assets, but should also bear in mind the currently existing rules, looking for the possible accommodation of the *Principles* in the prior law of the jurisdictions.

In reality, there are several closely related aspects to this provision, albeit on different grounds. Firstly, the so-called "principle of the application of pre-existing

digital assets across a variety of use cases". Cf. UNIDROIT 2020 - Study LXXXII - W.G.1 - Doc. 2, p. 5 (https://www.unidroit.org/english/documents/2020/study82/wg01/s-82-wg01-02-e.pdf).

[3] *See* https://www.unidroit.org/wp-content/uploads/2024/01/Principles-on-Digital-Assets-and-Private-Law-linked-1.pdf.

law" or "prior law", which was formulated as a principle of electronic commerce (electronic contracting). The aim was to expressly recognise that the rules of each legal system would continue to be applicable to new technical realities, insofar as the latter were included in the natural scope of application of each rule, with the corresponding reinterpretation of its foundations and mandate. The foundations were thus laid for the so-called "principle of functional equivalence", which is essential in all areas in which new technologies seem to question previous models when, in reality, they can in most cases be brought back to the already known institutions. This principle of electronic contracting, however, has been largely ignored (at least, there is no express reference to it) in the *Principles*. One of the applications of this principle of attention to pre-existing law would be to prevent classic institutions and concepts, rooted in the legal systems, from "contaminating" the drafting of the *Principles,* inclining their mandate towards the legal positions of a certain model of legal system. In short, it is a matter of paying due attention to the *principle* of "neutrality" in relation to the various jurisdictions (this principle is indeed included in the *Principles*), to which we will return later[4]. Secondly, in a more specific area, it is a matter of ensuring the consistency of the *Principles* with the rules of jurisdictions specifically dealing with other types of assets, not necessarily digital (or, at least, not in the sense in which they are contemplated in the *Principles*).[5] This task is particularly complex, as it does not seem easy to identify (ideally, in all jurisdictions) the domestic rules on the recognition and negotiation of the various possible models of "assets", ensuring such coordination in each jurisdiction. To further complicate matters, the international perspective (a regulation aligned with international requirements) is often not present (or duly addressed) in national regulations. In this area, the experience of the members of the working group would be particularly relevant, applying their own knowledge of the most widespread national and international models. Thirdly and finally, at the time of drafting the *Principles*, some texts, or initiatives, of specific national rules on digital assets or other forms of electronic "records" or "goods" were already available; without prejudice, moreover, to other texts of an international nature which, directly or indirectly, should be projected on the *Principles.*

In this regard, it was specifically noted that coordination with some of the Institute's other work was necessary. The reference to various previous UNIDROIT texts seemed to be a necessary strategy for the work that was beginning; not only to ensure internal coherence between the Institute's texts and instruments and their contents, but also for the purely formal aspects of the methodology and development of the work (taking advantage of the experience in the drafting of other instruments), the approaches and principles followed, etc. In this respect, the reference texts expressly

---

[4] "It would take a functional approach, neutral as to legal culture. It would therefore seek to identify the rights and obligations arising, without giving bundles of rights and obligations labels, such as 'property', which vary between jurisdictions" (*ibid.*).

[5] "It would be necessary to consider how far the principles developed by the project are consistent with existing law. Despite the fact that tokens are a 'new' type of asset, consistency with legal treatment of other types of asset could be seen as important, and consideration will need to be given to what extent existing legal principles can apply by analogy, and what modifications are required" (*ibid.*).

called for were the UNIDROIT *Principles on the Operation of Close-Out Netting Provisions* and the UNIDROIT *Legislative Guide on Intermediated Securities* ("Geneva Securities Convention")[6]. It should be noted that such works were not appealed to because of their proximity in content and regime to the *Principles* (from which they differ in terms of subject matter), but rather as models or "templates" for the work to be carried out[7]. Other UNIDROIT texts which, at least by reason of their mere name, could also have served as a reference to the *Principles* (I refer in particular to the UNIDROIT *Principles on International Commercial Contracts*[8]), were not expressly called for in this work. The choice is, in fact, logical (probably the only possible one), since both texts differ considerably in their object, purpose, scope, projection .... even in their very conception. Thus, the name (in both cases, Principles) does not reflect an attempt to draft similar instruments, and should be seen as the result of a mere terminological coincidence.[9] Therefore, perhaps, and looking to the future, it would be advisable for UNIDROIT to define the model of instrument it wishes to promote under the label of *principles*.

The work undertaken by UNIDROIT was also to be aligned with other texts of international organisations and institutions close to the subject matter of the *Principles* or some of their aspects. In general terms, and given the close ties of joint work between UNIDROIT and UNCITRAL, in addition to the prestige and the undoubted value of the instruments of the aforementioned UN Commission, reference to several of its texts seemed unavoidable. Regardless of the influence of the UNCITRAL instruments on the activity of the working group, the *Principles* themselves expressly call for some of these works in their *Commentaries*. These are particularly recent texts, with

---

[6] *See* https://www.unidroit.org/work-in-progress/digital-assets-and-private-law/#1488897069871-af7a84cf-bd9a. *See* also, among other texts, the *Guide on Best Practices for Electronic Collateral Registries* (available at https://unidroitfoundation.org/e-registry-best-practice/).

[7] *See* UNIDROIT 2020 - Study LXXXII - W.G.1 - Doc. 2, number 19, p. 5.

[8] *See* https://www.unidroit.org/wp-content/uploads/2021/06/Unidroit-Principles-2016-Spanish-i.pdf, for the fourth edition, 2016 (in Spanish); for the same edition in English *see* https://www.unidroit.org/english/principles/contracts/principles2016/principles2016-e.pdf.

[9] Although the two texts are similar *in form* (both texts are integrated with *principles* and *commentaries*), the differences between the two texts are substantial. The principles on international contracts have sought to define an extensive body of private law (in a broad sense), capable of forming a *system* to which the interested parties (businessmen, but also legislators, arbitrators, etc.) can have recourse in order to adjust their actions to a complete international contractual model. Hence its claim (not yet achieved) to even be considered part of the *new lex mercatoria* (or, at least, a relevant manifestation of the so-called *soft law*). For this reason, the text has so far undergone four *editions* (in 1994, 204, 2010 and 2106), which have involved both the revision of the original text and the addition of new chapters (and "precepts"). The drafting of these principles is based on experience and institutions (and on legal systems) that enjoy decades (even of almost ancestral origins) of international acceptance: the aim is more an orderly systematisation (unification) than the *ex novo* creation of precepts (because no new legal realities, institutions or figures are regulated, but rather the classic ones of all national legal systems, which are now synthesised in *blackletters*). Finally, the commentaries to these principles follow the American model of *restatements* (explanations or glosses of the main text, which have full "authority" in delimiting the ends of the mandate; they are not, therefore, examples and mere clarifications). These considerations cannot be formulated with equal propriety or rigour with respect to the *Principles* discussed in this chapter.

specialised content that overlaps with sections of the *Principles.* Thus, some prior concepts in relation to the subject of insolvency expressly call for the *UNCITRAL Legislative Guide on Insolvency Law*[10]; for example, when defining the insolvency proceedings that the *Principles* take into consideration (*see Commentary 2.28*). Similarly, in relation to the collateral regime that is contemplated, the experience of the *UNCITRAL Model Law on Secured Transactions* (2016) (*see comment 14.3* and, in general, the *Commentaries* to *Principles 14* to *17*, Section V of the *Principles*, regulating the possibility of creating collateral over digital assets) provided the Working Group with a solid basis for its approaches[11] (even if they did not limit the objectives of the *Principles*). Coordination was also sought with other more "general" UNCITRAL texts, with cross-cutting application to legal institutions. This would be the *UNCITRAL Model Law on Electronic Transferable Records 2017)*[12]. However, what is missing in the *Principles* is an express reference to other UNCITRAL texts, relevant because of their content and with a direct impact on the work of UNIDROIT. Thus, for example, the *UNCITRAL Model Law on Electronic Commerce (1996) with its new article 5 bis adopted in 1998*[13], whose points (coinciding with the *Principles* in essential aspects) extend to any electronic transaction, and likewise, other subsequent UNCITRAL texts that assume the principles of electronic contracting, albeit applied to specific matters.[14]

---

[10] https://uncitral.un.org/en/texts/insolvency/legislativeguides/insolvency_law.

[11] Although the aforementioned *Model Law* is claimed insofar as it represents the culmination of UNCITRAL's work on the subject, the reference should be understood as being made to what I have elsewhere descriptively called UNCITRAL's "security system" (*vid.* PENDÓN, "El "sistema uniforme de operaciones garantizadas" de la CNUDMI. Antecedentes y aspectos relevantes para la elaboración de la ley modelo sobre garantías mobiliarias", in *De Iure Mercatus. Libro Homenaje al Prof. Dr. Dr.h.c. Alberto Bercovitz Rodríguez-Cano*, coord. J.A. García-Cruces González; 2023, pp. 3487–3529). These are the *guides* accompanying the aforementioned 2016 Model Law: the *UNCITRAL Legislative Guide on Secured Transactions* (2007); the *UNCITRAL Legislative Guide on Secured Transactions: Supplement on Security Interests in Intellectual Property* (2010); the *UNCITRAL Guide on the Establishment of a Security Interest Registry* (2013); the *UNCITRAL Model Law on Secured Transactions: Guide to Enactment* (2017); and the *UNCITRAL Practice Guide on the Model Law on Secured Transactions* (2019). All the above texts are available on the UNCITRAL *website*: www.uncitral.org; page https://uncitral.un.org/es/texts/securityinterests for the Spanish version; page https://uncitral.un.org/en/texts/securityinterests for the English version.

This precision is appropriate because, although the *Model Law* synthesises (in the form of "model laws" for states) the experience accumulated during the years of work of UNCITRAL Working Group VI and its results, the text that required the most reflection and elaboration, the basis and foundation of the others, was the *UNCITRAL Legislative Guide on Secured Transactions* (2007). Its analysis will allow the reader to justify many of the proposals in the mandates of the Model Law.

[12] *See* https://uncitral.un.org/en/texts/ecommerce/modellaw/electronic_transferable_records, for the English version; for the Spanish version *see* https://uncitral.un.org/es/texts/ecommerce/modellaw/electronic_transferable_records.

[13] *See* https://uncitral.un.org/es/texts/ecommerce/modellaw/electronic_commerce, for the Spanish version; and https://uncitral.un.org/en/texts/ecommerce/modellaw/electronic_commerce, for the English version.

[14] "E. Terminology Use of Standard Definitions 22. One of the objectives of the project is to come up with a legal taxonomy relating to digital assets which is to be developed in coordination

These absences are not merely a question of reference, but probably should have been rigorously projected onto the *Principles.* This is the case, for example, with the principle of functional equivalence (to which we will make several references in these pages), which could perhaps have been expressly formulated; or, where appropriate, a reflection on its meaning, scope and usefulness (if necessary, adapting these points in relation to how it is formulated by UNCITRAL) could have been incorporated in the *Introduction*; this, as will be explained, would imply its extension to the whole text. However, references to "equivalence" are only included, with varying meanings, in some *Commentaries* to certain *Principles*, probably without the scope they deserve.

In short, the UNCITRAL texts provide a twofold reference. On the one hand, of "material" content, which guarantees coherence between the provisions of the documents of both organisations, given the notable international acceptance that the UNCITRAL and UNIDROIT texts enjoy in the legal community, in a broad sense, and among the States, when using them as a model for drafting their internal rules. On the other hand, "formal" drafting also influences the new texts, as it is a matter of incorporating the terminology already established in other previous instruments; especially if they were the result of joint work between the two organisations. Naturally, incorporating and sharing the terminology (formal aspect) implies, at the same time, participating in the regime and the institutions that derive from it (material aspect). The sum of UNCITRAL's and UNIDROIT's different works, therefore, are new and coherent perspectives on the development of international normative models, facilitating their orderly and coordinated incorporation into national law.

This does not imply, however, conditioning the new texts by earlier texts, which may have become "outdated" or overtaken by technology[15] or simply by the opportunity of a new approach to electronic commercial transactions. In this sense, it is possible that the *Principles* present a partially different approach (although, functionally, they may lead to the same result), with respect to other texts, in some of

with UNCITRAL. Accordingly, it is important that care be taken to ensure accuracy as well as uniformity and consistency across the terms used by both organisations. Consistency of terminology with existing instruments 23. Existing instruments use different terminology for related concepts. The Working Group will need to consider which terminology the guidance document should use. Particular attention will be paid to the terminology used in key instruments of reference such as the UNCITRAL Model Law on Electronic Records (e.g., "electronic transferable record" and "control") as well as the UNIDROIT Convention on Substantive Rules for Intermediated Securities (2013) and the UNIDROIT Legislative Guide on Intermediated Securities (2017)"; cfr. UNIDROIT 2020 - Study LXXXII - W.G.1 - Doc. 2, p. 6; *see* further references *ibid.* at p. 8, under Relationship with existing instruments and other projects of the current Work Programme.

[15] This is the case, for example, in the *UNCITRAL Model Law on Electronic Commerce*, with the concepts of "acknowledgement of receipt" and "data message". The former, to a large extent already obviated by the technique. The second, superseded by the broader (and more appropriate) concept of "electronic document" (article 2 of the *UNCITRAL Model Law on Electronic Transferable Records*), to the extent that the latter is a suitable medium for collecting the relevant information (in essence, the data message is information, the effectiveness of which depends on the context in which it is generated and transmitted). This is, of course, without prejudice to the fact that these concepts may be useful (perhaps sometimes "forced"), being taken up in other more recent texts (although perhaps anchored in techniques that have already been superseded); for example, in the recent *UNCITRAL Model Law on Automated Contracting* (https://uncitral.un.org/en/mlac).

their paragraphs. This issue is reflected upon in some of the UNIDROIT documents generated in the course of its work.[16]

Finally, in view of the history of joint work by both international organisations, the lack of reference in the text (perhaps of consideration, although it was announced otherwise) to other instruments that are currently being drafted in collaboration between UNCITRAL and UNIDROIT seems a notable absence. In this respect, it is worth recalling the work on warehouse receipts, which has already been expressed in a model law and a legal guide[17]. This work, together with other UNCITRAL work, would perhaps have allowed complementary reflections in the *Principles*, for example in relation to linked digital assets (*Principles 4* and *14*) with which the text of the *Principles* should be consistent.

In the same way, the need to take into consideration the legislative work already initiated in some countries has become evident; experiences that were contributed to the working group by some of its members.[18]

---

[16] "*Consistency of terminology with existing instruments.* 24. Existing instruments use different terminology for related concepts. The Working Group will need to consider which terminology the guidance document should use. Particular attention will be paid to the terminology used in key instruments of reference such as the UNCITRAL Model Law on Electronic Records (e.g., "electronic transferable record" and "control") as well as the UNIDROIT Convention on Substantive Rules for Intermediated Securities (2013) and the UNIDROIT Legislative Guide on Intermediated Securities (2017)" [cfr. UNIDROIT 2021 - Study LXXXII - W.G.2 - Doc. 2 (rev. 1), p. 6].

[17] "33. Another area which presents an opportunity for cross-cutting work is the joint UNIDROIT - UNCITRAL project concerning a Model Law on Warehouse Receipts. There is a direct relationship with this project which examines the issuance and transfer of electronic warehouse receipts for goods stored in warehouses. In this connection, one of the categories of digital assets to be examined in the Digital Assets project concerns digital tokens which are linked to an external non-digital asset. By fostering exchanges between the two Working Groups, the legal analysis undertaken in the context of both projects would be mutually enriched. Moreover, should the work in the project to draft a Model Law on Factoring cover receivables issued in the form of digital assets, the crossfertilisation between both projects would also bring about important benefits"; [UNIDROIT 2020 - Study LXXXII - W.G.1 - Doc. 2, p. 8].

On the basis of a *webinar* jointly organised by UNCITRAL and UNIDROIT to assess the feasibility of a Model Law on Warehouse Receipts (https://www.unidroit.org/unidroit-and-uncitral-host-warehouse-receipts-webinar/; and https://www.unidroit.org/english/news/2020/200326-warehouse-receipts/report-e.pdf), the two organisations agreed to jointly draft a Model Law on *Warehouse Receipts*, based on a *Draft Model Law on Warehouse Receipts*, accompanied by an Implementation *Guide*, prepared by UNIDROIT. After review by UNCITRAL, the two organisations approved the final text in May (UNIDROIT) and July (UNCITRAL) 2024. The Model Law is a "modern" uniform text (in line with international models and practices) on the regime of warehouse receipts, paying special attention to the issuance and transfer of documents in both electronic and paper format (principle of functional equivalence). In this scenario, the relationship between these documents covered by the Model Law (warehouse receipt and guarantee receipt) and, in particular, with digital assets linked (*principle 14*) is evident.

[18] *Vid.* for example in UNIDROIT 2020 - C.D. (99) A.4, p. 5. "The swift development of token technology has led many jurisdictions to consider whether national private law provides a sufficient framework for the realisation of the economic benefits. Some countries have introduced proposals to amend national legislation (e.g., Russia, Japan, Switzerland), others have brought in completely new codes (e.g., Malta, Liechtenstein, or the US State of Wyoming) and some common law countries are allowing the law to develop through case law (e.g., UK, Singapore,

These reflections would also underpin the Working Group's necessary attention to the so-called "principle of technological neutrality", also formulated when defining the principles of electronic commerce. On this occasion, the final version of the *Principles* does expressly state the adoption of this form of neutrality. However, as will be explained below, it has perhaps not been applied with the desired decisiveness and rigour[19]; basically because the relevance of the technical model implied by the system of decentralised registers, DLT/blockchain, is currently exerting a force on technical and commercial models that is difficult to overcome.

Finally, the same document included other indications that should guide the Working Group's activity, delimiting some of its initial objectives. All these guidelines were eventually addressed in the final document, as will be explained in the corresponding section of these comments. Thus, it was indicated that the project should focus its proposal on private law issues, excluding regulatory aspects. The reference, therefore, does not contemplate the distinction (generally difficult, often blurred in many scenarios) between public and private law, which each jurisdiction can define and embellish with very different nuances. In the aforementioned document (also, finally, in the text of the *Principles*), "private law" (the actions of individuals) was opposed to "regulation", in the sense of rules which, being of a mandatory public nature, affect individuals (conditions of access or exercise of the

---

New Zealand). Not surprisingly, different jurisdictions have taken different approaches, partly through differences in legal culture and partly for other policy and contextual reasons." In several footnotes, the document cited reports on legislative initiatives in those countries, outlining the following: Russia has introduced a bill into parliament for second reading, Draft Law No. 419059-7 "On Digital Financial Assets", which contains a number of definitions, including "cryptocurrency", "token" and "digital wallet". For details on Japan's legislative activities in this area, see Sayuri Umeda, "Regulation of Cryptocurrency: Japan", Law Library of Congress Legal Report, June 2018, available at https://www.loc.gov/law/help/cryptocurrency/japan.php. For details on the Swiss Federal Council's Blockchain/DLT Draft Bill, see: https://www.admin.ch/gov/en/start/documentation/media-releases.msg-id74420.html#downloads. For Malta, see Malta Digital Innovation Authority Act, 2018, available at: http://justiceservices.gov.mt/DownloadDocument.aspx?app=lp&itemid=29080&l=1, sect. 2(1). For details on Liechtenstein's recently adopted Blockchain Act on tokens and trusted technology service providers, which established a legal framework for transacting in digital tokens, see: https://www.loc.gov/law/foreignnews/article/liechtenstein-parliament-adopts-blockchain-act/. For the US State of Wyoming, see United States, Wyoming Statutes, Title 34, Chap. 29, sect. 101(a)(i), available at: https://wyoleg.gov/Legislation/2019/SF0125. For the UK, see: High Court of England and Wales, AA v. Persons Unknown, Case No. CL-2019-000746, Judgment, 13 December 2019, reported in Weekly Law Reports, vol. 2020, No. 4, [2019] EWHC 3556 (Comm), para. 61. For Singapore, see: Quoine Pte. Ltd. v. B2B2 Ltd., Civil Appeal No. 81 of 2019, Judgment, 24 February 2020, [2020] SGCA(I) 02, para. 144. In New Zealand, a recent application was filed in the High Court of New Zealand by liquidators of the cryptocurrency exchange Cryptopia Limited, see: https://www.grantthornton.co.nz/globalassets/1.-member-firms/newzealand/pdfs/cryptopia/2020/d.submissions-for-the-liquidators-23-january-2020.pdf".

[19] "The project would also take a neutral approach, as far as possible, in relation to technology, so as to 'future proof' the principles. In other words, it would seek to develop principles that could apply to any system in which data could constitute a token (that is, an asset which could only be spent once), rather than being specifically applicable to systems based on DLT or blockchain. In this way, the danger that the work would be overtaken by technological or market developments would be minimised" (*ibid.*).

activity, control and supervision, etc.). In short, rules for the organisation of the activity. In order to avoid legal qualifications, which could lead to confusion in the actual wording of the *Principles* and in their interpretation, these regulatory rules, always emanating from the national public authority and, therefore, specific to each State, are generically referred to in a descriptive and functional way as *other law*.

Despite this working criterion, which could simply be added in the *Commentaries*, the final text of the *Principles* considered a specific formulation to be appropriate, drafting an ad hoc*principle* which, in the area it calls *procedural law, including enforcement* (section VI), leads to the area of national public rules of procedural regulation (rules of private law based on others of a procedural nature, the enforcement procedure). Apart from the *basic* national rules on which the regime for digital assets would necessarily be based, the draft should specifically address particular aspects of the regulation of digital assets. Without wishing to go into too much detail, early attention was given to insolvency law (specifically, section VII of the *Principles*; although references to this area are constant in other *Principles* and *Commentaries*); security transactions (section V), the determination of applicable law (section II, which contains the rules of private international law, *Principle* 5) and the legal position of intermediaries managing digital assets (in particular, custodians, section IV).

Some aspects that would eventually prove to be decisive for the *Principles*' regime were not initially foreseen, at least not expressly. This is the case, for example, of the notion of "control" of the digital asset (Section III, *Principle 6*). This is a fundamental concept for determining title ("ownership") of the asset and the entitlement to transfer, acquire and exercise it. Although it is based on technical issues, which are outside the natural scope of the *Principles* (as it should be due to the principle of technological neutrality), the relevance of control lies in the fact that it makes it possible to identify and legitimise the owner of the digital asset and, thereby, the exercise of the rights it confers. This includes digital asset transfer and, in relation to the acquirer (and vis-à-vis third parties) its investiture and legitimisation to exercise the rights. In short, it deals with questions of title and standing in terms functionally equivalent to the title and standing (in particular, standing by—physical—possession) of many legal systems (thus, in the area of *civil law*). In fact, this new concept of "control" goes beyond ensuring the protection of the holder of the digital asset, as it also touches upon questions of authenticity (of the so-called "singularity") of the assets. Several international texts (notably those of UNCITRAL) already provided useful and appropriate models and references on this complex and necessary concept of control.[20]

This broad approach (the perspective of "private activity" rather than the question of the strict nature of the rules) is, above all, useful for the conception and application of the text. It implies, in other respects, freeing the *Principles* from the constraints imposed in each jurisdiction by its own legal terminology, which necessarily calls for normative figures and legal institutions. In short, it is the presupposition for what is called "jurisdictional neutrality" as mentioned in the *introduction to* the

[20] *See* Article 11 of the *UNCITRAL Model Law on Electronic Transmittable Documents*.

Principles (we will return to this subject briefly below). An example may help to delimit the relevance of this approach which, in short, is a manifestation of the "functional approach" that presides over the entire text of the *Principles*. The Working Group, in its first session, discussed the scope of the contractual aspects related to the future treatment of digital assets. The experts' positions varied according to their own experiences: to distinguish between "contractual aspects in the narrow sense" (what some jurisdictions would call "general contract theory", albeit focusing on the speciality of the transactional aspects of digital assets) and "contract content" (the regime expressly agreed by the parties). This second perspective seemed preferable and indeed dominated the Working Group's reflections. This option did not exclude other issues, particularly linked to technical developments, but with direct effect on the transactions between the parties. For example, the possible relevance of "smart contracts" and the emergence of artificial intelligence in transactions had to be taken into account. These technical developments would be taken into account by attributing their real legal value to them. Thus, so-called "smart contracts" are not in fact true contracts in the sense of the general theory, but conditional clauses of "automatic execution" (when the foreseen and programmed circumstances occur), by means of which the effects contemplated in the contract will be executed. In short, in addition to the above, the need was repeatedly raised to address the most recent experiences and technical developments in the dematerialisation or digitisation of goods and rights, the new digital goods (ultimately, "digital assets") and the transactions in which they are transmitted and acquired.[21]

2 The Meaning of the *Principles* and Their Expression (the *Blackletters*)

A first note, of a purely formal nature, must be made, which nevertheless affects the structure and meaning of some parts of the UNIDROIT text. The *Introduction* to the *Principles* is the only part of this instrument that is essentially expository, it has no dispositive content. This means that the *Introduction* does not express *principles* or *rules* in a separate, closed formulation. The *Introduction* is composed exclusively of *commentaries*, although, as will be shown, its tenor is not merely descriptive, but sets out very relevant fundamentals that are projected over the whole text. In fact, part of its content must be taken into account not only to ensure a correct understanding of the text (*interpretative purpose*), but also to provide States with a guide for eventual implementation of the *Principles* (*normative purpose*); these issues will be discussed separately in further detail in the following sections. As a consequence of this "strange" arrangement of the text, the *Commentaries* in the *Introduction* are not numbered, strictly speaking, like the rest of the *Commentaries* accompanying each *Principle*: the numbering of the *Principles*, from 1 to 19, is projected onto the arrangement of their *Commentaries*, which are listed by reference

[21] *See* UNIDROIT 2021 - Study LXXXII - W.G.1 - Doc. 4, Nos. 139 et seq. at pp. 27 et seq.

to the number of the *Principle* they relate to (thus, *Commentary* 1.1; this numbering, which is the one used in the UNIDROIT text, will be followed in the following pages). For their part, the "reflections" (as noted, they are in fact much more than mere reflections) in the *Introduction* are ordered from 0.1 to 0.20, even though formally the *Introduction* is not (and is not presented as such) section 0 of the *Principles*. This is probably a conscious decision (not the mere result of the development of the works), which implies questioning (at least, leaving with a certain degree of uncertainty) the material meaning and real effectiveness of the *Introduction*: It does not share the format of the *Principles*, either in form or in substance, because it does not formulate any *principles*. Perhaps these specialities are the consequence of a certain lack of definition as to the intended effectiveness of the *Introduction*, because, although as such it does not formally express *principles*, in reality it contains substantive *rules* that condition the totality of the *Principles* themselves.

The essential objective of the work undertaken by UNIDROIT was "to develop a legal taxonomy relating to digital assets in coordination with UNCITRAL"[22]. The concept of "legal taxonomy" is perhaps difficult to precisely delimit in many jurisdictions, where the term "taxonomy" remains anchored in its classical meaning (linked to classification and hierarchisation in biology) and does not represent a defined technique for application in the legal world. The experience of applying a method for ordering and classifying sources and other legal resources (in a broad sense) is therefore not available[23]. The working group undertook the task of analysing the available legal instruments (including those in the drafting stage), the most relevant international practices, studies and proposals formulated by industry, international organisations and regulatory authorities etc., and to identify the most significant

[22] Cf. UNIDROIT 2021 - Study LXXXII - W.G.1 - Doc. 4, number 153, at p. 29. Although only this document is cited, the reference to this guideline is constant in the different documents that reflect the evolution of the work.

[23] A starting point for these states, which perhaps contributes to a better understanding of the *Principles*, may be the reflections of DUBOVEC: "157. Mr Marek Dubovec raised several queries relating to taxonomy: (1) whether the terms should be related only to the principles rather than a broader general taxonomy; he favoured including terms related to the principles as this would help to narrow the scope; (2) whether the principles themselves would include terms (e.g., what is a digital asset, what is control, etc.), noting there could be some degree of overlap between the principles and the legal taxonomy; (3) he underscored the importance of how this was presented to States, in particular, the importance of avoiding inconsistencies or gaps, and to this end, he invited the WG to consider as a potential source of inspiration the UNCITRAL Legislative Guide which contained a series of recommendations on what the law ought to contain, alongside a series of key terms. The Chair concurred with Mr Dubovec's three points. He noted that the modest approach would be to limit the taxonomy to the principles, and a more ambitious one would be broader"; cf. UNIDROIT 2021 - Study LXXXII - W.G.1 - Doc. 4, nos. 139 et seq. at p. 29. As to the application of the method, it was specified: "165. Ms Louise Gullifer understood a taxonomy as less akin to a dictionary and more of a map of legal concepts which helped in drawing lines between categories, which went hand in hand with a legal analysis. It was more than a list of definitions as it sought to ascertain how those definitions fit together. She emphasised that any lists of definitions should be specifically targeted for private law purposes, rather than a much broader audience (e.g., technologists, economists)". However, as the UNIDROIT secretary stated (*ibid*., p. 30), "158. Mr Ignacio Tirado (UNIDROIT) clarified that the project's mandate was to establish principles rather than a legislative guide, but that an expanded mandate could be sought from the Governing Council at the next session".

elements for regulating certain aspects of digital assets. This process would make it possible to formulate rules to guide the regulation of assets which, due to their recent appearance on the markets, required an initial classification and systematisation, an initial proposal for regulating some of their aspects. In short, it would be a matter of identifying and classifying "sources" in order to decant the relevant foundations around the legal question. Along these lines, the *Principles* therefore respond both to the idea of "initiating" that proposal for regulation, drafted by an international body that contributes decisively to the formulation of uniform (commercial or at least private) law, and to the idea of expressing normative values and regulatory guidelines that can contribute to security and predictability in national and international transactions with digital assets.

It should be borne in mind that neither industry nor private individuals require legal concepts in the strict sense for their own actions, which are, however, required by jurists. Only on the basis provided by the rules (whatever their nature or rank) can legal certainty be built, which also makes it possible to satisfactorily resolve the problems that arise in relation to these transactions (formal requirements for their validity, registration, third party protection, effectiveness of the transaction, and even cases of insolvency). However, the market creates its own concepts and practices, which do not always fit into the legal categories to which they apparently pertain (e.g. the so-called "smart contracts", briefly mentioned above: being contractual clauses subject to "conditions", their execution will only produce the intended effect—never a "new" one, by independent decision of their "programmers"—depending on the circumstances). The terminology or, in this field, the "taxonomy" of digital assets must take into account the technology being used and its actual social and professional implementation; but it must not be conditioned or limited by it. This perspective is a requirement of the so-called "principle of technological neutrality", expressly called for by the *Principles* in the *Introduction* (and which is reiterated throughout the text, although we will return to that issue later).[24]

These reflections lead to the question of the nature of the *Principles.* This instrument, a priori, does not correspond to any of the usual instruments of uniform law in the strict sense, particularly those used by the international bodies most involved in its formulation. In general, the works presented in the form of "principles" do not aspire to become a text with the aim of being applied (effective adoption by States), but are usually a study or a proposal (often with a notable academic profile) setting out the status of the issue being analysed, with references to professional systems and models, and which ideally could inform, or precede, an ad hoc regulation.[25] This is because, as a starting point, principles are the abstract formulation of rules

---

[24] *See* further reflections on this, and the approaches proposed and adopted in relation to the *Principles,* in *UNCITRAL Exploratory work on legal issues related to the digital economy - reports of events,* Fifty-third session New York, 6–17 July 2020, https://docs.un.org/en/A/CN.9/LIII/INF/2; and in *JOINT UNCITRAL/* UNIDROIT *WORKSHOP Rome, Seat* UNIDROIT *6 and 7 May 2019 Summary of the Discussion and Conclusions,* https://www.unidroit.org/english/news/2019/190506-unidroit-uncitral-workshop/conclusions-e.pdf.

[25] The work of The Hague Conference on Private International Law can be cited as a model; among the numerous instruments it produces, including conventions (with uneven success in effective

that synthesise previous norms, the expression of the foundations of a regulation. Principles set out the common and fundamental substratum of the rules and, once formulated, inform subsequent rules (and societal action). In general, they are the end of a process of reflection on rules or institutions, for which the common and shared fundamental aspects (in short, their orientations) are fixed. The UNIDROIT *Principles*, on the other hand, are conceived as the beginning of a regulation (proposals for the future): the substantive aspects of digital assets have not been decided, because there were neither sufficient rules (nor practices) to do so, nor national texts that set out models for competing practices. It is therefore an *ex novo* formulation, the result of a process of reflection that is more attentive to existing systems (pre-existing law, which must be preserved and applied to new realities) than to recent technological developments in the strict sense (the drafters were aware that the technology is not yet fully defined and is likely to continue to evolve). The *Principles* are pioneering rules, conceived with the intention of influencing the interpretation and application of existing rules (the "classic" law enshrined in the legal systems), and of leading to the drafting of new ones to regulate ad hoc the management of digital assets (the regime called for by the "digital economy").

These texts cannot, of course, be equated to an international convention. It was never UNIDROIT's objective to draw up an international convention or, at least, such was not stated in the most relevant texts of the work. Therefore, the method of drafting the *Principles* was not adapted to the procedure required for an international convention, which, among other things, requires a different form of participation by the States (exercise of sovereignty) and the convening of a diplomatic conference, resulting in a text submitted for signature and ratification by the States. No such procedure is envisaged in the *Principles*. Likewise, UNIDROIT ruled out other flexible formulae that traditionally lead to the elaboration of uniform law texts (of international trade, in the strict sense, or of private law matters, in a broader sense). The most widespread formulae include *model laws*, *legislative guides* (often with *recommendations* facilitating the implementation of their content), *model provisions*, *legal guides*

implementation; *see* https://www.hcch.net/en/instruments/conventions; also, its studies and publications, available at https://www.hcch.net/en/publications-and-studies/publications2), there are also the *Principles on Choice of Law in International Commercial Contracts* (https://www.hcch.net/en/instruments/conventions/full-text/?cid=135). The Conference is a reference body in the elaboration of uniform texts, frequently participating in the work of UNCITRAL and UNIDROIT: *UNCITRAL, HCCH and* UNIDROIT *Legal Guide to Uniform Instruments in the Area of International Commercial Contracts, with a Focus on Sales* (https://uncitral.un.org/sites/uncitral.un.org/files/media-documents/uncitral/en/tripartiteguide.pdf).

An origin closer to academic activity (without prejudice to other institutions that participated as founders) and with more determined aims (in relation to European law) can be found in the *European Law Institute* (https://www.europeanlawinstitute.eu/) which, among its many activities (see https://www.europeanlawinstitute.eu/projects-publications/), has published the *ELI Principles on the Use of Digital Assets as Security* (https://www.europeanlawinstitute.eu/fileadmin/user_upload/p_eli/Publications/ELI_Principles_on_the_Use_of_Digital_Assets_as_Security.pdf).

and *practical guides*, among others[26]. The available examples of these instruments correspond neither to the form nor to the purpose of the UNIDROIT Principles.

However, among the usual techniques and working models, there is no generally accepted protocol for the elaboration of texts that are called "principles"[27]; although there are many institutions and bodies, both public and private, that formulate general rules or principles on an issue (which often do not transcend sufficiently in space or time). In fact, all these instruments (with the exception of conventions) are susceptible to being part of what is known as *soft law*. This (relatively) new concept refers to normative models, contractual forms and clauses, and guidelines and regulatory proposals that do not emanate from States, but from specialised bodies and institutions (of any nature: public, or above all, private). Their usefulness, their acceptance and, where appropriate, their consolidation, is due to the impact they create among professionals, who rely on these texts because of the prestige of the forum provided by these institutions and that of the drafters. It is not, therefore, a question of simply compiling the result of generally accepted professional practice in a text, which would lead us to the sphere of *the lex mercatoria* (the expression of established practices), but to the sphere of the regulatory ("normative") proposal. Obviously, the line between the two forms of promoting or recognising uniformity is often tenuous; it can even be seen that the concept of *lex mercatoria* is nowadays questioned or, at least, is more difficult to appreciate in the new instruments, in view of the flexibility and breadth attributed to the concept of "soft law". In any case, and whatever the denomination under which they are identified, consolidated practices (the so-called "best practices") are one of the elements taken into account in the drafting of *soft law* texts, in addition to being part of the *lex mercatoria*. The *Principles* aim to reflect and align themselves with these established practices, whatever the name or formal classification given to them.

From the beginning of UNIDROIT's work, it was proposed that the result of the activity should be the elaboration of "principles" which, as such, could serve as a model for national legislators when regulating this matter in their own legal systems. The incorporation of the *Principles* can be carried out either with regard to national transactions (thus achieving uniformity via an indirect route, by approximating the rules governing the corresponding transactions), or by expressly contemplating international transactions. The eventuality of this incorporation into domestic law required

---

[26] UNCITRAL's working methods (which constitute a reference in the field) and their results, all accessible on its *website*, can be consulted in summary and expository form in the *UNCITRAL Guide Basic Facts and Functions of the United Nations Commission on International Trade Law* (available at https://uncitral.un.org/sites/uncitral.un.org/files/media-documents/uncitral/es/12-57494-guide-to-uncitral-s.pdf for its Spanish version; at https://uncitral.un.org/sites/uncitral.un.org/files/media-documents/uncitral/en/12-57491-guide-to-uncitral-e.pdf for its English version. The working methods of UNIDROIT, which have led to the elaboration of the *Principles*, are accessible on its *website*, https://www.unidroit.org/.

[27] As indicated above, the UNIDROIT *Principles of International Commercial Contracts*, because of their special circumstances (essentially, scope and content), do not seem to serve as a model for this new text.

the formulation of general rules, which would enable legislators to familiarise themselves with these new models of goods and business, bringing them closer to international practice without the need to question their own legal systems. Due to their very conception and development, technological issues are beyond the national perspective and require attention to the internationality of their foundations (technological supports) and of the business deals they conclude on the resulting assets. This *soft law* instrument should be formulated with respect for what would be called "jurisdictional neutrality" (to which we will return later). Only as the work progressed and the actual scope of the document being drafted became clearer, could the UNIDROIT Governing Council propose (or, as the case may be, amend) a different name for the text and thus its formal nature.[28]

The choice of drawing up "principles", while rulng out other methods of standardising the law on digital assets, is coherent (probably the best option) at this initial stage of consolidation of digital asset trading practices. The aim is to formulate "first" rules that form the fundamental bases for subsequent (more complete) regulation, with a view to an approximation of national legislation (the path to uniformity). These rules are formally expressed in each *Principle*, highlighting in the text their synthetic formulation (almost in the form of articles, like those of any standard), and their formal presentation (ordered, numbered, highlighted in bold: *blackletters*). Their non-binding nature and their usefulness in informing rules of a private nature in legal systems, where necessary, make the *Principles* a flexible instrument, synthesising the current state of affairs in many of the world's States (in particular in relation to traditional law) and modern commercial practices. The variety and diversity of the participants in the working group guaranteed that broad spectrum and neutral vision (universal, contemplating the main legal systems and models of practice) that the document requires. It is, therefore, a "normative model" project which, unlike model laws, does not imply (or impose) systematic drafting of precepts in ad hoc norms, which may strain the mandates of national legal systems. A model law implies, at least initially, a tighter and more refined text, which will often require further revisions of the national rules (as the different degree of adaptation of the articles for some States will mean a break with the required uniformity). With the instrument drawn up by UNIDROIT, it will be the legislators who eventually lead the integration of its "mandates" into national law, without being subject to, or conditioned by, the limits which, to a greater or lesser extent, are imposed by the "pre-drafted" precepts.

On the other hand, the *Principles* also aim to inform the actions of professionals (in a broad sense: judges, arbitrators, mediators, practitioners, advisors, etc.) who have to be familiar with and resolve issues related to digital assets. The *Principles* offer "templates" for the drafting of contracts, for defining practices, for assessing business transactions... from a uniform international perspective. The nature of this instrument allows such "application" between individuals and professionals at their

---

[28] In this sense *vid.*, for all, UNIDROIT 2021 Study LXXXII - W.G.2 - Doc. 2 (rev. 1) (available at https://www.unidroit.org/english/documents/2021/study82/wg02/s-82-wg02-02rev-01-e.pdf), number 22 (D. Title of the instrument), at p. 6.

own choice, without any requirement of "validity" or State implementation, beyond its publication by UNIDROIT.

These reflections are merely descriptive, and do not imply that I necessarily agree with the model instrument chosen by UNIDROIT.[29] Model laws, even if they are not considered for direct enactment into national laws, can fulfil a similar function as principles, as they equally serve as examples for practitioners, lawyers and governments and legislators; even more so when, as is increasingly the case, these model laws are accompanied by *guides* for implementation (transposition) into national law. Such guides can be instrumental in supporting the work of the legislator. Even the *legal guides* themselves offer, both in their *text* (explanatory and with examples of application) and through their *recommendations*, the advantages of flexibility, coherence and reflection on international models, to the extent that *guides* have sometimes preceded (and subsequently accompanied and supplemented) model laws. The result is therefore a complex and extensive body of all-encompassing norms on an issue; although it may require projecting itself on matters and institutions already consolidated in international juridictions and practice, of which an orderly updating is offered to facilitate their incorporation into national law.[30]

3 About *the Commentaries* on*the Principles*

Formally, the *Principles* (apart from their *introduction*) are published in two distinct parts; the *Principle* in the strict sense (a total of 19) and its (often extensive) *Commentaries*. The *Principle* formulates a basic, abstract rule or idea, which cannot, however always be incorporated as a precept in a legal system. In this respect it differs from the proposed articles of model laws, where national legislators are provided with a

[29] For some good reflections on the possible instruments in this field, focusing on the UNIDROIT *Principles, see.* BAZINAS, S.V., "Digital assets and private law: is there a need for a uniform law?", *Uniform Law Review*, Volume 28, Issue 3–4, December 2023, pages 381–389.

[30] The reference in this case is to the *UNCITRAL Model Law on Secured Transactions (2016)*, expressly called for in several sections of the *Principles* (in its *commentaries*) and in the different documents produced during the development of the work. Although the "final" document is the aforementioned Model Law, this text was the result of the work carried out for years by UNCITRAL Working Group VI, which resulted in some previous instruments [the *UNCITRAL Legislative Guide on Secured Transactions* (2007); the *UNCITRAL Legislative Guide on Secured Transactions: Supplement on Security Interests in Intellectual Property* (2010); the *UNCITRAL Guide on the Establishment of a Security Interests Registry* (2013)]; texts available on the UNCITRAL *website*: www.uncitral.org; page https://uncitral.un.org/es/texts/securityinterests, for the Spanish version; page https://uncitral.un.org/en/texts/securityinterests for the English version] and subsequent to (or accompanying) the Model Law [the *UNCITRAL Model Law on Secured Transactions: Guide to Enactment* (2017); and the *UNCITRAL Practice Guide on the Model Law on Secured Transactions* (2019)]. The Guide published in 2007 is the basic text of the "system", both for its detailed and precise recommendations and for its "didactic" purpose, as it gathers the debates, examples and foundations of the proposals for a modern security system, which states could use as a reference for the implementation, or revision, of their legal systems. For some reflections on this set of norms, *see.* PENDÓN.

reference text, with a refined formulation, which is useful for the drafting of the corresponding mandate in the national law. The *Commentary* helps to clarify the scope of the mandate (justification, purpose, timeliness and orientation of its normative content), expressing reflections that can contribute to the modification that, where appropriate, the precept requires in each national system. When appropriate, they reflect the debate held within the working group, and when necessary, warn of the limits (delimitation) of the mandate, of the problems that may arise through adoption by the systems, and the purpose for which it should be incorporated into the systems (interpretation).

In general, it seems that the choice for the *Principle/Commentary* duality is based on the American model of the *restatements of the law*, particularly those that make up the *Uniform Commercial Code.* UNIDROIT had already expressly resorted to this technical model when drafting the UNIDROIT *Principles of International Commercial Contracts.* It should be noted that the Institute's option here was well received by the commentators on the work.

This North American "regulatory model" has no equivalent in most States, and requires special technical conditions to ensure its drafting and rigour[31], which in many respects are probably unrepeatable today in other settings (we will return to this issue later, taking up some of the criticisms of the drafting process of the *Principles*). Like the *restatements*, the *Principles* (and the *Commentaries*) are an example of the collaboration and interaction between academic rigour and practical utility that the text pursues, a model of theoretical coherence closely connected to the real world. The perspective provided by the different jurisdictions that participated in the elaboration of the *Principles* undoubtedly contributes to their uniformity, based on the agreement, attentive to reality, that has been achieved. All of this probably underlies the usefulness and projection in the case of *restatements.* Their recognition is particularly strong in academia and, by extension, in other specialised legal fields (arbitration, international commercial practices, etc.), largely because the academic

[31] *Restatements* (particularly in the *Uniform Commercial Code*) play a significant role in the US legal system. Although they lack normative force in the strict sense, they have a decisive influence on the interpretation, application and even the evolution of commercial law. Restatements contribute to the harmonisation of the law between states, insofar as they constitute a recognised synthesis of *common law* principles and the interpretation of the rules that make up that legal system; they thus contribute to the systematic organisation of legal doctrine in a broad sense. For this reason, courts of justice frequently resort to the support offered by restatements, as they make it possible to fill possible gaps or inaccuracies in the legal terms of the rules, to make up for the absence of previous judgments that resolve and clarify an issue or to coordinate variations between judgments (restatements are largely based on the most relevant judicial precedents). These *qualified commentaries* are prepared under the auspices of the American Law Institute (ALI), with the participation of judges, practitioners and academics. The collaboration of these professionals, each of whom brings his or her own vision to the drafting of the texts, ensures the technical coherence of the *restatements*, as well as their practical application, in which the legal community at large participates. The permanent revision to which they are subjected, both in their drafting and in their application and, where necessary, their modification or updating, guarantees the rigour and prestige of the texts, which thus command a high degree of consensus among specialists. This explains their clarity and usefulness, their de facto authority and their academic use.

contributions highlight the usefulness of the instrument and make it possible to verify the adequacy of the experience they bring to national systems.

If this is, very briefly, the relevance of the *restatements*, it seems obvious that the effectiveness (the legal projection) of the *Commentaries* to the *Principles* is not comparable with them, lacking the recognition and position in the legal systems (at present, only derived from academic reflections) that the American text enjoys in the United States. No general UNIDROIT document seems to be available that explains, as the Institute's own working method, the procedure to which the elaboration of this special instrument (principles and their commentaries) would be subjected; without prejudice to the fact that the study of the drafting process of the text (the *travaux preparatoires*) makes it possible to follow and legitimise each decision adopted, endorsed by the competent bodies (as is the case of these *Principles*; see above in the summary of this process and the official reference documents). The *Commentaries*, then, lack a clear position in the structure of the appropriate instruments envisaged by UNIDROIT to promote uniformity of international trade law. Their value, in any case, is that of a privileged source of reflections on digital assets, an indispensable text in the coming years to inform the work of lawyers in this area.

The absence of a prior procedure to guide and "legitimise" the nature of the work carried out is not only a formal (and relevant) issue, it also affects the assessment and acceptance that the *Principles* will project. Therefore, the participatory or collaborative model of professionals followed by UNIDROIT, although broad and generous in its conception, does not seem to have sufficiently responded to the sensitivities of some qualified actors on the international scene. Hence some of the criticisms already formulated, both from a strictly legal and opportunity perspective and from the assessment of its usefulness (and professional projection).[32]

At present, therefore, the *Commentaries* cannot be considered to reach the standard of the *restatements* (if indeed the *Commentaries* are based on that working model). However, it can be argued that they will be the core element of the reflections promoted by the *Principles*. Moreover, to the extent that the eventual incorporation of the *Principles* into national laws is based on the flexibility they provide (as *rules* or

[32] The relevance that UNIDROIT attaches to the composition of the working group is evident in each official document published, both in the documents prior to the sessions and in the report drafted afterwards. Thus, the list of participants in each case is not only given as a control and expression of attendance, but also highlighting the value of their participation and contributions: in the margin of the list of members of the group, it is stated "23. UNIDROIT also invited a number of organisations with expertise in the field of digital assets and private law to participate as observers in the Working Group. Participation of these different organisations will ensure that different regional perspectives are considered in the development and adoption of the instrument. It is also anticipated that the cooperating organisations will assist in the regional promotion, dissemination, and implementation of the guidance document once it has been adopted. The following organisations have been invited to participate as observers in the Working Group: […]. 24. Finally, UNIDROIT may also invite a number of industry associations to participate as observers in the Working Group to ensure that the guidance document will address the private sector's needs. The latter will also assist in promoting the implementation and use of the guidance document. The following private sector association has been invited to participate as an observer in the Working Group, but more may be invited: […]"; cf. UNIDROIT 2021 - Study LXXXII - W.G.3 - Doc. 2 (rev. 1), pp. 5 and 6 (). 5 and 6 (https://www.unidroit.org/english/documents/2021/study82/wg03/s-82-wg03-02-rev01-e.pdf).

foundations), the interpretation and adaptation they require to ensure their adequacy with domestic norms must necessarily be consistent with the *Commentaries*. This perspective enhances the value of the *Commentaries* and the role they are called upon to play in the extension of the *Principles*. We will return to the criticisms raised in relation to the composition of the UNIDROIT working group below.

4 The Value of the *Introduction*

Many of these preliminary reflections were essential to assess the meaning and scope of the *Introduction* to the *Principles*. Structurally, the *introduction* appears "at the beginning of the *Principles*", as a general presentation; but formally it neither lists any rule (or principle; it lacks *blackletters*) nor does it appear as a *Commentary*. It is then a question of determining its usefulness in the text (it claims a different treatment from the rest of the *Commentaries*, which do deal with the *Principles*) and its value in the UNIDROIT instrument (its application and projection on future rules and practices). A reading of the *Introduction* shows, at first glance, that it contains some general rules that explain the drafting of the *Principles* and guide the interpretation thereof; but these "instructions" are not formulated in a synthetic or abstract way, but as expository reflections that aim to project themselves on each *Principle*, on all the *Principles*. They are therefore commentaries that are superimposed on each *Principle* and its *Commentary*. In the absence of an express acknowledgement to this effect, it would at least be an "introductory or justificatory report" of the instrument.

Looking for a similar model, one could think of the *Introduction* as a kind of "explanatory memorandum" or preamble, which is typical of laws. This is a common formula in some *civil law* systems, with different specialities (for example, the explanatory memorandum would refer to the draft law prepared by the government, while the preamble refers to the law itself), the purpose of which is to present the "normative" part of the text. In itself it would have no legal value, without prejudice to the fact that on occasions it is sometimes attributed, erroneously in many cases (its content is often not reviewed after the parliamentary procedure), a certain interpretative value of the legal text. For all these reasons, the preamble should, at most, have a reference function.[33] Consequently, for these explanatory statements or preambles, it has even been considered advisable to omit their publication in the official gazettes, thus avoiding the debate on their scope and the possibility that the parliamentary procedure would not also be reflected in this presentation of the law. In short, they have no normative value per se.

The *Introduction* to the *Principles* is not preceded by a principle (rule) or summary. It does not have the value that would be attributed to principles, nor is it formulated as a mandate that can (or should) be expressly included in a future rule. It does

---

[33] The Spanish Constitutional Court has issued several rulings on which these ideas are based; among others, SSTC 36/1981, of 12 November; 150/1990, of 4 October; 90/2009, of 20 April. A doctrine that coincides with the one already expressed by our Supreme Court.

not therefore serve as a model for a precept, without prejudice to the fact that it could inspire the drafting of a precept *ex novo* (not provided for in the *Principles*) or revise the wording of the 19 principles that are expressly formulated. Nor is the *Introduction* called a *Commentary*, as *commentaries* necessarily refer back to the *Principle*, in the sense set out above. The *Introduction* does not therefore follow the structure of the rest of the *Principles*, nor does it take on the common name. A brief reflection is therefore necessary on the meaning (and perhaps the "value"), scope and effectiveness of the *Introduction* in the *Principles*.

It should be reiterated that the *Introduction* does not contain "mandates" (principles intended to become mandates or to formulate a rule), nor does it develop rules (clarifications or developments of the ideas underlying the mandates). Its structure (and thus its purpose) is different from that of the rest of the *Principles*. Two distinct parts can be distinguished in the *Introduction*. The *first* is the part in which reflections on the UNIDROIT instrument itself, as a whole, are formulated. These ideas are formulated "free of conditioning factors" or limiting criteria (beyond those deriving from the *Principles* themselves as a whole), as they are not delimited by a prior *principle* that is formulated. We will refer to this part as the *foundations*. The *second* part synthesises the organisation and content of the *Principles* themselves (a preview of all the *Principles*). We will call this part a *summary*. In this case, it is only a summary, with a brief commentary, of the various *Principles*, sometimes grouped into chapters.

The *foundations* are projected over the whole text of the *Principles*, guiding its reading, interpretation and application. It also sets out some of the criteria that were taken into account by the drafters and, therefore, to a large extent condition the proper usefulness that the UNIDROIT instrument should provide. It was not considered appropriate to translate its content into other *principles*, strictly speaking (although it probably should have been done). Perhaps this cannot be seen as a good thing. As will be discussed, these *fundamentals* impose a regulatory and implementation perspective on legislators and practitioners that needs to be taken into account in each *Principle* separately, in the instrument as a whole and in the legal environment that each State may adopt in application of the *Principles*. Excluding the "normative value" (or "regulatory value") from the *rationale* of the *Introduction* may cast doubt on its real effectiveness, even though it formulates general ideas which, in a proper overall interpretation of the text, can be deduced.

In these notes, the idea of the "obligatory nature" of the *foundations* of the *Introduction* is assumed, even though, formally, its formulation might indicate otherwise. We consider that the *foundations* do not only try to explain the setting of the *Principles*, but also advance and expose previous and necessary notions of the text. Likewise, they express interpretative and conceptual criteria of the instrument, which adequately situate the analysis of each *Principle*, contributing to its better understanding and application. In this scenario, however, analysing the *summary* of this *Introduction* is less useful, since the mere list of the sections and *Principles* included can easily be substituted (and improved) by the Commentary, *in extenso*, on each *Principle*. Therefore, in this area we refer to the considerations of the other authors who comment on the *Principles*.

From this perspective, the interest of the commentary to the *Introduction* is to highlight some assumptions of the *Principles* which, despite their relevance, are not expressly formulated elsewhere (the *foundations*). These preliminary ideas may contribute to overcoming some of the difficulties presented by the UNIDROIT text. In any case, assessments will be made that may contribute to the debate on the relevance of these UNIDROIT *Principles*. For this exposition, an outline similar to the account in the *Introduction*, which refers in general to all the *Principles*, will be followed.

5 Purpose of the *Principles*

The UNIDROIT *Principles* are initially conceived to serve the same purpose as any other regulation (or proposal for regulation) that is presented: to design a regulatory framework that, in addition to regulating the subject matter of the text in an orderly fashion, provides legal (and social and economic) security to the activities and transactions that fall within its scope of application. Compared to a "rule" in the strict sense (or to other instruments that seek to become a rule), which requires its formulation under certain rules of organisation (for example, by presenting the text in titles, chapters, etc. up to the articles) and normative coherence (by specifying the scope of application), the *Principles* are drafted with greater flexibility, due to their very nature. Their purpose, therefore, is not to become a norm, even with a cross-cutting or general scope, affecting different sectors of a State's legal system. The *Principles* are intended to be projected onto country-specific rules, where necessary to ensure alignment with the requirements of a regime for transactions in digital assets in an international market (without prejudice, where appropriate, to the national market) that calls for the greatest possible uniformity. Thus, for example, the *Principles* on collateral issues (numbers 14 et seq.) cannot (and are not intended to) define a complete regime on digital assets and their use in the market as collateral, but only specifically address those aspects that should be assessed for the application of previous, amended or revised national rules in the context of such assets and their transactions.

Like any instrument prepared within the framework of the so-called uniform international commercial (or trade) law, the UNIDROIT *Principles*, like the Institute itself, are conceived to promote uniformity of international commercial (or private) law as their ultimate purpose. In particular, the scope of application of the *Principles* delimits the projection of this commitment to uniformity to transactions in digital assets (*Introduction 0.1*). Notwithstanding this prior and common objective and the delimitation of the commercial transactions that define the subject matter of the *Principles,* other specific purposes are called for in several paragraphs, two of which are worth highlighting.

The *first* of these specific aims is to promote maximum efficiency in international transactions in digital assets (*Introduction 0.2*). This is a general and broad objective, for which no clear indicators are provided for its assessment. The digital assets taken as a reference are those defined, in very broad terms, in *Principle 2*;

although it is inevitable to appreciate throughout the text the influence that the most modern techniques that make electronic records possible (decentralised records, or DLT, in the framework of blockchain technology) have had on the work.[34] This technique is relatively recent and, as a result, the relationships and the transactions that can be carried out, for example, through the use of *tokens*, have yet to be defined. This objective is therefore proposed as a "maximum" proposal, extending the scope of application of the *Principles* as far as possible to allow them to be applied to forthcoming developments. In any case, the difficulty of specifying international transactions that are made possible through new technologies makes it difficult to assess the real effectiveness of this specific objective at this stage.

Maximum efficiency is achieved primarily by ensuring that transactions involving these digital assets (initially domestic transactions and, by extension under uniform law, also international transactions) are carried out at the lowest possible cost. Reducing the cost of transactions is an objective in itself of any transaction (national or international), as it means the most favourable economic conditions for the parties involved in a commercial transaction, while at the same time optimising the profitability of the transactions. However, it is not an objective that can be expressed in isolation, but one based on the prior formulation (and achievement) of other objectives. Confidence in transactions (and thus their use in the market) is essentially based on the predictability of the applicable regime and the outcome that will result from its application. This is an aspiration of any rule: that the consequences of its application are predictable and therefore guide the decisions of individuals and their effects in advance. In the framework of international transactions, where elements of internationality converge and often affect the conceptual unity of a transaction (derived from the specificities of each operator and each applicable legal system), the need to build certainty into the consequences of actions holds particularly significant value. The diversity of practices and rules, supported by different national regulations, affects the desired predictability. This fragmentation of a transaction is particularly significant in markets where digital transactions are involved—markets that have demonstrated extraordinary speed in incorporating new technologies and a particular agility in devising new transaction models. Such transactions are often not catered for by the classical institutions of national legal systems: the professional market is ahead of its regulation. Uniform law, constructed in this case on the basis of the "proximity" or similarity of national systems, offers a scenario of security and standardisation for the legal assessment of the various transactions. To this end, the *Principles* propose complementary and "corrective" models for the national legal

[34] A broad concept of "digital assets" is embraced in all the work that has been done in this area. Various technologies are creating, transforming or enabling the trading of different assets; these new "forms of property" (they are, at least in appearance, without prejudice to the fact that we are redirecting most of their regime to already known institutions) force us to consider existing technologies and products (digital files, digital records, all types of tokens, domain names, financial assets, digital carbon credits, NFTs, crypto-assets, non-fungible tokens, etc.) without excluding the possibility of new developments. The near future is really impossible to foresee and digital assets may undergo any evolution that the rules and principles we are preparing in various fora must be able to contemplate and include in their scope.

regime of classic transactions (generally on the basis of the *principle of functional equivalence* which, although essential in the digital world, is not expressed in the *Principles*).

Predictability and security are built on the basis of a regime that underpins the extremes of digital asset transactions with sufficient breadth and certainty. However, UNIDROIT ruled out (because of its complexity and, perhaps, its inappropriateness in these times of insufficiently settled technological change) the design of a comprehensive regime for digital assets (the initially envisaged taxonomy, which was subsequently narrowed down during the materialisation of the project). Instead, a (perhaps overly) broad definition of "digital asset" was chosen (see *Commentary* on *Principle 2(2)*)[35]: the *Principles* focus on the (broad) subject matter of transactions, without limiting either the nature or the typology of these transactions (which are in fact not defined by themselves, but by the generic reference to their proprietary purpose). At this stage, without a detailed analysis of each "asset" that can be qualified as a digital asset within the scope of *the Principles*, it is not possible to determine whether the UNIDROIT's work can be applied to the full range of possible assets or whether some of them will require specific exceptions or provisions (specific criteria will probably be needed for some of them, for example, some of those that make up the "category" of linked assets, *Principle 4* and *Principle 14*). The *Principles* provide rules, both summary and conceptual, which will help to define the basis for a complete system, although at this stage of affairs it is apparently a work in progress, meaning that we only have a basis or principles because such was deemed appropriate. To a large extent, this is due to the insufficiency of practices and models available in international markets to serve as examples for analysis, given the recentness of this technology, and with it, of the operations that can use them.

In the light of these considerations, the goal of predictability and efficiency (in the terms set out above) is more an expectation of the *Principles* than a reality. Thus, for example, the *Principles* purport to be based on, and to embrace, international best practice in digital asset transactions. However, it does not appear that UNIDROIT had any ad hoc studies that analysed the models used in professional practice and their efficiency. Any assessments that could be made were based on the personal (or professional) experience of the members of the Working Group. Therefore, it is impossible at present to assess the possible effective impact of the *Principles*, even though thoughtful, consensual and legally effective rules are logically put forward. Although during the drafting of the Principles, attention to best market practices was considered fundamental, the lack of participation of enough professionals who could contribute their own experiences and provide their business models and proposals

---

[35] The consideration that the concept of *digital asset* is extremely broad, as a consequence of its extension to numerous market practice models, is a conclusion shared by the studies carried out on the issue. *See* the work of the Law Commission of England and Wales https://webarchive.nationalarchives.gov.uk/ukgwa/20250109172211mp_/https://s3-eu-west-2.amazonaws.com/cloud-platform-e218f50a4812967ba1215eaecede923f/uploads/sites/30/2023/06/Final-digital-assets-report-FOR-WEBSITE-2.pdf. Similarly, the *Report of the European Law Institute* entitled *ELI Principles on the Use of Digital Assets as Security* (https://www.europeanlawinstitute.eu/fileadmin/user_upload/p_eli/Publications/ELI_Principles_on_the_Use_of_Digital_Assets_as_Security.pdf).

has been criticised in some forums (we will return to this issue below). Doubts about the efficiency *desideratum* that the *Principles* would promote are opportune[36] and force us to take a closer look at the interpretation of the *Principles* in order to ensure their effectiveness.

The second specific purpose stated in the *Principles* is to provide guidance to persons directly or indirectly involved in international transactions in digital assets (*Introduction 03*). The parties to the transaction in the strictest sense and the authorities that, where appropriate, supervise it (under the generic name of '*principals'*, protagonists of the transactions) are expressly cited as 'recipients' of the *Principles.* Likewise, the *Purpose of the Principles* is to support legal and economic professionals (who trade on the markets) and the specialists who inform the transactions (advisors, consultants, lawyers), providing them with an instrument to improve the design of the transaction itself and to resolve, where appropriate, any doubts and problems that may arise. The *Principles* also provide rules and reasoning to support the actions of the people and institutions responsible for resolving any disputes that may arise (arbitrators, mediators, judges and courts of law). Finally, the *Principles* encourage their dissemination among national legislators, who would thus have guiding criteria for the regulations they approve.

The aforementioned number of the *Introduction* lists all the addressees, albeit in a somewhat confusing way. At first glance, it appears that there are different levels of "responsibility" or participation among the possible addressees of the *Principles*, which would probably call for a separate treatment (and perhaps a clarification of the purpose of the claim). A first level would consist of private professionals, in the narrow sense (essentially, the conduct of commercial transactions). A second level would consist of supervisory authorities. The third level covers the exercise of jurisdictional functions in the strict sense (judicial and arbitration or mediation). Finally, the fourth level is exclusively for the national legislator. The impact of the *Principles* is different in each case: from the (almost full) freedom provided by the autonomy of will (freedom of contract) in the first level and the flexibility of the arbitration institution to the subjection to law imposed on judges and supervisory authorities. The reference to national legislators deserves a separate mention, to the extent that the *Principles* themselves devote a specific commentary to it (*Introduction 0.4*), under the formula of the adaptation of the *Principles* by the States; which shows the incovenience of its reference in *Introduction 0.3*.

It should be noted that the *Principles* can develop their effectiveness at certain levels (the contractual level in the strict sense, that of professional advisors, arbitration...) regardless (and independently) of the fact that the States (legislators) promote the revision of their rules on the basis of the *Principles.* And in this way, the contractual (professional and practical) acceptance of the *Principles* can contribute to (and

[36] Comment 3, by David GIBBS-KNELLER, University of East Anglia, pp. 18–19: "There is no guarantee that the model will produce predictable results, free from inherent inefficiencies that would otherwise appear in the regulatory market. Better outcomes may be produced by leaving the majority of matters covered in the Principles to regulatory competition. For example, the principle that a good faith purchaser without notice should take title over the original owner may be a certain rule, but it may introduce inefficient credit terms into digital assets".

also confront) the reception of the *Principles* in the rules of a State. That is, the application of the *Principles* takes place through different channels (and, perhaps, with different effectiveness) at different levels. Thus, even domestic law may reject, or ignore, *Principles* that may nevertheless be effective when nationals engage in international transactions with digital assets, under the protection of party autonomy.

The different projection of the *Principles* at the proposed levels (which do not exhaust the question) would recommend making the commentary in the *Introduction* more extensive and precise, since these are questions that affect the "value" of the *Principles* as an instrument for uniformity. In fact, as remarked in several sections of these notes, the *Introduction* to the *Principles* contains reflections (even real "informal" principles, which would be projected on all the *Principles*) which would probably deserve more attention and, in any case, a more detailed and careful drafting[37]; this matter is one of them.

6 *Objectives* of the *Principles*

Closely linked to the question of the aims of the *Principles* is the question of the objectives pursued. Again, as a starting point, the general objective is to contribute to international uniformity in the field of digital asset transactions by making an ad hoc instrument backed by the prestige and standing of the Institute available to stakeholders. These objectives can essentially be summarised in two respects.

First, the *Principles* are intended to *inform* the laws of States in all aspects that may be related to their scope of application. Although the *Principles* are few and very concise, they are intended to apply to all national laws insofar as they regulate international (including national) transactions involving digital assets. The *Principles* are too brief and conceptual to be expressed in normative mandates regulating a subject matter; therefore, they can only aspire to guide the interpretation and application of existing rules, in an attempt to define a specific field. This is a difficult goal to achieve.

The uniformity promoted by the *Principles* is thus based on their postulates permeating a system, not on their adoption "as is" by States. As noted elsewhere in these notes, it falls short of the precision and development that a model law requires (such was never intended). This is the only way to ensure the coherence of national norms with the *Principles*, keeping each national system's own postulates updated in the light of the *Principles*. The national rules will then require only a few new provisions or, where necessary, minimal corrections, which can even be resolved by promoting the functional interpretation of the precepts.

This objective of conformity is generally difficult to achieve for any *soft law* instrument, and is even more difficult to achieve for the instrument developed by

[37] A close reflection on the value of the *Introduction of* the *Principles* was proposed by S.V. BAZINAS, Kozolchyk National Law Center, in the document submitted for public consultation (UNIDROIT 2023 Study LXXXII - W.G.8 - Doc. 4, 43 COMMENT.2, p. 18).

UNIDROIT. It is not a matter of defining an institution, a figure, a contract or a practice; it is more a matter of influencing all the rules of a State (its legal system) that may be applicable to these transactions with digital assets (if necessary, while maintaining their own scope of application). This influence would at least apply to transactions of a private nature involving such assets. But this implies its application to transactions (in principle all types of transactions) in assets and, where appropriate, to the "securities" they represent, which are themselves subject to their own rules. The case of linked assets (*Principle 4*) is even more complex. The broad concept of "digital asset" on which the work is based, the huge quantity of possible transactions and the regulatory specialisations required may mean that a large number of different rules will have to be reviewed in each legal system, sometimes with different regulations in different countries, and this will inevitably lead to conflicts between jurisdictions and reduce the chances of achieving uniformity.

7 The Question of Ownership in the *Principles*

One of the most complex (and controversial) aspects that the *Principles* have addressed in their regulation is the question of digital assets as "objects" of property law (or, in broader, more flexible and therefore less binding terms, "objects of economic rights"). This question arises in particular because of the projection of the Principles into the area of private law, where ownership is inevitably a central issue. The *Principles* have been conceived and drafted on the premise that "(1) A digital asset can be the subject of proprietary rights", (*Principle 3*, which is headed *General principles*) and that "These Principles cover the set of transactions most important in commerce—transfers of proprietary rights in a digital asset and the creation of a security right in a digital asset (see Principle 2(5))" (*Introduction 0.16*).[38]

This approach promotes the debate on whether it is a "new type of property", or a revision or extension of the concept of property that each State has already defined

[38] The focus of the project is on private law, and, in this context, this implies, generally though not exclusively, property law (widely construed). Therefore, in the first instance, this project is concerned with digital assets that are plausibly objects of property rights, or perhaps rights similar to property rights. The focus on proprietary rights, however, presents a difficulty in terms of distinguishing cause and effect. Current principles of property law in different jurisdictions yield contradictory answers to the question whether any particular type of electronic data can be the object of proprietary rights, and indeed suggest quite different approaches to conceptualising intangible representations of value generally. Not all types of electronic data that the project will examine are considered as "property" in some jurisdictions. As part of its mandate, the project may consider surveying the variety of approaches typically found across national jurisdictions in order to identify common problems with a view to assisting in the development of appropriate Principles. While it might be possible to make a catalogue of the "property status" of electronic data under the current law of any number of jurisdictions, this would not per se yield workable Principles for the development and harmonisation of private law. It would therefore be necessary to take a broader view of the subject matter to define the scope of this project, whose purpose is to develop a set of Principles, at the transnational level, that courts and legislatures can use to guide legal interpretation and reform. cfr. UNIDROIT 2020 - Study LXXXII - W.G.1 - Doc. 2.

in its legal system, or finally a "functional property", with only certain effects and limited scope, expressly conceived for the *Principles*. The latter seems to be the option followed by the drafters, as it is stated that the aim is neither to question nor to alter the ownership regime of each State, but rather to ensure that some of the effects of the ownership regime are applied to digital assets: in particular, in relation to the protection of the third party acquirer in good faith of a digital asset (*Principle 8*) and the use of these assets as collateral (*Principle 14*)[39]. Of course, this option does not imply excluding that States may equate (recognise) the full ownership regime over digital assets; but the perspective of the *Principles* only requires a similar treatment for the situations or transactions that they expressly contemplate.

Both *common law* and *civil law* systems have norms or rules designed to ensure the effectiveness of certain transactions, limiting (even excluding) the possibility of claims when the acquirer acts in good faith; although each legal model affords some specialities or demands certain requirements. In both cases however, it is recognised that these are exceptions to the principle *nemo dat quod non habet*. This exceptional character requires their appropriate formulation and their limited application, as it is also generally considered that the rule is not absolute[40]. The diversity of assets that can be considered as digital assets makes it difficult to formulate a descriptive definition, taking into account the nature of the thing and the right, the relations between them (e.g. linked digital assets), registration and publicity of ownership and asset transactions or the dematerialisation of the title in which the asset is incorporated. The foregoing is considered without addressing the different technologies that underpin them. Hence the broad concept of digital asset that is formulated in *Principle 1*, given the impossibility of a concept that includes all possible forms of assets (tangible or intangible, fungible or infungible, etc.)[41]. Over the centuries, legal

[39] "Proprietary aspects 0.13. These Principles establish that digital assets (as defined in Principle 2(2)) are susceptible to being the subject of proprietary rights, without addressing whether they are considered 'property' under the other law of a State. See Principle 1 and Principle 3(1). As being the subject of proprietary rights, it is appropriate to fashion rules applicable to digital assets that provide for the protection of innocent acquirers and for security rights in digital assets, taking into account the particular characteristics of a digital asset. See Principle 8 and Principle 14".

[40] Perhaps, in the UNIDROIT *Principles* it would be more appropriate to express the principle *in extenso*, under the formula *nemo plus iuris ad alium transferre potest, quam ipse haberet*, as it contemplates "rights", making it clear that it does not only refer to things (often, the Roman maxim is linked, and justified, on the basis of possessory relationships, which call for a different perspective when it comes to rights and their ownership).

[41] "The application of property law rules generally depends on the identifiability of property and some form of publicity, as well as the following of transfers of interests in property from one person to another. The application of property rules also sometimes requires "tracing" of interests, which may require formulas or other methodologies. These concepts are particularly challenging in the context of digital assets. Moreover, some digital assets are fungible, and some are not. Ether and Bitcoin are fungible, for example. Non-fungible digital assets represent a unique asset that cannot readily be interchanged with other digital assets, even if two non-fungible digital assets seem similar to one another. Non-fungible digital assets can include metadata, visuals, serial numbers and other characteristics that make them unique, and, thus, uniquely valuable. Examples of a non-fungible digital asset would include unique digital items like crypto art, crypto-collectibles, and crypto-gaming tokens." cfr. UNIDROIT 2020 - Study LXXXII - W.G.1 - Doc. 2, pp. 13–14. 51.

systems have incorporated the specialities required by the different forms of property as new objects or rights that have appeared, that could benefit from the regime of a "special" property. It seems impossible to take advantage of all this heritage without an extraordinary effort of reflection and search for functional equivalence.

Each legal system will have the means to extend, if it so wishes, its own rules to certain types of digital assets (for example, those which, applying the principle of functional equivalence, do not present particular difficulties, such as those involving the dematerialisation of securities, the incorporation of certain rights and properties into NFTs, among others) or to the whole (the latter seems to be the initial option for England and Wales, as set out in the report drawn up by the Law Commission of England and Wales, mentioned above). In any case, all scenarios will need specific rules or interpretations adapting traditional concepts, such as possession and its acquisition (in line with what the principle of functional equivalence allows, e.g. the concept of "control" of digital assets as equivalent to possession, *Principles 6* and *7*; and the UNCITRAL Model Law on Transferable Records).[42]

8 Limits of the *Principles*

As is the case with any newly conceived normative (or regulatory) text, the *Principles* are "limited" by the law that makes up the legal system of each State (prior law). Every national legal system has been built on the basis of its own experiences, institutions and terminologies, integrated in an orderly and harmonious manner to transmit the required coherence between its provisions and its capacity for self-integration. The law of each State remains faithful to its own legal figures, and revising them requires a demanding conceptual (and normative) effort, which will only be faced when it is perceived that the national legal institutions will be able to assume the new perspectives (in this case, of uniform rules). The prior national assessment of the appropriateness and usefulness of the *Principles* is the challenge that this UNIDROIT instrument will face. Only to the extent that there is certainty as to their effectiveness, will States be willing to assume the "cost" of their implementation (the complex process of revising their own legal system). Such an analysis is a difficult task, as the *Principles* employ their own terminology which, however *neutral* it may claim to be (see below the reflections on the different concepts of "neutrality" that would have led to the elaboration of the *Principles*), is inevitably based on previously established legal concepts, which will not always be easy to "translate" and transpose into the legal systems. This difficulty is exacerbated by the fact that the *Principles*

[42] In this sense, the *Introduction* also focuses on the treatment of these issues on the occasion of "control": "Control 0.15. The Principles have developed a concept of 'control', consisting of a number of factual abilities that a person must have in order to have control of the digital asset, as discussed in Commentary 0.11. The concept of 'control' plays a critical role in the rules included in the Principles, in particular for the innocent acquisition rule and making a security right effective against third parties (see discussion of transfer below), as well as for the definition of a custody agreement. See Principles 6 and 7, and Principle 10".

are not accompanied by a terminology of their own which could facilitate this task of incorporation (we will return to this question later).

The regime proposed by the *Principles* is characterised, inter alia, by the idea of "minimum intervention", since it is based on the prior normative framework of States ("other law", in the terminology of the *Principles*). For this prior law, States are provided with interpretative rules (allowing the adoption of the UNIDROIT *Principles*) or, where appropriate, new rules (when required by the novelty of the subject, due to its technological connotations, which generally, could not be taken into account at the time of drafting). This contributes to the revision of national regulations, supporting their adaptation to a modern and uniform legal system[43]. The effort made revolves around the concept of "digital assets" *[Principle 2(2)*]; also, with the connotations that will be pointed out, "private law", as expressed by its own denomination.

This can lead to a high degree of indeterminacy: the scope of application of the *Principles* is only broadly described (on the basis of private law and digital assets), but the nature of the transactions that would be subjected to them is not identified, while it is noted that there are different areas of law that could be subject to review, with the exclusion of some (consumers, intellectual property, etc.). In reality, the *Principles* do not establish a true scope of application (*Principle 1).* The margin of interpretation for States is therefore undefined (even confusing), as each State will be able to decide which digital assets (and in which circumstances and transactions) would be (fully or partially) subject to the *Principles*; which of its rules could be applied to digital assets, whether or not they are aligned with the *Principles*; which of the existing rules could be reviewed in the light of the *Principles*, without prejudice to the other provisions of its law; and finally, in which cases, and to what extent (whether or not to adapt its own law), new rules specifically designed for digital assets and inspired by the *Principles* would be needed.

One of the issues that apparently creates uncertainty in relation to the *Principles* is the lack of any prior generic terminology, which would help to clarify the goals of their mandate. It is not a question of expanding the number of definitions (*Principle 2*), as these would in fact help to delimit the scope of application of the mandates and, with them, of the UNIDROIT instrument itself. The aim would be to provide a "glossary" that sets out the starting points of the discussions on which work has been built. Digital assets are defined in the *Principles* by their nature—electronic—and their use—control—but not what they actually are (in an attempt not to exclude any currently known in the state of the art or future forms thereof) or the transactions in which they may be involved. This "aseptic" or neutral construction is built on concepts,

---

[43] "This explains, naturally, the prudent approach adopted by the Principles, which only cover those areas where the nature and characteristics of digital assets required legal clarification or where ad hoc solutions were demanded. The rest - the majority - of private law matters are left to domestic law, although, even where reference is made to "other law" (as it is called), helpful guidance and legal analysis is provided in the Commentary, a part of the instrument which is almost as important as the blackletter Principles themselves. Rather than providing a comprehensive, new private law framework, the purpose of the instrument is to fill existing gaps and add legal certainty in the application to digital assets of a pre-existing national private law regime" (cf. foreword to the *Principles*).

techniques, realities and practices that are not always standardised or uniformly defined across borders. In short, UNIDROIT's work is based on assumptions by the drafters (the Working Group), which have not, however, been compiled anywhere, since they are taken for granted. This wealth of technologies and practices, of terms and experiences, is not reflected either in the *Principles* or in their *Commentaries*.

If we consider the text of the *Principles* themselves, they are the result of debates and consensus in drafting that faced the challenge of the conceptual linguistic barrier; the assumptions from which the members (participants and guests) of the Working Group started, each of them conditioned by their own technological, legal or economic language (according to their own speciality). If agreements were reached by adopting the terminology specific to each of these fields, a channel should be found to reflect these consensuses, which would now allow for appropriate interpretation of the *Principles* according to the will and the compromises reached within the Working Group (there were many meetings, debates, complementary activities... which involved presentations and agreements at different linguistic levels).

In short, the absence of a glossary explaining the terms and the agreements reached on them is, in my view, a notable shortcoming of the *Principles*. This situation should be redressed, including (if necessary) by drafting a new UNIDROIT instrument to supplement (or accompany, or integrate with) the *Principles*.

This glossary should define general and prior aspects, referring to technology and assets (the taxonomy initially envisaged, which in the end, is missing from the *Principles)*. At the very least, it seems essential to define concepts that are expressly used in the *Principles* or in their *Commentaries*. Thus, it should be clarified what is meant by "distributed ledger technology" and "blockchain technology" (*Introduction 0.5*)[44]; the special features of the concept of "possession" in relation to control (*Introduction 0.6*); the meaning of "private law", in particular in relation to "property

[44] The *Introduction*, at the indicated place, warns that the reference to these technologies does not limit, or sufficiently limit, the type of digital assets covered by the *Principles*: "However, this has been done only to clarify the application of the Principles and is not meant to favour assets that employ these types of technology, or to modify or undermine the applicability of these Principles to digital assets that employ other technologies. Importantly, this is not meant to impair the technology neutrality of these Principles. Thus, these Principles are intended to apply to all digital assets (as defined in Principle 2(2)), whether or not the record of these digital assets is on a blockchain. On the scope of these Principles, and more specifically, the type(s) of digital assets these Principles cover, see Commentary 0.11 and 0.12 and Principle 1.

Precisely for this reason it is desirable (perhaps necessary) to clarify the scope and meaning of the technology used as a reference. As a starting point, DLT can be considered as the "genus" or general category of a technology, while blockchain is a kind or application ("species") of decentralised record-keeping. From a technical descriptive point of view, DLT is a decentralised database (ledger or accounting record, it is often said, somewhat imprecisely); that is, there is no central "authority" to manage and verify entries, or to resolve disputes between participants in the transactions being documented. Distributed recording is intended to increase the transparency of records; in theory, by excluding (or at least making it extraordinarily difficult) fraud and manipulation, as each transaction is validated by a large number of participants. In any case, the traceability of transactions is guaranteed. In this previous scenario, blockchain is an application of DLT, with its own specialities: a shared database made up of blocks grouped in "chains", i.e. linked together by a "hash" that allows the cryptographic encryption ("signature") of the information (which, therefore, cannot be manipulated once it has been "encrypted"). Recent initiatives seem to lead these technical

rights" ("property" or "title"; "*derechos patrimoniales*", in Spanish), for example in *Introduction 0.9*, among other sections),[45] aspects that probably go beyond the provisions of *principle 3, 3.4*; the precise scope of "security rights" (*Introduction 0.10*); and elsewhere in the *Principles*, the concepts of "fungible assets" (*Principle 2, 2.21*), "White Paper" (*Principle 4, 4.2*), "System / platform" (*Commentaries* on *Principle* 5), "NFT" (*Principles 4, 4.*164), "multi-signature (multisig) arrangement" (*Principle 6, 6.10*), "full node" and "light node" (*Principle 10, 10.10*), "cold wallet storage" (*Principle 10, 10.15*), "crypto-lending market" (see para. 2 of *Principle 15, 15.2*), "close-out netting" (*Principle 17, 17.2*), among others. Having such a glossary would contribute to the understanding of the *Principles* by States and practitioners, allowing them to incorporate these concepts into their own legal system in the appropriate form (practice and regulatory review, as appropriate), in a uniform and generally accepted manner by international operators.

A second notable limitation of the *Principles* is the paucity of available models of international practice. Few practical examples could serve as references for the drafters of the instrument to abstract principles and rules from the practices and solutions tested professionally and most widely accepted in the markets. The initiatives that have been undertaken by relevant business groups, either in networks or consortia, are still at the conception (gestation) stage; and respond to special purposes (those specific to the business model of their promoters, e.g. in financial markets, in "paperless" international trade, etc.). While embracing some of these practices, the *Principles* are the result of a complex conceptual and creative process (largely driven by academic criteria) by individuals who had limited access to international "best practices". Although the work was carried out in the privileged forum provided by UNIDROIT, they had no (or at least no record of) economic analysis and data on international practices. They relied essentially on the expertise (and assessment) of the drafters and institutions invited to the Working Group. They were representative of activities, backgrounds, countries and jurisdictions. However, several voices have criticised that the Group's composition did not sufficiently take into account certain legal sensitivities and their practical models (especially from the French legal system). Although it can be proved that, at least in principle, the composition of the working group maintained an adequate balance between authors and institutions and, above all, between "representatives" of the two classical models of jurisdictions (*civil law* and *common law*). There has been some criticism on how the *Principles*

---

means towards networks with certain access "restrictions" (DLT networks), which make it possible to define the type of operations (and thus the classes and conditions of the participants) that are executed on the network (optimising their use at all levels). A basic reference (definition) of all these (and many more) extremes seems necessary in this possible glossary that financial institutions, consultancies, etc., generally formulate for their own initiatives.

[45] For example, within the *Introduction* itself: "*Proprietary aspects* 0.13. These Principles establish that digital assets (as defined in Principle 2(2)) are susceptible to being the subject of proprietary rights, without addressing whether they are considered 'property' under the other law of a State. See Principle 1 and Principle 3(1). As being the subject of proprietary rights, it is appropriate to fashion rules applicable to digital assets that provide for the protection of innocent acquirers and for security rights in digital assets, taking into account the particular characteristics of a digital asset. See Principle 8 and Principle 14".

are mostly inclined towards Anglo-Saxon models (and terminology). Thus, the functional perspective that characterises the *Principles* is probably more easily accepted, in general, in common law countries than in civil law countries; although the latter are applying the principle of functional equivalence which can sometimes lead to similar results. However, some problems are still claimed, because of the acceptance of a model of legal institutions, such as the Anglo-Saxon perspective on property, which differs from that of civil law countries in relevant aspects.[46]

Closely related to this question is that of how the text is drafted. The difficulties involved in drafting international texts (in this case, texts aiming at uniformity) so that they are sufficiently adapted to the particularities of the legal systems, but without the technique of one or another jurisdiction predominating, are well known. Apart from the question of the so-called "jurisdictional neutrality" in the *Principles* (to which we will return later), the legal drafting technique has also been the subject of reflection. The *Principles* often state to which issues a law other than the *Principles* themselves would apply; when perhaps it would be more correct to rectify this "intrusion" by simply clarifying the issues to which the *Principles* do not apply ("negative" delimitation of their scope of application, rather than claiming other rules to regulate certain aspects of digital assets), although it is true that this approach does not solve all interpretative issues either. For example, it is neither possible, nor appropriate, to attempt to list all the issues that, according to each legal system, can be classified as public law rules; but in this case the *Principles* have preferred the option of determining their scope of application: the private law of transactions with digital assets. In any case, the use of the novel expression "other law" to call for the application of national (or "domestic") rules is surprising. Time will tell whether this new terminology will find its way into future international instruments.

---

[46] Legal systems often have different rules depending on whether property concepts apply to tangible or intangible assets; sometimes even intangible assets are denied the property regime, based on a tradition that shaped property over tangible assets. Digital assets do not fit well into this normative reality, and countries are making efforts to incorporate the digital reality into traditional legal conceptions or, where appropriate, to issue ad hoc rules to accommodate it. In some legal systems, however, there are fewer difficulties in extending the classical regime to intangible assets (in common law, through *actio in personam* and *actio in rem*), making the intangible assets regime more flexible. Although legal systems have techniques to regulate or treat rights in a generic framework of incorporeal goods that they treat as things, the variety and complexity of digital assets makes them difficult to define and classify, and thus impossible to locate in known figures of the legal system. Thus, for example, it may be possible to reconduct tokens with some ease, on the basis of the nature of the good or right that they "represent"; experience may even be available in the dematerialisation of certain securities, which will also communicate their traditional regime on their digital or immaterial representation. Greater difficulties may be encountered either when the digital asset relates to qualified rights (e.g. shares) or when it is a title representing goods (bill of lading, warehouse receipt, etc.), which require the regime of the asset, the regime of the title, the regime of the underlying causal relationship - transport, deposit - and the speciality, deriving from all this, of its use in traffic to transfer ownership or other rights in rem. If we were to add to these issues the complexity that the technology used may entail (perhaps not enough thought has been given to the differences that the use of DLT-based or other technologies may entail for digital assets), it seems desirable that the *Principles* would have provided a classification of digital assets and the terminology that defines them.

9 *Rules* that Inspire the *Principles*

A novel section (in its conception and content) in the *Introduction* refers to some objectives or *rules* from which the whole text draws, although they are not expressly formulated in its sections. These *rules* (we shall call them so, in order to differentiate them from the *principles* of the text) play a dual role. *First*, they guided the work of the drafters of the *Principles*, so that they remained attentive to their prevalence during the debates and the drafting of the text. These *rules* therefore explain to a large extent the expression used and, sometimes, the technical choice made in the instrument. *Second*, these *rules* will be projected on the application (to whatever extent) of the *Principles* (their use by the addressees of the *Principles*): legislators, practitioners, advisors, etc. In short, these *rules* are presuppositions of the *Principles* (in their conception) and requirements of the *Principles* (in their application).

The first of the *rules* called for corresponds to the so-called *principle of technological neutrality* (set out in *Introduction 0.5*). This principle is considered fundamental from the moment of its definition within the "principles on electronic commerce" (or "on electronic contracting"). The reference to its formulation is found in the *UNCITRAL Model Law on Electronic Commerce with Guide to Enactment 1996 through its new article 5 bis adopted in 1998* (New York, 1999).[47] Essentially, this principle implies that the rules formulate their mandates in unbiased terms with respect to the technology covered by the rule itself, with a willingness to apply equally to developments that may occur in the future. It is therefore a standard that is not conditioned by technical progress. Since its definition, this principle has served as a guide for the "standardisation" of the digital phenomenon in commerce (both national and international) and the "standardisation" (drafting of rules) by national legislators and institutions. However, this is a principle of electronic contracting that is not fully effective if it is not complemented by others to which it is closely related. Hence, the *principle of non-discrimination* (difficult to separate from that of technological neutrality; see articles 5 and 5.*bis* and 9 of the aforementioned Model Law); the *principle of functional equivalence* (articles 6, 7 and 8 of the aforementioned standard); the principle that calls for the *survival of prior law*; and the principle that, in application of the previous ones, requires the *useful interpretation of the rules*.

The integration of these principles is a requirement of the rules, so that without the concurrence of the others, the principle of technological neutrality is largely devoid of meaning. In particular, functional equivalence is essential to give content to the principle of technological neutrality, as it justifies its usefulness and, above all, its effectiveness. Once discrimination between technologies has been ruled out (this is another of the projections of technological neutrality), it must be verified whether the existing rule is applicable to the new reality, due to the equivalence between the figures or institutions. Sometimes, in some jurisdictions, it may not be possible to determine functional equivalents between new and older technologies; for example,

---

[47] Available at https://uncitral.un.org/en/texts/ecommerce/modellaw/electronic_commerce, for the English version; and at https://uncitral.un.org/es/texts/ecommerce/modellaw/electronic_commerce, for the Spanish version.

in property matters, if the rules remain closely attached to paper-based or face-to-face transactions. In such cases, it may not be possible to maintain technological neutrality in relation to new technologies (different techniques and nuances will be required), but it will always be possible to recognise functional equivalence.

It is easy to state the relevance of the principle of technological neutrality, but it is difficult to maintain it in any policy instrument. It is not easy for drafters to detach themselves from its constraints. Their reflections, even the experiences and examples on which they are based and proposed, have the technology they know as a reference, the technology in the making and the "past" technology (which, in reality, claims the principle of functional equivalence and, where appropriate, the principle of non-discrimination). The mandate of some of the *Principles* may be justified and conditioned by the technology being referred to. It is clear that technology related to blockchain and distributed registration, tokenisation, etc. have been inescapable references in UNIDROIT's work. This had to be the case, because it was necessary to verify (as a "test bench") that the work would be consistent with current technology and directly applicable to the transactions being carried out; also, to the foreseeable forms of business and to the evolution of the state of the art. The envisaged scope of technology thus delimits the regime of the *Principles*, but may also limit them.[48]

Thus, for example, the mandate taking into account a DLT (Distributed Ledger Technology), authorised (and supervised) or not by the public authority (depending on the type of transactions involved) may require a greater or lesser degree of definition and, where appropriate, attribution of liability, which must be known by the users of the platform. This is a particularly relevant issue in insolvency cases, as liability may be diluted in the shared system if no express provision is made. However, in cases where such technology is dispensed with, the mandate, drafted ad hoc for that technology, may be empty. *Commentary* is essential to overcome these (and other) drawbacks, as the formulation of the "mandate" must avoid the casuistry of specific techniques. Moreover, such clarifications require recourse to functional equivalence (which, unfortunately, is not expressly called for in the *Principles*).

The second *rule* that is formulated (*Introduction 0.5*) to guide the drafting, interpretation and application of the *Principles* is "Neutrality in relation to the business models" that would define their scope of application. The mention is almost incidental (the quoted *Commentary* merely states: "First, these Principles are technology and business model neutral") and is not repeated elsewhere in the text; notwithstanding

---

[48] In this regard, *see* the comment of the World Bank Group, on the occasion of the document submitted by UNIDROIT for public exposure: "Despite this, we are not clear (in particular from the definition of Digital Asset and definition of Control in Principle 6) how can the Principles be applicable to other than unique non-duplicable "tokens" based on a DLT/blockchain or similar technology. A proper definition of Digital Asset including DLT/blockchain (see below for definitions) with the addition of "similar technologies" (as for example the definition of crypto-asset used at EU's MiCA) would, in our opinion, be broad enough to accommodate future developments while, at the same time, in line with the spirit and wording of the Principles. On this regard to be noted that "system" and "platform", referred to in Principle 5, are not defined while apparently pointing to DLT/blockchain platforms" (cfr. UNIDROIT 2023 - Study LXXXII - W.G.8 - Doc. 4, Comment 21, p. 11).

the fact that, as intended, the idea is present in its mandates and reflections. Formulated in such simple terms, without any further precision, it is an unnecessary rule, as it does not add any idea or limit to the scope of the *Principles*. If it was intended to emphasise the idea that the *Principles* are designed to be effective in any kind of transaction, the reference is of little use. Any "rule" is intended to be drafted in objective terms, within the scope of application that is established. Within that scope, the rule is intended to regulate all relationships that meet the requirements laid down. In the case of the *Principles*, these relationships (transactions) must occur in the context of commercial transactions ("business") between private parties (more precisely, subject to the private law regime). The *Principles*, like all rules, aspire to objective wording, devoid of the limits and conditions imposed by casuism; an aspiration of general projection within the framework of its own scope of application. It is not usual for the rules to express this question, which perhaps belongs to the field of normative technique, and consequently that is why it is particularly striking in the *Principles*. Its usefulness is probably to be found in its connection (which is why it is presented together) with the principle of technological neutrality, which it would aim to complement. The *Principles* are meant to apply irrespective of the technology that enables (creates) digital assets and underpins their transactions; and, equally, irrespective of the legal transaction that articulates those transactions or their denomination or treatment in different legal systems (in this sense, this rule is closely connected with jurisdictional neutrality).

In order to verify effective application of the *Principles* on Transactions in Digital Assets, it should be noted that the best international practices have been taken into consideration when drafting the text.[49] The result is a set of standardised *Principles* that are adequately aligned with international models. This objective, and this protocol of action for the conception and drafting of a uniform international instrument, is customary: to assess the existing practical models and to select the most general and uniform aspects from all of them, in order to facilitate their adoption by the States. This involves a task of systematisation and identification, in order to synthesise rules. Nevertheless, the novelty of the subject matter regulated by the *Principles* is evident, closely linked to recent technological innovations; therefore, to a certain extent innovative or even unknown in some legal systems. DLT technology is relatively recent, and along with it, the very concept of digital assets (in a broad sense), which is not yet refined in view of the variety of forms in which they are presented in the markets. As a result, the implementation of digital asset transaction models is still in the definition and testing stage. There are limited international standardised models of digital asset transactions that can serve as reliable examples of international practice, as standardisation has not yet been achieved. This calls for a broad formulation of *principles* in anticipation of new transaction models to be defined by practitioners and markets. This limited list of available practice models

[49] "These Principles are meant to serve as guidelines for States to enable their private laws to be consistent with best practice and international standards in relation to the holding, transfer and use as collateral of digital assets, as defined in Principle 2(2)".

also posed a challenge for the UNIDROIT Working Group. If proposals for uniformity are normally formulated by abstracting and synthesising the fundamentals of the multiplicity of practices under analysis (selecting "best practices"), the absence of sufficient references meant that the proposal of new and innovative criteria and concepts had to be risked to a large extent.[50]

Thirdly, the *Principles* advocate a new perspective of neutrality, equally novel in its formulation: the so-called "jurisdictional neutrality". Moreover, this form of neutrality offered in the *Principles* is conceived from two different perspectives, or applications.

The *first* is jurisdictional neutrality in the strict sense (*Introduction 0.6*), which means dissociating the *Principles*, their rules or even their terminology from the institutions and figures of a particular legal system. This reflection is essentially redirected to the permanent debate between the perspectives, approaches and solutions sought by the *civil law* and *common law* systems. It should be stressed that this *rule* implies a working line and criteria, it does not mean (or, at least, it should not mean) conditioning the result.

It is not common for uniform texts to express this idea, as it is considered an assumption in works that seek to approximate the legislation of States (and, with it, international uniformity). It is not a question of transferring ("imposing") the rules and practical models of one country, or one system, on the other countries, but of finding the institution, the regulation, that can satisfy the approaches and interests of the States and jurisdictions. Sometimes, the balance between institutions will be found somewhere in the middle of the proposals (consensus solutions). In other cases, a new perspective will be chosen, specifically in the service of the uniform text (hence the importance of definitions and, beforehand, of terminology). On other occasions, however, "best practices" will tip the balance in favour of one option or one system, which will generally require recourse to a specific legal terminology, and partially, to the institutions on which it is based. None of the options, a priori, is preferable to the others, notwithstanding the diversity of criteria (not only that of efficiency, but also that of consensus, opportunity, balance and proximity to other figures in international trade, among others). It is not always a question of projecting one's own experience onto international texts, but rather of sharing the result that derives from these texts, making it possible to adopt them (perhaps after adapting them) to national perspectives. In this complex balance between systems, interests, practices and rules, it is easy to identify the content that is closer to the *civil law* or *common law* systems in the *Principles*. Other times though, it is more a question of

---

[50] This is rightly stated by the Secretary-General and the President of UNIDROIT in the *Foreword* to the *Principles*: "A classic transnational law instrument codifies best practices. An initial step of this codification consists of identifying those legal regimes that have proved to work better in practice. This project was also different in this regard. The novelty of the subject matter was such that no specific private law rules had emerged, anywhere, as the best solution. Hence, the discussion at the Working Group level was in good part an original attempt at creating - not merely identifying - an international standard on the proprietary aspects of digital assets. UNIDROIT has served, thus, as the venue where experts from all representative legal families and systems converged to determine the most adequate solutions, an extraordinary service to the international legal community".

reflecting on the possibility that the rules adopted can be made compatible, with the necessary conceptual effort, with the rules of one's own system.[51]

These reflections are timely for an assessment of the orientation of the *Principles*. As has been explained, the *Principles* opt for a "functional perspective", more attentive to the functioning and results of the figures than to their classification according to the traditional principles of legal systems. It is, perhaps, an essential perspective in the face of new technical realities, far removed from the conceptions on which the legal traditions are based. The *Principles* require the jurist of civil law tradition to make a conceptual effort, and frequently, to renounce his own terminology and method of expression of the mandates, all of which is in favour of functional criterion.[52] Also practitioners and academics from other jurisdictions undergo the

[51] "Target Audience. As consistent with all UNIDROIT instruments, the prospective guidance document should be relevant for both common law and civil law States and would aim to reduce legal uncertainty which practitioners, judges, legislators and market participants would face in the coming years in dealing with digital assets" cfr. UNIDROIT 2020 - Study LXXXII - W.G.1 - Doc. 2, p. 5.

"Composition of the Working Group Consistent with UNIDROIT's established working methods, the Working Group is composed of experts selected for their expertise in the fields of property law, secured transactions, and digital technology and the law. Experts participate in a personal capacity and represent the world's different systems and geographic regions. 25. 26. The Digital Assets and Private Law Working Group Working Group is composed of: - Hideki Kanda, (Chair), Professor, Gakushuin University (Japan) - Jason Grant Allen, Senior Research Fellow, Humboldt University of Berlin (Australia) - Reghard Brits, Professor, University of Pretoria (South Africa) - Marek Dubovec, Executive Director, Kozolchyk National Law Center (NatLaw) (United States) - David Fox, Professor, University of Edinburgh (United Kingdom) - Louise Gullifer, Professor, University of Cambridge (United Kingdom) - Matthias Haentjens, Professor of Private Law at Leiden University (Netherlands) - Charles Mooney, Professor, University of Pennsylvania (United States) - Philipp Paech, Associate Professor at LSE (Germany) - Carla Reyes, Assistant Professor, Southern Methodist University (United States) - Nina-Luisa Siedler, Partner at DWF (Germany) - Luc Thévenoz, Professor, Université de Genève (Switzerland) - Jeffrey Wool, Senior Research Fellow, Harris Manchester College, University of Oxford (United States) - Mimi Zou, Fellow, Oxford University (China) UNIDROIT also invited a number of organisations with expertise in the field of digital assets and private law to participate as observers in the Working Group. Participation of these different organisations will ensure that different regional perspectives are considered in the development and adoption of the instrument. It is also anticipated that the cooperating organisations will assist in the regional promotion, dissemination and implementation of the guidance document once it has been adopted. The following organisations have been invited to participate as observers in the Working Group: - The World Bank Group - The United Nations Commission for International Trade Law (UNCITRAL) - The Hague Conference on Private International Law (HCCH) - The European Central Bank (ECB) - The European Banking Authority (EBA) - The American Law Institute (ALI) 27. Finally, UNIDROIT may also invite a number of industry associations to participate as observers in the Working Group to ensure that the guidance document will address the private sector's needs. The latter will also assist in promoting the implementation and use of the guidance document. The following private sector association has been invited to participate as an observer in the Working Group, but more may be invited: - The International Swaps and Derivatives Association (ISDA)" [UNIDROIT 2020 - Study LXXXII - W.G.1 - Doc. 2, pp. 6–7]; *see* the Institute's *website* for background information.

[52] A new example can be proposed, which accompanies some of those already set out in other pages of these reflections. In recent years, various texts (in particular those produced within UNICTRAL, to which reference has been made) have made it possible to adapt the rigid (but reliable and complete) regime of possession, as conceived in *civil law* countries, to the needs of the new forms of

tension of valuing and taking on board the perspective of other legal systems that are shaped by different principles. It is likely that the conceptual character and the principles on which *civil law* systems are based allow for such an evolution with some flexibility, whereas, in the *common law* system in England and Wales such a conclusion has already been expressly formulated.[53] But recourse to the principle of functional equivalence seems indispensable; and the place to verify the adequacy of the tradition to the novelty would have been the *Commentaries* (which, as has been stated on other occasions, do not address this matter).

There are several authors who, having analysed the work, consider that the text of the *Principles* does not achieve the desirable balance between systems. Thus, criticisms have emerged regarding the form and substance of the *Principles*, which have been considered to be biased in favour of a normative model of Anglo-Saxon style.[54] More expressive have been the criticisms of a possible "Anglo-Saxon bias", which leads us back to the starting point with regards to the composition of the Working Group (and thus, more or less indirectly, the apparent legitimacy of the result).[55] Certainly, the formal composition of the Working Group is striking, notably

---

commerce. There is a relatively peaceful doctrinal position on the concept of "control" (defined in several UNCITRAL texts, with adaptations according to the nature and scope of the text), which is considered sufficient (subject to some mismatches) to satisfy the requirements of possession (thus, in the Model Law on Electronic Transferable Records (MLETR); always, on the basis of functional equivalence). This "new model" of equivalent possession makes it possible, in turn, to review other legal figures, such as the legitimation by possession, typical of the title deeds in those systems of civil law tradition. Although, of course, not all the differences between these systems are resolved; for example, in relation to the protection of the bona fide acquirer of a *document of title to* the goods against whoever claims a "better right" (for example, for having been illegitimately deprived of the goods by the transferor of the title). In short, the concepts of incorporation and autonomy (among others; also, for example, literalness) that characterise securities have not been sufficiently revised.

It may be argued, moreover, that in some cases the adaptation of the terminology in the *Principles* was easy, but the language has remained too attached to techniques that the *civil law* jurist would find striking. *Innocent acquisition* which, in reality, regulates not the transaction, but the position of the "innocent acquirer"; that is, the acquirer in good faith (who is required by virtue of *Principle 8.1(b)* "(b) comply with requirements equivalent to those found in the relevant good faith acquisition (…)"). Moreover, such an acquirer is afforded the protection of a bona fide acquirer of a "negotiable instrument" in *civil law* systems: "*Principle 8* […] *(2) An innocent acquirer takes a digital asset free of conflicting proprietary rights ('proprietary claims'). (3) No rights based on a proprietary claim relating to a digital asset can be successfully asserted against an innocent acquirer of that digital asset.* […]".

[53] *See* the conclusions of the Law Commission on *Digital Assets* (cited above).

[54] *See* CAVALLER VERGÉS, M., "En busca de un marco legal para los activos digitales: Los principios UNIDROIT sobre activos digitales y derecho privado", *Cuadernos de Derecho Transnacional* (March 2024), Vol. 16, Nº 1, pp. 113–130; 22. Also, for example, C. Vassilopoulos & M. Kepeneghian Kriptown: "The Principles are too much inspired by common law. They do not take sufficient account of the specificities of the civil law tradition. As a result, it is difficult to see how they can be used in civil law countries. However, the Principles should not favour one part of a country over another" (cf. DIGITAL ASSETS AND PRIVATE LAW CONSULTATION SUBMISSIONS, UNIDROIT 2023 Study LXXXII - W.G.8 - Doc. 4 (February 2023), comment 22 C, p. 12).

[55] This was the understanding of the *Association française des marchés financiers* (AMAFI): "These principles have been developed without the participation or invitation of all Member States. This is a critical governance issue, in particular considering the UNIDROIT's foundational principles

the absence of permanent representation of countries that have traditionally played an important role in the drafting of uniform law, not only because of the "weight" of their own legal systems and their prominence in various forums (e.g. France), but also because of the influence they have exerted over the course of history on the shaping of other legal systems (e.g. Spain). The presence and contributions of experts and professionals from other countries, such as those indicated, would imply the participation (to some extent, the indirect "representation") of other geographical areas and countries with special circumstances (e.g. Latin American countries). The result is that prominent "economies" would seem to be under-represented; thus, the European Union because, regardless of the relevance of the contributions and perspectives that the participation of Germany and the Netherlands could entail, they neither exhaust the representation of the legal systems present in Europe nor exercise that sort of indirect representation that has been mentioned. In short, perhaps different and enriching approaches to the debates were lost.

In any case, the "extreme" positions that value participation in the work are excessive, even from a formal point of view (since the procedure seems to be in line with the provisions of the statutes and working systems of the Institute). On the other hand, the *Principles* may lead (or not) to the revision of the legal texts adopted in the future, providing a uniform international framework of reference which, at the very least, would provide the usefulness that derives from a comparative analysis. In any event, given the objective value of these critical evaluations[56] and the influence that

according to which Member States are to be consulted and shall participate and contribute. AMAFI deems that this deprives the proposed principles of any legitimacy and these principles should not find their way into applicable European legislation. It appears therefore highly inappropriate to expect States to adapt their legislation to comply with these principles. On the substance itself, our general view, as an association representative of capital markets, is that there is no clear view on the type of assets that may be captured by these principles whose key concepts are neither clearly defined nor aligned with existing notions, making it impossible to assess their consequences. The interdependencies of these principles with private and securities law are so important that it is absolutely critical to consider, in an appropriate manner, the collateral effects any such changes may have" [cf. UNIDROIT 2023 - Study LXXXII - W.G.8 - Doc. 4, pp. 9–10 (comment 17)]. It is likely that the criticism would have been formulated in other terms if the meaning and functions that the *Principles* are called upon to perform, which does not imply questioning established models of law or practice, had been made clearer.

In similar critical terms, *see.* Comment 5, by S. Saint Pé, France Post Marché, *ibid.* pp. 20 and 21: "The preparation of these principles has not been made with the participation/contribution of all members' representatives. This is a strong governance issue (in particular considering the UNIDROIT foundational principles according to which members are to be consulted and shall participate and contribute) which minimizes the legitimacy of the proposed principles and the opportunity to present these principles to EU authorities. It appears therefore impossible/useless/utopic to expect States to adapt current legislation in a view to comply with these principles". And further on it continues: "Section 2 of the document evidences tangible limits in the construction of these principles from a general/governance viewpoint. The approach is likely to be utopic and this is largely due to the absence of consultation of numbers of members including France (and associations involved in securities law). We raise this point as a major/critical one and hereby strongly challenge the merits of the principles. We strongly disapprove the process".

[56] The *Haut Comité Juridique de la Place Financière de Paris* [created at the initiative of the French Financial Markets Authority (AMF) and the Bank of France], *High* Committee for Financial Market

the *Principles* may have on national (or European) standards,[57] they certainly merit future reflection, which will allow us to overcome these positions of maximums.

The *second* way in which the so-called "jurisdictional neutrality" is conceived in the *Principles* refers to the way in which States may choose to implement them into their own legal systems (*Introduction 0.7*): "The jurisdictional neutrality of these Principles as explained above also means that it is for the jurisdiction in question to decide how to implement these Principles into its own law(s) and legal system". Thus formulated, this *rule* of the *Introduction* is probably the weakest of those formulated in this part of the *Principles.* It should be noted that the possible confusion caused by the use (the perhaps inopportune splitting) of the term "jurisdiction", used for a purpose which is not that of a consolidated term with other meanings in legal systems, is to be noted (this new meaning is therefore unnecessary). On the other hand, it addresses an issue that, being consistent, the *Principles* will refer to "other law" (to each State's own legal system). Indeed, each State has its own rules, its own organisation of its legal system and, consequently, its own channels for adopting the (sovereign) decision on the effectiveness it decides to give (in whole or in part) to the *Principles* and the form or method of doing so. Presenting this option as an input or *rule* of the Principles is unnecessary. The issue lies precisely in the (partly undefined) nature of the *Principles.* If it were an international convention, as is well known, the subject matter would be redirected to well-defined procedures[58] of signature, ratification, accession….[59] Similarly, a model law precisely requires the adoption of an appropriate instrument (according to the appropriate legal channel),

---

Legal Studies (HCJP) contacted UNIDROIT "to request that two of its members be accepted as observers in ongoing work on digital assets, given the lack of French experts on the subject" (cfr. UNIDROIT 2023 - Study LXXXII - W.G.8 - Doc. 4, p. 11, comment 20), highlighting the absence in the working group of members from some EU countries, in particular France, which "is in our view an important issue to the credibility of these Principles, in particular due to the fact that France was one of the few State who has implemented since 2019 a legal framework for digital assets. In our view, the composition of the working group could affect the legitimacy of the proposed principles".

[57] The criticism is due to the expectation that countries with more advanced legislation, already adapted to the digital reality (as was the case in France) would have been able to contribute their experiences directly to the working group. There was also a clear interest in coordinating UNIDROIT's initiatives with the (at the time, projected) European regulation (the MiCA Regulation, REGULATION (EU) 2023/1114 OF THE EUROPEAN PARLIAMENT AND OF THE COUNCIL of 31 May 2023 on markets in crypto-assets, and amending Regulations (EU) N° 1093/2010 and (EU) N° 1095/2010 and Directives 2013/36/EU and (EU) 2019/1937 (https://eur-lex.europa.eu/legal-content/EN/TXT/HTML/?uri=CELEX:32023R1114), as well as Regulation (EU) 2022/858 of the European Parliament and of the Council of 30 May 2022 on a pilot regime for market infrastructures based on distributed ledger technology ('Pilot Regime).

[58] Under the terms of the *Vienna Convention on the Law of Treaties*, adopted at Vienna on 23 May 1969.

[59] In times long past, it was customary for conventions to include a signing protocol with a mandate reminiscent of the reflection of the *Principles*, stating that "The High Contracting Parties may give effect to this Convention either by giving it the force of law or by including in their national legislation in a form appropriate to that legislation the rules adopted under this Convention" [this is the International Convention for the Unification of Certain Rules of Law relating to Bills of Lading (Brussels, 25 August 1924)].

whatever its rank in the legal system of a country. UNIDROIT has opted for a different (partly undefined) instrument for the sake of flexibility, which involves formulating indications accompanied by reflections, rather than mandates, rules or provisions that can be transposed into a standard. The *Principles* could even inform an order (for example, through the "formation" of the "promoters" of the rules or precepts) without any act of claim or recognition of formal incorporation of the *Principles* being evident. It seems, in short, an unnecessary *rule*.

Finally, the *Principles* declare their "organisational neutrality" (*Introduction 0.08* to *0.10*). The precise meaning of this *rule* is partly diluted among the numerous consequences that are predicated on its application, which make it somewhat vague. Formally, the *rule* is defined in the sense that the *Principles* do not presuppose or formulate indications (do not interfere) about in which "part" of the law (of the legal system) of a State these *Principles* should be included[60]; although from this perspective the rule shares areas (and is partly confused) with the previous one: when a State decides how to transpose the *Principles* it is deciding at the same time in which branch or sector of the legal system it considers that they should have their effects. It is therefore a matter of looking at the set of special rules that define a conceptual unit within a legal system; hence, reference is made either to the private law aspect of the legal system, or to commercial law (as a special part of it), or to a more specific branch (endowed with particular protective rules), such as consumer law.

The *Principles* advocate maintaining the conceptual integrity of their scope of application which, extended to private matters in general, would not contemplate the exclusion of areas traditionally ascribed to this generic concept (private as opposed to public, private activity as opposed to regulatory and supervisory activity).[61] For this reason, it should be noted at the same time that the *Principles* do not include what in some States is called "regulatory law" within their scope of application (e.g. administrative and economic law).[62] It is obvious that the precise determination of one or the other scope will be a complex issue, to be resolved within each State.

---

[60] "Third, these Principles are organisationally neutral. This means, as already stated above, that they take no position as to in what part of the laws of a State their rules should be included. Thus, a State may implement these Principles into a specific law on digital assets, but a State may also consider one or more of these Principles to follow from rules of general private law, commercial law, or consumer law" (cfr. *Introduction 0.08*).

[61] "However, the organisational neutrality of these Principles does not mean that they can be implemented in such a way that their scope is more limited than that defined in these Principles. For instance, if a certain jurisdiction considers 'commercial law' to apply to entrepreneurs/businesses only and not to consumers, these Principles should not be implemented only into that jurisdiction's commercial law, because their scope does not exclude consumers. Vice versa, these Principles should not be implemented only into a jurisdiction's consumer law, because their scope is not limited to consumers" (cf. *Introduction 0.08*).

[62] "As a matter of principle, they do not cover rules that are to be enforced by public authorities which in many jurisdictions would be called 'regulation' or 'regulatory law'. For instance, these Principles do not cover such matters as when, or whether, a person must obtain a licence for engaging in activities that concern digital assets. However, jurisdictions may wish to adopt rules of 'regulatory law', i.e., rules that are to be enforced by public authorities, to accompany and operate in tandem with these Principle" (cfr. *Introduction 0.09*).

It is not a simple question to address, because the *Principles* contemplate different perspectives, which cannot always be brought back to a unity of criteria. Thus, although the starting point is the regime for digital assets and its effectiveness in relation to rights of a proprietary nature or content ("property"), other more specific issues are called for, such as attention to operations (transactions with assets), the protection of the parties, and where appropriate, the position of bona fide third parties (private law issues). But all of this is conflated with pseudo-regulatory aspects (see *Introduction 0.09*), complicating the analysis with perhaps unnecessary casusism (as they are the subject of specific *principles*: thus, for procedural, or procedural aspects, *principle 18*).

The difficulty surrounding the meaning of this *rule* can be seen when it is stated that "there are many issues of private law which are not addressed by the Principles", without it always being clear what these exceptions are. The problem is the number of ramifications that, within the legal system of each State, exist between the different sections that may be affected by the *Principles*; in addition to those indicated, the rules on securities law, on guarantees, insolvency law, the consumer regime... The regulatory complexity of each legal system leads to uncertainty as to the relevance of the *Principles* in each area, making it impossible to foresee a priori how the modification of the rules in certain aspects can be carried out, avoiding possible collateral effects that will even be difficult to foresee. In short, it is not easy to accurately identify the uniform scope of application of the *Principles*, which refers to the issues of economic (property) rights over digital assets,[63] when exceptions continue to be established on closely connected issues and regulations.[64] Perhaps,

---

[63] *Introduction 0.9*: "These Principles cover only private law issues relating to digital assets and, in particular, proprietary rights. Thus, they specifically address digital assets where these are the object of dispositions and acquisitions, and where interests in those assets are to be asserted against third parties. [...]".

[64] *Introduction 0.10*: "Moreover, these Principles intend to cover only a specific area of private law, and there are many issues of private law which are not addressed by the Principles. These issues concern, for instance, rules of private law relating to intellectual property or consumer protection. As a matter of principle, these areas of law are not addressed by these Principles, and national intellectual property and consumer protection laws therefore remain unaffected by them. Also, these Principles do not address many issues of national private law relating to contract and property law". The confusion caused by this game of generalities and exceptions has already been pointed out; in this regard, *see*, for example, the comment by Dr. Gizem Alper (UNIDROIT 2023 - Study LXXXII - W.G.8 - Doc. 4, p. 20): "Moreover, these Principles intend to only regulate a specific area of private law, and there are many issues of private law which are not addressed by the Principles. These issues concern, for instance, rules of private law relating to intellectual property or consumer protection. As a matter of principle, these areas of law are not addressed by these Principles, and national intellectual property and consumer protection laws therefore remain unaffected by them. Also, these Principles do not address many issues of private law relating to contract and property law. Examples of these issues not addressed by these Principles include whether a proprietary right in a digital asset has been validly transferred to another person, whether a security right in a digital asset has been validly created, the rights as between a transferor and transferee of a digital asset, the rights as between a grantor of a security right in a digital asset and the relevant secured creditor, many of the legal consequences of third-party effectiveness of a transfer of digital assets and some of the requirements for, and legal consequences of, third-party effectiveness of a security right in a digital asset, etc. etc.".

to a large extent, the difficulty stems from the approach followed in the scope of application of the *Principles,* which although formally stated to deal with digital assets and their regulation (*Principle 1:* "These Principles deal with the private law relating to digital assets"), in reality regulate the contractual and proprietary (thus ownership) aspects of digital assets. By focusing on the contractual rather than the regulatory issue, it would perhaps be more feasible to delimit the meaning of the intended "private law".

10 Final Reflections and Criticisms on the *Principles*

Some final assessments of the *Principles* are summarised below. In some cases, these considerations are formulated on the basis of what has been set out in the previous pages, while in other cases they will be conclusive reflections, and may take into account *principles* beyond those set out in these notes (assessments therefore subject to the best judgement of the author commenting on the *principle* below).

I should start by acknowledging the extraordinary effort made by the working group within UNIDROIT and the usefulness of having a basic and harmonised set of "norms" (rules or principles) on the new forms of commercial activity enabled by digital assets.

The *Principles* address a relatively new issue (derived from the continuous changes and opportunities offered by new technologies) and a complex one (due to the variety of business models involved in the new forms of dematerialisation of economic rights and their circulation), which makes it necessary to review the fundamental principles on which the legal systems are based. New businesses are emerging under the protection of this new reality more and more frequently, which incorporates all kinds of goods into new transactions, under different forms of technology. The reaction of States to these new activities is, for the moment, slow, largely because they are carried out in international markets, outside the control of a State (and outside the conception of legal systems). The "new digital economy" must be built on a solid, reliable and predictable legal basis, with the best international recognition (and participation in its design), to ensure its implementation and uniform and harmonised treatment.[65] These needs are the focus of the UNIDROIT *Principles,* whose vision precisely addresses the elements of so-called private law (transactions

---

[65] It cannot be taken as a premise that technological advances have taken the jurist (society) by surprise: the reality is that it has taken decades to come to terms with the technical changes that have occurred and the regulatory developments that have accompanied them. Without prejudice to the general substratum provided by "electronic commerce" (essentially linked to the emergence of the Internet, reflected in the UNCITRAL model laws on electronic commerce, electronic signatures and electronic communications, of high impact in many countries), the technical-theoretical foundations (e.g., and without wishing to be exhaustive, public-key cryptography, public-key cryptography, electronic signatures and electronic communications, etc.) have been developed: public key cryptography in the 1960s and the foundations of digital signatures in the 1970s; the formulation of blockchain theory in the late 1960s; the concept of the "smart contract" in the mid-1990s; or the foundations of cryptocurrencies in 2008 and blockchain a few years later) have been established

between private parties), excluding public law issues (the organisation of the activity) that each State can regulate according to its own needs.

In this atmosphere of novelty, diversity and internationality that characterise the digital transactions scenario, it seems appropriate for an ambitious project such as the *Principles* to define and focus its objectives. For this reason, the delimitation of the scope of application established by the *Principles* (under an undeclared formula of "minimum intervention" in national systems), defined by transactions subject to private law with property consequences (and excluding the regulatory sphere), seems equally appropriate. However, expressing their desire for maximum application and usefulness, the *Principles* enshrine a broad concept of "digital assets" (the basis of all the work), with the aim of applying not only to current assets (and transactions), but also to those that new technologies may develop in the coming years.

The first question concerns the nature of the instrument that UNIDROIT has opted for: *Principles*, supplemented (or developed) by *Commentaries*. In general, this model instrument lacks sufficiently established recognition as a technique for promoting uniformity in international trade law. Some instruments commonly used by international organisations and institutions have their own precise regime, e.g. for international conventions, the Vienna Convention on the Law of Treaties, adopted in Vienna on 23 May 1969. This is the first example of what UNCITRAL calls legislative texts or techniques[66]; in the same group of techniques, but without the legal value of conventions, are model laws, legislative guides (with their recommendations) and model provisions. These instruments, which are very formal because of the result itself (international conventions) or because they are intended to become formal legal texts, are also complemented by so-called "explanatory techniques" (legal and practice guides, interpretative declarations and, with a different value, compilations of jurisprudence).[67] None of these techniques or models of instruments alone defines the *Principles*, which seem to share elements of some of them and would appear to form a category of their own.

The *Principles*, if anything, represent a significant exercise in reflection to bring coherence and uniformity to a new form (perhaps not "objects") of commercial

---

and even put into practice for years (bitcoin started operating in 2009, Digicash in 1992). Undoubtedly, the most important step since the internet has been taken with the generalisation of DLT and *blockchain* technologies, which make it possible to overcome the problems of identity, legitimacy, traceability and originality (the uniqueness of the document, or of the asset) that previously seemed insurmountable (or very limitedly addressable, based on closed registry systems managed by ad hoc closed consortia). The opportunities offered by new techniques will provide the decisive impetus for the public or "open" management of digital asset transactions. In this emerging scenario, the initiative that the *Principles* represent is not only pioneering, but necessary. The regulation of this matter is, at present, a necessity in the international trade scenario, as the states are generally only partially assuming it, if at all (*see* the aforementioned European regulations).

[66] Article 1 of the Organic Statute of UNIDROIT (https://www.unidroit.org/wp-content/uploads/2021/05/statute.pdf) first of all lists among the means for the harmonisation of private law between states.

[67] *Vid. supra* the reference to the UNCITRAL publication on the working methods and modernisation techniques it employs; while the numerous results of the activity carried out can be freely consulted *on the web page* of the aforementioned Commission.

reality, defined by new forms of technology. These reflections and the *Principles*' commitment to international uniformity represent a major achievement in promoting the harmonisation of national laws in the field of digital transactions. Their formal framing within UNIDROIT's own methods does not seem problematic.[68] However, as discussed above, the material value of the instrument remains unanswered. Principles formulated in the terms in which UNIDROIT has opted for seem to have little chance, at this stage, of making a significant contribution to the uniformity of the matter. Although it may partially achieve this through indirect academic channels, and eventually through contractual channels. After its analysis, ruling out the possibility of the *Principles* being drafted in the form of a convention, and assuming that at the very least they constitute a study on a topical subject with projection on international digital transactions, it could be agreed that they fall halfway between a legal guide and a "preliminary draft" (due to the lack of sufficient definition of its structure) of a model law. As a future model law, they would, of course, require further elaboration. UNIDROIT seems to have no intention at this stage to undertake such a revision.

In the event that it is decided to continue the work already embarked upon, the drafting of a Model Law could be addressed; an instrument that would probably be better suited to the objectives pursued, but which would require more time and effort than the Working Group was able to devote to it. From this (future) perspective, the *Principles* provide a solid basis for incorporating the study of some aspects of transactions in digital assets at a later date that were not included in the approved instrument; revising the *Principles*, to draft them in the form of precepts or articles (to serve as a model for national legislators); and using the *Commentaries* to develop the meaning and scope of the proposed mandates. This revision of the *Commentaries* would require either drafting them as *recommendations*, following the UNCITRAL models, or clearly resolving the question of their value and relevance in the text.

In any case, continuation of the studies (including the assessment of the *Principles* in their current state) seems to require the incorporation of the professional experiences of the sector, the contractual and practice models that employers are entering into. These experiences will sometimes be reflected in the recent national regulations that are starting to be consolidated, whether of a private nature (contractual) or of a public nature (regulatory rules, which impose models of activity). Only then will it be possible to analyse the actual business models, select the "good practices", and take on board and propose the "best practices" in the text (on the basis, for example, of their greater efficiency on the international scene and their compliance with the principles of the national systems—jurisdictional neutrality—among other criteria).

In this vein, as future work, revising (and expanding) the *Principles* could be considered, in order to give them a more classical or "familiar" structure and form of presentation, following the models of other international instruments. Such a possible

---

[68] Undoubtedly, the work carried out could be understood, without difficulty, to fall within some of the work formulas expressly provided for in its organic statute; in particular, "[...] (c) undertake studies in comparative private law; [...] (e) organise conferences and publish works which the Institute considers worthy of wide circulation" (*ibid.*, Article 1.º).

revision would, for example, resolve the question of the value of the *Principles*, as indicated above (the value of the *Principle*, the value of the *Commentary*). This would also require revising the structure of the text itself. For example, resolving the usefulness, placement and value of the *Introduction*; probably, incorporating some of its postulates as general *principles*, with express projection over the whole text. As for the content of the *Principles* themselves, a revision might be needed to precisely define their scope (*Principle 1*). In their present formulation, the *Principles*: *(a)* only deal with a few specific aspects of the private law of digital assets (not, therefore, with the entire "branch" of that law; this has never been the focus); *(b)* sometimes call de facto (because it is essential) for regulatory or market and transaction aspects (public law); and *c)* in reality, the aim of the *Principles* is to cover transactions with digital assets (not the digital assets themselves), but such transactions are neither listed in *Principle 1* nor defined in the corresponding place (*Principle* 2), which leaves some room for uncertainty. Therefore, it would be a matter of redirecting some items of the *Principles* to a "visible" (highlighted) first or *preliminary* Chapter (*section*, in current terminology), which accentuates their value and their projection on the whole text.[69]

Much of the critical issues surrounding the *Principles* derive from the deliberately broad (and, as a consequence, difficult to encompass) concept of "digital assets". UNIDROIT has opted for generalisation, i.e. to consider any digital asset conceivable in practice, without offering (perhaps necessary) differentiation criteria between assets "specific" to commercial activities and other digital assets; or, for example, "professional" assets and assets linked to individuals, without sufficient projection on complex commercial transactions (which require different treatment, for example, taking into account the consumer's right of withdrawal). The concept of a digital asset (*Principle 2*) is based on two "factual" elements: its very "existence", i.e. the record in electronic form; and its subjection to a qualified form of "control". This concept does not address the "connected" or underlying property rights, which are generally those that will provide commercial utility in transactions (the object and purpose of a transfer of property). The differences between "types" of digital assets can be very significant, depending on their nature. For example, digital assets incorporating shares, or security rights, are not only common in international business transactions, but also need to be compatible with a well-defined substantive national

[69] Similar reflections were already formulated in the assessments to the public exposure of the *Principles* [UNIDROIT 2023 Study LXXXII - W.G.8 - Doc. 4 (February 2023)]: "36. Comment 9 Finance, Competitiveness & Innovation Global Practice World Bank Group "It would be beneficial to relocate the definitions from Principle 2 to a separate section prior to the Introduction in order to provide a clear and comprehensive understanding of key concepts, such as digital assets, from the onset of the document rather than delaying their inclusion until Principle 2 (see in General comments our suggestions in terms of new definitions). Given the extensive and intricate subject matter covered within the nineteen outlined principles, it is recommended that an Executive Summary be included at the beginning of the document, providing a succinct overview of the key elements and recommendations within the principles. This approach can be similar to that utilised in the World Bank Principles for Effective Insolvency and Creditor/Debtor Regimes (see p. 5) and will aid policymakers in quickly gaining a comprehensive understanding of the key concepts and recommendations, facilitating ease of navigation within the document".

(sometimes international: see the work of UNCITRAL) regime. Other digital assets are still awaiting definition and uniform treatment, for example, the so-called crypto currencies; for which we still do not have complete and clear regulations in the legal system, despite the fact that they are frequently the object of transactions in markets in which consumers negotiate (sometimes, as protagonists).[70] These reflections are particularly relevant in relation to some "linked assets", which present particular complexities, that are very frequent in commercial transactions and have very well defined international rules and models (and may not have been adequately addressed in these *Principles*; see *Commentaries* on *Principles 4* and *14*). Domestic rules of any nature applicable to transactions, called for in the *Principles* under the general "other law" rubric, may entail different treatment of digital assets and transactions under those rules and with regard to the nature of the asset on which the digital asset is created, particularly where they involve consumer transactions.

The scope at which digital assets are contemplated implies, in turn, breadth (or lack of definition) of the types of transactions that the *Principles* seek to regulate. Since the intention is to apply the *Principles* "universally", it is necessary to consider future studies that review the new practices and business models that arise, and ensure that they correspond to the provisions of the text already approved (and, where appropriate, promote their revision).

In short, the relevant concept of a digital asset could perhaps be more specific in future versions or amendments of *the Principles*. Such a revision should address the nature of the asset and the nature and types of envisaged transactions. It should then entail a different definition of the asset that goes beyond the limited perspective of its recording data (digital nature) and its operation (control). These two criteria may be affected by the evolution of technology (straining the principle of technological

[70] As indicated above, one of the elements on which the *Principles* base the concept of a digital asset is "control", a technical characteristic (*principle 6*). It is difficult to formulate a broad concept and, above all, to assess its appropriateness, without having analysed and classified the models already in use in practice (and, as far as possible, to "anticipate" those that may be forthcoming: in general, linked to any form of ownership or title). This is why the *Principles* opt for maximum breadth; but it may not be a valid option in all cases. Where there are existing regulations, it will be difficult to project the *Principles* onto rules that do provide a more precise definition of the assets they regulate. In the framework designed by other instruments, for example MiCA, or in that of MiFID financial instruments, it will not be easy to determine the kind of digital assets that could fall within the concept formulated by the *Principles* (nor, therefore, will it be feasible to facilitate their adoption or their promotion, except in very vague terms, given the risk of affecting the regulation itself, which will often be conditioned by regulatory issues -excluded from the *Principles*-).

In any case, the concept of digital asset to be formulated must be careful to keep its wording "open", in the terms required by the principle of technological neutrality (a concept willing to incorporate new techniques). The one proposed by the *Principles* is very attached to a technology and a technique (which translates into control, *principle 8*). The question that arises is what happens if the system of control of assets is modified, if the technique finds other, more effective ways that are not expressed through control. At the present time, digital assets are "goods" still to be defined, they are in the process of gestation and subject to the evolution and possibilities offered by technology. Going beyond the technique of control would leave these digital assets outside the scope of application of the *Principles*; this would be a violation of the technological neutrality that underpins the UNIDROIT rules. The solution is, as has been pointed out before, a strong recognition of the principle of functional equivalence.

neutrality). A different approach may need to take into account the (property) effects of transactions with digital assets.

The conception of the *Principles* as basic and fundamental rules implies, to a certain extent, that UNIDROIT has opted for a "minimum intervention" approach. This principle has two perspectives: the (small) number and (synthetic) formulation of the *Principles* themselves (the minimum of common fundamental rules) and their interaction with the law of States. As the *Principles* are formulated as "minimum rules", the counterbalance provided by the legal systems clearly tips the balance in favour of national laws in the event of conflict. While the *Principles* save and reclaim national rights ("other law"), perhaps too much prominence has been left to national laws to the detriment of the *Principles*, i.e. there are too many issues on which the UNIDROIT instrument offers neither regime nor perspective. Often, the only function that the *Principles* will be able to perform in some States will be to inform (set interpretative criteria for) the law itself. However, the limited material scope of the *Principles* complicates their very application (probably less in contractual transactions between private parties and more in the judicial sphere). The *Principles* do not give any indications in this respect[71]; thus an excessively wide scope is given to States (unregulated and unresolved issues, unmentioned issues, without any instructions on the effective application of the Principles) to resolve issues in accordance with their own national law, without ensuring their harmonisation with the international practices and models that the *Principles* wish to promote. Perhaps there has been an over-reliance on the real possibility that all States will have the means and effective channels to incorporate complex technological solutions, both from a technical and legal point of view, into their legal systems.

In short, the imbalance between national law (supposedly complete and integrated systems, with their own interpretative criteria and conditioning factors) and the *Principles* (scarce and partial "minimum standards") may be a serious obstacle to the uniformity sought. Academic work and their use as a reference by individuals (their projection on practices and contracts) is for the moment the best opportunity for application of the *Principles*; without prejudice to the fact that, at a later moment in time, they will also be useful for the "authorities", valuing them as reflections on the ways of incorporating the *Principles* into domestic law.

The normative effectiveness (implementation) of the *Principles* will face considerable challenges and difficulties. One of them is the continued claim of the *Principles* on the domestic law of States (in the terminology of the Principles, "other law"); an expression that implies, at the same time, the negative delimitation of the scope of application of the *Principles*. Differences in the rules that exist between States on the same issue, whether private law or regulatory law, will result in a different treatment of the same transaction, depending on the State whose law is applicable. Even if

---

[71] The (deliberately) limited scope of the *Principles* implies recourse to national rules, which may be inconsistent with the UNIDROIT instrument or simply lack the necessary agility to reformulate themselves, aligning their provisions with the *Principles*. Naturally, UNIDROIT has been aware of this difficulty: "As States may have a wide range of other laws (in statutes and court decisions), there is no attempt to identify the specific law that may apply" (cf. paragraph *0.10* of the *Introduction*). Studying and following the *Principles* may help to overcome this difficulty.

States opting for the adoption of the *Principles* undertake a diligent exercise (with a view to joining the uniformity postulated by UNIDROIT) to determine whether the *Principles* fit with their regime (or, as the case may be, how it should be adopted), international uniformity is very difficult to achieve through a *soft law* instrument. It is even more complex if the instrument chosen for its promotion leaves many issues to be decided by States. In such cases, flexibility comes at a high cost for uniformity.[72]

Moreover, as noted in several sections of these notes, it seems necessary to supplement the *Principles* with the addition of an ad hoc "terminology" or "glossary" to assist in the interpretation of the *Principles* (the form and terms of their drafting) and their future application. The need for such a glossary is evident given the extraordinary diversity of "assets" that can be represented and traded through digital assets and the variety of techniques that can underpin such transactions.[73] Such a glossary would make it possible, inter alia, to differentiate and classify digital assets, to verify the appropriateness and effectiveness of the *Principles* on each of them and, if necessary, to adapt (or "dictate") the specific rules required.

Moreover, for the reasons set out in several points of these reflections, the convenience of making explicit the claim to the principle of functional equivalence in an eventual revision of the *Principles* is once again reiterated.

The ultimate (or first and foremost) purpose of the *Principles* is to contribute, from a "neutral" (as noted, this neutrality offers different projections) and uniform perspective, to "facilitating transactions in digital assets". Such transactions, and their treatment, define a novel area of commercial transactions, where there is a high degree of uncertainty. States have become aware of the volume of transactions that can be accessed in this new digital market, of the value of the transactions, of the tensions they generate in the traditional rules and concepts of the legal systems and, in short, of the insecurity in the face of the apparent regulatory vacuum; circumstances that multiply in international transactions. As a result, States are looking for ways to adapt their own legislation to the new practical and professional model that

---

[72] Strictly speaking, however, it is not left to state law to decide the actual scope of the Principles: whether or not they refer to private law issues, Irrelevance (and difficulty) of the distinction which, moreover, may have different meaning and scope depending on the states (which may prejudice the introduction of the Principles in their own legal system). A better approach would be to refer to the issues covered by the Principles directly (e.g., rights of custodians and proprietary rights, including their enforcement within and outside insolvency), without attempting to categorise them under private or public law. If that approach were followed, paragraph 10 would not need to refer to issues of private law not covered in the Principles. It would avoid clashes with national legal categories that are conceptual (even dogmatic); when in fact such a distinction could be dispensed with by delimiting the scope of application (to which issues they would apply). This would also not have constrained the Principles, which could have been extended to other issues.

[73] Some "types" of digital assets have been described in the previous pages, which are worth repeating in part, by way of example: digital assets linked to games (generically, *online*), books and other electronic intellectual property, digital securities, databases, digital images, DLT tokens (access, identification, legitimisation, etc.), social network data, digital files of any kind, linked assets (with transferable securities, securities and commodity-backed securities), etc. An appropriate glossary would make it possible to classify all types of digital assets, defining categories and, where appropriate, the specialisations that each of them requires.

"digital assets" represent. From these considerations, the usefulness of the *Principles* is unquestionable, contemplating international uniformity on the basis of prior national uniformity.

UNIDROIT has laid the foundations for promoting the international uniformity required by this business model. It now remains to participate in its further development, its international dissemination, its analysis from the point of view of each State, and if necessary, to contribute to its further development and eventual revisions.

Reflections on Section I: Scope and Definitions

Principle 1
Scope

Teresa Rodríguez de las Heras Ballell

These Principles deal with the private law relating to digital assets.

1 Official Commentary

Commentary

1.1. These Principles are meant to serve as guidelines for States to enable their private laws to be consistent with best practice and international standards in relation to the holding, transfer and use as collateral of digital assets, as defined in Principle 2(2). The Principles cover only private law issues relating to digital assets and, in particular, proprietary rights. Thus, they specifically address digital assets where these are the object of dispositions and acquisitions, and where interests in those assets are to be asserted against third parties. As a matter of principle, they do not cover rules that are to be enforced by public authorities (which in many jurisdictions would be called 'regulation' or 'regulatory law'). For instance, these Principles do not cover such matters as when or whether a person must obtain a licence for engaging in activities that concern digital assets. In the same vein, they do not cover rules for how persons should hold digital assets, if compliance with those rules is required by public authorities.

This work was financed within the framework of the Prometeo 2023 project of the Regional Ministry of Innovation, Universities, Science and Digital Society (CIPROM/2022/26) "Present and future of the regulation of cryptoassets in the EU [LegalCripto]", whose principal investigator is Carmen Pastor Sempere. The basic ideas contained herein were presented in the author's paper with the same title, given on November 13, 2024 at the IV International Congress on "UNIDROIT Principles on Digital Assets and Private Law: Context, Content, Perspectives", organized also by BAES Research Group of the University of Alicante on November 13 and 14, 2024.

Likewise, the Ministry of Science and Innovation's research project PDI2023-149583-C21, "Adaptación del Derecho Español para la adquisición, transmisión, gravamen y ejecución de los activos digitales en los negocios" (P.I. Teresa Rodríguez de las Heras Ballell/Manuel Alba Fernández).

T. Rodríguez de las Heras Ballell (✉)
Universidad Carlos III de Madrid, Madrid, Spain
e-mail: tla@der-pr.uc3m.es

C. Pastor Sempere and D. A. Morán Bovio (eds.), UNIDROIT *Principles on Digital Assets and Private Law*, Law, Governance and Technology Series 80,
https://doi.org/10.1007/978-3-032-11001-5_7

1.2. Moreover, these Principles intend to address only a specific area of private law, and there are many issues of private law which are not addressed by the Principles. These issues concern, for instance, rules of private law relating to intellectual property or consumer protection. As a matter of principle, these areas of law are not addressed by these Principles, and national intellectual property and consumer protection laws therefore remain unaffected by them. Also, these Principles do not address many issues of private law relating to contract and property law, for the reasons set out in Commentary 1.3. Examples of these issues not regulated by these Principles include whether a proprietary right in a digital asset has been validly transferred to another person, whether a security right in a digital asset has been validly created, the rights as between a transferor and transferee of a digital asset, the rights as between a grantor of a security right in a digital asset and the relevant secured creditor, the legal consequences of third-party effectiveness of a transfer of digital assets, some of the requirements for, and legal consequences of, third-party effectiveness of a security right in a digital asset. See also Principle 3(3) and Principle 4.

1.3. These Principles address situations where gaps may exist in current (private) laws, and also where traditional approaches would not be appropriate and should be modified. However, these Principles take a practical and functional approach in that they are intended to facilitate the private law treatment of digital assets in all technological and legal systems. Thus, the internationality of the Principles will enable jurisdictions to take a common approach to legal issues arising out of the holding, transfer and use of digital assets as collateral across a variety of use cases. On the technological, jurisdiction, and organisational neutrality of these Principles, see the discussion in Commentary 0.5 to 0.9.

2 Reflections

2.1 Introduction

2.1.1 The Role of the Principle

Principle 1 is the gateway to the UNIDROIT DAPL, serving the main introductory approach to the instrument. As concisely as possible, it seems to be limited to reproducing the title of the instrument (UNIDROIT Principles on Digital Assets and Private Law). It states that 'these Principles deal with the private law relating to digital assets'. With this succinctness nonetheless, Principle 1 encapsulates the main policy decisions underpinning the instrument. Firstly, it outlines the scope of application of the instrument. Secondly, it delimits and manages the interaction with other instruments. Thirdly, it evidences how the instrument articulates the functional and neutral approach.

Principle 1 of the UNIDROIT DAPL primarily plays a key role in limiting the scope of application of the Principles. In this respect, Principle 1 not only introduces the instrument, but it essentially outlines the profiles of the UNIDROIT DAPL sphere of application: private law relating to digital assets. See 2.3.2 below.

By delimiting the scope of the instrument to certain aspects of private law relating to digital assets, as defined in Principle 2(2), Principle 1 also reflects the interplay of the UNIDROIT DAPL with other instruments. In outlining the scope of the UNIDROIT DAPL, Principle 1 articulates how it coordinates with other instruments, adopted by or promoted under the auspices of either UNIDROIT or other organisations, and situates the UNIDROIT DAPL in the global legal harmonisation context. See 2.2 below.

Yet, Principle 1 is framed by the functional and neutral approach adopted by the UNIDROIT DAPL in three aspects: technology and business model neutrality, jurisdiction neutrality, and organisation neutrality. How private law is understood for the purposes of the UNIDROIT DAPL and how digital assets are defined highlight that approach. See 2.3.1 below.

2.1.2 The Location of the Principle and its Evolution Through Legislative History

Principle 1 is located in Section I on scope and definitions. Given its role in delimiting the scope, coordination with other instruments, and the crystallisation of the instrument's approach, it is placed as the first provision of the instrument. That location demonstrates and endorses its role as a gateway to the UNIDROIT DAPL. Nevertheless, as Principle 1 is strongly dependent upon Principle 2 on definitions, it was discussed whether the former should be located before or after the definitions.[1] There were reasons supporting either of the drafting options.

The first formulation of Principle 1 is incorporated into the black-letter principles[2] in February 2022 to be discussed at the fifth session on 7–9 March 2022. Its initial drafting differed from the current wording in two main points. On the one hand, the Principle was titled 'scope [of the Principles]'. On the other hand, the wording of the Principle was 'These Principles deal with the private law relating to [transactions in] digital assets'.

[1] Digital Assets and Private Law Working Group // Fifth session (hybrid) // Rome, 7–9 March 2022 1. //// UNIDROIT 2022 // Study LXXXII–W.G.5–Doc. 4 // English only // February 2022, pars. 17–20.

[2] Digital Assets and Private Law Working Group // Fifth session (hybrid) // Rome, 7–9 March 2022 1. //// UNIDROIT 2022 // Study LXXXII–W.G.5–Doc. 2 // English only // February 2022.

Before the formulation of the Principle as a black-letter rule, the WG had nonetheless discussed the scope of the instrument in depth. From the outset,[3] the WG had been invited to focus on private law issues relating to digital assets and in particular proprietary interests. The aim of the project was not only to provide solutions where there are gaps in legal systems, but also to signal where legacy rules prove not to be appropriate and may need to be adapted to cover digital assets. Therefore, once the main issues were identified, the WG was entrusted with the mandate putting forward principles that private law regime should incorporate to deal with digital assets. Hence, from the beginning, the project was intended to focus on private law issues. Such a scoping decision did not ignore the potential interactions with regulatory issues, which frequently came to light when dealing with aspects relating to custody. Although it was clear that regulation is outside the scope of the project, separating private law issues from regulatory issues was often a complex matter, and a number of aspects to be tackled in the project bordered on regulatory issues.[4]

The focus on private law issues, and primarily proprietary interests, was not abandoned[5] by the WG in subsequent sessions and finally crystalised in the drafting of Principle 1.[6]

While the approach to the scope of the UNIDROIT DAPL did not substantially change throughout the process of developing the instrument, the drafting of Principle 1 did evolve. Basically, there were two versions of the Principle. The first one was presented to the WG at its fifth session,[7] as follows:

Principle 1: Scope [of the principles].

These Principles deal with the private law relating to [transactions in] digital assets

[3] Digital Assets and Private Law Working Group // First session (remote) // Rome, 17–19 November 2020 1. //// UNIDROIT 2020 // Study LXXXII–W.G.1– Doc. 2 // English only // November 2020, par. 35.

[4] Digital Assets and Private Law Working Group // First session (remote) // Rome, 17–19 November 2020 1. //// UNIDROIT 2020 // Study LXXXII – W.G.1 – Doc. 2 // English only // November 2020, par. 35.

[5] Digital Assets and Private Law Working Group // Second session (remote) // Rome, 16 –18 March 2021 1. //// UNIDROIT 2021 // Study LXXXII – W.G.2 – Doc. 2 (rev. 1) // English only // March 2021, par. 38; Digital Assets and Private Law Working Group // Third session (remote) // Rome, 30 June – 2 July 2021 1. //// UNIDROIT 2021 // Study LXXXII – W.G.3 – Doc. 2 (rev. 1) // English only // June 2021, par. 34; Digital Assets and Private Law Working Group // Fourth session (hybrid) // Rome, 2 – 4 November 2021 1. //// UNIDROIT 2021 // Study LXXXII – W.G.4 – Doc. 2 // English only // October 2021, par. 34.

[6] Digital Assets and Private Law Working Group // Fifth session (hybrid) // Rome, 7 –9 March 2022 1. //// UNIDROIT 2022 // Study LXXXII – W.G.5 – Doc. 2 // English only // February 2022.

[7] Digital Assets and Private Law Working Group // Fifth session (hybrid) // Rome, 7 –9 March 2022 1. //// UNIDROIT 2022 // Study LXXXII – W.G.5 – Doc. 2 // English only // February 2022.

The second one was presented to and agreed on by the WG at the sixth session after the changes made by the Drafting Committee (hereinafter, DC) in its sessions 5, 6, 7, 8 and 9 during the intersession period between March 2022 and August 2022.[8] This second wording comprised the final drafting of Principle 1 through to adoption of the UNIDROIT DAPL.

Principle 1: Scope

These Principles deal with the private law relating to digital assets

Likewise, the Commentary to Principle 1, as it was drafted by the Drafting Committee (DC) at sessions 5 to 9 and agreed by the WG at its sixth session, was essentially the final drafting until the adoption of the instrument.

Whereas the change in the title of Principle 1 by removing the text in brackets ([of the Principles]) does not seem to have any relevant impact on the meaning, the change in the wording of the black-letter Principle is more substantial. It was decided to remove the text initially in brackets ([transactions in]). The rationale behind this drafting change is related to the actual scope of the UNIDROIT DAPL. By limiting the scope to transactions in digital assets, it was stressed that the instrument was focused on core commercial transactions in digital assets and was not aimed at addressing any private law issues relating to digital assets. Actually, as the Commentary to Principle 1 highlights, the instrument does specially address digital assets where these are the object of dispositions and acquisitions. Hence, it seemed that the scope was limited to such transactions, in particular, as far as proprietary interests are concerned. However, and without prejudice to the foregoing, it was noted[9] that the instrument also covered static situations such as custody. Thus, limiting the scope in Principle 1 to 'transactions in digital assets' might have been too restrictive.

Consequently, Principle 1 was finally drafted in a broader manner by focusing the scope on the key words: 'private law relating to digital assets'. As further explained below (see 2.3.2), this broad formulation does not mean that the instrument intends to cover general private law on digital assets. There are exceptions and limits as clarified and specified in the Commentary to Principle 1.

[8] Digital Assets and Private Law Working Group // Sixth session (hybrid) // Rome, 31 August – 2 September 2022 1. //// UNIDROIT 2022 // Study LXXXII – W.G.6 – Doc. 3 // English only // August 2022, pp. 1–2.

[9] Digital Assets and Private Law Working Group // Fifth session (hybrid) // Rome, 7 –9 March 2022 1. //// UNIDROIT 2022 // Study LXXXII – W.G.5 – Doc. 4 // English only // February 2022, par. 18.

2.2 *Relationship with other Instruments*

Given the inherently international scope of the market and the natural cross-border aspects of many transactions involving digital assets, a response based on common principles and internationally harmonised solutions is instrumental to enhance predictability, stability, and certainty in the global market. Thus, along with certain domestic and regional[10] legislative and regulatory responses, that vary substantially among each other and oftentimes differ in policy goals, harmonised principles and best practices are starting to emerge and become established as a result of various initiatives led by international organisations and formulating agencies for the unification of international trade law–UNCITRAL (United Nations Commission for International Trade Law),[11] UNIDROIT (International Institute for the Unification of Private Law),[12] HCCH (Hague Conference on Private International Law).[13] In these harmonisation efforts, the UNIDROIT DAPL project plays a pivotal role.

In parallel, the very notion of digital assets as a 'controllable electronic record' (as per Principle 2(2) UNIDROIT DAPL) entails a conceptual demarcation of the instrument that make it border with (or overlap with) other initiatives on data contracts,[14] or on electronic transferable records.[15]

Hence, the UNIDROIT DAPL has to fit into this legislative and regulatory ecosystem on digital assets and related aspects. Therefore, besides delimiting the scope of the

---

[10] Regulation (EU) 2023/1114 of the European Parliament and of the Council of 31 May 2023 on markets in crypto-assets, and amending Regulations (EU) No 1093/2010 and (EU) No 1095/2010 and Directives 2013/36/EU and (EU) 2019/1937 (Text with EEA relevance). PE/54/2022/REV/1; OJ L 150, 9.6.2023, p. 40–205.

[11] UNCITRAL: www.uncitral.org.

[12] UNIDROIT: www.unidroit.org.

[13] HCCH: www.hcch.net.

[14] Initiatives on data transactions are significantly diverse in terms of scope, policy objectives, and formulating agency. But they are all aimed to provide rules for certain data contracts considering their particular features as public goods (and non-excludable) or club goods (and excludable) - Duch Brown N, Martens B, Muller-Langer F (2017) The economics of ownership, access and trade in digital data, JRC Digital Economy Working Paper 2017–01, European Commission, 2017, JRC104756. Among these initiatives to provide rules for data contracts, three of them are highlighted and referred to below. First, ALI-ELI *Principles for a Data Economy: Data Transactions and Data Rights,* https://principlesforadataeconomy.org/ and https://www.europeanlawinstitute.eu/projects-publications/publications/ali-eli-principles-for-a-data-economy-data-transactions-and-data-rights/. Second, in the European Union, the Data Act - Regulation (EU) 2023/2854 of the European Parliament and of the Council of 13 December 2023 on harmonised rules on fair access to and use of data and amending Regulation (EU) 2017/2394 and Directive (EU) 2020/1828 (Data Act), PE/49/2023/REV/1, *OJ L, 2023/2854.* Third, the UNCITRAL Project on default rules for data provision contracts – United Nations Commission on International Trade Law // Working Group IV (Electronic Commerce) // Sixty-eight session // New York, 24–28 March 2025 /// A /CN.9/WG.IV/WP.188 // 20 January 2025.

[15] Notably, UNCITRAL Model Law on Electronic Transferable Records, 2017 (hereinafter, MLETR). Text available at https://uncitral.un.org/en/texts/ecommerce/modellaw/electronic_transferable_records.

instrument, Principle 1 also plays a key role in carving out a place for UNIDROIT DAPL in the international legal harmonisation context dealing with digital assets or related aspects. The project leading to the adoption of the UNIDROIT DAPL instrument benefits from other instruments, interacts with existing UNIDROIT texts, as well as creating synergies with ongoing, and concluded, works both at UNIDROIT and at other international formulating agencies (or international legal standard setters).

There are multiple points of interaction with other instruments. Some of them are linked to the definition of digital assets and its relationship with other similar or related concepts (data, electronic transferable records, intermediated securities, crypto assets, etc.). Others are associated with rules governing the holding, transfer, encumbering, and use of digital assets.

In closely assessing these relationships between the UNIDROIT DAPL and other instruments and projects, three criteria need to be considered.

First, the character of the instruments in comparison. From the outset,[16] the project on Digital Assets and Private Law[17] was proposed as a Guidance document. Thus, the Working Group was mandated to prepare a set of Principles with commentary, instead of, at least at that stage, a model law or convention. Hence, the envisaged output was not expected to be one of binding character. In the form of Principles, the expected instrument would embody best practices and international standards for States to follow as guidance when adopting legislation and so take a common approach to the legal issues covered by the instrument (0.4 UNIDROIT DAPL). Therefore, when interplaying with other instruments, that non-binding character (legislative guidance) should be taken into account, while the character of other instruments may be varied. Interplays can occur with binding instruments such as Conventions, as well as with Model Laws, best practices and recommendations. Consequently, the type of interaction will first depend upon the character of the interplaying instruments.

Second, the scope of the instruments. As stated in the concise wording of Principle 1, the scope of UNIDROIT DAPL is focused on certain private law issues related to digital assets, particularly regarding proprietary interests. Both key scope-delimiting elements are defined by the instrument with a specific extent. Thus, the UNIDROIT DAPL interacts with instruments that generally deal with similar private law issues but not in relation to digital assets, as well as with instruments that are designed to apply to digital assets but cover other legal issues or the same private law issues in more detail and extension. Therefore, the relationship established between the UNIDROIT DAPL and each of the instruments and projects with which it interacts may be complementary, partially overlap, cross-fertilising or synergistic. Sometimes the scopes of both instruments complement each other, while overlapping with others.

[16] Digital Assets and Private Law Working Group // First session (remote) // Rome, 17–19 November 2020 1. //// UNIDROIT 2020 // Study LXXXII – W.G.1 – Doc. 2 // English only // November 2020, pars. 1–18.

[17] The title of the project as 'Digital Assets and Private Law' was adopted (initially as a temporary change of name) by the Governing Council in its 99th session (B), held in Rome from 23 to 25 September 2020, Governing Council // 99th session (B) // Rome, 23 –25 September 2020 //// UNIDROIT 2020 // C.D. (99) B Misc. 2 // English/French // October 2020, par. 8.

Therefore, these interactions have to be visualised as a network of relationships which the UNIDROIT DAPL benefits or is benefited from, complements or is supplemented by, or aligns with or is inspired by other various instruments and projects.

Third, the organisation which adopts or under whose auspices the instrument is adopted. These interactions and synergies emerge at three different levels: with existing UNIDROIT instruments, with ongoing UNIDROIT projects of the Work Programme, and with instruments and projects led by other institutions and organisations–UNCITRAL (United Nations Commission for International Trade Law),[18] HCCH (Hague Conference on Private International Law),[19] EU (European Union), ELI (European Law Institute),[20] ALI (American Law Institute),[21] as well as other national initiatives.

Under the above-outlined three-criterion scheme, the following interactions with selected instruments and projects are detailed and further elaborated.

2.2.1 Digital Assets and Intermediated Securities

There is a natural link between the UNIDROIT DAPL and the Institute's work on the capital market. Both the Geneva Convention on Substantive Rules for Intermediated Securities[22] and the UNIDROIT Legislative Guide on Intermediated Securities implementing the Principles and Rules of the Geneva Securities Convention interact with the UNIDROIT DAPL in those aspects related to transfer, secured transactions and custodians. Whereas UNIDROIT DAPL needed to envisage important issues related to the transfer and secured transactions of digital assets and the notion of custodian, its duties, and the insolvency of the custodian, the Geneva Convention on Substantive Rules for Intermediated Securities had already addressed primary issues related to transfer, and collateral transactions over intermediated securities and to intermediaries.[23] Therefore, and not surprisingly, in the drafting of UNIDROIT DAPL, the Geneva Convention on Substantive Rules for Intermediated Securities provisions were considered as policy options and taken into account as an inspiration in the drafting. A meaningful example is the evolution of Principle 19 on the effect of insolvency on proprietary rights in digital assets that was finally aligned with Article 14 of the Geneva Convention over other alternative policy and drafting options. But it is not the only one, several of the UNIDROIT DAPL Principles (namely Principle 8(5),

[18] https://uncitral.un.org/.

[19] Hhtps://www.hcch.net.

[20] https://www.europeanlawinstitute.eu/.

[21] https://www.ali.org/.

[22] Geneva Convention on Substantive Rules for Intermediated Securities, UNIDROIT, Geneva, 9 October 2009.

[23] Kanda H et al. (2012), Official Commentary on the UNIDROIT Convention on Substantive Rules for Intermediated Securities, Oxford University Press, Oxford.

Principle 13(5 to 7), the approach followed by Principle 16, *inter alia*) are clearly based on and/or are consistent with Geneva Convention rules.

Acknowledging the relationship between the UNIDROIT DAPL and the rules on intermediated securities reveals interesting conceptual and policy assumptions. On the one hand, the commonalities in legal issues arising from the intermediated holding system (custodian and intermediary). On the other hand, the impact on the rules applicable to the transfer, and the creation and third-party effectiveness of security interests in digital assets. As Commentary 14.4 noted, where a digital asset is linked to another asset, that other asset may fall within existing categories of assets, such as securities.

Consistency and alignment between two UNIDROIT instruments would seem advisable and expected. But we should not lose sight of the fact that the spheres of application are not full matches. Precisely, the merit of the UNIDROIT DAPL is that it provides guidance for transactions on those assets, the digital assets as defined by the instrument–'an electronic record which is capable of being subject to control', Principle 2(2)–to which existing rules do not apply, or where legislators, courts, arbitrators, practitioners, and market players encounter difficulties or uncertainties in regulating or interpreting, or applying existing rules to transactions in digital assets. Where a digital asset is linked to another asset, that other asset may fall within a specific category in the domestic law of a State or pursuant to an international instrument. As a matter of this other law, either a domestic law or an international one, the linked digital asset may fall into a specific category, such as negotiable instruments or, in particular, securities. Therefore, according to other law, some linked digital assets may be included in the category of securities, pursuant to the Geneva Convention on Substantive Rules for Intermediated Securities, in which case the latter applies. Otherwise, the scope of the UNIDROIT DAPL goes much further than the conventional text.

2.2.2 Enforcement Against Digital Assets

As the market for digital assets grows in size and in diversity, transactions, commercial practice and also litigation involving digital assets are equally expanding and increasing. In such circumstances, creditors want, and need to be reassured that they can effectively enforce their rights, even if such rights are related to this type of assets. In practice, enforcement on digital assets proves to be challenging due to specific complexities arising from the functional, structural and operational characteristics of digital assets. As a consequence, in addition to the factors that may traditionally render enforcement proceedings costly, ineffective, or unsuccessful, creditors may face additional costs, uncertainties or inefficiencies in enforcing their rights against digital assets. Therefore, although new enforcement rules covering digital assets might not be necessary in all cases, there is a need to ensure the effectiveness of the enforcement of rights on digital assets. Best practices for helping courts, enforcement agents, legislators, practitioners, and parties can facilitate the accommodation of existing rules, measures, and procedures to the digital-assets realm. This is the main goal of the ongoing project at UNIDROIT on *Best Practices for Effective Enforcement*[24] (hereinafter, BPEE),[25] as well as the work of ELI on *Access to Digital Assets* (hereinafter, ELI ADA).[26]

The complementarity between the UNIDROIT DAPL and the UNIDROIT project on BPEE,[27] which was still in progress when the UNIDROIT DAPL was adopted, was natural and evident.[28] The BPEE was not only seriously and extensively addressing the impact of technologies on enforcement, as one of its main objectives, but it also dedicates a separate Part of the final instrument to best practices on enforcement against digital assets.[29] Multiple opportunities for cross-fertilisation between the two projects were seized. Joint workshops and joint drafting committees were enabled to exploit the synergies and to ensure coherence between the two projects. The BPEE elaborate on the succinct Principle 18 UNIDROIT DAPL with which they fully align, as well as building on their main concepts–digital assets, control, custodian pursuant to Principles 2, 6 and 10 UNIDROIT DAPL–and integrating some of their rules in their recommendations (such as Principle 17(2) UNIDROIT DAPL).

[24] For information on this project, and on the members and observers of the Working Group see https://www.unidroit.org/work-in-progress/enforcement-best-practices/.

[25] The author is an expert member of the UNIDROIT Working Group on Best Practices for Effective Enforcement - https://www.unidroit.org/work-in-progress/enforcement-best-practices/# 1644493658788-9cb71890-334f. All views and opinions expressed in this paper are the personal ones of the author and do not represent the opinions of neither the Working Group nor any of its members.

[26] This ELI project began as a broad initiative - Council Decision CD 2019/4 of 1 March 2019 on the Approval of a New Project on Access to Digital Assets - focusing on various aspects of the law relating to digital assets at a time when both digital assets and access to them were becoming increasingly important. In a first phase, the ELI Principles on the Use of Digital Assets were adopted and approved in February 2022 - ELI Principles on the Use of Digital Assets as Security, https://www.europeanlawinstitute.eu/fileadmin/user_upload/p_eli/Publications/ELI_Principles_on_the_U.se_of_Digital_Assets_as_Security.pdf. As a second phase, ELI Principles and Implementation Guidance on Enforcement against Digital Assets were approved by the ELI Council on 3–4 March 2025, Vienna. Update of the ELI project on Access to Digital Assets available at https://www.europeanlawinstitute.eu/projects-publications/current-projects/current-projects/eli-access-to-digital-assets/. The author is the co-reporter with Jos Huitdehaag of the ELI Project. All views and opinions expressed in this paper are the personal ones of the author and do not represent the opinions of neither ELI or its bodies nor any of the members of the project team and related committees.

[27] For more information on the work in progress, https://www.unidroit.org/work-in-progress/enforcement-best-practices/.

[28] Veneziano A, Rodríguez de las Heras Ballell T (2025) Digital Assets in Insolvency and Enforcement Proceedings: Some Insights from UNIDROIT's Work. In: Koller C, Lehmann M (ed) Digital Assets in Enforcement and Insolvency Securing Creditor Access and Protecting Customer Interests in the Crypto World, Hart Publishing, Oxford, p 27–43.

[29] Rodríguez de las Heras Ballell T (2024a, b) The Emergence of Principles and Best Practices on Digital Assets: Proprietary Rights, and Enforcement. European Journal of Risk Regulation 2024: 1–12. http://doi:10.1017/err.2024.55.

The synergic relation between these two UNIDROIT projects provides interesting insights.

On the one hand, both instruments–BPEE still an ongoing project when the UNIDROIT DAPL were approved–are of a non-binding character. The interplay between principles and best practices is easy and fluid, as the aim and the tone are similar.

On the other hand, the subject matters are complementary but largely diverse in both projects. While the BPEE are focused on enforcement, both judicially and extrajudicially, and cover all classes of assets, the UNIDROIT DAPL's scope is materially delimited to digital assets and only incidentally addresses enforcement-related issues through two Principles–Principle 17 on enforcement of security rights in digital assets, and Principle 18 on procedural law including enforcement. Accordingly, BPEE largely supplement the UNIDROIT DAPL by providing numerous and detailed recommendations for both judicial enforcement against digital assets and enforcement of security rights in digital assets. The latter covers both enforcement of security rights in digital assets by way of authority as well as nonjudicial enforcement of security rights in digital assets.

Given the complexities arising from enforcement against digital assets due to their distinctive features–functional, structural, and operational features -,[30] the BPEE provide specific recommendations for legislators, courts, practitioners, and market participants on enforcement against digital assets. To that end, Part III on Digital Assets Enforcement has been elaborated. Interestingly, Part III is intended to provide additional guidance to 'controllable digital assets', deemed as the most common digital assets in the commercial context. Thus, not surprisingly, the BPEE align with UNIDROIT DAPL's definition of digital assets. That means that the recommendations in Part III BPEE complement, specifically apply, or adapt general recommendations on enforcement (as provided for in Part I and Part II BPEE) to this notion of digital assets. Beyond the perimeters of this definition, other data assets, linked digital assets, and digital assets not falling under the notion of Principle 2(2) UNIDROIT DAPL, would nonetheless be covered by Part I and Part II BPEE.

Yet, the second phase of the ELI ADA also focuses on enforcement against digital assets. The instrument, adopted by the ELI Council in March 2025, provides Principles and Implementation Guidance on enforcement against digital assets (hereinafter, ELI P&G). It is well worth noting that the ELI text defines 'digital assets' as 'an electronic record that represents a value, a right, or a legally protected interest and which is capable of being subject to control' (B.1 ELI P&G). With this definition, the ELI P&G depart from the definition of digital assets used in the first phase of the ELI ADA (ELI Principles on the Use of Digital Assets as Security),[31] with the aim of accommodating the definition to the scope and purpose of the second phase. For the

[30] Rodríguez de las Heras Ballell T (2025) Foreword. In: Koller C, Lehmann M (ed) Digital Assets in Enforcement and Insolvency Securing Creditor Access and Protecting Customer Interests in the Crypto World, Hart Publishing, Oxford, p vii–xi.

[31] ELI Principles on the Use of Digital Assets as Security (2022), Definitions, b):

'digital asset' means any record or representation of value that fulfils the following criteria:

purposes of enforcement, a broad definition of digital assets was advisable. With a primary, albeit not exclusive, European approach,[32] and with the original Principle-Implementation Guidance structure, the ELI P&G also contribute to completing the UNIDROIT DAPL and elaborate on aspects related enforcement against digital assets.

2.2.3 Digital Assets Linked to other Assets

UNIDROIT DAPL cover linked assets (Principle 4). Linked assets are digital assets linked to another asset that may be tangible or intangible, including another digital asset. In this regard however, the UNIDROIT DAPL takes a neutral position and refers to the other law of the State to determine (or establish the minimum legal requirements) that the link between the digital asset and the other asset exists and what the legal effects are. Accordingly, and pursuant to applicable law, the other asset may fall under specific categories of assets, such as securities, bonds, invoices, warehouse receipts, or, other negotiable instruments.

From that perspective, UNIDROIT DAPL would interact, in the conditions laid down in Principle 4, with other pieces of legislation or instruments governing such specific categories of assets. Such interaction may be potentially materialised with a variety of instruments both at a domestic and at an international level. More interesting to be spotlighted is the interplay with other UNIDROIT instruments. Specifically, the UNCITRAL-UNIDROIT Model Law on Warehouse Receipts (2024)[33] allows for the issuance and transfer of both paper-based and electronic warehouse receipts

---

(i) it is exclusively stored, displayed and administered electronically, on or through a virtual platform or database, including where it is a record or representation of a real-world, tradeable asset, and whether or not the digital asset itself is held directly or through an account with an intermediary;
(ii) it is capable of being subject to a right of control, enjoyment or use, regardless of whether such rights are legally characterised as being of a proprietary, obligational or other nature; and
(iii) it is capable of being transferred from one party to another, including by way of voluntary disposition. It is irrelevant, for the purposes of this definition, what the design and operational features of the relevant platform or database are, or whether the relevant digital asset's protection against undue replication, transmission and/or use is dependent on the use of cryptography, or whether the relevant digital asset represents a monetary claim on (and, correspondingly, a liability of) an identifiable party as issuer, custodian or controller thereof or whether the asset in question fulfils the functions of money or currency

.

[32] Along with the UNIDROIT DAPL, the ELI P&G have taken into consideration the following sources: Recommendation Rec (17) 2003 of the Committee of Ministers to Member States on Enforcement, Council of Europe, adopted on 9 September 2003; CEPEJ Guidelines for a better implementation of the existing Council of Europe's Recommendation on Enforcement, European Commission on the efficiency of Justice (CEPEJ); Good practice guide on enforcement of judicial decisions adopted by CEPEJ in 2015; International Union of Judicial Officers (UIHJ) Global Code of Enforcement, 2024.

[33] Text available at https://www.unidroit.org/instruments/wr/. The author was an expert member of the Working Group on UNCITRAL-UNIDROIT Model Law on Warehouse Receipts. All views

on a medium-neutral and technology-neutral basis including in the form of digital assets.[34] Besides, should receivables be issued in the form of digital assets, there are also synergies with the UNIDROIT Model Law on Factoring,[35] adopted in 2023, whose Guide to Enactment is still work in progress, with expected date of adoption in 2025.[36]

2.2.4 Digital Assets and Private International Law

Given the natural cross-border nature of digital assets holding, transfers, and enforcement, and their inherent 'digital character' that challenges traditional connecting factors, in particular, the role of location–such as *lex res sitae* -, private international law (PIL) rules are also challenged and are facing a profound review and consideration to ensure their adequacy or adaptability. UNIDROIT DAPL Principles (Principle 5) devises a 'waterfall' model headed by party autonomy (UNIDROIT DAPL 0.14). On private international law matters, cooperation with HCCH (Hague Conference with Private International Law) is a natural alliance. In fact, joint work on Law Applicable to Cross-Border Holdings and Transfers of Digital Assets and Tokens between the two institutions (two of the 'three sisters') was explored.[37] Nevertheless, consensus was not reached to mandate future joint work on the matter.[38] Nonetheless, in Conclusion and Decision (C&D) No 12, according to which '(r)ecognising the importance of avoiding fragmentation among legal instruments developed by different intergovernmental organisations on related subject matters, including the *UNIDROIT Principles on Digital Assets and Private Law*, in March 2024 the Council on General Affairs and Policy of the HCCH (CGAP) mandated the PB, in partnership with relevant subject-matters experts and Observers, to study the PIL issues relating to digital

---

and opinions expressed in this paper are the personal ones of the author and do not represent the opinions of neither the Working Group nor any of its members.

34 https://unis.unvienna.org/unis/en/pressrels/2024/unisl358.html. The UNCITRAL-UNIDROIT Model Law on Warehouse Receipts was adopted in 2024. Text available at https://www.unidroit.org/wp-content/uploads/2025/01/2024-uncitral-unidroit-mlwr.pdf

35 The UNIDROIT Model Law on Factoring (MLF) was adopted by the UNIDROIT Governing Council at its 102nd session (Rome, 10–12 May 2023), https://www.unidroit.org/instruments/factoring/.

36 https://www.unidroit.org/work-in-progress/model-law-on-factoring-guide-to-enactment/.

37 "Proposal for Joint Work: HCCH-UNIDROIT Project on Law Applicable to Cross-Border Holdings and Transfers of Digital Assets and Tokens (DAT Joint Project)", Prel. Doc. No 3C of January 2023 for CGAP 2023, para. 17, available at www.hcch.net, Governance/Council on General Affairs and Policy/Archive (2000–2023).

38 The HCCH-UNIDROIT *Digital Assets and Tokens Project* was concluded as it was unlikely that a mandate for further work to be undertaken in the framework of the DAT Joint Project would find with consensus among HCCH Members, as Conclusions & Decisions, HCCH Council on General Affairs and Policy (CGAP), 5 to 8 March 2024, on the basis of Prel. Doc. No 3 of January 2024, par. 26, https://assets.hcch.net/docs/efce41ca-1c8c-4d61-9d8b-9348df9303a0.pdf.

tokens. The PB will report to CGAP 2025 on the outcomes of this study, including next step proposals'.[39]

The CGAP decided in March 2025 to establish an Expert Group on Digital Token Project to study the private international law issues raised by digital tokens. The interaction between Principle 5 UNIDROIT DAPL and the expected outcome of this HCCH project will be intense and close. Nothing else can be anticipated at this stage until the scope, the subject-matters, and the policy solutions finally adopted by the HCCH in this Digital Tokens Project are confirmed in due course.

2.2.5 Digital Assets and Data

The concept of 'digital asset' is neither uniformly defined nor clearly delimited at a global level. The UNIDROIT DAPL opts for a definition anchored on the notion of 'electronic record' and the concept of 'control'–'electronic record which is capable of being subject to control' as per Principle 2(2).

As electronic records, it becomes rather challenging to distinguish them from mere information, data sets, digital content, or a variety of digital realities with economic value (from social media accounts to transmissible files and electronic communications). Demarcating the perimeters of the 'digital assets' category is, however, particularly relevant and pressing in the face of the expanding data economy.[40] As non-rival (and non-excludable or excludable) goods, data can expand and replicate their value and utility for multiple purposes and unlimited uses and reuses without losing quality or dwindling quantity, whereas the notion of digital assets does strongly depend upon the concept of 'control'.

Therefore, in the first place, the UNIDROIT DAPL interplays with various instruments and projects on data.[41] It is first and foremost a relationship of mutual exclusion. Either it is a controllable electronic record under the UNIDROIT DAPL, or it is data

---

[39] HCCH, "Proposal for a Normative Project: Private International Law Issues Relating to Digital Tokens", Prel. Doc. No 5B REV of March 2024, available on the HCCH website www.hcch.net under "Governance" then "Council on General Affairs and Policy"; once the HCCH-UNIDROIT *Digital Assets and Tokens Project* was concluded, Conclusions & Decisions, HCCH Council on General Affairs and Policy (CGAP), 5 to 8 March 2024.

[40] ALI-ELI *Principles for a Data Economy: Data Transactions and Data Rights,* https://principlesforadataeconomy.org/, traces an interesting distinction between data representing information, functional data, and representative data. The latter sub-category comprises 'digital assets.Principle 2: Scope of the Principles "The primary focus of the Principles is on records of large quantities of information as an asset, resource or tradeable commodity. The Principles do not address functional data, e.g. data the main purpose of which is to deliver particular functionalities (such as a computer program), and representative data, e.g. data the main purpose of which is to represent other assets or value (such as crypto-assets)."

[41] Digital Assets and Private Law Working Group // First session (remote) // Rome, 17 –19 November 2020 1. //// UNIDROIT 2020 // Study LXXXII – W.G.1 – Doc. 2 // English only // November 2020, pars. 37–46.

falling under other instruments. The latter group of instruments comprises the ALI-ELI Principles for a Data Economy,[42] the European Union Data Act[43] with its Model Contractual Terms[44] on B2B Data Sharing,[45] and the UNCITRAL Project on default rules for data provision contracts.[46] Interestingly, in defining its scope,[47] the ALI-ELI Principles for a Data Economy masterly outline a typology of data: data representing information, functional data, and representative data. ALI-ELI Principles are aimed to apply to the first category, data representing information, records of large quantities of information as an asset, resource or tradeable commodity. However, they do not address functional data, e.g. data whose main purpose is to deliver particular functionalities (such as a computer program), and representative data, e.g. data whose main purpose is to represent other assets or value (such as crypto-assets).

---

[42] ALI-ELI *Principles for a Data Economy: Data Transactions and Data Rights,* https://principlesforadataeconomy.org/ and https://www.europeanlawinstitute.eu/projects-publications/publications/ali-eli-principles-for-a-data-economy-data-transactions-and-data-rights/.

[43] Regulation (EU) 2023/2854 of the European Parliament and of the Council of 13 December 2023 on harmonised rules on fair access to and use of data and amending Regulation (EU) 2017/2394 and Directive (EU) 2020/1828 (Data Act), PE/49/2023/REV/1, *OJ L, 2023/2854* -, aims to repair data market failures, allocating proper incentives, and deactivating counterproductive practices to combat unfairness. To that end, the Data Act provide for rules on unfair contractual terms in (B2B) data sharing contracts between enterprises (Article 13 Data Act) and non-binding model contractual terms on data access and use for B2B data sharing contracts to be developed and recommended by the Commission (Article 41 Data Act)*22.12.2023.*

[44] Rodríguez de las Heras Ballell T (2024a, b) Drafting Model Contractual Terms for Voluntary B2B Data Sharing: A Tool to Deal with Unfairness. In: Lohsse S, Schulze R, Staudenmayer D (ed) Private Law and the Data Act. Münster Colloquia on EU Law and the Digital Economy VIII. Nomos/Hart-Bloomsbury Publishing, Baden-Baden, p 127–148.

[45] The Expert Group on B2B data sharing and cloud computing contracts (E03840) – https://ec.europa.eu/transparency/expert-groups-register/screen/expert-groups/consult?lang=en&groupID=3840—has the mission of assisting the Commission in its work on developing model contractual clauses for B2B data sharing and standard contractual clauses for cloud computing contracts. On 19 November 2025, the Commission has adopted the Communication C(2025) 7750 final—to approve Draft Commission Recommendation on non-binding model contractual terms on data accessand use and non-binding standard contractual clauses for computing contracts (with Annexes). The author is member of the Expert Group. All views and opinions in this contribution are personal and do neither bind nor represent the European Commission or the Expert Group.

[46] United Nations Commission on International Trade Law // Working Group IV (Electronic Commerce) // Sixty-eight session // New York, 24–28 March 2025 /// A /CN.9/WG.IV/WP.188 // 20 January 2025. Draft Article 1(a) defines 'data' as *a representation of information in electronic form or other form suitable for processing in an information system.*

[47] Principle 2 ALI-ELI Principles for a data Economy: Scope of the Principles.

> 'The primary focus of the Principles is on records of large quantities of information as an asset, resource or tradeable commodity. The Principles do not address functional data, e.g. data the main purpose of which is to deliver particular functionalities (such as a computer program), and representative data, e.g. data the main purpose of which is to represent other assets or value (such as crypto-assets).'

On the other hand, by employing the notion of 'controllable electronic record' the UNIDROIT DAPL honours and connects to UNCITRAL work on electronic transferable records–Articles 2, 10 and 11 MLETR (2017).[48] The pivotal concept of 'control'[49] establishes bridges with other instruments and is placed at the heart of the private-law legal regime over digital assets. As a functional equivalent of possession, 'control' is decisive for the creation and the exercise of proprietary rights over digital assets, for enforcement, or for tracing and recovery in insolvency proceedings. This definition of digital assets as electronic records capable of being subject to control is paving the way for the deployment of a globally harmonised set of private-law rules. It is jurisdiction-agnostic, is independent from regulatory considerations, and is solidly rooted in the uniform notions of electronic records and control as developed by the texts on electronic commerce and electronic transferable records.

[48] See and compare Art. 11 MLETR; and Principle 6 DAPL Principles as for the extent of the 'exclusive ability' requirement. Article 11 MLETR traces the functional-equivalence link with possession by setting out two requirements to meet 'where the law requires or permits the possession of a transferable document or instrument' with respect to an electronic transferable: a reliable method to establish exclusive control of that electronic transferable record by a person; and a reliable method to identify that person as the person in control. UNIDROIT DAPL Principles provides for a more elaborate framework for digital assets that rightly differ from the MLETR standard in those specific points where the characteristics of the underlying assets (digital assets) call for. In Principle 6, three factual abilities of a person – who is allowed to identify itself as having such abilities – having 'control' of the digital asset are required: the exclusive ability to prevent others from obtaining substantially all of the benefits from the digital asset; the ability to obtain all such benefits; and the exclusive ability to transfer these abilities to another person. The element of exclusivity is relaxed in the UNIDROIT DAPL (Principle 6.3) and acknowledge situations where the digital asset, or the relevant protocol or system, limits the use of, or is programmed to make changes to, the digital asset, including change or loss of control, or the person in control has agreed, consented to, or acquiesced in sharing that ability with one or more other persons, such as in multiple-signature arrangement.

[49] The 'controllability' – 'capability of being subject to control' - is also a definitory and scoping element in the UCC § 12–102(a)(1) "Uniform Commercial Code-Controllable Electronic Records". C.R.S. § 4–12-101. Added by 2023 Ch. 136,§ 89, eff. 8/7/2023.2023 Ch. 136, passed without a safety clause. Upon the Amendments, Article 12 UCC defines 'Controllable electronic record' as 'a record stored in an electronic medium that can be subjected to control under Sect. 4–12-105. The term does not include a controllable account, a controllable payment intangible, a deposit account, an electronic copy of a record evidencing chattel paper, an electronic document of title, investment property, a transferable record, or an electronic record that is currently authorized or adopted by a domestic or foreign government and is not a medium of exchange that was recorded and transferable in a system that existed and operated for the medium of exchange before the medium of exchange was authorized or adopted by a government'. As per the *TriBar Report on Opinions Under 2022 Amendments to the Uniform Commercial Code Regarding Emerging Technologies, The Business Lawyer*, Spring 2024, Volume 79, Issue 2, '(t)he 2022 amendments (the "Amendments") to the Uniform Commercial Code (UCC) add a new Article 12 to the UCC and amend most of the other Articles of the UCC, in particular Article 9, to provide new and specific rules for sales of and security interests in certain types of digital assets'.

2.3 *Analysis of Principle 1*

2.3.1 Principle 1 and the Neutral Approach

In its conciseness, Principle 1 UNIDROIT DAPL is a complete expression of the neutral approach adopted by the instrument (0.5 to 0.10 UNIDROIT DAPL).

Firstly, the UNIDROIT DAPL is technology neutral. They are intended to apply to all digital assets meeting the definitory elements laid down in Principle 2(2) irrespective of the technology used. Despite that the instrument has been inspired by use cases and even provides illustrations based on distributed ledger technology, although the UNIDROIT DAPL is not technology-specific. On the contrary, as per Principles 1 and 2, a functional and technology-neutral approach is used to define the material scope of the instruments.

Secondly, the UNIDROIT DAPL is jurisdiction-agnostic. The Principles have been drafted and are intended to be applied to any legal system or culture. As in other international legal harmonisation instruments, their terms and rules should be interpreted having regard to the international character and the need to promote uniformity. That means that, on the one hand, the notions used in the UNIDROIT DAPL should not be deemed as carrying over a specific understanding of certain concepts grounded in legal traditions (such as control, possession, proprietary rights, security interest). To facilitate such a uniform approach, the UNIDROIT DAPL does not only use concepts in a jurisdiction-neutral manner, but they also leverage existing harmonised rules governing the main legal issues addressed by the instrument. A meaningful example is the frequent recourse to the solutions provided for by the UNCITRAL Model Law on Secured Transactions (2016)[50] when dealing with security interest in digital assets.

Thirdly, the UNIDROIT DAPL is organisationally neutral. As Principle 1 states that the 'principles deal with private law relating to digital assets' and, within such a realm, they are meant to serve as guidelines for States to adapt, adopt, or reform their laws in relation to the holding, transfer and use as collateral of digital assets to be consistent with best practices and international standards (1.1 UNIDROIT DAPL). But the instrument neither prejudges nor mandates how each State may implement the Principles in its legal system. Implementation options may range from specific law on digital assets to one or several provisions in general rules of private law, commercial law or consumer law. Regardless of how private law rules are organised in a specific jurisdiction, the UNIDROIT DAPL are only intended to apply to private law and, more specifically, to a specific area of private law–areas such as intellectual property or consumer law, that belong to private law, are not addressed by the instrument.

Under the same organisational neutrality, the UNIDROIT DAPL does not cover rules that are to be enforced by public authorities. Independently of how these rules are

[50] UNCITRAL Model Law on Secured Transactions, 2016, https://uncitral.un.org/en/texts/securi tyinterests/modellaw/secured_transactions.

called in each jurisdiction (regulation, regulatory law) and where they are located (as separate regulations, or as provisions of this character in private-law legislation), the UNIDROIT DAPL do not aim to cover such issues.

2.3.2 Principle 1 and the Scope of the Principles

Pursuant to Principle 1, the scope of the UNIDROIT DAPL is underpinned by two primary elements: private law, and digital assets. While Commentary to Principle 1 elaborates on the extent of private law and explains which issues of private law are addressed and unaddressed by the instrument, the pivotal concept of 'digital assets', the subject matter, is simply mentioned with no further comments under Principle 1. Thus, Principle 1 can only be fully construed when paired with Principle 2 on definitions.

To a certain extent, both elements–private law and digital assets–are inter-dependent in jointly delimiting the scope of the instrument. By confining the private law issues primarily, albeit not exclusively, to proprietary rights, the instrument builds on the more fundamental question of whether digital assets can be the object of disposition and acquisitions or collateral in secured transactions. Without answering the question on the 'property status', and, therefore, without prejudging the possible diverging response of legal traditions and systems, a pragmatic stance pervades the instrument–'a digital asset can be the subject of proprietary rights' (Principle 3 (1) UNIDROIT DAPL). The stance adopted over digital assets, approached as 'assets', has a profound and decisive conceptualising effect. It looks at what 'digital assets' are and what they are not by drawing a clear line between digital assets and data or pure information. The legal treatment of digital assets is then primarily approached from a property-law framework and sharply departs from a general narrative on the value of data and data transactions in today' s economy. The merits of such a pragmatic, but nonetheless decisive, courageous, and substantially prescriptive solution, is that it eludes the amply differing domestic approaches to property and avoids pronouncing on the elusive and dogmatically complex conundrum. Nevertheless, by affirming that digital assets can be the subject of proprietary rights, susceptible to enforcement, or relevant in insolvency proceedings, the hampering obstacle of the immobilism due to legal uncertainty is overcome. This is a contribution of paramount importance.

How to solve the question of the concept (and the definition) of digital assets pervades the current, multifaceted legal and policy discussion of whether the notion should be uniform and internationally harmonised, or is better left to domestic law. Conceptualising the new phenomena as 'digital assets' may be a way of justifying the analogous application of the rules governing other assets, or of stressing their differences to these assets, which would call for a different treatment. It also raises the question whether, and if so, to what extent, the regulatory concepts and rules[51] should influence the rules of private law, including private procedural law.

The UNIDROIT DAPL wisely evade the complex and hampering dogmatic issues to functionally and pragmatically address digital assets as susceptible of being subject to proprietary rights. All the provisions of the instruments hang on that assertion.

Also rather pragmatic is the position of UNIDROIT DAPL in defining which legal issues of private law are covered or are excluded. Private law relating to digital assets is successively narrowed down in three concentric circles.

First, private law covered by the UNIDROIT DAPL is confronted with regulation. Rules to be enforced by public authorities are not covered by the instrument. This clarification is highly relevant insofar as the issuance, transfer or negotiability of digital assets and the activities performed by intermediaries and custodians may fall under the perimeter of financial regulation. 'Same risk, same regulation' exerts a force of attraction of sub-classes and related activities to the perimeter of financial regulation and supervision. That could entail that an intermediary engaged in activities related to digital assets may need to obtain a licence, or that the issuance or the transfer of digital assets are subject to regulatory requirements. Therefore, digital assets either amount to existing products and services or they are assimilated or treated under analogous conditions. Regulatory responses such as the EU Regulation on Markets in Crypto-Assets[52] follow this path. The regulatory treatment does not, however, exhaust, the legal treatment of digital assets. Therefore, best practice and uniform rules on private law issues are crucial. The UNIDROIT DAPL are focused on those.

Second, only a specific area of private law is covered by the UNIDROIT DAPL. Rules on corporate law, consumer law, intellectual property or general contract law are not addressed by the instrument. In such cases, other law will apply. The instrument is primarily focused on legal issues arising out of the holding, transfer and use of digital assets as collateral in secured transactions.

Third, even within the remit of proprietary interests in digital assets as described above, many issues are not addressed either. Commentary 1.2 non-exhaustively lists a few issues that are excluded: whether a proprietary right in a digital asset has been validly transferred to another person, whether a security right in a digital asset has been validly created, the rights as between a transferor and transferee of a digital asset, the rights as between a grantor of a security right in a digital asset and the relevant secured creditor, the legal consequences of third-party effectiveness of a transfer of digital assets, some of the requirements for, and legal consequences of, third-party effectiveness of a security right in a digital asset.

---

[51] Zatti F, Barresi R G (ed.) (2024) Digital Assets and the Law. Fiat Money in the Era of Digital Currency. Routledge, Oxford.

[52] Regulation (EU) 2023/1114 of the European Parliament and of the Council of 31 May 2023 on markets in crypto-assets, and amending Regulations (EU) No 1093/2010 and (EU) No 1095/2010 and Directives 2013/36/EU and (EU) 2019/1937 (Text with EEA relevance). PE/54/2022/REV/1; OJ L 150, 9.6.2023, p. 40–205.

The UNIDROIT DAPL does not nor is intended to provide for a complete legal framework for digital assets, not even a complete body of rules governing the holding, the transfer and the use of digital assets as collateral. The ultimate aim is to provide guidance where gaps may exist in legacy private laws or where traditional approaches do not prove to be appropriate to digital assets. Only then, the UNIDROIT DAPL aim to provide a solution.

References

Duch Brown N, Martens B, Muller-Langer F (2017) The economics of ownership, access and trade in digital data, JRC Digital Economy Working Paper 2017–01, European Commission, 2017, JRC104756

Kanda H et al (2012), Official Commentary on the UNIDROIT Convention on Substantive Rules for Intermediated Securities, Oxford University Press, Oxford

Rodríguez de las Heras Ballell T (2024) Drafting Model Contractual Terms for Voluntary B2B Data Sharing: A Tool to Deal with Unfairness. In: Lohsse S, Schulze R, Staudenmayer D (ed) Private Law and the Data Act. Münster Colloquia on EU Law and the Digital Economy VIII. Nomos/ Hart-Bloomsbury Publishing, Baden-Baden, p 127–148

Rodríguez de las Heras Ballell T (2024) The Emergence of Principles and Best Practices on Digital Assets: Proprietary Rights, and Enforcement. European Journal of Risk Regulation 2024: 1–12. https://doi.org/10.1017/err.2024.55

Rodríguez de las Heras Ballell T (2025) Foreword. In: Koller C, Lehmann M (ed) Digital Assets in Enforcement and Insolvency Securing Creditor Access and Protecting Customer Interests in the Crypto World, Hart Publishing, Oxford, p vii–xi

Veneziano A, Rodríguez de las Heras Ballell T (2025) Digital Assets in Insolvency and Enforcement Proceedings: Some Insights from UNIDROIT's Work. In: Koller C, Lehmann M (ed) Digital Assets in Enforcement and Insolvency Securing Creditor Access and Protecting Customer Interests in the Crypto World, Hart Publishing, Oxford, p 27–43

Zatti F, Barresi R G (ed.) (2024) Digital Assets and the Law. Fiat Money in the Era of Digital Currency, Routledge, Oxford

Legal documents and legislation

ALI-ELI *Principles for a Data Economy: Data Transactions and Data Rights,* https://principlesforadataeconomy.org/ and https://www.europeanlawinstitute.eu/projects-publications/publications/ali-eli-principles-for-a-data-economy-data-transactions-and-data-rights/.

CEPEJ Good practice guide on enforcement of judicial decisions adopted by CEPEJ in 2015

CEPEJ Guidelines for a better implementation of the existing Council of Europe's Recommendation on Enforcement, European Commission on the efficiency of Justice (CEPEJ)

Digital Assets and Private Law Working Group // First session (remote) // Rome, 17 – 19 November 2020 //// UNIDROIT 2020 // Study LXXXII – W.G.1 – Doc. 1 //English only // November 2020

https://www.unidroit.org/english/documents/2020/study82/wg01/s-82-wg01-01-e.pdf last visited 9 March 2025

Digital Assets and Private Law Working Group // First session (remote) // Rome, 17 – 19 November 2020 //// UNIDROIT 2020 // Study LXXXII – W.G.1 – Doc. 2 //English only // November 2020

https://www.unidroit.org/english/documents/2020/study82/wg01/s-82-wg01-02-e.pdf last visited 9 March 2025

Digital Assets and Private Law Working Group // First session (remote) // Rome, 17 – 19 November 2020 //// UNIDROIT 2020 // Study LXXXII – W.G.1 – Doc. 4 //English only // March 2021
https://www.unidroit.org/english/documents/2021/study82/wg01/s-82-wg01-04-e.pdf last visited 9 March 2025
Digital Assets and Private Law Working Group // Fifth session (hybrid) // Rome, 7 – 9 March 2022 / /// UNIDROIT 2022 // Study LXXXII – W.G.5 – Doc. 2 //English only // March 2022
https://www.unidroit.org/wp-content/uploads/2022/03/W.G.5.-Doc.-2-Master-Copy-of-the-Black-Letter-Principles-Comparison.pdf last visited 9 March 2025
Digital Assets and Private Law Working Group // Sixth session (hybrid) // Rome, 31 August – 2 September 2022 //// UNIDROIT 2022 // Study LXXXII – W.G.5 – Doc. 2 //English only // March 2022
Digital Assets and Private Law Working Group // Sixth session (hybrid) // Rome, 31 August – 2 September 2022 //// UNIDROIT 2022 // Study LXXXII – W.G.6 – Doc. 1 //English only // August 2022
https://www.unidroit.org/wp-content/uploads/2022/08/W.G.6.-Doc.-1-Annotated-Agenda-Web site-1.pdf last visited 9 March 2025
Digital Assets and Private Law Working Group // Sixth session (hybrid) // Rome, 31 August – 2 September 2022//// UNIDROIT 2022 // Study LXXXII – W.G.6 – Doc. 3 //English only // August 2022
https://www.unidroit.org/wp-content/uploads/2022/08/W.G.6-Doc.-3-Tracked-Principles-and-Iss ues-Paper.pdf last visited 9 March 2025
Digital Assets and Private Law Working Group // Sixth session (hybrid) // Rome, 31 August – 2 September 2022 //// UNIDROIT 2022 // Study LXXXII – W.G.6 – Doc. 4 //English only // November 2022
https://www.unidroit.org/wp-content/uploads/2022/12/W.G.6-Doc.-4-Summary-Report-of-the-6th-Session.pdf last visited 9 March 2025
Digital Assets and Private Law Working Group // Seventh session (hybrid) // Rome, 19 – 21 December 2022 //// UNIDROIT 2022 // Study LXXXII – W.G.7 – Doc. 2 //English only // December 2022
https://www.unidroit.org/wp-content/uploads/2022/12/W.G.7-Doc.-2-Draft-Principles-and-Com mentary.pdf last visited 9 March 2025
Digital Assets and Private Law Working Group // Seventh session (hybrid) // Rome, 19 – 21 December 2022 //// UNIDROIT 2022 // Study LXXXII – W.G.7 – Doc. 3 //English only // December 2022
https://www.unidroit.org/wp-content/uploads/2022/12/W.G.7-Doc.-3-Issues-Paper.pdf last visited 9 March 2025
Digital Assets and Private Law Working Group // Seventh session (hybrid) // Rome, 19 – 21 December 2022 //// UNIDROIT 2022 // Study LXXXII – W.G.7 – Doc. 5 //English only // February 2023
https://www.unidroit.org/wp-content/uploads/2023/03/W.G.7-Doc.-5-Summary-Report-of-the-7th-Session-1.pdf last visited 9 March 2025
Digital Assets and Private Law Working Group // Eighth session (hybrid) // Rome, 8 – 10 March 2023 //// UNIDROIT 2023 // Study LXXXII – W.G.8 – Doc. 3 //English only // February 2023
https://www.unidroit.org/wp-content/uploads/2023/03/W.G.8-Doc.-3-Draft-Principles-and-Com mentary-Compared.pdf last visited 9 March 2025
ELI Principles and Implementation Guidance on Enforcement against Digital Assets, approved by the ELI Council on 3–4 March 2025, Vienna. Update of the ELI project on Access to Digital Assets available at https://www.europeanlawinstitute.eu/projects-instruments/instruments/eli-enforcement-against-digital-assets/
ELI Principles on the Use of Digital Assets as Security, https://www.europeanlawinstitute.eu/fil eadmin/user_upload/p_eli/Publications/ELI_Principles_on_the_Use_of_Digital_Assets_as_ Security.pdf.

Geneva Convention on Substantive Rules for Intermediated Securities, UNIDROIT, Geneva, 9 October 2009
Governing Council // 99th session (B) // Rome, 23 –25 September 2020 //// UNIDROIT 2020 // C.D. (99) B Misc. 2 // English/French // October 2020, par. 8
International Union of Judicial Officers (UIHJ) Global Code of Enforcement, 2024
Recommendation Rec (17) 2003 of the Committee of Ministers to Member States on Enforcement, Council of Europe, adopted on 9 September 2003
Regulation (EU) 2023/1114 of the European Parliament and of the Council of 31 May 2023 on markets in crypto-assets, and amending Regulations (EU) No 1093/2010 and (EU) No 1095/2010 and Directives 2013/36/EU and (EU) 2019/1937 (Text with EEA relevance). PE/54/2022/REV/1; OJ L 150, 9.6.2023, p. 40–205.
Regulation (EU) 2023/2854 of the European Parliament and of the Council of 13 December 2023 on harmonised rules on fair access to and use of data and amending Regulation (EU) 2017/2394 and Directive (EU) 2020/1828 (Data Act), PE/49/2023/REV/1, *OJ L, 2023/2854*
UCC § 12–102(a)(1) "Uniform Commercial Code-Controllable Electronic Records". C.R.S. § 4–12–101. Added by 2023 Ch. 136,§ 89, eff. 8/7/2023.2023 Ch. 136, passed without a safety clause.
UNCITRAL Model Law on Electronic Transferable Records, 2017. Text available at https://uncitral.un.org/en/texts/ecommerce/modellaw/electronic_transferable_records.
UNCITRAL Model Law on Secured Transactions, 2016, https://uncitral.un.org/en/texts/securityinterests/modellaw/secured_transactions.
UNCITRAL Project on default rules for data provision contracts – United Nations Commission on International Trade Law // Working Group IV (Electronic Commerce) // Sixty-eight session // New York, 24–28 March 2025 /// A /CN.9/WG.IV/WP.188 // 20 January 2025
UNIDROIT Model Law on Factoring (MLF), adopted by the UNIDROIT Governing Council at its 102nd session (Rome, 10–12 May 2023), https://www.unidroit.org/instruments/factoring/

Principle 2
Definitions

Carmen Pastor Sempere

(1) **'Electronic record' means information which is (i) stored in an electronic medium and (ii) capable of being retrieved.**

(2) **'Digital asset' means an electronic record which is capable of being subject to control.**

(3) **'Principles law' means any part of a State's law which implements or is consistent with these Principles.**

(4) **'Other law' means a State's law to the extent that it is not Principles law.**

(5) **In relation to a transfer of a digital asset:**

   (a) **'transfer' of a digital asset means the change of a proprietary right in the digital asset from one person to another person;**

   (b) **the term 'transfer' includes the acquisition of a proprietary right in a resulting digital asset;**

   (c) **'transferor' means a person that initiates a transfer, and 'transferee' means a person to which a proprietary right is transferred;**

   (d) **the term 'transfer' includes the grant of a security right in favour of a secured creditor, and 'transferee' includes a secured creditor.**

(6) **'Insolvency-related proceeding' means a collective judicial or administrative proceeding, including an interim proceeding, in which, for the purpose of reorganisation or liquidation, at least one of the following applies to the assets and affairs of the debtor:**

This work was financed within the framework of the Prometeo 2023 project of the Regional Ministry of Innovation, Universities, Science and Digital Society (CIPROM/2022/26) "Present and future of the regulation of cryptoassets in the EU [LegalCripto]", whose principal investigator is Carmen Pastor Sempere. The basic ideas contained herein were presented in the author's paper with the same title, given on November 13, 2024 at the IV International Congress on "UNIDROIT Principles on Digital Assets and Private Law: Context, Content, Perspectives", organized also by BAES Research Group of the University of Alicante on November 13 and 14, 2024.

C. Pastor Sempere (✉)
University of Alicante, Alicante, Spain
e-mail: carmen.pastor@ua.es

C. Pastor Sempere and D. A. Morán Bovio (eds.), UNIDROIT *Principles on Digital Assets and Private Law*, Law, Governance and Technology Series 80,
https://doi.org/10.1007/978-3-032-11001-5_8

(a) **they are subject to control or supervision by a court or other competent authority;**

(b) **the debtor's ability to administer or dispose of them is limited by law;**

(c) **the debtor's creditors' ability to enforce on them is limited by law.**

(7) **The meaning of the following terms is specified elsewhere in these Principles:**

(a) **'issuer' (Principle 5(2)(f), for the purposes of Principle 5(1)(c));**

(b) **'control' (Principle 6);**

(c) **'change of control' (Principle 6(2));**

(d) **'resulting digital asset' (Principle 6(2));**

(e) **'proprietary claims' (Principle 8(2));**

(f) **'custodian', 'sub-custodian', and 'client' (Principle 10(1));**

(g) **'maintain' (Principle 10(2));**

(h) **'custody agreement' (Principles 10(3) and 10(4);**

(i) **'shortfall' (Principle 13(5)).**

(8) **Words in the singular include the plural and those in the plural include the singular.**

1 Official Commentary

Commentary

Electronic record

2.1. 'Electronic records' comprise a class of which 'digital assets' (as defined in Principle 2(2)) form a subset. As defined, an 'electronic record' consists of information stored in an electronic medium, which is capable of being retrieved. 'Electronic medium' must be understood in a broad sense. Thus, the definition is intended to include any type of digital technology, even if the storage itself may not rely on electrons, such as hard disks using magnetic fields, and DVDs using physical changes in the material. It is implicit in the requirement that the information be retrievable that the information also must be retrievable in a form that can be perceived. It follows that an electronic record would not include, for example, oral communications that are not stored or preserved or information that is retained only through human memory.

2.2. This definition is consistent with the definition of the term 'electronic record' found in various national laws, insofar as the term is defined as 'information'. Were it not for this provenance of the definition it might seem odd that the term 'electronic record' is defined as 'information' and not as a 'record' of information (except as might be implicit in the requirement that the information be stored and retrievable). If one were writing on a clean slate, perhaps it would make sense to use the 'record of information' formulation. However, the role of this term is solely as a component of the definition of 'digital asset'. As explained in Commentary 2.3 to 2.17, the determinative factor is whether an 'electronic record' 'is capable of being subject to control'. It follows that either formulation of the definition of 'electronic record' would produce the same result. Therefore, the definition of the term has been chosen that already has been generally accepted.

Digital asset

2.3. The definition of 'digital asset' includes an electronic record only if it is 'capable of being subject to control' – as 'control' is defined in Principle 6. For example, some electronic records might be described colloquially as 'digital assets', but normally could not be subjected to 'control', as defined, and consequently would not be digital assets as defined here. While reference is made to Principle 6 for a detailed explanation of the concept of control, it should already be stated here that 'control' as defined in these Principles means exclusive control (subject to qualifications in the definition).

2.4. Consider a simplified example: three sets of information compose an electronic record. One set is 'Info Alpha' and a second set is 'key information' that, pursuant to public-key cryptography, renders these two sets of information capable of being subject to control by means of the associated private key. This does not mean, however, that the key information necessarily contains the private key itself, but only the information that makes it controllable with the private key. These two sets of information compose the digital asset 'Digital Asset Alpha'. The third set of information is 'Info Beta'. Although Info Beta is associated with and included in the same electronic record as Digital Asset Alpha, a change of control of Digital Asset Alpha so that it becomes subject to control through the different key information of the transferee would not transfer control of Info Beta. Indeed, Info Beta is not (it is assumed) capable of being subject to control. This example is not unrealistic. For example, an interest in bitcoin is composed of an unspent transaction output (UTXO). The UTXO might be associated with information, such as information included in a header, that is a part of the same electronic record as the UTXO but which is not capable of being subject to control. The header information would not necessarily be transferred as a result of spending the UTXO. The information included in a digital asset must also be distinguished from associated information such as Info Beta or any other asset in any way linked or associated with the digital asset. Principle 4 addresses such linked assets, for example, gold or securities linked to a digital asset. See discussion in Commentary 4.13 to 4.15 and 4.21.

2.5. Continuing with the example of Digital Asset Alpha described in Commentary 2.4, pursuant to Principle 8 an innocent acquirer (X) of the Digital Asset Alpha would acquire it free of conflicting proprietary claims. But this would not mean that X acquires Info Alpha (e.g., that X 'owns' Info Alpha, even if that information could be 'owned' under the applicable law). Instead, X acquires the Info Alpha only insofar as it is associated with the key information as a part of Digital Asset Alpha. Info Alpha exists not only as a component of Digital Asset Alpha but also independently and separate and apart from Digital Asset Alpha. Info Alpha is the same – 'Info Alpha' is 'Info Alpha' – however or wherever that information might be stored, existing, or perceived. Digital Asset Alpha is distinct, however, because it is composed not only of the Info Alpha but also of the key information.

2.6. Info Alpha might be an image, poem, book, video, song, database, a combination of 1s and 0s without any inherent value, or any other type of information. But whatever its content or characteristics, under Principles law (see Principle 2(3), defining 'Principles law') the information would remain subject to other law. If Info Alpha were subject to valid copyright protection, for example, the rights of the holder of the copyright would not necessarily be affected by the creation, acquisition, or transfer of Digital Asset Alpha. On the other hand, it is possible that inclusion of Info Alpha in Digital Asset Alpha, or the use, transfer, or acquisition of Digital Asset Alpha, could violate, or infringe upon, rights under such laws. Even if Info Alpha (or any other information included in a digital asset) were not subject to any protection under intellectual property or other laws, the existence, use, or rights (if any) in respect of that information outside of and other than as a part of Digital Asset Alpha would not be affected by Principles law.

2.7. The information such as Info Alpha included in a digital asset must also be distinguished from associated information such as Info Beta. The following Illustrations to Principle 1 (scope), Principle 2(1) (definition of 'electronic record'), and Principle 2(2) (definition of 'digital asset') provide additional examples of the application of the definition of digital asset and the scope of these Principles.

2.8. ***Illustration 1: Virtual (crypto) currency on a public blockchain (e.g., bitcoin) is a digital asset****. In a public blockchain no one person controls the underlying protocol (software) i.e., the blockchain that tracks transactions in the digital assets. A consensus mechanism embedded in the protocol verifies the validity of transactions that users attempt to effect through the protocol. No one individual user has control over the protocol or its consensus mechanism. The underlying protocol (system) for the public blockchain itself would not be capable of being subject to 'control' (as defined in Principle 6). However, an individual user does have control over a private key, which allows the individual user to obtain 'control' (as so defined) over a digital asset within the protocol (i.e., over a UTXO (unspent transaction output) in the caseof bitcoin).*

2.9. Although other public blockchains may differ from the bitcoin blockchain as to the applicable consensus mechanism and the manner that transactions are tracked, the foregoing description would apply nonetheless. An individual user could not, alone, control the underlying protocol (the database or blockchain), but could control its own private key and thereby have 'control' (as defined) over the digital assets held through the protocol. A protocol within which a digital asset exists is not itself a digital asset within the scope of these Principles; however, an asset controlled by a private key is a digital asset within the scope.

2.10. The analysis and discussion in Illustration 1 also Informs the following illustrations

2.11. ***Illustration 2: A CBDC may be a digital asset.*** *A State wishing to issue a central bank digital currency (CBDC) could do so in a number of ways. One possibility is that the State issues a digital asset as defined in Principle 2(2). In that case, units of the CBDC could correspond to an electronic record that is subject to control as defined in Principle 6.*

2.12. The relevant monetary statute of the issuing sovereign State (or monetary union) would define the legal relationship between the holder of the CBDC and the issuing central bank. It would also govern the legal nature of the CBDC as a currency, including its name and its convertibility with physical currency at par. Monetary law (lex monetae) would also decide whether the use of the CBDC is open to everyone (retail CBDC) or only to certain institutions (wholesale CBDC), and whether, and to what extent, it is legal tender amongst its users.

2.13. However, depending upon the CBDC's design features, and as for all digital assets (as defined in Principle 2(2)), these Principles could inform the private law rules applying to proprietary issues and transactions involving a CBDC such as a transfer from one person to another (whether as payment of a debt or as creation of a security right). Transactions in a CBDC issued in the form of a digital asset could require protection of innocent acquirers in the same way as transactions in tangible currency (see Principle 8 and Commentary 8.7).

2.14. ***Illustration 3: If a digital asset contains information that is a valuable dataset or database (e.g., a dataset that is the basis for the operation of an artificial intelligence (AI) system), image, or textual expression, the information is subject to applicable intellectual property laws and the information existing outside of the digital asset is not part of the digital asset.*** *As discussed in Commentary 2.6, if the information included in the digital asset is itself subject to protection under intellectual property law (presumably copyright law, in this example), the rights of the holder of the intellectual property would be preserved notwithstanding the inclusion of the information in the electronic record or the transfer of the digital asset to an innocent acquirer. To the extent permitted by the applicable intellectual property law, the transferee of the digital asset might be entitled to the use and enjoyment of the information (not unlike the lawful purchaser of a book protected by copyright). Alternatively, if the information or its functionality were protected by patent law, for example, then the acquirer of the digital asset could be infringing the patentee's rights by using the information.*

2.15. Although the particular facts of this illustration may not be realistic or reflect common practice, it is intended to illustrate and underscore the point that Principles law and other law relating to digital assets should be subject to any applicable intellectual property laws. It also illustrates the broader point that a digital asset comprises only the package of information that includes the information necessary to make it capable of being subject to control. As discussed above in Commentary 2.4 and 2.5, the same information that is included in a digital asset, and that exists outside of and separate and apart from the digital asset, is not a part of the digital asset.

2.16. ***Illustration 4: A social media page with password for access is not a digital asset.*** *Generalisations about social media or social networking platforms are difficult. But social media platforms generally involve licensing arrangements with users that do not permit the users to acquire 'ownership' of 'pages' or the data stored on the platform. This is so even though, colloquially, users may refer to 'their' pages and information that 'belongs' to them. In general, these platforms do not allow users to acquire the exclusive abilities contemplated by the definition of 'control' in Principle 6. Consequently they do not constitute or involve digital assets within the scope of these Principles.*

2.17. ***Illustration 5: Although an Excel or Word file with password protection could be a digital asset, Principles law may have no material impact or utility for such assets.*** *A Word, Excel, or similar data file recorded in a hard drive is an electronic record as defined in Principle 2(1). If access to viewing the contents of the file is password protected, then it is possible that one who has both knowledge of the password and direct access to the hard drive in which the file is stored would have the exclusive abilities necessary to obtain control under Principle 6. Because the file would be capable of being subject to control, the file would be a digital asset as defined in Principle 2(2) and within the scope of these Principles. That said, unless the digital asset were associated with a protocol that facilitates the acquisition and disposition of such assets, Principles law would not have any material utility or impact for these assets. For example, in order to transfer control of a password protected Word file that is stored in a hard drive, it would be necessary to hand over not only the password to the file but also the hard drive in which the file is recorded. If a person in control of the file were to send the file, for example as an email attachment, to another person who is given the password, that would not amount to a change of control. The file received would be an entirely new electronic record – albeit an exact copy of the material information. Moreover, as discussed in Commentary 2.6, control of the file would not impair rights existing under any applicable intellectual property laws. One might view this circumstance as indicating that the scope of the Principles is overbroad. However, this circumstance is better characterised as merely an example of digital assets that would not normally be disposed of and consequently would not benefit from or involve the need for the legal regimes that the Principles contemplate. On the other hand, an attempt to narrow the definition of digital asset to exclude such digital assets might risk the exclusion of assets that would (or could) benefit from inclusion.*

Principles law and other law

2.18. Under Principle 1, these Principles cover private law issues relating to digital assets. Therefore, these Principles provide rules for issues such as the custody and transfer of, and the provision of security rights in, digital assets. Under Principle 2(3), all the rules provided by the Principles qualify as 'Principles law' once they have been adopted and implemented into the law of a State. For the avoidance of doubt, 'Principles law' thus also includes the private international law rules provided in Principle 5, once these rules have been implemented into the law of a State. Notably, these Principles take no position as to whether its rules should be included in a State's special law on digital assets, should be incorporated into more general laws, already follow from general laws, or are addressed by a combination of these approaches. On the technological, jurisdiction, and organisational neutrality of these Principles, see more extensively Commentary 0.5 to 0.9.

2.19. 'Principles law' may or may not already follow from general private law rules in a specific jurisdiction. If, in a specific jurisdiction, the law following from general private law rules is consistent with these Principles, then under these Principles such general private law rules are considered to be 'Principles law', but only to the extent they apply to digital assets as covered by these Principles.

2.20. Pursuant to their principles of functionality and neutrality, these Principles do not prescribe a specific classification of digital assets. However, they do require that digital assets can be the subject of proprietary rights (see Principle 3(1)). This may mean, in certain jurisdictions, that digital assets must be classified as 'property', 'good', 'thing', or similar concept, but this would depend on the applicable law in question and is left for each specific State to decide. If the law of a State includes a classification of different categories of assets which can be subject to proprietary rights, and these different categories have different consequences, it is recommended that the State's law should specify which category or categories of assets digital assets are. This is so that digital assets can be subject to proprietary rights. This could mean the introduction of a new category of asset, but again, this is left for each specific State to decide.

2.21. More generally, if, in a specific State, it is unclear, which (if any) of its existing rules or standards of general application apply to digital assets, it is recommended that this is clarified. This is specifically relevant where it concerns the acquisition and disposition of proprietary rights in digital assets. This may also mean, for instance, that a State should specify which (if any) of its existing rules or standards of general application govern the provision of security rights in digital assets. It does not mean that the law of a State needs to list every rule or standard which applies to digital assets. Not only would this be far too complicated, it would also be unnecessary as hese Principles are concerned with private law rules only, and proprietary rights in particular. See also Commentary 3.1 to 3.4.

2.22. Within the law of a State, all law that is not 'Principles law' as defined here is referred to as 'other law' in these Principles (see Principle 2(4)). 'Principles law' and 'other law' as defined here together form 'the law'. Other law includes administrative rules and judicially determined law, as well as legislation.

Transfer

2.23. A transfer as defined here, i.e., a change of a proprietary right (discussed in Commentary 3.4) in a digital asset, must be distinguished from a change of control of a digital asset (as defined in Principle 6(2)). A change of control may or may not be associated with a transfer of proprietary rights (See Commentary 2.26). In some situations, and depending on the applicable other law, a change of control will not result in a transfer of proprietary rights. A custodian (as defined in Principle 10(1)), for instance, may obtain control of a digital asset for a client, but will typically not acquire 'ownership' (as defined under the applicable national law) of that digital asset. Vice versa, whilst in many situations a transfer of proprietary rights will be accompanied by a change of control, in some situations it may not. The law of a State, for instance, may provide that under certain circumstances a proprietary right (such as ownership) in a digital asset may pass to another person, whilst control stays with the transferor.

2.24. A transfer, as defined in Principle 2(5), includes not only the transfer of a digital asset from one person to another person but a transfer that results in the acquisition of a resulting digital asset that is not the same digital asset that was transferred by the transferor (see Principle 6(2)). An example of such a resulting digital asset is the UTXO (unspent transaction output) generated by a transaction in bitcoin. Another example might be adjustments in balances in accounts resulting from transactions in ether on the Ethereum platform, as to which the digital asset that is disposed of and the digital asset that is acquired are fungible assets and not necessarily the 'same' asset.

2.25. In these Principles, the term 'transfer' is also used to denote the grant of a security right in favour of a secured creditor, and a 'transferee' includes a secured creditor. This use of the term transfer is for definitional purposes only, and does not mean that, pursuant to these Principles, a grant of a security right must be identified with a transfer of ownership or of any other proprietary right under the applicable law. See, e.g., Convention of 5 July 2006 on the Law Applicable to Certain Rights in Respect of Securities held with an Intermediary ('Hague Securities Convention'), Article 1(1)(h) (defining 'disposition' as 'any transfer of title whether outright or by way of security and any grant of a security interest, whether possessory or non-possessory').

2.26. These Principles do not prescribe the conditions for a proprietary right in a digital asset to be validly transferred to another person. Although Principle 3(1) does require that digital assets must be susceptible to proprietary rights, and Principle 8 that a transferee must have obtained control to qualify as an innocent acquirer, these Principles do not prescribe the requirements for a valid transfer of a digital asset. For instance, they do not prescribe whether a change of control suffices or is required for a change of a proprietary right to be valid. This is left to other law. See also Principle 3(3).

2.27. The term 'transferor' is defined as 'a person that initiates a transfer' because that person may have the power to transfer greater rights than that person has. Indeed, a person in control of a digital asset may have no rights at all but has the power to transfer rights to an innocent acquirer. See Principle 8(4) and Commentary 8.9.

Insolvency-related proceeding

2.28. The definition of 'insolvency-related proceeding' is not meant to provide a general definition of insolvency proceedings but defines the concept only for the purpose of these Principles. A general definition of 'insolvency proceedings' can be found in the UNCITRAL Legislative Guide on Insolvency Law and subsequent insolvency law texts. The definition in Principle 2(6) seeks to include all forms of collective, insolvency-related procedures, which may take place in court or out of court, so long as the procedure is aimed at dealing with a debtor's current or immediate financial or economic distress and some legal effect is attached to the commencement of that procedure. This definition captures the new generation of insolvency proceedings whose legal design, often labelled as 'hybrid', features characteristics of both formal, in court proceedings and out of court contractual, collective workouts. The term 'insolvency related proceeding', as defined in Principle 2(6), would include full in court proceedings; proceedings the opening of which entails a limitation in the debtor's ability to manage and/or dispose of its assets outside the ordinary course of its business; or proceedings which merely trigger a temporary stay of enforcement against the debtor's assets necessary for the continuation of the business activity. Hence, unlike in other legal texts such as the 2009 UNIDROIT *Convention on Substantive Rules for Intermediated Securities ('Geneva Securities Convention') (Article (1)(h)), a debtor would find itself in an 'insolvency-related proceeding' for the purpose of these Principles even where its assets are not subject to control or supervision of the court or an administrative authority.*

2.29. The word 'control' used in Principle 2(6)(a) must be understood in its common meaning given under insolvency law, not in the sense specified in Principle 6 of these Principles.

Other definitions

2.30. Principle 2(7) contains a list of terms used in the Principles the meaning of which is specified elsewhere in the Principles, and is for the purpose of cross-reference

Rule of interpretation

2.31. Principle 2(8) contains a general rule of interpretation that applies to the whole of the Principles. For example, if a digital asset is generally understood to be fungible (i.e., of the same description), a reference to 'a digital asset' or 'the digital asset' includes a reference to a certain quantity of digital assets of the same description, see Commentary 11.6.

2 Reflections

2.1 Introduction and Background

2.1.1 Purpose and Nature

I. From an economic point of view, Blockchain, Distributed Ledger Technology (hereinafter DLT),[1] is an important step in the Digital Economy because of its ability to record information digitally in a decentralised manner, practically preventing this information from being copied or manipulated and ensuring that it can be transferred securely between different people. Security is exclusively ensured through mathematical procedures (e.g. encryption technology, cryptography) and defined rules. The encryption and decryption of data is a mathematical and computational discipline known as cryptography. The study of mathematical models of strategic interaction between rational decision-makers is known as game theory. This provides the possibility of creating a digital record of means of payment or assets and the possibility to conduct transactions with no direct intermediary being responsible for the execution of such transaction. This capability is usually attributed to physical tokens which have a unique physical existence, such as those used in arcade machines or bumper cars. The decentralised technology implements this capability in a purely digital domain and solution. For several reasons this is a solution for many problems, including the ease of creating an exact replica of any piece of digital data, the lack of recipient particularity in the digital domain, and the possibility of double spending by payers.

The applications of technology are not restricted to simple transactions of coins or tokens with an exchangeable value between private individuals. Rather, they provide the option for a wide range of economic services, as assets or rights can also

[1] A distributed ledger is essentially an asset database that can be shared across a network of multiple sites, geographies or institutions. All participants within a network can have their own identical copy of the ledger. Any changes to the ledger are reflected in all copies in minutes, or in some cases, seconds. The assets can be financial, legal, physical or electronic. The security and accuracy of the assets stored in the ledger are maintained cryptographically using 'keys and signatures to control who can do what within the shared ledger. Entries can also be updated by one, some or all the participants, according to rules agreed by the network. Underlying this technology is the 'blockchain', which was invented to create the peer-to-peer digital cash Bitcoin in 2008. Block chain algorithms enable Bitcoin transactions to be aggregated in 'blocks' and these are added to a 'chain' of existing blocks using a cryptographic signature. The Bitcoin ledger is constructed in a distributed and 'permissionless' fashion, so that anyone can add a block of transactions if they can solve a new cryptographic puzzle to add each new block. The incentive for doing this is that there is currently a reward in the form of Bitcoins awarded to the solver of the puzzle for each 'block'. Anyone with access to the internet and the computing power to solve the cryptographic puzzles can add to the ledger and they are known as 'bitcoin miners. The mining analogy is apt because the process of mining bitcoin is energy intensive as it requires very large computing power. (See, Distributed Ledger Technology: beyond blockchain (Report by the UK Government Chief Scientific Adviser), Government Office for Science (UK). January 2016. Archived from the original on 16 March 2018. Retrieved 29 August 2016. https://web.archive.org/web/20180316224959/https://www.gov.uk/government/uploads/system/uploads/attachment_data/file/492972/gs-16-1-distributed-ledger-technology.pdf.

be recorded in technology systems in general. Thus, companies offering financial services on Blockchain systems generally use an available digital infrastructure to provide their services, such as digital wallets, custodial services for crypto-currencies and exchanges for virtual currencies. However, it is also possible to record a much broader range of assets and other rights on blockchain systems, and several additional services related to these rights will be offered. In particular, the low cost of digital transactions is likely to open new opportunities beyond financial services, in fields such as logistics, mobility, energy, industry, media, and many more. All these potential applications are grouped together under what are now known as "Digital Assets".

Moreover, the BIS (Bank for International Settlements), proposes the concept of the "Unified Ledgers", as an important building block of the Finternet (multiple interconnected financial ecosystems, much like the internet, designed to empower individuals and businesses by placing them at the centre of their financial lives), and as a vehicle to turn their vision of an efficient future financial system into reality. They consist of digital platforms that bring together multiple financial asset markets—such as for wholesale tokenised central bank money, tokenised commercial bank deposits and other tokenised assets, including company shares, corporate or government bonds and real estate, to name just a few—as executable objects on common programmable platforms. In doing so, unified ledgers would provide the necessary economic and financial architecture to realise the full potential of tokenisation and other novel financial technologies, supported by robust legal and governance arrangements and modern technological underpinnings. Once on a ledger, assets could be transferred immediately, safely and securely, with less reliance on external verification processes or messaging systems that make today's financial system so costly, slow, and in some cases, unreliable. Based on a digital-first approach and leveraging tokenisation, unified ledgers would improve existing financial transactions, by making them cheaper, faster and safer.[2] The adoption of ISO 20022 by these cryptocurrencies demonstrates their capacity to bridge the gap between traditional finance and Distributed Ledger Technology. This facilitates cross-border financial transactions that are faster, more secure, and more cost-effective.[3]

---

[2] By Carstens. A, Nilekani. N (2024).

[3] ISO 20022 is an international standard that regulates the digital transfer of financial information between financial institutions. Developed by the International Organization for Standardization (ISO), ISO 20022 improves the interoperability and efficiency of banking and financial transactions by providing a consistent and adaptable approach to financial messaging. By standardising financial communications, ISO 20022 improves the orderliness and interoperability of the cryptocurrency sector, enabling reliable interaction between different platforms and networks. This standard meets the financial sector's need for a universally recognised communication language. See https://www.iso20022.org/. It enables these organisations to interact with partners and conduct business on a global platform. An example of this growing demand for adaptation is Ripple, the company behind the XRP cryptocurrency, has joined the ISO 20022 standards body. The cryptocurrency issued by Ripple Labs reached a market capitalisation of more than $170 billion for the first time in its history. Ripple's cryptocurrency ranks as the 85th most valuable financial asset in the world. in the world as of 16 January 2025, Source: CoinMarketCap, https://coinmarketcap.com/.

As seen below, the EU has already adopted new laws resulting from this initiative. The Regulation on Markets in Crypto-assets is establishing a new legal environment for DLT-based 'coins' with a stable value ('stablecoins'); another regulation will provide a framework for the monitoring and control of digital operational resilience for the financial sector. More legislative procedures are ongoing in the fields of open finance and the digital euro. New directions are being suggested, such as the establishment of a 'unified ledger', to smoothen transfers between instruments using different DLT market infrastructure.[4]

The UNIDROIT Principles (UNIDROIT Principles on Digital Assets and Private Law) can help encourage wider use of Digital Assets across the economy (Unified Ledgers or Distributed Ledger Technology), and this can result in significant gains in liquidity, cost reduction and enhanced security. It can also foster the technological development of Digital Assets, which in turn may result in significant economic benefits. Legislators should pay particular attention to the importance of coherence of legal frameworks in supporting innovative technologies. The UNIDROIT Principles can help them achieve this, but not in the problematic areas, such as open questions related to customer and asset protection or the misuse of this technology for money laundering or other criminal purposes.[5]

The UNIDROIT Principles connect Digital Assets with the traditional doctrine of commercial electronic instruments, services and professionals. By identifying the fundamental principles that originated in commercial practice with the incorporation of rights to negotiable instruments and services, we analyse to what extent Digital Assets can perform functionally equivalent roles to those of the existing instruments in commerce and finance. These Principles cover the most important set of transactions in commerce: transfers of proprietary rights in a Digital Asset and the creation of a security interest in a Digital Asset.

II. From a legal point of view, guaranteeing legal security for the use of any type of technology is of vital importance, since this will help develop the new business of Digital Assets regardless of the future development of new technologies and legal categories. Different legal systems and technologies offer different solutions to the same de facto situations, as we shall see below and in the successive Reflections on the different Principles included in this volume.

Technology neutrality requires the adoption of legal provisions that are neutral with respect to the technologies, methods and products used. This means that if technology advances, no further legislative work is needed. However, the emergence of digital assets and the complexity of the technologies needed to realise them now presents regulators with the question of how to address and respond coherently to the big question of how to capture and recognise ownership through their legal systems, and how to transfer and regulate digital assets appropriately.

---

[4] Digital finance legislation: Overview and state of play, EPRS | European Parliamentary Research Service. PE 762.308 – May 2024.

[5] KYC and CDD: Know your Customer and Customer Due Diligence are measures required by governments to comply with laws against money laundering, tax evasion and the financing of terrorism.

This poses a challenge in international markets and across regions, where digital assets may be defined differently depending on the legal tradition (e.g. civil law or common law) and practices, or the purposes and views of the institutions and authorities that regulate these assets.

Unlike other tools, there is no taxonomy as such, although the members of the UNIDROIT Principles working group initially set out to develop a taxonomy for Digital Assets,[6] they soon realised that the characteristics of these assets differed depending on stakeholder intent and application. It was also aired that there were differences in the use of the technology and associated challenges as outlined in point 5: Consideration of the issues identified in the Issues Paper (Study LXXXII - W.G.1 - Doc. 2)[7] which reflects the remarks of Mr. Jason Grant Allen warning about the existence of other ongoing projects, both in UNIDROIT and in other organisations, which could have an impact on the work of the taxonomy project. In addition, another challenge was taken into account, stemming from the presence of terminologies belonging to very different disciplines (e.g. technical versus legal). He noted that the section on scope was mainly concerned with the question of which digital assets the project should examine, how that subset of digital assets should be circumscribed, and how to find a definition of digital assets that was interoperable with other relevant definitions.

In classifications of Digital Assets, they are often referred to as native or non-native. This classification mainly depends on the value creation process, i.e. whether there is an issuer or not. Typical examples of native digital assets are Bitcoin and Ether. In the context of UNIDROIT Principles, non-native digital assets can be described as 'Linked Assets'. Common examples of non-native digital assets are security tokens (i.e. a device that tokenises assets such as debt securities) and so-called linked tokens (the linkage is to an underlying asset). It should also be noted that the concept of Digital Asset in the UNIDROIT Principles does not comprise 'all data linked to it', thus the concept of Digital Asset is composed only of information that can be subject to control (see Principle 6), and the other linked asset (even if composed only of information) is not a component of the digital asset and does not fall within the scope of these Principles (see Principle 4, 15).

The security and integrity of the data contained in the Digital Asset is not discussed either, nor the identification of the parties (signatory)—i.e. that changes in their status are digitally signed. Therefore, these Principles state that digital assets (as defined in Principle 2(2)) are susceptible to proprietary rights, without addressing whether they are considered 'property' in the other rules of a State—see Principle 1 and Principle 3(1). The project team also concluded that the use of cryptographic or blockchain technology should also not be the determining condition for digital assets. Thus, these Principles are intended to apply to all digital assets (as defined in Principle 2(2)), whether the record of these assets is on a blockchain. As they are the subject of economic rights, they elaborate rules applicable to digital assets that provide for the

[6] As part of the intersessional work that the WG agreed upon at its first session, Sub-Group 4 was established with a dual focus (taxonomy and PIL). At the second meeting, the WG analysed the first draft of the Tentative Principles on PIL.

[7] (Study LXXXII - W.G.1 - Doc. 2). UNIDROIT 2021 - Study LXXXII - W.G.1 - Doc. 4.

protection of bona fide acquirers and security interests in digital assets, considering the characteristics of a Digital Asset—see Principle 8 and Principle 14.

These definitions therefore specifically cover cases where these digital assets are subject to disposition and acquisition, and the interest in those assets is enforceable against third parties. In other words, they are limited to the discipline of transfers and collateral transactions of a subset of digital assets. They are also distinguished from the definitions of other digital assets by identifying them as digital assets that are capable of being controlled and uniquely identified. For these Principles, ‘control’ refers to a digital asset over which a person can establish that it has (i) the exclusive ability to prevent others from obtaining substantially all of the benefits of the digital asset, (ii) the ability to obtain substantially all of the benefits of the digital asset, and (iii) the exclusive ability to transfer control of the digital asset to another person. See Principle 6.

It is therefore important to note at the outset that while control is the keystone on which the UNIDROIT Principles rest (as defined in Principle 6), it is also the keystone of the definition of ‘digital asset’ in Principle 2(2). As mentioned above, the actual definition of Control is provided in the Reflection on Principle 6, according to which a “digital asset” can only be an electronic record that is capable of being subject to control. Consequently, the issue of taxonomy was gradually given a back seat, and was finally eliminated. Its place, at the heart of the UNIDROIT Principles was taken by the importance of clearly defining a digital asset and articulating the relevant criteria, be it transferability, control or exclusivity (i.e. avoiding the problem of double-spending). Ultimately, the UNIDROIT Principles are evolving and focusing more on how to ensure legal certainty and predictability by bridging the gap between existing digital assets and new emerging assets.

In Prof. Hideki’s words, at the IV International Congress held in Alicante,[8] many interesting, and sometimes difficult, legal issues are likely to arise in the coming years in relation to digital assets in many jurisdictions. Legal certainty will be provided by legislation, court decisions or a combination of both. The UNIDROIT Principles on Digital Assets and Private Law are useful for all jurisdictions to examine this area and reflect on the appropriate interpretations of their existing private law and the need for new legislation.

III. The definition of a digital asset in Principle 2 of the UNIDROIT 2023 Principles,[9] is the most comprehensive to date. It includes not only newly emerging crypto assets, but also electronic records such as electronic payments, dematerialised securities, and provides a possible link for digital assets to existing legal frameworks within the concept of linked assets. As stated in Principle 4, digital assets can be linked to other tangible and intangible assets for which specific legal practices already exist. In

[8] IV INTERNATIONAL CONGRESS 2024 UNIDROIT DAPL. KEYNOTES BY Hideki Kanda y Ignacio Tirado. ENGLISH, Available; https://www.youtube.com/watch?v=rHTbSup3MXM.

[9] A ninth ad hoc session of the WG was held online on 5 April 2023, where the draft Principles and Commentaries submitted by the Drafting Committee were reviewed, which implemented a limited number of final comments. The approval was carried out for adoption at its 102nd session- UNIDROIT 2023– C.D. (102) 6, April, para. 19- held in Rome from 10 to 12 May 2023 UNIDROIT 2023– C.D. (102) Misc. 2, May, para. 7. UNIDROIT 2023– C.D. (102) 25, August, par. 106.

the context of the UNIDROIT Principles, non-native digital assets can be described as 'Linked Assets'. Common examples of non-native digital assets are 'security tokens' (i.e. a device that tokenises assets such as debt securities) and so-called linked tokens (the linkage is to an underlying asset). Therefore, businesses related to Digital Assets can be openly promoted with foreseeable legal constraints, as well as flexibility in the case of native assets (e.g. bitcoin) and the concept of 'Resulting Asset', as discussed below.

Principle 2 essentially lays down the key definitions, which cover the most important set of transactions in commerce: transfers of proprietary rights and the creation of a security interest in digital assets. At the same time, not all relevant definitions are contained in Principle 2; instead, many of the definitions of terms are provided in the context of the Principle in which they play a role. Thus Principle 2 itself expressly refers us to the respective Principles for definitions of, 'issuer' (Principle 5(2)(f), for the purposes of Principle 5(1)(c)); 'control' (Principle 6); 'change of control' (Principle 6(2)); 'resulting digital asset' (Principle 6(2)); 'proprietary claims' (Principle 8(2));) 'Custodian', "sub-custodian" and "client" (Principle 10(1)); "manage" (Principle 10(2)); "custody arrangement" (Principles 10(3) and 10(4)); all of which will be the subject of Reflection in this work, as will the definition of (6) "Insolvency-related proceeding", which will be discussed in the Reflections on Principles 13 and 19.

Our Reflection on Principle 2, examines digital assets from a legal perspective, defining a digital asset as an electronic record subject to control, and defining an electronic record as information stored in an electronic medium capable of being retrieved. As mentioned above, the definitions of these terms in the UNIDROIT Principles remain neutral as to the type of asset and the technology by means of which such an electronic record is stored. However, some of the other technical terms defined in the UNIDROIT Principles follow the conventional interpretation of those terms as they are already used for these actions or functions in the capital market. Examples include 'transfer' (of a digital asset, including the use of 'transferor' and 'transferee'); 'issuer' (of a digital asset); 'custodian'; 'sub-custodian'; and 'custody arrangement'. Therefore, in our Reflection we will necessarily refer to conventional, not necessarily neutral, technologies and concepts.

In short, due to the limits of the length of this volume, we will limit ourselves to reflect on the Definitions of: (1) 'Electronic record' (2) 'Digital asset' (3) 'Principles law' (4) 'Other law' (5) Transfer of a digital asset.

2.1.2 Context—Relationship with Other Instruments

The DAPL Principles and the UNIDROIT Project on "Best Practices for Effective Enforcement" (BPEE) address the need for more clarity and predictability of the legal regime applicable to the enforcement of rights in digital assets outside insolvency and, as regards the UNIDROIT Principles, also within insolvency.[10] They do so by offering soft-law guidance to legislators and other stakeholders, which can then be adapted to the specificities of each legal system while preserving the objectives and the harmonised legal framework introduced with the uniform law instrument. While the UNIDROIT Principles have just been adopted and the BPEE project is still awaiting completion, they appear to be well suited to serve their respective aims, and, in relation to the specific topic of enforcement of rights in digital assets, to contribute to increasing certainty and effectiveness of the legal framework within domestic laws and across borders. Once formally adopted such global instruments face the challenge of being (correctly) implemented and accepted by their intended addressees.[11]

The participants who worked on the UNIDROIT Principles were aware at all times of the complexity and intricacies of the definitions. Thus point 5: Consideration of the issues identified in the Issues Paper (Study LXXXII - W.G.1 - Doc. 2)[12] welcomes the comments of Mr Jason Grant Allen[13] which pointed out the difficulty of the Issues Paper in providing definitions or classification and their contextualisation. Hence, the existence of other ongoing projects, both in UNIDROIT and in other organisations, was pointed out from the outset, which could have an impact on the work of the project, especially on taxonomy, as we have mentioned previously.[14]

At present, we must highlight the effort and importance of avoiding fragmentation between the legal instruments elaborated by different intergovernmental organisations on issues related to Digital Assets, thus creating a global framework that will favour their development. Both the HCCH (Hague Conference on Private International Law), as well as UNCITRAL (United Nations Commission for International Trade Law), refer to the UNIDROIT Principles on Digital Assets and Private Law in their respective texts, the complementarity, and cooperation between them. In particular, the Hague Conference is mandated to collaborate with UNCITRAL and other organisations with relevant expertise on issues relating to the private international law (hereinafter 'PIL') aspects of the digital economy,[15] as well as the American Law Institute (hereinafter Ali) and the European Law Institute (hereinafter Eli) who have adopted the *Principles for a Data Economy - Data Transactions and Data Rights-*,[16] whose Part V ("*Multi-State Issues*") provides principles on conflicts of

[10] The seventh session of the Working Group established to prepare Best Practices for Effective Enforcement (hereinafter "the Working Group") was held in hybrid format – in person in Rome and remotely via Zoom – from 15 to 17 April 2024.

[11] T Rodríguez de las Heras Ballell, (2024).

[12] Point 5: Consideration of the issues identified in the Issues Paper, Study LXXXII - W.G.1 - Doc. 2. UNIDROIT 2021 - Study LXXXII - W.G.1 - Doc. 4.

[13] Nº. 12.

[14] (Study LXXXII -W.G.1 - Doc. 2). UNIDROIT 2021 - Study LXXXII - W.G.1 - Doc. 4.

[15] Conclusions & Decisions of the Council on General Affairs and Policy (CGAP) (C&D of March 2024), No 11(b), available on the HCCH website at https://www.hcch.net under 'Governance' and then 'Council on General Affairs and Policy'.

[16] American Law Institute and European Law Institute, *Principles for a Data Economy. Data Transactions and Data Rights*, adopted by the ALI on May 18, 2021, and by the ELI on September

laws, See UNIDROIT's Reflection on Principle 5 in this volume. During the working sessions of the WG on the Digital Assets Project, discussions were initiated to shape a Joint HCCH-UNIDROIT Project on Applicable Law to Cross-Border Holdings and Transfers of Digital Assets and Tokens.[17]

The exploratory and preparatory work of the Joint HCCH-UNIDROIT Project was formally approved by the CGAP of the HCCH in March 2023 and by the Governing Council of UNIDROIT in May 2023, based on the Project Proposal presented at its 102nd Session.[18] Following the approval, the participants designated by the two Secretariats explored the feasibility of joint work on the occasion of two preparatory meetings: the first was held on 12 June 2023 at the HCCH premises in The Hague; the second was held in a hybrid format from 2 to 4 October 2023 at UNIDROIT headquarters in Rome.[19] At its 2024 meeting,[20] the CAGP took note of the report of the HCCH-UNIDROIT Project on Digital Assets and Tokens,[21] the summary conclusions on possible future work on PIL in relation to digital assets, and decided to conclude the work on the Project, thanking the experts and the UNIDROIT Secretariat for their continued cooperation and coordination with the Permanent Bureau. The Tokens Project was launched in March 2024 under a mandate from the General Affairs and Policy Council (see Conclusion and Decision No. 12). In the framework of this project, the PO, in collaboration with experts and observers specialising in the field, is studying the private international law issues raised by tokens. The CAGP mandated the PO to collaborate with experts and observers to study the private international law issues raised by the tokens. The PO will submit a report to the CAGP 2025 on the findings of this study, with proposals for next steps.

1, 2021. Available in: https://principlesforadataeconomy.org/fileadmin/user_upload/p_principlesforadataeconomy/Files/Principles_for_a_Data_Economy_ELI_Final_Council_Draft.pdf.

[17] HCCH- Prel. Doc. No 3C Rev of January 2023. Available in: https://assets.hcch.net/docs/a91fd233-acf7-4c42-9aad-a426c4565068.pdf

[18] HCCH-UNIDROIT Project on Law Applicable to Cross-Border Holdings and Transfers of Digital Assets and Tokens, UNIDROIT 2023– C.D. (102) 6, April. Available in: https://www.unidroit.org/wp-content/uploads/2023/05/C.D.-102-12-Proposal-for-Joint-Work-HCCH-UNIDROIT.pdf.

[19] HCCH-UNIDROIT Joint Project on Applicable Law to Cross-Border Holdings and Transfers of Digital Assets and Tokens, UNIDROIT 2023, Study LXXXIIA – P.M.2 – Doc. 3, November, Second Preparatory Meeting (hybrid), Rome, October 2023, para. 47.

[20] HCCH- Conclusions & Decisions, Council on General Affairs and Policy, March 2024. Available in: https://assets.hcch.net/docs/7d647a6f-b927-4c1a-a837-d0846fbacca1.pdf

[21] HCCH-UNIDROIT Digital Assets and Tokens Joint Project: Report, Prel. Doc. No 3 of January 2024. Available in: https://assets.hcch.net/docs/efce41ca-1c8c-4d61-9d8b-9348df9303a0.pdf.

The work by UNCITRAL plays a central and coordinating role in the UN system in addressing legal issues related to the digital economy and digital commerce (A/74/17, para. 211). At its fifty-fifth session, in 2022, the Commission requested the secretariat to prepare a guidance document on legal issues relating to the use of distributed ledger systems in commerce, within existing resources and in cooperation with other interested organisations, as appropriate (A/77/17, paras. 22(f) and 169).[22] The Commission's request stems from the preparation of a section on distributed ledger *Systems in the Taxonomy of Legal Issues in the Digital Economy* (hereinafter the 'Taxonomy').[23]

At its fifty-sixth session, in 2023, the Commission was provided with a note by the Secretariat on legal issues related to the use of distributed ledger technology in commerce (the 'background paper') (A/CN.9/1146). The Commission expressed broad support for the work to be carried out in close coordination with other interested international organisations, and its relevance to several projects recently undertaken by the Hague Conference on Private International Law was noted (A/78/17, paras. 200–202).

Indeed, the 'Taxonomy' itself recognises (see paras. 81–116, p. 43/60), that States have different approaches to the definition of 'digital asset'. For example, the US Commodity and Futures Trading Commission (hereinafter 'CFTC') seems to emphasise the control and transferability of digital assets, whereas the EU seems to focus on what the asset 'represents', i.e. the rights embodied in the token. The Taxonomy acknowledges the lack of consensus on the definition of digital assets; however, it states that, in its ordinary meaning, the term 'digital asset' connotes a collection of data, stored electronically, that is of use or value (Taxonomy, paragraph 82). By focusing on data as a representation of 'information', the working definition allows certain types of data to be distinguished, including software (i.e. data comprising computer code) and digital assets (i.e. data comprising an electronic record that is capable of being controlled and uniquely identified, as defined in part three of this Taxonomy).

[22] UNCITRAL notes cited are available, https://uncitral.un.org/es/commission.

[23] Taxonomy of Legal Issues related to the Digital Economy Prepared by the Secretariat of the United Nations Commission on International Trade Law, Viena 2023, UNITED NATIONS PUBLICATION, 2024, e-ISBN 978-92-1-358507-8, available, https://uncitral.un.org/sites/uncitral.un.org/files/media-documents/uncitral/en/digitaleconomytaxonomy.pdf.

Thus, at the fifty-seventh session, New York, 24 June–12 July 2024,[24] the secretariat intends to further expand this Note, through cooperation with relevant organisations and the help of experts, to include information on complementary issues such as the interaction between DLT and free trade agreements. In addition to the above, two aspects are particularly relevant for the purposes of this Reflection on Principle 2 (UNIDROIT Principles). The Note "Legal issues relating to the use of distributed ledger technology" contains, firstly, in its annex, a glossary of technical terms and, secondly, its express pronouncement on the principle of technological neutrality and functional equivalence as a cornerstone of the UNCITRAL texts on electronic commerce and on DLT.[25] Technology neutrality, will require the adoption of legal provisions that are neutral with respect to the technologies, methods and products used. This means that even if technology advances, no further legislative work is needed, as the text is technologically neutral. The rules already accommodate any future developments. Thanks to technological neutrality, the UNCITRAL texts generally support the use of DLT. As these technologies use a private key to sign transactions, anyone with the public key can verify the signatory. Digital signatures detect any tampering with information. Furthermore, since the encrypted data is also signed, digital signatures guarantee unity. Consequently, any tampering will invalidate the signature. The data cannot be revealed because it is encrypted. It cannot be tampered with again, even if it is revealed. The identity of the sender or owner is

---

[24] *Legal issues relating to the use of distributed ledger technology in trade Note by the Secretariat*, A/CN.9/1175, https://uncitral.un.org/sites/uncitral.un.org/files/1175_for_submission1.pdf. At the time of revising this paper, we can state with certainty that the Guide on Legal Issues Relating to the Use of Distributed Ledger Technology in Trade was adopted by the United Nations Commission on International Trade Law (UNCITRAL) at its fifty-eighth session in 2025 and authorised for publication in electronic form in all official languages of the United Nations (A/80/17, para. 161). The Guide is published as a United Nations publication (Sales No. E.26.V.2, ISBN 978-92-1-157732-7, e-ISBN 978-92-1-154683-5). Building on Part Five of the UNCITRAL Taxonomy of Legal Issues Related to the Digital Economy (Sales No. E.12.V.11), the Guide provides guidance on legal issues relating to the use of DLT in trade from the perspective of commercial operators. It consists of three parts—background on DLT, legal issues relating to the use of DLT in trade, and application of UNCITRAL texts on electronic commerce—and a glossary. With regard to the definition of 'digital asset', paragraph 83 of the Guide expressly references Principle 2 of the UNIDROIT Principles on Digital Assets and Private Law (DAPL), adopted by the UNIDROIT Governing Council at its 102nd session (Rome, 10–12 May 2023). The Guide states: 'According to Principle 2 of the UNIDROIT Principles on Digital Assets and Private Law (DAPL), which is in turn inspired by the definition of "controllable electronic record" contained in Section 12-102 of the Uniform Commercial Code (UCC) of the United States of America, "digital asset" means an electronic record which is capable of being subject to control'. The Guide further notes (para. 83) that other definitions of 'digital asset' focus on what the asset 'represents', that is the rights that the digital asset incorporates. Additionally, paragraph 85 of the Guide refers to Principle 3(1) of the DAPL regarding proprietary rights in digital assets, acknowledging that laws have been drafted on the regime applicable to digital assets which 'may also specify if digital assets may be the subject of proprietary rights (see Principle 3(1) of the DAPL)'. Available at https://uncitral.un.org/sites/uncitral.un.org/files/mediadocuments/EN/Texts/UNCITRAL/2516855e-ebook-accessible.pdf. See also the preparatory documents: A/CN.9/1146 (scoping paper, 2023), A/CN.9/1175 (background paper, 2024), and A/CN.9/1222 (draft guidance document, 2025).

[25] 9/37.

also protected by a digital signature. As a result, a signature is legally binding for its owner and cannot be ignored.

Thus, with regard to the identification requirement set out in Article 9 of the Model Law on Electronic Transferable Documents (hereinafter 'MLETR')[26] for electronic signatures used in electronic transferable documents, 'identification, and the possibility of linking pseudonym and real name, even on the basis of factual elements outside distributed ledger systems, could satisfy the requirement to identify the signatory' (MLETR Explanatory Note, paragraph 78). The definition of 'electronic document' in Article 2 of the MLETR has been extended to cover 'all information logically associated or otherwise linked together in such a way that it becomes part of the document, whether or not it was generated contemporaneously' to confirm its application to DLT-based applications. This definition is closely related to the definition of 'data message', which ensures the technological neutrality of the UNCITRAL texts on electronic commerce. Controllability and singularity are the defining features of an 'electronic transferable record' under the MLETR, which is a particular type of digital asset. As noted, in the *Legal issues relating to the use of distributed ledger technology*, the technologies and methods used by a DLT system to implement the distributed ledger make the data recorded therein 'immutable' in the sense of remaining complete and unchanged from the time it was first entered into the ledger.

These qualities correspond to the concept of 'integrity' in the UNCITRAL texts on electronic commerce, which is relevant to certain rules of functional equivalence: (a) Article 8 of the Model Law on Electronic Commerce (hereinafter 'MLEC') prescribes integrity as one of the functions that a data message containing information must fulfil to satisfy the legal requirement that the information be presented or preserved in its original form. The function is fulfilled if the information remains 'complete and unaltered' from the time it was first generated in its final form, apart from the addition of any annotations and any changes arising in the normal course of communication, storage and display. The same requirement is contained in Article 9(4) of the United Nations Convention on the Use of Electronic Communications in International Contracts (hereinafter 'CEC').[27] Methods using DLT can provide a higher level of reliability with respect to integrity assurance.[28] As stated in the

[26] UNCITRAL Model Law on Electronic Transferable Records, 2017 (hereinafter, MLETR). Text available at https://uncitral.un.org/en/texts/ecommerce/modellaw/electronic_transferable_records.

[27] See also art. 17(3) of the MLEC, which establishes a "guarantee of singularity" to permit the use of electronic transport documents: UNCITRAL Model Law on Electronic Commerce with Guide to Enactment 1996 with Additional Article 5 bis as Adopted in 1998 (United Nations publication, Sales No. E.99.V.4), para. 115.

[28] DLT Act was enacted for the first time in the Principality of Liechtenstein: The "Token- und VT Dienstleister-Gesetz" (TVTG, Token and DLT Service Provider Act), and define, Art.2, ""vertrauenswürdige Technologien (VT)": Technologien, durch welche die Integrität von Token, die eindeutige Zuordnung von Token zu VT-Identifikatoren sowie die Verfügung über Token sichergestellt wird;"Gesetz vom 3. Oktober 2019 über Token und VT-Dienstleister (Token- und VT-Dienstleister-Gesetz; TVTG), https://www.gesetze.li/konso/2019301000.

(hereinafter eIDAS2) Regulation[29] in Whereas: 68, electronic records are a sequence of electronic data records which must ensure their integrity and the accuracy of their chronological order.[30]

As discussed under the following heading, a more commonly called P2PKH transaction (Pay To Public Key Hash)[31] meets the definition of an account-based system 'links ownership to an identity' in such a way that 'claims are represented in a database that records the value together with a reference to the identity' and 'transactions are authorised by identification'—in Principle 7, Identification of a person in control of a digital asset, (....)(2) and the identification mentioned in Principle 6(1)(b-) may be by a reasonable means, including (but not limited to) an identifying number, a cryptographic key, an office, or an account number, even if the means of identification does not indicate the name or identity of the person to be identified.

The Bitcoin blockchain can be seen as a distributed version of the reference database for recording bitcoins (value) and their properties as referenced by the public keys (identities) of the owners. We can consider signing a message with a private key for verification by others using the corresponding public key as proof of knowledge of a secret (and thus classify the method as token-based). However, the creation of a digital signature with the respective private keys to initiate a bitcoin payment can be better seen as an identification process because this is a common realisation of the well-known 'something you know' authentication factor that has been widely used for entity authentication, along with 'something you have' and 'something you are', and public keys are generally considered identities in cryptography. One possible

---

[29] Regulation (EU) 2024/1183 of the European Parliament and of the Council of 11 April 2024 amending Regulation (EU) No 910/2014 as regards establishing the European Digital Identity Framework, ELI: http://data.europa.eu/eli/reg/2024/1183/oj, "Electronic ledgers are a sequence of electronic data records which should ensure their integrity and the accuracy of their chronological ordering. Electronic ledgers should establish a chronological sequence of data records.(…). Qualified electronic ledgers should establish a legal presumption for the unique and accurate sequential chronological ordering and integrity of the data records in the ledger. Due to their specificities, such as the sequential chronological ordering of data records, electronic ledgers should be distinguished from other trust services such as electronic time stamps and electronic registered delivery services. To ensure legal certainty and promote innovation, a Union-wide legal framework that provides for the cross-border recognition of trust services for the recording of data in electronic ledgers should be established. This should sufficiently prevent the same digital asset from being copied and sold more than once to different parties. The process of creating and updating an electronic ledger depends on the type of ledger used, namely whether it is centralised or distributed. This Regulation should ensure technological neutrality, namely neither favouring, nor discriminating against, any technology used to implement the new trust service for electronic ledgers.(…)..".

[30] See, Article 45k.

[31] Public key hash payment (P2PKH) transactions are the most common Bitcoin transactions. These transactions contain a blocking script that locks the output with a public key hash. They require proof of ownership of the public key to spend bitcoins. A P2PKH output can be unlocked (spent) using a public key and a digital signature created with the corresponding private key. The blockchain nodes would verify the correctness of this signature with the public key in the blockchain script. Considering public keys as identities, creating a digital signature in the unlocking script to spend bitcoins would be equivalent to proving identity to the blockchain nodes to request them to update ownership records as payment is processed. In other words, the operation of P2PKH transactions is like a typical account-based system.

argument against this view is that public keys are not linked to real identities and the transfer of ownership of bitcoins takes place anonymously. In these cases, the signing of a transaction is simply considered proof of knowledge, rather than proof of identity.

In other words, submitting a signature or password through a challenge-response protocol is widely considered as proof of identities online. As an illustrative example at the European level, the European Digital Identity (eIDAS2), as we will see below, enables the mutual recognition of electronic identification systems in different EU countries and allows European citizens and businesses to identify themselves and verify their personal information online, without having to use commercial providers, regardless of where they are in the European Union. This ensures that all EU citizens and businesses resident in the EU can use a personal digital wallet. Article 5 expressly recognises the use of pseudonyms in electronic transactions: 'Without prejudice to specific rules of Union or national law requiring users to identify themselves or to the legal effect given to pseudonyms under national law, the use of pseudonyms chosen by the user shall not be prohibited'. We should not forget its close connection to privacy and that the principles of data minimisation and data protection by design and by default are essential when processing involves significant risks to the fundamental rights of individuals. Considering the state of the art, all parties to the data exchange, even when they are within the scope of this GDPR Regulation,[32] must implement technical and organisational measures to protect these rights. Such measures include not only pseudonymisation and encryption, but also the use of increasingly available technology that allows algorithms to be embedded in the data and enables valuable information to be obtained without the transmission between parties or the unnecessary copying of the raw, structured and standardised data itself.[33] We highlight the inherent trade-offs between privacy, auditability and performance in digital payment systems. For example, zero-knowledge proofs

[32] Regulation (EU) 2016/679 of the European Parliament and of the Council of 27 April 2016 on the protection of natural persons with regard to the processing of personal data and on the free movement of such data, and repealing Directive 95/46/EC (General Data Protection Regulation) (Text with EEA relevance), ELI: http://data.europa.eu/eli/reg/2016/679/oj.

[33] The 'Legal Entity Identifier of the offeror or person seeking admission to trading, where available' referred to in Commission Implementing Regulation (EU) 2024/2984 of 29 November 2024 laying down implementing technical standards for the application of Regulation (EU) 2023/1114 of the European Parliament and of the Council as regards forms, formats and templates for crypto-asset white papers. In the future, there could be an electronic declaration of attributes with the LEI, which would be issued to the Legal Entity Identifier (LEI) and is a global and unique code based on the ISO 17442 standard, which is used to identify legal entities that are parties to financial transactions and to comply with reporting requirements in the financial markets. However, official information on companies is not always readily available on a cross-border basis. Directive 2012/17/EU set out provisions for the mandatory interconnection of the central, commercial and companies registers (typically referred to as business registers) as a measure required to create a more business-friendly legal and fiscal environment. The new system, known as Business Registers Interconnection System (BRIS) became a reality on 8 June 2017. On 29 March 2023, European Commission published a proposal for a directive amending Directives 2009/102/EC and (EU) 2017/1132 as regards further expanding and upgrading the use of digital tools and processes in company law. https://eur-lex.europa.eu/legal-content/EN/TXT/?uri=CELEX%3A52023PC0177&qid=1708001464894.

can verify information without revealing it, offering strong privacy protection. We emphasise the importance of both "hard privacy" (achieved through cryptographic methods and user-controlled data) and "soft privacy" (enforced through institutional controls and data protection policies).[34]

2.2 *Definitions (1) 'Electronic Record' (2) 'Digital Asset' (3) 'Principles Law'(4) 'Other Law' (5) Transfer of a Digital Asset*

To understand the definitions contained in Principle 2, we will start with five central considerations.

I. First, from a substantive perspective, the UNIDROIT Principles adopt a functional approach to digital assets, drawing significant inspiration from recent developments in American uniform law. The definition of 'digital asset' in Principle 2(2)—*"an electronic record which is capable of being subject to control"—reflects a conception that finds its closest parallel in the 2022 Amendments to the Uniform Commercial Code (hereinafter UCC),*[35] adopted by the Uniform Law Commission (hereinafter ULC) and the American Law Institute. The new UCC Article 12 introduces the concept of 'controllable electronic record', defined as "a record stored in an electronic medium that can be subjected to control".[36] This characterisation, centred on the factual ability to exercise control over an electronic record, constitutes the conceptual foundation of DAPL Principle 6, which establishes the criteria for control: (I) the exclusive ability to prevent others from obtaining substantially all of the benefit from the digital asset; (II) the ability to obtain substantially all the benefit; and (III) the exclusive ability to transfer these abilities to another person. On the relationship between the DAPL Principles and the UCC reform, see, in this volume, Steven Weise / Edwin Smith, 'UNIDROIT DAPL Principles: Highlights and Points of Comparison with UCC Reform'.

II. Secondly, the definitions in Principle 2 are drafted taking into account the future development of new technologies and legal categories. That is, to follow the principles of functionality and neutrality, thus, the definitions are written to be

---

[34] Privacy-enhancing technologies for digital payments: mapping the landscape BIS Working Papers | No 1242 | 23 January 2025 by Raphael Auer, Rainer Böhme, Jeremy Clark and Didem Demirag https://www.bis.org/publ/work1242.htm.

[35] Uniform Commercial Code Amendments (2022), adopted by the Uniform Law Commission and the American Law Institute. As of December 2025, over 25 US jurisdictions have enacted these amendments. https://www.uniformlaws.org/viewdocument/final-act-with-comments-40?CommunityKey=f7237fc4-74c2-4728-81c6-b39a91ecdf22&tab=librarydocuments.

[36] National Conference of Commissioners on Uniform State Laws (Uniform Law Commission) y American Law Institute, *Uniform Commercial Code Amendments* (2022), approved in July 2022. Available in: https://www.uniformlaws.org/viewdocument/final-act-164?CommunityKey=1457c422-ddb7-40b0-8c76-39a1991651ac&tab=librarydocuments.

technology and business model neutral, jurisdiction neutral (e.g., they can be applied in both civil law and common law jurisdictions) and organisation neutral.

III. Thirdly, while UNIDROIT is neutral, to understand the comments it is necessary to consider the Governance and layered structure of the computer system. Without the supervision of a central authority, distributed ledger technology (DLT) holds cryptographically verified information among a group of users who have agreed on a predetermined network protocol. The content of the blockchain is stored on a server located in a data centre somewhere on the planet. Clients request content or data from application servers while browsing the Internet or using any relevant application, known as client-server architecture. Clients can connect to other clients and share data. A peer-to-peer (hereinafter P2P) network is a large group of computers sharing data. Blockchain is a peer-to-peer network of computers that computes, validates and records transactions in an orderly fashion on a shared ledger. As a result, a distributed database is created that stores all data, transactions and other relevant data. Layers in blockchain are fundamental to overcoming the limitations of earlier generations of this technology, allowing for greater scalability, efficiency and interoperability. As blockchain technology evolves, we are likely to see the development of more solutions in each of these layers. Interoperability between different blockchains and layers can be introduced through blockchain bridges that facilitate the transfer of assets between chains.

Furthermore, in terms of computing, the global and representative systems are different. In a token system, as is true in the case of cash, the recording system is individual in each asset. (i.e. tokens), each of which has a corresponding owner (whose real identity may or may not be known) who can spend (or control) the asset. Each of these tokens has a specific value, which does not change. When two tokens, in the same way as banknotes of the same nominal value, are received from different payers, their values would not be aggregated and the tokens would still be distinguishable from each other, i.e. the beneficiary can still distinguish the tokens received from different payers (e.g. via the serial numbers of the banknotes). In other words, tokens are uniquely distinguishable, but fungible. In contrast, an account-based system records the state of the system as a list of accounts, each of which is under an account holder and has a corresponding balance.

IV. Fourthly, Digital Assets are thus not only the object that is traded, but also the way in which transactions are settled. A salient feature of the economic notion of distributed ledger technology (DLT) is the sufficiency to verify the authenticity of an electronic entry, as well as to confirm the validity of a payment, the ownership of a token or the transfer of value. This contrasts sharply with an account-based system that requires an intermediary to record and update account balances. This sufficiency condition of some distributed ledger technology (DLT) allows for decentralised, peer-to-peer settlement of payments without relying on any intermediary. A common confusion is that Bitcoin, which claims to be a peer-to-peer payment system, is considered to support peer-to-peer exchange of value without the need for any intermediary. However, as we shall see, the peer-to-peer environment in Bitcoin refers to a computer science model that contrasts with the typical financial client-server model, as the Bitcoin white paper puts it: '… we propose a solution to the double-spending problem by using a peer-to-peer distributed timestamp server to generate a computational proof of time-ordering of transactions'. But the above implies that we are dealing with an account-based, if you will, mixed system. The UNIDROIT Principles Commentary (2.24.) explains that a transfer as defined in Principle 2(5) includes not only the transfer of a digital asset from one person to another, but also a transfer that results in the acquisition of a 'resulting digital asset' that is not the same digital asset that was transferred by the transferor (see Principle 6(2)), but is of the same value (we add). An example of such a resulting digital asset, might be adjustments in balances in accounts resulting from transactions in ether on the Ethereum platform, as to which the digital asset that is disposed of and the Digital Asset that is acquired are fungible assets and not necessarily the 'same' asset. Another example given in UNIDROIT Principles Commentary (2.24.) is the UTXO ('unspent output transaction', hereinafter UTXO) generated by a transaction.[37] However, an individual user does have control over a private key, which allows the individual user to obtain 'control' (as so defined) over a digital asset within the protocol (i.e., over an UTXO). In the case of UNIDROIT Principles Commentary (2.9.) it is stated that although other public blockchains may differ from the Bitcoin blockchain as to the applicable consensus mechanism and the manner that transactions are tracked, the foregoing description would apply, nonetheless. An individual user could not, alone, control the underlying protocol (the database or blockchain), but could control its own private key and thereby have 'control' (as defined) over the digital assets held through the protocol. A protocol within which a digital asset exists is not itself a digital asset within the scope of these Principles; however, an asset controlled by a private key is a digital asset within the scope thereof.

Furthermore, verification of the real identity of the owner of a public key is a system design choice, rather than an inherent property of the UTXO design. As we will see, anonymity should not be a defining characteristic for defining DLT-based systems in the digital domain. Therefore, we believe that the creation of Digital Assets markets—sectoral or not—for the use of digital tools and processes, at least in Europe, could use pseudonyms and be coordinated with the digital identity of citizens and businesses as proposed in eIDAS2, as well as payments (wholesale/retail) and e-procurement.

V. Public and private money can coexist in the digital age, as means of settling commercial transactions. However, depending upon the CBDC's design features, and as for all digital assets (as defined in Principle 2(2)), these Principles could inform the private law rules applying to proprietary issues and transactions involving a central bank digital currency (CBDC), such as a transfer from one person to another (whether as payment of a debt or as creation of a security right). Transactions in a CBDC or stablecoins and e-money tokens (digital private currencies) issued in the form of a digital asset could require innocent acquirers to be protected in the same way as transactions in tangible currency (see Principle 8 and Commentary 8.7).

---

[37] Nakamoto. S (2019) Bitcoin: A Peer-to-Peer Electronic Cash System, https://bitcoin.org/bitcoin.pdf.

At the time of writing, this work is shrouded by a certain degree of uncertainty following the signing of an executive order by the President of the United States, Donald Trump, which, among other things, prohibits the development of a (CBDC) in the United States,[38] and the European Union (EU) responded to the new president, emphasising the 'need' for a digital euro. It remains to be decided whether the next step is the addition of central bank digital currencies (CBDC, digital euro[39]) and/or stablecoins and e-money tokens (digital private currencies), whether the technology could enable instant transfer of 'digital cash or banknotes' without the need to go through any clearing mechanism—requiring an intermediary to record and update account balances-. If these decentralised exchanges were regulated, this would confer a better structure to the Digital Assets markets, far removed from the current confusing cryptocurrency trading (exchanges). Furthermore, the portability of data and assets in the European Digital Single Market (of Digital Assets) could be made effective, in which 'almost all its pieces (tokens)' would be regulated and have a

---

[38] On Thursday 23 January 2025, President Donald Trump signed an executive order which, among other measures, expresses support for stablecoins such as USDT to strengthen the dollar and establishes a ban on central bank digital currencies (CBDC). Section 5, which seeks to 'take steps to protect Americans from the risks of central bank digital currencies (CBDCs), which threaten the stability of the financial system, individual privacy, and the sovereignty of the United States'. Explicitly, the order lists that the prohibition touches on the 'establishment, issuance, circulation, and use of a CBDC within the jurisdiction of the United States'. Executive orders signed by the White House are administrative directives issued by the President of the United States for the purpose of directly managing and guiding the operations of the federal government. These orders 'act with the force of law', allowing the president, in this case Donald Trump, to implement policies, regulate administrative matters and direct federal agencies without going through the congressional legislative process. https://www.whitehouse.gov/presidential-actions/2025/01/strengthening-american-leadership-in-digital-financial-technology/. The Guiding and Establishing National Innovation for U.S. Stablecoins Act (GENIUS Act), Public Law 119–27, was signed into law by President Donald Trump on 18 July 2025, becoming the first major federal cryptocurrency legislation in the United States. The Act establishes a comprehensive regulatory framework for 'payment stablecoins', defined as digital assets designed for payment or settlement that issuers are obligated to redeem at a fixed monetary value. Key provisions include: (I) a requirement that stablecoins be backed one-for-one by US dollars or other low-risk assets (such as Treasury bills, insured deposits, and money market funds); (II) a dual federal and state supervisory regime, whereby issuers with less than $10 billion in market capitalisation may opt for state-level regulation; (III) consumer protection measures, including disclosure requirements, redemption procedures, and priority of stablecoin holders over other claims in bankruptcy; (IV) anti-money laundering provisions subjecting issuers to the Bank Secrecy Act; and (V) rules for foreign stablecoin issuers participating in the US market. The Act defines 'digital asset' as 'any digital representation of value which is recorded on a cryptographically-secured distributed ledger' (Section 2(6)). The primary federal payment stablecoin regulators—the Office of the Comptroller of the Currency (OCC), the Federal Deposit Insurance Corporation (FDIC), the Federal Reserve, and the National Credit Union Administration (NCUA)—are required to promulgate implementing regulations within one year. The Act takes effect on the earlier of 18 months from enactment or 120 days after the issuance of final regulations. See S.1582, 119th Congress (2025–2026), available at https://www.congress.gov/bill/119thcongress/senate-bill/1582.

[39] The digital euro is at an advanced stage of research and preparation. The ECB is currently at the stage of phased pilots, with a decision pending by 2025 or 2026 on whether to deploy CBDC. This project adds to the dozens of other CBDC initiatives currently under development around the world. https://www.ecb.europa.eu/press/inter/date/2025/html/ecb.in250109~f88fb55cf4.es.html.

defined scope, function and market. And this, due to its intrinsic 'plasticity', allows it to move forward from financial instruments, to digitise ('tokenise') any single real asset and use it as a representation and/or backing for financial assets, intellectual property rights, and an endless list of illiquid (non-market) assets.

Finally, from this perspective of the Geopolitics of digital assets we must consider the vision of the BRICS countries. From 22 to 24 October 2024, the Tatar city of Kazan hosted the sixteenth BRICS summit, attended by representatives and heads of state from some thirty countries: Brazil, Russia, India, China and South Africa, of course, but also Egypt, Iran, Turkey, the United Arab Emirates and Saudi Arabia. The result was the 'Kazan Declaration' on strengthening multilateralism. Among the proposals that were made, BRICS will experiment with distributed ledger technology (DLT, such as blockchain), promoting the use of central bank digital currencies (CBDCs) so that nations can settle trade imbalances directly, without the need for the SWIFT system and correspondent banks located in third countries. There are also plans for the establishment of a BRICS Grain Exchange and an associated pricing agency, with hubs for trading commodities such as grain, oil, natural gas and gold, which can also be used to resolve trade imbalances.[40]

2.2.1 'Electronic Record' (1) 'Digital Asset' (2)

In its ordinary meaning, the term "digital asset" connotes a collection of data, stored electronically, that is of use or value. The concept has already been well discussed in UNCITRAL texts on electronic commerce. In this sense, a digital asset is essentially a collection of "data messages" within the meaning of the MLETR (The Model Law on Electronic Transferable Records) or an "electronic record" within the meaning of the MLETR (Transferable documents or instruments typically include bills of lading, bills of exchange, promissory notes and warehouse receipts). For instance, in the context of DLT systems, the ISO (the International Organization for Standardization)[41] defines a "digital asset" as an asset, i.e. "anything that has value to a stakeholder", that "exists only in digital form or which is the digital representation of another asset".[42] The most expansive notion is chosen by the UCC and the UNIDROIT Principles. The UCC is concerned with "controllable electronic records", while the

---

[40] https://www.baeslegalcripto.eu/legalcripto/principios-unidroit-activos-digitales-y-derecho-privado/.

[41] ISO (the International Organization for Standardization) is a worldwide federation of national standards bodies (ISO member bodies). The work of preparing International Standards is normally carried out through ISO technical committees. ISO defines basic terms relating to blockchain and distributed ledger technologies to clarify the meaning of terms and concepts used in other document within the domain of ISO/TC 307 standards. This document was prepared by Technical Committee ISO/TC 307, Blockchain and distributed ledger technologies.

This second edition cancels and replaces the first edition (ISO 22739:2020), which has been technically revised. This international standard applies to all types of organisations (e.g., commercial enterprises, government agencies, not-for-profit organisations).

[42] See https://www.iso.org/obp/ui/en/#iso:std:iso:22739:ed-1:v1:en.

UNIDROIT Principles focus on "digital assets". Both notions are very similar since the UNIDROIT Principles define a digital asset as "an electronic record which is capable of being subject to control". The notion of control is also defined very similarly in both texts. They thus comprise every type of controllable asset recorded on a blockchain, whether centralised or decentralised, with or without an issuer. They cover cryptocurrencies, such as or, as well as tokens, including stablecoins. The Executive Order signed on Thursday 23 January 2025, and "in order to promote United States leadership in digital assets and financial technology while protecting economic liberty",[43] Sec. 2. Definitions. (a) For the purpose of this order, the term "digital asset" refers to any digital representation of value that is recorded on a distributed ledger, including cryptocurrencies, digital tokens, and stablecoins. (b) The term "blockchain" means any technology where data is: (i) shared across a network to create a public ledger of verified transactions or information among network participants; (ii) linked using cryptography to maintain the integrity of the public ledger and to execute other functions; (iii) distributed among network participants in an automated fashion to concurrently update network participants on the state of the public ledger and any other functions; and (iv) composed of source code that is publicly available, (c) "Central Bank Digital Currency" means a form of digital money or monetary value, denominated in the national unit of account, that is a direct liability of the central bank.

UNIDROIT Principle 2, defines digital assets from a purely legal perspective, breaking down a digital asset as an electronic record subject to control, and an electronic record is defined as information stored in an electronic medium capable of being retrieved. The definitions of these terms in the UNIDROIT Principles remain neutral as to the type of asset and the technology by means of which such an electronic record is stored. However, some of the other technical terms defined in the UNIDROIT Principles and their commentaries closely follow the DLT technology that addresses the recording of digital records in very different ways, depending on whether they are token-based or account-based, as follows.

There is no widely accepted definition of a digital asset, for which various names exist. However, the UNIDROIT Principles consider that digital archives fit sufficiently well with property law, as they are capable of ensuring exclusive control, (as defined and contextualised in the Principles and commentaries to Principle 6 and Principle 3). In other words, the definition of 'digital asset' includes an electronic record only if it is 'capable of being subject to control'—as 'control' is defined in Principle 6. For example, some electronic records might be described colloquially as 'digital assets' but could not normally be subjected to 'control', as defined, and consequently would not be digital assets as defined here. While reference is made to Principle 6 for a detailed explanation of the concept of control, it should be stated here that 'control' as defined in these Principles means exclusive control (subject to qualifications in the definition). That said,—2.17. Illustration 5: Although an Excel or Word file with password protection could be a digital asset, Principles law may have no material

[43] https://www.whitehouse.gov/presidential-actions/2025/01/strengthening-american-leadership-in-digital-financial-technology/.

impact or utility for such assets—unless the digital asset were associated with a protocol that facilitates the acquisition and disposition of such assets. Consequently, Principles law would not have any material utility for or impact on these assets. For example, to transfer control of a password protected Word file that is stored in a hard drive, it would be necessary to hand over not only the password to the file but also the hard drive in which the file is recorded. If a person in control of the file were to send the file, for example as an email attachment, to another person who is given the password, that would not amount to a change of control. The file received would be an entirely new electronic record—albeit an exact copy of the material information.

Digital assets are sometimes referred to as “cryptoassets” in reference to the cryptographic techniques used to authenticate transactions involving the digital asset. They are sometimes also referred to as “tokens”. A digital token is simply a piece of digital data.[44] Like any digital data, it can be easily copied and replicated at virtually no cost, implying that there is no ‘unique’ virtual existence of a digital token. After a payer passes a digital token to a payee, the payer would still have a copy of it. Ownership of the token cannot be proven simply by possession of a copy of the token; the transfer of ownership of a digital token is not as clearly resolved as that of a physical token. The transfer of ownership of a physical token can be confirmed easily and quickly due to its unique physical existence. When a payer transfers a physical token to a payee, he no longer owns it and there is no ambiguity as to the ownership of the token. Therefore, without a physical dimension or contextual factor, it is impossible to prevent others from receiving the same digital object and thus claiming ownership. Anyone in possession of a copy of a digital token can claim ownership. When multiple exact replicas of a digital token are presented, determining which of these replicas or copies is truly original and carries or inherits the underlying (monetary) value of the asset represented by the token is no trivial matter. In the trade context, it has been suggested that the feature of legal significance that distinguishes these types of digital assets—i.e. cryptocurrencies and asset-backed digital tokens—from a mere collection of data messages or an electronic record is their transferability.

This in turn presupposes that the digital asset is supported by a system that provides control over the asset, in the sense that the asset is capable of being controlled (whose control may be transferred from one person to another). It also presupposes that the system provides some guarantee as to the singularity or rivalrousness of the digital asset,[45] in the sense that the digital asset can be singled out and secured against replication. Several legislative initiatives have identified controllability, singularity

[44] Pastor, C, (2017). The bitcoin unit of account is originally called a cryptocurrency, because the vision of the creator of the Bitcoin protocol was to create a decentralized payment system managed by a community, without the need for a central body (in this case a central bank). Since then, all successive decentralized protocols have called their protocol units of account ‘cryptocurrencies’, ‘cryptocurrencies’, ‘tokens’.

[45] In UK framework, ‘rivalrous’ use is all that distinguishes a bitcoin unit from a digital media file—and yet items can have multiple uses, and also different degrees of ‘rivalrousness’ (for example multiple ‘identical’ copies of an NFT, or a single copy of the master of an unreleased film—in the former another blockchain based seems to not be rivalrous to the other NFTs, and in the latter, a

and rivalrousness as defining features of digital assets. This does not mean, however, that the key information necessarily contains the private key itself, but only the information that makes it controllable with the private key. Continuing with the example of Digital Asset Alpha described in Commentary 2.4 Info Alpha exists not only as a component of Digital Asset Alpha but also independently and separate and apart from Digital Asset Alpha. Info Alpha is the same—'Info Alpha' is 'Info Alpha'—however or wherever that information might be stored, exists, or perceived. Digital Asset Alpha is distinct, however, because it is composed not only of the Info Alpha but also of the key information. These two sets of information compose the digital asset 'Digital Asset Alpha', as referred to in the UNIDROIT Principles. The third set of information is 'Info Beta'. Although Info Beta is associated with and included in the same electronic record as Digital Asset Alpha, a change of control of Digital Asset Alpha, whereby it becomes subject to control of the transferee through the different key information, would not transfer control of Info Beta.

Bitcoin [to continue with the example in UNIDROIT Principles, 2.8. Illustration 1: Virtual (crypto) currency on a public blockchain (e.g.,) is a digital asset], has mixed characteristics, partly of token-based systems and partly of account-based systems. Bitcoin handles record keeping using Bitcoin addresses that are known as 'unspent transaction outputs' (UTXO), which are a data structure that shares many similarities with objects in a token-based system. On the other hand, a Bitcoin address is in essence an account and the private key associated with the Bitcoin address is the proof of identity required to transact through that account. Funds are not stored as objects in the user's software wallets but are recorded in a ledger (which is the public Bitcoin blockchain), and the process of moving funds requires intermediation through the collective work of Bitcoin miners.

For the purposes of the definition of Digital Asset the above has consequences. First, in an account system such as Bitcoin, digital assets are not objects, and this is a critical element of the economic notion of tokens. The Bitcoin account number is the public key under which the "bitcoins are stored" (more precisely, P2PKH transaction—in the formal definition, the processing of a split transaction and a merge transaction for P2PKH transactions). Second, while the value of a payment object in a pure token-based system remains the same when transferring ownership from one owner to another, UTXO-based implementations often allow for splits and merges to occur in the transfer, which can result in a change in the value of a resulting UTXO and a change in the total number of UTXOs in the overall system.

Bitcoin is truly a system of record-keeping that holds accounts in the name of payers and payees, represented by their public keys. As argued above, these public keys are Bitcoin account numbers. The difference is that instead of registering a single balance under one account number, Bitcoin maintains multiple separate UTXOs under one account number. When someone wants to spend a bitcoin or UTXO, the protocol verifies a signed transaction (in essence, an instruction) from him using his public key. Considering public keys as identities, this signature generation could be

---

second leaked copy of the film could be very rivalrous to it). See https://www.gov.uk/government/publications/property-digital-assets-etc-bill/property-digital-assets-etc-bill-factsheet.

seen as his proof of identity for blockchain miners who can then determine the link between the transactor and the histories (i.e., the ownership records on the blockchain linked to his public key) before the transaction is processed. In the case of Bitcoin, no aggregation occurs, whereas, in the case of cryptoassets in Ethereum, aggregation occurs for each defined asset.

Notwithstanding the above, token-related terminology in the cryptocurrency community, including the concept of tokenisation, often refers to an implementation that is unambiguously an account-based system. For example, the Ethereum community proposed a standard for fungible units of value called ‘tokens’, which was introduced in the Ethereum White Paper. The adopted standard, widely known by its proposal identifier ERC-20, is arguably the main reference point for the concept of tokens in Ethereum and other public blockchains today. Although referred to as tokens, ERC-20 tokens are recorded in the form of an account balance (under an account address) in copies of smart contracts hosted in replicated databases on the public blockchain, not stored as digital ‘objects’ in the user’s software wallet. The wallet only stores the private key used to sign the instructions sent to the smart contract. In essence, it is an account-based system.

As a result, the definition of digital assets in the Principles remains technology neutral, and at the same time, opens up opportunities for the consideration of new legislation in relation to securities as electronic records in jurisdictions that do not have such frameworks in place. Furthermore, given the principle of neutrality on which the UNIDROIT Principles are based, as we have seen, Principle 4 refers to the question of the existence, requirements and effects of the link to the other law of the State (‘other law’, Principle 4, sentence 3). By recognising the functional equivalence of digital assets to ‘digital things’, UNIDROIT has acknowledged that digital assets, in the abstract, can be the subject of property rights, regardless of whether they are considered ‘property’ under national law. However, from the Private International Law (PIL) perspective, the absence of a characterisation of what we should understand by “property issues” and what legal nature the different “digital assets” have, makes it difficult to develop uniform PIL rules valid for the different legal systems in the contemporary world (See Principle 5).

2.2.2 ‘Principles Law’ (3) ‘Other Law’(4)

According to Principle 2 (4) on definitions, ‘other law’ means ‘the law of a State to the extent that it is not the Law of Principles’ and, according to Principle 2 (3), ‘law of the Principles means ‘any part of a State’s law to the extent that it is not the law of the Principles’. Therefore, according to Principle 2 (3), all rules provided for by the Principles qualify as ‘Principles law’ once they have been adopted into the law of a State. Consequently, within the law of a State, all law which is not ‘law of the Principles’ as defined in Principle 2 (3) is referred to as ‘other law’ in these UNIDROIT Principles. Thus, the ‘law of the Principles’ and the ‘other law’ together form ‘the law’. Furthermore, it is specified that ‘other law’ includes administrative rules and judicially determined rules as well as legislation (Comment 2.22).

In other words, to ensure legal certainty, digital assets and their transfer must be effective vis-à-vis third parties and bona fide acquisition must be possible. Therefore, the UNIDROIT Principles only address situations where there may be loopholes in existing private law or where traditional approaches in certain jurisdictions need to be modified. Issues that are not directly covered by the Principles are left to 'other law', i.e. the applicable private law of the relevant jurisdiction. However, many of these issues are explicitly identified in the Principles and their Commentary, which provide guidance and direction for possible modifications that a jurisdiction may need to make to its existing law. Thus, Commentary 2.20. By virtue of their principles of functionality and neutrality, these Principles do not prescribe a specific classification of digital assets. However, they do require that digital assets can be the subject of economic rights (see Principle 3(1)). Specifically continuing with Commentary 2.20. UNIDROIT Principles, this may mean, in certain jurisdictions, that digital assets should be classified as 'property', 'good', 'thing' or similar concept, but this would depend on the applicable law in question and is left to the decision of each individual State. If the law of a State includes a classification of different categories of assets that can be the subject of economic rights, and the different categories entail different consequences, it is recommended that the law of the State specifies to which category or categories of assets the digital assets belong. In this way, digital assets may be subject to economic rights. This could mean the introduction of a new category of assets, but again this is a matter for each individual state to decide.

In the initial versions of the draft Principles, there was no Principle 4 as such, but linked assets (referred to at the time as 'digital assets "linked" to another asset') were simply defined and commented on in the Principle on definitions (Principle 2 in the final version); and in particular they were presented as an example of the general concept of 'digital asset'. It was not until in later versions of the draft Principles that Principle 4 emerged for the autonomous and independent treatment of linked assets. The reason for this stand-alone treatment, as explained in the introductory section of the preparatory *iter* of the Principles, is that in this way the Principle contains a considerable amount of Commentary providing examples of linked assets. After the creation of Principle 4, the concept of Digital Asset became clear, and that the digital asset is composed solely of information that can be subject to control and the other asset (even if composed of information) is not a component of the digital asset and does not fall within the scope of these Principles. The effects of the links on the underlying other linked asset will depend not on the Principles but on the law applicable to the other linked asset (digital or not): whether there is a property right or whether the transfer of the former implies the transfer of the latter is a matter to be resolved on a case-by-case basis depending on the law of each State applicable to that other asset (see Principle 4).

The 'Law of Principles' may or may not be derived from general rules of private law in each jurisdiction. If the law derived from general rules of private law in each jurisdiction is consistent with these Principles, then, under these Principles, such general rules of private law are 'Principles law', but only to the extent that they apply to the digital assets covered by these Principles.

This does not mean, however, that all rules provided for in the Principles are considered 'Principles law' once they have been adopted and implemented in the law of a State. For the avoidance of doubt, the 'law of the Principles' also includes the rules of private international law provided for in Principle 5, once these rules have been incorporated into the law of a State (we refer to its Reflection in this same volume).

As seen below, regarding the characterisation of digital assets, the UNIDROIT Principles deal with digital assets based on the control criterion included in the recent amendments to the Uniform Commercial Code, and this can be considered 'Principles law'. Unlike the UNIDROIT Principles, the European Union has considered the dissociation of the legal nature of digital assets characterised as securities or financial guarantees[46] and those other assets registered in a distributed registry.[47]

The European Union has put together a complex and exhaustive regulatory package (digital finance package[48]), 'Other law' in the field of digital finance that pursues a dual objective: on the one hand, to transpose the obligations derived from European law into national legislation (transposition of Directives and adoption of certain national decisions mandated by Regulations); and, on the other hand, to complete and update national legislation in order to mitigate the possible risks that new technologies may bring, while taking advantage of the opportunities they offer to improve the provision of financial services. Thus, in the European Union, the European Commission describes crypto-assets as a subset of digital assets and provides a comprehensive definition of crypto-assets in its Regulation on crypto-asset markets MiCA, (Regulation (EU) 2023/1114 of the European Parliament and of the Council of 31 May 2023 on crypto-asset markets): 'Crypto-assets are digital representations of securities or rights, which can be transferred and stored electronically, using a specific technology (known as distributed ledger technology or similar technology). The space covered by MiCA in this new market is that of means of payment, in which current accounts held with banks are not used, but instead Wallets and fungible crypto-assets for payment (privately issued money), of two types: 'Asset-Referenced Token' (ART), which is intended to hold a stable value by referencing the value of several currencies that are legal tender (fiat currencies), one or more commodities, or one or more cryptoassets, or a combination of such assets; and "electronic money

---

[46] Digital assets classified as securities or financial guarantees are likely to have a different legal nature and, consequently, be subject to different conflict of laws rules. For example, securities deposited with an intermediary covered by the 2006 Hague Convention or financial instruments on stock exchanges and other trading systems, governed by Article 4(1)(h) of the Rome I Regulation.

[47] As noted in the Reflection of Principle 5, France addresses this issue by distinguishing the category of digital assets provided for in financial instruments from those others, which it breaks down into two categories: tokens, classified as intangible assets for the purposes of applying the token issuer status, and digital assets representing securities with an "exchange" function. See Haut Comité Juridique de la Place Financière de Paris, *Report on the determination of the law applicable to assets registered in distributed ledgers*, May 2024. Available in: https://www.banque-france.fr/fr/system/files/2024-07/Rapport_63_A.pdf.

[48] The Digital Finance Package, which includes a digital finance strategy, a renewed retail payments strategy and legislative proposals on (i) crypto-assets; and (ii) digital resilience, was adopted by the European Commission in 2020.

tokens" (EMT) which are a type of cryptoasset that is intended to be a medium of exchange and holds a stable value by referencing the value of a fiat currency that is legal tender. Finally, it deals with utility tokens, which are intended to provide digital access to a good or service, available on DLT, and only accepted by the issuer of that token. MiCA also establishes issuance requirements and the reservation of activity for cryptocurrency service providers.

Since 2024, the EU has been aiming to implement a sound legal framework enabling the use of interoperable digital identity solutions which should render customer onboarding much quicker and easier, as discussed later on. With this priority in mind, the strategy points towards achieving greater harmonisation in the fields of Anti-Money Laundering (AML) and Combatting the Financing of Terrorism (CFT), as seen below.[49] Indeed, the revised framework for electronic identification and trust services for electronic transactions eIDAS2 seeks to enhance trust in electronic transactions in the internal market by recognising the 'uniqueness of the data message' and the pseudonymous systems of DLTs regulated under eIDAS2. As already seen, in general terms this would support a broad space for the verification of the autonomy of will in the registration and transaction of commercial Digital Assets that have not been regulated as unique (Non fungible Tokens -hereinafter NFT-), which are linked to goods or other digital products that are purported to be unique or identifiable.

Unlike cryptocurrencies, NFTs are not traded or exchanged in equivalence, a characteristic that, a priori, seemed to exclude them from any financial operation and functionally destine them to the registration of ownership of unique assets, suitable, for example, for digital works of art to which they give 'uniqueness' and, therefore, value and the opportunity to fully automate markets and resale royalties for secondary sales. Certain markets already use DLTs and Registries (such as EUIPO) which recognise them for authenticating luxury goods.[50]

[49] On 19 March of 2024, the European Parliament approved a package of laws establishing new anti-money laundering rules in the European Union (EU) that in some way touch on the cryptocurrency sector. All financial institutions, including cryptocurrency exchanges (cryptoasset service providers or CASPs) are obliged entities. So are non-financial institutions such as football clubs or gambling services that could be prone to the risk of money laundering. This accordingly excludes hardware and software providers and providers of self-custody wallets that do not have control over cryptoassets (such as, for example, Metamask). This was already in line with the Funds Transfer Regulation and the eurozone implementation of the Financial Action Task Force (FATF) travel rule. Alongside MiCA, the so-called 'travel rule' also comes into force on 30 December 2024 through the new Transfer of Funds Regulation (TFR). It consists of a set of recommendations put forward by the Financial Action Task Force (FATF) since 2019 to counter money laundering and terrorist financing (AML/ CFT). They were updated in June 2022 and revised at the plenary that concluded on 23 June 2023. They will now be mandatory in the EU, following the guidelines of the European Banking Authority (EBA). This means that exchanges must store customer data and keep track of their cryptocurrency movements. They will have to share that information when required by the authorities, if transactions exceed €1,000. Companies will also be responsible for compliance when using third-party providers.

[50] See, EUROPEAN UNION INTELLECTUAL PROPERTY OFFICE (EUIPO), Trademark guidelines for examination FINAL VERSION 1.2 31/03/2024, hhttps://guidelines.euipo.europa.eu/2214311/2215372/trade-mark-guidelines/4-4-3-non-fungible-tokens--nfts-.

It could be said that the criterion that defines the 'unregulated zone' in the EU lies in fungibility. That is, those that are not regulated because they are non-fungible tokens (NFT-), and/or because, despite being fungible, they are algorithmic (decentralised issuances, such as Bitcoin, referred to in the DAPL as native). However, the plasticity of DLT to which we alluded earlier,[51] means a token issued as an NFT, despite having a unique identifier, can be fractioned and divided into aliquots, a 'resulting asset' in the terms of the Principles. As we shall see, this raises serious doubts about the impossibility of becoming a financial instrument, or a fungible with attribution of payment by the parties (commodity money), and could even be used as an instrument for money laundering and money evasion, so that guidelines have been provided in this regard by the European Securities and Markets Authority (ESMA).[52] Here as we see with algorithmic assets, it may be necessary to confirm the existence of a third category of personal property to better recognise and protect the unique characteristics of certain digital assets, as we shall discuss below on Common Law systems.

It has been pointed out that this approach would coincide with the position of Liechtenstein,[53] which the Liechtenstein Parliament introduced in October 2019 passing the Token and Trusted Technology Service Provider Act (TVTG), with the law coming into force on January 1st 2020—although tokens were recognised as sui generis assets in its legal system.[54] However, if tokenised securities were to be offered publicly in Liechtenstein or if the offer were to be extended to the entire European Economic Area (EEA), it might be necessary to prepare and publish a

[51] Let's take the example of crypto assets such as UNI or LINK, i.e. the ERC20 tokens of the Ethereum-based protocols Uniswap or Chainlink. Each of these tokens is fungible because a UNI or LINK token will always be equivalent to any other UNI or LINK token. The ability to propose and establish new token standards creates more room for new use cases for the Ethereum network. The ERC20 and ERC721 standards is that they do not allow a smart contract to support more than one type of fungible or non-fungible token. Therefore, every time you want to implement a new token, you must write a new smart contract. Moreover, with the two previous standards, it is not possible to create semi-fungible tokens. This is why the ERC1155 token standard was established, which allows Ethereum developers to create fungible, semi-fungible and non-fungible tokens with the same standard. In addition, with the ERC1155 standard, a single contract can be created that supports multiple, individually configurable token types, reducing the complexity of the token creation process.

[52] See, 3.9 Guideline 8 (classification as crypto-assets which are unique and not fungible with other crypto-assets—NFTs). Final Report, Guidelines on the conditions and criteria for the qualification of cryptoassets as financial instruments, 17 December 2024 ESMA75453128700-1323, https://www.esma.europa.eu/document/final-report-guidelines-conditions-and-criteria-qualification-crypto-assets-financial.

[53] *Taxonomy of Legal Issues related to the Digital Economy Prepared by the Secretariat of the United Nations Commission on International Trade Law*, Viena 2023, UNITED NATIONS PUBLICATION, 2024, e-ISBN 978-92-1–358507-8, available, https://uncitral.un.org/sites/uncitral.un.org/files/media-documents/uncitral/en/digitaleconomytaxonomy.pdf.

[54] The first countries in the world to adopt special legislation on blockchain, namely the Token and Trusted Technology Service Provider Act (also TVTG or Liechtenstein Blockchain Act), which has been enforced from the beginning of 2020, creating one of the world's first safe and regulated environments for token-related services. Gesetz vom 3. Oktober 2019 über Token und VT-Dienstleister (Token- und VT-Dienstleister-Gesetz; TVTG), aviable: https://www.gesetze.li/konso/2019301000.

securities prospectus. In Liechtenstein, as part of the EEA, both the EEA Prospectus Implementation Act (EWR-WPPDG) and Delegated Regulations (EU) 2017/1129, supplemented by Regulations (EU) 2019/979 and 2019/980, apply to security tokens that meet the three criteria of transferability, standardisation and tradability.[55]

It can therefore be pointed out, as was argued by Prof. Hideki Kanda at the IV International Congress held in Alicant,[56] "that we could point out as examples of 'Principles law', (the reforms are consistent with the UNIDROIT Principles): The Private Law Reform in the U.S. and the U.K. on Digital Assets U.S.: New Article 12 was added to the Uniform Commercial Code (2022), and in the U.K.: the Property (Digital Assets etc.) Bill was introduced into Parliament (September 2024)".[57]

Regarding the *characterisation* of digital assets, as we saw, the UNIDROIT Principles deal with digital assets based on the control criterion included in the recent amendments to the Uniform Commercial Code. In 2022, the Uniform Law Commission introduced a new article to the Uniform Commercial Code (hereinafter "UCC") regarding "controllable electronic records". As with all the UCC, this article is a recommendation addressed to the federal states of the US; in other words, it is soft law. Nevertheless, it is very significant, given that most states follow the UCC as a model (see also, in this volume, Steven Weise / Edwin Smith, *UNIDROIT DAPL Principles highlights and those points on UCC reform treatment).*

In the U.K., the government and the Financial Conduct Authority recently provided updates on the proposed new U.K. crypto-asset regulatory regime that is now intended to take effect in 2026. On 11 September 2024, the UK government introduced the Property (Digital Assets etc.) Bill, which provides that digital assets can be personal property under the laws of England and Wales and could therefore be afforded the same legal protections as other, traditional categories of personal property.[58] The Bill is concerned with the law of personal property in England and Wales. It provides that something may be capable of attracting property rights even if

---

[55] Detailed clarifications are provided in the FMA's instructions and communication to be found at the FMA's https://www.fma-li.li/en.

[56] IV INTERNATIONAL CONGRESS 2024 UNIDROIT DAPL. KEYNOTES BY Hideki Kanda y Ignacio Tirado. ENGLISH, Aviable; https://www.youtube.com/watch?v=rHTbSup3MXM.

[57] At the time of revising this paper, the Property (Digital Assets etc.) Bill has completed its passage through Parliament. Introduced in the House of Lords on 11 September 2024 (HL Bill 31), it passed third reading in the Lords on 8 May 2025 and was subsequently considered by the House of Commons. The Bill received Royal Assent on 2 December 2025 and is now the Property (Digital Assets etc.) Act 2025 (c. 29). Based closely on Law Commission recommendations published in June 2023, the Act establishes that digital assets, such as crypto-tokens and non-fungible tokens (NFTs), may constitute a 'third category' of personal property, distinct from things in possession and things in action. The Act extends to England and Wales, and Northern Ireland (following agreement from the Northern Ireland Assembly in March 2025); Scotland has introduced separate legislation owing to differences in its property law system. Full text available at https://www.legislation.gov.uk/ukpga/2025/29/enacted. See also Law Commission, 'Digital Assets: Final Report' (Law Com No 412, 2023).

[58] The Property (Digital Assets etc.) Bill is very short. Its single substantive clause reads: Objects of personal property rights, A thing (including a thing that is digital or electronic in nature) is not prevented from being the object of personal property rights merely because it is neither (a) a thing in possession, nor (b) a thing in ction.

does not fit into either of the 2 categories of personal property that have traditionally been recognised under the law of England and Wales. These categories are things in possession (generally, tangible things) and things in action (personal property that can only be claimed or enforced through a court action).

As precedents, the English Courts decided in several cases that digital assets are capable of being property as a matter of common law, and many decisions of Courts considered the English decision of AA v Persons Unknown [2019] EWHC 3556, [2020] 4 WLR 35,[59] which also treated cryptocurrencies as "property" by granting an interim proprietary injunction against a cryptocurrency exchange over the disputed assets. Along similar lines, on 8 April 2020, the High Court of New Zealand issued a judgment concluding that cryptocurrencies are a species of intangible personal property capable of being the subject matter of a trust (See, Ruscoe v Cryptopia Ltd (in liq.),[60] a judgement which follows on from a long series of previous pronouncements and concludes that cryptocurrencies are a kind of intangible personal property that can be the subject of a trust. The International Commercial Court of Singapore of B2C2 Ltd v Quoine Pte Ltd [2019] 4 SLR 17 at [142, had concluded that they were intangible property, as they passed the Ainsworth test.[61]

The Bill gives effect to recommendations of the Law Commission for England and Wales. The Commission recommended statutory confirmation that a thing will not be deprived of legal status as an object of personal property rights merely by reason of the fact that it is neither a thing in possession nor a thing in action. This recommendation responds to the development of new types of assets such as crypto tokens which challenge the traditional categories. The Bill would establish that things can be property, even if they do not meet the traditional definitions of property established in case law. The Bill is designed to clarify that assets such as crypto-tokens, crypto-currency and non-fungible tokens could be capable of attracting property rights. However, it does not establish that any category of thing is property.

We note that the Bill does not define the boundaries of the "third category" of property; nor does it define "things in action" or "things in possession". We agree that such determinations are likely to be complex and that the Bill should not attempt to exhaustively define the boundaries of property rights. However, given the novel and complex nature of the issues, we welcome the government's announcement that the UK Jurisdiction Taskforce (hereinafter "UKJT") will act as an expert body to provide guidance to industry and the courts. It is important that the UKJT's remit should be wide enough to consider any aspect of property rights attaching to digital assets, and this should not be limited to issues relating to "control" of digital assets.

While new legislation in the UK aims to confirm the existence of a third category of personal property to better recognise and protect the unique characteristics of certain

---

[59] See https://www.bailii.org/ew/cases/EWHC/Comm/2019/3556.html.

[60] Ruscoe v Cryptopia Ltd (in liq.) [2020] NZHC 728 at [55–69]. See https://www.courtsofnz.govt.nz/cases/ruscoe-v-cryptoia-ltd-in-liquidation.

[61] B2C2 Ltd v Quoine Pte Ltd [2019] 4 SLR 17 at [142. The Judge accepted that "there may be some academic debate as to the precise nature of the property right", see https://www.elitigation.sg/gd/s/2020_SGCAI_2.

digital assets, the commission also recommended that the UK government create a panel of industry experts to provide guidance on technical and legal issues related to digital assets. The recommendations also included providing market participants with new ways to take collateral on crypto-tokens and tokenised securities, which do not yet exist in England and Wales.[62]

2.2.3 Transfer of a Digital Asset (5)

The UNIDROIT Principles on Digital Assets do not prescribe the conditions for a proprietary right in a digital asset to be validly transferred to another person. Although Principle 3(1) requires that digital assets be capable of economic rights, and Principle 8 requires that a transferee has obtained control to be considered a bona fide acquirer, these Principles do not prescribe the requirements for a valid transfer of a digital asset. Whether with or without direct human intervention i.e. where the contracts in question were concluded by the parties' respective algorithms, as is typical in algorithmic trading, or transfer is a dataset that is the basis for the operation of an artificial intelligence (AI) system. In other words, they do not prescribe whether a change of control is sufficient or necessary for a change of an economic interest to be valid. This is left to 'other law', see also Principle 3(3).

Consistently, and seeking to draw parallels with other instruments developed by UNIDROIT, which deal with transferable assets and assets used in commerce, Mr Jason Grant Allen pointed out that the concept of transferability generally connotes a 'thing' that is transferred, whereas in the context of digital assets, depending on the technical system used, there may not be a 'thing' that is transferred. In addition, other questions could be raised, such as whether certain systems underlying certain digital assets have the capacity to transfer legal rights. Ms. Carla Reyes[63] confirmed that the meaning of transferability should cover 'transfers' that contemplate the disappearance, destruction, cancellation or deletion of a digital asset and the subsequent and corresponding derivative acquisition of other digital assets. Citing the operation of Bitcoin, she stressed that the operation of a technical system underlying a digital asset should not be a reason to remove a given digital asset from the scope of DAPL.[64] "Transfer" of a digital asset means the change of a proprietary right in the digital

---

[62] The public consultation on the draft Cryptoasset Service Providers (Due Diligence and Reporting Requirements) Regulations 2025 closed on 10 January 2025. The draft regulations, published by HM Revenue & Customs on 30 October 2024, implement the Organisation for Economic Cooperation and Development (OECD) Cryptoasset Reporting Framework (CARF). They set out reporting and due diligence requirements for reportable cryptoasset service providers (RCASPs), penalties for non-compliance, and requirements for cryptoasset users to provide valid self-certification. The final regulations are expected to come into force on 1 January 2026. See https://www.gov.uk/government/consultations/draft-regulations-the-cryptoasset-service-providers-due-diligence-and-reporting-requirements-regulations-2025.

[63] Nº 13.

[64] Punto 5: Examen de las cuestiones identificadas en el documento de debate (Estudio LXXXII-W.G.1 - Doc. 2). UNIDROIT 2021 - Estudio LXXXII - W.G.1 - Doc. 4.

asset from one person to another person; and includes the granting of a security right in favour of a secured creditor, and 'transferee' includes a secured creditor, and the acquisition of a proprietary right in a resulting digital asset.

The rules of the system determine how the digital asset is created and transferred. These rules are encoded in the software that runs the system and may be put on a contractual footing by agreement between the administrator and the person holding the digital asset.

In an account-based system, the crucial issue for the receiver is the identity of the payer, whereas, in a token-based system, the identity of the payer is irrelevant. Instead, the crucial issue for the receiver is the authenticity of the object received, whether real or fake. The same dichotomy is commonly applied to discussions of digital currencies and cryptoassets, including bitcoin. It defines token-based systems as value storage systems (such as cash, fiat money and stored-value cards) that 'rely on the transfer of some payment object (whether coins, banknotes or stored electronic value) between the payer and the payee and depend critically on the payee's ability to verify the payment objects'. 'A payment is made by a transfer of a claim on a security existing elsewhere' and'therefore, a payment requires giving instructions to transfer ownership of a claim on the security from one person to another '. In other words, to sufficiently verify the validity of a payment transaction, a token-based system requires verifying the validity of the object used to pay, whereas an account-based system requires verifying the identity of the payer.

In a token-based system, the payment object (i.e. the cash) is the record that summarises past production, trading and consumption decisions. Possession of the object is generally considered proof of ownership of the cash because each object has a unique physical existence (i.e. the same object can only be owned by one entity at any given time). Once the payer delivers it to the payee, the payer no longer owns it, but the payee possesses it. The authenticity of the object being transferred is all that a payee needs to verify to confirm the validity of the transfer of ownership. No trusted party is required to attest to this transfer of ownership. The beneficiary assumes full responsibility if the cash is counterfeit. When funds are transferred, the system record is updated by increasing and decreasing the balances in the relevant account. When two payments are received on an account, their transaction values would be added to the existing balance to update the system register with a new balance. The values of the two payments are included in the new account balance, and no one can tell from the account balance whether it is the total result of a single payment or of several previously received payments.

Both token-based and account-based systems are record-keeping mechanisms for recording ownership of an asset. The difference between them lies in how the records are maintained and who maintains and updates them. In short, in a token-based system, the registry is maintained and updated by the owners of the tokens, whereas in an account-based system, the registry is typically maintained and updated by an operator of a system infrastructure who plays the role of a trusted intermediary.

In decentralised systems that run on open-source software, the only contract may be the end-user agreement to use the software (the governance of DLT systems). In other systems, including centralised systems, the contract may be more prescriptive on matters relating to the administration of the system. The transfer of a digital asset will generally be done under a contract. Similarly, any dealings in the linked asset will also generally be done under a contract (e.g., a sales agreement or security agreement). There may also be a contract between the person who holds the digital asset and the person on whose behalf the digital asset is held (e.g., a custodian agreement)[65] or without direct human intervention where the contracts in question were concluded by the parties' respective algorithms, as is typical in algorithmic trading, where the buy and sell contracts on the Platform were concluded without any direct human intervention other than that involved in the creation of the algorithmic processes that led to their formation. That was the case in 2020, when the Singapore Court of Appeal considered whether Bitcoins were assets which could be held on trust.[66] To solve the problem of ambiguity of ownership of digital tokens, a Bitcoin transaction generally includes the identity of the payee to specify the designated recipient of a payment. A payment-to-public-key-hash (P2PKH) transaction is the most common form of Bitcoin transaction—it includes (the hash of) the payee's public key and the amount to be paid to the payee in a transaction format called UTXO. As discussed above, the public key (or its hash) is a form of identity for the beneficiary. In this way, the transfer of value is explicitly addressed to the intended beneficiary in an unambiguous way, and the legitimate ownership of a UTXO can be correctly corroborated by looking at the specified public key hash.

As with any other account-based electronic money transfer, the transfer of bitcoins depends on compliance with the transfer protocols of a payment scheme, which requires an infrastructure of hardware, software, standards and supporting financial arrangements. Consequently, the information package that makes up the Digital

---

[65] Liechtenstein's Blockchain Act, Art. 6 Disposal of tokens

(1) A disposal is deemed to be

   (a) the transfer of the right to dispose of the token; or
   (b) the creation of a security or a usufructuary right to a token.

(2) The disposal of a token requires that:

   (a) the transfer of the Token has been completed in accordance with the rules of the TT System, whereby a limited right in rem to a Token can also be created without a transfer, provided that this is recognisable to third parties and the time of the creation is clearly established.
   (b) the transferor and the transferee unanimously declare their intention to transfer the right to dispose of the token or to establish a limited right in rem to it; and
   (c) the transferor is authorised to dispose of the token in accordance with Art. 5; Art. 9 remains reserved.
   (3) If a token is disposed of without legal grounds or if such grounds subsequently cease to exist, reversal shall be affected in accordance with the provisions of the law of enrichment (Sections 1431 et seq. ABGB).

[66] B2C2 Ltd v Quoine Pte Ltd [2019] 4 SLR 17 at [142]. The Judge accepted that "there may be some academic debate as to the precise nature of the property right", see https://www.elitigation.sg/gd/s/2020_SGCAI_2.

Asset itself needs to be differentiated. For these reasons, we must focus our analysis on a specific factual scenario in which party B excludes party A from access to a digital file, which gives rise to a dispute in which A seeks to recover the file or receive compensation from B. An example would be a case where cloud provider B excludes customer A from a digital file, stored on B's servers, which A has uploaded to the cloud, and which is vital to A's business. Focusing on another specific scenario also allows us to test the argument that other areas of the law already protect information, making property rights over digital files unnecessary. Multisig or multisignature wallets afford an additional layer of protection where multiple individuals would need to sign a transaction to move any Bitcoin within the underlying wallets. These are standard measures in cryptocurrency project treasuries or decentralised autonomous organisations (DAOs) to protect against the compromising of a single wallet or individual. However, they can be adopted by security-conscious retail users who may include family, friends and transfers to oneself to provide an additional layer of security.

To illustrate our analysis, as mentioned above, different layers are needed for this. Layer 0 components include the Internet, the hardware and the connections that will allow layer one to run smoothly. The Ethereum network, layer one, is responsible for consensus processes, programming languages, block timing, dispute resolution, and the rules and parameters that maintain the basic functionality of a blockchain network. It is also known as the implementation layer. Bitcoin is an example of a layer one blockchain, layer two is a third-party integration that is used in conjunction with layer one to increase the number of nodes, and consequently the performance of the system. Smart contracts in the primary blockchain protocol only deal with deposits and withdrawals and ensure that off-chain transactions follow the rules. Bitcoin's Lightning Network is an example of a layer two blockchain. The application layer is often referred to as layer three or L3 (DApps[67]). L3 projects act as a user interface while masking the technical aspects of the communication channel. Many Layer 2 and Layer 3 solutions are developed and maintained by third parties. This introduces a dependency on the security and reliability of those external entities. If a Layer 2 solution suffers a security breach, it could compromise the funds or data managed through it, even if the base layer remains secure. Transactions and data that are processed outside the main chain (e.g. in Layer 2 solutions) may not benefit from the same security inherent in the blockchain. This separation can introduce vulnerabilities if the security measures implemented in these layers are not as robust as those of the main chain. Bitcoin and Lightning Network: Bitcoin is a clear example of Layer 1, while Lightning Network is a Layer 2 implementation designed to allow near instantaneous and very low-cost transactions. Ethereum and Layer 2 solutions: Ethereum, like Layer 1, has seen the development of multiple Layer 2 solutions to improve its scalability. An example of Layer 2 in Ethereum is Arbitrum, and two

---

[67] The term DApp stands for 'decentralized application'. DApps are, therefore, autonomous applications that function in a decentralized way. They do not depend on company servers but use a peer-to-peer network distributed in a decentralized way. Data storage, communications and transactions are based on the blockchain technology. Furthermore, DApps use transparent open-source code that can generally be seen by users and can be used free of charge.

examples of implementations that use rollups to process transactions more efficiently are Polkadot and Cosmos. Although they do not strictly conform to the layered nomenclature, they are examples of projects that seek to address interoperability issues (an aspect of what a Layer 3 would be) by allowing different blockchains to interact with each other.

It is therefore more appropriate to view Bitcoin as account-based, rather than token-based in the economic sense, as payments involve the verification and updating of accounting entries (in the form of UTXO representations) on a blockchain or distributed ledger. Unlike a typical account-based system (which records System state as a list of accounts, each with a corresponding balance), the Bitcoin blockchain records System state as a list of individual bitcoins (more precisely, UTXOs), each of which has a corresponding owner who can spend the bitcoins. Each UTXO has a specific value. To initiate a transfer, the holder of a UTXO must prove that he or she owns it by signing a payment transaction (which is essentially an instruction) using the private key associated with the UTXO record on the blockchain. An individual UTXO cannot be partially spent; instead, the UTXO that is transferred is generally destroyed and replaced with two newly created smaller UTXOs (which add up to the same total value), one goes to the payee and the other is returned to the payer as change. In other words, each currently active UTXO on the blockchain inherits its value from one or more UTXOs it consumes. There are exceptions though, such as the process known as Bitcoin mixing or Coin-Join, which consists of exchanging UTXOs with other anonymous network users. It would be like a group of people putting notes in a big jar, mixing them up and then each taking out exactly the same amount they contributed minus commissions, but receiving different notes. Of course, the Coin-Join process is much more complex. The randomness of the process makes each UTXO more difficult for the government and Chainalysis or similar companies to track, although this can be done through Blink. The Lightning Network is a Layer 2 solution where you can execute a virtually unlimited number of transactions without touching the main chain. However, when you finally want to send funds on the chain, that transaction will generate a single UTXO. Therefore, you can use the Lightning Network and Blink to DCA or accumulate Bitcoin by any means you prefer and, when you are ready, consolidate UTXOs directly with that single transaction.

Consequently, in our view, the UNIDROIT Principles' provision on digital assets has a significant loophole, which needs to be filled by "other law", in cases where there is no oversight, and neither the registrar nor the issuer is identifiable or has a discernible seat. This concerns, for example, widespread digital assets such as bitcoin or ether (see Principle 5). For these and similar situations, States have tried to provide solutions such as the Liechtenstein Blockchain Act, which is formulated in a sufficiently abstract manner to ensure that it remains applicable to subsequent generations of technology. This is why the law uses the term 'transaction systems based on trusted technologies (TT-systems)'.[68] On the other hand, the option of registered assets or, more generally, rights in tokens, raises essential legal issues that

---

[68] Liechtenstein's Blockchain Act, Art. 5, Power of disposal and authorisation to dispose
1) The holder of the TT Key has the power of disposal over the Token.

need to be clarified in the interest of the overall legal certainty for users of 'transaction systems based on trusted technologies (TT-systems)' and of TT service providers. An example is the legal effect of the transfer of tokens on the right represented. Liechtenstein law makes it possible to register the 'real' world in TT-systems in a legally secure way to exploit the full potential of the token economy.

As we have seen, Liechtenstein law focuses on a notion of 'tokens' in a broad sense and covers native tokens, which do not embody any rights. However, by its substantive provisions, the Liechtenstein law appears to be limited to digital assets that have an issuer, thus excluding fully decentralised blockchain networks such as Bitcoin. However, those issues are not addressed in the UNIDROIT Principles on Digital Assets. They need to be addressed through clear regulation. Since blockchain technology is also actively used and has become generalised in the global economy, the" other law" should clarify which requirements apply to significant activities in the systems. In any case, it should consider the protection of customers and the application of due diligence obligations to ensure compliance with international standards and a comprehensive and effective fight against money laundering. In 2021 the Financial Action Task Force (FATF) published a set of recommendations for cryptocurrency platforms, stating that what is known as KYC (know your customer) user verification should be applied. The measures recommended by this transnational group are so far-reaching that they even indicate that they should be applied in decentralised exchanges (DEX).

Consequently, in line with other FATF recommendations, the 'travel rule' has been widely implemented across jurisdictions. In the European Union, this principle is enshrined in the Transfer of Funds Regulation (TFR), which requires that for any transfer of funds exceeding EUR 1,000—including transfers involving cryptocurrencies—the originator's identifying information must accompany the transaction from initiation to completion. In practice, this necessitates the systematic sharing of customer data between platforms involved in the transfer chain. It should be noted that the monitoring and enforcement of the 'travel rule' specifically targets exchanges and other cryptocurrency platforms operating as 'virtual asset service providers' (VASPs), rather than peer-to-peer transactions conducted without intermediaries.[69]

However, the Gordian knot in this law is self-custodial wallets, as their use does not require KYC user verification. The application of VASP has, for now, only been applied to exchanges and centralised platforms.[70] The use and exchange of Bitcoin

---

2) The person who has the power of disposal is also presumed to be the person authorised to dispose of the Token. For each previous holder of the power of disposal, it is assumed that he was authorised to dispose of the token at the time of his ownership.

3) If a person holds the power of disposal without intending to be authorised to dispose of it, he may rely on the fact that the person from whom he received the token in good faith is authorised to dispose of it.

[69] Regulation (EU) 2023/1113 of the European Parliament and of the Council of 31 May 2023 on information accompanying transfers of funds and certain crypto-assets and amending Directive (EU) 2015/849 (Text with EEA relevance) PE/53/2022/REV/1, ELI: http://data.europa.eu/eli/reg/2023/1113/oj.

[70] See, ut supra, in this paper nº, 51.

through self-custodial wallets can be considered anonymous, if none of the exchanged Bitcoins have interacted with the fiat system through any exchange operating with VASP mechanisms. In other words, the rules do not apply to person-to-person transfers made without a provider or between providers acting on their own behalf, or transfers to oneself.

One solution could be to implement a 'digital duty to cooperate' in the UNIDROIT Project on 'Best Practices for Effective Enforcement' (BPEE), which at the time of revising this work is in its final stages of adoption, having completed its public consultation (1 July – 15 September 2025) and its eleventh and final Working Group session. In reference to Prof. Hideki's comments at the IV International Congress held in Alicante,[71] regarding two typical situations involving Digital Assets, which require the "Duty to cooperate": A general creditor obtains a court judgement against the debtor, and attempts to seize the debtor's assets, which happen to include digital assets. A creditor who took the debtor's digital assets as collateral attempts to realise its security right where the creditor tries to sell the digital assets to satisfy its claim. The UNIDROIT Digital Assets Principles do not provide specific rules on this issue, and delegate the issue to each jurisdiction's national law (or "other law"). The UNIDROIT Project on "Best Practices for Effective Enforcement" is expected to propose some basic rules on this issue. Duty to cooperate of the debtor (or the third party) for seizure and transfer. Cooperation by the debtor (or the third party) may be required to effectively and efficiently seize digital assets. Seizure of digital assets for the purposes of enforcement may require cooperation by the debtor (or the third party) to disclose or make available relevant information for the enforcement agents or authorities to gain control over the digital assets—private key, recovery phrase, or access data to the device or system where it is stored, and/or to convey the control over the digital assets. The law shall provide for effective, proportionate, and adequate sanctions in case the debtor (or the third party) refuses to cooperate, without legitimate reason not to do so, or if it provides inaccurate, false or partial information.

References

Carstens. A and Nilekani.N (2024), Finternet: the financial system for the future BIS Working Papers | No 1178 | 15 April 2024. https://www.bis.org/publ/work1178.htm

Chan, A. (2021). UTXO in Digital Currencies: Account-based or Token-based? Or Both?. https://doi.org/10.48550/arXiv.2109.09294

Nakamoto. S (2019) Bitcoin: A Peer-to-Peer Electronic Cash System, https://bitcoin.org/bitcoin.pdf.

Pastor Sempere, C, 2017. Cryptocurrencies: would a legal disruption in the eurozone?, Revista de Estudios Europeos Nº 70, julio-diciembre, 2017-284-318 Monográfico-Economía colaborativa ISSN: 2530-9854. https://uvadoc.uva.es/handle/10324/28425

[71] IV INTERNATIONAL CONGRESS 2024 UNIDROIT DAPL. KEYNOTES by Hideki Kanda y Ignacio Tirado. ENGLISH, Aviable; https://www.youtube.com/watch?v=rHTbSup3MXM.

Rodríguez de las Heras Ballell,T (2024) "The Emergence of Principles and Best Practices on Digital Assets: Proprietary Rights, and Enforcement". European Journal of Risk Regulation. https://doi.org/10.1017/err.2024.5.

Principle 3
General Principles

David Amable Morán Bovio

(1) A digital asset can be the subject of proprietary rights.

(2) Principles law takes precedence over other law to the extent that they conflict.

(3) Except as displaced by these Principles, other law applies to all issues, including:

> **(a) whether a person has a proprietary right in a digital asset;**
>
> **(b) whether a proprietary right in a digital asset has been validly transferred to another person;**
>
> **(c) whether a security right in a digital asset has been validly created;**
>
> **(d) the rights as between a transferor and transferee of a digital asset;**
>
> **(e) the rights as between a grantor of a security right in a digital asset and the secured creditor to whom the security right is granted;**
>
> **(f) the legal consequences of third-party effectiveness of a transfer of a digital asset;**
>
> **(g) the requirements for, and legal consequences of, third-party effectiveness of a security right in a digital asset.**

This work was financed within the framework of the Prometeo 2023 project of the Regional Ministry of Innovation, Universities, Science and Digital Society (CIPROM/2022/26) "Present and future of the regulation of cryptoassets in the EU [LegalCripto]", whose principal investigator is Carmen Pastor Sempere. The basic ideas contained herein were presented in the author's paper with the same title, given on November 13, 2024 at the IV International Congress on "UNIDROIT Principles on Digital Assets and Private Law: Context, Content, Perspectives", organized also by BAES Research Group of the University of Alicante on November 13 and 14, 2024.

D. A. Morán Bovio (✉)
University of Cádiz, Cádiz, Spain
e-mail: david.moran@uca.es

C. Pastor Sempere and D. A. Morán Bovio (eds.), UNIDROIT *Principles on Digital Assets and Private Law*, Law, Governance and Technology Series 80,
https://doi.org/10.1007/978-3-032-11001-5_9

1 Official Commentary

Commentary

Principle 3(1)

3.1. As stated in Principle 1, these Principles cover private law issues and, in particular, proprietary rights relating to digital assets. Principle 3(1) therefore provides, as a matter of principle, that Principles law (as defined in Principle 2(3)) should provide that digital assets can be the subject of proprietary rights. All rules provided in these Principles are built on this premise. However, the question of whether digital assets can be the subject of proprietary rights has been controversial in several jurisdictions. As courts in multiple high-profile cases have considered that digital assets are the subject of proprietary rights, and several authoritative authors have expressed that digital assets should be the subject of proprietary rights, these Principles advise States to increase legal certainty on this issue and make explicit that digital assets can be the subject of proprietary rights. What is meant by 'proprietary rights' is discussed in Commentary 3.4.

3.2. Whether digital assets can be the subject of proprietary rights (a legal consequence) must be distinguished from the classification of digital assets. As explained in the Commentary to Principle 2(3), these Principles do not prescribe a specific classification of digital assets. That digital assets must be susceptible to proprietary rights, as Principle 3(1) requires, may mean, in certain jurisdictions, that a digital asset must be classified as 'property', 'a good', 'a thing', or a similar concept, but this would depend on the applicable law in question and is left for each specific State to decide. If the law of a State includes a classification of different categories of assets which can be subject to proprietary rights, and these different categories have different consequences, it is recommended that the law of that State should specify which category or categories of assets digital assets are. This is in order that digital assets can be subject to proprietary rights in that State. This could mean the introduction of a new category of asset, but again, this is left for each specific State to decide.

3.3. Principle 3(1) also leaves to other law (as defined in Principle 2(4)) issues such as whether a person has a proprietary right in a digital asset and whether a proprietary right in a digital asset has been validly transferred to another person. Whilst Principle 3(1) does require that digital assets must be susceptible to proprietary rights, it does not prescribe, for instance, the specific requirements for a valid right of ownership in a digital asset or for a valid transfer of the same. These issues are left to other law. See also Principle 3(3) and Commentary 3.8 to 3.12.

3.4. The phrase 'proprietary rights' in these Principles is used in a broad sense, in that 'proprietary rights' include both proprietary interests and rights with proprietary effects. This broad definition reflects the functional approach of these Principles, which intend to cater for the largest variety of jurisdictions possible. Also, the definition of proprietary rights intends to express that persons can have rights or interests in digital assets, which rights or interests can be asserted against third parties, i.e., against persons that are not necessarily contractual parties. This may be particularly relevant in the context of insolvency, where an insolvency representative might assert rights or interests in digital assets on behalf of the insolvency estate against third parties, and where third parties might assert rights or interests in digital assets against the insolvency representative.

Principle 3(2)

3.5. These Principles provide specific rules for the holding, transfer and use of digital assets, taking into account the specific nature of this asset class. This means that the rules of these Principles may supplement, or derogate from, State laws. To give the rules of these Principles full effect, Principle 3(2) provides that they should take precedence over State laws wherever they conflict. Consequently, once they have been adopted and implemented into the law of a State, these Principles (by then 'Principles law' as defined in Principle 2(3)) must take precedence over other law (as defined in Principle 2(4)).

3.6. As already stated above, these Principles take no position as to whether their rules should be included in a special law on digital assets enacted by a State, should be incorporated into more general laws of a State, already follow from the general law of a State, or are addressed by a combination of these approaches. However, Principles law (as defined in Principle 2(3)) takes precedence over other law (as defined in Principle 2(4)) (see also Commentary 2.18 to 2.22, especially Commentary 2.19). This may be achieved in a State as a result of generally applicable rules that grant precedence to specific laws over general laws, or to later laws over earlier laws. A State may need to specify the laws and sections or articles in other laws that are repealed or superseded.

3.7. It is possible that a State has, or decides to enact, a law that is even more specific than the Principles, such as a law that relates to a particular type of linked asset (see Principle 4). In that situation, the State should ensure that, as far as possible, Principles law in relation to that type of digital asset is consistent with the specific law. For example, a State might want to adopt a slightly different innocent acquisition rule for that type of digital asset (see Commentary 8.7), or it might want to ensure that the secured transactions rules specific to that category of asset apply as appropriate (see Commentary 14.4). To the extent that any conflict remained, the specific law would have precedence over Principles law. An example of such a specific law is the UNCITRAL Model Law on Electronic Transferable Records, which gives functionally equivalent legal effect to electronic equivalents of transferable paper documents and instruments. Such an electronic equivalent could be in the form of a digital asset as defined in Principle 2(2) (see Commentary 4.22 for an example). In a State where the UNCITRAL Model Law on Electronic Transferable Records has been implemented, that law, and the law of that State governing the relevant functional paper equivalent, would have precedence over Principles law in the event of a conflict. However, as mentioned earlier, it is recommended that a State should take steps to avoid inconsistency wherever possible.

Principle 3(3)

3.8. Principle 3(3) makes it explicit that other law (as defined in Principle 2(4)), continues to apply to digital assets. For this purpose, Principle 3(3) lists several examples of issues of property law, but also of contract law, that may continue to be addressed by a State's other law, because these Principles do not cover those issues, nor do they intend to change or derogate from that other law. The list is not intended to be exhaustive or limitative. It is reiterated that, first, these Principles cover only private law issues relating to digital assets, so that they do not cover rules that are to be enforced by public authorities which in many jurisdictions would be called 'regulation' or 'regulatory law'. Secondly, these Principles cover only a specific area of private law, and there are many issues of private law which are not addressed by the Principles. These issues concern, for instance, rules of private law relating to intellectual property or consumer protection. As a matter of principle, these areas of law are not addressed by these Principles, and national intellectual property and consumer protection laws therefore remain unaffected by them. Finally, as mentioned above, there are several issues of property and contract law that these Principles do not cover, important examples of which are listed in Principle 3(3). Strictly speaking, 'Except as displaced by these Principles' is redundant, because 'other law' (as defined), is, by definition, law that is not covered by these Principles. It is for the avoidance of any doubt that Principle 3(3) says that 'except as displaced by these Principles', other law continues to apply. It is not intended to mean that a specific State law continues to apply only to the extent that these Principles (as contrasted with Principles law) explicitly displace such State law. Although Principle 2(5) defines 'transfer' (as used in these Principles) as including the grant of a security right in favour of a secured creditor, the list in Principle 3(3) refers separately to transfers and security rights. This is for clarity of exposition, and because Principle 3(3) lists matters to which other law applies.

3.9. The examples in Principle 3(3) of issues that continue to be addressed by other law, can be categorised as follows. First, Principle 3(3)(a) concerns the static situation in which it must be determined whether a person has a proprietary right in a digital asset. Pursuant to Principle 3(3)(a), the requirements for a (valid) right or interest in a digital asset that can be asserted against third parties continue to be a matter of other law. Therefore, and by way of example, whether a person holds a valid right of ownership in a certain digital asset, is, as a matter of principle, not regulated by these Principles.

3.10. Second, Principles 3(3)(b) and 3(3)(c) concern dynamic situations of acqui-

sition and disposition of a digital asset from the perspective of the transferor and security right provider respectively. If the question arises whether a person has validly transferred a proprietary right, or validly created a security right, in a digital asset, Principles 3(3)(b) and 3(3)(c) make it clear that the requirements for a (valid) transfer or creation of a security right continue to be, as a matter of principle, a matter of other law. However, these Principles do provide some specific rules regarding the transfer of, and third-party effectiveness of a security right in, a digital asset. For example, Principle 15 provides that control (as defined in Principle 6) must be an available method of making a security right in a digital asset effective against third parties, but other law may provide for other means of achieving effectiveness. Moreover, Principle 8 provides that an innocent acquirer takes free from conflicting proprietary rights and Principle 12 provides similar protection to a client for whom a custodian maintains a digital asset. Whenever it is unclear whether existing rules or standards of general application apply to digital assets, and whenever Principles law derogates from other law, it is recommended that State law make this explicit.

3.11. Principles 3(3)(d) and 3(3)(e) make explicit that the relationships between a transferor and a transferee, and between a grantor of a security right and the relevant secured creditor, respectively, continue to be a matter of other law and are not, as a matter of principle, dealt with by these Principles. In some situations and some jurisdictions, these relationships are characterised as primarily contractual in nature. Principles 3(3)(d) and 3(3)(e) provide that the rights between a transferor of a digital asset and the transferee, and between a grantor of a security right in a digital asset and the secured creditor, are left to be dealt with by other law, whatever the qualification of the relationships between those parties.

3.12. As explained above, Principles 3(3)(d) and 3(3)(e) concern, respectively, the (contractual) relationships between a transferor and a transferee, and between a grantor of a security right and the relevant secured creditor. These provisions thus concern inter se relationships, i.e., relationships between (contracting) parties. Principles 3(3)(f) and 3(3)(g), on the other hand, concern erga omnes relationships, i.e., the relationships with third parties. Pursuant to Principles 3(3)(f) and 3(3)(g), whether a transfer and a security right, respectively, can be asserted against third parties, continues to be, as a matter of principle, a matter of other law. In some jurisdictions, the 'assertability' of a right or interest against third parties follows from the concept of 'effectiveness'. Principles 3(3)(f) and 3(3)(g) provide that, whatever the doctrinal context, the requirements for such effectiveness or assertability continue to be, as a matter of principle, a matter of other law, except where the Principles provide other rules (see Commentary 3.10 and Principle 15).

2 Reflections

2.1 Introduction

To aid in the understanding of Principle 3 of the UNIDROIT Principles on Digital Assets and Private Law (DAPL) within the context of this common task, it seems preferable to divide the exercise into two sections: the first (Sect. 2.2) will present the formation process of the DAPL Principle 3 *General Principles*, the second (Sect. 2.3) will provide some insight into its purpose.

The analysis will rely exclusively on the documents available on the UNIDROIT website, specifically those listed in the right-hand column of the DAPL Principles page under the tab "Preparatory Work" and within the "Working Group Meetings" section, where documents from the first to the eighth session of the Working Group can be found in consecutive order. Two additional documents have also been consulted: two General Council reports (also publicly accessible via the UNIDROIT website by browsing to the top menu "meetings" and clicking "Governing Council").

The method employed to achieve this aim using the aforementioned sources is to highlight those passages deemed most relevant to the objective, bringing them (partially) into the footnotes of the following pages (primarily).

These pages will have fulfilled their intended purpose if the reader learns (in Sect. 2.2) how DAPL Principle 3 was developed and why it was drafted in that particular way, and (in Sect. 2.3) what objectives it seeks to achieve.

The sequence (Sect. 2.2) will follow a reverse chronological order: from the UNIDROIT DAPL Principles edition to the documents containing the DAPL Principles origins. This approach allows one to observe when, how, and why Principle 3 and its Commentary were finalized, as well as the history behind the inclusion of its various elements, with references provided to the documents where each detail can be traced according to the reader's interest (as the limitations of these pages allow for the discussion of only selected aspects).

To approach the clarification of the objectives of Principle 3 (Sect. 2.3), another plan ought to be followed. This section will be structured in two steps. Firstly, a broader overview will highlight the common understanding that underpinned the drafting of Principle 3. Secondly, the focus will shift to the specific rationale behind the three key issues whose explanation may contribute to a full understanding of Principle 3's purpose (fully in parallel with its three main sections). These are: "Proprietary rights" applicable to digital assets, "Principle's law" precedence, and "other law".

That different approach is also applied to the apparently preferable sequence in this Sect. 2.3: it will proceed from the earliest documents and ideas toward the later evolution of the Working Group, allowing the reader to engage with the original formulations of the ideas behind Principle 3, and then follow how they were refined over time. Perhaps, it seems obvious that the pages in Sect. 2.3 should be considerably shorter than in Sect. 2.2, as it benefits from cross-referencing and a more direct focus on purpose, while changes in the wording are less significant (if present at all).

In opposition to the order of Sect. 2.3 described two paragraphs above, Sect. 2.2 is at first sight preferable as a single, undivided narrative in order to maintain the natural sequence to explore the principle's origins.

As a consequence of the considerations (Sects. 2.2 and 2.3), several brief concluding remarks will be presented (Sect. 2.4).

2.2 DAPL Principle 3 and Its Commentary Formation Process

The public version of DAPL Principle 3[1] was adopted by the UNIDROIT Governing Council four months earlier.[2] The text (always in relation to Principle 3 and its Commentary) used for the adoption[3] is practically identical to the one examined by the Working Group in its last session (the eighth).[4] This version, in turn, follows the draft prepared for review[5] by the preceding Working Group meeting at the seventh session,[6] during which several modifications were introduced, mostly affecting the Commentary, while the text of Principle 3 itself underwent only a minor revision.

Before delving further, one point about the general structure of the Principles should be mentioned: the Working Group agreed to insert the Commentary only after the final version of each Principle was completed.[7] Each Principle will show first its text (the so-called black letter text, because it is in bold type) and afterwards its Commentary (and Examples, eventually).[8] Though this change is purely stylistic, it signals a high degree of evolution in the Working Group's process at that stage, suggesting, so to speak, that "the hard work had been done".

---

[1] The book published by the International Institute for the Unification of Private Law (UNIDROIT) Via Panisperna, 28 - 00184 Rome – ITALY, with ISBN: 978-88-86449-49-6 and Copyright © UNIDROIT 2023, has a President (M.C. Malaguti) and Secretary General (I. Tirado) foreword dated on September 2023.

[2] In its 102 session (10–12 May 2023) [UNIDROIT 2023 – C.D. (102) 25 – Report, para.106 for the decision, para.92–105 for the discussion at that instance].

[3] UNIDROIT 2023 – C.D. (102) 6, April 2023.

[4] Held in Rome 8–10 March 2023. UNIDROIT 2023 – Study LXXXII – W.G.8 – Doc. 2.

[5] UNIDROIT 2022 – Study LXXXII – W.G.7 – Doc. 2.

[6] A hybrid (remote and with presence) session (still COVID restrictions affects diversely the world) held in Rome 19–21 December 2022, UNIDROIT 2022 – Study LXXXII – W.G.7 – Doc. 1, for the agenda where timing and links are detailed.

[7] At UNIDROIT 2023 – Study LXXXII – W.G.7 – Doc. 5, para.11: "The [Working Group] Chair [Hideki Kanda, according to ibid. para.3; to be distinguished from the Chair of the Drafting Committee: DC Chair, Louise Gullifer, ibid. para.6] invited comments on the style of the Principles, and particularly on whether the Commentary should appear after each sub-provision, or at the end of each Principle. Several Members of the Working Group and Observers agreed that the Commentary should follow each Principle, rather than each sub-provision".

[8] That template follows indications expressed at the first steps on "Format of the Guidance Document", suggested in first place by the UNIDROIT Principles on the Operation of Close-Out Netting Provisions: UNIDROIT 2020 – Study LXXXII – W.G.1 – Doc. 2, para.19.

That 'doing' is manifested on the Working Group agreement on a slight alteration to Principle 3(1)[9]: the final version uses the singular form to facilitate interpretation.[10]

The modifications introduced in the Commentary reflects the Working Group's indications: the adding of clarity in relation with the area covered by domestic law to both the classification of digital assets and the meaning of proprietary rights.[11] These refinements are particularly evident in the new elements of Commentary 3(2) and 3(3)—the former addressing the classification of digital assets,[12] and the latter

[9] See UNIDROIT 2023 – Study LXXXII – W.G.7 – Doc. 5, para.97 and 98.

[10] The singular form of the text eases interpretation, at least by setting aside the question of whether multiple digital assets are required to be subject to proprietary rights, or if the mere presence of one digital asset is sufficient to establish such rights: The version revised by the Working Group in its sixth session said: "Digital assets can be the subject of proprietary rights". While the one adopted by the Working Group's seventh session (which ends up as the final one) said: "A digital asset can be the subject of proprietary rights". As a result from intersessional activities, this is a case of text amendment without an express opinion from the Working Group, but with its final approval (see UNIDROIT 2022 – Study LXXXII – W.G.7 – Doc. 3, p. 21).

[11] "All of the changes in this Principle provide additional clarity on the previous draft, as requested at the Working Group's sixth session. Additional guidance has been provided on the issue of classification of digital assets, which is a matter for domestic law. Additionally, further clarity has been provided on the matter that the Principles do not prescribe what constitutes a proprietary right, which is a matter for domestic law." UNIDROIT 2022 – Study LXXXII – W.G.7 – Doc. 3, para.32.

[12] To facilitate text comparison, the version received during the sixth Working Group session is written before the version resulting from the instructions of that session (summarized in the previous footnote) and adopted during the seventh Working Group session. The received text: "If a specific State law includes classification of different types of property or assets which can be subject to proprietary rights which have different consequences, and it is unclear how digital assets as defined in these Principles must be classified, it is recommended that such States specify which type or types of property digital assets are" (UNIDROIT 2022 – Study LXXXII – W.G.6 – Doc. 2, p. 11). The resulting text (which would be the final one: "Whether digital assets can be the subject of proprietary rights (a legal consequence) must be distinguished from the classification of digital assets. As explained in the commentary to Principle 2(3), these Principles do not prescribe a specific classification of digital assets. That digital assets must be susceptible to proprietary rights as this Principle 3(1) requires, may mean, in certain jurisdictions, that digital assets must be classified as 'property', 'good', 'thing', or similar concept, but this would depend on the applicable law in question and is left for the specific States to decide. If a State's law includes a classification of different categories of assets which can be subject to proprietary rights, and these different categories have different consequences, it is recommended that the State's law should specify which category or categories of assets digital assets are. This is so that digital assets can be subject to proprietary rights. This could mean the introduction of a new category of asset, but again, this is left for the specific States to decide" (UNIDROIT 2022 – Study LXXXII – W.G.7 – Doc. 2, p. 13).

defining the role of domestic law in determining proprietary rights.[13] The Commentary also received some additional improvements to settle internal cross-references and text alignments.

With that slight text evolution in relation to Principle 3 and its Commentary between the two last Working Group sessions (eighth and seventh), the sixth Working Group meeting[14] emerges as especially relevant.

This importance is directly tied to the quantity and quality of work conducted between the fifth and the sixth Working Groups sessions: five Drafting Group meetings were held,[15] the Steering Committee responded to a mandate from the Working Group,[16] the project was reviewed by the UNIDROIT Governing Council,[17] and a special (although focused) workshop was convened.[18] All that meant an additional task for the Drafting Group and the Secretariat in order to "prepare a more consistent and cleaner set of Draft Principles, with a view to moving towards finalisation of the document".[19]

---

[13] Which entirely new text it's a result of intersessional activities. These have consistently been an intense part along all the DAPL previous work. In this episode (between sixth and seventh Working Groups), intersessional activities are presented in UNIDROIT 2023 – Study LXXXII – W.G.7 – Doc. 5, para.7 as an invitation of the Chair to the Drafting Committee Chair ("The Drafting Committee had met thrice during the intersessional period. Its main focus had been to address and incorporate the feedback received from the previous Working Group session and to restructure the Draft Principles accordingly") and to the Steering Committee one (Ms. Monika Paurnekova), whose detail can be seen in *ibid.* para.8–9.

[14] Another hybrid session from 31 August to 2 September 2022 (see UNIDROIT 2022-Study LXXXII – W.G. 6 – Doc. 1, for the agenda).

[15] See UNIDROIT 2022 – Study LXXXII – W.G.6 – Doc. 4, para.6, where the Chair invited the Drafting Committee Chair to present the results of their intersessional work. See also UNIDROIT 2022 – Study LXXXII – W.G.6 – Doc. 3, pp. 1–2 at 2.b), which offers dates and outlines summary of the meetings. All of them are one day meetings with the following dates (in 2022): March 25th, April 8th. and 25th., June 24th. and August 12th.

[16] UNIDROIT 2022 – Study LXXXII – W.G.6 – Doc. 3, para.2.c., which may be partially copied: "a draft of the Principles was shared with the Steering Committee in March–April 2022 alongside questions for which feedback was requested. 24 experts from 14 countries and one Regional Economic Integration Organisation provided comments. All of these can be found in Annex 1 of this document". The compiled responses are contained in UNIDROIT 2022 – Study LXXXII – W.G.6 – Doc. 3 – ANNEX, an eighty-six-page text.

[17] "The comments received as part of the discussions at the 101st Session of the UNIDROIT Governing Council, where the Principles were presented", so at UNIDROIT 2022 – Study LXXXII – W.G.6 – Doc. 3, para.2.d.

[18] "A Special Workshop on Issues Related to Enforcement in Digital Assets, which took place as a side event to the 101st Session of the UNIDROIT Governing Council in Rome and on Zoom on 10 June 2022. The Workshop was attended by Members of the UNIDROIT Governing Council, the UNIDROIT Working Group on Digital Assets and Private Law, the UNIDROIT Working Group on Best Practices in the Field of Effective Enforcement, as well as Members of the Steering Committee of the Working Group on Digital Assets", in UNIDROIT 2022 – Study LXXXII – W.G.6 – Doc. 3, para.2.e. That focusing didn't reduce the effect on all the Project: the DAPL Principles are so intertwined that it seems rather difficult to touch any (even little) aspect without the need to revise almost everything.

[19] UNIDROIT 2022 – Study LXXXII – W.G.6 – Doc. 3, para.2.f.

Regarding the black letter of Principle 3, the agreements reached during the sixth session marked a significant turning point.[20] The revised text of Principle 3(1) clarified the potential of a digital asset to be the object of proprietary rights, and that the Principles' basic rule would be firm from now on.[21] This same Working Group session,[22] helped to delineate the boundaries between Principles law and other law in that section, in response to feedback received prior to the meeting.[23]

A second notable update in the black letter appears in Principle 3(3), having two objectives: to enhance the Principles law pre-eminence (as prior to other law), and to offer a more abstract composition within two other law aspects.

The Principles pre-eminence derives from a subtle alteration in the text of 3(3).[24] The more abstract form for 3(3)(b) and 3(3)(c) stems from the shift to impersonal phrasing, replacing earlier formulations that relied on personal references.[25] Thus,

---

[20] From: "The law should provide that digital assets can be the subject of proprietary rights", to: "Digital assets can be the subject of proprietary rights" (UNIDROIT 2022 – Study LXXXII – W.G.6 – Doc. 3, p.19).

[21] Supra fn. 11–12 for the following amendment. The Working Group decision possesses several aspects that deserve to be underscore, i.e., the notion of property and how digital assets might fit within it, both of which were alluded to during the discussion: "Another Member of the Working Group highlighted the difference between using the term 'property', and the concept of 'proprietary rights', adding that the draft Principles did a good job at using language which dealt with rights with proprietary effects, rather than property, which differed from state to state [sic]. The DC Chair and a Member of the Working Group agreed with this, noting that Paragraph 20 of the Commentary of Principle 3 could be clarified further. However, the word 'property' should still be avoided." (at UNIDROIT 2022 – Study LXXXII – W.G.6 – Doc. 4, para.25). It seems then more interesting to pay attention to this point evolution within the Working Group session because one of the documents in front of the Working Group (UNIDROIT 2022 – Study LXXXII – W.G.6 – Doc. 3, para.35) states: "Additionally, consideration is also being given to defining the term 'proprietary' as part of this Section."

[22] When discussing Principle 5 and its relationship with Principle 16, the proprietary rights issue came back to the discussion and the way to solve it seems conclusive: "The DC Chair noted that Principle 16 was the equivalent of Principle 3(1), whereby it simply indicated that digital assets could be the subject of security rights. It was not intended to detail how creating a security right in a digital asset would operate. It was noted that the matter of what a proprietary right was remained an issue of [sic] for the forum, and the Principles had originally not dealt with this. It was added that the Commentary could explain what the meaning of proprietary right was, should the Working Group decide this would be useful. An Observer from NatLaw agreed with these comments" (at UNIDROIT 2022 – Study LXXXII – W.G.6 – Doc. 4, para.48).

[23] A representative from Japan to the Steering Committee wrote: "Principle 3 does not have clear definition or the list of proprietary issues that the Principle intend to cover, but only has the list of issues that will not be covered by the Principle [...] if you want to clarify the content of some specific proprietary rights under the Principles regardless of the laws of the countries concerned, it seems better to not only list the matters to which the Principles do not apply, but also the matters to which the Principles do apply..." (UNIDROIT 2022 – Study LXXXII – W.G.6 – Doc. 3, para.32).

[24] Instead of affirming at the Principle 3.3 *chapeau*: "Other law applies to all issues not dealt with in these Principles, including ...", the Principle will be read (and that formula also will be maintained): "Except as displaced by these Principles, other law applies to all issues, including ..." (UNIDROIT 2022 – Study LXXXII – W.G.6 – Doc. 3, p.20).

[25] Where it was said: "whether a person has validly transferred a proprietary right in a digital asset to another person" [3(3)(b)] or "whether a person has validly created a security right in a digital

a clear formula establishing the precedence of Principles law was agreed[26] and also the language of 3(3)(b) and 3(3)(c) was modified.[27]

The Commentary on Principle 3 received different modifications on style but only one underlining the private law nature of the projected Principles and the relationship between the Principles law and the other law.[28]

The fifth session of the Working Group[29] encircles an important collection of events for Principle 3. Perhaps, the first to be mentioned should be Principle 4 stemming from Principle 3 that the Working Group Members approved.[30] Secondly, it was

---

asset" [3(3)(c)], it will appear: "whether a digital asset has been validly transferred to another person" [3(3)(b)] and "whether a security right in a digital asset has been validly created" [3(3)(c)] (UNIDROIT 2022 – Study LXXXII – W.G.6 – Doc. 3, p. 20).

[26] In Drafting Committee sixth (UNIDROIT 2022 – Study LXXXII – W.G.6 – Doc. 3, para.31).

[27] "Additional parts of Principle 3(3) have been redrafted in a more passive style for consistency and to suit the nature of the Principles document" (also at UNIDROIT 2022 – Study LXXXII – W.G.6 – Doc. 3, para.31).

[28] The following addition is proposed for the first Commentary number 3(3): "It is reiterated that, first, these Principles cover only private law issues relating to digital assets, so that they do not cover rules that are to be enforced by public authorities which in many jurisdictions would be called 'regulation' or 'regulatory law'. Moreover, these Principles intend to only regulate a specific area of private law, and there are many issues of private law which are not addressed by the Principles. These issues concern, for instance, rules of private law relating to intellectual property or consumer protection. As a matter of principle, these areas of law are not addressed by these Principles, and national intellectual property and consumer protection laws therefore remain unimpaired by them. Finally, there are several issues of property and contract law that these Principles do not cover, and this Principle 3(3) lists important examples those issues. Strictly speaking, 'Except as displaced by these Principles' is redundant, because 'other law' (as defined), is, by definition, law that is not covered by these Principles. It has been for the avoidance of any doubt that Principle 3(3) says that 'except as displaced by these Principles', other law continues to apply. It is not meant to say that a specific State law continues to apply only to the extent these Principles (as contrasted with Principles law) explicitly displace such State law." [UNIDROIT 2022 – Study LXXXII – W.G.6 – Doc. 3, Commentary (then) num.7 (that would become finally 3.8)].

[29] A hybrid session was again developed between 7 and 9 March 2022 (see UNIDROIT 2022 – Study LXXXII – W.G.5– Doc. 1, for the meeting agenda). The Drafting Committee (having hold four meetings since Working Group fourth session: two in January and another two in February, see UNIDROIT 2022 – Study LXXXII – W.G.5– Doc. 4, para.7) got two documents ready for the Working Group session: UNIDROIT 2022 – Study LXXXII – W.G.5– Doc 2, a "Master Copy of Black Letter Principles", and UNIDROIT 2022 – Study LXXXII – W.G.5– Doc.3, a "Master Copy of the Principles and Comments". The last one inserts questions to the Working Group at the end of each Commentary section (29 questions numbered consecutively) in order to attract Working Group's attention on points where answers were convenient.

[30] In UNIDROIT 2022 – Study LXXXII – W.G.5 – Doc. 4, para.11, the Drafting Committee Chair (Louise Gullifer) presented the Principle 4 as "an entirely new Principle". During the session, however, some consideration was given to this issue of introducing a new Principle. So can be read in para.44 (ibid.): "Sub-Group 4 Co-Chair Elisabeth Noble queried whether Principle 4 ought to become Principle 3(4) to retain consistency in terms of overall structure. The DC Chair acknowledged this point and noted that the reason for potentially retaining Principle 4 as a separate Principle was because it contained a considerable amount of commentary providing examples of linked assets." What is now Principle 4 was previously part of Principle 3.

decided for the title for Principle 3 as "General principles"[31] to remain.[32] Thirdly, the new formula for 3(2) was raised during the discussion.[33] Fourthly, indications on the nature of 3(3) as an open list of items[34] and about its aims was decided.[35]

Although the Commentary was rather new[36] and opinions had been requested,[37] the Working Group focused on the black letter of Principle 3 leaving the Commentary almost without any additional attention or direction.[38]

---

[31] Although the intervention by the UNCITRAL representative regarding Principle 3(3) raised a question of scope, suggesting that Principle 3(3) "would ordinarily say something along the lines of "these Principles do not do this", or "nothing in these Principles affects", etc.", and perhaps ought to be relocated, "the Working Group discussed a possible rearrangement of Principle 3(3) into Principle 1 to reflect it being a scope provision." However, it was apparently concluded that Principle 3(3) was appropriately placed and that the title of Principle 3 adequately encompassed the content of 3(3).

[32] In its "introduction" as Chair of the Drafting Committee, Louise Gullifer informs of that, as well as the reception in Principle 3 of new items ("a number of principles considered to be of a broader relevance were shifted to Principle 3, now called General Principles", see UNIDROIT 2022 – Study LXXXII – W.G.5– Doc. 4, para.9). Later in the session the Drafting Committee Chair insists on the issue: "The DC Chair presented Principle 8, flagging that most of the Principle's previous substance had been moved to Principle 3." (UNIDROIT 2022 – Study LXXXII – W.G.5– Doc. 4, para.103, and see also para.104 almost with the same wording but in relation with Principle 9).

[33] In UNIDROIT 2022 – Study LXXXII – W.G.5– Doc. 4, para.41, it is alluded the Sub-Group 2 Co-Chair Matthias Haentjens intervention about Question 9 (in UNIDROIT 2022 – Study LXXXII – W.G.5– Doc.3, p.13), that is rephrased so: "to what extent general principles would apply to digital assets as defined in the Principles." The ALI (American Law Institute) representative (Steven Weise) reply succeeded and framed Principle 3(2) for the future. He "proposed a concise generic statement that dealt with the interaction between the Principles and digital assets law in different jurisdictions. It was further suggested that this generic statement should be expressed as an operative Principle (perhaps using words similar to those used in the US Uniform Laws such as "to the extent displaced by this law"), which would then be supplemented with supporting commentary." This approach was followed by the Working Group agreement: "it should be made explicit where the "Principles Law" took precedence over the "other Law" and where that "other Law" derogated from these Principles" (at UNIDROIT 2022 – Study LXXXII – W.G.5– Doc. 4, para.42).

[34] It was enhanced during the discussion the open character of the list included in Principle 3(3): "It was clarified that the list of not covered issues in Principle 3(3) was non-exhaustive but gave guidance to the audience on the matters not covered by these Principles." (at UNIDROIT 2022 – Study LXXXII – W.G.5– Doc. 4, para.46).

[35] Words from the Drafting Committee Chair presenting that rule as: "clarifying that these Principles did not deal with every single proprietary aspect of control and transfer, and noted that the list from (a) to (g) was not an exclusive list, but was merely indicative." (at UNIDROIT 2022 – Study LXXXII – W.G.5– Doc. 4, para.39). And adding (ibid. para.40): "Principle 3(3) concerned the interaction between digital assets law and Principles law and the rest of the legal system."

[36] So affirmed by Louise Gullifer at the Working Group session first steps: "In terms of the commentary [...] were few changes made to what was already drafted by the time of the last Working Group session, with the major exceptions of new commentary to Principle 1 and Principle 3" (at UNIDROIT 2022 – Study LXXXII – W.G.5– Doc. 4, para.11).

[37] The Drafting Committee Chair "queried whether more commentary and guidance were required for this Principle." (UNIDROIT 2022 – Study LXXXII – W.G.5 – Doc. 4, para. 40).

[38] One exception is counted on Marek Dubovec, Sub-Group 3 Chair. He "remarked that the commentary could be amended to suggest a State might want to specify which general rules did not apply to DAs [sic] (rather than list all the rules which did)", ibid., at para. 47.

The Working Group's fourth session took place again in a hybrid form.[39] This was the last session with the prior sub-groups structure.[40] Under the title: "Acquisition and Disposition ('Transfer') of Digital Assets",[41] Principle [X.2] was the rule closest to the future Principle 3 among those revised by the Working Group. Principle [X.2] containing partly and roughly what would eventually be found in Principle 3: the applicability of proprietary rights to digital assets,[42] the need to specify which law governs that issue,[43] and the specification of the law governing related questions about proprietary rights in digital assets.[44]

---

[39] 2–4 November 2021, see the agenda at UNIDROIT 2021 – Study LXXXII – W.G.4 – Doc. 1.

[40] The purpose of that structure was to order and to make to progress faster the intersessional work. The four working areas' titles were (as listed in UNIDROIT 2021 – Study LXXXII – W.G.4 – Doc. 1): Control and Custody (Sub-Group 1), Control and Transfer (Sub-Group 2), Secured Transactions (Sub-Group 3), Taxonomy and Private international law (Sub-Group 4). That work order generated some overlapping as two Sub-Groups could deal with the same point (an evidence, for instance, in UNIDROIT 2021 – Study LXXXII – W.G.4 – Doc. 2, p. 43, fn. 19, where it is said: "This comment is similar to [Control] Principle X.1D, Explanation and commentary, paragraph 2. Ultimately the point of these comments might be made as a part of only one of the Principles with that Principle containing only a cross-reference to other relevant Principles."). Precisely, when the Working Group session was ending, a proposal from the Working Group Chair for a change of method reached consensus: to establish a little Drafting Group with the Sub-Groups Co-Chairs, that the Sub-Groups should sent "revised versions of the explanations and illustrations accompanying the draft Principles at the next Working Group session", the set-up of workshops on detailed questions (UNIDROIT 2021 – Study LXXXII – W.G.4 – Doc. 3, para. 164 to 166 respectively, para.167 for the Secretary General endorsement).

[41] In Annex III, Appendix 2 – SUB-GROUP 2 – Control and Transfer, at UNIDROIT 2021 – Study LXXXII – W.G.4 – Doc. 2, p.41.

[42] Appears (ibid.) in Principle [X.2] (2) with the following wording: "The law should provide that digital assets may be the subject of proprietary rights."

[43] As (ibid.) Principle [X.2] (1) with the text: "The applicable law other than law governing digital assets contemplated by these principles (ie, the digital assets law) should specify which (if any) of its existing rules or standards of general application govern the acquisition and disposition of proprietary rights in digital assets. (As used in these Principles references to proprietary rights include proprietary interests and rights with proprietary effects.)"

[44] At (ibid.) Principle [X.2] (4): "Except as otherwise provided in these Principles, the applicable law other than the digital assets law governs issues relating to proprietary rights, such as: // (a) whether a person has a proprietary right in a digital asset; // (b) whether a person has validly transferred a proprietary right in a digital asset to another person and the requirements for any such transfer; // (c) the rights as between a transferor and transferee of digital assets and derivative digital assets inter se; and // (d) the requirements for and legal consequences of a transfer of digital assets vis-à-vis third parties (ie, "third-party effectiveness")."

Reactions to the projected rule stemmed from the same document, presented under the section titled "Key considerations in respect of this Principle",[45] followed by another section entitled "Explanation and commentary".[46]

Perhaps the wide scope of work faced by the Working Group, along with the limited session time, resulted in only a very restricted reference to Principle [X.2] during the meeting. The substance of the discussion could be summarised as difficulties in defining the notion of "applicable law" and how to reflect that within the Principle, particularly considering the Principle's two-fold approach to the law: whether, over time, there will be a distinction between "other law" and the "Principles law." However, that clarity had still not emerged months later.[47]

---

[45] There were two of them (and both are interesting). The first one said: "This Principle addresses several substantive provisions [...]. But it also is very much directed to the scope of the issues relating to proprietary rights in digital assets—ie, matters that are and that are not covered by the Principle—and thus to the scope of the digital assets law" (UNIDROIT 2021 – Study LXXXII – W.G.4 – Doc. 2, p.43). The second one is more explicative about the understanding of some Principle [X.2] used terms (part of them will appear further within the Principle 7 Commentary): "References in this Principle to "the law" or to "the digital assets law" contemplate positive legal rules that would address specifically digital assets. However, this Principle takes no position as to whether those rules should be included in a special law on digital assets, incorporated into more general laws, or addressed by a combination of these approaches. References in this Principle to applicable law other than law governing digital assets contemplated by these Principles (ie, the digital assets law) are to laws of general application that do not address specifically digital assets."

[46] From that section, it could be extracted its number two [as it can illuminate the future Principle 3(3)]: "The deference to other law mentioned in subparagraph (a) of paragraph (4) [its text appears above at fn. 44] is consistent, for example, with the approach in the Cape Town Convention, which defers to other law as to whether a person has a "power to dispose" of an interest in mobile equipment. The deference to other law mentioned in subparagraph (b) contemplates, for example, that a transfer may require an agreement or manifestation of intention by a transferor or that such an agreement might by itself result in a transfer of proprietary rights (whether or not limited in effect to the parties as contemplated by subparagraph (c) and subject to the digital assets law, including, but not limited to, paragraph 8(c)).", at UNIDROIT 2021 – Study LXXXII – W.G.4 – Doc. 2, p.43.

[47] It began with Sub-Group 4 Co-Chair Philipp Paech's proposition: "that the reference to the "applicable law other than law governing digital assets contemplated by these principles" in the first sentence of Principle X.2, para. 1. be simplified to refer to 'the law' for the time being, as previous experience had shown the difficulty in clarifying which law was being referred to, e.g. material law, substantive law, conflict-of-laws, etc." (at UNIDROIT 2021 – Study LXXXII – W.G.4 – Doc. 3, para.36). It was followed by another expert's suggestion: "that the commentary should simply state: "the applicable law contemplated by these principles should specify which, if any, of its existing rules or standards of general application govern the acquisition and disposition of proprietary rights of digital assets". Taking this approach, the domestic legal system could then decide whether it wanted to do this via the general rules of application, or whether they contemplated specific rules for property in digital assets." (ibid. para.37) With a third group of interventions that clarifies that opened end discussion: "Several experts remarked that it was often impossible to determine the applicable law, especially within permissionless open systems. An expert suggested that in these instances, a court may simply adopt broad rules that apply to the area of law in question – a technique which already existed in France, among other legal systems" (ibid. para.38).

The Third Working Group session was also held in a hybrid format.[48] The document guiding the Working Group's discussion[49] included a draft of Principle [X.2], which was almost identical to the version presented during the Group's fourth session.[50]

During the third Working Group's session, it became evident how the Chair of the Working Group emphasised the importance of intersessional work.[51] In relation with what would be the future of Principle 3, the discussion was quite short (there was limited time and a significant number of topics to address).[52] Although short, the discussion was substantial in content, particularly when the Chairs of Sub-Group 2[53] presented the origins and reasons for the draft proposal on Principle [X.2]. In relation to Principle 3, the idea of seeking the basic points (referred to as "building block")[54] comes out, as well as the relationship between the law proposed in the Principles and the local law and the pattern selected for that interaction.[55]

The second session of the Working Group was also conducted remotely.[56] The "issues paper"[57] for that session shows how the project's object had matured surprisingly. In this regard, it is worth emphasising the timeframe of this meeting: held from 16 to 18 March 2021[58]: only six months (22–24 September 2020) after the Governing

---

[48] See UNIDROIT 2021 – Study LXXXII – W.G.3 – Doc. 1 (rev. 1) for the session's agenda taking place from 30 June to 2 July 2021.

[49] UNIDROIT 2021 – Study LXXXII – W.G.3 – Doc. 2 (rev. 1).

[50] See supra fn. 42–44 for the alluded one. The difference is strictly formal: what it is "General comment" for the Working Group's third session partly constitutes "Key considerations in respect of this Principle", and what are now Comment 1 and Comment 2 appears as "Explanation and commentary" for the following session.

[51] In UNIDROIT 2021 – Study LXXXII – W.G.3 – Doc. 4, para.7 (as a response to the presentation of the "Outcomes and reflections from the "Digital Twins" Workshop (31 May 2021) and future work"), he proposed: "that additional Special Workshops be organised to examine other cross-cutting matters which concerned multiple Sub-Groups such as the control principle and custody of digital assets, with the first to be held before the next Working Group session".

[52] In UNIDROIT 2021 – Study LXXXII – W.G.3 – Doc. 4, where the Working Group's third session Summary Report figures, there are ten paragraphs devoted to the point: para. 41 to 51, pp. 6–7.

[53] Charles Mooney. Jr., and Matthias Haentjens (ibid, para.41).

[54] Ibid, para.42, where it is written: "the Sub-Group had sought to consider the most basic building block principles of property law, referred to as proprietary interests, including interests which have proprietary effects under the relevant law, while questioning which of these building block principles the digital asset law (provisions of law dealing directly with digital assets) should address and in what manner. Moreover, this was considered with respect to law other than "digital assets law", i.e., the general law of the State which did not directly address digital assets."

[55] Ibid, para.43, records the following clarification: "The Co-Chairs remarked that this pattern was previously adopted in the Geneva Securities Convention, where the impossibility of harmonisation of numerous legal principles relating to intermediated securities in a hard law document was noted. Accordingly, when such harmonisation was not possible, an explicit reference was made to so-called non-Convention law, i.e., the law of the Contracting State other than Convention law. As the DAPL Project was a soft law instrument, there was more flexibility in the development of the Principles."

[56] UNIDROIT 2021 – Study LXXXII – W.G.2 – Doc. 1, displays the Working Group's agenda.

[57] UNIDROIT 2021 – Study LXXXII – W.G.2 – Doc. 2 (rev. 1).

[58] Supra fn. 57.

Council[59] decided to change the name of this project, to clarify its object and the manner to carry it out,[60] transforming what was initially labelled "Work on Artificial Intelligence, Smart Contracts and DLT (Distributed Ledger Technology)".[61]

These new directions were the result of extensive work, to offer more ground to the Governing Council's decision: two joint workshops to narrow down the subject, ending up in a document for the Spring Governing Council meeting.[62] This document set out various aspects of the project: emphasising key principles in the field of private law, with a focus on digital assets (referred to as tokens), the need to clarify essential topics such as property rights, secured transactions, exchanges and custodians, insolvency, and the applicable law in cross-border activities, and the need to emphasise a technology-neutral approach.[63]

The Spring (2020) Governing Council confirms this approach and the Secretariat with its mandate nominated Professor Hideki Kanda as Chair of the Exploratory Working Group. This group held five meetings between May and September, in addition to organising two Exploratory Workshops on Digital Assets and Private Law, which culminated in a Preliminary Issues Paper.[64]

The expected content for the work was also presented to the Governing Council: the idea of principles with commentaries and its denomination as "The UNIDROIT

---

[59] In its second session of that year, the other one was in Spring, as usual (April/May 2020, a remote session in the wake of the COVID-19), see UNIDROIT 2020 – C.D. (99) B.21 – Report.

[60] Ibid, para.91: "The Governing Council approved the temporary change of name of the project to "Digital Assets and Private Law" and decided in favour of an "enhanced" structure for the project which would entail setting up a Steering Committee composed of additional experts from different technical and legal fields and reflecting a diversity in terms of legal systems background and geography." In para.90, the allowance to the Secretariat for the Working Group establishment and the confirmation for the high priority status given to the Project appears.

[61] Ibid, Agenda Item 4(b).

[62] Ibid, para.60, with a document submitted to the Spring Governing Council meeting.

[63] What it is said in para.60 deserves to be partially copied: "the project would aim to develop principles relating to the legal nature, transfer and use of tokens. It would focus on private law, and not regulation. It would consist of a legal taxonomy, along with consideration of specific issues arising in various contexts, such as insolvency, secured transactions, identification of the applicable law in cross-border transactions, and the legal position of intermediaries involved in the token markets, such as exchanges and custodians. It would take a functional approach, neutral as to legal culture and seek to identify the rights and obligations arising from transactions in digital assets in different jurisdictions. Further, it would consider how far the principles developed by the project were consistent with existing law. While tokens were a new type of asset, consistency with legal treatment of other types of assets would be important, and consideration would need to be given to what extent existing legal principles could apply by analogy, and what modifications would be required. The project would also take a neutral approach, insofar as possible, in relation to technology, so as to "future proof" the principles. As such, it would seek to develop principles that could apply to any system in which data could constitute a digital asset, rather than being specifically applicable to systems based on DLT or blockchain. In this way, the danger that the work would be overtaken by technological or market developments would be minimised."

[64] Ibid., para.61.

Principles and Legislative Guidance on Digital Assets and Private Law".[65] The refinement of the scope proposed within the Spring Governing Council led to a proposal "to focus on private law issues relating to digital assets, with particular emphasis on proprietary interests".[66]

UNIDROIT's President then gave the floor to Professor Kanda who, with the recent (September 17–18) Exploratory Workshop on digital assets and private law results, stated the goal of the project,[67] the difficulty of the notion of digital assets,[68] and affirmed a collection of principles as the instrument's prospective nature.[69] Ms. Pauknerová, as Czech representative on the Governing Council, recalled that her country sent the first proposal for working on this issue and consequently expressed her congratulations to the Secretariat for the Exploratory Workshop and Mr. Kanda's election as its Chair. She noted that she had attended the Exploratory Workshop and praised its high quality, outlining eight key issues the project should address,[70] among others. She supported the Working Group's establishment.[71]

The previously mentioned intervention was followed by a series of others. Their addition offered more acute profiles on the importance of the subject matter of this work, and consequently its high priority within UNIDROIT's agenda, the need to compose a balanced Working Group and the desirability of paying attention to other organisations' work on the issue.[72] The Secretary General's intervention, summarising the main arguments, marked an end to the discussion[73] and grounded the decision.[74]

Two months later,[75] the aforementioned Governing Council agreement took place at the Working Group's First session. The "issues paper" for this Working Group's

---

[65] Ibid., para.62.

[66] Ibid., para.63.

[67] "[T]o reduce legal uncertainty which judges, lawyers, and market participants would face in the coming years in dealing with digital assets", ibid., para.69.

[68] Ibid., para.70.

[69] Ibid., para.71.

[70] Ibid., para.72. Those points deserve to be mentioned: "(i) contract law and digital assets and related questions of acquisition, ownership, and control over digital assets, and disposal thereof; (ii) the relationship between digital assets and other assets in the legal sense; (iii) principles of private law as they applied to digital assets; (iv) the involvement of third parties as intermediaries to digital assets transactions; (v) the provision of custody services; (vi) the treatment of digital assets in insolvency proceedings and possible impact of such proceedings on the digital assets; (vii) protection of the ownership or control of digital assets (the question of remedies and enforceability of rights in digital assets); and (viii) the applicable law in international situations involving digital assets."

[71] Ibid., para.73.

[72] Other Governing Council member interventions: Ms Broka, Mr Gabriel, Ms Sabo, Ms Dacoronia, Mr Meier, Ms Villata, Mr Leinonen, Ms Fauvarque-Cosson, and the UNCITRAL representative (Mr Estrella Faria), at ibid, para. 75 to 86.

[73] Ibid., at. para.87 to 89.

[74] Supra fn. 61.

[75] UNIDROIT 2020 – Study LXXXII – W.G.1 – Doc. 1, from 17 to 19 November 2020, for the meeting's agenda.

meeting reveals different items of the work extremes that would be maintained throughout the process of forming the DAPL Principles: the document's objectives and methods[76] are taken from the Governing Council's decision. Notably, the emphasis was placed on proprietary rights[77] and technological neutrality.[78] That document also includes questions to the Working Group in order to clarify the path for the evolution of the future project.[79]

The election of Professor Kanda as Chair was the Group's first decision.[80] The discussions then followed the structure of the "issues paper" order.[81] The conclusions on that discussion show how the Working Group's task was then orientated. The Chair proposed four Sub-Groups, each with two Co-Chairs (one for each major law system) plus another devoted to Private International Law issues. All Working Group

---

[76] So, "a set of Principles with commentary [...] which would include a legal taxonomy relating to digital assets, plus consideration of legal issues arising in particular contexts. A functional approach to legal concepts was deemed to be most appropriate [...] which could be applied and reflected in any given legal system or culture. The Principles would embody best practice and international standards and would enable jurisdictions to take a common approach to legal issues arising out of the holding, transfer and use of digital assets across a variety of use cases" at UNIDROIT 2020 – Study LXXXII – W.G.1 – Doc. 2, para.18.

[77] Then, "proprietary interests" (ibid., para.35), although it is further indicated later: "digital assets that are plausibly objects of property rights, or perhaps rights similar to property rights." (ibid., para.40).

[78] Ibid., para.42.

[79] "Should the scope of the project be limited to digital assets that are transferable? // If so, what is the meaning of transferability? Would this encompass "transfers" that contemplate the disappearance, destruction, cancellation, or elimination of a digital asset and the resulting and corresponding derivative acquisition of other digital assets? // Should tradeability be another element that determines or affects the scope of the Principles? // Should the Principles reflect other specific criteria to carefully exclude certain digital assets from the scope (i.e. electronic data such as digital images)? // Would it be helpful to conduct a brief survey regarding the variety of approaches regarding the "property status" of electronic data typically found across national jurisdictions in order to identify common problems? // Should the concept of "control" be regarded (to the extent possible) as a factual state of affairs (or a functional concept), rather than as a legal concept?" (ibid., para.46).

[80] At UNIDROIT 2021 – Study LXXXII – W.G.1 – Doc. 4, para.9.

[81] Ibid, para.10. That "issues paper" identifies the document: UNIDROIT 2020 – Study LXXXII – W.G.1 – Doc. 2, which Section II under de title: "Scope of the Guidance Document" (pp. 8–22) introduces the key aspects for the work to begin: "(A) Relationship with existing instruments and other projects of the current Work Programme", "(B) General: Private law relating to Digital Assets, in particular proprietary interests", "(C) The subject matter of the project", and "(D) Identify specific areas/issues of private law to be addressed". Nine numbers are distinguished within this group: "Issues relating to the contract involving digital assets. Acquisition, disposition, and competing claims. The legal nature of a proprietary connection between digital data and another asset. Accommodation of disparate types of assets and technologies. Provision of digital asset custody services. Taking of security over digital assets. The legal treatment of digital assets in relation to insolvency proceedings. Remedies and Enforcement. Law applicable to issues relating to digital assets." The study of that document and its echoes in Working Group would be interesting as a further research subject.

members were invited to participate in the Sub-Groups of their preference.[82] Sub-Groups were conceived to facilitate a draft for the next Working Group session.[83] That meant a considerable amount of work between the first Working Group session and the following one.

In relation with Sub-Group 2—Control and transfer, the following "issues paper" informs of three intersessional meetings.[84]

Thus, it is clear why a draft of Principle [X.2] could be presented at the second session of the Working Group.[85]

After this section, reading it makes one point unmistakably clear: the quantity and the quality of the work developed. The huge number of hours devoted to the project by (mainly) the Working Group members, the UNIDROIT Secretariat and (also by) all the people close to them meaning they were able to achieve something that can only be described as a piece of extremely valuable work. That picture explains the results, (I would say) absolutely unexpected.

2.3 DAPL Principle 3 Aims

Before progressing any further, it is important to highlight that Principle 3 perhaps conveys more clearly than the other Principles,[86] what might be called the UNIDROIT DAPL Principles "targeted audience and intended purpose".[87]

---

[82] "[A] number of subgroups be established with two co-chairs to represent both common law and civil law jurisdictions. The four subgroups would address the following topics: (1) holding (including custody); (2) transfer; (3) secured transactions; and (4) taxonomy (in coordination with UNCITRAL) and private international law issues (in coordination with HCCH). All members and observers were welcome to participate in all groups." At UNIDROIT 2021 – Study LXXXII – W.G.1 – Doc. 4, para.188. Further it is said that the Secretariat will arrange a system of communication to avoid overlapping (ibid, para.192).

[83] Ibid., para.188.

[84] 20 January and 10 and 24 February [at UNIDROIT 2021 – Study LXXXII – W.G.2 – Doc. 2 (rev. 1), p. 46, in which the working plan for those sessions (two hours each but evidently quite focused) appears.

[85] Ibid., p. 19.

[86] And it may be an interpretation key for Principle 3 and, perhaps, for all DAPL UNIDROIT Principles.

[87] To follow the terms already established in the main document (issues paper) presented to the first Working Group: UNIDROIT 2020 – Study LXXXII – W.G.1 – Doc. 2, para.20. There, it can be read: "the prospective guidance document should be relevant for both common law and civil law States and would aim to reduce legal uncertainty which practitioners, judges, legislators and market participants would face in the coming years in dealing with digital assets." This statement rephrases, almost without modification, what was said during the Governing Council, which formally marked the beginning of the work: see above fn. 67, and accompanying text and notes.

A previous footnote underscores two central axes of UNIDROIT work on digital assets and private law. First, a community of users broadly referred to as "law professionals" (and others in the digital assets marketplace). Second, the overarching goal of increasing legal certainty in this area of private law.

As a consequence, the UNIDROIT DAPL Principles ought to deal with private law, of course, but they do so, so to speak, at a legislative level. The DAPL Principles are in fact private law, but they are almost *constitutional* private law, as they contain indications for legislators and States, rather than dealing solely with what is traditionally understood as private law: regulating relationships among citizens, ordinary people, with a (normally) dispositive frame. This perspective is substantial for a better understanding of Principle 3.

The idea that Principle 3 is drafted in the language of constitutional private law, insofar as it offers indications to legislators on how to arrange private law on digital assets,[88] is nevertheless enlightened by the approach to digital assets made by the Principles: the neutrality on technology, the functionality on legal concepts.[89]

When this perspective remains clear and well established, the three sections of Principle 3 can be better understood, as they did not delve into private law concepts,[90] but they set private law fences (between the national law where the Principles law is adopted and the general national law) with additional indications about what ought to be on each side of the division.

From Principle 3 title, "*General principles*",[91] the general category which inspires the rule is declared. This generality unfolds in three points: a digital asset is suitable to be the subject of property rights (2.3.1), a law based on the DAPL Principles has priority (2.3.2), and the issues outside of the Principles ought to be governed by each national law (2.3.3).

---

[88] This is perhaps more important for those familiar with other UNIDROIT works, where the Rome's Institute focuses on the private law (business) relationships instead of the private law (business) legislation (with the idea of indicating how a specific rule ought to be designed).

[89] Also, from the first "issues paper": UNIDROIT 2020 – Study LXXXII – W.G.1 – Doc. 2, para.12 (coming from the Exploratory Group previous to the Working Group): "The project would also take a neutral approach, as far as possible, in relation to technology, so as to 'future proof' the Principles. In other words, it would seek to develop Principles that could apply to any system in which data could constitute a token (that is, an asset which could only be spent once), rather than being specifically applicable to systems based on DLT or blockchain. In this way, the danger that the work would be overtaken by technological or market developments would be minimised". And ibid. at para.18: "A functional approach to legal concepts was deemed to be most appropriate in order to produce a set of Principles which would not be jurisdiction specific, but which could be applied and reflected in any given legal system or culture." It is also important to recall the inspiration for these words from the previous UNIDROIT Governing Council, as can be seen before in fn. 67 and the corresponding text and notes.

[90] Exploring private law concepts and attempting to define them seems to contradict the aim and philosophy of UNIDROIT DAPL Principles, particularly Principle 3, as suggested by the text of the above document at the beginning, in fn. 87 and fn. 89 (and it will be orderly discussed below).

[91] For that title origin, supra fn. 32.

2.3.1 "Proprietary Rights" Applicable to Digital Assets

The first rule on Principle 3 appears as a very basic one, but it is precisely in its simplicity that its importance lies: proprietary rights can encompass a digital asset.

It can be seen as a "foundation principle". It was formulated[92] and reiterated right from the beginning of the project.[93] It stands as an "*instruction*" to the Working Group.[94]

There are good reasons to develop the Principles starting with this idea. In some States, when Judges were required to decide on the applicability of proprietary rights to digital assets, those decisions were not in the line of enshrining digital assets into proprietary rights.[95]

Also, from that starting point, there were references to legal reforms in some States. Along these lines, the need to clarify the possibility for digital assets to be the object of proprietary rights was highlighted.[96]

Acknowledging the difficulties arising from a traditional legal understanding,[97] early in the discussions the notion of digital assets as a manifestation of proprietary

---

[92] "The focus of the project is on private law, and, in this context, this implies, generally though not exclusively, property law (widely construed). Therefore, in the first instance, this project is concerned with digital assets that are plausibly objects of property rights, or perhaps rights similar to property rights", at UNIDROIT 2020 – Study LXXXII – W.G.1 – Doc. 2, para.40. But see also before fn. 77 and fn. 60 (then as "proprietary interests", at the Spring Governing Council).

[93] Even literally: see UNIDROIT 2021 – Study LXXXII – W.G.2 – Doc. 2 (rev. 1), para.44 (below fn.104 its full text).

[94] "It [the Working Group in defining the scope of the project] may wish to further specify that it is limited to digital data which can or should be the subject of property rights (or analogous rights)", at UNIDROIT 2020 – Study LXXXII – W.G.1 – Doc. 2, para.46.

[95] During the first Working Group discussions, a case from Japan, Mt. Gox case, attracted attention as it was clear that the Court didn't recognize proprietary rights to digital assets. The following is a presentation during the first Working Group meeting: "Mr Morishita examined the Mt. Gox case to identify the rights of customers who deposited virtual currencies in digital exchanges which had later become bankrupt. In this case, the Tokyo District Court held that customers were not entitled to Bitcoin they had deposited since they were not deemed to own them, as under Japanese law, 'ownership' could only exist in assets which were tangible and subject to exclusive control. This judgment did not explore the legal nature of Bitcoin itself or its return based on other grounds.", at UNIDROIT 2021 – Study LXXXII – W.G.1 – Doc. 3, para.9.

[96] In UNIDROIT 2020 – Study LXXXII – W.G.1 – Doc. 2, para.46, its fn. 7 declares: "It is noted that there are jurisdictions where tokens and other digital assets are not currently treated as property, but there is a growing consensus that they should be. See, for instance, Germany's recent draft bill which proposes to deem electronic securities without a paper certificate as objects of property pursuant to art. 90 of the BGB."

[97] "Nevertheless, the problem of mapping digital assets onto existing notions of patrimony or things continued to exist, especially since they were incorporeal but might not represent a right to performance of an obligation owed by another party, but merely had value by virtue of the willingness of people to accept them in exchange for other things of value. In this regard, these types of digital assets fell into the category of things that many systems would only accept if they were corporeal." so at UNIDROIT 2021 – Study LXXXII – W.G.1 – Doc. 3, para.12.

rights became apparent.[98] Consequently, the need to follow a practical and functional approach to evade formal concepts that could oppose the construction of digital assets as another manifestation of proprietary rights became clear.[99] Proceeding in this methodological manner during the discussions was reinforced by the Chairman of the Working Group through very clear statements.[100] It was soon recognised as a point of agreement.[101]

[98] "He [Mr. Allen] noted that most legal systems offered different rules for tangible and intangible objects, with some legal systems not recognising intangible objects as the subject of property rights. Legal systems also worked with a positive–negative binary approach which distinguished between fixed categories such as real and personal property (with anything not being real property being personal property), or moveable and immovable property (where anything which was not immovable was moveable). These types of approaches failed to align with the technical and legal realities towards which digital asset taxonomies pointed and had resulted in domestic civil law legislations trying to incorporate digital assets into traditional legal theories and conceptualisations", so at UNIDROIT 2021 – Study LXXXII – W.G.1 – Doc. 3, para.17.

[99] (With the same starring that in precedent footnote): "He [Mr. Allen] underscored the importance of adopting a functional approach and a technologically neutral perspective in undertaking this work, while at the same time ensuring that relevant applicable legal doctrines were adequately considered." at UNIDROIT 2021 – Study LXXXII – W.G.1 – Doc. 3, para.16.

[100] See UNIDROIT 2021 – Study LXXXII – W.G.1 – Doc. 4, para.28, with Paech and Weise concurrent opinion (ibid. para.31) and additional nuances from the last one (ibid. para.44).

[101] See UNIDROIT 2021 – Study LXXXII – W.G.2 – Doc. 2 (rev. 1), para.52, where it is used a clear expression "a descriptive, neutral approach to scope is preferable" together with another one at the same line of thought: "rather than get attached to terms which presupposed certain definitions, the WG should focus on a factual description of very practical cases it wished to examine".

That pragmatic path led to the notion of "control" as an alternative to physical possession.[102] It was repeatedly stated[103] from different perspectives[104] and there was eventually (at a very early stage) a consensus.[105]

Perhaps Principle [X2][106] should be recognised as the formal starting point for this issue. This is the evolution of the "building block", as presented in the early documents.[107]

How the rule evolved, from its initial form in the plural to the singular as it stands today[108] was in order to avoid, as suggested, interpretation hurdles derived from a hypothetical requirement involving more than one digital asset, seems to indicate the Working Group's deep knowledge about how the rule would work in different jurisdictions. Nonetheless, the foundation was solid almost from the outset: digital assets are able to be the object of proprietary rights. This statement is written to help the world's legal community and digital assets marketplace to add further evidence (certainly quite important as sufficient to help States, legislators and tribunals to

---

102 Also, very soon in the deliberations: "What are the factual features which distinguish those digital objects that should be recognised as objects of proprietary rights from those which should not? In this context, a functional approach could be called for, and the object's amenability to control would seem of paramount importance" [and follow with the statement] "In previous work on the harmonisation of private law (for example the UNCITRAL Model Law on Electronic Transferable Records) the concept of control has been adopted as an analogue of possession, given that electronic records are not capable of possession in the ordinary legal sense, which implies amenability to physical possession in the factual sense". At Unidroit 2020 – Study LXXXII – W.G.1 – Doc. 2, para.44.

103 For instance: "Since digital assets form the basic units of digital transacting, the fundamental question was whether private law recognised such assets as patrimonial assets, or as things which were the subject of real rights (or proprietary interests in common law), as these were transactional units recognised by all systems of private law. Mr Fox noted that digital assets shared many of the general characteristics of other assets currently recognised as property. This included their ability to be specifically individuated and exclusively controlled. Additionally, transactions with digital assets often also took place on a publicly discoverable ledger", at Unidroit 2021 – Study LXXXII – W.G.1 – Doc. 3, para.12.

104 "The focus of the project is on private law, and, in this context, this implies, generally though not exclusively, property law (widely construed). Therefore, in the first instance, this project is concerned with digital assets that are plausibly objects of property rights, or perhaps rights similar to property rights. The focus on proprietary rights, however, presents a difficulty in terms of distinguishing cause and effect. Current principles of property law in different jurisdictions yield contradictory answers to the question whether any particular type of electronic data can be the object of proprietary rights, and indeed suggest quite different approaches to conceptualising intangible representations of value generally. Not all types of electronic data that the project will examine are considered as "property" in some jurisdictions", at Unidroit 2021 – Study LXXXII – W.G.2 – Doc. 2 (rev. 1), para.44.

105 "The Working Group agreed that "subject to control" denoted the correct proprietary aspect to the assets with which the Project was concerned.", at Unidroit 2021 – Study LXXXII – W.G.3 – Doc. 4, para.19.

106 See fn. 42 for its content in relation with Principle 3(1) and origins, as well as fn. 49 with their texts of reference.

107 See fn. 54 to realize when the graphic expression was used.

108 See fn. 9-fn.10.

assert) that proprietary rights are applicable to digital assets.[109] Additionally, the penultimate modification of Principle 3(1) illustrates the same aspect, changing from "The law should provide that digital assets can be the subject of proprietary rights", to "Digital assets can be the subject of proprietary rights".[110]

What the understanding of "proprietary rights" would be was a matter of discussion for the Working Group that (also quite early on) confirmed its standpoint through different assertions set forth in the documents throughout the years of work. Two key points clearly emerged from those discussions: the DAPL Principle clear boundaries: "what constitutes a 'proprietary right' is a matter of domestic law",[111] and the reiteration that digital assets are the object of proprietary rights.[112]

2.3.2 "Principle's Law" Precedence

The Principle 3(2) rule clarifies the primacy of the law derived from the UNIDROIT DAPL Principles in the legal framework governing digital assets. In a national law context, this functions as a mechanism to ensure the validity of the law with that origin. This is a way to protect "DAPL Principle's law" and it can also be seen as an invitation to States to adopt UNIDROIT DAPL Principles in its domestic law and to adapt their private law in order to avoid inconsistencies between the national law system in private law and digital assets as a new element in the equity world that ought to be assumed and ordered within the law system.

These ideas could be seen as latent from the beginning of the works, although the pattern was not defined until the Working Group fifth session. One of the questions put forward by the Working Group was: "To what extent general principles would apply to digital assets as defined in the Principles",[113] which gave rise to a reply from the ALI (American Law Institute) representative, Steven Weise, who offered a solution. He "proposed a concise generic statement that dealt with the interaction between the Principles and digital assets law in different jurisdictions [...] this generic statement should be expressed as an operative Principle (perhaps using words similar to those used in the US Uniform Laws such as "to the extent displaced by this law"), which would then be supplemented with the supporting Commentary."[114] That approach was upheld by the Working Group: "it should be made explicit where the "Principles law" took precedence over the "other Law" and where that "other Law" derogated from these Principles".[115] An additional consideration was made when preparing

[109] See UNIDROIT 2021 – Study LXXXII – W.G.2 – Doc. 3, para.54.

[110] Copying in the text what have been written on fn. 20 (see there the documentary reference).

[111] See previously fn. 11, but also fn. 22 (among other references).

[112] Supra on fn. 20 and fn. 21.

[113] Raised by Sub-Group 2 Co-Chair Matthias Haentjens (in UNIDROIT 2022 – Study LXXXII – W.G.5– Doc.3, p. 13).

[114] At UNIDROIT 2022 – Study LXXXII – W.G.5– Doc. 4, para.42.

[115] Ibid. para.43. The reader would realize that the paragraph is composed with the previous indications on fn. 33 lightly redrafted to fit in the text.

the Working Group's sixth session to narrow down the text, but it was not finally adopted.[116]

That pre-eminence for the Principles law (i.e., the national law that has adopted the law suggested within the UNIDROIT DAPL Principles, as Principle 2(3) defines it) over the national law ("other law" as defined in Principle 2(4): a law alien to Principles law) assures the integrity and effectiveness of the DAPL UNIDROIT Principles when they are incorporated into national law, by avoiding any conflict between the Principles law and other law (again as defined in 2(3) and 2(4) respectively).

It can also be seen as a consequence of the (perhaps it can be said) universal "*lex specialis*" dogma, that can be seen in many legal systems. In accordance with that dogma, the "*special law*" supersedes the "*general law*". The Principles law as "*lex specialis*" should have priority over other law, the general law.[117]

Principle 3(2) is particularly appropriate, because it could disregard any conflict between the Principles law and other law.

The Commentary draws particular attention to two key points: the indifference about how the national law adopt and adapt UNIDROIT DAPL Principles (in a special rule or in a general one) to construe the Principles law, and the importance to check that the Principles law is actually aligned with UNIDROIT DAPL Principles.[118]

2.3.3 "Other Law" on Digital Assets

From the core objective of the UNIDROIT DAPL Principles, which is to affirm that digital assets fall under proprietary rights and the subsequent reliance on national law even to clarify what ought to be understood by proprietary rights, Principle 3(3) stems as a consequence. It is designed to clarify that the proprietary rights meaning, content and implications ought to be found in the national law.

Hence, in the draft of Principle [X2](4) it is only natural to mention something along those lines.[119] The Working Group was aware of the difficulties on that issue,

---

[116] Precisely, it was too strict on the understanding: "For Principle 3(2), consideration was given at DC7 [Drafting Committee 7] to including the terms '…other law relating to private law matters …'. However, this was considered to be too narrow and later removed from the draft", at UNIDROIT 2022 – Study LXXXII – W.G.6 – Doc. 3, para.30 (at p. 23).

[117] Commentary 3.6 devotes an interesting statement to the point that deserves to be brought here: "This may be achieved in a State as a result of generally applicable rules that grant precedence to specific laws over general laws, or to later laws over earlier laws."

[118] Commentary 3.7 expands a case that possibly could occur in different jurisdictions that have adopted the UNCITRAL Model Law on Electronic Transferable Records. Since that Model Law is more specific than the UNIDROIT DAPL Principles, conflicts may appear. The suggestion for legislators from the final words of Commentary 3.7 is to carefully review any potential clashes that may arise with the Principles law.

[119] For its content, see above fn. 44.

particularly if one follows the slippery slope of the applicable law debate[120] so in line with the substance of Principle 3(3).

The pattern followed in UNIDROIT's previous instruments[121] to solve the interaction between the uniform rule and the national law helped to clarify the DAPL Principles' scope during the structuring of Principle 3(3), and what falls outside it and is thus left to national law. This allowed the documents to clearly state that Principle 3(3) addresses "issues relating to proprietary rights in digital assets [...] matters that are and that are not covered by the Principle."[122]

This context enabled Louise Gullifer (the Chair of the Drafting Group) at the fifth Working Group session to establish the nature and aims of Principle 3(3): an open list of items to offer some guidance on what national law should rule (because the DAPL Principles do not cover those items)[123] and therefore "the list from (a) to (g) was not an exclusive list, but was merely indicative", because "these Principles did not deal with every single proprietary aspect of control and transfer".[124]

The following steps taken by the Working Group on Principle 3(3) were mainly formal in content: a discussion on the wording of its *chapeau* text: "except as displaced by these Principles" because it was considered redundant, though the Working Group wished to leave no room for doubt.[125] That path of objectivity and

---

[120] When considering Commentary to 3.3: see above fn. 47, deserving to be extracted the following: "the commentary should simply state: "the applicable law contemplated by these principles should specify which, if any, of its existing rules or standards of general application govern the acquisition and disposition of proprietary rights of digital assets". Taking this approach, the domestic legal system could then decide whether it wanted to do this via the general rules of application, or whether they contemplated specific rules for property in digital assets." (at UNIDROIT 2021 – Study LXXXII – W.G.4 – Doc. 3, para.37). Another group of interventions, instead, insisted that that was an opened end discussion: "Several experts remarked that it was often impossible to determine the applicable law, especially within permissionless open systems. An expert suggested that in these instances, a court may simply adopt broad rules that apply to the area of law in question – a technique which already existed in France, among other legal systems" (ibid., para.38).

[121] There are references to the Geneva Securities Convention (at UNIDROIT 2021 – Study LXXXII – W.G.3 – Doc. 4, para.43) and to the Cape Town Convention (at UNIDROIT 2021 – Study LXXXII – W.G.4 – Doc. 2, p. 43), references that have been cited within fn. 55 and fn. 46 respectively. The first one, although already copied in fn. 55, deserves to be partially repeated: "The Co-Chairs remarked that [...] where the impossibility of harmonisation of numerous legal principles relating to intermediated securities in a hard law document was noted. Accordingly, when such harmonisation was not possible, an explicit reference was made to so-called non-Convention law, i.e., the law of the Contracting State other than Convention law. As the DAPL Project was a soft law instrument, there was more flexibility in the development of the Principles." Later, on the Working Group's fourth occasion, consistency with the Cape Town Convention on International Interests in Mobile Equipment was expressed, because it "defers to other law as to whether a person has a "power to dispose" of an interest in mobile equipment".

[122] See UNIDROIT 2021 – Study LXXXII – W.G.4 – Doc. 2, p.43, already cited in a more complete form in supra fn. 45.

[123] See supra fn. 34 and accompanying text for the full reference.

[124] At UNIDROIT 2022 – Study LXXXII – W.G.5– Doc. 4, para.39.

[125] Details supra fn. 28, three last phrases.

clearness drove a text reform: to remove any reference to persons (contracting) and, instead, keep to the contract or the transaction itself.[126]

Almost at the end of the text's evolution, a criticism emerged,[127] but the Working Group was convinced about the quality of Principle 3(3) and chose to keep it as it was.

Notwithstanding their nature as examples, the seven sections with letters (a) to (g) in Principle 3(3) deserve a brief mention, as they help clarify the aim of Principle 3(3): to indicate what falls outside the scope of the Principles and, consequently, what must be addressed by national law. National law must examine how these aspects function within its own legal system once a digital asset is subject to consideration with UNIDROIT DAPL Principles as a supporting tool. This pre-eminence of the Principles justifies the opening words in the *chapeau* of 3(3): "Except as displaced by this Principles", indicating that even regarding the content of 3(3) letters (a) to (g), the Principles may contain their own specific rules.

The first statement (Principle 3(3)(a)) makes it clear that the relationship between proprietary rights and a digital asset through the owner's perspective is the first duty of the national law. In other words, once the proprietary rights on a digital asset have been assumed (Principle 3(1)), it is up to national law to determine the conditions under which someone may acquire such rights.

The second point of attention for national law to address in the context of digital assets (if the UNIDROIT DAPL Principles are used) is transferability: when a digital asset has been validly transferred from one person to another.

Lastly, the third item to be addressed by national law (when using the UNIDROIT DAPL Principles) is focused on the use of a digital asset as a security right. Principle 3(3)(c) emphasises that it is a task for the national law to identify when (and how) a digital asset can be fully employed as a security right.

If the previous sections of Principle 3(3) identify the basic proprietary rights aspects that national law should address, the following provisions go further by pointing to the contractual consequences between the parties involved in the transfer and its security relationships.

Thus, Principle 3(3)(d) indicates the rights between a transferor and a transferee of a digital asset as a task to be carried out by national law when it has been decided that the UNIDROIT DAPL Principles should rule that issue.

Meanwhile, Principle 3(3)(e) contemplates the rights between the grantor and the secured creditor when a digital asset is the good granted as a security right. National law should therefore clearly define the rights between the two (grantor and secured creditor).

The last two sections (letters (f) and (g)) on Principle 3(3) focus on third-party effectiveness in relation to digital asset transfers and the use of digital assets as security rights. National law should govern the legal consequences for third parties arising from the transfer of a digital asset, as well as the legal implications for third parties when a digital asset is used as the object of a security right.

---

[126] See above, fn. 25 and fn. 27.

[127] It can be read at fn. 23, with corresponding text to clarify the observations timeframe.

3 Conclusions

It was announced at the start that these pages would follow a specific plan, I hope this has been observed. Under Sect. 2.2, the formation of UNIDROIT DAPL Principle 3 can be seen in reverse order: from its publication back to its inception, in order to more clearly and easily reveal the different text layers and their timing, always with due reference to the UNIDROIT documents. In Sect. 2.3, first, a general statement on the orientation of Principle 3 was provided; second, a collection of ideas on the aims of Principle 3, aligned with its three sections: the digital asset as the object of proprietary rights, the pre-eminence of the Principles law, and the broad scope covered by national law: from defining proprietary rights as applicable to digital assets regarding transferability, the construction of security rights and third-party effects (although details in the content of each Principle 3(3) always need further development). This Sect. 2.3 is also based exclusively on UNIDROIT documents (almost all the references were extracted from Sect. 2.2 footnotes and eventually repeated), starting with the inception of Principle 3 (mainly Principle [X2]) and tracing its aims and limited evolution.

If Sect. 2.2 serves to affirm the considerable quantity and quality of the work carried out by the Working Group members and UNIDROIT Secretariat personnel, as evidenced by the high quality of the resulting text, then Sect. 2.3 could be written only with the references to Sect. 2.2 documents. As this section draws to a close, the value of the work performed by the Working Group members and the Secretariat staff should be emphasised. There is a word in the German language that combines the ideas of work and time: a task done and its lapse: "*leistung*". "Achievement" is one of the suggested translations closest to the meaning: great achievement for the UNIDROIT DAPL Working Group. "Performance" and "attainment" are also fitting options. Yet, the German word encompasses these and more English words as a translation. Thus, it is fitting to conclude: "*großartige Leistung!*" with congratulations to all of those whose hard work brought us to that point.

What the impact of UNIDROIT DAPL Principles will be remains to be seen (although some insights can be read within this volume), but it seems beyond any doubt that Principle 3 stands out as a remarkable landmark, particularly for legislators.

References

GOVERNING COUNCIL / 102nd session / Rome, 10–12 May 2023 // UNIDROIT 2023 / C.D. (102) 25 / Original: English / August 2023 // REPORT // (prepared by the Secretariat).

GOVERNING COUNCIL / 102nd session / Rome, 10–12 May 2023 // UNIDROIT 2023 / C.D. (102) 6 / Original: English / April 2023 // Item No. 4 on the agenda: Adoption of Draft UNIDROIT Instruments // (c) Principles on Digital Assets and Private Law (prepared by the Secretariat).

Digital Assets and Private Law Working Group / Eighth session (hybrid) / Rome, 8–10 March 2023 / UNIDROIT 2023 / Study LXXXII - W.G.8 – Doc. 2 / English only / February 2023 // DRAFT UNIDROIT PRINCIPLES ON DIGITAL ASSETS AND PRIVATE LAW.

Digital Assets and Private Law Working Group / Seventh session (hybrid) / Rome, 19–21 December 2022 / UNIDROIT 2022 / Study LXXXII – W.G.7 – Doc. 1 / English only / December 2022 // ANNOTATED AGENDA.
Digital Assets and Private Law Working Group / Seventh session (hybrid) / Rome & Zoom / 19–21 December 2022 // UNIDROIT 2023 / Study LXXXII – W.G.7 – Doc. 5 / English only / February 2023 // SUMMARY REPORT OF THE SEVENTH SESSION / (Hybrid, 19–21 December 2022).
Digital Assets and Private Law Working Group / Seventh session (hybrid) / Rome, 19–21 December 2022 // UNIDROIT 2022 / Study LXXXII – W.G.7 – Doc. 3 / English only / December 2022 // ISSUES PAPER.
Digital Assets and Private Law Working Group / Sixth session (hybrid) / Rome, 31 August – 2 September 2022 // UNIDROIT 2022 // Study LXXXII – W.G.6 – Doc. 2 / English only / August 2022 // MASTER COPY OF THE DRAFT PRINCIPLES AND COMMENTS.
Digital Assets and Private Law Working Group / Seventh session (hybrid) / Rome, 19–21 December 2022 // UNIDROIT 2022 / Study LXXXII – W.G.7 – Doc. 2 / English only / December 2022 / MASTER COPY OF THE DRAFT PRINCIPLES AND COMMENTS.
Digital Assets and Private Law Working Group / Sixth session (hybrid) / Rome, 31 August – 2 September 2022// UNIDROIT 2022 / Study LXXXII – W.G. 6 – Doc. 1 / English only / August 2022 // ANNOTATED AGENDA.
Digital Assets and Private Law Working Group / Sixth session (hybrid) / Rome & Zoom 31 August – 2 September 2022 // UNIDROIT 2022 / Study LXXXII – W.G.6 – Doc. 4 / English only / November 2022 // SUMMARY REPORT OF THE SIXTH SESSION.
Digital Assets and Private Law Working Group / Sixth session (hybrid) / Rome, 31 August – 2 September 2022 // UNIDROIT 2022 / Study LXXXII – W.G.6 – Doc. 3 / English only / August 2022 // ISSUES PAPER.
Digital Assets and Private Law Working Group / Sixth session (hybrid) / Rome, 31 August – 2 September 2022 // UNIDROIT 2022 / Study LXXXII – W.G.6 – Doc. 3 / Annex /English only / August 2022 // Comments Received by the Steering Committee.
Digital Assets and Private Law Working Group / Fifth session (hybrid) / Rome, 7 – 9 March 2022 // UNIDROIT 2022 / Study LXXXII – W.G.5 – Doc. 1 / English only / February 2022 // ANNOTATED AGENDA.
Digital Assets and Private Law Working Group / Fifth session (hybrid) / Rome, 7 – 9 March 2022 / / UNIDROIT 2022 / Study LXXXII – W.G.5 – Doc. 4 / English only / April 2022 // SUMMARY REPORT OF THE FIFTH SESSION / (Hybrid, 7 – 9 March 2022).
Digital Assets and Private Law Working Group / Fifth session (hybrid) / Rome, 7 – 9 March 2022 / / UNIDROIT 2022 / Study LXXXII – W.G.5 – Doc. 2 / English only / February 2022 // MASTER COPY OF BLACK LETTER PRINCIPLES.
Digital Assets and Private Law Working Group / Fifth session (hybrid) / Rome, 7 – 9 March 2022 / / UNIDROIT 2022 / Study LXXXII – W.G.5 – Doc. 3 / English only / February 2022 // MASTER COPY OF THE PRINCIPLES AND COMMENTS.
Digital Assets and Private Law Working Group / Fourth session (hybrid) / Rome, 2 – 4 November 2021 // UNIDROIT 2021 / Study LXXXII – W.G.4 – Doc. 1 / English only / October 2021 // ANNOTATED DRAFT AGENDA.
Digital Assets and Private Law Working Group / Fourth session (hybrid) / Rome, 2 – 4 November 2021 // UNIDROIT 2021 / Study LXXXII – W.G.4 – Doc. 2 / English only / October 2021 // ISSUES PAPER.
Digital Assets and Private Law Working Group / Fourth session (remote) / Rome, 2 – 4 November 2021 // UNIDROIT 2021 / Study LXXXII – W.G.4 – Doc. 3 / English only / December 2021 / / SUMMARY REPORT OF THE FOURTH SESSION // (Videoconference, 2 – 4 November 2021).
Digital Assets and Private Law Working Group / Third session (remote) / Rome, 30 June – 2 July 2021 // UNIDROIT 2021 / Study LXXXII – W.G.3 – Doc. 1 (rev. 1) / English only / June 2021 // ANNOTATED DRAFT AGENDA.

Digital Assets and Private Law Working Group / Third session (remote) / Rome, 30 June – 2 July 2021 // Unidroit 2021 / Study LXXXII – W.G.3 – Doc. 1 (rev. 1) / English only / June 2021 / ANNOTATED DRAFT AGENDA.

Digital Assets and Private Law Working Group / Third session (remote) / Rome, 30 June – 2 July 2021 // Unidroit 2021 / Study LXXXII – W.G.3 – Doc. 4 / English only / July 2021 // SUMMARY REPORT OF THE THIRD SESSION / (Videoconference, 30 June – 2 July 2021).

Digital Assets and Private Law Working Group / Second session (remote) / Rome, 16 – 18 March 2021 // Unidroit 2021 // Study LXXXII – W.G.2 – Doc. 1 / English only / March 2021 // ANNOTATED AGENDA.

Digital Assets and Private Law Working Group / Second session (remote) / Rome, 16 – 18 March 2021 // Unidroit 2021 / Study LXXXII – W.G.2 – Doc. 2 (rev. 1) / English only / March 2021 / ISSUES PAPER.

GOVERNING COUNCIL / 99th session (B) / Rome, 23 - 25 September 2020 // Unidroit3 2020 C.D. (99) B.21 / Original: English / November 2020 // REPORT / (prepared by the Secretariat).

Digital Assets and Private Law Working Group / First session (remote) / Rome, 17 – 19 November 2020 // Unidroit 2020 / Study LXXXII – W.G.1 – Doc. 1 / English only / November 2020 // ANNOTATED AGENDA.

Digital Assets and Private Law Working Group / First session (remote) / Rome, 17 – 19 November 2020 // Unidroit 2020/ Study LXXXII – W.G.1 – Doc. 2 / English only / November 2020 // ISSUES PAPER.

Digital Assets and Private Law Working Group / First session (remote) / Rome, 17 – 19 November 2020 // Unidroit 2021 / Study LXXXII – W.G.1 – Doc. 4 / English only / March 2021 // SUMMARY REPORT OF THE FIRST SESSION.

Unidroit *Principles on Digital Assests and Private Law*, International Institute for the Unification of Private Law (Unidroit) Via Panisperna, 28 - 00184 Rome – ITALY, ISBN: 978-88-86449-49-6, foreword President (M.C. Malaguti) and Secretary General (I. Tirado), September 2023.

Unidroit PRINCIPLES ON THE OPERATION OF CLOSE-OUT NETTING PROVISIONS / / International Institute for the Unification of Private Law (Unidroit) / Via Panisperna, 28 - 00184 Rome - ITALY / ISBN: 88-86449-26-7 / Unidroit 2013.

Principle 4
Linked Assets

Apol·lònia Martínez Nadal

The digital assets to which these Principles apply include a digital asset linked to another asset. The other asset may be tangible or intangible (including another digital asset). Other law applies to determine the existence of, requirements for, and legal effect of any link between the digital asset and the other asset, including the effect of a transfer of the digital asset on the other asset.

1 Official Commentary

Commentary

4.1. As provided in Principle 4, a digital asset may be linked to another asset or assets. Principles law takes a neutral stance as to whether this link is sufficiently established and what, if any, the legal effect of the link may be. These matters are instead left to the other law of the State, including its regulatory law, to determine. The operation of the link may depend on other law already in force in the State or on new rules specially developed for linked assets. Consequently, the link between the digital asset and the other asset may operate in a variety of different ways depending on the other law applicable to it.

4.2. One common reason for linking a digital asset to another asset is to enable transactions with the other asset to be effected by a transfer of the digital asset. The intention in creating the link may be to enable the holder of the digital asset to alter a person's rights in relation to the other asset or in relation to a person who issued

This work was financed within the framework of the Prometeo 2023 project of the Regional Ministry of Innovation, Universities, Science and Digital Society (CIPROM/2022/26) "Present and future of the regulation of cryptoassets in the EU [LegalCripto]", whose principal investigator is Carmen Pastor Sempere. The basic ideas contained herein were presented in the author's paper with the same title, given on November 13, 2024 at the IV International Congress on "UNIDROIT Principles on Digital Assets and Private Law: Context, Content, Perspectives", organized also by BAES Research Group of the University of Alicante on November 13 and 14, 2024.

A. Martínez Nadal (✉)
University of the Balearic Islands, Palma, Spain
e-mail: apollonia.martinez@uib.es

C. Pastor Sempere and D. A. Morán Bovio (eds.), UNIDROIT *Principles on Digital Assets and Private Law*, Law, Governance and Technology Series 80,
https://doi.org/10.1007/978-3-032-11001-5_10

it. The intention may be that a transfer of the digital asset should have the effect of transferring rights in the other asset.

4.3. The 'other asset' referred to in Principle 4 may be tangible or intangible, and it may be another digital asset or one created under other law, such as a share or bond. The other asset is one which exists contemporaneously with, but separately from, the digital asset. It does not include a 'resulting digital asset', within the meaning of Principle 6(2). which only comes into existence to give effect to some change in the control of an original digital asset.

Existence and effect of the link

4.4. The operation of linked assets depends on two distinct questions: (1) whether there is any link at all between the digital asset and the other asset; and (2) whether the link has a legal effect on the parties' rights in relation to the other asset. Both questions depend on the other law of the State.

4.5. Whether the link is proved to exist is primarily a question of fact. Its existence depends on all the circumstances of the case and the intentions of the parties who created the digital asset. The link may be apparent from the coding of the digital asset or from any related system protocols applying to it. It may also be apparent from any published documentation relating to the digital asset or the other asset, such as a white paper or the terms of issue applying to them. The other law of the State may also be relevant to the existence of the link. The other law (including its regulatory law) may define minimum legal standards for recognising that the link exists. A link which failed to satisfy those standards would be ineffective whatever the intentions of the parties who created the digital asset might have been.

4.6. Even where the factual existence of the link between the digital and the other asset is satisfactorily established, its legal effect depends on other law. 'Legal effect' is to be understood broadly. It includes, most importantly, the effect of any transaction with the digital asset on the parties' rights in relation to the other asset, and the effect of those transactions in insolvency. One consequence of giving legal effect to the link may be that rights in the digital asset and the other asset are transferred synchronously with each other. It may also enable a change in any contractual rights between the holder of the digital asset and the holder of the other asset.

4.7. Consistently with the primacy of other law under this Principle, the parties who issue or transact with the digital asset cannot confer any greater legal effect on the link than the other law of the State would allow. It may not be sufficient, for example, simply for them to provide by a contract between them that a transfer of the digital asset will necessarily transfer proprietary rights in the other asset. The other law of the State would need to permit or provide for this effect. The contractual agreement may only apply between the parties to it.

Comparison with registry systems

4.8. Transactions with linked digital assets do not always have the same legal effect as transactions with conventional assets, such as securities recorded in a legally constituted registry system. A change in the recorded holding of a digital asset is legally neutral in relation to the other asset unless other law confers a legal effect on the link. Where the other law does so provide, the consequence may be that a transfer of proprietary rights in the digital asset and the other asset would be synchronised.

4.9. With a conventional securities registry, a transfer recorded in the registry has the legal effect of transferring the proprietary interest in the debt or equity securities that it relates to. The reason is that other law, typically legislation, confers legal effect on the registry system. Similarly, it would be open to the other law of a State to provide that a recorded transfer of a digital asset had the effect of transferring the proprietary interest in the other asset, such as a share, that it was linked to. The reason would be that the other law defined the link in such a way that the transfer of digital asset was directly constitutive of the parties' proprietary interests in the other asset.

Form of other law

4.10. The legal effect may be determined by existing rules of other law, or a State may provide for it in special rules developed for linked assets. Other law may recognise the existence of the link without also recognising that a disposition of the digital asset has any legal effect at all on the parties' rights in relation to the other asset. A separate legal act may be required to change the parties' rights to the other asset. Thus, the legal effect of holding and transferring linked assets depends on a combination of these Principles and any rules of other law relevant to the other asset.

Innocent acquisition

4.11. It would be open to the other law of a State to provide that the benefit of any innocent acquisition rule applied to a digital asset in accordance with Principle 8 should also apply to the other asset linked to it. Consistently with the primacy of other law, however, the simple proof of the link between the digital asset and the other asset would not necessarily mean that the holder of the other asset took the benefit of the innocent acquisition rule. The other law of the State would need to provide for this result. See Commentary 4.29 to 4.32: Illustration 8.

4.12. As illustrations of the different legal effects of a link between the digital asset and the other asset, eight examples follow.

4.13. ***Illustration 1****. The rules of other law already in force may apply to the parties' transaction with the digital asset and determine the legal effect on the other asset linked to it.*

4.14. For example, a system may be established for trading quantities of tokenised gold. An investor may hold a digital token which evidences a proprietary right in a fractional share of specifically identified gold. Whether a sale and transfer of the token passes the seller's proprietary right in the gold depends on the rules that apply to the gold in the relevant State's other law. In some legal systems, the other law may treat the parties' dealings with the digital token as the outward expression of their intention to transfer the proprietary right in the gold. The proprietary right in the gold would pass to the buyer of the token. The State would not need to enact any new rule of other law for this to happen (as an aside, it should be noted that even if the other law of the State permitted this effect, it would not necessarily preclude the parties from transacting directly with the gold separately from the digital token. If so, the effect would be that the proprietary interests in the gold and the token would become desynchronised.)

4.15. In other States, other law may provide that the seller must deliver the gold to the buyer in order to pass the proprietary right in it. In that case, a sale and transfer of the token would not pass the proprietary right in the gold. A new rule of other law might need to be enacted to synchronise the transfer of the proprietary rights in the two assets.

4.16. **Illustration 2.***One digital asset may be linked to another digital asset and the legal link between them would depend on the effect of any legal relations between the holders of the two assets.*

4.17. For example, an issuer may create a digital asset which is a 'wrapped' version of another digital asset on a different protocol. Like the 'stable coin' in Illustration 6, only one 'wrapped' digital asset would be created for every other digital asset on the other protocol. The white paper may provide that the holder of the wrapped digital asset is entitled to redeem the other digital asset. In return, the holder's wrapped digital asset would be 'burned'. The effect of this 1:1 relationship is that the value of the wrapped digital asset should correspond to the value of the other digital asset. When the wrapped digital asset is transferred, the transferee should receive the same value as if the other digital asset had been transferred between them. The rights of the holder of the wrapped asset in relation to the other asset would depend on the legal effect of the link between them. The terms of a contract between the issuer and holder of the wrapped digital asset would determine if the holder had a right to regain control of the other digital asset and have the wrapped asset 'burned' at that point. It should be noted that in Illustrations 2, 6 and 7, the word 'issuer' is not used with the limited meaning set out in Principle 5(2)(f).

4.18. **Illustration 3.***The rules of other law already in force may govern all proprietary aspects of an asset linked to a digital asset, regardless of the representations and intention of the parties dealing in these assets.*

4.19. For example, a person (Alpha) may create a non-fungible digital asset (A-NFT) that is recorded in a blockchain ledger maintained and operated through a public, permissionless, distributed network. Alpha may make written and verbal representations that she intends for A-NFT to embody all her copyrights relative to a musical work of her creation. Moreover, Alpha may enter into a transaction with another person (Beta) in which they agree that, by transferring the A-NFT, Alpha assigns her copyrights to Beta and that Beta may subsequently re-assign these copyrights to others by transferring to them the A-NFT. Regardless of Alpha's intention to tokenise her copyrights, the applicable copyright law will determine whether the link between the A-NFT and her copyrights has any legal effect. Analogously, the applicable copyright law will determine whether transferring the A-NFT constitutes a valid assignment of the copyrights in question, as well as whether Beta can subsequently reassign these copyrights by re-transferring the A-NFT.

*4.20.**Illustrations 4 and 5.**A State may choose to enact special legislation to make the link between the token and the other asset legally effective.*

4.21. For example, a company may raise finance from investors by issuing debt securities on a blockchain ledger. Each investor holds a transferable digital token representing their claim against the company. The terms of issue purport to give the investor a right to payment by the company who has issued the debt securities. When the token is transferred on the ledger, the transferee acquires the right against the company. The company which issued the debt security gets an effective discharge if it pays the current holder of the token. Special legislation may be needed to effect this result if it cannot be achieved, for example, by the State's existing other law of contract, assignment, novation, or securities transfer.

4.22. As a further example, a State may enact special legislation that creates digital equivalents to paper negotiable instruments or documents of title to goods. The legislation may provide that a change of control of the digital asset has the same legal effect as the delivery of possession of the paper document to which it is equivalent. Depending on the State's existing other law, the effect may be that the transferee of the digital asset would acquire the right to claim on a monetary debt or a title to the goods linked to the digital asset. The special legislation would define minimum criteria that the digital asset would need to satisfy if it were to serve as a legal equivalent to the paper documents in the existing other law of the State.

*4.23. **Illustration 6.**The precise legal effect of any link between the digital asset and another asset may depend as much on ascertaining the parties' intentions from any system coding, protocols, and documentation as it does from the operation of the other law. Thus, the terms of a white paper accompanying the issue of a digital asset may be relevant to inferring the nature and value of the legal right, if any, that the holder of the digital asset was intended to have in relation to the other asset.*

4.24. For example, an issue of stable coins may take the form of transferable tokens which are denominated in the units of a fiat currency, such as USD. For each USD unit of stable coins created, the issuer creates a 1:1 reserve of liquid assets denominated in USD. The reserve is held by an intermediary, separately from the issuer's own assets. The white paper may provide that any holder of the stable coin is entitled to re-sell it to the issuer at par value in USD. The effect of this right to resale is to stabilise the transfer value of the coin as it circulates in payment transactions.

4.25. The legal effect of transferring the stable coin and any rights it may appear to confer against the issuer may depend as much on the other law of assignment or novation of contractual rights as it does on the terms of the white paper. The terms of the white paper may show that each holder of the coin was primarily intended to have a contractual right against the issuer. The transfer of the stable coin may operate as an assignment or novation of that right. Even if the holder of the token had a proprietary right in the stable coin, it may be apparent from other law or from the terms of the white paper that the holder would not also have a proprietary right in the other assets held in the reserve. It would be for the insolvency rules of the applicable other law to determine how, if at all, this right might take priority over any other claims enforceable against the issuer.

4.26. ***Illustration 7.****Digital assets may be used to create transferable portions of value derived from other assets which exist off the blockchain. Even where the link between the digital assets and the other assets is clear, the precise effect of the holders' rights will be determined by the other law of the State. The parties' intention to link the assets cannot override the other law that applies to those assets.*

4.27. For example, an issuer may sell digital assets that purport to give the holder a claim in relation to real estate. The assets are transferable on a blockchain ledger. On closer analysis, most tokenised real estate actually involves the establishment of a company to which ownership of the real estate is transferred. The shares in the company are then 'tokenised' and made transferable on the ledger. The transfer of the token may not be sufficient in law to transfer the shares in the company or any proprietary interest in the real estate. These may be questions for the system of other law where the company is registered, or the real estate is located. The relevance of the digital asset is to illustrate (i) the 'chain' of legal relations between the holder and the shares and the real estate, and (ii) steps that may need to be taken by the acquirer of the token to update a company register; or update a register of real estate.

4.28. This illustration shows that the mere fact of the transfer of the token from one person to another may not effect the transfer of shares or the real estate. Nor may one person's control over the token be sufficient to prevent the shares or the real estate from being transferred independently of any dealing with the token.

4.29. ***Illustration 8.****The other law of a State may recognise a good faith acquisition rule in relation to the other asset linked to the digital asset. The effect may be that* *both the digital asset and the other asset would benefit from a good faith acquisition rule.*

4.30. For example, as in Commentary 4.13 to 4.15, a system may be established for trading quantities of tokenised gold and an investor may hold a digital token which evidences a proprietary right in a fractional share of specifically identified gold. A hacker may unlawfully obtain control of the token and transfer it by sale to an innocent buyer. Under Principle 8, the buyer would acquire a proprietary interest in the token which was free from the claims of the original investor who once held the token. It would be, however, for the other law of the State to determine whether the innocent buyer would also acquire a proprietary right in the 'linked' share of the gold and also take it free of the original investor's claims.

4.31. The other law of a State may provide similar consequences for a linked asset subject to a security right. A security right may be granted in a digital token that purports to evidence a proprietary right in a fractional share of gold. Whether the security right extends to the gold is a matter of other law. Developing the example in Commentary 4.20 to 4.22, the other law may, for instance, treat the digital token evidencing a proprietary right to gold as a document of title, in which case a security right in the token would extend to the gold. Any such system would have to consider carefully how to address rights in the linked asset so that all rights 'reside' in the token.

4.32. If other law provides similar consequences for the good faith acquisition of the other asset, then the innocent acquirer of a digital asset may take both assets free of the security right. Consistently with the primacy of other law, the rights of any innocent acquirer in relation to the other asset may be determined by legal rules which are different from the Principles law relevant to the digital asset itself. States may therefore need to enact special legislation to ensure that the rights of a third-party acquirer in relation to the digital asset and the other asset remain in line with each other.

2 Reflections

2.1 Introductory: Context and Evolution of the Preparatory Works for the Development of the UNIDROIT Principles on Digital Assets and Private Law

Principle 4 is the last of the four included in Section I of the UNIDROIT Principles on digital assets and private law. It discusses the purpose and definitions of the Principles. Principle 4 is dedicated to so-called linked assets, which are digital assets linked to another tangible or intangible asset and to which the UNIDROIT Principles also apply. However, the existence of the link, its requirements and effects, will be regulated by another law (a national law other than any national law that implements or is consistent with these Principles, in accordance with Principle 2 (2) and (3)).

Linked assets have been the focus of attention by UNIDROIT's working group since the beginning of its activity, even in the initial preparatory phases. Thus, in the Exploratory Workshop that was held on September 17 and 18, 2020 by the Working Group on Digital Assets and Private Law, one of the sessions was dedicated to this subject. In particular, session 3 examined the issue of "Digital assets linked to real-world assets (digital twins): implications for civil law and private international law." That session focused on exploring the issues of "digital twins" that represented a real-world asset and typically faced issues on how to prevent the "digital twin" from being separated from the real-world asset it represented. The speakers explained how their respective jurisdictions addressed these issues.

Issues such as the legal aspects of tokenizing real-world assets were discussed in more detail at that session, noting that several types of risks arise at multiple stages of the asset life cycle. These stages covered a wide range of issues relating to the asset's ideation and creation, its existence, its authenticity, ownership of the asset, its provenance, its inherent properties, its quality, its function, custody issues, its transferability, activities, and end of life. It was noted that tokenization of assets involved the digital representation of real (physical) assets on distributed ledgers, or the issuance of traditional asset classes in tokenized forms. This was not a new concept and was simply a mechanism to record certain rights and interests related to an asset. It is also noted that while private law issues existed throughout the life cycle of an asset, it was also important to examine issues regarding the existence of the asset in the context of tokenization, such that the tokenized asset accurately represented the rights relating to the real-world asset. Additionally, issues of ownership and transferability were also relevant and closely linked, with the mechanics of transferability (of the tokenised asset, as well as the real-world asset) carrying a high degree of importance.

2.1.1 First Meeting of the Working Group (November 2020)

Later, when the Working Group began its activity, in order to establish its objectives in the preparatory documents, it is noted that DLT-based digital data can alternatively be analysed as either (a) a record of the transfer of an asset, or (b) as a separate asset in its own right. Whether this analysis is suitable, in what situations it could apply, and the legal ramifications of this analysis are all considered issues that the project will have to address. This distinction between DLT-based digital data that does not relate to an asset that exists irrespective of that data, and DLT-based digital data that does relate to such an asset is considered a very difficult question, and not one that can be decided at this stage. This distinction is a matter which the Working Group will discuss in relation to the taxonomy of digital assets rather than the scope of the project.

Following on from that, the central question of the legal nature of a proprietary connection between digital data and another asset is addressed.[1] It is noted that some types of digital data can be structured so as to represent other assets, in such a way that the holder of the digital data purports to have a proprietary right to that other asset. When the process of transfer of the digital asset takes place, the proprietary right to that other asset is transferred from A to B. The mechanism of linking one asset to another is sometimes called tokenisation. The other asset will generally (but not necessarily) be an asset (tangible or intangible) that is not a digital asset. This type of digital asset is colloquially known under a number of different terms, including "token" and "coin". However, it is clarified that the connection under this heading does not include at least one other type of possible connection between a digital asset and another asset. With this exclusion, reference is expressly made for the first time to what will later be the linked assets of the current Principle 4, the subject matter of this work. The excluded case when the value of the digital asset is "backed by" or "pegged to" one or more other assets but the holder of that digital asset does not have any proprietary rights to those other assets (e.g. certain kinds of stablecoins). Stablecoins are defined as a kind of cryptocurrency designed to minimize the volatility of the price of the stablecoin, relative to some "stable" asset or basket of assets. A stablecoin can be pegged to a cryptocurrency, fiat money, or to exchange-traded commodities (such as precious metals or industrial metals).

In the first session of the Working Group, held on November 17 to 19, 2020,[2] the Working Group referred to the question regarding the link between a digital asset and "other assets", noting it was a good illustration of the larger discussion as to whether the project should only seek to identify problems and desired outcomes, or additionally provide indications as to the best ways of resolving the practical problems. The Working Group queried whether there was a consensus among the Working Group that rights in the digital asset ought to affect the rights in the linked or underlying 'real-world' asset, and, if so, how that desired outcome could be reached.

It was also noted that much work was required on the issue of "digital twins", where the goal of a system might be to effect the transfer of a digital asset together with the transfer of another accompanying asset. In this regard, it was queried whether all aspects of the rights in the digital asset transferred or mirrored exactly the status of the rights in the other asset. The key question to provide guidance on was with regard to a law governing proprietary rights in a digital asset and, what exactly that law should say about the other assets which were 'linked' or 'tethered' to that digital asset. While the project's advice on digital assets could go beyond advice on a law on digital assets and seek to give advice on how to achieve the desired outcomes, the Working Group noted that it could not realistically provide advice on every other related area of law (e.g., law of intangibles, rights to payment, etc.), so that even if comprehensive advice could not be provided for this reason, important guidance could be given regarding the relationship between the digital asset and other assets.

[1] UNIDROIT 2020 - Study LXXXII – W.G.1 – Doc. 2 November 2020, Issues paper, par. 59 a 64.

[2] UNIDROIT 2021 - Study LXXXII – W.G.1 – Doc. 4, March 2021, par. 50 to 56.

To round off that first session, the Working Group pointed out that the discussion surrounding link was paradigmatic of the distributive nature of property law and insolvency law, which were ultimately concerned with the question of determining who the rightful owner of a given asset was. Consequently, there is a need for some decisions to be made, such as deciding whether the real-world asset should "beat" the digital twin, or vice versa. The Working Group therefore urged that care be taken to ensure consistency and coherence in the logic behind the various decisions on where assets should end up.

2.1.2 Second Meeting of the Working Group (March 2021)

At the second session of the Working Group, the discussion was initially limited to digital assets such as Bitcoin and Ether (what are sometimes called cryptocurrencies), which have no link to other assets (not digital twins). Subsequently, the work could then be expanded to consider the application of conclusions on digital twins. Therefore, the discussions did not initially deal with digital twins at all but rather focused on the 'cryptocurrency' paradigm. The following questions specifically dealing with "tethering" or "digital twins" were also raised: 1. Should a law on DAs (main focus of the work) provide that transfer of a DA ipso facto may transfer rights in tethered assets? 2. If so, under what circumstances/conditions? 3. If so, how are rights of third parties under other applicable law addressed? 4. Should takes-free rule for DAs extend to tethered assets? 5. If so, under what circumstances/conditions? 6. Should ipso facto treatment be left to other law outside of law on DAs?

During the second session of the Working Group,[3] it was suggested that the UNIDROIT Secretariat conduct research into use cases regarding "digital twins" to provide a factual basis as to the current products currently available in the market and how it fits in with the work done so far. He recommended that the following meeting focus on defining digital assets and ensuring it was not personal data or music. Related to these objectives, and on the topic of "digital twins", a "Digital Twins" Workshop was held on May 31 (May 31, 2021).

2.1.3 Third Meeting of the Working Group (June–July 2021)

In the preparatory documentation for the third session of the Working Group,[4] in which the next steps were examined, building on the examples discussed at the 'Digital Twins' workshop, and wider desk-based market analysis, it was suggested that the Sub-Group provide further examples of 'digital assets'. As to the categories of "digital twins", at that time, the following broad types were identified for the purposes of further discussion: (a) Non-fungible tokens (NFTs); (b) Digital assets associated

[3] UNIDROIT 2021 - Study LXXXII – W.G. 2 – Doc. 3, April 2021, par. 81.

[4] UNIDROIT 2021 - Study LXXXII – W.G.3 – Doc. 2: Revised Issues Paper (rev. 1), par. 61.

with external art or other objects by a technical pointer and/or by a licensing agreement; (c) Digital Asset backed by Real-World Assets; (d) Digital Assets backed by Digital Assets; (e) Decentralized Finance (DeFi).[5]

During the deliberations of the Working Group's third session, Sub-Group 3 (Secured Transactions) explained that it had begun exploring several issues concerning digital twins, particularly the legal aspects of digital twins where a State has recognised that an asset might embody rights to another asset and how that recognition occurred: through case law or statutory treatment. It was noted that secured transactions law did not create, but rather recognised, the digital twin; otherwise, it was provided for in the relevant applicable law. For a secured transaction to work in this context, the law needed to recognise the link between the digital asset and the underlying asset. The Subgroup compared this with concepts relating to documents of title, as this was perhaps the closest analogy, considering different jurisdictions, especially English law bills of lading and how they came to be recognised as documents of title.

The basic conclusion was that there were two ways to envisage the current law to recognise a document or record that represented title, ownership, or some other proprietary interest in the underlying asset. The first was by codifying the principles as in German law, Dutch law, or the UCC. The second method entailed establishment of a practice as in English law in which a bill of lading, recognised by the courts, represented rights to goods. In the current context, the easiest and most obvious solution would be for the existing law to recognise, through one of the two mechanisms, that certain assets could be represented by a digital asset in the same manner as bills of lading in many jurisdictions.

From the secured transactions perspective, the Sub-Group 3 Chair noted that a Principle would ultimately involve a statement suggesting that, if the underlying law recognised that certain digital assets could represent a title or some other proprietary interest in an underlying asset, then it should also be possible to create a security right in the "digital twin" that extended to the underlying asset. He noted that there was a difference between the market developing a solution where a certain digital asset represented another real-world asset, especially a physical object, such as gold in a vault, and the question of whether a legal system would recognise that as truly representing rights in the gold. The Chair noted that the document of title was brought into existence because a special statute recognised it as such. He observed that in the case of digital twins there would usually be no such special statutes and so he queried what the legal principles should be.

Finally, a Sub-Group member queried what would occur in the case of a divergence between the digital asset and the actual asset, especially where the two were transferred separately creating a conflict of priority. The Sub-Group 3 Chair confirmed that the Principle did not directly deal with the question of priority between person A, who might have acquired a tangible object, and person B who acquired the linked digital asset. He suggested that Sub-Group 3 should clarify where the priority conflict

[5] UNIDROIT 2021 - Study LXXXII – W.G.3 – Doc. 2: Revised Issues Paper (rev. 1), par. 68.

may lie and how it might be resolved, depending on whether the State had recognised this type of a digital asset as a twin or not.

2.1.4 Fourth Meeting of the Working Group (November 2021)

In the preparatory documentation for the fourth session of the Working Group, the same four categories of "digital twins" already mentioned are maintained in the document.[6] In addition, a special section on "Digital twins" and commercial paper is included in the document in Annex III.[7]

In summary, it is noted that there are two ways in which a document can become a document of title, which may provide the basis for conceptualizing a digital asset as a "digital asset of title" (digital twin/tethered asset). The first is through statutory recognition. Codified civil law systems usually take this approach, examples being Germany and the Netherlands. Even in such cases, legislative recognition was usually preceded by mercantile practice and other developments. The second method, which is best illustrated by English law, is where a document is recognised by the courts as a document of title, without any statutory definition, typically because, over many years, participants in that market have come to treat the documents in that way.

In the same sense, the Secured Transactions Sub-Group co-chairs confirmed the following: the secured transactions principles enable the creation and perfection (by control) of a security right in the digital asset, but defer to the applicable law that establishes whether a digital asset embodies a right to any tethered asset. The secured transactions law does not create what we colloquially refer to as a "digital twin". If the applicable law provides that a digital asset embodies a right to the tethered asset (e.g., the Pax Gold token could be recognized as a type of a document of title), then the security right would extend to the gold as well. The secured transactions principles thus do not require any modification, at this point.

The examples of definition of "digital asset" include the case of "digital asset tethered to another asset", as follows: "This Illustration contemplates that, pursuant to law other than a digital asset law and any applicable contractual arrangements, an acquirer of a digital asset will, ipso facto, acquire another asset. That other asset might be entirely exogenous (e.g., a physical commodity such as a precious metal) or one that is inherently connected to the digital asset (e.g., a security that by its terms may be acquired and disposed of only in connection with the acquisition and disposition of a digital asset within the relevant protocol/platform). The digital asset is composed only of information capable of being subject to control, and the other asset (even if it is itself composed of information) is not a component of the digital asset and does not fall within the scope of these Principles".[8]

---

[6] Annex III – Appendix 3 – SUB-GROUP 3 – Secured transactions Sub-Appendix A – Digital Assets and Security Rights – Special Sections "Digital twins" and commercial paper.

[7] Annex III – Appendix 3 – SUB-GROUP 3 – Secured transactions Sub-Appendix A – Digital Assets and Security Rights – Special Sections "Digital twins" and commercial paper.

[8] UNIDROIT 2021 - Study LXXXII – W.G.4 – Doc. 2, page 38.

The Discussions Questions on Principles on Scope, Definitions, and Controls state the position that the Principles on "tethered" assets should adopt: a. Should the Principles explicitly address the potential role of digital assets in transferring rights in exogenous assets "tethered" to digital assets? If so, what should the content of principle(s) relating to tethered assets be? b. Should the Principles provide that, whether the acquisition of a digital asset ipso facto results in rights in any other asset, will depend on the application of other law, including any relevant contractual arrangements, and the relevant facts? c. Should the Principles instrument include commentary and illustrations of tethered assets? If so, what would be the best examples?[9]

In the discussions of session 4 of the Working Group, some relevant formal and substantive considerations regarding linked digital assets were made.[10] Thus, first of all, from the formal point of view, a terminological point was raised regarding the use of the word 'tethered': it was suggested that it be avoided because it carried connotations to the existing digital currency "Tether". The word "linked" as well as "referenced" asset were proposed as potential substitutes. An expert encouraged the Working Group to agree on an appropriate term to describe this important category of assets, noting that the existing literature had not yet settled on any standard terminology. It was noted that a list of examples in the Commentary could also be useful in this regard, a task which could perhaps be delegated to Sub-Group four on taxonomy.[11]

Secondly, in terms of content, several experts likewise agreed upon the importance of taking a careful approach to how the issue of 'linked' assets was presented, and that it should be clarified that the question of the effect on linked assets was based on the relevant applicable law, not the Principles of this Project.[12] On the other hand, a member of the Working Group raised a point in relation to the custody principle and 'linked' assets (i.e. digital assets linked with another, non-digital asset), noting that whether the effect of custody was 'linked' depended on how that link was made. Noting that Sub-Group 3 had already done some work on this question, she encouraged the taxonomy Sub-Group to develop a list of examples showing how this link could be established.[13] Finally, the Chair raised a query concerning the term 'linked' digital asset, observing that it might seem confusing if the law applicable to the link was different from the law applicable to the proprietary interest of the digital asset. He queried whether it would make more sense if the applicable law was identical.[14]

---

[9] Annex III – Appendix 2 – SUB-GROUP 2 – Control and Transfer Sub-Appendix A Discussion Questions: Principles on Scope, Definitions, and Controls.

[10] UNIDROIT 2021 - Study LXXXII – W.G.4 – Doc. 3: Summary Report of the 4th session.

[11] UNIDROIT 2021 - Study LXXXII – W.G.4 – Doc. 3: Summary Report of the 4th session, par. 40–41-

[12] UNIDROIT 2021 - Study LXXXII – W.G.4 – Doc. 3: Summary Report of the 4th session, par. 80.

[13] UNIDROIT 2021 - Study LXXXII – W.G.4 – Doc. 3: Summary Report of the 4th session, par. 123.

[14] UNIDROIT 2021 - Study LXXXII – W.G.4 – Doc. 3: Summary Report of the 4th session, par. 156.

2.1.5 Fifth Meeting of the Working Group (March 2022)

The fifth meeting of the Working Group took place from March 7 to 9, 2022. For the first time, the precedent of the current Principle 4 appears, as an autonomous and separate principle from that dedicated to the notion of digital assets.[15] Specifically, in the document "Master copy of the principles, plus commentary (with questions)" the first draft of Principle 4 appears as follows (accompanied by various comments and examples):

Principle 4: Digital Assets 'Linked' to Other Assets

(1) Where a digital asset, or any related system protocols or documentation, appears to confer a right to another asset, which can be tangible or intangible (the other asset'), the legal effect (if any) is a matter for the law, [other than the digital asset law,] [and is not addressed in these principles].

(2) The law specifies the requirements to be met, including as regards the form and content of the information to be provided, for any legal effect to occur.

Alternative formulation for discussion: The requirements to be met for any legal effect to occur (including as regards the form and content of the information to be provided) are a matter for the law to specify.

The enunciation of this Principle 4 is followed by 7 Comments in which it is explained that the purpose of this principle is to identify the limit of the Principles as regards digital assets 'linked' to other assets. And it is also clarified that the Principle makes clear that the legal effect of the link (if any) is not addressed in these Principles, in particular because: (i) the nature of the link may vary from case to case depending on the facts and on the law, and (ii) the issue of proprietary rights in the 'other asset' is a matter that is to be determined in accordance with the law applicable to that asset. Four examples of 'linked' assets are also included, as an illustration of the fact that the link between a digital asset and another asset may operate in various ways, depending on the intention of the parties to the transaction and the effect given to it by the general law.

Finally, this document concludes the treatment of the new Principle 4 with different questions: Q.10. Does the Working Group agree to leave the requirements for documentation demonstrating the link between the assets to the scope of regulation of the other law or the law? Is Principle 4(2) satisfactory to achieve this goal? Q.11. In a static situation of custody, would the holding of a digital asset have an effect on the other linked asset? Q.12. Could the Working Group provide additional examples (to be included in the commentary) of linked assets of various types; particularly, stablecoins and NFTs? Q.13. What, apart from the digital asset itself, should be referred

[15] UNIDROIT 2022 - Study LXXXII – W.G.5 – Doc. 2: Master Copy of the Black Letter Principles (Comparison) and Study LXXXII – W.G.5 – Doc. 3: Master Copy of the Principles, plus Commentary (with Questions).

to in Principle 4(1) as a possible source of the appearance of linkage between the assets?

This new Principle 4 is the object of analysis in session 5 of the Working Group, with the following contributions and reflections.[16] As a general overview of the Drafting Committee's work, in terms of changes to the structure of the Principles, the Working Group noted the addition of two entirely new principles: Principle 4 on "linked assets" and Principle 5 on conflict of laws. The reason for potentially retaining Principle 4 as a separate Principle was because it contained a considerable amount of commentary providing examples of linked assets.[17]

A detailed analysis of Principle 4 begins below. Sub-Group 4 Co-Chair presented the newly drafted Principle 4. She noted that it referred to "digital assets linked to other assets", instead of the shorter "linked digital assets" or similar. The reason was because what were promoted as "linked assets" may, for all purposes under the law, in fact not be a linked asset. Hence the longer formulation to achieve greater neutrality.[18]

Principle 4(1) provided that a legal effect will depend from case to case, and the issue of proprietary rights in the other assets was a matter to be determined in accordance with the law applicable to that asset, namely the State's law. Principle 4(1) confirmed that the Principles cannot determine whether or not there was a proprietary effect achieved in practice because this varied from case to case and had to be determined in accordance with the law applicable to that asset (par. 49). Regarding the language "appear to confer a right to another asset", she explained that whether or not there was indeed a right to another asset had to be determined, taking account of the facts and, ultimately, the law of the State.[19]

Regarding Principle 4(2), the State's law specified the requirements to be met, including as regards the form and content of the information to be provided for any legal effect to occur. The reason for including Principle 4(2) was to address a very real problem in the market where in many cases there was an insufficient evidentiary basis to determine the intentions of the parties. Accordingly, it was deemed to be helpful to include an express signal in the Principle that it would be helpful for States to include something in the law to specify what requirements were to be met in order for a legal effect to occur.[20]

The Working Group Members were broadly in agreement that the underlying policy intention of the Principle had merit. The representative of the UCC queried whether the current formulation of Principle 4 may be overly complicated. He proposed a simpler formulation, along the lines of: "a digital asset cannot give a right to another asset unless". Sub-Group 4 Co-Chair suggested that the Principle should retain its current structure, emphasising the importance of retaining the substance of

---

[16] UNIDROIT 2022 - Study LXXXII – W.G.5 – Doc. 4: Summary Report of the 5th session.

[17] UNIDROIT 2022 - Study LXXXII – W.G.5 – Doc. 4: Summary Report of the 5th session, par. 8 and 44.

[18] UNIDROIT 2022 - Study LXXXII – W.G.5 – Doc. 4: Summary Report of the 5th session, par. 48.

[19] UNIDROIT 2022 - Study LXXXII – W.G.5 – Doc. 4: Summary Report of the 5th session, par. 51.

[20] UNIDROIT 2022 - Study LXXXII – W.G.5 – Doc. 4: Summary Report of the 5th session, par. 43.

sub-paragraph 2. Finally, the Chair captured the Working Group's consensus, noting that there were no substantive disagreements, and that it was a matter for further drafting to clearly reflect the underlying policy intention behind the Principle.[21]

2.1.6 Sixth Meeting of the Working Group (August–September 2022)

The sixth meeting of the Working Group took place from 31 August to 2 September 2022. In the new version of the Draft Principles a new wording of Principle 4 appears, accompanied by 9 comments and 6 examples, in the following terms[22]:

Principle 4: Linked assets

Other law applies to determine the existence of, requirements for, and legal effect of any link between a digital asset and another asset, whether the other asset is tangible or intangible.

Regarding the existence of Principle 4 as an autonomous principle, it is noted that incorporating Principle 4 on Linked Assets to Principle 3(3) was considered. However, it was recommended to retain it as a separate Principle to highlight this important point separately and with specific detailed commentary.[23]

The Chair opened the discussions on Principle 4 noting that this principle must be read in conjunction with Principle 3(3). It was recalled that the substance of Principle 4 related to a conclusion which the Working Group had reached in its earlier sessions, whereby the Principles did not apply to how a digital asset was/could be linked to another asset, or any of the legal characteristics or rights related to that link. The Commentary for this Principle clearly explained how/why this was the case, as well as providing guidance on this matter for all readers.[24]

An observer queried the reasoning behind Principle 4. Several Members of the Working Group and Observers clarified that a large number of market participants understood that the law governing, or related to a digital asset, would also have an impact on any linked assets. As such, the confusion needed to be addressed. The Chair noted that additional guidance behind the reasoning for Principle 4 could be added to the Commentary. Other Members of the Working Group also confirmed that it was important to clearly indicate that other law applied to the existence of, requirements for, and legal effect of any link between a digital asset and another asset, whether the other asset was tangible or intangible. It was also added that the illustrations were an important factor in explaining the need for the Principle.[25]

---

[21] UNIDROIT 2022 - Study LXXXII – W.G.5 – Doc. 4: Summary Report of the 5th session, par. 56, 58 and 62.

[22] UNIDROIT 2022 - Study LXXXII – W.G.6 – Doc. 2: Master Copy of the Draft Principles and Comments.

[23] UNIDROIT 2022 - Study LXXXII – W.G.6 – Doc. 3: Tracked Principles and Issues Paper.

[24] UNIDROIT 2022 - Study LXXXII – W.G.6 – Doc. 4: Summary Report of the 6th session, par. 41.

[25] UNIDROIT 2022 - Study LXXXII – W.G.6 – Doc. 4: Summary Report of the 6th session, par. 53.

The Deputy Secretary-General and an observer proposed considering the Principle being expressed in a positive tone, rather than a negative one. It was noted that the Drafting Committee would explore this option.[26]

Finally, a Member of the Working Group noted that the scope of the Principles was limited to digital assets, however, additional guidance on linked assets could be included in the Commentary to cover some of the points raised, including where a digital asset was linked to another digital asset.

2.1.7 Seventh Meeting of the Working Group (December 2022)

The seventh meeting of the Working Group took place from 19 to 21 December 2022. The new version of the Draft Principles[27] includes a new wording of Principle 4, which, in line with the suggestions brought forward at the previous session, now has a positive wording. The principle, written as follows, is accompanied by 10 comments and 7 examples[28]:

Principle 4: Linked assets

These Principles apply to a digital asset linked to another asset, whether the other asset is tangible or intangible. Other law applies to determine the existence of, requirements for, and legal effect of any link between the digital asset and the other asset.

The revisions made were to draft the Principle in a positive tone, rather than a negative one. Additionally, an example of legislation that created a digital equivalence of paper assets was inserted into the Commentary. A few sentences had been moved from the Principle to the Commentary, and the language had generally been improved. The Working Group supported the draft of Principle 4 and requested the Drafting Committee to continue to further develop the Commentary.[29]

2.1.8 Eighth Meeting of the Working Group (March 2023)

At the request of the Working Group, the UNIDROIT Secretariat launched an online public consultation on 10 January 2023, which was open until 28 February 2023.[30]

---

[26] UNIDROIT 2022 - Study LXXXII – W.G.6 – Doc. 4: Summary Report of the 6th session, par. 55.

[27] UNIDROIT 2023 - Study LXXXII – W.G.7 – Doc. 2: Draft Principles and Commentary.

[28] UNIDROIT 2023 - Study LXXXII – W.G.7 – Doc. 2: Draft Principles and Commentary, par. 4 and 37.

[29] UNIDROIT 2023 - Study LXXXII – W.G.7 – Doc. 5: Summary Report of the 7th session.

[30] UNIDROIT 2023 – Study LXXXII – W.G.8 – Doc. 4, February, par. 4. UNIDROIT 2023– C.D. (102) 6, April, par. 16.

Of the total comments received, comments 11 to 137 are devoted to the issue of Principle 4 on linked assets.[31]

The eighth meeting of the Working Group was held from 8 to 10 March 2023. The WG discussed the final version of Principle 4,[32] fleshed out on the basis of comments received at the sixth meeting of the WG, intersessional work and comments to the public consultation.[33] Finally, after the debate, the WG adopted the final version.[34]

The session also addressed comments received through the online public consultation. The Working Group deliberated on the comments received in a Principle-by-Principle format. The Group expressed its agreement with the final structure of the Principles, concluded that the draft instrument was close to completion and should be submitted to a ninth ad hoc session for adoption.[35]

2.1.9 Ninth Meeting of the Working Group (April 2023)

Finally, a ninth ad hoc session of the Working Group was held online on 5 April 2023, where the draft Principles and Commentaries submitted by the Drafting Committee were reviewed. In addition, the Working Group discussed comments from observers participating on behalf of UNCITRAL and HCCH and called for some changes. The adoption took place at the 102nd session held in Rome from 10 to 12 May 2023.[36]

2.2 Reflections on Principle 4 and Its Commentaries

This section analyses the structure and content of Principle 4. In order to achieve this, the elaboration procedure that has been presented in summary in the previous section is of special interest since its precedents and antecedents give meaning to the final version of the Principle.

As we advanced in the introductory section, Principle 4 is the last of the four that form part of Section I of the UNIDROIT Principles on Digital Assets and Private Law. Section I is dedicated to the scope and definitions of the Principles. Specifically, Principle 1 establishes that the Principles deal with the private law relating to digital assets. Principle 2 establishes various definitions, including the central notion of digital asset which means "an electronic record which is capable of being subject to control".

---

[31] UNIDROIT 2023 Study LXXXII – W.G.8 – Doc. 4: Public Consultation Comments,.

[32] UNIDROIT 2023 - Study LXXXII – W.G.8 – Doc. 2, February 2023.

[33] UNIDROIT 2023 - Study LXXXII – W.G.8 – Doc. 4, February 2023.

[34] UNIDROIT 2023 - Study LXXXII – W.G.8 – Doc. 6, February 2023.

[35] UNIDROIT 2023 – C.D. (102) 6, April, par. 18.

[36] UNIDROIT 2023 – C.D. (102) Misc.2, May, par. 7. UNIDROIT 2023– C.D. (102) 25, August, par. 106.

In this context, Principle 4 is dedicated to so-called linked assets, which are digital assets linked to another tangible or intangible asset, to which the UNIDROIT Principles also apply. However, the existence of the link, its requirements and effects will be ruled by another law (a national law other than any national law that implements or is consistent with these Principles, in accordance with Principle 2, paragraphs 2 and 3).

In fact, in the initial versions of the draft Principles, there was no principle 4 as such but rather linked assets (referred to at the time as "digital asset 'tethered' to another asset") were simply the subject of definition and commentary in the dedicated Principle on definitions (Principle 2 in the final version); and, specifically, they were presented as an example of the general concept of "digital asset". It is in later versions of the draft Principles that Principle 4 emerges for the autonomous and independent treatment of linked assets. The reason for this autonomous treatment, as explained in the introductory section on the preparatory iter of the Principles, is that in this way the principle contains a considerable amount of commentary providing examples of linked assets. After the creation of Principle 4, incorporating its content into Principle 3 was considered. However, it was recommended to retain it as a separate Principle precisely to highlight this important point separately and with specific details.

In the initial versions of the draft Principles, the "digital asset" definition examples include and describe the case of "digital asset tethered to another asset", as follows: "Illustration 3: Digital asset is 'tethered' to another asset. This Illustration contemplates that pursuant to law other than a digital asset law and any applicable contractual arrangements, an acquirer of a digital asset will, ipso facto, acquire another asset. That other asset might be entirely exogenous (e.g., a physical commodity such as a precious metal) or one that is inherently connected to the digital asset (e.g., a security that, by its terms, may be acquired and disposed of only in connection with the acquisition and disposition of a digital asset within the relevant protocol/platform. The digital asset is composed only of information capable of being subject to control and the other asset (even if it is itself composed of information) is not a component of the digital asset and is not within the scope of these Principles. For example, under a law conforming to Principle [X.2], an innocent acquirer of the digital asset may take the digital asset free of competing proprietary claims. But other law (and the relevant facts, including the applicable contractual arrangements) would determine whether (and the extent to which) or not the acquirer would take free of (or subject to) competing proprietary claims to the other asset".[37]

Likewise, the title of the Principle and the name of this category of digital assets have also changed. Initially the name was "tethered assets". Such denomination was replaced because it was suggested that the use of the word 'tethered' should be avoided because it carried connotations to an existing digital currency ("Tether"). The words "linked" as well as "referenced" asset were proposed to describe this important category of assets, noting that the existing literature had not yet settled on any standard terminology. The expression initially chosen was "assets linked to other assets". Finally, in the definitive version, simply "linked assets". However, it

[37] UNIDROIT 2021 - Study LXXXII – W.G.4 – Doc. 2, page 38.

was considered that this last expression ("linked digital assets" or similar) may be confusing because what were promoted as "linked assets" may in fact for all purposes under the law not be a linked asset; hence a preference was expressed for the longer formulation to achieve greater neutrality.

The final version of the Principle is structured in a single section, followed by the corresponding Commentaries (4.1 to 4.12). Additionally, for clarification purposes, 8 Illustrations are included (Sects. 4.13 to 4.32). In the initial version of the first draft there were two sections in the wording of Principle 4, and during the preparation procedure a third section was even included with an alternative wording, although in the final version they were reduced to a single section. On the other hand, during the process of developing the Principle, the number of comments and examples increased because, due to the complexity of the topic, the intention was to broadly expose the different cases of linked assets and, as a guide, offer proposals of solutions that may be applicable in the other law of the States.

Finally, in the first draft of Principle 4, negative wording was used, to indicate that the Principles did not apply to the linking of the digital asset with another asset. Finally, on accepting different suggestions in this regard, the current positive wording was established: the Principles apply to the digital asset while the existence and legal effects of the link will be ruled by the other law of the State.

2.2.1 Linked Asset. Concept; Problem and Solution in Accordance with Principle 4

The purpose of Principle 4 is to identify the limit of the Principles as regards digital assets 'linked' to other assets. To understand the meaning and purpose of this Principle 4, it is necessary to relate the principles that precede it. Indeed, Principle 1 provides that the purpose of the UNIDROIT Principles is to "deal with the private law relating to digital assets". However, the Principles intend to address only a specific area of private law, and there are many issues of private law which are not addressed by the Principles (Commentary to Principle 1). The central notion of the Principles is, therefore, digital assets, defined in Principle 2 (2) as "an electronic record which is capable of being subject to control".

In commercial practice, what are called, in short, "linked digital assets" have appeared. As digital assets, linked digital assets are included in the general concept defined in Principle 2 (2). Due to its complexity though, Principle 4 addresses this class of digital assets separately. They would more accurately be "digital assets linked to other assets". It is a name that, in commercial practice, includes many and diverse products, as shown in the Illustrations that complement this principle. Indeed, given the breadth of this product in commercial practice, on several occasions members of the Working Group requested that examples be provided of products that could be considered linked assets. Initially, based on a market analysis, within the category of "digital twins", the Working Group identified the following general types: non-fungible tokens (NFTs): digital assets associated with external art or other objects using a technical indicator and/or through a license agreement; digital asset backed by real-world assets; digital assets backed by digital assets; decentralized Finance (DeFi).

More simply, examples of "linked digital assets" would be those digital assets linked or referred to another asset, whether material (e.g., gold, oil) or immaterial (e.g., a credit right, a share). There is no limitation on the nature of the 'other asset'. The concept is to be interpreted broadly and may be intangible or tangible. That other asset might also be exogenous (e.g., a physical commodity such as a precious metal), or one that is inherently connected to the digital asset (e.g., a security that by its terms may be acquired and disposed of only in connection with the acquisition and disposition of a digital asset). The digital asset is composed only of information capable of being subject to control and the other asset (even if it is itself composed of information) is not a component of the digital asset and is not within the scope of these Principles.

The so-called "stablecoins" are also included in the preparatory works of the UNIDROIT Principles among the examples of "linked digital assets" because they are referenced or linked to other assets (e.g., an official currency such as the dollar, or a commodity of stable value like gold) to minimize the volatility of the price of the stablecoin and avoid large fluctuations and oscillations. In fact, from a legal point of view, in recent regulatory initiatives of the European Union such as Regulation (EU) 2023/1114 of the European Parliament and of the Council of 31 May 2023 on markets in crypto-assets, the denomination "stablecoins" is avoided because, as the European Central Bank points out, they are neither currencies nor stable.[38] The aforementioned Regulation prefers to call them precisely "asset-referenced tokens" which are those whose purpose is to stabilize their value by referring to another security or right, or a combination thereof, including one or more official currencies.[39]

The question of the legal nature of this link or connection between the digital asset and the other asset (digital or not, endogenous or exogenous) and its scope is of special relevance. Its clarification is important because in practice different situations arise. Sometimes the linked asset can be structured so as to represent other assets, in such a way that the holder of the digital assets purports to have a proprietary right to that other asset (tangible or intangible). In that case, when the digital asset is transmitted, the proprietary right to that other asset is transferred from A to B. In other cases, there may be another type of possible connection between a digital asset and another asset: it may occur that the value of the digital asset is "backed by" or "pegged to" one or more other assets but the holder of that digital asset does not have any proprietary rights to those other assets (e.g. certain kinds of stablecoins can be pegged to a cryptocurrency, fiat money, or to exchange-traded commodities in order to minimize the volatility of the price of the stablecoin).

[38] European Central Bank, "Stablecoins – no coins, but are they stable?" IN FOCUS I Issue no 3 I November 2019.

[39] Regulation (EU) 2023/1114 of the European Parliament and of the Council of 31 May 2023 on markets in crypto-assets, and amending Regulations (EU) No 1093/2010 and (EU) No 1095/2010 and Directives 2013/36/EU and (EU) 2019/1937, Official Journal of the European Union L 150/40, 9.6.2023.

Therefore, the common characteristic is the existence (real or apparent) of a link, of a relationship between a digital asset and another asset (digital or not). Given this apparent or real link, from the legal point of view, the problem is the existence of the link and its legal effectiveness. That is to say, if this apparent link actually exists and what requirements are necessary; and, once that link does exist, what legal effects does it have.

This is not a merely a theoretical issue but one of great practical importance that confronts us with the problem of dissociation that would arise when the digital asset and the linked asset (digital or not) follow different and unrelated paths. As an example, in the case of transmission of the digital asset, the question is whether it also involves the transmission of the other linked asset. Furthermore, the question arises of what happens in the event of a distinct and separate transmission of the other linked asset (digital or not). In short, the conundrum is what would occur in the case of a divergence between the digital asset and the other asset, especially where the two were transferred separately creating a conflict of priority. The same problem of dissociation arises in cases of insolvency of the holder of the linked digital asset. The question then is whether or not insolvency extends to the other linked asset (digital or not).

During the preparation of the UNIDROIT Principles on digital assets, the importance of the issue of linked assets and the legal problems they raise were detected from the beginning. Thus, in the first exploratory works, the problem of "digital twins" had already been raised. They were described as digital assets linked to real-world assets and posed problems such as preventing the "digital twin" from being separated from the real-world asset it represented. The Working Group noted that there was a difference between the market developing a solution where a certain digital asset represented another real-world asset, especially a physical object, such as gold in a vault, and the question of whether a legal system would recognize that as truly representing rights in the gold. In the initial documents of the Working Group, these assets were called "tethered digital assets", although this name was later ditched due to its coincidence with a well-known commercial product (Tether).

Once the problem was detected, the next question that was also raised right from the outset was whether these UNIDROIT Principles should address and resolve the question of the existence and effects of the link, thus extending their scope not only to the digital asset but also to the other asset (digital or not) linked. Or whether this issue should be resolved by other instruments (the internal law of each state, the courts, commercial practices and uses or contractual clauses).

The solution to this question is found in the principle of neutrality that inspires the content of the UNIDROIT Principles on digital assets. As we have already noted, in accordance with Principle 1, the purpose of these Principles is to "deal with the private law relating to digital assets". However, the Principles intend to address only a specific area of private law, and there are many issues of private law which are not addressed by the Principles (Commentary to Principle 1). Among these unaddressed issues is precisely that relating to the existence and effects of the link in the case of linked assets. The reason is the principle of neutrality: the effects of the links on the other underlying linked asset will depend not on the Principles but on the law applicable to the other linked asset (digital or not): whether there is a property right or whether the transfer of the first implies the transfer of the second is a question that will have to be resolved on a case-by-case basis depending on the law of each state applicable to that other asset.

In this way the Principle makes clear that the legal effect of the link (if any) is not addressed in these Principles. This neutral solution of the Principles on the question of the nature of the legal relationship between the digital asset and the underlying asset is justified because, to a large extent, the solution depends on the different jurisdictions and how they treat such other assets: the nature and effects of the link may vary from case to case and will have to be determined in accordance with the law applicable to that asset (the other law of the State).

Therefore, the final solution is that the Principles do not apply to the other linked asset (digital or not) nor to the existence and effects of the link. They do apply though to the linked digital asset. The way this solution is expressed in the Principles is relevant: it should be presented in such a way that it is clear that the question of the nature and effects of the linked assets will be resolved in accordance with the relevant applicable other law of the State, not in accordance with the UNIDROIT Principles, and, at the same time, that these Principles will be applicable to digital assets. This clarification is important because, as the Working Group noted, a large number of market participants understood that the law governing, or related to a digital asset, would also have an impact on any linked assets. Therefore, the confusion needed to be addressed.

In the early drafts of the Principles, Principle 4 had negative wording in the sense that it was limited to indicating its inapplicability to other assets linked to the digital asset. Following a suggestion to this effect within the Working Group, it is changed to the current positive wording in which, on the one hand, it is established that the Principles apply to a digital asset linked to another asset (as a digital asset in accordance with the Principle 2): "The digital assets to which these Principles apply include a digital asset linked to another asset." (initial sentence of Principle 4). On the other hand, it is provided that "other law" will apply to the existence of, requirements for and legal effects of any link between the digital asset and the other asset (including the effect of a transmission of the digital asset on the other asset) (third and final sentence of Principle 4).

However, although Principle 4 does not regulate this issue of the existence of, requirements for and legal effects of the link (which will be resolved in accordance with other law of the State), the intention of the Principles is to serve as a guide for the resolution of this issue, as is made clear in the Comments and Illustration that accompany Principle 4, which are extensively dedicated to the form and content of the "other law".

The question about the link between a digital asset and "other assets" is a good example of the broader discussion about whether the UNIDROIT Principles should seek only to identify problems and desired results, or also provide guidance on the best ways to solve the problems raised. In this sense, Principle 4 does not apply to the question of the existence and effects of the link, which is referred to the other State law, but rather possible solutions to this issue are offered in the Comments that accompany Principle 4. In these comments, as we will see, the issue of the form and content of this other State law is extensively addressed. Therefore, although Principle 4 does not regulate this issue, which is referred to other law of the State, the underlying policy intention behind the Principle 4 is to serve as a guide for the resolution of this issue by the different States.

2.2.2 About the Existence, Requirements and Effects of the Link

As we have just seen, the existence of the link and its effects depend on the other law of the State. Although the scope of the Principles is limited to digital assets, however, additional guidance on linked assets is included in the Commentaries to provide solution proposals for some of the points raised, including where a digital asset was linked to another asset (digital or not) and the effects of such link.

Existence of the link. In principle, the existence of the link can be considered a question of fact, depending on the circumstances of the case and the intentions of the parties. The link may arise from the coding of the digital asset, from a white paper or from the issuance conditions. However, the truth is that in practice there is the problem that in many cases there was an insufficient evidentiary basis to determine the intentions of the parties. Therefore, the other law of the State can also be decisive for the existence of the link, establishing minimum requirements for its existence. Therefore, any links that fail to comply with such requirements will be ineffective, regardless of the more or less clear intentions of the parties, due to the principle of primacy of the other law that presides over the UNIDROIT Principles.

Legal effects of the link. A different issue from the factual existence of the link is that related to its effects that depend on the other law of the State. The legal effects of the link refer to issues such as the effect of a transmission of the digital asset on the other asset, to which Principle 4 expressly refers. But those effects also extend to situations of insolvency of the holder of the digital asset or cases of constitution of warranty rights. In such cases, making the link fully effective could mean that the transmission of the digital asset implies the simultaneous transmission of the other linked asset. It would also imply that the insolvency of the holder of the digital asset extends to the other linked asset and that the guarantee intended for that digital asset also extends to the other underlying asset.

In accordance with Principle 4, these legal effects do not depend on the UNIDROIT Principles but on the other law of the State, which, where appropriate, will be the one that will regulate such effects. Consequently, and given the principle of primacy of the other State law, the contractual agreement of the parties who issue, transmit, give as guarantee or carry out any other act or legal transaction on the linked asset will depend on what is established by the other State law. Therefore, the parties cannot grant the link an effect greater than that established by the other law of the State. Thus, for the transmission of the digital asset to imply the transmission of the economic rights over the other asset, the agreement of the parties would not be enough, but it would be necessary for the other State law to establish or allow it (Comment 4.7).

2.2.3 Form and Content of the Notion "Other Law"

Given the principle of neutrality on which the UNIDROIT Principles are based, as we have seen, Principle 4 refers the question of the existence, requirements and effects of the link to the other law of the State ("other law", Principle 4, sentence 3).

Given the importance of this reference, it is necessary to delimit the concept of "other law" and distinguish it from other different concepts. According to Principle 2 (4), relating to definitions, "other law" means "a State's law to the extent that it is not Principles Law". According to Principle 2 (3) "Principles Law" means "any part of a State's law which implements or is consistent with these Principles. Therefore, under Principle 2 (3), all the rules provided by the Principles qualify as "Principles Law" once they have been adopted into the law of a State. Consequently, within the law of a State, all law that is not "Principles Law" as defined in Principle 2 (3) is referred to as "other law" in these UNIDROIT Principles. Therefore, "Principles Law" and "other law" together form "the law". Furthermore, it is specified that "other law" includes administrative rules and judicially determined rules, as well as legislation (Commentary 2.22).

There are several possibilities as to the form that the provisions of this "other law" could or should take. They may be existing rules of other law or special rules provided by a State and specifically developed for linked assets. Furthermore, both the pre-existing rules and the new rules may be contained in a general law (which is applicable to linked assets) or in a special law specifically intended to regulate linked assets. It is even possible that other law may recognise the existence of the link but without recognising any legal effect to the disposition of the digital asset in relation to the other asset, which in turn may depend on a separate legal act. The Illustrations accompanying Principle 4 show these different possibilities regarding the form and content of other law; we will refer to them in summary at the end of these reflections.

In the case where the other law of State recognizes the link between the digital asset and the underlying asset, this situation has been compared to documents of title and especially bills of lading in English Law. The basic conclusion of the Working Group was that there were two ways of conceiving the current law to recognize a document or record that represented title, ownership or some other property interest in the underlying asset. The first was by codifying the principles as in German law, Dutch law or the UCC (statutory recognition). The second method detailed the establishment of a practice as in English law where a bill of lading, recognized by the courts, represented rights in property: the courts in England have given legal recognition to an established mercantile practice or custom. In this case, the courts in England have given legal recognition to an established mercantile practice or custom, without any statutory definition. The easiest solution would be for the existing law to recognize that certain assets could be represented by a digital asset in the same way as bills of lading in many jurisdictions through one of two mechanisms.

2.2.4 Innocent Acquisition

The possible dissociation between the digital asset and the other linked asset (digital or not) also raises problems in the event of the transfer of the digital asset by a transferor who is acting wrongfully and has no proprietary right in the digital asset to a third party acting in good faith (innocent acquirer).

For digital assets in general, under Principle 8(2), an innocent acquirer would acquire a right to a digital asset free of conflicting proprietary rights (proprietary claims). Similarly, Principle 8(3) provides that no right based on a proprietary claim relating to a digital asset can be successfully asserted against an innocent acquirer of that digital asset.

This innocent acquisition rule set out in Principle 8 is an exception to the basic rule *nemo dat quod non habet* (one cannot give what one does not have). In the UNIDROIT Principles on digital assets and private law the innocent acquisition rule represents a policy balance in favour of an innocent acquirer, mainly in the case of digital assets. For that reason: a person who has an owner right in a digital asset is considered to be in a better position than a transferee to protect its property from wrongful activity by taking steps to safeguard its proprietary rights.

In the case of linked digital assets, the question that arises is whether the application of the innocent acquirer rule provided for digital assets in general extends equally to the other asset (digital or not) linked to it. Certainly, Principle 4 on linked assets does not expressly contemplate the case of acquisition by innocent acquirers. However, following the principle of neutrality that inspires Principle 4, the solution should be the non-application of the UNIDROIT Principles to this issue and the consequent reference to the other law of each State. This is confirmed by Commentary 4.11, which does expressly address this issue and provides that the other law of a State could provide that the benefit of any innocent acquisition rule applied to a digital asset in accordance with Principle 8 should also apply to the other asset linked to it.

However, in accordance with the primacy of the other law, it is specified that merely proving the link between the digital asset and the other asset would not necessarily mean that the holder of the other asset took the benefit of the innocent acquisition rule. To achieve this result, a specific provision in the other law of the State is necessary. In such a case, if the other law of the State provides an innocent acquisition rule in relation to the other asset linked to the digital asset, the effect would be that both the digital asset and the other asset would benefit from such a rule (Example 8, Comment 4.29 to 4.32, where this issue of the innocent acquisition rule is discussed at length).

Consequently, States may need to enact special legislation, different from the Principles Law relevant to the digital asset itself, to ensure that the rights of a third-party acquirer in relation to the digital asset and the other asset remain in line with each other. This solution is not only consistent with the principle of neutrality and primacy of the other law, but is justified because, as we have already explained, the application of this rule represents a policy balance and each State must be able to decide whether such policy balance is made in favour of the holder of the digital asset or the acquirer depending on who is in the best position to defend itself from wrongful activity based on the circumstances of each case.

2.2.5 Summary of the Comments and Illustrations

Following on from Principle 4, there are 12 paragraphs of comments (4.1 to 4.12) that, due to their content, we group as follows, with a brief description of their content.

Introductory (4.1.–4.3). The notion of a digital asset linked to another asset is introduced. Its usual purpose is explained. The "other asset" is described. The neutrality of the Principles is established with respect to the existence and effects of the link. The solution to these issues is referred to the other law of the State.

Existence and effect of the link (4.4.–4.7). How linked assets work depends on two distinct questions: (1) whether there is any link between the digital asset and the other asset; and (2) whether the link has any legal effect on the parties' rights in relation to the other asset. Both issues depend on the other law of the State. In accordance with the primacy of the other law under this Principle, the parties cannot confer a legal effect on the link greater than that permitted by the other law of the State.

Comparison with registration systems (4.8.–4.9). Transactions with linked digital assets do not always have the same legal effects as transactions with conventional assets, such as securities registered in a legally constituted registry system. The reason is that another law, usually legislation, confers legal effect on the registration system.

Form of other law (4.10.). The legal effect may be determined by existing rules of other law, or a State may provide for it in special rules developed for linked assets.

Innocent acquisition (4.11.). It would be open to the other law of a State to provide that the benefit of any innocent acquisition rule applied to a digital asset in accordance with Principle 8 should also apply to the other asset linked to it.

Illustrations (4.12. a 4.32.). Eight examples are included as illustrations of the different legal effects of a link between the digital asset and the other asset.

Illustration 1 (4.12. a 4.15.). The rules of other law already in force may apply to the parties' transaction with the digital asset and determine the legal effect on the other asset linked to it.

Illustration 2 (4.16. a 4.17.). One digital asset may be linked to another digital asset and the legal link between them would depend on the effect of any legal relations between the holders of the two assets (provisions of white paper or the contract between the issuer and the holder of digital asset).

Illustration 3 (4.18. a 4.19.). The rules of other law already in force may govern all proprietary aspects of an asset linked to a digital asset, regardless of the representations and intention of the parties dealing in these assets.

Illustrations 4 and 5 (4.20. to 4.22.). A State may choose to enact special legislation to make the link between the token and the other asset legally effective (e.g., to create digital equivalents to paper negotiable instruments or documents of title to goods or issue debt securities on a blockchain ledger).

Illustration 6 (4.23. a 4.25.). The precise legal effect of any link between the digital asset and another asset may depend as much on ascertaining the parties' intentions from any system coding, protocols, and documentation as it does from the operation of the other law. Thus, the terms of a white paper accompanying the issue of a digital asset may be relevant to inferring the nature and value of the legal right, if any, that the holder of the digital asset was intended to have in relation to the other asset.

Illustration 7 (4.26. to 4.28.). Digital assets may be used to create transferable portions of value derived from other assets which exist off the blockchain. Even where the link between the digital assets and the other assets is clear, the precise effect of the holders' rights will be determined by the other law of the State. The parties' intention to link the assets cannot override the other law that applies to those assets.

Illustration 8 (4.29.). The other law of a State may recognise a good faith acquisition rule in relation to the other asset linked to the digital asset. The effect may be that both the digital asset and the other asset would benefit from a good faith acquisition rule.

2.3 *Relationship of Principle 4 with other Principles*

The question of the legal effects of the link in the case of linked assets affects very diverse issues. Most importantly, as we have anticipated, issues such as the acquisition and transfer of these assets, the establishment of security rights over them or the situations of insolvency of the owner. In these cases, it is decisive to know who is the rightful owner of a given asset.

Therefore, Principles other than Principle 4 also refer to linked assets. Those other Principles resolve the question of the existence and effects of the link in coherence with the solution of referral to "the other law of the State" of Principle 4 or even expressly refer to Principle 4.

This is the case of Principle 5, on Applicable Law. In Commentary 5.24 (on linked assets) it is established that where a digital asset is linked, or purports to be linked, to another asset, other law (in this case, the conflicts of law rules contained in other law) determines the law applicable to determine the existence of, requirements for, and legal effect of any link between the digital asset and the other asset; A final reference is made to Principle 4, stating that "These matters are determined by other law under Principle 4."

In the case of Principle 8 on "Innocent acquisition", in Commentary 8.6, in relation to the operation of the innocent acquirer rule in Principle 8 to linked assets,

Commentary 4.11 and 4.29 to 4.32 of Principle 4 are referred to directly for the treatment of this issue.

Finally, Principle 14 on "Secured transactions", after establishing that "(1) Digital assets can be the subject of security rights", it provides that "(2) If a digital asset is linked to another asset, other law applies to determine the legal effect on that other asset of the creation of a security right in that digital asset. (3) If a digital asset is linked to another asset, other law applies to determine the legal effect on that other asset of a security right in that digital asset being made effective against third parties." Therefore, it adopts the approach of Principle 4 of referring the solution of these issues to "the other law of the State".

2.4 Relationship of Principle 4 with other instruments

2.4.1 United Nations Commissions on International Trade Law: Model Law on Secured Transactions

The UNCITRAL Model Law on Secured Transactions, approved on 5 July 2006, deals with security interests in all types of tangible and intangible movable property, such as goods, receivables, bank accounts, negotiable documents, non-intermediated securities and intellectual property rights, with some exceptions, such as intermediary securities. This Model Law adopts a unitary approach using a single concept for all types of security interests under which the Model Law applies to all types of transactions serving security purposes, such as secured loans, retention-of-title sale or financial lease, and a comprehensive approach under which the Model Law on Secured Transactions applies to all types of assets, secured obligations, borrowers and lenders.

Article 16 of this Model Law is dedicated to negotiable documents and tangible assets covered by negotiable documents. This article states that "A security right in a negotiable document extends to the tangible asset covered by the document, provided that the issuer of the document is in possession of the asset at the time the security right in the document is created." In accordance with the Guide to Enactment of this Model Law, article 16 reflects the generally accepted principle that a negotiable document is treated as embodying rights in the tangible assets covered by the document. As a result, a security right in those tangible assets may be created by creating a security right in the document. For example, a security right in cargo covered by a negotiable bill of lading issued by the carrier or in assets covered by a negotiable warehouse receipt issued by the operator of the warehouse in which those assets have been deposited may be created by creating a security right in the bill of lading or warehouse receipt. According to the Guide to Enactment, under article 16, a security right in a negotiable document extends to the assets covered by the document only if the issuer of the document is in possession of the assets when the security right is created. If this condition is satisfied, the security right in the tangible assets covered by the document continues to exist even after the assets are no longer in the possession of the issuer of the negotiable document. However, under article 26, paragraph 2, the effectiveness of the security right in the assets against third parties that was achieved by possession of the document applies while the document covers the assets and lapses once possession of the assets is relinquished by the issuer.

Article 17 is dedicated to tangible assets with respect to which intellectual property is used. In this case it is stated that "A security right in a tangible asset with respect to which intellectual property is used does not extend to the intellectual property and a security right in the intellectual property does not extend to the tangible asset". According to the Guide to Enactment, article 17 is based on recommendation 243 of the Intellectual Property Supplement. It is intended to recognize the distinction between a tangible asset with respect to which intellectual property is used and the intellectual property (e.g. a motor vehicle that incorporates features that rely on the manufacturer's right to use a patented invention or copyrighted software as distinct from the patent or copyright itself). As a result, a secured creditor who has a security right in a tangible asset with respect to which intellectual property is used does not acquire a security right in the intellectual property, unless the intellectual property is included in the description of the encumbered assets in the security agreement and then only if the grantor has rights, or the power to create a security right, in the relevant intellectual property.

2.4.2 European Law Institute: Principles on the Use of Digital Assets as Security

The European Law Institute has developed the Principles on the Use of Digital Assets as Security (2022).[40] The Principles have no bearing on the legal characterisation of a digital asset and, in particular, on whether a given asset embodies a contractual, proprietary or other, *sui generis* right. Indeed, the novelty of digital assets makes it difficult to apply a classic property or contract law analysis to them.

The types of assets falling within the proposed definition include social media and other online accounts, cryptocurrencies and stablecoins, uncertificated financial assets that only exist electronically, in the form of tokens, such as security tokens, Moreover, the proposed definition captures both 'pure' digital assets (i.e. digital assets that have been created and only exist in the digital world, in the form of tokens representing a unique set of valuable attributes, such as cryptocurrencies, security tokens, and social media accounts) and asset-backed tokens (i.e. digital representations of already existing, valuable attributes, such as cryptocurrencies, security tokens, and social media accounts) and asset-backed tokens (i.e. digital representations of already existing, physical assets, such as tokenised securities or bonds, tokenised gold-bullion, tokenised real estate or patents) and so-called 'non-fungible tokens' (NFTs), such as tokenised works of art or collectibles.

---

[40] European Law Institute, *Principles on the Use of Digital Assets as Security*, 2022. Available in: https://www.europeanlawinstitute.eu/fileadmin/user_upload/p_eli/Publications/ELI_Principles_on_the_Use_of_Digital_Assets_as_Security.pdf.

Principle 2 is dedicated to "Digital Assets as Security", stating that a digital asset can be used as security in accordance with the terms of a security agreement between a security provider and a secured creditor (Principle 2(1)). Furthermore, it is added that the use of a digital asset as security is subject to compliance with the provisions of the law governing the creation of security interests, under Principle 3, and to the law governing the effectiveness of security interests against third parties, under Principle 4 (Principle 2(2)).

Principle 3(4) addresses the specific case of digital assets that represent real-world assets, whether tangible or intangible. The question of whether, and under which conditions, a security interest created in the digital asset would also result in the creation of a security interest in the underlying real-world asset is to be decided by reference to the substantive law to which the ordinary conflict of laws rules governing the proprietary aspects regarding the underlying real-world asset would point (for example, the *lex rei sitae* rule or the *lex registrationis rule*). This solution strikes a balance between legal certainty, on the one hand, and facilitating the use of assets created by new technologies, on the other hand, and it is also mindful of the dichotomy that the literature makes between the law of the token and the law of the main (underlying) asset as regards the conflicts of laws treatment of so-called 'exogenous tokens'.

Principle 4(4) shares the same philosophy and is motivated by the same public as those underlying Principle 3(4). Thus, in common with Principle 3(4), Principle 4(4) points to the ordinary conflict of laws rules governing the proprietary aspects of the real-world asset referenced by a token as decisive on the question of whether, and subject to which conditions, third-party effectiveness achieved with respect to a security interest in the token would also result in third-party effectiveness of a security interest in the underlying real-world asset.

2.4.3 European Union: Regulation 2023/1114 of the European Parliament and of the Council of 31 May 2023 on Markets in Cryptoassets

Regulation 2023/1114 of the European Parliament and of the Council of 31 May 2023 on markets in cryptoassets[41] (MiCA) establishes uniform rules for issuers of cryptoassets and for crypto-asset service providers. The Regulation applies to the issuance, offering to the public, and admission to trading of Crypto-assets and the provision of certain crypto-asset services in the EU.

This Regulation aims to apply to all cryptoassets not already covered by other financial services legislations. According to art. 3.1, 'cryptoasset' means a digital representation of a value or of a right that is able to be transferred and stored electronically using distributed ledger technology or similar technology. MiCA classifies

[41] Regulation (EU) 2023/1114 of the European Parliament and of the Council of 31 May 2023 on markets in crypto-assets, and amending Regulations (EU) No 1093/2010 and (EU) No 1095/2010 and Directives 2013/36/EU and (EU) 2019/1937 (OJ L 150, 9.6.2023, p. 40–205).

cryptoassets into three types, which should be distinguished from one another and subject to different requirements depending on the risks they entail. The classification is based on whether the cryptoassets seek to stabilise their value by reference to other assets.

The first type is ‘electronic money token’ or ‘e-money token’, that means a crypto-asset that purports to maintain a stable value by referencing the value of one official currency (art. 3.1.7). The second type of cryptoassets is ‘asset-referenced token’ that means a type of crypto-asset that is not an electronic money token and that purports to maintain a stable value by referencing another value or right or a combination thereof, including one or more official currencies (art. 3.1.6). This second type covers all other cryptoassets, other than e-money tokens, whose value is backed by assets. Finally, the third type is a catch-all category of cryptoassets other than asset-referenced tokens and e-money tokens, which covers a wide variety of cryptoassets, including ‘utility token’, a type of crypto-asset that is only intended to provide access to a good or a service supplied by its issuer (art. 3.1.9).

2.4.4 Joint HCCH-UNIDROIT Project on Applicable Law to Cross-Border Holdings and Transfers of Digital Assets and Tokens

During the working sessions of the WG on the Digital Assets Project, discussions were initiated to shape a Joint HCCH-UNIDROIT Project on Applicable Law to Cross-Border Holdings and Transfers of Digital Assets and Tokens.[42] At its 2024 meeting,[43] the CAGP took note of the report of the HCCH-UNIDROIT Project on Digital Assets and Tokens,[44] in particular the summary conclusions on possible future work on PIL in relation to digital assets, and decided to conclude the work on the Project.

“Linked assets” were identified as the main area of work, with consensus on the desirability to conduct work on “linked assets”, which were not defined or considered in Principles 4 and 5 of the UNIDROIT DAPL Principles. The necessity of working on appropriate connecting factors to identify the law applicable to the determination of whether a valid link exists between the digital asset and the asset to which it purports to be linked, and the legal nature of the link, if any, was identified.

[42] HCCH-UNIDROIT Project on Law Applicable to Cross-Border Holdings and Transfers of Digital Assets and Tokens, UNIDROIT 2023– C.D. (102) 6, April. Available in: https://www.unidroit.org/wp-content/uploads/2023/05/C.D.-102-12-Proposal-for-Joint-Work-HCCH-unidroit.pdf.

[43] HCCH, Conclusions & Decisions, Council on General Affairs and Policy, March 2024. Available in: https://assets.hcch.net/docs/7d647a6f-b927-4c1a-a837-d0846fbacca1.pdf

[44] HCCH-UNIDROIT Digital Assets and Tokens Joint Project: Report, Prel. Doc. No 3 of January 2024. Available in: https://assets.hcch.net/docs/efce41ca-1c8c-4d61-9d8b-9348df9303a0.pdf.

Reflections on Section II: Private International Law

Principle 5
Applicable law

Ángel María Ballesteros Barros

(1) Subject to paragraph (2), proprietary issues in respect of a digital asset are governed by:

(a) the domestic law of the State expressly specified in the digital asset, and those Principles (if any) expressly specified in the digital asset; or, failing that,

(b) the domestic law of the State expressly specified in the system on which the digital asset is recorded, and those Principles (if any) expressly specified in the system on which the digital asset is recorded; or, failing that,

(c) in relation to a digital asset of which there is an issuer, including digital assets of the same description of which there is an issuer, the domestic law of the State where the issuer has its statutory seat, provided that its statutory seat is readily ascertainable by the public; or.

(d) if none of the above sub-paragraphs applies:

OPTION A:

(i) those aspects or provisions of the law of the forum State as specified by that State;

(ii) to the extent not addressed by sub-paragraph (d)(i), those Principles as specified by the forum State;

This work was financed within the framework of the Prometeo 2023 project of the Regional Ministry of Innovation, Universities, Science and Digital Society (CIPROM/2022/26) "Present and future of the regulation of cryptoassets in the EU [LegalCripto]", whose principal investigator is Carmen Pastor Sempere. The basic ideas contained herein were presented in the author's paper with the same title, given on November 13, 2024 at the IV International Congress on "UNIDROIT Principles on Digital Assets and Private Law: Context, Content, Perspectives", organized also by BAES Research Group of the University of Alicante on November 13 and 14, 2024.

Á. M. Ballesteros Barros (✉)
University Pablo de Olavide, Sevilla, Spain
e-mail: ambalbar@upo.es

C. Pastor Sempere and D. A. Morán Bovio (eds.), UNIDROIT *Principles on Digital Assets and Private Law*, Law, Governance and Technology Series 80,
https://doi.org/10.1007/978-3-032-11001-5_11

(iii) to the extent not addressed by sub-paragraphs (d)(i) or (d)(ii), the law applicable by virtue of the rules of private international law of the forum State.

OPTION B:

(i) those Principles as specified by the forum State;

(ii) to the extent not addressed by sub-paragraph (d)(i), the law applicable by virtue of the rules of private international law of the forum State.

(2) In the interpretation and application of paragraph (1), regard is to be had to the following:

(a) proprietary issues in respect of digital assets, and in particular their acquisition and disposition, are always a matter of law;
(b) in determining whether the applicable law is specified in a digital asset, or in a system on which the digital asset is recorded, consideration should be given to records attached to, or associated with, the digital asset, or the system, if such records are readily available for review by persons dealing with the relevant digital asset;
(c) by transferring, acquiring, or otherwise dealing with a digital asset a person consents to the law applicable under sub-paragraph (1)(a), (1)(b) or (1)(c);
(d) the law applicable under paragraph (1) applies to all digital assets of the same description;
(e) if, after a digital asset is first issued or created, the applicable law changes by operation of sub-paragraph (1)(a), (1)(b) or (1)(c), proprietary rights in the digital asset that have been established before that change are not affected by it;
(f) the 'issuer' referred to in sub-paragraph (1)(c) means a legal person:

(i) who put the digital asset, or digital assets of the same description, in the stream of commerce for value; and
(ii) who, in a way that is readily ascertainable by the public,

(A) identifies itself as a named person;
(B) identifies its statutory seat; and
(C) identifies itself as the person who put the digital asset, or digital assets of the same description, into the stream of commerce for value.

(3) The law applicable to the issues addressed in Principles 10 to 13, including whether an agreement is a custody agreement, is the domestic law of the State expressly specified in that agreement as the law that governs the agreement, or

if the agreement expressly provides that another law is applicable to all such issues, that other law.
(4) Paragraphs (1) and (2) are subject to paragraph (3).
(5) Other law applies to determine:

(a) the law applicable to the third-party effectiveness of a security right in a digital asset made effective against third parties by a method other than control;
(b) the law applicable to determine the priority between conflicting security rights made effective against third parties by a method other than control.

(6) Notwithstanding the opening of an insolvency-related proceeding and subject to paragraph (7), the law applicable in accordance with this Principle governs all proprietary issues in respect of digital assets with regard to any event that has occurred before the opening of that insolvency-related proceeding.
(7) Paragraph (6) does not affect the application of any substantive or procedural rule of law applicable by virtue of an insolvency-related proceeding, such as any rule relating to:

(a) the ranking of categories of claims;
(b) the avoidance of a transaction as a preference or a transfer in fraud of creditors;
(c) the enforcement of rights to an asset that is under the control or supervision of the insolvency representative.

1 Official Commentary

Commentary

General

5.1. It is recognised that a conflict-of-laws rule will always be imperfect. The aim of Principle 5 is therefore to improve the clarity and legal certainty surrounding the issue of conflict-of-laws to the greatest possible extent.

5.2. Principle 5 addresses the applicable law for proprietary issues in general and is not limited to those issues that are covered by the Principles. The law of the forum determines what would qualify as 'proprietary issues'. This broad scope of Principle 5 is to prevent the issues covered by these Principles, which are limited in scope, being governed by laws different from those governing proprietary issues that are closely connected with the issues covered by these Principles, but fall outside its scope. See, e.g., the issues listed in Principle 3(3).

5.3. Principle 5 concerns only choice-of-law issues and does not address the question of the jurisdiction of any tribunal over a party or the subject matter at issue.

5.4. Principle 5 recognises that the usual connecting factors for choice-of-law rules (e.g., the location of persons, offices, activity, or assets) usually have no useful role to play in the context of the law applicable to proprietary issues relating to digital assets. Indeed, adoption of such factors would be incoherent and futile (except in the limited case where there is an identified issuer, see Principle 5(1)(c)) because digital assets are intangibles that have no physical situs. Instead, the approach of this Principle is to provide an incentive for those who create new digital assets or govern existing systems for digital assets to specify the applicable law in or in association with the digital asset itself or the relevant system. This approach would accommodate the special characteristics of digital assets and the proprietary questions concerning digital assets that may arise.

Principles 5(1)(a) and 5(1)(b)

5.5. Principle 5(1) provides a 'waterfall' of factors for the determination of the applicable law. Under Principle 5(1)(a), the applicable law is the domestic law of the State specified in the digital asset itself, together with any of the Principles that are specified. If Principle 5(1)(a) does not apply, the applicable law is that of the State specified in the system in which the digital asset is recorded, together with any of the Principles that are specified (Principle 5(1)(b)) (for a discussion of the notion of 'system' see Commentary 5.6). The choice of-law rules in Principles 5(1)(a) and 5(1)(b) are based on party autonomy, for the reasons given in Commentary 5.4 and also because Principle 5(2)(c) treats every person dealing with a digital asset, and who could be affected by a determination of a proprietary issue, as consenting to the choice-of-law rules in Principle 5(1) (see also Commentary 5.16). Such persons will know about the specification of the applicable law, since it will be in records readily available for review by such persons (see Principle 5(2)(b) and Commentary 5.16). Moreover, although many digital assets, or systems, currently do not include a specification of applicable law, the rules in Principles 5(1)(a) and 5(1)(b) provide an incentive for such a specification to be included. This reliance on party autonomy is consistent with Article 3 of the Hague Conference Principles on Choice of Law in International Commercial Contracts ('Hague Conference Principles'). It would also be possible for a digital asset, or a system, to specify that these UNIDROIT *Principles or some of them (supplemented where necessary by the specified domestic law) would be the law applicable to proprietary issues.*

5.6. The notion of 'system' in Principle 5(1)(b) should be considered technology neutral and construed broadly and functionally. It includes any type of protocol, platform, application, transfer arrangement, and network in so far as it has the capabilities necessary to record digital assets. It should be noted that networks are generally built in layers (e.g., physical layer, data link layer, network layer, transport layer, session layer, presentation layer, and application layer), so that a digital asset can be recorded in an application that operates and relies on a platform which, in turn, operates and relies on a protocol. It is possible that a different applicable law is specified for two or more layers. To address the ensuing uncertainty, a State might consider adopting a specific rule to determine which law applies in these circumstances. An example of such a rule could be that the applicable law specified by the layer closer to the digital asset prevails. The question of which layer is closer is a matter of fact which will need to be determined by the competent court. The uncertainty identified in this paragraph would, however, not arise if the applicable law were specified in the digital asset (Principle 5(1)(a)).

5.7. As stated above, Principle 5(1) provides a 'waterfall' of connecting factors for the determination of the applicable law. Under Principle 5(1)(a), the applicable law is the domestic law of the State specified in the digital asset itself. The digital asset can also specify all or some of the Principles as the applicable law: in that case, these would take precedence over the specified domestic law (see Principle 3(2)). However, even if all the Principles were specified, a domestic law would also need to be specified as this would apply to issues which are, under the Principles, a matter of other law. If Principle 5(1)(a) does not apply, the applicable law is the domestic law of the State specified in the system on which the digital asset is recorded, plus all or some of the Principles if specified, as discussed above. If a choice of law has been made neither in the digital asset itself, nor in the system on which it is recorded, the law of the issuer's State applies as per Principle 5(1)(c). The law so determined, i.e., the issuer's law, governs not only the specific digital asset that may be the object of a concrete case, but all digital assets that are 'of the same description' (see Principle 5(2)(d)). 'Of the same description' means, in these Principles, digital assets that are treated by market participants as fungible. See also Commentary 11.6.

Principle 5(1)(c)

5.8. Principle 5(1)(c), i.e., the third step down the waterfall provided by Principle 5, is of limited scope. The scope is limited, first, because not all digital assets will have an issuer (as defined in Principle 5(2)(f), see Commentary 5.10). In all those instances, this rule will not apply, and the applicable law is to be determined under Principle 5(1)(d). See, however, for examples of digital assets that are typically issued, Commentary 4.23 to 4.28.

5.9. Second, the connecting factor of the issuer is qualified in multiple ways. Importantly, Principle 5(1)(c) refers to the State where the issuer has its statutory seat. If one must determine an issuer's location, its statutory seat is the connecting factor that gives most certainty as it is most easily identifiable by third parties. Other possible connecting factors, such as the place of 'central administration', the 'principal place of business', or the 'centre of main interest' cannot be identified with the same level of certainty and would therefore introduce an unwarranted measure of uncertainty. Under Principle 5(1)(c), the issuer's statutory seat must be 'readily ascertainable by the public'. If, for instance, the issuer does not have a statutory seat because it is an informal partnership, there would be no statutory seat that is 'readily ascertainable by the public' as per Principle 5(1)(c). Also, if it were unclear which issuer issued a specific digital asset because the digital asset is issued by different persons or in different layers, the statutory seat of the issuer of this digital asset would not be readily ascertainable by the public. In all those instances, Principle 5(1)(c) will not apply and the applicable law is to be determined under Principle 5(1)(d).

5.10. Third, 'issuer' is defined in Principle 5(2)(f), and a person must meet no less than five cumulative criteria to qualify as an issuer. First, for a person to qualify as an issuer, it must be a legal person. Natural persons are therefore excluded from qualifying as an 'issuer' under these Principles. This criterion could already be inferred from Principle 5(1)(c), where reference is made to the issuer's statutory seat, which logically can only refer to a legal person. Also, from Principle 5(1)(c), read in conjunction with the chapeau of Principle 5(2)(f), it must be inferred that if the relevant issuer does not qualify as a legal person (for instance, because an informal partnership is not recognised as a legal person under the applicable law), Principle 5(1)(c) does not apply. In all these instances, the applicable law must be determined under Principle 5(1)(d). Second, the issuer must have put the digital asset, or digital assets of the same description, in the stream of commerce for value as per Principle 5(2)(f)(i). This criterion is meant to exclude instances in which a digital asset is created by a person who has no further commercial interest in it. On the concept of 'the same description', see Commentary 5.17 and Commentary 11.6). Third, for a person to qualify as an issuer, that person must have identified itself as a named person in a way that is readily ascertainable by the public as per Principle 5(2)(f)(ii)(A). This means that the name of the issuer must be easily identifiable by third parties. Fourth, the issuer must have identified its statutory seat in a way that is readily ascertainable by the public as per Principle 5(2)(f)(ii)(B). This criterion seems self-explanatory. Finally, the issuer must have identified itself, in a way that is readily ascertainable by the public, as the person who put the digital asset, or digital assets of the same description, into the stream of commerce for value as per Principle 5(2)(f)(ii)(C). This means that not only must the issuer have put the digital asset in the stream of commerce for value as a matter of fact (as per Principle 5(2)(f)(i)), it also must have identified itself as such (in a way that is easily identifiable by third parties). Again, should a person not comply with any (or all) of the criteria for qualification as issuer under this Principle 5(2)(f), the applicable law must be determined under Principle 5(1)(d).

Principle 5(1)(d)

5.11. At the bottom of the 'waterfall', in the absence of a specification made in the digital asset or the system as contemplated by Principle 5(1)(a) and Principle 5(1)(b), and if Principle 5(1)(c) does not apply, Principle 5(1)(d) provides a State with a considerable degree of freedom to choose the appropriate rules for a forum sitting in that State. An overarching consideration is the fact that in many cases the digital asset may have no significant connection with any State. It is not feasible to specify in Principle 5(1)(d) a definitive, 'one size fits all' approach to be applied by the forum to proprietary questions in respect of a digital asset. Principle 5(1)(d) therefore provides for two options (Option A and Option B): each includes the application of some or all of the Principles (as specified by the forum State) to such questions. Because these Principles are generally accepted on an international level as a neutral and balanced set of rules, their application at the bottom of the waterfall is appropriate (see Article 3 of the Hague Conference Principles that 'allows the parties to choose not only the law of a State but also 'rules of law', emanating from non-State sources.'). It is important to emphasise that the Principles applicable under each option are only those specified by the forum State.

5.12 Within each option in Principle 5(1)(d), there is a 'waterfall' set out in sub-paragraphs, based on specifications made by a State when adopting Principle 5.

Option A

5.13. Option A is suitable if a State decides that it is appropriate for the forum sitting in that State to apply some aspects of its own domestic law in respect of proprietary issues in relation to a digital asset. This might be the case, for example, if the State has adopted laws that deal specifically with proprietary issues relating to digital assets. One example of this would be where the State has already adopted some aspects of these Principles as part of its domestic law. These aspects of domestic law specified by the forum State form the first part of the waterfall (Principle 5(1)(d)(i) of Option A). The second part of the waterfall (Principle 5(1)(d)(ii) of Option A) relates to matters not addressed by Principle 5(1)(d)(i) of Option A, and is comprised of either the (entire) Principles, or some Principles or some aspects of the Principles, according to the choice, and consequent specification, of the forum State. The third part of the waterfall (Principle 5(1)(d)(iii) of Option A), which applies to the extent not addressed by other clauses, requires the forum to apply the law otherwise applicable under its private international law rules.

Option B

5.14. Option B consists of the second and third parts of the waterfall set out in Option A. It therefore is suitable for a State which determines that proprietary issues relating to digital assets should be determined only by the Principles or some portions thereof, without any reference to substantive domestic laws. This might be the case, for example, if the State has not adopted laws that deal specifically with proprietary issues relating to digital assets. Again, the applicable Principles are those specified by the forum State. The third part of the waterfall applies as set out in Commentary 5.13.

5.15. By making reference to these Principles, Principle 5(1)(d) provides an innovative means of permitting a forum to adopt the Principles for persons and matters subject to its jurisdiction where none of Principles 5(1)(a), 5(1)(b) or 5(1)(c) applies. The adoption of Principle 5 would accommodate the wish of a forum to adopt the Principles in such situations. In particular, the forum would apply the Principles even where the substantive law of a forum State itself would otherwise apply, without the potential delay and complexity in making substantial revisions of otherwise applicable local private law. Indeed, a forum State might choose this approach either as its primary means of adopting the Principles or as an interim approach, pending their full adoption. Of course, if the relevant digital asset or system specified the substantive law of the forum State (which would thereby apply under Principles 5(1)(a) or 5(1)(b)) it is reasonable to assume that the forum State would have adopted acceptable substantive rules such as those exemplified by these Principles. Principle 5 leaves considerable flexibility for a State to craft choice-of-law rules that conform to its policy judgments and are compatible with its domestic law.

Principle 5(2)

5.16. Paragraph (2) provides additional guidance on the interpretation and application of Principle 5(1). Principle 5(2)(a) confirms that proprietary issues are subject to law regardless of whether (i) the participants in the relevant network refute the application of any law and exclusively want to rely on code, and (ii) the application of the law is said to be too complex or to produce unclear outcomes or to disrupt the functioning of the network, as a consequence of the nature of the technology, or of the international character of the network. Principle 5(2)(b) makes it clear that a specification of applicable law in a digital asset, or in a system, can be determined by looking at records (in the sense of information recorded electronically or by other means) attached to or associated with the digital asset, system, but only if such records are readily available for those dealing with the asset. Persons dealing with the asset, who will be able to view these records, are treated, by virtue of their dealing, as having consented to the specified applicable law: this is the effect of Principle 5(2)(c).

5.17. The effect of Principles 5(2)(d) and 5(2)(e) is that the specified applicable law applies to all digital assets of the same description from the time the digital asset is created or issued, but if the applicable law changes from a later time, pre-existing rights in the digital asset are not affected. It is particularly important that the same applicable law govern all digital assets of the same description. Changes in the applicable law should be avoided if at all possible. If such changes were to occur, transitional provisions that ensure that the same law applies to all such digital assets at all times would be essential. Principle 5(2)(f) is discussed in Commentary 5.10.

Principles 5(3) and 5(4)

5.18. Principles 5(3) and 5(4) make it clear that Principle 5(1) does not determine the law applicable to the relationship between a custodian and its client. This question is determined by the choice-of-law rule in Principle 5(3), namely, that the applicable law is the law expressly stated in the custody agreement as governing that agreement or, if different, the law expressly stated as governing the issues addressed in Principles 10 to 13. This rule would typically result in the application of a single law to those matters. It is appropriate for one law to apply to the custody relationship, rather than different laws, as might be specified in different digital assets or different systems as contemplated by Principles 5(1)(a) and 5(1)(b).

5.19. The specific conflict of laws rule provided in Principle 5(3) determines the applicable law in the relationship between a custodian and its client, but it is limited in scope. This rule only concerns the issues addressed in Principles 10 to 13, including whether the agreement is a custody agreement. Principle 13 addresses issues arising if a custodian enters into an insolvency-related proceeding. As is shown by Principles 5(6) and 5(7), the conflict of laws rule in Principle 5(3) applies to contractual and proprietary issues addressed in Principles 10 to 13, but the applicable insolvency law will govern insolvency law issues.

5.20. The issues covered by the choice-of-law rule in Principle 5(3) are generally considered to be issues of private law. This rule therefore does not prejudice the application of any rule of regulatory law that may concern the custodian - client relationship. See, for examples of such regulatory rules, Commentary 10.21. Moreover, a custodian may be a regulated entity, and regulatory authorities may wish to restrict a custodian's choice of law for the custody agreement or for the issues covered by Principles 10 to 13. Principle 5(3) does not set aside any such rule of regulatory law restricting the custodian's choice of law.

5.21. By excluding the custody relationship from the application of Principles 5(1) and 5(2), it is not suggested that those Principles do not apply to proprietary issues such as where a custodian acquires, or disposes of, a digital asset.

Principle 5(5)

5.22. Principle 5(5) recognises that the approach taken in Principle 5(1) would be inappropriate to determine the law governing a registration system for security rights, which must be based on objective indicia (such as the location of the grantor) that a third-party searcher of the registry could determine.

5.23. For the reason given in Commentary 5.22, Principle 5(5) provides that other law (in this case, the conflicts of law rules contained in other law) determines the law applicable to third-party effectiveness of a security right in a digital asset made effective against third parties by a method other than control. In addition, because the same law also needs to govern priority between two or more such security rights, Principle 5(5) provides that other law determines the law applicable to determine priority between such conflicting security rights. If one conflicting security right is made effective against third parties by control (even if it is also made effective against third parties by a method other than control), Principle 5(1) does apply to determine the applicable law. See also Commentary 16.5.

Linked assets

5.24. Where a digital asset is linked, or purports to be linked, to another asset, other law (in this case, the conflicts of law rules contained in other law) determines the law applicable to determine the existence of, requirements for, and legal effect of any link between the digital asset and the other asset. These matters are determined by other law under Principle 4.

Principles 5(6) and 5(7)

5.25. Principle 5(6) makes it clear that in an insolvency-related proceeding Principle 5 should be applied to proprietary questions in respect of a digital asset relating to events occurring before the opening of the insolvency-related proceeding. Principle 5(7) provides the usual exceptions that defer to the applicable insolvency law. These exceptions are discussed in Commentary 19.9 to 19.12. It should be noted that the term 'control' in Principle 5(7)(c) is used in a broad sense, and not as defined in Principle 6 (see Commentary 19.4).

2 Reflections

2.1 Context

Principle 5 ("Applicable Law") is the only principle contained in Section II ("Private International Law"). Private International Law (hereinafter PIL) issues can relate to the determination of applicable law, jurisdiction, and to the extraterritorial recognition of foreign judgments. The only issues to fall within this UNIDROIT Project's scope are the issues relating to applicable law, with the specification that "the other issues are likely to be explored by the Hague Conference on Private International Law or other organizations."[1] This delimitation limits the scope of application of the Principles to the conflict of laws domain, excluding matters of international jurisdiction and the recognition and enforcement of foreign judicial decisions.

Principle 5(2)(a) sets out rules for determining the law applicable to "property issues in respect of digital assets, and in particular their acquisition and disposition". Its scope of application is broader than that of the substantive rules set out by the Principles, which exclude a number of matters listed in Principle 3(3). According to Commentary 5.2, this broad scope is designed to prevent matters covered by these Principles and which have a limited scope of application from being governed by laws other than those governing property matters which are closely related to the matters covered by these Principles but which fall outside their scope of application [for example, matters listed in Principle 3(3)].

[1] UNIDROIT 2020 // Study LXXXII – W.G.1 – Doc. 2 // November 2020, 20, marg. 80.

From the PIL perspective, the main consequence of the generalist approach adopted to define the Principles is the absence of a uniform solution to the *characterisation* problem. The decision to develop common rules for "property issues relating to a digital asset" without first characterising (i) what we should understand by "property issues" and (ii) the legal nature of the different "digital assets" makes it difficult to develop uniform PIL rules valid across different legal systems in the contemporary world. Unlike comparative PIL instruments, the project does not address the main problems of conflict of laws rules (public order and *renvoi*[2]).

2.2 *Purpose and Nature*

As indicated in the Introduction, "these Principles are designed to facilitate transactions in digital assets" (paragraph 0.1) and "aim to reduce the legal uncertainty which practitioners, judges, arbitrators, legislators and market participants would otherwise face in the coming years in dealing with digital assets" (paragraph 0.3). Substantive rules in national law have not been hitherto developed in a coordinated or uniform manner, leading to legal fragmentation.

The Principles, however, do not contain any provisions or comments which help to clarify the nature of the text[3]—unlike other similar instruments such as the UNIDROIT Principles of International Commercial Contracts[4] and the Hague Principles on the Choice of Law Applicable to International Contracts ("Hague Principles").[5] The recommendation made to States to adopt legislation consistent with these Principles (Introduction, paragraph 0.4) infers that the Principles are designed to serve as a model for legislators, conditioning their outcome to their implementation in domestic regulations. Consequently, the aim is not to provide a complete and systematic body of rules to be respected by digital asset transactions but to inspire the national legislator to take these Principles into account when implementing them into domestic law. The

---

[2] UNIDROIT 2020 // Study LXXXII – W.G.1 – Doc. 2 // November 2020, 20, marg. 84.

[3] European Association of Private International Law (Eapil), Position Paper, UNIDROIT 2023 // Study LXXXII – W.G.8 – Doc. 4, Annex II // February 2023, p. 118–133.

[4] UNIDROIT, Principles on International Commercial Contracts, approved in May 1994. According to its Preamble, *"these Principles set forth general rules for international commercial contracts. They shall be applied when the parties have agreed that their contract be governed by them. They may be applied when the parties have agreed that their contract be governed by general principles of law, the lex mercatoria or the like."*

[5] HCCH, Principles on Choice of Law in International Commercial Contracts, approved on 19 March 2015. According to its Introduction, *"the Principles do not constitute a formally binding instrument such as a Convention that States are obliged to directly apply or incorporate into their domestic law. Nor is this instrument a model law that States are encouraged to enact. Rather, it is a non-binding set of principles, which the Hague Conference encourages States to incorporate into their domestic choice of law regimes in a manner appropriate for the circumstances of each State. In this way, the Principles can guide the reform of domestic law on choice of law and operate alongside existing instruments on the subject."*

Principles are a soft law document and are not binding. They, therefore, accentuate the fragmentation of State regulations.

From the PIL perspective, Principle 5 does not seek to unify the applicable conflict of laws rules to determine the law that should govern digital asset property issues, particularly their acquisition and disposition. There are two reasons for this: (i) due to the nature of the chosen instrument ("Principles"), which by no means replaces the function of an international convention or a harmonising model law, and (ii) because of the cascade of connections used, expressly providing for different legislative options. Consequently, resulting national implementations will not reflect a desirable homogeneity for international trade. This contradicts the intended objective of reducing legal uncertainty in digital asset transactions.

2.3 *Preparatory Works*

2.3.1 First Working Group Meeting (November 2020)

In its first session,[6] the Working Group (hereinafter WG) raised the issue of the law applicable to digital assets to explore whether existing rules determining the law applicable to transactions could apply to digital assets. If they could not be applied, the question was whether the Principles should be applied to all types of digital assets uniformly or should instead establish a set of general rules or specific approaches for certain types of digital assets like the United Nations Model Law on International Trade Law (hereinafter UNCITRAL) on secured transactions. It also questioned whether conflict of laws rules already provided for in international standards should be applied to certain types of digital assets.[7]

At that first meeting, the WG analysed a summary report of the exploratory workshop held in September 2020. The 3rd workshop session was entitled "Digital Assets Linked to Real-World Assets (Digital Twins): Civil Law and Private International Law Implications."[8]

The Final Report of the first meeting contains an interesting debate among experts on the questions raised by the UNIDROIT Secretary-General. Particularly relevant was the intervention by G. GOH ESCOLAR, on behalf of the Hague Conference on Private International Law (hereinafter HCCH), who noted that this organisation had received a mandate from their Council to work on digital assets in the digital economy. HCCH surveyed the law applicable to digital asset transfers, confirming that existing rules did not meet the sector's expectations, significantly diverging from regulatory expectations. The HCCH was mandated to address the possibility of a new normative project which would focus on applicable law, jurisdiction, recognition and enforcement, choice of law, and choice of forum, focusing on proprietary effects

---

6 UNIDROIT 2020 // Study LXXXII – W.G.1 – Doc. 2 // November 2020, p. 20–22, marg. 80–87.

7 UNIDROIT 2020 // Study LXXXII – W.G.1 – Doc. 2 // November 2020, p. 21–22, marg. 87.

8 UNIDROIT 2020 // Study LXXXII – W.G.1 – Doc. 3 // November 2020, p. 11–16, marg. 50–74.

and what impact they would have on party autonomy, choice of law, and choice of forum. G. GOH ESCOLAR added that the HCCH was also considering incorporating applicable law, such as integrating choice of law in Distributed Ledger Technology (hereinafter DLT) protocols. Given the uncertainty as to which State would have jurisdiction to solve disputes, they looked at connecting factors concerning digital assets created and transferred for centralised and decentralised systems. Finally, G. GOH ESCOLAR added that the HCCH also examined existing regulation and its impact on PIL.[9]

2.3.2 Second WG Meeting (March 2021)

As part of the intersessional work that the WG agreed on during its first session, Sub-Group 4 was established with a dual focus (taxonomy and PIL). At the second meeting, the WG analysed the first draft of the Tentative Principles on PIL,[10] with a proposal based on party autonomy and, in the absence of a choice of law, on applying fallback rules (transferor or transferee law) and special rules for insolvency cases.

At its second session, the WG agreed on three issues to be addressed in the Tentative Principles: (i) the law applicable within the digital assets platform (network) and, in particular, the law covering acquisitions and dispositions (the same law should apply to transfers and collateralisation on a given network); (ii) the conflict of laws concerning "digital twins"; and (iii), the conflict of laws with insolvency-related issues. On this last point, the WG noted that for legal certainty, the law applicable to a transaction in question should be given preference over insolvency proceedings law. However, this may conflict with other principles of different legal systems. The WG agreed to consider a hybrid approach.[11]

2.3.3 Third WG Meeting (June–July 2021)

The third session addressed for the first time a draft of Tentative Principles on PIL Issues Applicable to Digital Assets and Enforcement in the Context of Insolvency.[12]

The first issue concerns the law applicable to the acquisition and disposition (including the provision of collateralisation) of digital assets amongst adherents to the relevant digital-asset platform, which participants may choose. If no choice is explicitly made, reverting to interpretation and implicit choice principles is possible. If no result is reached, fallback rules (such as transferor law, transferee law, etc.) can determine the applicable law.

Concerning the different laws that may be relevant in an insolvency scenario, as a general principle, it is the law of the jurisdiction (*lex fori*) of the territory in which

---

[9] UNIDROIT 2020 // Study LXXXII – W.G.1 – Doc. 4 // November 2020, p. 26, marg. 134.

[10] UNIDROIT 2021 // Study LXXXII – W.G.3 – Doc. 2 (rev 1) // June 2021, p. 54–56, marg. 131–132.

[11] UNIDROIT 2021 // Study LXXXII – W.G.3 – Doc. 2 (rev 1) // June 2021, p. 54–56, marg. 131–132.

[12] UNIDROIT 2021 // Study LXXXII – W.G.3 – Doc. 2 (rev 1) // June 2021, p. 55–56, marg. 132.

the insolvent debtor is located which is adopted. Where the insolvency law differs from the law applicable to acquisitions and dispositions on the platform, a general risk arises: a rule favouring insolvency law and its overriding powers could disrupt the integrity of the digital asset platform operation, especially if participants are located in different jurisdictions. In this respect, a rule favouring the law applicable to acquisitions and dispositions on that platform would leave the internal functioning of the platform intact. Still, it could empty the insolvency principles of the forum law of content and result in unequal creditor treatment. This conflict of laws could be eliminated through the material harmonisation of the acquisition and disposition rules of the digital asset platform.

2.3.4 Fourth WG Meeting (November 2021)

In this session, four draft rules on applicable law and enforcement in the context of insolvency were revised.[13] The overall objective of the digital asset insolvency rules was to encourage the adoption of a common policy concerning DLT blockchain networks. Specifically, they were intended to ensure that an uneven application of national laws, particularly national insolvency laws, did not severely disrupt their functionality concerning property.

Rule 1 introduced some general principles to be observed by States to define the scope of application of the Principles clearly. The following limitations to the scope of application were identified: first, certain aspects of the rules would inevitably overlap with property issues. It was considered that PIL rules and choice of law rules should only refer to aspects of property since it would be too ambitious to provide any guidance beyond this scope.[14]

Regarding the application of mandatory conflict of laws rules, it was explained that two additional aspects had to be reconciled: one concerned the law applicable to property aspects, while the other concerned the law applicable to insolvency proceedings. The mandatory application of these law domains needed to be revised regarding the points where these laws clashed. The question was, therefore, how to reconcile the potential conflicts between these laws. It was noted that the Hague Securities Convention offered a solution: the intermediated securities followed specific rules, with certain safeguards, the proprietary effect prevailing over any local insolvency law. It was argued that a similar solution should be adopted for the core insolvency rule in the Draft.[15]

The choice of applicable law was particularly relevant where network operators were regulated, incorporated, or linked to a particular State. Different solutions could be found in the EU Settlement Finality Directive (i.e., the applicable law can be imposed by the court of the State in question) and the Hague Securities Convention (i.e., the parties can choose the law themselves, provided they present a factual

[13] Annex III, Appendix 4 of the revised Subgroup 4 Paper.

[14] UNIDROIT 2021 // Study LXXXII – W.G.4 – Doc. 3 // December 2021, p. 15, marg. 131.

[15] UNIDROIT 2021 // Study LXXXII – W.G.4 – Doc. 3 // December 2021, p. 15–16, marg. 134–135.

connection to the place and the chosen law). Rule 3 concerned insolvency recognition and was taken directly from the Hague Securities Convention.

2.3.5 Fifth WG Meeting (March 2022)

In its fifth session, the WG analysed a first draft of the Principles on the law applicable to digital assets, which had yet to be commented on, followed by several issues. The WG held an extensive discussion on the waterfall structure of Principle 5(2). WG members presented their concerns on the re-drafted waterfall's connecting factors, commenting that they may not reflect current market practices. The Chair suggested an ad hoc workshop be set up and held before the next WG session to finalise Principle 5 on Conflict of Laws.

The WG agreed on the overall waterfall structure of the Principle but raised concerns regarding the following: (a) Connecting factors relating to a network location and any possible location alternatives in the context of DLT operation; (b) Scoping of the Conflict of Laws Principle, particularly its interaction with other insolvency laws; (c) The coverage of different types of digital assets by these Principles; (d) How issuers could be incentivised to choose a digital asset law concerning the same issue; (e) Including the choice of applicable law in the digital assets code; and (f), Whether the waterfall structure sequence should be reversed or rearranged. The WG discussed potential solutions for the bottom of the waterfall structure such as the Principles themselves or some other law of a State based on those Principles.[16]

2.3.6 Sixth WG Meeting (September 2022)

The WG discussed a new draft of Principle 5, with a more developed waterfall structure than the previous one and based on comments received at the fifth WG meeting and on intersessional work. First, a preference was set for the choice of law specified in the digital asset; second, the law specified in the network/platform was examined; and finally, at the bottom of the waterfall, it was noted that States would eventually adopt their own private law rules, which were expected to be consistent with the Principles, thus producing more predictable outcomes.

An observer noted that the HCCH would use Principle 5 as a starting point for further work it intended to undertake on the digital economy and conflicts of laws domains. It was noted that the Council on General Affairs and Policy (hereinafter CAGP) of the HCCH was in the process of determining its specific mandate for work in the near future and would keep UNIDROIT informed in this regard. It was equally indicated that UNIDROIT and HCCH could collaborate in this area, possibly in the form of a joint project. The UNIDROIT Secretary-General expressed his appreciation for the updates shared by HCCH. He proceeded to remark that a joint project between the two organisations would need to be approved by the UNIDROIT Governing Body,

[16] UNIDROIT 2022 // Study LXXXII – W.G.5 – Doc. 4 // April 2022, p. 10, marg. 84–87.

which would probably welcome it, given the excellent track record of cooperation and collaboration between the two organisations.[17]

Due to the WG's broad consensus, it was considered that Principle 5 would be retained in its current form. It was agreed that more attention would be paid to exceptions, custody situations, and, more generally, to the lower part of the waterfall, especially in relation to connecting factors and situations where a State has already adopted the Principles and a digital asset did not refer to any applicable law. Furthermore, the principles should distinguish between contractual and ownership issues. It was noted that the Drafting Committee would undertake further work on this Principle and report back to the WG at its next meeting.

2.3.7 Seventh WG Meeting (December 2022)

In its seventh session, all changes introduced during the intersessional work were discussed. The waterfall structure was maintained and guided in the same way by Principle 5 as in the previous WG session. Moreover, two options were drafted for States to choose from when applying these Principles in their domestic law. These options (A and B) were explained in the Commentary. They contained several bracketed points, and these latter points were suggested to be kept in the final draft, as they constituted instructions to be taken into account by States. It was added that Principle 5(5) still needed to be finalised. Furthermore, it was noted that several changes had been proposed in the Commentary and that the WG was invited to provide its views on them. This included additional guidance on whether Principle 5 referred only to property issues covered by the Principles or to all property issues in general. Also commented was the fact that some additional text could be included to cover the relationship between Principle 4 and Principle 5. The WG concluded that the Drafting Committee would maintain and refine the current approach based on the input received.[18]

2.3.8 Eighth WG Meeting (March 2023)

The WG discussed the final version of Principle 5,[19] which had been developed based on comments received at the sixth WG meeting, intersessional work, and public consultation comments.[20] The WG adopted the final version following the debate.[21]

---

[17] UNIDROIT 2022 // Study LXXXII – W.G.6 – Doc. 4 // November 2022, p. 7, marg. 31–32.

[18] UNIDROIT 2023 // Study LXXXII – W.G.7 – Doc. 5 // February 2023, p. 4–6, marg. 15 and 24.

[19] UNIDROIT 2023 // Study LXXXII – W.G.8 – Doc. 2 // February 2023.

[20] UNIDROIT 2023 // Study LXXXII – W.G.8 – Doc. 4 // February 2023.

[21] UNIDROIT 2023 // Study LXXXII – W.G.8 – Doc. 6 // February 2023.

2.3.9 Ninth WG Meeting (April 2023)

A ninth ad hoc WG session was held online on 5 April 2023. The draft Principles and Commentaries submitted by the Drafting Committee, which implemented a limited number of final comments, were reviewed. The draft was submitted for adoption at the 102nd session[22] held in Rome from 10 to 12 May 2023.[23]

2.4 *Relationship with Other Instruments*

2.4.1 The Hague Conference on Private International Law

Among the precedents worth citing related to the study subject is the Convention of 5 July 2006 on the Law Applicable to Certain Rights in respect of Securities held with an Intermediary (hereinafter CH 2006).[24] This convention provides legal certainty regarding the law applicable to clearing, settlement and transactions with cross-border secured credits. The Convention only determines the applicable law: it does not address the regulation of substantive law. This convention was taken as a reference during the UNIDROIT Principles debates on two issues which had to be reconciled: the law applicable to property matters and the law applicable to insolvency proceedings. As regards the applicable law, the main rule is based on the relationship between account holders and their intermediaries, giving preference to the express agreement of the parties over the account contract. As regards the second, CH 2006 offered the following solution: the intermediated securities would follow specific rules, the patrimonial effect prevailing over any insolvency law. For this reason, it was considered that a similar solution should be applied to the basic insolvency rule in the Principles of this project. In accordance with the CAGP's decision in March 2020,[25] the Permanent Bureau had been studying the impact of developments in the domains of distributed ledger technology and financial technology (Fintech) with a view to identifying potential PIL issues for future works.[26] Subsequently, in March 2021, the CAGP confirmed the Permanent Bureau mandate to continue studying the implications for PIL related to DLT-domain developments.[27]

---

[22] UNIDROIT 2023– C.D. (102) 6, April, marg. 19.

[23] UNIDROIT 2023– C.D. (102) Misc. 2, May, para. 7. UNIDROIT 2023– C.D. (102) 25, August, marg. 106.

[24] Approved on 5 July 2006, entering into force on 1 April 2017 following ratification by the three States to which it applies (United States, Mauritius and Switzerland).

[25] HCCH, Conclusions & Decisions, Council on General Affairs and Policy, March 2020. Available in: https://assets.hcch.net/docs/70458042-f771-4e94-9c56-df3257a1e5ff.pdf

[26] HCCH, Permanent Bureau, Developments with respect to PIL implications of the Digital Economy (Prel. Doc. No 4 of November 2020). Available in: https://assets.hcch.net/docs/8bdc7071-c324-4660-96bc-86efba6214f2.pdf

[27] HCCH, Conclusions & Decisions, Council on General Affairs and Policy, March 2021. Available in: https://assets.hcch.net/docs/94e2d886-1cbf-4250-b436-5c1899cb942b.pdf.

This work was organised within the Digital Economy Project framework in 2021. The Permanent Bureau has been monitoring and reporting on major developments in the digital economy area with implications for PIL, for example, on topics such as decentralisation, distributed ledger technology, digital platforms, artificial intelligence and automated contracting, asset tokenisation, digital currencies, immersive technologies, big data and fintech.

Researching and monitoring Digital Economy Project developments have led to new projects relating to PIL implications: central bank digital currencies, tokens, and voluntary carbon markets.

In accordance with the CAGP's mandate in March 2024, the Permanent Bureau has been monitoring developments relating to the digital economy to identify potential PIL issues to address in future work. The mandate also includes digital platforms, artificial intelligence, automated contracting, and immersive technologies in collaboration with UNICITRAL.

At that same 2024 meeting, the CAGP also tasked the Permanent Bureau with exploring jurisdiction determination and applicable law in the securities markets domain—taking into account distributed ledger technology—and assessing the ramifications of the increasing focus of the financial services and securities industry on technological developments. The Permanent Bureau was also tasked with identifying opportunities in the context of the digital economy and with exploring the appropriateness and feasibility of future regulatory guidance in securities matters.

Regarding the HCCH project on tokens, the March 2024 CAGP acknowledged the importance of avoiding the fragmentation of the legal instruments developed by different intergovernmental organisations on related topics, mentioning in particular the UNIDROIT Principles on Digital Assets and Private Law. It accordingly mandated the Permanent Bureau to engage with experts and observers to study the PIL issues relating to tokens. It will begin with a general study of existing international and regional instruments, as well as of previous and ongoing work, in order to form a basis for discussions. Questions will be posed to experts and observers, who will be offered the opportunity to submit papers exposing their position on the topic. To this end, the Permanent Bureau will submit a report to the CAGP in March 2025 on the findings of this study, with proposals regarding the next steps to be taken. Within this framework, a working document entitled "Proposal for a Normative Project: Private International Law Issues Relating to Digital Tokens" has been prepared.[28]

---

[28] HCCH, Prel. Doc. No 5B Rev of March 2024. Available in: https://assets.hcch.net/docs/d6e2d062-7cd0-4f3d-be96-189c12164ab6.pdf

2.4.2 UNIDROIT/HCCH

During the WG working sessions on the Digital Assets Project, discussions were initiated to shape a Joint HCCH-UNIDROIT Project on Applicable Law to Cross-Border Holdings and Transfers of Digital Assets and Tokens.[29]

The exploratory and preparatory work of the Joint HCCH-UNIDROIT Project was formally approved by the CGAP of the HCCH in March 2023 and by the Governing Council of UNIDROIT in May 2023, based on the Project Proposal presented at its 102nd Session.[30] The instrument which the two organisations intended to jointly develop would be based on Principle 5 of the Principles on Digital Assets and Private Law, complementing UNIDROIT's work with additional guidance.

Following the approval, the participants designated by the two Secretariats explored the feasibility of joint work during two preparatory meetings: the first was held on 12 June 2023 at the HCCH premises in The Hague; the second had a hybrid format and was held from 2 to 4 October 2023 at UNIDROIT headquarters in Rome.[31]

At its 2024 meeting,[32] the CAGP took note of the report of the HCCH-UNIDROIT Project on Digital Assets and Tokens,[33] in particular the summary conclusions on possible future PIL work in relation to digital assets. The CAGP decided to conclude the work on the Project, thanking the experts and the UNIDROIT Secretariat for their continued cooperation and coordination with the Permanent Bureau.

2.4.3 United Nations Commission on International Trade Law

The United Nations Convention on the Assignment of Receivables in International Trade of 12 December 2001[34] contains a Chapter V on the conflict of laws. Article 28 provides that the rights and obligations of the transferor and the transferee shall be governed by the law of their choice; in the absence of a choice of law, they shall be governed by the law of the State to which the transfer contract is most closely connected.

---

[29] HCCH, Prel. Doc. No 3C Rev of January 2023. Available in: https://assets.hcch.net/docs/a91fd233-acf7-4c42-9aad-a426c4565068.pdf

[30] HCCH-UNIDROIT Project on Law Applicable to Cross-Border Holdings and Transfers of Digital Assets and Tokens, UNIDROIT 2023– C.D. (102) 6, April. Available in: https://www.unidroit.org/wp-content/uploads/2023/05/C.D.-102-12-Proposal-for-Joint-Work-HCCH-UNIDROIT.pdf.

[31] HCCH-UNIDROIT Joint Project on Applicable Law to Cross-Border Holdings and Transfers of Digital Assets and Tokens, UNIDROIT 2023, Study LXXXIIA – P.M.2 – Doc. 3, November, Second Preparatory Meeting (hybrid), Rome, October 2023, marg. 47.

[32] HCCH, Conclusions & Decisions, Council on General Affairs and Policy, March 2024. Available in: https://assets.hcch.net/docs/7d647a6f-b927-4c1a-a837-d0846fbacca1.pdf

[33] HCCH-UNIDROIT Digital Assets and Tokens Joint Project: Report, Prel. Doc. No 3 of January 2024. Available in: https://assets.hcch.net/docs/efce41ca-1c8c-4d61-9d8b-9348df9303a0.pdf.

[34] Adopted on 12 December 2001. It has not yet entered into force.

The UNCITRAL Model Law on Secured Transactions (hereinafter MLST)[35] deals with security interests applied to all types of tangible and intangible movable property, such as goods, receivables, bank accounts, negotiable documents, non-intermediated securities, and intellectual property rights, with some exceptions, such as intermediary securities. The MLST adopts a unitary approach using a single concept for all types of security interests. Following this approach, the Model Law applies to all types of transactions serving security purposes, such as secured loans, retention-of-title, sales, or financial leases. Moreover, it adopts a comprehensive approach according to which the MLST applies to all types of assets, secured obligations, borrowers, and lenders. The MLST contains a number of Model Registry Provisions that may be implemented in a statute or other type of legal instrument. The Model Provisions deal with the registration of a notice of security interests in a publicly accessible Registry to make a security interest effective against third parties and to provide an objective basis for determining the priority of a security interest over the rights of competing claimants.

The MLST is based on the United Nations Convention on the Assignment of Receivables in International Trade, the Uncitral Legislative Guide on Secured Transactions, and the UNCITRAL Guide on the Establishment of a Security Rights Registry. Chapter VIII deals with Conflict of Laws. Article 84 provides that the law applicable to the mutual rights and obligations of the grantor and the secured creditor arising from the security agreement between them shall be the law of their choice and, in the absence of a choice of law, the law governing the security agreement. With regard to security interests in intangible assets, Article 86 provides that the law applicable to the creation, effectiveness against third parties, and priority of a security right in an intangible asset shall be the law of the State in which the grantor is located. Article 94 provides that the commencement of insolvency proceedings in respect of the grantor shall not displace the law applicable to security rights under the provisions of the MLST, in the same way as that provided for in CH 2006 on the Law Applicable to Certain Rights on Securities held with an Intermediary.

In line with its central and coordinating role within the United Nations system in addressing legal issues related to the digital economy,[36] UNCITRAL continues its efforts to legally enable emerging technologies and their business applications, such as dispute settlement, security interests, insolvency, and the international transport of goods. In 2022, UNCITRAL approved the publication of a Taxonomy of Legal Issues Related to the Digital Economy,[37] which records the secretariat's exploratory

[35] Approved on 5 July 2006.

[36] UNCITRAL, A/CN.9/1012, *Legal issues related to the digital economy*. Fifty-third session, New York, July 2020. Available in: https://documents.un.org/doc/undoc/gen/v20/024/68/pdf/v2002468.pdf

[37] UNCITRAL, *Taxonomy of legal issues related to the digital economy*, p. 35-50, New York, 2023. Available in: https://uncitral.un.org/sites/uncitral.un.org/files/media-documents/uncitral/en/digitaleconomytaxonomy.pdf.

work on the topics of artificial intelligence, data, online platforms, digital goods[38] and decentralised systems and is intended to guide proposals for future legislative work on e-commerce.

2.4.4 European Union

Regulation 593/2008 on the law applicable to contractual obligations (hereinafter Rome I)[39] provides for the parties' free choice of the applicable law as a general rule (Article 3). In the absence of a choice of law, Article 4 establishes a number of presumptions for certain types of contracts (paragraph 1) and a connection based on the characteristic performance of the contract (paragraph 2). Article 14(1) regulates the law applicable to the assignment of receivables and conventional subrogation, stating that "the relations between the assignor and the assignee, under a voluntary assignment or contractual subrogation of a claim against another person (the debtor) shall be governed by the law that applies to the contract between the assignor and assignee under this Regulation." Secondly, the relations with the assigned debtor are governed by the law applicable to the assigned receivable [Art. 14(2)]. This law governs issues such as credit transferability, the relationship between the assignee and the debtor, the conditions for assignment enforceability to the debtor, and the liberating nature of the payment made by the latter. The concept of assignment of credit includes outright transfers of claims, transfers of rights by way of security, as well as pledges or other security rights over claims [Art. 14(3)]. This regime will be completed by the future Regulation on the law applicable to the third-party effects of assignments of claims, for which the European Commission has already presented a Proposal.[40] This instrument establishes a general rule based on the application of the law of the country in which the assignor has its habitual residence [Art. 4(1)]. The assignor and assignee may choose the law applicable to the assigned claim as the law applicable to the third-party effects of an assignment of claims in view of a securitisation [Art. 4(3)].

In the field of insolvency, Article 7(1) of Regulation 2015/848[41] provides that "the law applicable to insolvency proceedings and their effects shall be that of the

---

[38] UNCITRAL, A/CN.9/1012/Add.3, *Legal issues related to the digital economy – digital assets.* Fifty-third session, New York, July 2020. Available in: https://documents.un.org/doc/undoc/gen/v20/025/48/pdf/v2002548.pdf

[39] Regulation (EC) No 593/2008 of the European Parliament and of the Council of 17 June 2008 on the law applicable to contractual obligations (OJ L 177, 4.7.2008, p. 6–16). Available in: https://eur-lex.europa.eu/legal-content/EN/ALL/?uri=CELEX%3A32008R0593.

[40] European Commission, Proposal for a Regulation of the European Parliament and of the Council on the law applicable to the third-party effects of assignments of claims (COM/2018/096 final, of 12 March 2018). Available in: https://eur-lex.europa.eu/legal-content/EN/TXT/?qid=1520854606250&uri=COM:2018:96:FIN.

[41] Regulation (EU) 2015/848 of the European Parliament and of the Council of 20 May 2015 on insolvency proceedings (OJ L 141, 5.6.2015, p. 19–72). Available in: https://eur-lex.europa.eu/legal-content/EN/TXT/?uri=CELEX%3A32015R0848.

Member State within the territory of which such proceedings are opened" (*lex fori concursus*). However, Regulation 2015/848 provides exceptions to this general rule by laying down special conflict of laws rules for certain issues. For example, Article 7 shall not apply where the person who benefited from an act detrimental to all the creditors provides proof that such an act is subject to the law of a Member State other than the State of the opening of proceedings and that the law of that Member State does not allow any means of challenging that act in the relevant case [Art. 16]. Article 8 on third parties' rights in rem provides that "the opening of insolvency proceedings shall not affect the rights in rem of creditors or third parties in respect of tangible or intangible, movable or immovable assets, whether specific or indefinite sets of property which vary from time to time, belonging to the debtor which are situated within the territory of another Member State at the time of the opening of the proceedings."

Regulation 2023/1114 of the European Parliament and of the Council of 31 May 2023 on markets in cryptoassets[42] establishes uniform rules for issuers of crypto-assets and for crypto-asset service providers. The Regulation applies to the issuance, offering to the public, admission to trading of crypto-assets, and provision of services related to crypto-assets. In particular, the Regulation sets out: (a) transparency and information requirements in relation to the issuance, public offering and admission to trading of crypto-assets on a crypto-asset trading platform; (b) requirements for the authorisation and supervision of crypto-asset service providers; issuers of asset-referenced tokens and issuers of electronic money tokens, as well as for their operation, organisation and governance; (c) requirements for the protection of crypto-asset holders in the issuance, public offering and admission to trading of crypto-assets; (d) requirements for the protection of customers of crypto-asset service providers; and (e) measures aimed at preventing insider dealing, unlawful disclosure of inside information and market manipulation concerning crypto-assets, to ensure the integrity of crypto-asset markets. This instrument regulates substantive law and does not establish provisions on the conflict of laws.

This regime will be complemented in the future by the Regulation of a pilot regime for market infrastructures based on decentralised ledger technology, on which the European Commission has already submitted a Proposal.[43]

[42] Regulation (EU) 2023/1114 of the European Parliament and of the Council of 31 May 2023 on markets in crypto-assets, and amending Regulations (EU) No 1093/2010 and (EU) No 1095/2010 and Directives 2013/36/EU and (EU) 2019/1937 (OJ L 150, 9.6.2023, p. 40–205). Available in: https://eur-lex.europa.eu/legal-content/EN/TXT/HTML/?uri=CELEX:32023R1114.

[43] European Commission, Proposal for a Regulation of the European Parliament and of the Council on a pilot regime for market infrastructures based on distributed ledger technology (COM/2020/594 final, 24 September 2020). Available in: https://eur-lex.europa.eu/legal-content/EN/TXT/HTML/?uri=CELEX:52020PC0594.

2.4.5 Uniform Law Commission

The *Uniform Fiduciary Access to Digital Assets Act*,[44] adopted by the Uniform Law Commission (hereinafter Ulc), defines in its Sect. 2–10 the Digital asset as "an electronic record in which an individual has a right or interest. The term does not include an underlying asset or liability unless the asset or liability is itself an electronic record." The definition of "digital asset" expressly excludes underlying assets such as funds held in an online bank account. Because records may exist in electronic and non-electronic formats, this definition clarifies the scope of the act and the limitation on the type of records to which it applies. The term includes types of electronic records currently in existence and yet to be invented. It consists of any electronically stored information, such as (1) information stored on a user's computer and other digital devices, (2) content uploaded onto websites, and (3) rights in digital property. It also includes records that are either the catalogue or the content of an electronic communication. This text does not contain any conflict of law provisions.

The *Uniform Commercial Code Amendments* (2022),[45] adopted by the Ulc and the American Law Institute, provides in its *Sect. 12–107* the law applicable to "Controllable Electronic Records", establishing, as a general rule, that the local law of a controllable electronic record's jurisdiction governs a matter covered by this article. For a controllable electronic record that evidences a controllable account or controllable payment intangible, the local law of the controllable electronic record's jurisdiction governs a matter covered by Sect. 12–106 unless an effective agreement determines that another jurisdiction's local law governs.

From a material perspective, the UNIDROIT Principles adopt a form-based approach to electronic registration, strongly inspired by the American uniform law, which subjects all types of registered securities or rights to the same body of substantive rules. This unique characterisation derives from the possibility of exercising control over the right or security contained in the electronic medium. Principle 6 maintains the criterion of control included in the recent amendments to the Uniform Commercial Code.

2.4.6 American Law Institute /European Law Institute

The American Law Institute (hereinafter ALI) and the European Law Institute (hereinafter ELI) have adopted the *Principles for a Data Economy - Data Transactions and*

[44] National Conference of Commissioners on Uniform State Laws (Uniform Law Commission), *Uniform Fiduciary Access to Digital Assets Act* (2015), approved in July 2015. Available in: https://www.uniformlaws.org/viewdocument/final-act-with-comments-40?CommunityKey=f7237fc4-74c2-4728-81c6-b39a91ecdf22&tab=librarydocuments.

[45] National Conference of Commissioners on Uniform State Laws (Uniform Law Commission) y American Law Institute, *Uniform Commercial Code Amendments* (2022), approved in July 2022. Available in: https://www.uniformlaws.org/viewdocument/final-act-164?CommunityKey=1457c422-ddb7-40b0-8c76-39a1991651ac&tab=librarydocuments.

Data Rights-,[46] whose Part V ("*Multi-State Issues*") provides principles on conflicts of laws.

According to Principle 38 ("Application of Established Choice-of-Law Rules of the Forum"), data contracts should be governed by the law chosen by the parties in accordance with the forum's conflict of laws rules on contractual matters. For any other issue arising under these Principles, the law applicable to that issue should be (a) the law of the State that would be selected under the forum's choice-of-law rules if those rules provide a clear rule for determining the law applicable to that issue; or (b) if the forum's choice-of-law rules do not provide a clear rule for determining the law applicable to that issue, the law determined by application of Principle 39.

Principle 39 provides that, in the absence of a choice of law, the applicable law should be the law of the State having the most significant relationship with the legal issue in question. Contracts to be taken into account in determining which State has the most significant relationship include: (a) the place where data activities (i) are designed to produce effects on relevant interests, or (ii) actually produce effects; (b) the domicile, residence, nationality, place of incorporation and place of business of the party asserting a right and the party against whom it is asserted; and (c), the law of the State that governs a pre-existing legal relationship, if any, between the party asserting a right and the party against whom it is asserted; and (d), the place where the data is generated.

Finally, Principle 40 addresses the relevance of the place of storage as a connecting factor only when the issue in question relates to storage or to rights in the medium. Thus, the location of data storage may be relevant for the choice of law purposes as a connecting factor of a residual nature, such as in the absence of other connecting factors or when the consideration of other connecting factors is indeterminate. The fact that data is stored outside a State does not, in itself, ordinarily, raise issues of extraterritorial exercise of jurisdiction or application of law, provided that there are sufficient links between the State and the activities with respect to the data it seeks to regulate or the entitlements with respect to the data it seeks to enforce.

More recently, the ELI developed the *Principles on the Use of Digital Assets as Security*.[47] Principle 3(2) addresses conflict of laws, stating that the applicable law is the law of the State in which the security provider has, at the time of the creation of the security interest, its place of business, or its central administration (if it has a place of business in more than one jurisdiction) or the law of the jurisdiction in which the security provider has its habitual residence (in the absence of a place of business). However, in cases where the digital asset itself is clearly connected with one particular jurisdiction, the law of that jurisdiction is deemed to be the applicable law [Principle 3(3)].

---

[46] American Law Institute and European Law Institute, *Principles for a Data Economy. Data Transactions and Data Rights*, adopted by the ALI on May 18, 2021 and by the ELI on September 1, 2021. Available in: https://principlesforadataeconomy.org/fileadmin/user_upload/p_principlesforadataeconomy/Files/Principles_for_a_Data_Economy_ELI_Final_Council_Draft.pdf.

[47] European Law Institute, *Principles on the Use of Digital Assets as Security*, 2022. Available in: https://www.europeanlawinstitute.eu/fileadmin/user_upload/p_eli/Publications/ELI_Principles_on_the_Use_of_Digital_Assets_as_Security.pdf.

2.5 *Final Considerations*

2.5.1 Characterisation of Digital Assets

From the PIL perspective, it is difficult to develop uniform PIL rules which are valid for the different legal systems in the contemporary world. The reason is that no characterisation has been established of what we should understand by "property issues" nor of the legal nature of the different "digital assets".

(i) With respect to property issues, the scope of the law designated under the connections factors of Principle 5 covers a number of substantive issues formally excluded from the scope of the Principles, in particular all those excluded by Principle 3.
(ii) Regarding the *characterisation* of digital assets, the UNIDROIT Principles deal with digital assets based on the control criterion included in the recent amendments to the Uniform Commercial Code. Unlike the UNIDROIT Principles, the European Union has taken into account the fact that the legal nature of digital assets *characterised* as securities or financial guarantees[48] is dissociated from that of other assets registered in a distributed registry.[49]

2.5.2 Party Autonomy in the Choice of Applicable Law

Principle 5(1), paragraphs (a) and (b), provides that the applicable law governing property issues relating to digital assets should be specified in the digital asset itself or in the system or platform on which the asset is recorded. This rule is based on party autonomy, which is widely recognised in contractual matters but not in property issues. The fundamental reason is that property and rights in rem issues affect third parties, who should be able to recognise the law governing the property aspects of the assets.

As regards the protection of third parties, the choice of applicable law should only be effective with respect to third parties if they can clearly determine or verify that such a choice has been made. The choice of law applicable to a digital asset or a system should be verifiable by third parties. It should, therefore, be attached to the relevant asset in a format accessible to any third party wishing to investigate the status of the asset or, in the case of choice made in systems or platforms, it should be accessible to all participants in the system or platform.

---

[48] Digital assets classified as securities or financial guarantees are likely to have a different legal nature and, consequently, be subject to different conflict of laws rules. For example, securities deposited with an intermediary covered by the 2006 Hague Convention or financial instruments on stock exchanges and other trading systems, governed by Article 4(1)(h) of the Rome I Regulation.

[49] France addresses this issue by distinguishing the category of digital assets provided for in financial instruments from those others, which it breaks down into two categories: tokens, classified as intangible assets for the purposes of applying the token issuer status, and digital assets representing securities with an "exchange" function. See Haut Comité Juridique de la Place Financière de Paris, *Report on the determination of the law applicable to assets registered in distributed ledgers*, May 2024. Available in: https://www.banque-france.fr/fr/system/files/2024-07/Rapport_63_A.pdf.

Principle 5(2)(b) provides that "in determining whether the applicable law is specified in a digital asset, or in a system on which the digital asset is recorded, consideration should be given to records attached to, or associated with the digital asset, or the system, if such records are readily available for review by persons dealing with the relevant digital asset." This provision may, nevertheless, be confusing, as it does not require such records to be readily available, but that they should be taken into account if they are readily available for review. If no records are available for review, they cannot be taken into consideration, and it is therefore unclear how third parties will be able to recognise the applicable law.

Principle 5(1)(a) provides that the choice of law must be expressly specified in the digital asset. However, Principle 5(2)(c) appears to contemplate implicit consent to the choice of law by stating that any manner of dealing with a digital asset constitutes consent to the law declared for the purposes of Principle 5(1). It is submitted that, while the choice of law need not be expressed in the relations between the parties to a specific transaction involving a digital asset, the choice of law governing property issues must be expressed and public in order to be effective against third parties. Thus, the requirement that the choice of law be expressed should be addressed in the context of the rule requiring that such choice be recorded in the public register attached to or associated with the asset, system or platform in question. In our view, the formal and material requirements for a valid choice of law should be specified in the same sense as in Article 3 of Regulation 593/2008 (Rome I) on the choice of law applicable to contractual obligations.[50]

Finally, the rules do not provide for the exclusion of *renvoi* in the choice of law applicable to property matters involving digital assets. An exclusion clause should perhaps have been established in similar terms to those provided in Article 20 of Regulation 593/2008 (Rome I) or in Article 8 of the Hague Principles.

For the reasons set out above, the following solution might have been more in line with the legal nature of digital assets and the objectives pursued: determining the connection of the party autonomy as a connection only in matters so determined by the forum's conflict of law rules, as established by the Principles for a Data Economy developed by the ALI and the ELI (Principle 38), with the exception clause of the most significant relationship in the absence of choice.

2.5.3 Applicable Law in the Absence of Choice

We believe that the applicable law in the absence of a choice of law should be determined by uniform rules based on more foreseeable connecting factors. Further guidance on how States should determine the applicable law and specify the connecting factors in the absence of a choice of law would be desirable. The latter could be

[50] European Association of Private International Law (EAPIL), "Position Paper", UNIDROIT 2023 // Study LXXXII – W.G.8 – Doc. 4, Annex II // February 2023, p. 124–125, marg. 22.

accomplished perhaps by clearly establishing a general rule with its exceptions and an escape clause.[51]

Principle 5(1)(d), in both Option A(ii) and Option B(i), provides that in the absence of a specification of the applicable law in the digital asset or in the system/platform in which the digital asset is recorded, the Principles as specified by the forum State shall apply, in whole or in part. Commentary 5.5 clarifies that the objective of these provisions is not to provide for the application of a national law implementing the Principles, but rather the Principles themselves as "rules of law" or non-State law.

Regarding this application of the Principles as non-State law, no general acceptance of international instruments has been reached, allowing the courts to apply non-State law as a rule governing a given legal issue. In the European Union, the introduction of such a power was ultimately rejected in the legislative process, leading to the adoption of Regulation 593/2008 (Rome I).

Furthermore, both options A(iii) and B(ii) of Principle 5(1)(d) contain as a default rule a reference to the "law applicable by virtue of the rules of private international law of the forum State". Such a general reference might not be compatible with the objective of legal harmonisation pursued by draft rules of PIL.

From a comparative perspective, the waterfall structure of Articles 4(3) and 4(4) of Regulation 593/2008 (Rome I) could perhaps be used as a reference with the escape clause ("manifestly more closely connected"). In the same way, Article 28 of the 2001 United Nations Convention on Assignment of Receivables in International Trade provides that in the absence of a choice of law by the parties, the rights and obligations of the assignor and the assignee shall be governed by the law of the State with which the assignment contract is most closely connected. In similar terms, the Principles for a Data Economy adopted by the ALI and the ELI refer in Principle 39 to the connection of the closest links. Finally, the Principles on the Use of Digital Assets as Security adopted by the ELI also establish in Principle 3(3) an escape clause: "in those cases where the digital asset itself is clearly connected with one particular jurisdiction".

[51] European Association of Private International Law (EAPIL), "Position Paper", UNIDROIT 2023 // Study LXXXII – W.G.8 – Doc. 4, Annex II // February 2023, p. 125–126, marg. 24–34.

Reflections on Section III: Control and Transfer

Principle 6
Control

Marina Echebarría Sáenz

(1) A person has 'control' of a digital asset if:

(a) subject to paragraphs (2) and (3), the digital asset, or the relevant protocol or system, confers on that person:

(i) the exclusive ability to prevent others from obtaining substantially all of the benefit from the digital asset;

(ii) the ability to obtain substantially all of the benefit from the digital asset; and

(iii) the exclusive ability to transfer the abilities in subparagraphs (a)(i), (a)(ii) and (a)(iii) to another person; and

(b) the digital asset, or the relevant protocols or system, allows that person to identify itself as having the abilities set out in paragraph (a).

(2) A 'change of control' means a transfer of the abilities in subparagraph (1)(a) to another person, and includes the replacement, modification, destruction, cancellation, or elimination of a digital asset, and the resulting and corresponding derivative creation of a new digital asset (a 'resulting digital asset') which is subject to the control of another person.

This work was financed within the framework of the Prometeo 2023 project of the Regional Ministry of Innovation, Universities, Science and Digital Society (CIPROM/2022/26) "Present and future of the regulation of cryptoassets in the EU [LegalCripto]", whose principal investigator is Carmen Pastor Sempere. The basic ideas contained herein were presented in the author's paper with the same title, given on November 13, 2024 at the IV International Congress on "UNIDROIT Principles on Digital Assets and Private Law: Context, Content, Perspectives", organized also by BAES Research Group of the University of Alicante on November 13 and 14, 2024.

The chapter has been written in the framework of the research project funded by the Ministry of Science and Innovation entitled "The consolidation of the digital revolution and its challenges: adaptation of the competitive strategies of economic operators and the ordering rules of the markets". PID2022- 139741OB-C2. IP C.A. HERRERO SUÁREZ.

M. Echebarría Sáenz (✉)
Valladolid University, Valladolid, Spain
e-mail: marina.echebarria@uva.es

C. Pastor Sempere and D. A. Morán Bovio (eds.), UNIDROIT *Principles on Digital Assets and Private Law*, Law, Governance and Technology Series 80,
https://doi.org/10.1007/978-3-032-11001-5_12

(3) An ability for the purposes of sub-paragraph (1)(a) need not be exclusive if, and to the extent that:

> **(a) the digital asset, or the relevant protocol or system, limits the use of, or is programmed to make changes to, the digital asset, including change or loss of control of the digital asset; or**
>
> **(b) the person in control has agreed, consented to, or acquiesced in sharing that ability with one or more other persons.**

1 Official Commentary

Commentary
General

6.1. The concept of 'control' is of great importance in these Principles. Principle 6 contains a detailed definition of control of a digital asset. Although control is a factual concept that is separate from, and need not accompany, proprietary rights, the existence of 'control' pursuant to the definition in Principle 6 is a requirement for certain legal consequences in these principles (for example, as a condition precedent to qualification as an innocent acquirer, and for third-party effectiveness and priority of security rights). The exclusive ability requirements in Principle 6(1)(a) (as relaxed in Principle 6(3)) recognize that the ability to exclude is an inherent aspect of proprietary rights.

6.2. The exclusive ability requirements in Principle 6(1)(a) contemplate that 'control' assumes a role that is a functional equivalent to that of 'possession' of movables. However, possession' in this context is a purely factual matter and not a legal concept. Moreover, because a digital asset is intangible, this functional equivalence to possession involves only the dominion and power over a digital asset but does not involve the physical situs dimension applicable to possession of movables. Whether 'control', as defined in Principle 6, exists is a matter of fact and does not depend on a legal conclusion. However, as explained below, the presence of control gives rise to legal consequences. The exclusivity criterion of control (including the standards in Principle 6(3) for its relaxation) appears to reflect the norm in the relevant markets for digital assets. Acquirers expect and believe that they have obtained the relevant exclusive abilities with respect to a digital asset (subject to understood exceptions) and in fact that generally has been the case.

6.3. Although control assumes a role that is, as a purely factual matter, a functional equivalent to that of 'possession', control as used in these Principles must not be understood to be identical to 'possession' as a legal concept used in certain jurisdictions. In those jurisdictions, possession is a legal concept and a possessor may 'hold' possession of an asset through another person. However, under these Principles control is a factual matter and a person cannot control a digital asset unless the criteria of Principle 6 are met. On the custody of digital assets, see also below and Principle 10.

6.4. The concept of control in a law governing digital assets serves as a necessary (but not a sufficient) criterion for qualifying for protection as an innocent acquirer of a digital asset other than as a client in a custodial relationship), and as a method of third-party effectiveness and a basis of priority of security rights in a digital asset. States also may choose to adopt the concept of control as an element of third-party effectiveness of proprietary interests more generally. It is important to note that control (as defined in Principle 6) is also an element in the definition of 'digital asset' in Principle 2(2): only an electronic record which is capable of being subject to control is a 'digital asset' and therefore within the scope of the Principles.

6.5. The change of control from one person to another person must be distinguished from a transfer of a digital asset or an interest therein, i.e. a transfer of proprietary rights. See Principle 2(5) (defining 'transfer'). Whether there is a valid transfer of proprietary rights in a digital asset is a matter of other law and is not dealt with in these Principles (see Principle 3(3) and Commentary 2.26). Whilst in many situations a transfer of proprietary rights will be accompanied by a change of control, in some situations it may not. The law of a State, for instance, may provide that under certain circumstances 'ownership' (as defined by the applicable national law) in a digital asset may pass to another person, whilst control stays with the transferor. Vice versa, in some situations, and depending on the applicable other law, a change of control will not result in a transfer of proprietary rights. A custodian (as defined in Principle 10(1)), for instance, may obtain control of a digital asset for a client, but will typically not in that context acquire 'ownership' (as defined by the applicable national law) of that digital asset. This explanation reflects the understanding of control of a digital asset as a functional equivalent of possession. In an effort to highlight this distinction between changes of control and transfers of proprietary rights, instead of references to, e.g. a 'delivery', a 'delivery of control', or similar references, these Principles refer simply to a 'change of control'. 'Change of control' is defined in Principle 6(2) and two illustrations of change of control are given in commentary 6.14 to 6.17.

6.6. Control by a person of a digital asset as agent (for example, an employee may have control for their employer), is treated in these Principles as control by the principal, as an implementation of the law of agency. The concept of control is also relevant in the context of the custody of digital assets. As set out in Principle 10, under a custody agreement a service provider is obliged to maintain digital assets for its clients, either by controlling the digital assets itself or by entering into a custody agreement with a sub-custodian whereby the sub-custodian controls the digital assets for the service provider. This is an example of one person (the custodian) having control while proprietary rights are transferred to or remain with another person (the client). A thief of digital assets would be another example of the separation of control and proprietary rights.

'Ability' of a person with control

6.7. In Principle 6 the term 'ability' is used instead of the term 'power'. While the terms have identical meanings, 'ability' is more compatible with the concept of control as a factual standard and 'power' has a more 'legal' connotation. On the exclusivity aspect of required abilities, see commentary 6.10 to 6.12.

6.8. Principle 6(2) addresses the situation in which the change of control relates to a derivative digital asset over which control is acquired, inasmuch as the derivative digital asset is not the same digital asset as to which control was relinquished. An example of such a derivative digital asset is the UTXO (unspent transaction output) generated by a transaction in Bitcoin. Another example might be adjustments in balances in accounts resulting from transactions in ether on the Ethereum platform, as to which control is relinquished and acquired over fungible assets that are not necessarily the 'same' assets.

6.9. The requirements in Principle 6(1)(a) (as relaxed in Principle 6(3)), as noted above, reflect the ability to exclude as an inherent attribute of proprietary rights. However, it is possible that a person (other than a person rightfully in control) who has no proprietary rights might acquire these abilities without the consent of the rightful control person, such as by the discovery of relevant private keys through 'hacking', finding, or stealing a device or other record on which the keys are stored. This underscores the distinction between a change in control and a transfer of proprietary rights. Although control is functionally analogous to possession inasmuch as it is a condition for innocent acquisition under Principle 8 and for third-party effectiveness under Principle 15, and a person in control may or may not have proprietary rights in the digital asset, there are important differences.

Exclusivity of abilities

6.10. The exclusive abilities contemplated by Principles 6(1)(a)(i) and 6(1)(a)(iii) assume the existence of a system for digital assets that reliably establishes those abilities and their exclusivity. But the abilities and exclusivity are not negated by the possibility that such a reliable system might be compromised by a wrongful 'hacking'—even if such a wrongful compromise actually occurs. Such a possibility is an inherent, if unfortunate, attribute of any digital asset (as is the improper taking of physical possession of a tangible object from a person in physical possession of the tangible object). As a practical matter, however, past experience indicates that the occurrence of such a hack would be likely to result in a prompt change of control by the wrongdoer. See also Commentary 7.2. Moreover, even if another person were to obtain the relevant abilities without the affirmative consent of the rightful control person, the rightful control person would continue to have control until such time as it no longer has the requisite abilities (i.e. the abilities are lost because control had been transferred to another person). The rightful control person would not lose control merely because the other person obtained those abilities (as by discovering the private key associated with a digital asset) so long as the other person acquiring the abilities had not transferred control. The other person might acquire the abilities innocently and with no intention or reason to transfer control. A person acquiring the abilities wrongfully, however, presumably would not sit idly by while allowing the rightful control person to maintain the ability to deal with the digital asset. Such a wrongful acquirer presumably would promptly transfer control, as mentioned above. Were the rightful control person to discover that the other person had acquired the abilities, presumably it would either immediately transfer control to protect its interests or would acquiesce in the other person's shared control. It follows that it is unlikely that shared control with another person in the absence of the rightful control person's actual or implicit agreement, consent, or acquiescence would continue beyond a very short period of time.

6.11. Principle 6(3) provides explicit relaxation of the exclusivity requirements imposed by Principle 6(1)(a). Principle 6(3)(a) contemplates situations in which the inherent attributes of a digital asset or the system in which it resides may result in changes, including a change of control, which constitute exceptions to the exclusivity of a control person's abilities. Principle 6(3)(b) recognizes that a person who has control may wish to share its abilities with one or more other persons for purposes of convenience, security, or otherwise. For example, in a multi-signature (multi-sig) arrangement, if a person can identify itself under Principle 7(1)(b), it could have control even if it shares the relevant abilities with another person. This is so even if the action of the other person is a condition for the exercise of a relevant ability. See Illustration 1 at commentary 6.13. Another example is that of multi-party computation (MPC) in which the private key is split up into several shards, all of which are required to execute a transaction.

6.12. Principle 6(1)(a)(ii) does not require that the specified ability must be exclusive. Inasmuch as a control person must have the exclusive ability to prevent others from obtaining substantially all of the benefit of a digital asset, it would be of no (legal) consequence that a control person has elected to permit another person (or persons) to obtain the benefits (or some of them). It also may be that this situation is already covered by the exceptions provided in Principle 6(3)(b), which permits sharing of abilities. If so, whether or not the ability specified in Principle 6(1)(a)(ii) is required to be exclusive would be of little or no consequence. In any event, a control person need not prove a negative fact, as provided in Principle 7 and explained in the commentary thereto.

Shared control

6.13. ***Illustration 1: Shared control and multi-sig arrangements.*** *Investor acquires proprietary rights in a digital asset (cryptocurrency) held in a public blockchain platform. Investor holds through a multi-sig arrangement in which the two of three private keys—the Investor's private key and the private keys of X and Y, parties trusted by Investor—are required to change control of the digital asset. Assuming Investor has all of the abilities specified in Principle 6(1)(a) and can identify itself as provided in Principle 6(1)(b), Investor has control over the digital asset. Although Investor has shared the ability to change control specified in Principle 6(1)(a)(iii) and action by X or Y is a condition for Investor to exercise that ability, Principle 6(3)(b) provides an exception to the exclusivity requirement of Principle 6(1)(a)(iii).*

Change of control

6.14. ***Illustration 2: Change of control via PKI****: A public, permissionless, distributed network (Alpha) supports a virtual machine (Alpha-VM) that enables the creation and use of electronic records (Beta) in its database (Alpha-DB). Alpha implements a public-key cryptography system, whereby every Beta is associated with a public key and can be used only by a person who sends the appropriate instructions to the Alpha-VM validated by the corresponding private key. Alpha and the Alpha-VM support two uses for Betas. First, a person can actuate a Beta to record a small image file into the Alpha-DB permanently; each Beta can be actuated only once. Second, a person can change the public key with which a Beta is associated; after a Beta has been associated with a new public key, its corresponding private key is required to use that Beta.*

6.15. A Beta is a digital asset, as it satisfies all the requirements of Principle 2(2) and Principle 6. Person A changes control of a Beta to Person B by disassociating the Beta from a public key for which only Person A knows the private key, and associating it with a public key for which only Person B knows the private key.

6.16. ***Illustration 3: Change of control via OTP-Device****: A private, permissioned, distributed network (Gamma) supports a virtual machine (Gamma-VM) that enables the creation and maintenance of electronic records (Delta) in its database (Delta-DB). Deltas are records capable of storing only unformatted text. Gamma implements a form of hardware security, whereby each Delta is paired with a hand-held device that randomly generates one-time passwords (OTP-Device). To read, edit and delete text stored in a Delta, a person requires a one-time password generated by the OTP-Device paired with the Delta in question.*

6.17. A Delta is a digital asset, as it satisfies all the requirements of Principle 2(2) and principle 6. Person A changes control of a Delta to Person B by physically handing to them the OTP-Device paired with that Delta.

2 Reflections

2.1 Introduction and Background

The main problem for the jurist who deals with the principle of control is the risk of looking for a shelter in the legal categories with which he is familiar. Despite the clarity of the text and the commentary prepared by UNIDROIT, many readers will look for a correspondence with their knowledge of the basic institutions used by their State law which attribute the power to obtain the exclusive yield of an asset, to exclude third parties from such yields or to transfer it to a third party. The temptation to assimilate control to the powers attributed by the concept of property or patrimonial right immediately arises, and when dissociation between ownership of the asset or property itself and the capacity to dispose of it is observed, we quickly transpose the concepts of possession or the mechanisms of representation, agency or legitimisation that we are familiar with in other contexts. Similarly, when the assets represented by the token are themselves tangible assets or commodities, it is easy for the continental jurist to get carried away by the similarities with the notion of incorporation of a right into a title that is typical of traditional securities (such as warehouse receipts or letters of credit).

As jurists, we are accustomed to qualifying or "making fit" concepts into the legal categories of our legal system. This is certainly the right thing to do, because we need to respond to the conflicts that are submitted within the context of our legal system, but there are occasions when it is necessary to avoid "false friends" - and this is precisely one of those situations.

The genesis of the Principles dates back to 2015/2016 with two proposals for regulation of Blockchain and Smart Contracts from Hungary and the Czech Republic, as well as an attempt to work together with UNCITRAL in light of its model law on Electronic Transferable Records (2018), and its model law on secured transactions (2016).[1] Those initiatives led to the adoption of the harmonization project at two meetings in Rome in May 2019 and an expert group in Vienna in March 2020 to begin work on establishing a taxonomy of the digital asset market.[2] An exploratory group under the leadership of Dr Kanda presented its initial work in September

[1] UNCITRAL/UNCITRAL, Model Law on Electronic Transferable Records, (13 July 2017. https://uncitral.un.org/en/texts/ecommerce/modellaw/electronic_transferable_records

Model Law on secured transactions (2016).

UNCITRAL Model Law on Secured Transactions (2016) I United Nations Commission On International Trade Law.

[2] HCCH-UNIDROIT. STUDY LXXXII W.G.1, Doc 2. *DIGITAL ASSETS AND PRIVATE LAW, WORKING* GROUP 1ST SESSION ROME 17–19 NOVEMBER 2020 AND.

https://www.unidroit.org/english/governments/councildocuments/2019session/cd-98-17-e.pdf

2020,[3] Several consultations and analyses took place in 2021[4] and finally the work was finally approved in May 2022.[5]

The intent of this work was to develop this taxonomy of the concepts involved in the use of tokens and to develop a functional, technology-neutral approach, that can be applied to any context in which a data set becomes a valuable token or a digital asset.

The concept of control in this context is a Paramount concept that comes from UNICITRAL's *Model Law on electronic transferable records*[6] where it is adopted as an electronic synonym for physical possession which, by definition, is not possible in an electronic record.

The Principles should also be consistent in terminology with UNCITRAL's work on best enforcement practices,[7] its model law on warehouse deposit certificates, the guide on Best Practices in the field of electronic Registry Design and operation,[8] etc. Furthermore, they should also be consistent with other previous UNIDROIT works, such as the Principles on the Operation of close-out Netting Provisions (2013),[9] the Convention on substantive rules for intermediated securities (2013),[10] or the Legislative Guide on intermediate Securities (2017).[11] The objective of determining rules on custody and insolvency of digital asset operators and attempting to define the scope of these rules was also identified from the outset.

First of all, it should be recalled that the fact that an attempt is made to define control as a factual situation does not imply that the definition of control has no legal consequences. It obviously does, starting with the fact that the finding of control is one of the two necessary **factors that must be present for bona fide purchasers** to enjoy an irreclaimable situation.

The principle of control also has an important connection with the **definition** of digital assets. The concept of digital assets in these Principles is defined as an

---

[3] - HCCH-UNIDROIT. Study LXXXII W.G.1, Doc 2. Digital assets and Private LAW, WORKING Group 1st session Rome 17–19 November 2020.

- HCCH-UNIDROIT. Study LXXXII W.G.1, Doc 3. Digital assets and Private LAW, Exploratory workshop. Rome 17–18 September 2020. March 2021.

- HCCH-UNIDROIT. Study LXXXII W.G.1, Doc 4. Digital assets and Private LAW, WORKING Group. First session remote, 17-19 November 2020, March 2021.

[4] See note precedent and HCCH-UNIDROIT. STUDY LXXXII W.G.2, Doc 2. *DIGITAL ASSETS AND PRIVATE LAW, WORKING* GROUP. SECOND SESSION REMOTE, ROME, 16–18 MARCH 2021.

[5] HCCH-UNIDROIT. PRINCIPLES ON DIGITAL ASSETS AND PRIVATE LAW, Rome, 2023.

[6] "Control is a fundamental notion of the Model Law since it represents the functional equivalent of possession of a transferable document or instrument".

[7] UNCITRAL/UNCITRAL Arbitration rules, 2021. www.https://uncitral.un.org/sites/uncitral.un.org/files/media-documents/uncitral/en/21-07996_expedited-arbitration-e-ebook.pdf.

[8] UNCITRAL, Cape Town academic Convention project on Best Practices in the field of electronic Registry Design and operation.

[9] HCCH-UNIDROIT. PRINCIPLES ON THE OPERATION OF CLOSE-OUT NETTING PROVISIONS, Rome, 2013.

[10] tps://www.unidroit.org/instruments/capital-markets/geneva-convention/

[11] Legislative Guide - UNIDROIT.

electronic document that can be subject to control (*Principle 2*). It should be noted that here a process of conceptual inversion takes place: it is not that a digital asset can be subject to control, it is that if control cannot be exercised, it is not a regulated digital asset. Indeed, as we have stated before, not all digital data can be characterized as an "asset", and there are even some types that could plausibly be considered as an "asset" which are excluded from the scope of the Principles. It is understood that "asset" is a term that has several meanings and is generally used to describe an object with a value attached to it. Therefore, the Principles are only interested in those that have a value, are transferable and tradable and, as we can see, can be subject to control.

Finally, the Principles had to be neutral in terms of the technical system and the legal system employed, so that ownership of digital assets, let alone control over them, was not prejudged as property or property-like rights. It is true that it is plausible to identify ownership or property-like rights over digital assets in most legal systems, but focusing on this creates problems in the distinction between cause and effect. As we shall see, different legal systems offer different solutions to the same de facto situations.

2.2 The Notion of Control: Ownership, Possession, Legitimation and "Exclusive Capacities"

UNIDROIT's drafters have made a clear effort to configure the principle of control as a de facto issue; a representation of the technical operation, or better still, of the various technical operations existing in the crypto-assets and digital assets market. On the basis of these operations, they strived to establish clear rules for attributing legal consequences, compatible with different legal systems and different conceptual approaches in each State law. It is true that many of the situations that we will observe in the digital market can be included in a State system in the concepts of ownership or mediated possession. In other situations, we will be able to attribute a regulation to them specific to an operational scheme of agency. In other cases, we will resolve the issue by assimilating the conduct of an operator in accordance with the rules of legitimization or representation that we apply in other financial contexts (managing asset wallets) or through other instruments with a similar purpose, as may occur with securities. It is equally true however, that on other occasions this will not be the case. Acting automatically in a general transposition of concepts can lead to problems that are difficult to solve when faced with the examples provided by the market. As the preliminary studies show, the operation of digital assets is enormously varied in its protocols and content. In the market, we find digital assets that are placed in a fungible repository regime, as opposed to those that constitute a non-fungible repository, and identify and individualize each asset throughout its lifetime. Most digital assets represent a value in themselves, but others are linked to other types of tangible assets that they represent and to which they establish some kind of link.

We find digital assets that are backed by value, and others that are not. In terms of management, assets may be held in network wallets or on physical media such as computers or memory sticks. The access keys that facilitate the disposition of the assets may also be in the hands of the holder, the custodian of the assets, a custodian outside the asset, or may be shared among several parties (with joint use or indistinct use). The notion of control in this context is technologically neutral with respect to the computer systems and network designs used. It serves and applies to **transactional systems** such as Bitcoin or Ethereum as well as to **accounting/traceable systems of record**. So, for example, when I transfer 5 of the 20 bitcoins I own, being a transactional system, what happens is that my registered digital asset is replaced by various UTXO files necessary for the accounting registration of the transaction on a Blockchain, and the process concludes with the birth of a new digital asset of 15 bitcoins in my name and another new digital asset of five in the name of the acquirer. By contrast, in ***registry systems***, the asset remains unchanged, although its transfer to a third party is recorded and an accounting record of its traceability is kept: I retain ownership of 15 units and transfer, as a derivative acquisition, five units to a third party. In both systems, however, we will note the need to exercise control over the disposition of digital assets. Control operates with neutrality vis-à-vis the design of the registration and transfer system.

To put it in legal terms, a possessor in the legal sense may hold possession through a custodian, who is in control. For continental countries this would be a case of mediate possession, where it would be assumed that the custodian should follow the instructions of the owner or possessor, which may, or occasionally may not, be the case. This is why it is argued that control is a necessary, but not always sufficient requirement for the valid transfer of the digital asset. *Principle 10* identifies the person who receives the asset from the one who has control as a bona fide acquirer, and has standing under the applicable national law.

On the other hand, digital asset operators can play a wide variety of roles: they can be simple depositaries without control capacities, or simple custodians of the keys on behalf of a holder, but it is much more common to find custodians with relevant capacity and even with full capacity to dispose of the digital assets on behalf of their holders. Hence the drafters' insistence that "Control" is a factual term, which may or may not coincide with the legal qualification of "ownership" or "property right" or "right in rem" in some legal systems, especially when we think of the power of exclusive use. The operations of traders and crypto-asset exchanges are full of examples in which there is a separation between the proprietary rights over the digital asset and the capacity to control it, on the basis of a custody contract, agency, portfolio management, transfer of usufruct, management of trusts, pledging as collateral, etc. etc. The emergence of smart contracts equipped with artificial intelligence has a major impact here. As an example, in an increasingly widespread operating model for digital asset traders, an investor deposits FIAT currency with a custodian,[12] and in exchange obtains a digital asset that is subject to various smart

[12] The term deposit is used improperly here, as it is used in the European Union countries and other States which consider "deposit" only those realized in Credit Institutions, submitted to the financial

contracts. The value delivered may be subject to a mining process to increase its value or be delivered to a smart contract that manages the digital asset. This smart contract, depending on market developments, may promote various acts of disposal, such as its realization and replacement by another asset with better performance, the loan of the digital asset to a hedge fund that is leveraging its position against a rising or falling digital asset, or even, faced with the risk of loss of value due to a sudden drop in the price level on the exchange, it may liquidate the asset completely. When making the relevant legal qualifications, note that the first smart contract transfers control and "ownership" on behalf of a remote customer to a second smart contract. The smart contracts have a kind of "cyber personality" in that they can be registered and identified in an electronic ledger in accordance with various technical regulations in EU countries. Legally though, the two smart contracts may belong to the same natural or legal person (who is legally responsible) or to different persons (at which point we establish that there has been a transfer in the status of the customer-custodian relationship). All these operations can be carried out in fractions of a second through dialogue between several smart contracts, which in turn may belong to the same custodian or to different custodians (as possible sub-custodians or third parties). The speed at which the opportunity calculations are made totally excludes human intervention in the face of certain risks, and therefore, the entire operation can only be based on the transfer of control over the digital asset to a custodian.[13]

In the same way that the powers of exclusion bring us closer to the idea of "possession" in legal terms, an assimilation that occurs in the UNCITRAL model law, but equally the situation described as a control will apply to cases in which this assimilation will not be appropriate.

The important thing, therefore, is that the factual description of the capacities of control should have uniform legal consequences regardless of the legal framework applied to them a posteriori, as this is the only way to provide legal certainty and fair treatment in an essentially globalized and transnational market. This is why we are told that the existence of the regular exercise of "control" is a necessary factor for assessing the legitimacy of a *bona fide* acquirer or an acquirer *a non-domino*, without prejudice to the fact that the use of control may not be sufficient to acquire the legal status of a *bona fide* acquirer or innocent customer-acquirer. Control, in short, may be one of the factors to be assessed to determine the legitimacy of the transferor and the acquirer of an asset. A necessary factor, but not the only one or necessarily sufficient, because, as in the case of securities, the fact that the non-possessory purchaser's irrevocability is determined does not entail the loss of the dispossessed owner's economic rights, who may claim them from the dispossessor. Or, in the same way, the possession of control capacities may not be sufficient to realize a valid transfer of the asset or its capacities to a third party, as can be seen in the 11th principle or in the examples of shared control in the 6th principle.

---

system and offer a warranty or safety in case of Insolvency of the Credit Institution. But in all crypto-asset operations there is a common use of the language of the financial market that creates semantic conflicts.

[13] Another example by HINKES. UNIDROIT 2021 - Study LXXXII - W.G.1 - Doc. 3, p. 8.

The notion of control thus hinges on two basic ideas:

First, the controlling party has the exclusive ability to prevent others from obtaining the benefits of the digital asset. The one who has control can obtain all the benefits of the digital asset, and the controlling party can transfer these two capabilities to another person.

Second, the asset or its protocols allow identifying of the person possessing the above abilities.

Thus, in order to define whether control exists, we will have to be able to distinguish those cases in which a data unit can be individualized with respect to a larger body of data where the behaviour of that data unit can be controlled, including exclusion of access by third parties, or, if preferred, where "consumption" by one person precludes consumption by others. In addition, this data unit can be transferred within the system or between different systems.

The notion of ***exclusive use*** lends itself to some confusion, as it is usually the holder of an asset, the owner, who enjoys the benefits of the asset and excludes third parties from using it. With regard to control however, ownership of the asset is not jeopardised, but only the ability of the holder of control to obtain the benefits of the asset in its own interest or in the interest of others. The same applies to the ability to transfer this power to a third party.

Once again, there will be cases in which the ability to control is detached from the ownership of the digital asset, as an obvious example in cases of hacking, but also in cases where it is operated under a loan of assets, or where the exclusive capabilities are exercised under a portfolio management contract or similar, as in the example cited regarding the management of Wallets or Vaults by Smart Contracts.

The reason why the control holder enjoys these capabilities may have different origins. It may indeed be a consequence of ownership of the asset. But it may also be a right of possession by representative mandate or by agency, in the interest of the true owner or holder. That is why the Principles do not speak of owners or holders, but rather only mention the term "**customer**", which does not prejudge a legal qualification.

The most archetypical examples here would be trusts, digital asset loans, pledges, usufruct or contracts for the management of another's business (agency, representation) in which the holder of the asset transfers control capacities to the trustee, borrower, pledgee, usufructuary, etc. On the other hand, it could also be the case that it is a capacity that is misused against the interest or order of the real owner of the digital asset (interference, hacking). Also, in the context of digital asset markets one finds changes in control capacities resulting from void legal transactions. Once again, control only means that this capacity is available, it does not presuppose the title by which it is possessed. The holder of control often acts in the interest of, and as manager of, the holder of the digital asset. However, a client who provides a custodian with control over a digital asset may also be a holder of another type of right that legitimizes him despite not having ownership (pledgee, usufructuary, trustee, portfolio manager…).

That is why the official commentary indicates the usual functional equivalence between control and possession of movable property, but such equivalence does not exist in jurisdictions, such as Japan, that do not accept the concept of possession of movable property in relation to intangible assets.[14] As Dr Morishita points out, a distinction is made in Japan between digital assets that do not have a backing value and those that allow claims to be made on a tangible asset, including security tokens (shares, bonds, right of investment), and only the latter are linked to the concept of ownership. In these contexts, the holder of the digital asset without a material backing is linked to it only by a contractual relationship and not by a property right.[15] In contrast, in continental law the assimilation of the treatment of digital assets to that of traditional securities is common. In fact, when there have been doubts, as in the example provided in section 90 of the German BGB "Only corporeal objects are things as defined by law".[16] Reforms have been promoted establishing said equality.[17] On the continental scope of application however, we will find ourselves in a very similar situation to the Japanese example, with regard to customers who hold a share right to a pool of digital assets in community *pro indiviso* in a transactional system. Since it is not finally possible to identify a specific digital asset, as its identifiers change with each transaction, or a specific security, as it mutates within the joint exchange, all the customer really has is a claim on a share that we identify through the traceability of the digital asset. An analysis of each case or dispute is therefore important. In the bankruptcies of various crypto-asset exchange platforms as well as in the "*corralitos*" or freezing of operations carried out by others in the face of the loss of backing assets, different solutions were given to the same scenario in different national jurisdictions. Furthermore, an analysis of the cases clearly shows that the interests of the litigants were also at odds with each other. Thus, where digital assets had a backing value, the interest of the investors was to defend the existence of a proprietary interest in the asset, and thus in the material backing value, as the only means to minimize losses. However, where digital assets lacked a backing value, it was much more operational for claimants to assert a claim against the custodian for its management. Indeed, in crypto-asset trading, many investors do not really want to be credited with anything that resembles ownership, as this would mean having to file tax returns on the value of such holdings, and think of the up and down volatility of crypto-assets. On the contrary, if the assets are held in pledge, trust, usufruct or any other title, it is more likely that the economic purposes sought will be fulfilled and that there will only be an obligation to declare the materialized returns on the

---

[14] Art 85 Japanese Civil Code. See Kanda in, HCCH-UNIDROIT. STUDY LXXXIIW.G.1, Doc 2. *DIGITAL ASSETS AND PRIVATE LAW, WORKING* GROUP 1ST SESSION ROME 17–19 NOVEMBER 2020.

MORISHITA, in HCCH-UNIDROIT. Exploratory Workshop on Digital Assets and Private Law, Study LXXXII, Doc. 3. Rome, 2021 (17–18 September 2020).

[15] MORISHITA, in HCCH-UNIDROIT. Exploratory Workshop on Digital Assets and Private Law, Study LXXXII, Doc. 3. Rome, 2021 (17–18 September 2020).

[16] Note that art. 85 of Japanese Civil Code has its origin in the art. 90 of the German BGB.

[17] In Germany Gesetz zur Einfürung von Elektronischen Wertpapieren, 9 june 2021. https://www.bmj.de/SharedDocs/Gesetzgebungsverfahren/DE/2021_Einfuehrung_elektr_Wertpapiere.html?nn=17134. Y Kreditwesengesetz 2020 (Sec 1.11.4) In Japan Law of financial instruments and exchange 2017 and 2020. In UK new proposed Property Digital Assets Bill, 11 September 2024.

digital assets. Hence, applying a neutral notion of control to the different operations to promote uniform consequences is more interesting than trying to establish a single legal qualification of the positions of customers and custodians.

Let us assert once again that, although we are dealing with a de facto concept, it does not imply that possessing or exercising control has no legal consequences. Third parties usually identify the capacities inherent in economic rights with those of control in their legal system, and in any case, the acquirers of digital assets, when they receive the exclusive exploitation capacities of the person who holds control, and reasonably expect that the transaction is valid and that they have obtained the capacity to make use of the digital asset. This is normally the case, as evidenced by the innocent acquirer status in Principles 11 and 12. Acquirers commonly receive the digital asset from the person who owns and controls it, or from the person who holds it on behalf of the owner and controls it (a custodian, a manager, a nominee). Proving that the digital asset has been received from the person in control is therefore necessary in order to be *a bona fide* acquirer, to be able to oppose third parties and to be able to exercise its real prerogatives. However, a situation may also arise in which control of an asset is obtained in bad faith from someone who was knowingly not authorized to transfer it. While control at the time of transfer is a necessary requirement, it will not always be sufficient for the acquirer to be an innocent acquirer (Principle 11), and thus unassailable against the previous owner. Moreover, the way in which the innocent acquirer is defined in Principles 11 and 12 does not always meet with the same treatment in national law. By way of example, Principle 8.5 d) (Innocent Acquisition) excludes gratuitous transfers as a valid cause of transfer, following a tradition based on continental exchange law and Geneva Bill of Exchange Uniform Law. It is considered that a gratuitous cause in the assignment does not deserve the same level of protection as the onerous cause in the business that justifies the transfer. In many legal systems however, such as Spain's, the prejudice against gratuitous transfer operations has disappeared in national case law, as the donation is considered to be an efficient cause of transfer, the same as onerous transfers. In any case, the idea that should be pointed out here is that complying with the rules of the Exchange does not always imply that the rules of transfer of ownership or legal title of a State have been complied with.[18]

The notion of control in Principle 6.1 b) and 7 requires the protocol applicable to the digital asset clearly establishing who has exclusive rights over the digital asset and under what circumstances, as this results in a principle of legitimacy and a legal appearance. The above is an exception to the principle "*nemo dat quod non habet*", and this is important in order to assess the effects of possible transfers of all or some of the asset's properties. Digital assets certainly sometimes behave evanescently, change, mutate, multiply or circulate quickly, and it is therefore essential to be able to determine their traceability, for which it is essential to know who has control at any given time, and what use has been made of the exclusive abilities at any given time. When those exclusive capabilities are lost because control is transferred, it is

[18] FOX in HCCH-UNIDROIT. Exploratory Workshop on Digital Assets and Private Law, Study LXXXII, Doc. 3. Rome, 2021 (17–18 September 2020).

essential to know who acquired them. The mere fact of losing exclusive knowledge of the keys to a digital asset does not necessarily mean the loss of control over it, as that would only occur when the acquirer of those keys uses them in a way that results in a transfer of control to a person other than the original acquirer.

3 Change of Control and Transfer

Regarding this matter it is also necessary to distinguish between a change of control and a transfer of the asset or its proprietary rights (Principle 2). A change of control without a change of ownership or proprietary rights over the digital asset is entirely possible, and is also common, or conversely, a change of ownership without a change of control over the digital asset.

The two can certainly go together, and ownership, possession or a real right and the capacity to control can be transferred at the same time, but it may also be the case that they are not, such as when we only change the custodian of the digital asset (same owner, different holder of control). The opposite may also be the case; the owner of the digital asset may change and the custodian who has control over it may remain the same (hence again, the frequent assimilation between capacity to control and "possession"). In view of this diversity of possible situations, the Principles have avoided terms such as "delivery" and only use the term "**change of control**".

Moreover, an analysis of the case will force us to determine what we necessarily have control over, and in many cases we will conclude that the controlled object is not a "stable" or immutable asset, since, as we have already indicated, many crypto-assets "wear out", transform or mutate with each operation and give rise to constant transformations in the identification of the controlled asset. Similarly, some controlled assets constitute a pool of indistinct or fungible assets, closer to the concept of a quota than to that of an isolated and identifiable asset, which we usually use in the securities market.

In other operations, the asset does not mutate as such, but its owner does, and precise traceability of the asset is also maintained. In practical operations therefore, there are various systems that follow a registration system, usually decentralised (DLT). All of this may also mean that the transferred asset comes under the control of another custodian (e.g. another exchange platform), or that both transferred and non-transferred digital assets remain under the control of the same custodian.

Moreover, it can become even more complicated. Many cryptoassets are managed by platforms that, in an attempt to offer greater tax opacity, a behaviour closer to the circulation of physical money or less traceability of transactions, allow you to "flip", "churn" or "shake" your transactions in an exchange of similar operations, blurring the trace of the specific asset that you "owned" and transforming it into another resulting asset (e.g. Binance). Here, the digital asset clearly manifests a more fungible character than those that always remain unalterably identified. In fact, as we will see later on, when talking about the transfer of digital assets and the situation of insolvency of custodians (Principle 13), we must determine whether we are actually dealing with a situation of control on behalf of a holder, or whether we are dealing with an asset that is included in the custodian's balance sheet and the "Customer" only has a contractual right enforceable against the custodian, who is, in reality, the real owner of the digital asset. The Principles already contemplate the transformation, replacement by replacement of the digital asset by a derived asset, as this is necessary considering the various technical forms of articulation of the transfer of digital assets (transactional or accounting systems), but equally appropriate to cover cases in which the transformation of the asset is not due to a transfer. In those situations, the driving element of the holder's rights will not be the traceability of the asset itself, but rather the traceability of ownership of control.

As noted above, some of the contests of crypto-asset exchange platforms have had a major influence on the development of the Principles, as they readily manifested these issues regarding the actual control of digital assets. Sometimes it was decided that it was the trading platform or issuer of the digital asset itself that had control and ownership of the assets, with investors in those assets being recognized as having a mere contractual position.[19] This solution proved to be very unsatisfactory for investors, as it meant that they lost their rights in preference to creditors who had a direct security interest in the underlying tangible assets. In very similar contexts however, other national courts recognized the ownership of digital assets to investors, even though they clearly lacked the control capabilities. This solution largely treated digital assets in the same way as other securities in the ordinary financial market.[20] In any event, divergent solutions were affected by issues specific to the legal system used, such as whether the national law recognized a right of possession over intangible assets or a mere obligatory position. Or questions of fact, such as whether the digital asset was a stable or traceable identifiable asset, or a simple notation on a fungible pool also arose.

It is a fact that many cryptoassets owners do not have the capacity to control their cryptoassets, other than in the sense of being entitled to order the holder of control to carry out acts of disposition in their interest or to authorise the holder of control to manage and dispose of the cryptoassets in their interest and subsequently demand accountability. Changing the holder of control, therefore, does not necessarily imply a change in the ownership of the economic rights. Legally, we may be dealing with a simple change of possession or a simple transfer of agency duties to the new holder of the control capacities.

---

[19] Tokyo District Court confirmed in a 2015 decision in the MtGox case that Bitcoin could not be classified as a "thing" for the purposes of the property law regime under the Civil Code of Japan (Tokyo District Court, Plaintiff Z1 v. MtGox Co. Case No. 33320 of 2014, Judgment, 5 August 2015) (https://www.law.ox.ac.uk/research-subject-groups/commercial-law-centre/blog/2019/02/english-translation-mt-gox-judgment-legal).

[20] Without departing from the Japanese example, by application of the 2019 payment services law, the same Tokyo courts granted credit priority to the customer contracting with a custodian, giving it the same treatment as a traditional bond or financial security on the basis of its liquidity similar to that of a security. MORISHITA, in HCCH-UNIDROIT. Exploratory Workshop on Digital Assets and Private Law, Study LXXXII, Doc. 3. Rome, 2021 (17–18 September 2020).

Similarly, and once again, not every act of transfer of a cryptoasset is a transfer of ownership; it may be an act of partial disposal, splitting or transformation of the cryptoasset. As an example, let us take the situation that arises when a digital asset mutates the way it is treated and is split into two different ones (original and derivative) or a new digital asset is created to replace the previous one. This is what happens in a so-called "hard fork". A digital asset changes its issuing algorithm and its rules, resulting in a bifurcation of the chain of transmission or traceability thereof, between the "classic" line and the new line of the Blockchain. In regard to this matter, there are several examples of the division of digital assets, in which some national courts have determined the obligation of the holders of control to secure and provide the holders of the replaced digital asset with the resulting new assets. This would be a change of ownership of the asset itself, by mutation of the asset, but without a change of control. However, the various cases of Hard Fork that we have been able to study, also show situations in which the holder of control of the original asset did not have access to control of the new resulting assets.

Another situation that represents the concept explained here can be seen in cases of digital asset lending. For example, let's say I lend my digital assets to a custodian on a term loan, with the obligation to return the same quantity and quality plus an agreed return. This makes economic sense for those who do not want to hold property rights that need to be declared to the tax authorities, or to temporarily increase their position in an asset, obtain its speculative return and then abandon it. It is in fact a very common practice for crypto-asset hedge funds seeking to strengthen their position in the event of a possible rise or fall in the price of a crypto-asset.

Therefore, the transfer rules of the control principle, without considering the legal nature of the underlying transaction, only focus on establishing the rules for determining the regularity of the transfer made by the custodian, manager or whoever holds the capacity of control.

4 Exclusivity of Capacities and Shared Control

When assessing the content of the various exclusive capacities mentioned in Principle 6.1(a), it is necessary to differentiate between them, and essentially between those referred to in paragraphs 6.1(a)(II) and (III). Paragraph 6.1 a (II) refers to the "exclusive" use of the benefits or yields of a digital asset, as opposed to paragraph (III), which refers to the exclusive capacity to transfer it or, if preferred, to carry out an act of full disposal. In reality, paragraph (II) does not impose the economic exploitation of a digital asset being exclusive to one subject. What it tells us is that the holder of control must have the ability to prevent others from obtaining substantially the benefits of a digital asset, but not that it is not possible to voluntarily share those substantial benefits (or a part of them) by virtue of a covenant. An easy example of this would be the establishment of a usufruct relationship over a digital asset, where the usufructuary receives the returns from the asset. Another example is provided by situations of shared control (multi-signature systems, shared computing), which will be discussed below. In short, when we speak of exclusive capacity, it is perhaps necessary to assess which of the exclusive capacities we are talking about, as some of them can be shared without actually reducing the notion of control. However, the same problem does not arise when we talk about the exclusive capacity to transfer control.

Unfortunately, in the world of digital assets, it is not impossible to rule out the possibility of hacking due to the discovery of private keys and the consequent committing of unlawful asset transfers. This, once again, clearly marks the difference between change of control and transfer of proprietary rights. By stealing a customer's keys, a transfer of the digital asset can be triggered without altering the custodian's rules or changing control (illegitimate order). By stealing the keys of the custodian in control, an improper transfer of the digital asset can be triggered by feigning legitimate control (absence of legitimization and legitimate control). The possible status of the third party as a bona fide acquirer (Principle 8) or innocent customer (Principle 11) will depend on the knowledge or possibility of knowledge of such circumstances. But as we see, in practice, hacks only succeed to the extent that the control holder is persuaded to affect a transfer in the belief that it is legitimate, or the ability to control is transferred from the control holder. Simple key disclosure may not be effective as long as the person in control is the legitimate party. Theft or dispossession requires the legitimate holder of control to transfer it to a third party. These situations are occasional and very limited in time, as either the hacker proceeds to transfer control quickly, or the legitimate holder of control proceeds to defend the asset and renew the keys. Situations of shared control without the legitimate holder's consent are very rare.

However, and in apparent contradiction to paragraph 6.1 of the Principles, the "exclusive" and "exclusionary" ability to control can legitimately be shared between several subjects. In reality, exclusionary abilities do not necessarily imply the exclusive ability of a single subject, as it can be a shared capacity. This is true, obviously, in those cases where abilities of control shared between several subjects are established with the consent of the holder, but also in those cases where the configuration of the digital asset itself provides for the change or loss of control. There are many different situations and reasons for this. This loss of exclusivity may be due to security reasons, to reasons of economic convenience or to the consequences of the operation of the digital asset.

The first example would be cases in which, in order to exercise control over the asset and exploit its yields or dispose of it, the signature of several parties in a ***multi-signature*** or *multi-sig* system is required. These could be, for example, the owner and the custodian of the digital asset, who thus share the control capabilities. On the other hand, it could be the beneficiary of a loan or a pledgee, where the authorizing signature of a corporate officer or an oracle smart contract is needed for the release and provision of the asset or some of its substantive capabilities to the owner. Or they can be two smart contracts, which dialogue and act jointly when the protocol requires the joint action of them both. It could also work conversely, when the circumstances of the digital asset provide for the ability to revert or veto operations of disposal of the asset to a third party other than the person who ordinarily holds control.

Consider, for example, cases in which control over the digital asset is shared because it is delivered as collateral for a loan or a secured obligation, similar to the delivery of goods in an ordinary pledge. Thus, the asset holders establish a multi-sig system to dispose of the assets held in the wallet and establish rules on their use (escrow agent) so that in the event of the borrower's insolvency or default on the secured obligation, the agent passes full access to the keys to the lender or the holder of the secured obligation. Conversely, once the primary secured obligation is discharged, the pledge on the digital asset is released and the keys shared with the pledgee are revoked. We could imagine a wide range of business schemes in which this system, described as a factual situation in the description of the control principle, would operate.

Another relevant example is provided by ***multi-party computing*** (MPC) systems in which the control key is divided into fragments distributed or generated by several subjects, all of whom have to sign a transaction. A very common example of this type of situation is when a digital asset is deposited in the wallet of a custodian subject to smart contracts that act in an automated manner according to their protocol in various scenarios and perform operations that allow access to the returns or even disposition operations such as the sale, transformation or replacement of the digital assets themselves.

Situations similar to those that would arise if such digital assets were held in a trust or trustee regime, with behaviour dependent on the will of third parties or with automated behaviours through Smart Contracts.

In short, the ability to control may allow other persons to receive all or some of the benefits of the digital asset, as long as the exercise of the act of control is defined in its rules and the identification of its holder remains clear (Principle No. 6.1(a) III and 7).

The Principles themselves present another interesting example of these operations by showing an example of control by means of PKI or custody scenarios in which the disposition of the registered digital asset uses a **public key cryptography system** in which the public and private keys must necessarily coincide in order to carry out acts of control over the asset. Keys that may be distributed among different parties and keys that, with the acts of disposal of the asset, may be changed, giving a new holder control of the new public and private keys. Legally, multiple different legal transactions can be identified behind this type of operation. For example, we can give a key to a party to guarantee that we will not sell the digital asset without their consent in a kind of pledge, or to allow them to execute the digital asset given as a guarantee if the holder of the asset fails to fulfil their guaranteed obligation.

Security requirements also generate a variety of similar situations, and **OTP systems** are given as an example. Imagine a repository of digital files that are linked to specific electronic devices, such as your mobile phone, which generates single-use access keys. Each time you want to access the controlled digital asset in order to make it available, you will need to use the unique access key generated by the registered device. As a result, in order to truly have full control over the digital asset or to change the ownership of the digital asset by transfer, both the custodian's keys and the unique keys of the device should allow for key substitution or replacement of the linked device. Alternatively, the linked device owner should physically hand over the paired device to the new control holder. Note that in the latter case the control of the digital asset is linked to a tangible movable asset (a thing) circulating under the relevant national law and how this legal transaction of buying and selling a movable material asset would nevertheless have an impact on the change of control over the digital asset.

In the business world (and why not in public administration management), where power counterbalances are increasingly articulated against acts of disposition in the hands of a single responsible owner, and where there is a growing interest in behavioural oversight, such key-sharing operations, control devices and multi-signature systems are proliferating rapidly. They are also the most appropriate mechanism for the various combinations of asset disposition by artificial intelligence machines and the necessary human-in-the-loop oversight, or for articulating the decisions of different AI machines that collaborate or negotiate with each other. Also contributing to this is the fact that when a security is established, duties are usually established that exclude unilateral enforcement without notice to the parties or third parties. Moreover, it is even possible to imagine other scenarios, for example in the case of insolvency proceedings, in which acts of disposition of the insolvent party's assets are subject to the supervision of an insolvency administrator, etc. The UNCITRAL Model Law on Secured transactions in connection with the UCC (Art. 8–9) provides another interesting example. Under US law, a digital asset such as Bitcoin does not qualify for delivery as collateral, but in practice a similar effect is obtained by granting priority access to control to the lender to safeguard its interests in the event of the borrower's insolvency, which again is done with one of these shared control systems.

5 Conclusions

The control principle is a key concept for adapting traditional legal solutions to the new context of digital asset trading by offering uniform solutions to a global and transnational market. The control principle is also an essential tool for the legal adaptation to the increasing use of DLT technologies and artificial intelligence in the trading of digital assets and securities.

The notion of control firstly allows us to delimit a relevant field of digital assets for whose circulation it is possible to draw uniform legal consequences, regardless of the business scheme applied or the consistency of the conduct with the different perspectives of national tort law.

Given the proliferation of digital files produced in an electronic transaction, and which the Blockchain recording systems treat in an equivalent way, control allows us to select those files that will be endowed with a legal significance for the circulation of the value. Control will also provide us with an essential piece of information, which is the determination of the possible legitimacy of the parties involved in a transfer, and will also be a key factor in assessing the good faith or legitimacy of the expectation of those who claim to be innocent third parties or bona fide acquirers. In the face of the differences in semantic content that accompany the contracting instruments used in the digital asset markets, control provides us with a factual description of the relevant conduct and of the consequences that should legitimately occur, without considering whether the language used has the same content for all contracting parties, or in all States and jurisdictions involved.[21]

On the other hand, Control is a concept that enables adaptation to the volume, complexity and opacity of digital transactions carried out through smart contracts. More and more Exchange platforms use complex networks of smart contracts to manage and improve the performance of digital assets. The market for digital assets is often highly speculative and can be based on non-existent collateral or assets whose collateral can be rapidly devalued. The fluctuation of such collateral leads to the use of rapid settlement or realization mechanisms against the risk of loss of cover,[22] through disposition systems entrusted to a smart contract that acts as an oracle and whose execution order is automated and not subject to human intervention to prevent it. This means that some digital assets are transferred, transformed or exploited in fractions of a second in an incessant dialogue between several smart contracts, which follow a set of complex instructions. As noted above, this operation may have different legal consequences depending on the business model it represents, but also on the ownership of ultimate responsibility for the conduct of such smart contracts. For traditional law, it may have a different significance if the transfers occur within the scope of control of a custodian, regardless of the AI instruments it uses, or if they occur between AI machines belonging to sub-custodians or third-party custodians. Determining who has control at each operational stage will be essential for the subsequent attribution of legal consequences.

Control also has an important application to the assessment of the traceability of data on the digital asset; it allows us to determine the legitimacy of the process, to identify the responsible subjects and to attribute legal consequences to the chain of relevant facts, as well as to give us a final judgement on the outcome. The notion of control does not only allow us to focus on those data sets that are relevant and to discard complementary information without legal relevance. It also allows us to identify the relevant parties in each transaction or the holders of the relevant instruments in each transaction, with a view to subsequent attribution of responsibilities. In any cases in which the technical operation does not allow us to monitor the traceability of the digital asset, it will be possible to trace the control holders and their possible responsibilities. Likewise, in those cases in which the holders of the private keys might not be registered or identified, the ownership of control offers us an identifiable and relevant subject for the purposes of the application of public law (duties of collaboration with the administration) or private law. Finally, the principle of control offers us a contrast on the degree of compliance with the security protocols in the successive transfers or acts of exploitation of the digital asset, providing us with an essential criterion for validating or invalidating such operations.

[21] See also WEISE, S. UNIDROIT 2021 - Study LXXXII - W.G.1 - Doc. 3, p. 12 and sq.

[22] HINKES. UNIDROIT 2021 - Study LXXXII - W.G.1 - Doc. 3, p. 8.

Lastly, as we can see in Principle 13, Control can be a relevant issue to assign a credit preference between several creditors in conflict over a digital asset, understanding that creditors can trust the legitimacy granted by the control ability over other kinds of guarantees.

Principle 7 Identification of a Person in Control of a Digital Asset

Ignacio Alamillo-Domingo, María Cristina Timón-López, and Julián Valero-Torrijos

(1) In any proceeding in which a person's control of a digital asset is at issue:

(a) it is sufficient for that person to demonstrate that the identification requirement in Principle 6(1)(b) is satisfied in respect of the abilities specified in Principle 6(1)(a);

(b) if that person demonstrates that it has the abilities specified in Principles 6(1)(a)(i) and 6(1)(a)(iii), those abilities are presumed to be exclusive.

(2) The identification mentioned in Principle 6(1)(b) may be by a reasonable means, including (but not limited to) an identifying number, a cryptographic key, an office, or an account number, even if the means of identification does not indicate the name or identity of the person to be identified.

This work was financed within the framework of the Prometeo 2023 project of the Regional Ministry of Innovation, Universities, Science and Digital Society (CIPROM/2022/26) "Present and future of the regulation of cryptoassets in the EU [LegalCripto]", whose principal investigator is Carmen Pastor Sempere. The basic ideas contained herein were presented in the author's paper with the same title, given on November 13, 2024 at the IV International Congress on "Unidroit Principles on Digital Assets and Private Law: Context, Content, Perspectives", organized also by BAES Research Group of the University of Alicante on November 13 and 14, 2024.

I. Alamillo-Domingo (✉) · M. C. Timón-López · J. Valero-Torrijos
University of Murcia, Murcia, Spain
e-mail: ignacio.alamillod@um.es

M. C. Timón-López
e-mail: mariacristina.timon@um.es

J. Valero-Torrijos
e-mail: julivale@um.es

C. Pastor Sempere and D. A. Morán Bovio (eds.), Unidroit *Principles on Digital Assets and Private Law*, Law, Governance and Technology Series 80,
https://doi.org/10.1007/978-3-032-11001-5_13

1 Official Commentary

Commentary

7.1. Only in a litigation context (broadly construed) would an issue arise as to which person has control of a digital asset under a digital assets law that includes the criteria specified by Principle 7. If the control of a person is challenged, it would be impossible for the putative control person to prove with certainty a negative – that no person other than one permitted by the definition has the relevant abilities. Principle 7(1)(a) makes it clear (although it would be implicit in any event) that a person asserting that it has control of a digital asset establishes a presumption that it has the specified abilities. It need not prove the negative – that no one else has the abilities – in order to prove that it has control. Principle 7(1)(b) dictates a similar result in relation to exclusivity of abilities through the operation of a presumption, the operation of which would be governed by the applicable domestic procedural law. Of course, a person who previously (rightfully) had control may demonstrate under applicable domestic law that it has a better proprietary interest than the person who currently has control by proving that the change of control was wrongful. The presumption can be overcome by sufficient proof under the State's procedural rules.

7.2. As a practical matter, there is little chance that another person would appear in a contested proceeding to claim that it has the relevant exclusive abilities without the putative control person's consent. Under the criteria, that other person also would not have control. Any concern about such a person (e.g., hacker, thief, or finder) appearing to make such a claim seems unwarranted. Moreover, experience has shown that in situations in which the relevant abilities have been obtained wrongfully the abilities have quickly been exercised and the assets have been removed from the control of the original control person. This reflects a set of risks that are inherent in digital assets.

2 Reflections

2.1 Context and Evolution of the Preparatory Works for the Development of Principle 7

In the preparatory works, Principle 7, which pertains to the identification of a person in control of a digital asset, was initially conceived as part of the Principle of Control (now Principle 6). During the second session of the Working Group,[1] identification was still discussed as a component of this principle (control). This was notably reflected in the following formulation:

[1] Digital Assets and Private Law Working Group // Second session (remote) // Rome, 16–18 March 2021 //// UNIDROIT 2021 // Study LXXXII – W.G.2 – Doc. 2 (rev. 1) // English only // March 2021.

The digital asset or its associated records allows the person to identify itself as having the powers mentioned in (2)(a).

During the session, the Working Group explored several questions and additional considerations. One key issue was whether the process of identification should go beyond using a person's name and include other methods such as an identifying number, a cryptographic key, an office designation, or an account number. This reflects a broader understanding of identification, suggesting it could be achieved through alternative means that do not necessarily require disclosing a person's name or identity. This idea has been adopted in the final formulation of Principle 7, indicating that identification could be achieved without the need to disclose personal information.

In addition, during this session, it was discussed whether the Principles clearly address the possibility of an unauthorised individual (such as a hacker or someone who wrongfully acquires private keys) gaining control or the ability to transfer control. It was suggested that this should be explicitly clarified, a point that was later incorporated into the Commentary on Principle 7.

Later, during the third session of the Working Group,[2] the concept of identification remained part of the principle of control but was further expanded. Notably, what is now paragraph 1 of Principle 7 was already included at that stage, albeit in a redrafted form. At that point, it was articulated as follows:

In any proceeding in which a person's control of a digital asset is at issue, it is sufficient for that person to demonstrate that the identification requirement in paragraph (1)(b) is satisfied as to the abilities specified in paragraph (1)(a). It is not necessary for the person to prove the exclusivity of any ability specified in (paragraph 1) (a), i.e., that no person other than the person in control and those permitted by paragraph (3) has that ability.

Furthermore, at that time, paragraph 5 of the principle of control already stated that the identification referred to in paragraph (1)(b) could be achieved through reasonable means, such as an identifying number, a cryptographic key, an office designation, or an account number, even if the identification does not indicate the name or identity of the person to be identified.

Among the comments, it was noted that a person other than the rightful controller might gain these abilities without the consent of the person in rightful control. This could occur through methods such as hacking to discover relevant private keys, finding or stealing a device or record where the keys are stored, or by other similar means.

Similarly, the comments highlighted potential issues that could arise in legal disputes over who has control of a digital asset under the specified principles. It was noted that if someone's control is challenged, it would be impractical for them to

[2] Digital Assets and Private Law Working Group // Third session (remote) // Rome, 30 June–2 July 2021 //// UNIDROIT 2021 // Study LXXXII – W.G.3 – Doc. 2 (rev.1) // English only // June 2021.

prove a negative (that no other person possesses the relevant abilities). Paragraph (4) addresses this concern by clarifying that a person can establish control by demonstrating they have the specified abilities without needing to prove that no one else does.

Additionally, a person who was previously in rightful control can assert a superior proprietary interest if they can prove that the transfer of control was wrongful. In practice, it is unlikely that an unauthorised person, such as a hacker, thief, or finder, would appear in legal proceedings to claim they have exclusive abilities without the consent of the rightful controller. According to the criteria, such individuals would not be considered to have control. Concerns about these unauthorised persons making such claims are therefore seen as unwarranted. Furthermore, experience shows that when someone wrongfully acquires the relevant abilities, they typically act quickly to exercise them, often removing the assets from the original controller's possession. These aspects were later incorporated into the Commentary on Principle 7.

During the fourth session of the Working Group,[3] identification continued to be an integral part of the principle of control. However, it was during the fifth session of Working Group 5,[4] that the principle of identifying a person in control of a digital asset was distinguished as a separate principle from the, at that time, redrafted 'definition of control'. This newly established principle incorporated the commentary and discussions raised during the third session of Working Group 3, integrating them into a standalone principle that began to resemble the current version more closely.

During the sixth session of the Working Group,[5] the Principle underwent further redrafting, resulting in its current content. While the Commentary maintained the same overall structure, there were notable differences. For example, the phrase in lines 6 and 7, 'burdens of production and persuasion by showing (...)', was replaced with the 'establishment of a presumption'. Additionally, the term 'same result' was substituted with 'similar result', reflecting a refinement in the language to better align with the intended meaning.

At this point however, we already have the key elements of Principle 7; which focus on: firstly, control in legal proceedings where the control of a digital asset is contested; secondly, the requirement for a person claiming control of a digital asset to demonstrate their ability to both use or manage the asset and prevent others from accessing or using it; and thirdly, the presumption of exclusivity and the various reasonable means for identification, even if these do not reveal the person's civil identity. Likewise, the Commentary on Principle 7 addresses the impracticality of proving a negative (e.g., proving no one else has control), and emphasises the legal presumption of control for those demonstrating abilities under Principle 6. Finally,

---

[3] Digital Assets and Private Law Working Group // Fourth session (hybrid) // Rome, 2–4 November 2021 //// UNIDROIT 2021 // Study LXXXII – W.G.4 – Doc. 2 // English only // October 2021.

[4] Digital Assets and Private Law Working Group // Fifth session (hybrid) // Rome, 7–9 March 2022 //// UNIDROIT 2022 // Study LXXXII – W.G.5 – Doc. 2 // English only // February 2022.

[5] Digital Assets and Private Law Working Group // Sixth session (hybrid) // Rome, 31 August–2 September 2022 //// UNIDROIT 2022 // Study LXXXII – W.G.6 – Doc. 2 // English only // August 2022.

it describes real-world risks (e.g., theft or hacking) and notes that wrongful exercise of control typically results in rapid transfer or loss of assets.

During the seventh session of the Working Group,[6] the Principle underwent more redrafting, focusing on formatting and style improvements. The changes refined explanations, concentrated on procedural aspects and explicitly introduced terms like 'establishes a presumption' to highlight the procedural presumption of control. However, these adjustments did not result in any significant changes to the legal interpretation or application of the Principle.

Finally, during the eighth session of the Working Group,[7] various comments were raised. These notably emphasised the cross-referencing capability of the Principle, the importance of addressing situations involving possession, and the need to strengthen the connection between the concept of identity and the identification requirements under the principle of control.

2.2 *The Two Presumptions Embodied in Principle 7(1)*

Principle 7(1) deals with the establishment of two presumptions to alleviate the burden of proof regarding control of a digital asset, which would be twofold: first, identifying the person in control, and second, an exclusivity element in the ability to change control. Both these presumptions have the same purpose, which is to avoid imposing a burden of proof of a negative fact. Given the highly procedural nature of this approach, some of the comments received suggested referring this issue to Principle 18.

Under Principle 6(1)(a), a person has control of a digital asset if the digital asset or the relevant protocol or system confers three abilities (exclusively preventing third parties from substantially obtaining all of the benefit of the digital asset; substantially obtaining all of the benefit of the digital asset; and transferring the above capabilities to third parties); but only if the digital asset itself or the relevant protocol or system enables that person to be identified as "having" those abilities (Principle 6(1)(b)).

For its part, under Principle 7(1)(a), in case of doubt as to whether a person has control of a digital asset, it is sufficient for that person to identify himself or herself in respect of those abilities. Similarly, under Principle 7(1)(b), if that person demonstrates that it has the abilities specified in Principles 6(1)(a)(i) and 6(1)(a)(iii), those abilities are presumed to be exclusive.

As can be seen, the formulation is different in both cases: in Principle 6(1)(b), identification refers to "having" the capabilities, while in Principle 7(1), the identification requirement "in respect of" the capabilities of Principle 6(1)(a) must be

[6] Digital Assets and Private Law Working Group // Seventh session (hybrid) // Rome, 19–21 December 2022 //// UNIDROIT 2022 // Study LXXXII – W.G.7 – Doc. 2 // English only // December 2022.

[7] Digital Assets and Private Law Working Group // Eighth session (hybrid) // Rome, 8–10 March 2023 //// UNIDROIT 2023 // Study LXXXII – W.G.8 – Doc. 2 // English only // February 2023.

satisfied. It does not seem, in any case, that the drafters of the DAPL intended to establish a differentiated treatment, but simply to avoid the burden of a negative fact (that no one else has the capabilities in question, or that where he or she has a supposedly exclusive capability, there is no one else who has such capabilities).

However, this demonstration is actually in respect of "having" the capabilities, which goes beyond a simple declaration by the person, as could be deduced from the reading of comment 7.1, which would require the corresponding technical proof, as a condition for either presumption to operate. The drafters of the DAPL seem to consider that such proof will generally not be necessary in the case of fraud, since the malicious actor who has achieved an unauthorised change of control will most likely make a further change of control very quickly (as mentioned in comment 6.10), so that the protection of the innocent acquirer under Principle 8 will apply.

What the DAPL does not address are the safeguards for such assumptions to be acceptable, which would most likely be linked to the technical assurance of the digital asset (as an artefact), or of the underlying protocol or system, which are completely ignored. An example of this would be: if a system is used that ostensibly assures the three capabilities of Principle 6(1)(a) to a person identified in terms of Principle 6(1)(b) but this is not really true. In Commentary 6.10 it is explicitly mentioned that "The exclusive abilities contemplated by Principles 6(1)(a)(i) and 6(1)(a)(iii) assume the existence of a system for digital assets that reliably establishes those abilities and their exclusivity", without addressing the issue of reliability in the DAPLs, either directly or indirectly.

This is a different approach from UNCITRAL's approach, which usually provides for it, as for example in the MLETR, Article 11(1) of which states that "Where the law requires or permits the possession of a transferable document or instrument, that requirement is met with respect to an electronic transferable record if a reliable method is used: (a) To establish exclusive control of that electronic transferable record by a person; and (b) To identify that person as the person in control".

Article 12 MLETR sets out a general reliability standard based on two alternatives. First, in accordance with (a), a method must be used that is as reliable as appropriate for the fulfilment of the function for which the method is being used, in the light of all relevant circumstances. Furthermore, it points out which circumstances may be considered relevant for this purpose: (i) Any operational rules relevant to the assessment of reliability; (ii) The assurance of data integrity; (iii) The ability to prevent unauthorized access to and use of the system; (iv) The security of hardware and software; (v) The regularity and extent of audit by an independent body; (vi) The existence of a declaration by a supervisory body, an accreditation body or a voluntary scheme regarding the reliability of the method; (vii) Any applicable industry standard.

Secondly, Article 12(b) allows for a method proven in fact to have fulfilled the function by itself or together with further evidence, which will certainly have to be proved in the event of a dispute. Due to the complexity and unfamiliarity of most of the protocols and systems underlying digital assets, a significant degree of difficulty is to be expected.

Nevertheless, it appears that the drafters of the DAPLs deemed it unnecessary to establish a standard of trustworthiness, as the demonstration of skills is simply contingent upon the possession of the elements that enable control of the digital asset. In the case of cryptographic-based approaches, which represent the majority, the possession of a secret cryptographic material, such as a private key, is a prerequisite for demonstrating the ability to control the digital asset.

This approach is in contrast to the MLETR, under Article 10 of which any electronically transferable record would be considered a digital asset, requiring the implementation of a reliable method in this case: (i) To identify that electronic record as the electronic transferable record; (ii) To render that electronic record capable of being subject to control from its creation until it ceases to have any effect or validity; and (iii) To retain the integrity of that electronic record.

Despite the DAPL's reference to "private law relating to digital assets" and its omission to address "rules that are to be enforced by public authorities (which in many jurisdictions would be called 'regulation' or 'regulatory law')," as stated in Commentary 1.1, the utilization of underlying systems that provide adequate safeguards (in accordance with the general reliability standard of Article 12 MLETR) would be highly advantageous. One such example would be a qualified electronic distributed ledger in accordance with the amended eIDAS Regulation, in addition to the use of sound cryptography standards.

Regulation (EU) 2024/1183 of the European Parliament and of the Council of 11 April 2024 amending Regulation (EU) No 910/2014 as regards establishing the European Digital Identity Framework (eIDAS 2 Regulation) has expanded the catalogue of trust services it regulates, including the new electronic ledger trust service.

Recital 68 of the eIDAS 2 Regulation explains that electronic ledgers are a sequence of electronic data records with the aim of ensuring their integrity and the accuracy of their chronological order. The aforementioned Recital elucidates the interconnection of the newly introduced trust service with the digital assets domain, with the objective of ensuring legal certainty and fostering innovation. Consequently, it recognizes the necessity for a Union-wide legal framework that provides for the cross-border recognition of trust services for the recording of data in electronic ledgers. Furthermore, the co-legislators explicitly state that this framework should effectively prevent the same digital asset from being duplicated and sold to multiple parties.

Moreover, the proposal underscores the necessity of establishing a unified, pan-European framework to facilitate cross-border recognition of trust services that support the operation of electronic ledgers. This is of particular significance when the technical approach involves a distributed electronic ledger, such as blockchain.

This is not the first instance in which a general regulation of blockchain technology has been proposed. For instance, Italy's Decree-Law 135/2018 (validated by Law 12/2019) granted these technologies equivalent legal effect to the electronic time stamp. Similarly, Andorra's Law 29/2021 of April 29th, 2021, also granted legal recognition to blockchain technology. However, this is the first occasion on which a comprehensive regulatory framework has been proposed.

It is noteworthy that this proposal adopts a neutral stance, encompassing both decentralized and centralized solutions. The document introduces the concept of a trust service, defined as the recording of electronic data in an electronic ledger, where the role of trust service providers for electronic ledgers should be to ascertain the sequential recording of data into the ledger (Recital 69 of the eIDAS 2 Regulation). It further stipulates the requirements and legal consequences associated with such a service, in addition to the application of common requirements applicable to all trust services.

The definition of the electronic ledger refers to a sequence of electronic data records, ensuring their integrity and the accuracy of their chronological order (Article 3(52) of the amended eIDAS Regulation), in a technologically neutral approach, which allows for centralised and distributed systems, such as blockchain.

The recently amended eIDAS Regulation outlines the requirements for qualified electronic ledgers (Article 45l(1) of the amended eIDAS Regulation), including that such ledgers must be created and maintained by one or more qualified trusted service providers, that the origin of the records in the ledger must be established, that the ledger must ensure the unique sequential chronological order of the records, and that the data must be recorded in such a way that any subsequent changes to the data are immediately detectable, thereby ensuring the integrity of the data over time.

Compliance with these requirements shall be presumed where an electronic ledger complies with the standards, specifications and procedures to be established by the Commission by 21 May 2025. Consequently, certification of the technical conformity of the electronic ledger, which possesses indisputable factual value, engenders a presumption of compliance with the requirements of the electronic ledger. This, in turn, bolsters legal certainty for all parties involved and fosters the adoption of digital assets.

Following the normative logic and the two-tier approach of the eIDAS Regulation, it is firstly ensured that any electronic ledger will benefit from the principle of non-discrimination, thus being able to access the procedure and, where appropriate, produce legal effects; whereas, if the electronic ledger is qualified, it will enjoy the legal presumption of its unique and precise sequential chronological order and completeness. We are therefore faced with a standard that meets and even exceeds the general standard of reliability.

This framework may overcome some of the issues that are hindering the deployment of blockchain-based solutions, especially from the perspective of the use of blockchain as an instrument of accreditation and transfer of legal liability.

In contrast to the necessary judicial decision in case of dispute, based on the possible acceptance of the procedure "*ad matematicatem*", the amended eIDAS Regulation presents a radically different approach, which is aimed at fostering the adoption of these technologies by regulating them as a trusted service, and establishing the corresponding legal presumptions.

From a different perspective, regulation of the electronic ledger is also an imperative for its reliable use in business processes, in particular due to the replacement of proof-of-work based consensus protocols through protocols that are not based on intensive mathematical proof, which also pose environmental sustainability challenges, such as proof of authority or proof of stake.

Conversely, the eIDAS 2 Regulation addresses only a limited subset of the legal challenges posed by the utilization of these technologies. Consequently, as articulated in the eIDAS 2 Regulation, this pan-European directive shall be implemented without prejudice to other EU secondary legislation. In instances where electronic ledgers are employed to facilitate the issuance and/or trading of bonds or crypto-assets, the use cases must be compatible with all applicable financial regulations, including the Markets in Financial Instruments Directive, the Payment Services Directive, and the Crypto-assets Markets Regulation.

It is imperative to note that when use cases involve personal data, service providers are obligated to comply with the pertinent regulatory standards. This subject has been the focal point of extensive deliberation, particularly regarding the delineation of non-personal or pseudonymized data. This is of paramount importance when such data is to be stored on a public or permissioned public blockchain. Other salient discussions in this context pertain to the potential for redacting the blockchain to remove sensitive data.

2.3 *Principle 7(2): Are "Reasonable Means of Identification" Reasonable?*

Given the definition of digital asset as "an electronic record which is capable of being subject to control" (Principle 2(2)) and that the notion of control requires that the person controlling the digital asset can be identified as "having" the capabilities of control (Principle 6(1)(b)), it follows that any digital asset is necessarily linked to an identity, albeit a mathematical identity and not a "legal" or "civil" one.

This consideration derives from the fact that Principle 6(1)(b) is not really concerned with the legal identification of the person who has the control abilities, as a matter prior to the association of such personal identity to a digital asset, but on the contrary, it starts from the purely factual notion of proving the ability to control the digital asset. In the most common example, the "identity" of the person having the control abilities would be a key pair: the public key would act as the identity (actually identifier) of the person, which could be proved by using the private key, that is secretly stored in a digital wallet, to generate mathematical proof of possession (in this case, the most common form would be a digital signature).

Principle 7(2) endeavours to maintain technological neutrality by permitting the utilization of any reasonable means, including, but not limited to, identification numbers, cryptographic keys, and account numbers. Ironically, the application of this approach allows a person to be considered reasonably identifiable even if he or she uses a system that would normally qualify as pseudonymous or even anonymous.

This would be the case when utilizing zero knowledge proofs to demonstrate an individual's possession of the capabilities delineated in Principle 6(1)(a). These capabilities are considerably more advanced than the general public's comprehension of what constitutes a means of identification. As Commentary 7.2 indirectly acknowledges, while this may constitute a feature (a risk) inherent to digital assets, it shows the potential need to consider legally recognised electronic identification means. It is at this point where we need to turn our attention to the European digital identity ecosystem.

The eIDAS Regulation established a framework for the cross-border recognition of electronic identification schemes issued by Member States, if they meet certain conditions and have been notified. To this end, a federation of identities has been established in the Union, mainly based on a network of eID interoperability nodes underpinning the delegation of authentication, essentially geared towards cross-border and remote access by citizens to electronic public services.

Although the identity federation system has been deployed in recent years, and as the evaluation report foreseen in Article 49 of the eIDAS Regulation shows, the functioning of this system has several limitations. From the perspective of the effectiveness of the eIDAS Regulation, the report identifies shortcomings in the coverage of notified electronic identification systems (approximately 59%), in the acceptance of notified systems, in the lack of sufficient incentives to connect to the European infrastructure, in insufficient awareness of the system's use by citizens and private service providers, and in the complexity of the system's governance model.

From the perspective of the effectiveness of the eIDAS Regulation, the report details several issues. First, being in charge of the management of the system, national authorities, eIDAS node operators and electronic identification providers bear significantly higher costs than service providers. Second, the quantifiable costs are higher than the benefits due to a low uptake that has prevented these benefits from materialising. Third, for individual stakeholders, a considerable part is "expected" benefits (discounted as future benefits) and therefore hardly quantifiable. Finally, the reduction of uncertainty for the private sector, the centralisation of eIDAS node updates and outreach to end-users would lead to possible reductions in net costs.

From the perspective of the relevance of the eIDAS Regulation, the report considers that the current scope and focus on electronic identification schemes notified by Member States to enable access to online public services is too limited and inadequate. It also considers that the vast majority of eID and remote authentication needs are still found in the private sector, as the eIDAS Regulation does not address the needs of specific sectors (e.g. education, banking, travel, aviation), one of the limiting factors being the lack of domain-specific attributes. This is clearly true in the case of digital assets.

From a consistency perspective, the analysis identifies several issues. First, there is a lack of common understanding of the requirements of the assurance level framework. Second, there are limitations to the minimum data set for the identification of persons. This is a significant shortcoming for the implementation of eIDAS solutions in several sectoral EU legislations. Third, there is an absence of provisions for the mutual recognition of non-EU electronic identity documents.

In conclusion, although the eIDAS Regulation has incentivized Member States to implement an electronic identification solution, the added value regarding electronic identification is limited due to its low coverage, adoption, and use. Nevertheless, it is contended that the requisites initially identified for the implementation of the eIDAS Regulation remain pertinent, and the abrogation of the Regulation would result in fragmentation and deleterious ramifications for other legislative domains that are contingent on eIDAS.

The European Commission has identified four major issues in relation to the eID system. First, there has been a shift in focus from the provision and use of rigid digital identities towards the provision and reliance on specific attributes related to those identities. This shift is indicative of a new environment. Second, there is an increased demand for electronic identity solutions that can deliver these capabilities, providing enhanced efficiency and a high level of trust across the EU, both in the public and private sector. Third, the inadequacies of the current eIDAS Regulation must be addressed. It is noteworthy that the privacy and data protection issues of identity solutions that fall outside the scope of eIDAS (social media providers and financial institutions) have not been adequately addressed.

In response to this challenge, the eIDAS 2 Regulation has the establishment of a framework as its foundation that, by 2030, will lead to the widespread adoption of a trusted, voluntary, and user-controlled digital identity, recognized throughout the Union, thereby allowing each user to exercise control over their data in online interactions. This framework aligns with the objectives of the European Declaration on Digital Rights and Principles for the Digital Decade, which articulates the EU's vision for digital transformation, prioritizing the well-being of individuals, empowering citizens, and incentivizing innovative businesses.

In this context, the European Commission had four objectives when proposing the reform of the eIDAS Regulation: to ensure access to highly secure and reliable electronic identity solutions; to enable public and private services to rely on reliable and secure digital identity solutions; to empower natural and legal persons to use digital identity solutions; and finally, to ensure that these solutions are linked to a variety of attributes and allow for the specific exchange of identity data limited to the needs of the requested service.

A notable innovation in the eIDAS 2 Regulation is the establishment of a legitimate right for Union citizens to possess a digital identity under their exclusive authority. This provision empowers individuals to exercise their rights within the digital domain and to engage in the digital economy.

The eIDAS 2 Regulation aims to address the aforementioned challenges by augmenting the existing system. This reform is implemented through two different, yet closely related initiatives: the regulation of a new means of electronic identification and the issuance and validation of electronic attribute attestations, which are two new trust services.

2.4 The European Digital Identity Wallet

The primary innovation of the eIDAS 2 Regulation is the European digital identity wallet, which is defined as a new electronic identification means that enables the user to securely store, manage, and validate person identification data and electronic attestations of attributes. This facilitates the provision of these data to using parties and other users of European digital identity wallets. It also enables the signing of documents by means of qualified electronic signatures and the sealing of documents by means of qualified electronic seals (Article 3(42) of the amended eIDAS Regulation).

The objective of this initiative is to guarantee that all natural and legal persons possess secure, trusted, and seamless cross-border access to public and private services within the Union, while retaining full control over their data (Article 5a(1) of the amended eIDAS Regulation). Moreover, the European digital identity wallet can not only be used to communicate with third party systems, but also with other wallets.

The eIDAS Regulation stipulates that each Member State must provide at least one European identity wallet to natural persons, legal persons, and natural persons representing other natural persons or legal persons. These individuals are designated as "users" under the regulation (Article 3(5a) of the amended eIDAS Regulation). However, the provision of this wallet is contingent upon the individuals in question being citizens of the Union or residents of the Union, as defined in national law. The regulation further stipulates that "Member States should ensure equal access to electronic identification for all their citizens and residents" (Recital 15 of the eIDAS 2 Regulation).

The European digital identity wallet is legally configured as a service of strictly voluntary use by users. It does not impose any obligations on users to obtain it or, in the case of having it, to utilize it in their interactions with other users (who possess their own wallet) or with user entities, including public administrations. This distinction marks a significant departure from other personal identification systems, particularly the DNI or TIE implemented in Spain, which are mandatory in view of the public interests these instruments serve.

The amended eIDAS Regulation is unambiguous in stipulating that the wallet is to be provided by the Member State (cf. the revised wording of Article 2(1) of the Regulation). However, it should be noted that this provision can take place in various modalities. This was also the case in the eIDAS Regulation with regard to electronic identification means (cf. Article 7(a) of the eIDAS Regulation). These modalities include direct provision by a Member State, provision under a mandate by a Member State, or provision independently by a Member State, but with the recognition of that Member State (Article 5a(2) of the amended eIDAS Regulation). The primary objective of this provision is to provide flexibility to Member States and to take advantage of more advanced technologies (Recital 16 of the eIDAS Regulation 2).

As was previously established in the notification regime for electronic identification systems, the provision of the European digital identity wallet also reflects the public service nature that permeates the regulation of electronic identification in the eIDAS Regulation. Furthermore, it is indicative of the diversity of perspectives among the Member States of the European Union regarding the provision model, with varying degrees of market intervention.

Member States are subject to different legal obligations in relation to the provision of the European digital identity wallet. These obligations vary depending on the lifecycle of a wallet solution or the lifecycle of each wallet instance, as the case may be. The specific duties and obligations pertaining to the provision of the European digital identity wallet are contingent upon the applicable provision model, which can be categorized as direct, mandated, or recognition. In certain instances, the aforementioned duties may be incumbent upon the entity responsible for providing the European digital identity wallet.

First, prior to its provision, the Member State must assess the conformity of the European digital identity wallet with the functional requirements, common protocols and interfaces, and validation mechanisms, with the logical separation requirement, and, where applicable, with the technical standards and specifications to facilitate user on-boarding of the European digital identity wallet (Article 5c(1) of the amended eIDAS Regulation), including relevant cybersecurity requirements (Article 5c(2) of the amended eIDAS Regulation). This certification—although it would be more accurate to speak of certifications, or composite certification—refers to the European digital identity wallet solution, and has been further developed by Commission Implementing Regulation (EU) 2024/2981 of November 28, 2024, laying down detailed rules for the implementation of Regulation (EU) No 910/2014 of the European Parliament and of the Council as regards certification of European digital identity wallets.

Secondly, States are bound by legal obligations of an informative nature regarding the provision of the European digital identity wallet. Specifically, Article 5a(18) of the eIDAS Regulation stipulates that Member States are obligated to furnish the Commission with pertinent information without undue delay. This information encompasses the following: (a) the designated body responsible for establishing and maintaining the registry of registered parties utilizing European digital identity wallets, along with the location of said registry; (b) the bodies entrusted with the provision of European digital identity wallets; (c) the bodies responsible for ensuring that the person identifiers are associated with the European digital identity wallet; (d) the mechanism for validating the person identifiers and the identity of the using parties; and (e) the mechanism for validating the authenticity and validity of the European digital identity wallets. The aforementioned information shall be disseminated to the public by the Commission, employing a secure channel and in an electronically signed or sealed form that is suitable for automated processing (Article 5a.18 in fine of the amended eIDAS Regulation). These issues have been further elaborated in Commission Implementing Regulation (EU) 2024/2980 of November 28, 2024, which establishes comprehensive regulations for the implementation of Regulation (EU) No. 910/2014 of the European Parliament and of the Council with regard to notifications to the Commission concerning the European digital identity wallet ecosystem.

The Member State is also obligated to inform the Commission and the Cooperation Group without undue delay of the European Digital Identity Wallets that have been provided and certified by the Conformity Assessment Bodies. Furthermore, the Member State is required to notify the Commission and the Cooperation Group when any certification is cancelled, stating the reasons for the cancellation (Article 5d(1) of the amended eIDAS Regulation). In such instances, the Commission is tasked with establishing, publishing in the Official Journal of the European Union, and maintaining in a machine-readable format a register of certified European Digital Identity Wallets (Article 5d(3) of the amended eIDAS Regulation).

As long as it complies with its obligation to provide at least one European digital identity wallet (for each of the categories of users, or common to one or more categories of users), the State may decide to withdraw a European digital identity wallet solution by submitting a request to the Commission (Article 5d(4) of the amended eIDAS Regulation).

The eIDAS Regulation stipulates provisions for the suspension or withdrawal of a European digital identity wallet solution in the event of a security breach (Article 5e of the amended eIDAS Regulation). Additionally, it outlines the revocation of a specific instance of the European digital identity wallet upon the user's express request when their security has been compromised or in the event of their death or the cessation of activity of the legal person (Article 5a.(9) of the amended eIDAS Regulation).

2.5 The Contents of the European Digital Identity Wallet

2.5.1 Person Identification Data

The European digital identity wallet has the capacity to contain Person Identification Data (PID), which, in an ideal scenario, would enable highly secure identification and cross-border identity matching.

In regard to the identification of users to be provided with the European digital identity wallet, the eIDAS 2 Regulation acknowledges that only the competent authorities of Member States can provide a high level of confidence in the determination of a person's identity. Therefore, those authorities can ensure that the person claiming or representing a certain identity is actually the person they claim to be. This is due to the fact that, for the provision of European digital identity wallets, it is necessary to rely on the legal identity of citizens of the Union, residents of the Union, or legal persons (Recital 19 of the eIDAS 2 Regulation). Consequently, the Regulation alludes to the electronic identification system under which the European digital identity wallet is furnished (Article 5d(2) of the amended eIDAS Regulation), a function it implements during the process of issuing person identification data.

Only when the PID is issued can the European digital identity wallet be considered as a real means of electronic identification.

Person identification data, as delineated in Article 3(3) of the eIDAS Regulation, is defined as "a set of data which makes it possible to establish the identity of a natural or legal person, or of a natural person representing a legal person". Article 2 of the eIDAS Regulation has been amended regarding this definition to include a "set of data issued in accordance with Union or national law that establishes the identity of a natural or legal person, or of a natural person representing another natural person or a legal person". This amendment subjects the issuance of such data to Union or national law, extending the concept to include natural persons representing other natural persons (although the case of a legal person representing a natural person remains outside the scope of the concept).

Commission Implementing Regulation (EU) 2024/2977 of 28 November 2024 laying down detailed rules for the implementation of Regulation (EU) No 910/2014 of the European Parliament and of the Council as regards person identification data and electronic attribute declarations issued to European digital identity wallets has taken care of establishing the set of identification data of the natural person and the legal person, differentiating between mandatory and optional data, as well as metadata on the person identification data. Two technical encodings are also established for this information: the format specified in the ISO/IEC 18013-5:2021 standard and the "Verifiable Credentials Data Model 1.1", W3C recommendation of 3 March 2022. A similar provision is contained in Article 8 of Commission Implementing Regulation (EU) 2024/2979 of 28 November 2024 laying down detailed rules for the implementation of Regulation (EU) No 910/2014 of the European Parliament and of the Council as regards the integrity and core functionalities of European digital identity wallets.

2.5.2 Electronic Attestations of Attributes

Secondly, the European digital identity wallet may contain electronic attestations of attributes, where appropriate, qualified or issued by certain public sector bodies, with the same legal value as paper-based documents.

Indeed, among the newly established trust services is the issuance and validation of electronic attestations of attributes, which the Regulation defines as "an attestation in electronic form that allows attributes to be authenticated" and defines the concept of an attribute as a "characteristic, quality, right, or permission of a natural or legal person or of an object". Examples of attributes include academic qualifications, university degrees, and professional qualifications, as cited by the eIDAS 2 Regulation.

It is evident that this constitutes a novel category of electronic document, which integrates one or more identity attributes with a natural or legal person, thereby ensuring the veracity and authenticity of these attributes. According to the provisions outlined in the eIDAS 2 Regulation, a natural or legal person may utilize the services of a trust service provider to issue these attribute declarations. Upon acquiring these attestations, the data subject is empowered to employ them in transactions as required, thereby facilitating the emergence of a novel personal data market. This market is subject to the oversight and control of the data subject, offering high assurances of security and privacy.

The recently amended eIDAS Regulation establishes two distinct legal frameworks for the issuance of electronic attribute declarations. The first framework pertains to declarations issued by trust service providers, where qualified, and the second framework applies to declarations issued by or on behalf of public sector entities responsible for authentic sources.

One of the most significant innovations is the issuance of electronic attribute declarations by trust service providers, as it signifies a privatization of the legal activity of acts of constancy, which heretofore was exclusively reserved to the authorities and other entities maintaining legal and administrative registers. The second notable innovation is the introduction of regulations by the Council concerning the issuance of electronic attribute declarations by or on behalf of public sector bodies entrusted with the management of authentic sources.

Accordingly, the amended eIDAS Regulation stipulates the following legal consequences for electronic attestations of attributes. Firstly, the principle of non-discrimination is established, stipulating that an electronic attestation of attributes cannot be denied legal effect or admissibility as evidence in legal proceedings solely on the basis that it is in electronic form or does not meet the requirements applicable to qualified electronic attestations of attributes (Article 45b(1) of the amended eIDAS Regulation).

Secondly, on the basis of the principle of functional equivalence, qualified electronic attestations of attributes and attestations of attributes issued by or on behalf of a public sector body responsible for an authentic source shall have the same legal effect as attestations lawfully issued on paper (Article 45b(2) of the eIDAS Regulation as amended).

The Regulation establishes provisions for cross-border recognition of attestations, operating in a dual manner. First, Article 24a(9) of the amended eIDAS Regulation stipulates that a qualified electronic attesttion of attributes issued in one Member State must be recognized as a qualified electronic attestation of attributes in all other Member States. Second, according to Article 45b(3) of the amended eIDAS Regulation, an electronic attestation of attributes issued by or on behalf of a public sector body responsible for an authentic source in one Member State must be recognized as such in all other Member States. In both cases, the use of such declarations is to be ensured.

To ensure the reliability of information provided in attestations issued by trust service providers, the Regulation stipulates that these providers must have access to authentic sources containing the necessary attributes for matching (Article 45e(1) of the amended eIDAS Regulation). These sources are defined as repositories or systems managed by public sector bodies or private entities. These repositories or systems are required to contain and provide attributes on both natural and legal persons, and they are considered reliable sources of information under Union or national law, including administrative practices. According to the recently amended eIDAS Regulation, a registry or system is defined as a repository under the responsibility of a public sector body or private entity. This system contains and provides attributes on a natural or legal person. The registry is considered a primary source of such information or is recognized as authentic in accordance with Union or national law, including administrative practices.

Access is ensured at least for the following attributes, contained in Annex VI: address, age, gender, civil status, family composition; nationality or citizenship, educational qualifications, titles and licences, professional qualifications, powers and mandates to represent natural or legal persons, public permits and licences, and, for legal persons, financial and company data.

This list demonstrates the transformative capacity of the proposal, as it facilitates the establishment of a novel decentralized market for data utilization within business processes, under the control of the data subject. It is reasonable to hypothesize that this will also facilitate the use of digital assets, for instance when associated with legal entities.

Moreover, Article 8 of Implementing Regulation (EU) 2024/2979 requires European digital identity wallets to support the use of electronic attestations of attributes in the same formats as the person identifier data, i.e. the format specified in ISO/IEC 18013-5:2021 and the W3C recommendation "Verifiable Credential Data Model 1.1" of 3 March 2022, which is desirable in terms of interoperability.

2.5.3 User-created pseudonyms

Finally, the European Parliament has proposed an innovation regarding the European Commission's initial proposal, namely, the concept of a digital identity wallet. This wallet can contain user-created pseudonyms, which facilitate user authentication in an "anonymous"—although it would clearly be "pseudonymous"—manner for access to online services. Additionally, and although the Regulation does not expressly mention it, the wallet can also be used for relations between users in peer-to-peer, wallet-to-wallet communications.

In the words of Recital 19 of the eIDAS 2 Regulation, "the use of legal identity should not prevent users of European digital identity wallets from accessing services using a pseudonym where there is no legal obligation to use legal identity for authentication". That possibility is reiterated in Recital 60 of the eIDAS 2 Regulation when it states that "unless specific rules of Union or national law require users to identify themselves, access to services using a pseudonym should not be prohibited". This is the case for many types of digital assets. According to Recital 22 of the eIDAS 2 Regulation, "European digital identity wallets should include a functionality to generate pseudonyms chosen and managed by the user for authentication purposes when accessing online services", which reinforces Recital 57 of the eIDAS 2 Regulation itself in relation to the obligation for very large online platforms to accept the wallet, "while respecting the principle of data minimisation and the right of users to use freely chosen pseudonyms".

Accordingly, Article 5 of the amended eIDAS Regulation requires that "without prejudice to specific rules of Union or national law requiring users to identify themselves or to the legal effects of pseudonyms under national law, the use of pseudonyms chosen by users shall not be prohibited". That same provision is reiterated in Article 5b(9) of the amended eIDAS Regulation to some extent, whereby "user parties shall not refuse the use of pseudonyms where Union or national law does not require identification of the user", a real legal obligation enforceable under the law applicable to the service where such a pseudonym is to be accepted.

Article 14 of Implementing Regulation (EU) 2024/2979 develops this possibility through two rules. Firstly, wallet units shall support the generation of pseudonyms for users of a wallet in accordance with the technical specifications set out in Annex V, i.e. using WebAuthn - W3C recommendation of 8 April 2021, level 2.

Secondly, wallet units shall allow the generation, upon request, of a specific and unique pseudonym for a wallet user and shall provide it either on its own or together with the identification data of the person or the electronic attribute declaration requested by that wallet user party. In other words, a different pseudonym shall be available for each user party, but generally unique for all transactions with that user party.

2.6 The Functionalities of the European Digital Identity Wallet

Once the European digital identity wallet unit is available to the user, it must enable the user to perform a number of actions or functionalities, always in a way that is intuitive, transparent and traceable by the user. Furthermore, the functionalities referred to must be implemented in accordance with a number of additional requirements, including the use of common protocols and interfaces (Article 5a(5)(a) of the amended eIDAS Regulation), in order to ensure interoperability across the Union.

Other requirements for European digital identity wallets are that their use shall be voluntary (Article 5a(15) of the amended eIDAS Regulation), and that their issuance, use and revocation shall be free of charge for all natural persons (Article 5a(13) of the amended eIDAS Regulation).

In this regard, Article 5a(15) of the amended eIDAS Regulation mandates that access to public and private services, access to the labour market and the freedom to conduct a business shall not be restricted in any way or be detrimental to natural or legal persons who do not use European digital identity wallets, and access to public and private services shall continue to be possible through other existing means of identification and authentication.

The specific functionalities delineated in the amended eIDAS Regulation have been further elaborated in Implementing Regulation (EU) 2024/2979. In regard to the concept of exclusive user control, Article 3 of the aforementioned Implementing Regulation (EU) 2024/2979 stipulates that wallet units are prohibited from executing any of the functions enumerated in Article 5a(4) of the amended eIDAS Regulation, with the exception of user authentication for wallet access, until the wallet unit has successfully authenticated the user of the wallet. This protocol is designed to ensure that only the legitimate user can utilize these functionalities.

Firstly, the user must be able to request, obtain, store and delete personal identification data and electronic attribute declarations (Article 5a(4)(a) of the amended eIDAS Regulation), which is equally applicable to electronic attribute declarations.

The wallet must allow the user to request and obtain personal identification data, which, as previously mentioned, are necessary for the wallet to be considered a means of electronic identification. This implies that a wallet must be provided to the user before it contains personal identification data and that only from the wallet will it be possible to request and obtain personal identification data. However, as elucidated in Articles 5a(18) and 5d(2) of the amended eIDAS Regulation, the relationship between the European digital identity wallet and the electronic identification system is particularly pronounced. In practical terms, this relationship translates to the challenge faced by a Member State other than the State providing the European digital identity wallet in issuing its own electronic identification data within that wallet.

Secondly, the user must be able to securely select, combine, share and present, under the sole control of the user, personally identifiable data and, where appropriate, in combination with electronic attestations of attributes, authenticate to user parties for the purpose of accessing public and private services (Article 5a(4)(a) of the amended eIDAS Regulation).

In order to enhance users' privacy, Article 5a(16) of the amended eIDAS Regulation stipulates that the technical framework of the European digital identity wallet shall (a) not allow, subsequent to the issuance of the electronic attestation of attributes, electronic attestations of attributes providers or any other party to obtain data that would allow tracking, linking or correlating, or otherwise obtaining knowledge of the user's transactions or behaviour, unless explicitly authorized by the user. (b) shall enable privacy protection technologies that ensure non-linkage, where the attestation of attributes does not require identification of the user; requirements that do not appear to be required for the secure sharing and presentation of personally identifiable data.

The first requirement refers to unobservability, a concept that for the European Commission means that there should be no correlation of data between different services for the purposes of tracking or tracing users or for determining, analysing and predicting behaviour, interests or personal habits.

The second requirement refers to unlinkability, a concept that is widely addressed in international standards, defined in ISO/IEC TR 27550:2019 as "a property that ensures that a stakeholder can make multiple uses of resources or services without others being able to link these uses together".

Thirdly, the user must be able to use the European digital identity wallet online and, where applicable, in offline mode (Article 5a(4)(a) of the amended eIDAS Regulation), so that it can be used in face-to-face and remote relationships, which is a major innovation compared to the system initially foreseen in the eIDAS Regulation. Article 3(57) of the amended eIDAS Regulation defines the offline mode for the use of European digital identity wallets as the interaction between a user and a third party that takes place at a physical location using proximity first technologies, without the need for the European digital identity wallet to access remote systems via electronic communications networks for the purpose of the interaction.

This is therefore a proximity scenario, typical of face-to-face relationships, where the user's mobile device should not require connectivity for its use, but where it can be assumed that the user party (e.g. a merchant) should have connectivity, in order to perform the appropriate technical validations to be able to make use of the user's European digital identity wallet. This makes sense, for example, in order to be able to access the information necessary to verify that the wallet has not been suspended or revoked.

In particular, Recital 19 of the eIDAS 2 Regulation considers that "offline authentication will be important in many sectors, especially healthcare, where services are often provided through face-to-face interaction, and e-prescriptions should be able to use QR codes or similar technologies to verify their authenticity".

Fourthly, the user must be able to make targeted disclosure of personal identification data as well as other identity attributes, if necessary, in a combined form (Article 5a(4)(a) eIDAS Regulation as amended).

Although no legal definition of selective disclosure is provided, it is described in the eIDAS 2 Regulation as "a concept that empowers the data owner to disclose only certain parts of a larger data set so that the receiving entity obtains only the information that is necessary for the provision of a service requested by the user", requiring that it is "technically possible for the user to disclose these attributes in a selective manner, even from several different electronic attestations and to combine and present them seamlessly to the using parties", and should therefore "become a basic design feature of European digital identity wallets, thereby enhancing convenience and the protection of personal data, in particular data minimisation" (Recital 59 of the eIDAS 2 Regulation).

From a technical standpoint, there exist myriad mechanisms that facilitate the realization of this functional requirement, including atomic credential schemes, multi-message signature schemes, and the utilization of hashes of salted attributes or proofs for arithmetic circuits, as described in ETSI TR 119 476. Of these, it is preferable to employ those based on zero-knowledge proofs, as outlined in Recital 14 of the eIDAS 2 Regulation. These are characterized as cryptographic methods that "should allow a user party to validate whether a given attestation, based on the identification data and attribute declaration of the person, is true without revealing any data on which the attestation is based, thus preserving the privacy of the user." This vision represents a significant departure from a legislative perspective, albeit a reductionist one.

Fifthly, and as we have already seen, the user must be able to generate pseudonyms, store them encrypted and locally in his European digital identity wallet (Article 5a(4)(b) of the amended eIDAS Regulation), and use them in his relations with third parties, except when the law requires the identification of the user (Article 5b(9) of the amended eIDAS Regulation).

Sixth, in peer-to-peer communications, the user must be able to securely authenticate another person's European digital identity wallet, as well as receive and share person identification data and electronic attribute statements securely between the two European digital identity wallets.

Seventh, in web-server-wallet communications (such as a website of a private entity, or the electronic site of a public administration), the user must be able to verify the authenticity and validity of the identity of registered third parties requesting data from it.

Eighth, the user should be able to access a record of the transactions carried out with the European digital identity wallet, by means of a dashboard that allows the user to view an up-to-date list of the third parties with whom data has been exchanged, and, where applicable, all the data exchanged. This functionality has been specified in Article 9 of Implementing Regulation (EU) 2024/2979.

Ninth, the user should be able to ask a third party (who has interacted with the user, of course), using the European digital identity wallet, to delete personal data; and to notify the national data protection supervisory authority of any suspicious request for data by a third party.

Tenth, the European digital identity wallet must offer qualified electronic signatures and qualified electronic seals (Article 5a(4)(e) of the amended eIDAS Regulation), a function implemented by Articles 11 and 12 of Implementing Regulation (EU) 2024/2979. In the case of qualified electronic signatures, they will be offered by default and free of charge to natural persons for non-professional purposes (i.e. acting as a citizen or a consumer), thus maintaining healthy competition in relation to the market for trust services.

Eleventh, the European Identity Wallet must allow for downloading, as far as technically feasible, the data, the electronic attribute declaration and the user settings (Article 5a(4)(f) of the amended eIDAS Regulation). However, due to the existence of cryptographic security measures linking electronic attribute declarations to a specific device, it may not be technically feasible to comply with this obligation, in particular for qualified declarations issued by public sector bodies responsible for authentic sources.

Finally, the wallet should allow the user's rights to data portability to be exercised (Article 5a(4)(f) of the amended eIDAS Regulation). In this regard, Recital 48 of the eIDAS 2 Regulation states that "this Regulation should encourage the choice between European digital identity wallets and the possibility to switch between them when the Member State has endorsed more than one European digital identity wallet solution in its territory", so that "in order to avoid blocking effects in such situations, where technically feasible, European digital identity wallet providers should ensure effective data portability at the request of European digital identity wallet users, and should not be allowed to use contractual, economic or technical barriers to prevent or discourage effective switching between different European digital identity wallets". However, depending on the security measures outlined above, this provision may imply receiving documents that can no longer be used in relations with third parties, requiring their reissuance.

In this regard, Article 13 of Implementing Regulation (EU) 2024/2979 exempts from the possibilities of export and portability critical assets, i.e. assets contained in or related to a wallet unit which are of such extraordinary importance that if their availability, confidentiality or integrity were to be compromised, the effect on the ability to use the wallet unit would be very serious and debilitating.

2.7 Concluding Remarks

Principle 7 serves the dual purpose of relieving the burden of proof of negative evidence of control, if any, of a digital asset, and of establishing a standard of reasonableness with respect to means of identification.

The aforementioned principles presuppose that digital assets, along with the underlying protocols and systems, offer adequate reliability for the purpose of control. However, it should be noted that these principles do not establish a comprehensive reliability standard, a feature that is present in instruments such as the MLETR. The approach of the Principles may raise doubts about the appropriateness of adopting a weak legal approach supporting transfers of proprietary rights.

While it is true that the Principles are based on factual situations in which it is not always possible to establish high standards of protection, it is no less true that digital assets that use protocols or underlying systems with guarantees should develop under better conditions. It is conceivable that regulatory frameworks could evolve in this direction, incentivizing or mandating the utilization of qualified electronic ledgers in accordance with the amended eIDAS regulation.

With respect to the criterion of reasonableness in the means of identification, it is somewhat circular with respect to the concept of digital asset, which is directly linked to the identification, in a mathematical sense, of the person who controls it. Therefore, without identity, there is no attribution of control abilities and, consequently, no digital asset. In light of these considerations, it would have been prudent to explicitly underscore the necessity of authentication as a dynamic component of the identification process.

In many cases, however, it will be necessary to proceed with the use of legally required means of "civil" identification, in line with the new European digital identity framework foreseen in the amended eIDAS Regulation. The European Wallet is poised to play a pivotal role in ensuring the security of individuals who manage digital assets, while offering a substantial degree of privacy protection, particularly through the use of pseudonyms.

Principle 8
Innocent Acquisition

Alfonso Martínez-Echevarría y García de Dueñas

(1) In order to qualify as an innocent acquirer, a transferee must:

(a) obtain control of a digital asset; and

(b) comply with requirements equivalent to those found in the relevant good faith acquisition and take-free rules as specified by the relevant State.

(2) An innocent acquirer takes a digital asset free of conflicting proprietary rights ('proprietary claims').

(3) No rights based on a proprietary claim relating to a digital asset can be successfully asserted against an innocent acquirer of that digital asset.

(4) An innocent acquirer can acquire a proprietary right in a digital asset even if control of that digital asset is changed by a transferor who is acting wrongfully and has no proprietary right in the digital asset.

(5) If these Principles are applied pursuant to Principle 5(1), in addition to the requirement in sub paragraph (1)(a), the following requirements for a transferee to be an innocent acquirer apply with respect to a digital asset:

(a) A transferee of a digital asset is an innocent acquirer of a digital asset unless, at the time the transferee takes control of the digital asset, the transferee actually knows or ought to know that another person has an interest in the digital asset and that the acquisition violates the rights of that other person in relation to its interest;

This work was financed within the framework of the Prometeo 2023 project of the Regional Ministry of Innovation, Universities, Science and Digital Society (CIPROM/2022/26) "Present and future of the regulation of cryptoassets in the EU [LegalCripto]", whose principal investigator is Carmen Pastor Sempere. The basic ideas contained herein were presented in the author's paper with the same title, given on November 13, 2024 at the IV International Congress on "UNIDROIT Principles on Digital Assets and Private Law: Context, Content, Perspectives", organized also by BAES Research Group of the University of Alicante on November 13 and 14, 2024.

A. Martínez-Echevarría y García de Dueñas (✉)
Universidad San Pablo-CEU, CEU Universities, Madrid, Spain
e-mail: alfonso.martinezechevarria@ceu.es

C. Pastor Sempere and D. A. Morán Bovio (eds.), UNIDROIT *Principles on Digital Assets and Private Law*, Law, Governance and Technology Series 80,
https://doi.org/10.1007/978-3-032-11001-5_14

(b) In determining whether a person ought to know of an interest or fact:

(i) the determination must take into account the characteristics and requirements of the relevant market for the digital asset; and

(ii) the person is under no general duty of inquiry or investigation;

(c) An organisation actually knows or ought to know of an interest or fact from the time when the interest or fact is or ought reasonably to have been brought to the attention of the individual responsible for the matter to which the interest or fact is relevant; and

(d) A transferee of a digital asset is not an innocent acquirer if the transfer of the digital asset is made by way of gift or otherwise gratuitously and is not the grant of a security right.

(6) Except as provided in Principle 9, if a transferee is not an innocent acquirer under paragraph (1) or, if applicable, paragraph (5), other law applies to determine the rights and liabilities, if any, of that transferee.

1 Official Commentary

Commentary

General

8.1. As is made clear in Principle 9 and its Commentary, the basic rule of nemo dat quod non habet (one cannot give what one does not have) applies to digital assets. However, this is subject to the innocent acquisition rule set out in Principle 8, which is an exception to the basic nemo dat rule. As set out in Principles 8(2) and 8(3), an innocent acquirer takes free of conflicting proprietary rights, and no rights based on a proprietary claim can be asserted against an innocent acquirer.

8.2. The rights conferred on innocent acquirers in accordance with Principles 8(2) and 8(3) mean that digital assets will have attributes similar to those of negotiability under rules applicable to negotiable instruments, negotiable documents of title, and negotiable certificated securities in many common law and civil law jurisdictions.

8.3. It is recognised that the result of an innocent acquisition rule is that, in some circumstances, a person with a proprietary claim, who is the victim of wrongful activity, will not be able to assert that claim successfully against the innocent acquirer. The victim would have a claim against the wrongful actor, but that is unlikely to be effective. The innocent acquisition rule represents a policy balance, in this situation, in favour of an innocent acquirer for the reasons set out in Commentary 8.4 and 8.5.

8.4. Digital assets are often traded on a distributed ledger system or other electronic networks that permit near instantaneous transactions. The fluidity of the market allows for transactions that recognise the full value of these assets and transactions. This fluidity, and the fact that many transferors are pseudonymous and often based in different jurisdictions, makes investigations as to whether there are any conflicting proprietary rights in the asset being acquired highly impractical. A person who has a proprietary right in a digital asset is therefore in a better position than a transferee to protect itself from wrongful activity by taking steps to safeguard its proprietary rights. The availability of an innocent acquisition rule would facilitate the types of transactions referred to above and would contribute to legal certainty and efficient markets. In the absence of an innocent acquisition rule, the risk of third-party proprietary claims to a digital asset would be likely to be factored into, and reduce, the amount that a prudent buyer would be willing to pay for the digital asset or the value a secured creditor would assign to the digital asset as an encumbered asset. Moreover, the legal certainty provided by an innocent acquisition rule also benefits custodians of digital assets and their clients (see also Principle 12 and its Commentary). The availability of an innocent acquisition rule will reduce friction in transactions and reduce costs for all involved. The availability of innocent acquirer status in other areas, such as negotiable instruments and securities, has proved effective and safe for the operation of those markets. Digital assets are playing an important role in the current economy and are expected to play an even greater role over time.

8.5. Moreover, a digital asset can be coded in such a way that its negotiability is limited in fact. For example, a digital asset could either directly or indirectly display information that puts prospective purchasers on notice of the possible existence of conflicting claims. This would be the case, for example, if a digital asset were programmed so that its metadata clearly specified the identity of its legitimate owner and expressly stated that anyone considering acquiring it should deal with that person.

8.6. In relation to the operation of the innocent acquirer rule in Principle 8 to linked assets, see Commentary 4.11 and 4.29 to 4.32.

Principles 8(1) to 8(3)

8.7. Principle 8(1) sets out the requirements for a transferee to be an innocent acquirer. The first is that the transferee must obtain control, as defined in Principle 6. The second is that the innocent acquirer must comply with the requirements specified by the relevant State (that is, the State whose domestic law is the applicable law). As indicated by Principle 8(1)(b), a State has flexibility as to the precise contours of the requirements for innocent acquisition of digital assets that it adopts, given that such requirements need to be consistent with the good faith acquisition and take free rules of that State for other types of assets. A State might wish to adopt slightly different innocent acquisition rules for different types of digital assets (see also Commentary 3.7).

8.8. As discussed in Commentary 8.1 and 8.2 above, Principles 8(2) and 8(3) set out the consequences of a transferee being an innocent acquirer. Principle 8(4)

8.9. Principle 8(4) is intended to make clear that, for example, even if an acquirer receives control of a digital asset by a change of control made by a thief or a 'hacker', the acquirer may qualify as an innocent acquirer. See also the discussion in Commentary 6.6, 6.9 and 6.10.

Principle 8(5)

8.10. Principle 8(5) provides a default set of requirements for a transferee to be an innocent acquirer for use if, first, a State's court needs, in the course of litigation, to apply the Principles pursuant to one of the choice-of-law rules in Principle 5(1)(a), 5(1)(b) or 5(1)(d) and, second, that State has not yet adopted its own innocent acquisition rule for digital assets of the relevant type. If the State has adopted its own rule, that rule would apply as Principles law. Principle 8(5) is drawn substantially from the innocent acquisition rule in the Geneva Securities Convention.

Principle 8(6)

8.11. Principle 8(6) reflects Principle 3(3), which states that, except as displaced by these Principles, other law continues to govern issues relating to a digital asset. However, this is subject to Principle 9.

2 Reflections

2.1 Introduction—The Method Chosen for This Study

UNIDROIT Digital Assets and Private Law Principle 8 deals with the regulation of the innocent acquisition of digital assets and the determination of the applicable law to this institution.

The text of the UNIDROIT Principles on Digital Assets and Private Law is structured in such a manner that each Principle is followed by a Commentary by the members of the Digital Assets and Private Law Working Group for the preparation of the Principles on Digital Assets and Private Law.[1] Consequently, given that *ab initio* there are already commentaries to the Principles, in this paper we make some "considerations"

[1] The members of this *Working Group* are listed in one of the final sections of the document. (UNIDROIT *Principles on Digital Assets and Private Law*, p. I).

or analysis of both the text and the Commentaries to UNIDROIT Digital Assets and Private Law Principle 8.

From a methodological point of view, all the chapters of the work in which this paper is included basically use three sources: the first is the UNIDROIT Principles on Digital Assets and Private Law themselves; the second is the documents corresponding to the eight meetings held by the Digital Assets and Private Law Working Group, and the third comprises other international standards and instruments that also aim to regulate digital assets.

Consequently, the use of bibliographical sources, which only appear occasionally throughout the book, has been dispensed with. The intended audience of the work as a whole is not exclusively and primarily academic, but, as in the case of the Principles, "practitioners, judges, arbitrators, legislators, and market participants".[2] The author, the readers or any third party with an interest in the subject matter may carry out a study supported by legal literature and other speculations in a framework with a different purpose than that of this collective work.

2.2 *The Context of Principle 8 in the Framework of the UNIDROIT Principles on Digital Assets and Private Law*

Ownership over a digital asset can be achieved by means of the legal institution known as *innocent acquisition*. This is recognised in UNIDROIT Digital Assets and Private Law Principle 8.

As we will see, innocent acquisition makes it possible to recognise and protect the right of ownership over a digital asset of the person who acquires it, even from a hacker. Innocent acquisition is an exceptional situation that both tests and confirms the soundness of the legal regime for digital assets.

One of the main purposes of the innocent acquisition of digital assets is to create legal certainty and, more specifically, certainty in the legal-economic traffic and in the digital asset markets.

Before beginning the analysis of the innocent acquisition of digital assets regime contained in Principle 8, we put this Principle in context with other Principles that more directly help to understand, complement and integrate it.

Principle 8 is found in Section III of the UNIDROIT Principles on Digital Assets and Private Law, entitled "Control and Transfer". This section is composed of Principles 6 to 9. Innocent acquisition relates directly not only to the other three Principles that make up Section III, but also to other Principles to which the text of Principle 8 explicitly and implicitly refers.

Obviously, the concept of "digital asset" as formulated in Principle 2(2) is essential to the understanding of innocent acquisition of these assets.

[2] UNIDROIT *Principles on Digital Assets and Private Law*, p. 1, par. 0.3.

Among the general principles contained in Principle 3, of particular relevance to the innocent acquisition regime is Principle 3(1), which recognises that "a digital asset may be the subject of property rights".

The innocent acquisition regime is largely based on the concepts of "control" and "change of control" in Principle 6.

Principle 7 deals with the identification of the person who has control over a digital asset. This issue is clearly necessary for the innocent acquisition of digital assets regime.

Principle 8 sets out the requirements for such an acquisition to take place. A distinction is made between two categories of requirements. On the one hand, Principle 8(1) contains the requirements for the good faith acquisition of digital assets when the applicable law is the law of the State concerned. On the other hand, Principle 8(5) sets out the requirements that apply when, in accordance with Principle 5(1), the UNIDROIT Principles on Digital Assets and Private Law is the applicable law, rather than another law that could have been applied, such as the national law of a particular State.

Principle 9 provides for the application to digital assets of the *nemo dat quod non habet* rule. As we will see, this rule is directly related to the innocent acquisition regime and is expressed in Principle 9(1), which explicitly refers to Principle 8.

2.3 The Dual Purpose of Principle 8: Regulation of Substantive Law and Determination of Applicable Law

The aim of the UNIDROIT Principles on Digital Assets and Private Law is not to regulate substantive or material legal-economic relationships involving digital assets. This was stated by the members of the Working Group at its first meeting: "regulation *per se* is outside the scope of this project".[3] The main objective of the Principles is to establish rules that help the parties involved to determine which law is applicable to a legal relationship on digital assets in the field of international trade. The members of the Working Group are also clear on this point: "[o]nly the issues of the applicable law are within the scope of the UNIDROIT Principles on Digital Assets and Private Law".[4] Aware that there are other institutions at the international level and even other UNIDROIT projects on to digital assets, the Working Group members leave the substantive regulatory aspects to be dealt with by those institutions and projects.[5]

[3] Digital Assets and Private Law Working Group // First session (remote) // Rome, 17 – 19 November 2020 //// UNIDROIT 2020 // Study LXXXII – W.G.1 – Doc. 2 // November 2020, p. 9, par. 36.

[4] Digital Assets and Private Law Working Group // First session (remote) // Rome, 17 – 19 November 2020 //// UNIDROIT 2020 // Study LXXXII – W.G.1 – Doc. 2 // November 2020, p. 20, par. 80.

[5] "(T)he other issues are likely to be explored by the Hague Conference on Private International Law or other organisations" (Digital Assets and Private Law Working Group // First session (remote) // Rome, 17 – 19 November 2020 //// UNIDROIT 2020 // Study LXXXII – W.G.1 – Doc. 2 // November 2020, p. 20, par. 80).

Principles 8 and 9 are an exception, both of which contain substantive law issues. They deal with two issues that are considered essential to ensure a minimum of security in commercial relationships over digital assets. Moreover, both are accepted in their basic or essential aspects in the two major international legal cultures, civil law and common law. Those issues are innocent acquisition, covered by Principle 8, and the *nemo dat quod non habet* principle, contained in Principle 9.

Principle 8 was drafted to serve two purposes, as it seeks both to provide guidelines for the regulation of innocent acquisition and to establish criteria for the determination of the applicable law. In fact, since the Third Meeting of the Working Group, the documents of the meetings have enshrined the term "innocent acquisition rule" and the acronym IAR to refer to this part of the content of this Principle.[6] This dual purpose of regulation and determination of the applicable law is spread throughout the six paragraphs of Principle 8, which we will analyse in the subsequent sections of this study. We shall now briefly comment on how this dual purpose of Principle 8 is reflected in its six paragraphs.

From a substantive regulatory point of view, in order to facilitate the alignment of the Principles with other relevant standards, the "innocent acquisition rule" of Principle 8 has been modelled on the Geneva Securities Convention.[7]

Principle 8(1) deals with the requirements a person must meet to be an innocent acquirer. In this respect, firstly, it provides for a requirement that is inexcusable: acquiring "control" of the digital asset.[8] Secondly, if a State whose law is applicable has been established, Principle 8(1) refers to the law of that State for the determination of the other requirements.

In the next three paragraphs, (2) to (4), Principle 8 sets out provisions of a regulatory nature.[9]

Principle 8(5), as it occurs in the first paragraph, contains substantive regulatory and choice of law rules. In this case, the applicable law is that of the Principles and not that of a State. Principle 8(5) refers in its first lines to Principle 5(1) for the determination of the applicable law. The remainder of the broader text of Principle 8(5) sets out the requirements for a transferee to be considered an innocent acquirer, which

---

[6] *Vid.* Digital Assets and Private Law Working Group // Third session (remote) // Rome, 30 June – 2 July 2021 //// UNIDROIT 2021 // Study LXXXII – W.G.3 – Doc. 2 (rev. 1) // June 2021, *passim.*

[7] In particular, Article 18(1) of the UNIDROIT Convention on Substantive Rules for Intermediated Securities has been taken as a reference (2013) -Geneva Securities Convention- (available in https://www.unidroit.org/instruments/capital-markets/geneva-conguvention).

Digital Assets and Private Law Working Group // Seventh session (hybrid) // Rome & Zoom, 19 – 21 December 2022 //// UNIDROIT 2023 // Study LXXXII – W.G.7 – Doc. 5// February 2023, p. 7, par. 29.

[8] UNIDROIT Digital Assets and Private Law Principle 8(1)(a).

[9] Which fulfil the purpose of the Working Group formulated in the Digital Assets and Private Law Working Group // Fourth session (remote) // Rome, 2 – 4 November 2021 //// UNIDROIT 2021 // Study LXXXII – W.G.4 – Doc. 2 // October 2021, pp. 41–42, par. 6.

are in addition to the requirement established in Principle 8(1)(a), the acquisition of 'control' of the digital asset.[10]

Principle 8(6) also serves the dual purpose of substantive regulation and determination of the applicable law. It refers to the applicable law of the State to determine what rights and responsibilities, if any, are conferred on a transferee of digital assets who is not an innocent acquirer. From a regulatory point of view, Principle 8(6) provides that, in any event, the principle of *nemo dat quod non habet*, provided for in Principle 9, applies to a transferee who is not an innocent acquirer.

2.4 *The Internal Precedents: The Documents of the Eight Meetings of the Digital Assets and Private Law Working Group*

2.4.1 First Meeting of the Working Group (November 2020)

The first meeting of the Digital Assets and Private Law Working Group took place telematically from 17 to 19 November 2020.

The doctrines of good faith acquisition and similar innocent acquisition rules contemplated in UNIDROIT on Digital Assets and Private Law Principle 8 were the subject of discussion from the first meeting of the Working Group and are reflected in its Issues Paper.[11]

Issues relating to the regulation of digital assets are not the focus of the UNIDROIT Principles on Digital Assets and Private Law.[12] Their focus is on issues relating to the choice or determination of the applicable law to a relationship involving digital assets. Therefore, the members of the Working Group consider that the other issues should preferably be dealt with by other institutions that are working on them, such as the "Hague Conference on Private International Law" or other organisations.[13] However, there are two substantive or regulatory issues that are addressed by the UNIDROIT Principles on Digital Assets and Private Law. One is the innocent acquisition of digital assets, and the other is the recognition of the application of the *nemo dat quod*

---

[10] As provided in the Digital Assets and Private Law Working Group // Fourth session (remote) / / Rome, 2 – 4 November 2021 //// UNIDROIT 2021 // Study LXXXII – W.G.4 – Doc. 2 // October 2021, pp. 42–43, par. 8–10.

[11] Digital Assets and Private Law Working Group // First session (remote) // Rome, 17 – 19 November 2020 //// UNIDROIT 2020 // Study LXXXII – W.G.1 – Doc. 2 // November 2020, p. 13, par. 55.

[12] "(R)egulation per se is outside the scope of this project" (cfr. Digital Assets and Private Law Working Group // First session (remote) // Rome, 17 – 19 November 2020 //// UNIDROIT 2020 // Study LXXXII – W.G.1 – Doc. 2 // November 2020, p. 9, par. 36).

[13] Digital Assets and Private Law Working Group // First session (remote) // Rome, 17 – 19 November 2020 //// UNIDROIT 2020 // Study LXXXII – W.G.1 – Doc. 2 // November 2020, p. 20, par. 80.

non habet principle to digital assets.[14] These two issues are closely interrelated, as innocent acquisition is an exception to the *nemo dat* principle.

The members of the Working Group do not hesitate to include both rules in the Principles, as both common law and civil law systems provide for rules regulating the acquisition of property and other rights in rem free of third party claims, provided that certain requirements are met, as described by the "doctrines of good faith purchase or similar innocent acquisition rules".[15]

This first meeting of the Working Group already rightly states what the requirements for the innocent acquisition of digital assets could be. Two are mentioned, which would eventually be incorporated into the text of Principle 8: firstly, that the acquirer is unaware that his/her acquisition is detrimental to the rights or interests of a third party in the digital asset (i.e. that he/she is acting in good faith); secondly, that there is something analogous to the taking of possession or material delivery (the latter is also identified as *traditio*) of a tangible asset. With regard to this second requirement, it is considered that this analogous event can be the "control" of an electronically transferable intangible asset, as defined by the UNCITRAL Model Law on Electronic Transferable Records.[16]

Other considerations made by the members of the Working Group at its first meeting, and which will be confirmed as sound and desirable, concern the link between the rules on innocent acquisition of digital assets and the negotiability of these assets.[17] Negotiability is a feature of digital assets that would be impaired or diminished if innocent acquisition of these assets were not possible. On the contrary, recognition of the innocent acquisition rule enhances the security of legal transactions in these assets and, consequently, security in the market.[18]

---

[14] UNIDROIT Digital Assets and Private Law Principle 9.

[15] Digital Assets and Private Law Working Group // First session (remote) // Rome, 17 – 19 November 2020 //// UNIDROIT 2020 // Study LXXXII – W.G.1 – Doc. 2 // November 2020, p. 13, par. 55.

[16] Digital Assets and Private Law Working Group // First session (remote) // Rome, 17 – 19 November 2020 //// UNIDROIT 2020 // Study LXXXII – W.G.1 – Doc. 2 // November 2020, p. 14, par. 56.

[17] Digital Assets and Private Law Working Group // First session (remote) // Rome, 17 – 19 November 2020 //// UNIDROIT 2020 // Study LXXXII – W.G.1 – Doc. 2 // November 2020, p. 14, par. 56; Digital Assets and Private Law Working Group // First session (remote) // Rome, 17 – 19 November 2020 //// UNIDROIT 2021 // Study LXXXII – W.G.1 – Doc. 4 // March 2021, p. 9, par. 41.

[18] Digital Assets and Private Law Working Group // First session (remote) // Rome, 17 – 19 November 2020 //// UNIDROIT 2020 // Study LXXXII – W.G.1 – Doc. 2 // November 2020, p. 14, par. 55, where it is noted that "(s)ome digital assets are traded on platforms/exchanges while others in peer-to-peer markets".

Among the various documents and legal texts cited during the first meeting of the Working Group, of particular interest is The Liechtenstein Blockchain Act,[19] in which Article 9 protects the *bona fide* third-party acquirer of tokens.[20]

2.4.2 Second Meeting of the Working Group (March 2021)

At its second meeting, the members of the Working Group continued to consider the desirability and importance of including rules on the acquisition of property rights in digital assets free of third-party claims in the UNIDROIT Principles on Digital Assets and Private Law, because both common law and civil law systems provide for "doctrines of good faith purchase or similar innocent acquisition rules".[21]

A "Sub-group 2—Control and Transfer" is created, dedicated to the study of these matters.[22]

At this stage, the Working Group had already produced a preliminary draft of some of the Principles, including this one. The identification and title initially attributed to it is "Principle [X.2] Acquisition and Disposition ("Transfer") of Digital Assets".[23]

The concept of "control" is considered to be the functional or technical equivalent of the concept of "possession" and it is therefore considered that the former will be necessary for innocent acquisition to occur.[24]

It is proposed that the regulation of innocent acquisition in the Principles should be done using functional language, without imposing a particular legal terminology (e.g. using the term "control", instead of using the legal term "possession").[25] Such functional language should also be technology neutral, not exclusively linked to DLT (Distributed ledger technology) or blockchain based systems, so that it is valid for any system in which data can be considered a token.[26]

---

[19] Law of 3 October 2019 on Tokens and TT Service Providers (Token and TT Service Provider Act; TVTG), whose original German title is Gesetz vom 3. Oktober 2019 über Token und VT-Dienstleister (Token- und VT-Dienstleister-Gesetz; TVTG).

[20] Exploratory Workshop on Digital Assets and Private Law // Rome and Zoom (17 – 18 September 2020) //// UNIDROIT 2021 // Study LXXXII – W.G.1 – Doc. 3 // March 2021, p. 16, par. 72.

[21] Digital Assets and Private Law Working Group // Second session (remote) // Rome, 16 – 18 March 2021 //// UNIDROIT 2021 // Study LXXXII – W.G.2 – Doc. 2 (rev. 1) // March 2021, p. 17, par. 81.

[22] Digital Assets and Private Law Working Group // Second session (remote) // Rome, 16 – 18 March 2021 //// UNIDROIT 2021 // Study LXXXII – W.G.2 – Doc. 1 // March 2021, p. 1, par. 4.(a)iv.2.

[23] Digital Assets and Private Law Working Group // Second session (remote) // Rome, 16 – 18 March 2021 //// UNIDROIT 2021 // Study LXXXII – W.G.2 – Doc. 2 (rev. 1) // March 2021, p. 19.

[24] Digital Assets and Private Law Working Group // Second session (remote) // Rome, 16 – 18 March 2021 //// UNIDROIT 2021 // Study LXXXII – W.G.2 – Doc. 3 // April 2021, p. 9, par. 29.

[25] Digital Assets and Private Law Working Group // Second session (remote) // Rome, 16 – 18 March 2021 //// UNIDROIT 2021 // Study LXXXII – W.G.2 – Doc. 3 // April 2021, p. 12, par. 42.

[26] Digital Assets and Private Law Working Group // Second session (remote) // Rome, 16 – 18 March 2021 //// UNIDROIT 2021 // Study LXXXII – W.G.2 – Doc. 2 (rev. 1) // March 2021, p. 4, par. 13.

The determination of the types of digital assets to which the innocent acquisition rule can be applied is left to a later stage of the Working Group meetings. It is fitting that it should apply to digital assets having the nature of financial instruments (or securities). However, doubts arise as to the appropriateness of applying the innocent acquisition rule to other types of digital assets, such as NFTs (non-fungible tokens), for which, depending on the case, this form of acquisition may or may not be appropriate.[27]

The members of the Working Group consider it desirable that States adopt, or, if they already have one, maintain a principle of protection underpinning the regulation of innocent acquisition that the Principles will eventually contain.[28]

2.4.3 Third Meeting of the Working Group (June–July 2021)

On reaching the third meeting of the Working Group, innocent acquisition and innocent acquisition regulation had already been consolidated as subject matters of the UNIDROIT Principles on Digital Assets and Private Law and, as a manifestation of this fact, the acronyms IA (innocent acquirer) and IAR (innocent acquisition rule) appear in the Working Group documents to refer to these issues.

The Working Group agreed to further examine two issues already discussed in its previous meetings. On the one hand, whether the innocent acquisition rules should apply to digital assets, as they apply to other assets in different jurisdictions. On the other hand, to which types of digital assets the Principles should apply. The Working Group also reached a consensus that States should adopt (or maintain) a principle of protection that supports the innocent acquisition rule in the foreseeable event that the Principles contain harmonised innocent acquisition rules.[29] This last consideration significantly enriches the scope of the addressees of the UNIDROIT Principles on Digital Assets and Private Law, since, in addition to addressing lawyers, arbitrators, jurists and market operators, they are particularly addressed to the legislators of the States.

The text of the draft Principle [X.2] Acquisition and Disposition ('Transfer') of Digital Assets is expanded. Part of this expansion consists of the Commentary to the text of the Principle itself (this Commentary in the final version of the Principles is published after the paragraphs that, *stricto sensu*, make up each Principle).[30] Principle

[27] Digital Assets and Private Law Working Group // Second session (remote) // Rome, 16 – 18 March 2021 //// UNIDROIT 2021 // Study LXXXII – W.G.2 – Doc. 3 // April 2021, p. 12, par. 42.

[28] Digital Assets and Private Law Working Group // Second session (remote) // Rome, 16 – 18 March 2021 //// UNIDROIT 2021 // Study LXXXII – W.G.2 – Doc. 3 // April 2021, p. 13, par. 46, and p. 14, par. 54.

[29] Digital Assets and Private Law Working Group // Third session (remote) // Rome, 30 June – 2 July 2021 //// UNIDROIT 2021 // Study LXXXII – W.G.3 – Doc. 2 (rev. 1) // June 2021, p. 16, par. 75.

[30] Digital Assets and Private Law Working Group // Third session (remote) // Rome, 30 June – 2 July 2021 //// UNIDROIT 2021 // Study LXXXII – W.G.3 – Doc. 2 (rev. 1) // June 2021, pp. 16–18.

[X.2](5)(a) refers to the "shelter principle" which is desirable for all States to have.[31] Principle [X.2] paragraphs (6)(a), (8)(a) and (8)(e) refer specifically to the regulation of the innocent acquisition of digital assets.[32] In this latter regard, the Summary report of the third session notes that in some jurisdictions there is no regulation of innocent acquisition that comprehensively covers all non-digital assets and, consequently, a uniform rule on innocent acquisition of digital assets linked to non-digital assets could create anomalies in the laws of those States.[33]

2.4.4 Fourth meeting of the Working Group (November 2021)

The documents of the Fourth Working Group meeting note that the draft Principle [X.2] Acquisition and Disposition ("Transfer") of Digital Assets continues to be refined by "Sub-group 2—Control and Transfer".[34] The Working Group considers that the Commentary accompanying this Principle should include guidance on how different jurisdictions should apply the innocent acquisition rule, so that different legal systems can reflect the best use of applicable technologies.[35]

As the Working Group meetings progress, the desirability of excluding certain types of property from the scope of the Principles, such as photographs or social media postings, is confirmed.[36]

The concept of "control" is confirmed as a necessary, but not sufficient, requirement for the innocent acquisition of a digital asset to occur.[37] The subject protected by the innocent acquisition rule must have control over the digital asset.

It is important that the innocent acquirer must be unaware that his/her acquisition is detrimental to the rights of a third party in the acquired digital asset. Consequently, such unawareness will be included in the "innocent acquisition rule" (IAR) contained in the Principles as a condition for being considered an "innocent acquirer" (IA). However, the innocent acquisition rule should also specify the consequences of the fact that the transferee of a digital asset does have knowledge that his/her acquisition of that asset is detrimental to a third party. In particular, the Principles should specify

[31] Digital Assets and Private Law Working Group // Third session (remote) // Rome, 30 June – 2 July 2021 //// UNIDROIT 2021 // Study LXXXII – W.G.3 – Doc. 2 (rev. 1) // June 2021, p. 17.

[32] Digital Assets and Private Law Working Group // Third session (remote) // Rome, 30 June – 2 July 2021 //// UNIDROIT 2021 // Study LXXXII – W.G.3 – Doc. 2 (rev. 1) // June 2021, pp. 17 and 18.

[33] Digital Assets and Private Law Working Group // Third session (remote) // Rome, 30 June – 2 July 2021 //// UNIDROIT 2021 // Study LXXXII – W.G.3 – Doc. 4 // July 2021, p. 7, par. 48.

[34] Digital Assets and Private Law Working Group // Fourth session (remote) // Rome, 2 – 4 November 2021 //// UNIDROIT 2021 // Study LXXXII – W.G.4 – Doc. 3 // December 2021, p. 3, par. 6 and ss.

[35] Digital Assets and Private Law Working Group // Fourth session (remote) // Rome, 2 – 4 November 2021 //// UNIDROIT 2021 // Study LXXXII – W.G.4 – Doc. 2 // October 2021, p. 12, par. 51.

[36] Digital Assets and Private Law Working Group // Fourth session (remote) // Rome, 2 – 4 November 2021 //// UNIDROIT 2021 // Study LXXXII – W.G.4 – Doc. 2 // October 2021, p. 12, par. 52.

[37] Digital Assets and Private Law Working Group // Fourth session (remote) // Rome, 2 – 4 November 2021 //// UNIDROIT 2021 // Study LXXXII – W.G.4 – Doc. 2 // October 2021, p. 39.

whether the transferee loses the status of innocent acquirer altogether, and any rights to which it may have given rise, or whether, on the contrary, it will be considered an innocent acquirer, but will be subject to the claims that may arise from its knowledge of the detriment caused by the acquisition.[38]

2.4.5 Fifth Meeting of the Working Group (March 2022)

Two of the documents for the fifth meeting of the Working Group contain versions of the Principles. The *"Master copy of black letter Principles"*[39] shows the changes made to the text of each Principle up to the wording of that version. The other document, entitled *"Master copy of the Principles and Comments"*,[40] is more extensive and contains the text of the Principles, structured in eight sections and twenty principles, each of which is accompanied by an extensive Commentary. This document also includes questions that members of the Working Group put forward with a view to the drafting of the Principles, which is still under development.

In that version, "innocent acquisition" is dealt with in three Principles. First, a "Principle 9: Innocent Acquirer Rule" is foreseen. As we know, in the final version of the Principles, the number, title and text of this Principle would be changed to "Principle 8: Innocent acquisition". Secondly, a "Principle 10: Shelter principle" is envisaged. Thirdly, a "Principle 11: Application of Innocent Acquirer Rules to a Custody Relationship" is included. Principle 11 is kept in the version of the Principles for the Sixth meeting of the Working Group and in the version for the Seventh meeting of the Working Group, although, in this case, the Principle is renumbered and renamed "Principle 10: Innocent client rule". Both Principle 10 and 11 would eventually disappear from the final version of the Principles, where the specific issues of "custody" would be dealt with in a specific section[41] and those relating to innocent acquisition linked to custody are expressly mentioned in Commentary 8.4.

The principle of "innocent acquisition" was reaffirmed as a cornerstone of the UNIDROIT Principles, providing that an innocent acquirer of a digital asset or derivative asset acquires it free from conflicting proprietary claims. This protection extends

---

[38] Digital Assets and Private Law Working Group // Fourth session (remote) // Rome, 2–4 November 2021 //// UNIDROIT 2021 // Study LXXXII – W.G.4 – Doc. 2 // October 2021, p. 42, par. 9.

[39] Digital Assets and Private Law Working Group // Fifth session (remote) // Rome, 7 – 9 March 2022 //// UNIDROIT 2022 // Study LXXXII – W.G.5 – Doc. 2 // February 2022.

In this version with visible changes, much of the previously drafted text has been discarded. The discarded text of each Principle is struck through, so that the reader can be aware of it and appreciate the evolution of the resulting content.

[40] Digital Assets and Private Law Working Group // Fifth session (remote) // Rome, 7 – 9 March 2022 //// UNIDROIT 2021 // Study LXXXII – W.G.5 – Doc. 3 // February 2022.

[41] Section IV: Custody, UNIDROIT Digital Assets and Private Law Principles 10 to 13.

even in cases in which the asset was transferred without the authority of the legitimate owner. The Principle emphasizes that control over a digital asset is essential for establishing the status of an innocent acquirer.[42]

It is envisaged that the Principles contain a regulation of innocent acquisition based on the requirements that must be met by the innocent acquirer in order to be considered as such.[43]

It is specified that innocent acquisition may concern both digital assets and "derivative digital assets". The concept of "derivative digital assets", as explained in "Principle 6: Definition of Control",[44] relates to a change of control over a digital asset that results in the creation of a new digital asset (referred to as a "derivative digital asset").[45] The concept of "derivative digital asset" is retained in the final version of the UNIDROIT Principles on Digital Assets and Private Law.[46]

Principle 11 broadens the scope of the IAR by including clients in custodial arrangements within the scope of its protection. This ensures that a client acquiring digital assets through a custodian enjoys the same protection as a direct acquirer, even though the custodian retains control over the assets. The discussions by the members of Working Group highlighted the need to clarify the relationship between the custodian's rights and the client's rights under this principle.[47]

The Working Group addresses the complexities of distinguishing between on-chain and off-chain transfers in the context of the IAR. It was noted that off-chain transfers, such as physical transfers of hardware wallets, could still qualify as transfers of control under Principle 9. This recognition ensures that the IAR remains effective across diverse transaction mechanisms.[48]

2.4.6 Sixth Meeting of the Working Group (August–September 2022)

Among the documents taken to the Sixth Working Group meeting, as was the case for the Eighth meeting, one of them contains the comments sent to the Working Group members by third parties.[49]

---

[42] Digital Assets and Private Law Working Group // Fifth session (remote) // Rome, 7 – 9 March 2022 //// UNIDROIT 2022 // Study LXXXII – W.G.5 – Doc. 4 // April 2022, p. 12, par. 103–110.

[43] Digital Assets and Private Law Working Group // Fifth session (remote) // Rome, 7 – 9 March 2022 //// UNIDROIT 2022 // Study LXXXII – W.G.5 – Doc. 2 // February 2022, pp. 5–6.

[44] Digital Assets and Private Law Working Group // Fifth session (remote) // Rome, 7 – 9 March 2022 //// UNIDROIT 2022 // Study LXXXII – W.G.5 – Doc. 2 // February 2022, p. 4.

[45] An example of a "derivative digital asset" is the UTXO ("*unspent transaction output*") generated by a Bitcoin transaction.

[46] Commentary 6.8 of the UNIDROIT Digital Assets and Private Law.

[47] Digital Assets and Private Law Working Group // Fifth session (remote) // Rome, 7 – 9 March 2022 //// UNIDROIT 2022 // Study LXXXII – W.G.5 – Doc. 4 // April 2022, p. 13, par. 114–117.

[48] Digital Assets and Private Law Working Group // Fifth session (remote) // Rome, 7 – 9 March 2022 //// UNIDROIT 2022 // Study LXXXII – W.G.5 – Doc. 4 // April 2022, p. 12, par. 109–110.

[49] Digital Assets and Private Law Working Group // Sixth session (hybrid) // Rome, 31 August – 2 September 2022 //// UNIDROIT 2022 // Study LXXXII – W.G.6 – Doc. 3 – ANNEX.

At the time of the Sixth Working Group Meeting, the issue of innocent acquisition and its regulation had already been firmly established within the UNIDROIT Principles on Digital Assets and Private Law. The discussions during this session further refined the scope, applicability, and legal effects of the innocent acquisition rule.

In the Working Group's Sixth Meeting version of the Principles,[50] the concept of "innocent acquisition" continues to be addressed in three principles, the titles of which vary slightly from those of the Fifth Meeting version: "*Principle 9: Innocent Acquisition Rule*", "*Principle 10: Shelter rule*" y "*Principle 11: Application of innocent acquisition rule to a custody relationship*".

The Working Group acknowledged that for a transferee to qualify as an innocent acquirer, an element of good faith was necessary. However, it was also noted that the innocent acquirer rule varied across jurisdictions, which called for further elaboration in the Commentary to the Principle.[51]

The Drafting Committee sought to clarify the Principle by addressing the use of terms such as "proprietary claim" and "purchase".[52] The term "purchase" was particularly problematic in civil law jurisdictions, necessitating a reconsideration of its usage. The Committee thus committed to reviewing these terminological ambiguities to ensure clarity across different legal traditions.

The relationship between the innocent acquisition rule and control was explored, drawing parallels with the revised text of Article 12 of the Uniform Commercial Code (UCC) of the United States. Some observers cautioned that the definition of control in the Principles might be circular, as it required exclusive ability to change control while simultaneously using control as a defining criterion.[53]

Application of the innocent acquisition rule to custody relationships was also discussed under Principle 11.[54] The Working Group debated whether the rule should apply to the client, the custodian, or both, particularly in cases in which the custodian, rather than the client, had control over the digital asset. Some members suggested that a client who is an innocent acquirer should be protected from any adverse claims under the take-free rule, even when control is exercised by the custodian.

---

[50] Digital Assets and Private Law Working Group // Sixth session (hybrid) // Rome, 31 August – 2 September 2022 //// UNIDROIT 2022 // Study LXXXII – W.G.6 – Doc. 2 // August 2022.

[51] Digital Assets and Private Law Working Group // Sixth session (hybrid) // Rome & Zoom, 31 August – 2 September 2022 //// UNIDROIT 2022 // Study LXXXII – W.G.6 – Doc. 4 // November 2022, p. 23, par. 138.

[52] Digital Assets and Private Law Working Group // Sixth session (hybrid) // Rome & Zoom, 31 August – 2 September 2022 //// UNIDROIT 2022 // Study LXXXII – W.G.6 – Doc. 4 // November 2022, p. 23, par. 139.

[53] Digital Assets and Private Law Working Group // Sixth session (hybrid) // Rome & Zoom, 31 August – 2 September 2022 //// UNIDROIT 2022 // Study LXXXII – W.G.6 – Doc. 4 // November 2022, p. 24, par. 141.

[54] Digital Assets and Private Law Working Group // Sixth session (hybrid) // Rome & Zoom, 31 August – 2 September 2022 //// UNIDROIT 2022 // Study LXXXII – W.G.6 – Doc. 4 // November 2022, p. 30, par. 182.

Furthermore, the Working Group discussed whether the innocent acquisition rule should apply uniformly across different tiers in a sub-custody arrangement.[55] The Drafting Committee was tasked with refining these provisions to ensure consistency and practicality in application.

The interaction between the innocent acquisition rule and secured transactions was also a subject of debate. It was noted that a secured creditor would be covered by the take-free rule regarding the security interest in the asset when taking control of an asset as an innocent acquirer in good faith.[56] However, this raised questions regarding the extent to which innocent acquisition principles should override established security interests.

One key issue was whether the custodian or the client needed to be innocent for the rule to apply, particularly when a custodian had agreed not to create an additional security interest but subsequently did so.[57] The potential for conflicting claims between innocent acquirers and prior secured creditors highlighted the need for detailed guidance in the Commentary.

2.4.7 Seventh Meeting of the Working Group (December 2022)

One of the documents of the 7th meeting of the Working Group contains the *"Master copy of the draft Principles and Comments"*,[58] which changes the number of the Principle containing the "Innocent acquisition rule" from 9 to Principle 8.[59] This is the number in the final version of the Principles, although the title of the Principle would be shortened to "Innocent acquisition".

"Innocent acquisition" is no longer dealt with in three principles, as in the versions of the Fifth and Sixth Working Group meetings, but is dealt with specifically only in Principle 8 and cross-references are made from it to other Principles and vice versa. The "shelter rule", contemplated in the previous version in Principle 10, is included in this version in "Principle 9: Rights of transferees", specifically in the second paragraph.

---

[55] Digital Assets and Private Law Working Group // Sixth session (hybrid) // Rome & Zoom, 31 August – 2 September 2022 //// UNIDROIT 2022 // Study LXXXII – W.G.6 – Doc. 4 // November 2022, p. 30, par. 183.

[56] Digital Assets and Private Law Working Group // Sixth session (hybrid) // Rome & Zoom, 31 August – 2 September 2022 //// UNIDROIT 2022 // Study LXXXII – W.G.6 – Doc. 4 // November 2022, pp. 18–19, par. 109.

[57] Digital Assets and Private Law Working Group // Sixth session (hybrid) // Rome & Zoom, 31 August – 2 September 2022 //// UNIDROIT 2022 // Study LXXXII – W.G.6 – Doc. 4 // November 2022, p. 19, par. 110.

[58] Digital Assets and Private Law Working Group // Seventh session (hybrid) // Rome, 19 – 21 December 2022 //// UNIDROIT 2022 // Study LXXXII – W.G.7 – Doc. 2 // December 2022.

[59] Digital Assets and Private Law Working Group // Seventh session (hybrid) // Rome, 19 – 21 December 2022 //// UNIDROIT 2022 // Study LXXXII – W.G.7 – Doc. 2 // December 2022, p. 29.

This reorganisation seeks to align the innocent acquisition rule with the general structure of the Principles, in particular with Principle 5 on conflict of laws and the *nemo dat* rule of Principle 9.

The Working Group acknowledged that the Geneva Securities Convention[60] had served as a model for the innocent acquisition rule in the UNIDROIT framework[61] . However, application of this rule to digital assets presented unique challenges, necessitating further refinements in the Commentary.

A key issue raised during the session concerned the terminology used in the drafting of Principle 8. A Member of the Working Group suggested that the phrase "good faith purchases" be replaced with "good faith acquisitions", arguing that the latter terminology would be more broadly accepted across jurisdictions.[62] This adjustment was deemed necessary to ensure that the Principles were accessible to both common law and civil law systems. Additionally, it was suggested that the overall language of Principle 8 be harmonized with the rest of the instrument to maintain internal consistency.[63]

A significant discussion point at that session was the applicability of the innocent acquisition rule to non-fungible digital assets, such as NFTs. The Working Group noted that while the rule should apply equally to NFTs, additional clarification was needed to reassure stakeholders that this rule would not enable bad faith actors to exploit the digital asset economy. An Observer from the Uniform Law Commission (UCC) supported the notion that the rule should apply to NFTs in the same manner as to fungible assets, provided that the Commentary clearly explained this application.[64] This clarification was necessary to avoid ambiguity regarding whether NFTs could be acquired free of claims under the innocent acquisition rule.

The shelter principle, which allows a transferee to benefit from the rights of a prior innocent acquirer, was identified as an issue requiring further consideration.[65] While the principle is widely accepted in many legal systems, its application in the digital asset context was still under review.

---

[60] UNIDROIT Convention on Substantive Rules for Intermediated Securities, 2013 (Geneva Securities Convention) https://www.unidroit.org/instruments/capital-markets/geneva-convention.

[61] Digital Assets and Private Law Working Group // Seventh session (hybrid) // Rome & Zoom, 19 – 21 December 2022 //// UNIDROIT 2023 // Study LXXXII – W.G.7 – Doc. 5// February 2023, p. 7, par. 29.

[62] Digital Assets and Private Law Working Group // Seventh session (hybrid) // Rome & Zoom, 19 – 21 December 2022 //// UNIDROIT 2023 // Study LXXXII – W.G.7 – Doc. 5// February 2023, p. 7, par. 30.

[63] Digital Assets and Private Law Working Group // Seventh session (hybrid) // Rome & Zoom, 19 – 21 December 2022 //// UNIDROIT 2023 // Study LXXXII – W.G.7 – Doc. 5// February 2023, p. 7, par. 30.

[64] Digital Assets and Private Law Working Group // Seventh session (hybrid) // Rome & Zoom, 19 – 21 December 2022 //// UNIDROIT 2023 // Study LXXXII – W.G.7 – Doc. 5// February 2023, p. 7, par. 31.

[65] Digital Assets and Private Law Working Group // Seventh session (hybrid) // Rome & Zoom, 19 – 21 December 2022 //// UNIDROIT 2023 // Study LXXXII – W.G.7 – Doc. 5// February 2023, p. 7, par. 29.

The Working Group approved the draft of Principle 8, expecting the Drafting Committee to further refine the Commentary in subsequent sessions.[66]

2.4.8 Eighth Meeting of the Working Group (March 2023)

The Eighth Working Group meeting is the last meeting held by the Working Group. Consequently, unlike all previous meetings, the documents for this meeting do not include an "Issues paper" or a "Summary Report", but rather documents of a more conclusive nature. With regard to the issue at hand, Innocent Acquisition, three documents are of interest: two versions of the almost final draft of the "Principles and Commentary" (one with visible changes[67] and the other without them[68]) and the document entitled "Digital Assets and Private Law consultation submissions",[69] which contains the results of the second public consultation on the draft "Principles on Digital Assets and Private Law" carried out by the Working Group.

The wording of the final version of Principle 8 of the UNIDROIT Principles on Digital Assets and Private Law is slightly different from that contained in the draft Principles for the Eighth Meeting of the Working Group, although with only minimal differences.[70]

At the time of the Eighth Working Group Meeting, the Principle of Innocent Acquisition had already been solidified as a fundamental component of the UNIDROIT Principles on Digital Assets and Private Law. Principle 8 explicitly establishes the criteria for an "innocent acquirer" and provides a framework for determining whether a transferee can take a digital asset free of conflicting proprietary rights.[71]

---

[66] Digital Assets and Private Law Working Group // Seventh session (hybrid) // Rome & Zoom, 19 – 21 December 2022 //// UNIDROIT 2023 // Study LXXXII – W.G.7 – Doc. 5// February 2023, p. 7, par. 32.

[67] Digital Assets and Private Law Working Group // Eighth session (hybrid) // Rome, 8 – 10 March 2023 //// UNIDROIT 2023 // Study LXXXII – W.G.8 – Doc. 3 // February 2023.

[68] Digital Assets and Private Law Working Group // Eighth session (hybrid) // Rome, 8 – 10 March 2023 //// UNIDROIT 2023 // Study LXXXII – W.G.8 – Doc. 2 // February 2023.

[69] Digital Assets and Private Law Working Group // Eighth session (hybrid) // Rome, 8 – 10 March 2023 //// UNIDROIT 2023 // Study LXXXII – W.G.8 – Doc. 4 // February 2023.

[70] In the version from the Eighth meeting of the Working Group, Principle 8(1)(b) has a wording that is not definitive. The following text appears in brackets: "[a State should specify requirements equivalent to those found in its relevant good faith acquisition, finality, and take-free rules.]". This text is replaced in the final version by the following: "comply with requirements equivalent to those found in the relevant good faith acquisition and take-free rules as specified by the relevant State".

In the final version of Principle 8, paragraph (5) existing in the Eighth meeting version is removed, where it states that "(i)n this Principle, 'digital asset' includes a resulting digital asset".

[71] Paragraph (6) of the Eighth meeting version, which corresponds to paragraph (5) of the final version, has slight differences in its first paragraph, regarding the numbering of the internal reference to Principle 5 made in both versions.

The wording of paragraph (7) in the Eighth meeting version, which corresponds to paragraph (6) in the final version, is less detailed, but both versions convey the same idea.

Digital Assets and Private Law Working Group // Eighth session (hybrid) // Rome, 8 – 10 March 2023 //// UNIDROIT 2023 // Study LXXXII – W.G.8 – Doc. 2 // February 2023, p. 32.

By the Eighth Working Group Meeting, Principle 8 had been firmly established as a fundamental rule governing the innocent acquisition of digital assets. The innocent acquisition rule is formulated in a manner that aligns digital assets with negotiable instruments and other forms of property subject to good faith acquisition rules. This reflects a policy choice favouring transactional security over proprietary claims by prior owners who may have been victims of wrongdoing.[72]

The Principle sets forth that, in order to qualify as an innocent acquirer, a transferee must obtain control of a digital asset and comply with the requirements specified by the relevant jurisdiction regarding good faith acquisition, finality, and take-free rules.[73] It also recognizes that an innocent acquirer takes the asset free of conflicting proprietary rights and that no claims based on such rights can be successfully asserted against them.[74]

A notable aspect of Principle 8 is its provision that an innocent acquirer can acquire a proprietary right in a digital asset even if the transferor acted wrongfully or lacked proprietary rights.[75] This principle establishes a critical distinction from traditional *nemo dat* rules, reinforcing the negotiability of digital assets and the fluidity of their transactions.

The Commentary underscores that innocent acquisition confers characteristics similar to negotiability in the context of negotiable instruments and securities to digital assets.[76] However, it acknowledges that this rule may lead to situations where a rightful owner loses their proprietary claim due to an innocent acquisition, thereby striking a policy balance in favour of market efficiency over absolute property protection.[77]

The relationship between innocent acquisition and good faith acquisition is explicitly addressed. While Principle 8 adopts a standard of innocence, it gives States the flexibility to align the rule with their own good faith purchase and take-free rules.[78] The default requirements for innocent acquisition include an absence of actual or

[72] Digital Assets and Private Law Working Group // Eighth session (hybrid) // Rome, 8 – 10 March 2023 //// UNIDROIT 2023 // Study LXXXII – W.G.8 – Doc. 2 // February 2023, p. 33, par. 2.

[73] Digital Assets and Private Law Working Group // Eighth session (hybrid) // Rome, 8 – 10 March 2023 //// UNIDROIT 2023 // Study LXXXII – W.G.8 – Doc. 2 // February 2023, p. 32, Principle 8(1)(a)-(b).

[74] Digital Assets and Private Law Working Group // Eighth session (hybrid) // Rome, 8 – 10 March 2023 //// UNIDROIT 2023 // Study LXXXII – W.G.8 – Doc. 2 // February 2023, p. 32, Principle 8(2)-(3).

[75] Digital Assets and Private Law Working Group // Eighth session (hybrid) // Rome, 8 – 10 March 2023 //// UNIDROIT 2023 // Study LXXXII – W.G.8 – Doc. 2 // February 2023, p. 32, Principle 8(4).

[76] Digital Assets and Private Law Working Group // Eighth session (hybrid) // Rome, 8 – 10 March 2023 //// UNIDROIT 2023 // Study LXXXII – W.G.8 – Doc. 2 // February 2023, p. 33, par. 1.

[77] Digital Assets and Private Law Working Group // Eighth session (hybrid) // Rome, 8 – 10 March 2023 //// UNIDROIT 2023 // Study LXXXII – W.G.8 – Doc. 2 // February 2023, p. 33, par. 2.

[78] Digital Assets and Private Law Working Group // Eighth session (hybrid) // Rome, 8 – 10 March 2023 //// UNIDROIT 2023 // Study LXXXII – W.G.8 – Doc. 2 // February 2023, p. 33, par. 7.

constructive knowledge of conflicting proprietary rights, and the transferee is not under a general duty to investigate such claims.[79]

Additionally, the concept of "innocent client", introduced in Principle 12, adapts the innocent acquisition rule to custodial relationships. The principle establishes that a client for whom a custodian maintains a digital asset cannot be subject to proprietary claims unless the client had or ought to have had knowledge of conflicting rights at the time of acquisition.[80]

2.5 *Relationship with the Standards and Instruments of Other International Organisations or UNIDROIT Itself*

There are several bodies at the international level that have dealt with the regulation and legal treatment of digital assets. The Working Group has taken these standards and instruments of other institutions into consideration and makes explicit reference to them both in its meeting documents[81] and in the text of the Principles.

The regulation of innocent acquisition of digital assets is dealt with in some of these documents, which makes it possible to establish a relationship between them and the *UNIDROIT Principles on Digital Assets and Private Law.*

2.5.1 International Institute for the Unification of Private Law (UNIDROIT)

As mentioned above, the Working Group takes into account the work done within UNIDROIT itself on capital markets and, more specifically, in the area of intermediated securities.[82] This work resulted in the so-called Geneva Securities Convention.[83] In order to ensure that the regulation of innocent acquisition of digital assets receives harmonious treatment in both texts, Principle 8(5)(a) draws from the same criterion as that established in Article 18(1) of the Geneva Securities Convention to determine

79 Digital Assets and Private Law Working Group // Eighth session (hybrid) // Rome, 8 – 10 March 2023 //// UNIDROIT 2023 // Study LXXXII – W.G.8 – Doc. 2 // February 2023, p. 33, par. 6.

80 Digital Assets and Private Law Working Group // Eighth session (hybrid) // Rome, 8 – 10 March 2023 //// UNIDROIT 2023 // Study LXXXII – W.G.8 – Doc. 2 // February 2023, p. 45, par. 1.

81 In Annex I of the "Issues paper" from the first meeting of the Working Group, a comprehensive list of sources from the Institute itself and other organizations on digital assets is provided (Digital Assets and Private Law Working Group // First session (remote) // Rome, 17 – 19 November 2020 //// UNIDROIT 2020 // Study LXXXII – W.G.1 – Doc. 2 // November 2020, pp. 23–24).

82 Digital Assets and Private Law Working Group // First session (remote) // Rome, 17 – 19 November 2020 //// UNIDROIT 2020 // Study LXXXII – W.G.1 – Doc. 2 // November 2020, p. 8, par. 31.

83 UNIDROIT Convention on Substantive Rules for Intermediated Securities (2013) -Geneva Securities Convention- (available in: https://www.unidroit.org/instruments/capital-markets/geneva-con guvention).

one of the requirements to be met by the innocent acquirer,[84] which we will see below: whether the innocent acquirer knows or has an obligation to know that its acquisition is detrimental to the rights of a third-party over the digital asset.

Additionally, the Geneva Securities Convention has a complementary document, the Legislative Guide on Intermediated Securities,[85] whose Legislative Principle 6 deals with the "Protection of an innocent acquirer" in terms very similar to those of Principle 8 as regards the requirements that the innocent acquirer must meet and the consequences of such acquisitions.

2.5.2 United Nations Commission on International Trade Law (UNCITRAL)

There are many synergies between the UNIDROIT Principles on Digital Assets and Private Law and the UNCITRAL Model Law on Electronic Transferable Records.[86] However, in this UNCITRAL document, there is an explicit waiver of addressing the concept of "good faith", because it is considered that the meaning of the principle of good faith applied to the transfer of documents or instruments is different from the meaning of the same principle in international trade law.[87]

On the other hand, Principle 8(1)(b) does refer to good faith and resolves the existence of the different meanings of this concept in the international sphere by referring to the applicable State law for the specific regulation of good faith acquisition.[88]

---

[84] This is provided for in the "Issues paper" of the Fourth session of the Working Group (Digital Assets and Private Law Working Group // Fourth session (remote) // Rome, 2 – 4 November 2021 //// UNIDROIT 2021 // Study LXXXII – W.G.4 – Doc. 2 // October 2021, p. 42, par. 8(e)(viii)).

Accordingly, the final wording of Principle 8(5)(a) ("the transferee actually knows or ought to know that another person has an interest in the digital asset and that the acquisition violates the rights of that other person in relation to its interest") closely follows the wording of Article 18(1) of the Geneva Securities Convention ("an acquirer actually knows or ought to know, at the relevant time, that another person has an interest in securities or intermediated securities and that the credit to the securities account of the acquirer, designating entry or interest granted to the acquirer violates the rights of that other person in relation to its interest").

[85] UNIDROIT Legislative Guide on Intermediated Securities, 2017 (available in: https://www.unidroit.org/instruments/capital-markets/legislative-guide).

[86] UNCITRAL Model Law on Electronic Transferable Records, 2017 (available in: https://uncitral.un.org/sites/uncitral.un.org/files/media-documents/uncitral/en/mletr_ebook_e.pdf).

[87] UNCITRAL Model Law on Electronic Transferable Records, 2017, p. 28, par. 42 (available in: https://uncitral.un.org/sites/uncitral.un.org/files/media-documents/uncitral/en/mletr_ebook_e.pdf).

[88] Commentary 8.7 of the UNIDROIT Principles on Digital Assets and Private Law.

2.5.3 HCCH-UNIDROIT Digital Assets and Tokens Project (DAT Joint Project)

The Hague Conference on Private International Law - *Conférence de La Haye de droit international privé* (HCCH) and UNIDROIT are undertaking a joint project to build on the work done by the UNIDROIT Digital Assets and Private Law Working Group. The project is called HCCH-UNIDROIT Digital Assets and Tokens Project (DAT Joint Project).[89]

The objective of this project is to analyse the text of UNIDROIT Digital Assets and Private Law Principle 5, which was in draft form at the time of the initiation of this joint project, as well as to examine other issues relating to the applicable law to cross-border holdings and transfer of digital assets and tokens, including the "innocent acquisition rule".[90]

The Experts taking part in the DAT Joint Project take the UNIDROIT Principles on Digital Assets and Private Law as a reference for the study of the legal nature of issues such as "transfer", "control" and "acquisition".[91] The more advanced nature of the work carried out by the UNIDROIT Digital Assets and Private Law Working Group, together with the success of this work, confers an influential position to the text of the UNIDROIT Principles on Digital Assets and Private Law in the DAT Joint Project.

2.5.4 ALI-ELI Principles for a Data Economy

Special mention should be made of the joint project between the American Law Institute (ALI) and the European Law Institute (ELI), in the field of the data economy, which has resulted in the draft Principles for a Data Economy. Data Transactions and

[89] HCCH-UNIDROIT Digital Assets and Tokens Joint Project: Report; Prel. Doc. No 3 of January 2024, p. 1, par. 2 (available in: https://assets.hcch.net/docs/efce41ca-1c8c-4d61-9d8b-9348df9303a0.pdf).

See the document of the proposal for the constitution of this joint project, in which another name is used, which makes a more detailed reference to its object of study: Proposal for a Joint Work: HCCH-UNIDROIT Project on Law Applicable to Cross-Border Holdings and Transfers of Digital Assets and Tokens; Prel. Doc. No 3C of January 2023 (available in: https://assets.hcch.net/docs/a91fd233-acf7-4c42-9aad-a426c4565068.pdf).

[90] HCCH-UNIDROIT Digital Assets and Tokens Joint Project: Report; Prel. Doc. No 3 of January 2024, p. 10, par. 12 (available in: https://assets.hcch.net/docs/efce41ca-1c8c-4d61-9d8b-9348df9303a0.pdf).

[91] HCCH-UNIDROIT Digital Assets and Tokens Joint Project: Report; Prel. Doc. No 3 of January 2024, p. 10, par. 12 (available in: https://assets.hcch.net/docs/efce41ca-1c8c-4d61-9d8b-9348df9303a0.pdf).

Data Rights of 2021.[92] Through these Principles, both Institutes seek to facilitate commercial transactions between the United States and Europe involving data.[93]

The concepts "data" and "digital asset" are related. Principle 3(1)(a) of the Principles for a Data Economy. Data Transactions and Data Rights defines "data" as "information recorded in any machine-readable format suitable for automated processing, stored in any medium or as it is being transmitted".

The Principles for a Data Economy. Data Transactions and Data Rights do not expressly deal with innocent acquisition, but synergies can be established with regard to their treatment of "wrongful acquisition" and the concept of "good faith" related to this type of acquisition.

Principle 34 of the Principles for a Data Economy. Data Transactions and Data Rights deals with "Wrongfulness taking effect vis-à-vis downstream recipient".[94] It notes that, as in the UNIDROIT Principles on Digital Assets and Private Law, for this acquisition to take place, a number of requirements must be taken into consideration, such as the onerousness of the acquisition (or the existence of losses or gains) and the good faith of the transferee with regard to the lack of knowledge of the wrongfulness in the acquisition of the digital assets.[95]

2.5.5 Draft Common Frame of Reference (DCFR)

The Draft Common Frame of Reference (DCFR) is an academic study that was submitted to the Commission of the European Union in 2008 for consideration regarding its integration into a political Common Frame of Reference.[96] As an

---

92 American Law Institute and European Law Institute, *Principles for a Data Economy. Data Transactions and Data Rights*, adopted by the ALI on May 18, 2021 and by the ELI on September 1, 2021 (available in: https://principlesforadataeconomy.org/fileadmin/user_upload/p_principlesforadataeconomy/Files/Principles_for_a_Data_Economy_ELI_Final_Council_Draft.pdf).

93 Principle 1: Purpose of these Principles, *Principles for a Data Economy. Data Transactions and Data Rights.*

See American Law Institute and European Law Institute, *Principles for a Data Economy. Data Transactions and Data Rights*, adopted by the ALI on May 18, 2021 and by the ELI on September 1, 2021, p. 6 (available in: https://principlesforadataeconomy.org/fileadmin/user_upload/p_principlesforadataeconomy/Files/Principles_for_a_Data_Economy_ELI_Final_Council_Draft.pdf).

94 American Law Institute and European Law Institute, *Principles for a Data Economy. Data Transactions and Data Rights*, adopted by the ALI on May 18, 2021 and by the ELI on September 1, 2021, p. 218 (available in: https://principlesforadataeconomy.org/fileadmin/user_upload/p_principlesforadataeconomy/Files/Principles_for_a_Data_Economy_ELI_Final_Council_Draft.pdf).

95 American Law Institute and European Law Institute, *Principles for a Data Economy. Data Transactions and Data Rights*, adopted by the ALI on May 18, 2021 and by the ELI on September 1, 2021, pp. 225–227 (available in: https://principlesforadataeconomy.org/fileadmin/user_upload/p_principlesforadataeconomy/Files/Principles_for_a_Data_Economy_ELI_Final_Council_Draft.pdf).

96 European Parliament – Directorate General for Internal Policies – Policy Department C: Citizens' Rights and Constitutional Affairs – Legal Affairs, *The Common Frame of Reference: an optional instrument?*, Brussels, 2010, p. 5 (available in: https://www.europarl.europa.eu/document/activities/cont/201004/20100430ATT73925/20100430ATT73925EN.pdf).

academic document, it is an optional instrument, which serves to provide legal practitioners acting within the European Union with a basic legal basis to refer to when establishing transnational legal relationships that are not governed by the law of one State.[97] The DCFR is inspired by the *Restatements of the Law* and *Principles of Law* of the *American Law Institute*,[98] which serve a similar function for US lawyers when dealing with the law and not only with the rules applicable in a single US state.

The comparative study of the DCFR and the *UNIDROIT Principles on Digital Assets and Private Law* helps to contrast their value and usefulness in a legal and economic field as relevant as the European Union.

The DCFR devotes Chapter 3 of Book VIII to the "Good faith acquisition of ownership".[99] Its regulation of good faith acquisition is much more detailed than that of the innocent acquisition of UNIDROIT Digital Assets and Private Law Principle 8. To give an example, Article VIII.-3:1001 (Good faith acquisition of ownership), paragraph (1)(b) of the DCFR refers to "delivery or equivalent of delivery" which is something that ties in with the Roman '*traditio*', so deeply rooted in civil law legal cultures. This greater degree of detail in the DCFG is provided for by Principle 8 itself, since it refers to the law of States, where applicable, and although the DCFR is not the rule of a State, but an international instrument, because it is an instrument that refers to a smaller number of legal systems than the UNIDROIT Principles on Digital Assets and Private Law, a greater number of shared legal features appear in it. What is important though, is that all the requirements of Principle 8 are reflected in Chapter 3 of the DCFR.

2.5.6 Uniform Commercial Code Amendments (2022)

The Uniform Commercial Code Amendments (2022)[100] adopted by the Uniform Law Commission and the American Law Institute do not devote a specific provision to regulate innocent acquisition, but in its definition of "qualifying purchaser" of a "controllable electronic record", contained in Section 12–102(a)(2)[101] we find that the requirements that must be met by the "innocent acquirer" of "digital assets", in

---

[97] The version of the DFCRs that we have handled is contained in Jerez Delgado (2015). The translation contained in that edition has been made in the context of a project funded by the European Commission, although the European Commission does not accept any responsibility for the accuracy of the translated text.

[98] The various *Restatements of the Law* and *Principles of the Law* published by The American Law Institute are available in: https://www.ali.org/publications#publication-type-restatements.

[99] Jerez Delgado (2015), p. 355.

[100] National Conference of Commissioners on Uniform State Laws (Uniform Law Commission) and American Law Institute, *Uniform Commercial Code Amendments* (2022), approved in July 2022 (available in: https://www.uniformlaws.org/viewdocument/final-act-164?CommunityKey=1457c422-ddb7-40b0-8c76-39a1991651ac&tab=librarydocuments).

[101] Section 12–102(a)(2) Uniform Commercial Code Amendments (2022): "'Qualifying purchaser' means a purchaser of a controllable electronic record or an interest in a controllable electronic record that obtains control of the controllable electronic record for value, in good faith, and without notice of a claim of a property right in the controllable electronic record".

accordance with UNIDROIT Digital Assets and Private Law Principle 8, make it easier to understand the provisions of this Principle.

2.5.7 European Union

The EU's approach to the regulation of digital assets, which the EU commonly refers to as crypto-assets, is very different from that of the UNIDROIT Principles on Digital Assets and Private Law. The European Union regulates crypto-assets from a substantive point of view, whereas, as we know, the Principles seek to resolve the determination of the law applicable to legal relationships over digital assets and, exceptionally, deal with substantive regulation by addressing *innocent acquisition* and the *nemo dat* rule.

Interestingly, the EU regulation does not deal with the "innocent acquisition rule" contained in UNIDROIT Digital Assets and Private Law Principle 8. Perhaps the European Union delegates this matter to State regulation to an even greater degree than the UNIDROIT Principles because of its smaller geographical scope and the differences between the legal cultures concerned, in which innocent acquisition is satisfactorily regulated.

However, there is concern in EU law about the existence of fraud, cyber threats or negligence, which can lead to changes in ownership of crypto-assets. This can be seen in one of the most prominent EU rules on crypto-assets, Regulation (EU) 2023/1114 of the European Parliament and of the Council of 31 May 2023 on crypto-asset markets, amending Regulations (EU) No. 1093/2010 and (EU) No. 1095/2010, and Directives (EU) 2013/36/EU and (EU) 2019/1937 (known as the MiCA Regulation). Article 75(3) of the MiCA Regulation provides that crypto-asset service providers who provide custody and administration of crypto-assets on behalf of their customers must minimise the risk of loss of the crypto-assets themselves, or the rights to them, as a result of such fraud, hacking, cyber threats or negligence. This concern is also reflected in the obligation to refer to fraudulent acts, losses and unwanted changes of ownership of crypto-assets in the reports to be submitted to the European Parliament and the Council by the Commission,[102] the European Securities and Markets Authority (ESMA) and the European Banking Authority (EBA).[103]

Another important piece of legislation in this area is Regulation (EU) 2022/858 of the European Parliament and of the Council of 30 May 2022 on a pilot scheme for

---

[102] Article 140 of the MiCA Regulation requires the Commission to submit two reports, one in June 2025 and one in June 2027, on the implementation of the MiCA Regulation, accompanied, if appropriate, by a legislative proposal. Specifically, Article 140(2)(f) of the MiCA Regulation foresees that the report should cover the number of cases in which crypto-assets are subject to fraud, hacking, cyber-attacks, theft, etc.

[103] Article 141 of the MiCA Regulation requires ESMA and the EBA to submit from 2025 onwards a joint annual report on the implementation of the MiCA Regulation and on developments in crypto-asset markets. Article 141(k) of the MiCA Regulation refers to the need to report specifically on the number of fraudulent acts linked to crypto-assets.

market infrastructures based on decentralised registry technology, amending Regulations (EU) No. 600/2014 and (UE) n. 909/2014 and the Directive 2014/65/UE. It imposes an obligation on market infrastructure operators to ensure the technical security of IT systems so as to prevent risks of fraud, negligence, loss, unauthorised access, etc. affecting crypto-assets and their holders.[104]

2.6 *The Concepts of "Digital Asset" and "Control" as Essential Elements of the Innocent Acquisition Scheme*

Principle 2(2) contains a definition of "digital asset". According to this Principle, a digital asset is "an electronic record capable of being controlled".

In these lines, our interest focuses on highlighting the aspects of the concept of digital assets that are more directly related to their innocent acquisition.

First of all, it is worth considering that a digital asset has the status of property. Within this category, a digital asset is an asset with a proprietary content that can be the subject of property rights or rights in rem, as provided for in Principle 3(1). In innocent acquisition, the acquirer or transferee acquires ownership rights in the digital asset and, in the interest of market certainty, the previous legitimate owner of that digital asset is divested of those rights.

The Principles are not concerned with all types of digital data, but only those that can be characterised as an "asset", and there are even some types of "assets" that do not fall within the scope of the Principles.[105]

The term "asset" may encompass various meanings. However, for the purposes of the Principles, it refers to an object to which value is ascribed, meaning that individuals are willing to exchange other valuable objects (such as fiat currency) to acquire it. The Principles are concerned with assets that are transferable and, in many instances, specifically designed for trading. Consistent with UNIDROIT's objectives, the focus of the Principles is on digital assets that are created and transferred within the context of commercial transactions.[106]

---

[104] Art. 11.1.b) Regulation (EU) 2022/858 of the European Parliament and of the Council of 30 May 2022 on a pilot scheme for market infrastructures based on decentralised registry technology and amending Regulations (EU) n. 600/2014 and (EU) n. 909/2014 and Directive 2014/65/EU.

[105] Digital Assets and Private Law Working Group // First session (remote) // Rome, 17 – 19 November 2020 //// UNIDROIT 2020 // Study LXXXII – W.G.1 – Doc. 2 // November 2020, p. 9, par. 38.

[106] Digital Assets and Private Law Working Group // First session (remote) // Rome, 17 – 19 November 2020 //// UNIDROIT 2020 // Study LXXXII – W.G.1 – Doc. 2 // November 2020, p. 9, par. 39.

Accordingly, the Principles primarily concern digital assets that can plausibly be regarded as objects of property rights.[107] Some examples of digital data that do fall within the scope of the Principles are cryptocurrencies (e.g., Bitcoin) and digital assets that, in some manner, represent, are backed by, or are linked to other assets (e.g., commodities). Conversely, certain categories of electronic data, such as digital images, fall outside the scope of the Principles.[108]

Some types of digital data may be structured to represent other assets, such that the holder of the digital data claims to have a proprietary right in that other asset. Digital data in such a structure may be considered a digital asset in its own right or simply a digital record. The Principles assume the former characterisation for the sake of simplicity of terminology.[109] Accordingly, when the process of transferring the digital asset takes place, the proprietary right to that other asset is transferred to the acquirer.[110] From a terminological point of view, it is important to underline that, in the opinion of the members of the *Digital Assets and Private Law Working Group* the "mechanism of linking one asset to another is sometimes called tokenisation, but what matters is the mechanism itself, and focusing on 'tokens' may be misleading in a proper legal analysis".[111] Consequently, the terms "token" and "coin" are accepted by the members of the Working Group as "colloquial" terminology.

Secondly, the concept of control, which is part of the concept of "digital assets", is noteworthy. Principle 6 deals with the concept of "control" and its regime. Commentary 6.1 rightly emphasises that "control is a *factual* concept that is separate from economic rights and need not accompany them". One who has control over a digital asset enjoys two fundamental issues: first, a triple capacity over the digital asset, described in Principle 6(1)(a); second, to be identified as having that triple capacity, as provided for in Principle 6(1)(b). The three capacities with which a person in control of a digital asset is vested are: the exclusive ability to prevent others from

---

[107] Digital Assets and Private Law Working Group // First session (remote) // Rome, 17 – 19 November 2020 //// UNIDROIT 2020 // Study LXXXII – W.G.1 – Doc. 2 // November 2020, p. 9, par. 40.

[108] Digital Assets and Private Law Working Group // First session (remote) // Rome, 17 – 19 November 2020 //// UNIDROIT 2020 // Study LXXXII – W.G.1 – Doc. 2 // November 2020, p. 10, par. 41.

[109] Digital Assets and Private Law Working Group // First session (remote) // Rome, 17 – 19 November 2020 //// UNIDROIT 2020 // Study LXXXII – W.G.1 – Doc. 2 // November 2020, p. 14, par. 59.

[110] Examples of this type of structure are when a digital asset gives a right to physical goods such as gold (see e.g. https://www.gcoin.com) or art (see e.g. https://en.cryptonomist.ch/2020/07/04/tokenized-art/); or when a digital asset represents a debt security, such as 'tokenised' corporate bonds (see e.g. https://www.financemagnates.com/institutional-forex/exchanges/gibraltar-stock-exchange-tooffer-digital-debt-securities/)" (Digital Assets and Private Law Working Group // First session (remote) // Rome, 17 – 19 November 2020 //// UNIDROIT 2020 // Study LXXXII – W.G.1 – Doc. 2 // November 2020, p. 14, par. 59).

[111] Digital Assets and Private Law Working Group // First session (remote) // Rome, 17 – 19 November 2020 //// UNIDROIT 2020 // Study LXXXII – W.G.1 – Doc. 2 // November 2020, p. 14, par. 59.

obtaining the full benefits of the digital asset[112]; the ability to obtain the full benefits of the digital asset,[113] and the ability to transfer to another person the two capacities just mentioned.[114] This concept of control is more comprehensive and, in our view, more precise than that formulated in other international instruments.[115]

Principle 6(2) deals with the concept of "change of control", which will help us below when analysing the details of innocent acquisition.

2.7 The Requirements for the Innocent Acquisition of Digital Assets When the Applicable Law is the Law of the Relevant State

This category of requirements for the innocent acquisition of a digital asset is set out in Principle 8(1). As we shall see, Principle 8(5) also sets out another category of requirements, which apply when the circumstances described therein are met.

The first requirement is to obtain control of the digital asset.[116] The second is to comply with the essential requirements of the applicable legal system of the State concerned relating to "good faith acquisition and take-free rules".[117]

In relation to the first requirement, obtaining control of the digital asset, Principle 6(2) provides for what is meant by "change of control". Thus, control is changed when there is a transfer of the triple capacity referred to in Principle 6(1)(a) to another person, who, in this case, is the innocent acquirer.

Recall that control is a technical factual concept, largely separate and apart from economic rights, but it is a presupposition for the occurrence of legal consequences attached to digital assets.[118] Control is functionally equivalent to the possession of movable property. The digital asset is an intangible good, therefore, the functional equivalence of control with possession means that the person with control has exclusive power or capacity over the asset - an exclusivity that can be qualified, according to the rules of Principle 6(3).

---

[112] UNIDROIT Digital Assets and Private Law Principle 6(1)(a)(i).

[113] UNIDROIT Digital Assets and Private Law Principle 6(1)(a)(ii).

[114] UNIDROIT Digital Assets and Private Law Principle 6(1)(a)(iii).

[115] European Law Institute, *Principles on the Use of Digital Assets as Security*, 2022, p. 17 (available in: https://www.europeanlawinstitute.eu/fileadmin/user_upload/p_eli/Publications/ELI_Principles_on_the_Use_of_Digital_Assets_as_Security.pdf), in which "Definitions" it is provided that "'control' in respect of a digital asset means the legal power or factual capability of any natural or legal person to deal in and/or extinguish such assets, as the case may be".

[116] UNIDROIT Digital Assets and Private Law Principle 8(1)(a) and Commentary 8.5 of the UNIDROIT Principles on Digital Assets and Private Law.

[117] UNIDROIT Digital Assets and Private Law Principle 8(1)(b) and Commentary 8.7 of the UNIDROIT Principles on Digital Assets and Private Law.

[118] Commentary 6.1 of the UNIDROIT Principles on Digital Assets and Private Law.

The acquisition of control over the digital asset is a necessary, but not sufficient, precondition for achieving the legal status of innocent acquirer.[119] By means of control and the capacities it confers, the innocent acquirer can exclude other persons from enjoying the benefits of the digital asset. Among those persons excluded from enjoyment is the former rightful owner of the digital asset.[120]

The second requirement is compliance with the requirements of the applicable legal system of the State concerned that are essential for "good faith acquisition and take-free rules". By establishing this measure, Principle 8(1)(b) refers to two issues that may constitute the main rational reason behind the UNIDROIT Principles on Digital Assets and Private Law: the first is the existence of differences between the private law of different national States; the second is the need for the parties to an international legal relationship between private parties to choose a body of law or regulation that will help them to resolve those differences. Such applicable law or regulation may be the national law of a State[121] or it may be other types of provisions such as bilateral international treaties, multilateral international conventions or sources of non-governmental origin. When it is clearly established that the innocent acquisition of a digital asset is governed by the rules of a State, the other essential requirements of that State for the good faith acquisition and take-free rule of other types of assets must be met in addition to taking control. This is not the place for an exhaustive analysis of those requirements or the differences among different national legal systems. What we can point out, however, is that what is usually required by the laws of the States is that there must be good faith on the part of the acquirer in terms of his/her unawareness of the fact that there is a person who has been deprived of his/her legitimate ownership of the digital asset. On the other hand, there are dissimilarities in different legal systems as to whether it is strictly necessary for the innocent acquirer to have acquired the asset for valuable consideration or whether, on the contrary, acquisition also occurs if the acquirer obtained the asset free of charge.

2.8 The Rights and Entitlements of the Innocent Acquirer of Digital Assets

As far as the rights and entitlements of the innocent acquirer are concerned, the innocent acquirer is not affected by conflicting economic rights in the digital asset.[122] Moreover, if a person seeks to assert a claim based on an economic interest in the digital asset, he cannot successfully enforce it against the innocent acquirer.[123]

[119] Commentaries 6.4 and 6.9 of the UNIDROIT Principles on Digital Assets and Private Law.

[120] Commentary 6.1 of the UNIDROIT Principles on Digital Assets and Private Law.

[121] Commentary 8.7 of the UNIDROIT Principles on Digital Assets and Private Law.

[122] UNIDROIT Digital Assets and Private Law Principle 8(2) and Commentary 8.1 of the UNIDROIT Principles on Digital Assets and Private Law.

[123] UNIDROIT Digital Assets and Private Law Principle 8(3) and Commentary 8.1 of the UNIDROIT Principles on Digital Assets and Private Law.

The strength of the legal position of the innocent acquirer of digital assets under Principles 8(2) and 8(3) derives from the negotiability that characterises the nature of digital assets.[124] Negotiability is an essential feature of marketable securities, securities, book-entry securities and other assets that are traded in markets, especially markets in financial instruments. Negotiability, in turn, is based on autonomy, which is a characteristic feature of securities, whose legal regime is centuries-old and in some respects has served as the basis for the digital assets regime. If a person acquires an autonomous right, this means that he acquires it free of any rights and claims that third parties may have against the previous holder of that right. Autonomy and tradability are features of the rights contained in digital assets, which make their transfer and acquisition on the market secure.

2.9 Innocent Acquisition by an Intentional Transferor with no Proprietary Interest in the Digital Asset

Principle 8(4) recognises the extent of the legal effects of innocent acquisition, as it accepts that a proprietary right can be acquired even if the change of control over the digital asset is made maliciously by a transferor who has no proprietary right over the asset-Commentary 8.3.

This scenario is known as acquisition *a non domino*. In this case, a person, e.g. a hacker, wrongfully and maliciously changes control over a digital asset. By virtue of this change of control, the legitimate owner of the digital asset is deprived of his right over it and the innocent acquirer becomes the new owner. The wrongfully dispossessed owner will not be able to successfully enforce his claim against the innocent acquirer, but must direct his claim against the wrongdoer. The latter is rather difficult in the markets and systems in which digital assets are traded, as some of those involved in them act under pseudonyms-Commentary 8.4. However, the vast experience of the markets for financial instruments and the experience of the digital asset markets themselves make it advisable to exceptionally break with the *ubi rem meam invenio, ibi vindico* in this case, and thus to enhance traffic safety—Commentary 8.4-.

2.10 The Specific Requirements of Innocent Acquisition When the Principles are Applied in Preference to Other Law

The requirements of Principle 8(1) apply when innocent acquisition is governed by the national law of a State.

---

[124] Commentaries 8.2 and 8.5 of the UNIDROIT Principles on Digital Assets and Private Law.

When, under Principle 5(1), innocent acquisition is governed by the UNIDROIT Principles on Digital Assets and Private Law, innocent acquisition is achieved if the requirements of Principle 8(5) are met.

Principle 5 is entitled "Applicable law" and aims at improving clarity and legal certainty in the area of conflict of laws.[125] Principle 5(1) sets out criteria for determining the law applicable to property issues relating to a digital asset.[126]

The requirements contained in Principle 8(5) for the innocent acquisition of digital assets appear broader than those of Principle 8(1). This apparent broadness is due to the fact that Principle 8(1) refers to the law of the State whose law is applicable, whereas Principle 8(5) explicitly spells out the requirements under the Principles for the innocent acquisition of digital assets.

The first of the requirements is also the acquisition of control of the digital asset, and in this respect Principle 8(5) refers to Principle 8(1)(a).

This requirement is supplemented by the requirements listed below.

Principle 8(5)(a) deprives a person of the status of innocent acquirer when obtaining control of the digital asset, if he knew or ought to have known that there is another person with an interest in the digital asset and that the acquisition infringes that person's rights.

Principle 8(5)(b) sets out the criteria to be taken into account in determining whether a person should have known of an interest or fact about a digital asset. Thus, on the one hand, the characteristics of the relevant market for the digital asset should be taken into account. On the other hand, it must be clarified whether the person lacks a general duty to inquire or investigate. If the person in question is exempt from such a duty to inquire or investigate, the threshold is lowered for the purpose of determining whether he should have known that there was another person with an interest in the digital asset. In the same vein, it will be easier to presume that the innocent acquirer was unaware that its acquisition infringes the rights of that other person with an interest in the digital asset.

When it is an entity or organisation that should know of the interest or fact about a digital asset, Principle 8(5)(c) provides that knowledge is required from the time when the person responsible for the matter could reasonably have known of the interest or fact.

Principle 8(5)(d) provides that there is no innocent acquisition if the transfer of the digital asset is made by way of gift or otherwise gratuitously and is not the granting of a security right.

[125] Commentary 5.1. of the UNIDROIT Principles on Digital Assets and Private Law.

[126] Commentary 8.10. of the UNIDROIT Principles on Digital Assets and Private Law.

2.11 *The Rights and Responsibilities of the Transferee of a Digital Asset who is not an Innocent Acquirer (the Shelter Principle)*

If a transferee is not an innocent acquirer, the Principles will not apply, but another law will apply to determine what rights and liabilities it may have. However, Principle 8(6) provides that Principle 9 applies.

Principle 9(1) contains the *nemo dat quod non habet* rule. Principle 9(2) formulates the shelter principle: a "transferee of proprietary rights in a digital asset acquires all of the proprietary rights that its transferor had or had the power to transfer".[127] However, the 'shelter principle' is qualified by the second proposition of Principle 9(2), which provides that, if a transferor does not transfer all of his proprietary rights on the digital asset, the transferee acquires only the proprietary rights which the transferor transferred.[128]

Consequently, under the shelter principle of Principle 9, a transferee who is an innocent acquirer of proprietary rights in a digital asset and any subsequent transferees acquire the rights of the innocent acquirer, but no more. It will therefore be free from claims asserted against it by third parties who claim to have any rights in the digital asset. The transferee will benefit from the shelter principle even if, at the time of acquisition, it did not meet the requirements of an innocent acquirer (e.g. if it was aware that its acquisition would be detrimental to the rights of a third party in the digital asset[129]).[130]

References

Digital Assets and Private Law Working Group // First session (remote) // Rome, 17 – 19 November 2020 //// UNIDROIT 2020 // Study LXXXII – W.G.1 – Doc. 2 // November 2020.
Exploratory Workshop on Digital Assets and Private Law // Rome and Zoom (17 – 18 September 2020) //// UNIDROIT 2021 // Study LXXXII – W.G.1 – Doc. 3 // March 2021.
Digital Assets and Private Law Working Group // First session (remote) // Rome, 17 – 19 November 2020 //// UNIDROIT 2021 // Study LXXXII – W.G.1 – Doc. 4 // March 2021.
Digital Assets and Private Law Working Group // Second session (remote) // Rome, 16 – 18 March 2021 //// UNIDROIT 2021 // Study LXXXII – W.G.2 – Doc. 1 // March 2021.
Digital Assets and Private Law Working Group // Second session (remote) // Rome, 16 – 18 March 2021 //// UNIDROIT 2021 // Study LXXXII – W.G.2 – Doc. 2 (rev. 1) // March 2021.
Digital Assets and Private Law Working Group // Second session (remote) // Rome, 16 – 18 March 2021 //// UNIDROIT 2021 // Study LXXXII – W.G.2 – Doc. 3 // April 2021.

---

[127] Commentary 9.2 of the UNIDROIT Principles on Digital Assets and Private Law expresses the "shelter principle" more clearly: "a transferee acquires all the proprietary rights of the transferor that were transferred or that the transferor had the power to transfer".

[128] Commentary 9.2 of the UNIDROIT Principles on Digital Assets and Private Law.

[129] In this case, exceptionally, the provisions of UNIDROIT Digital Assets and Private Law Principle 8(5)(a) would not be fulfilled.

[130] Commentary 9.3 of the UNIDROIT Principles on Digital Assets and Private Law.

Digital Assets and Private Law Working Group // Third session (remote) // Rome, 30 June – 2 July 2021 //// UNIDROIT 2021 // Study LXXXII – W.G.3 – Doc. 2 (rev. 1) // June 2021.
Digital Assets and Private Law Working Group // Third session (remote) // Rome, 30 June – 2 July 2021 //// UNIDROIT 2021 // Study LXXXII – W.G.3 – Doc. 4 // July 2021.
Digital Assets and Private Law Working Group // Fourth session (remote) // Rome, 2 – 4 November 2021 //// UNIDROIT 2021 // Study LXXXII – W.G.4 – Doc. 2 // October 2021.
Digital Assets and Private Law Working Group // Fourth session (remote) // Rome, 2 – 4 November 2021 //// UNIDROIT 2021 // Study LXXXII – W.G.4 – Doc. 3 // December 2021.
Digital Assets and Private Law Working Group // Fifth session (remote) // Rome, 7 – 9 March 2022 //// UNIDROIT 2022 // Study LXXXII – W.G.5 – Doc. 2 // February 2022.
Digital Assets and Private Law Working Group // Fifth session (remote) // Rome, 7 – 9 March 2022 //// UNIDROIT 2021 // Study LXXXII – W.G.5 – Doc. 3 // February 2022.
Digital Assets and Private Law Working Group // Fifth session (remote) // Rome, 7 – 9 March 2022 //// UNIDROIT 2022 // Study LXXXII – W.G.5 – Doc. 4 // April 2022.
Digital Assets and Private Law Working Group // Sixth session (hybrid) // Rome, 31 August – 2 September 2022 //// UNIDROIT 2022 // Study LXXXII – W.G.6 – Doc. 2 // August 2022.
Digital Assets and Private Law Working Group // Sixth session (hybrid) // Rome, 31 August – 2 September 2022 //// UNIDROIT 2022 // Study LXXXII – W.G.6 – Doc. 3 – ANNEX.
Digital Assets and Private Law Working Group // Sixth session (hybrid) // Rome & Zoom, 31 August – 2 September 2022 //// UNIDROIT 2022 // Study LXXXII – W.G.6 – Doc. 4 // November 2022.
Digital Assets and Private Law Working Group // Seventh session (hybrid) // Rome, 19 – 21 December 2022 //// UNIDROIT 2022 // Study LXXXII – W.G.7 – Doc. 2 // December 2022.
Digital Assets and Private Law Working Group // Seventh session (hybrid) // Rome & Zoom, 19 – 21 December 2022 //// UNIDROIT 2023 // Study LXXXII – W.G.7 – Doc. 5 // February 2023.
Digital Assets and Private Law Working Group // Eighth session (hybrid) // Rome, 8 – 10 March 2023 //// UNIDROIT 2023 // Study LXXXII – W.G.8 – Doc. 2 // February 2023.
Digital Assets and Private Law Working Group // Eighth session (hybrid) // Rome, 8 – 10 March 2023 //// UNIDROIT 2023 // Study LXXXII – W.G.8 – Doc. 3 // February 2023.
Digital Assets and Private Law Working Group // Eighth session (hybrid) // Rome, 8 – 10 March 2023 //// UNIDROIT 2023 // Study LXXXII – W.G.8 – Doc. 4 // February 2023.
Jerez Delgado C (coord) (2015) Principios, definiciones y reglas de un Derecho Civil europeo: el Marco Común de Referencia (DCFR). Agencia Estatal Boletín Oficial del Estado, Madrid.

Principle 9
Rights of the Transferee

María José Vañó Vañó

(1) In accordance with Principle 8, a person may transfer only the ownership rights, if any, that it has in a digital asset, and no greater ownership rights.

(2) A transferee of ownership rights in a digital asset acquires all the ownership rights that its transfer or had or had the power to transfer, except that the transferee acquires rights only to the extent of the rights that were transferred.

1 Official Commentary

Commentary

Principle 9(1): nemo dat rule

9.1. Principle 9(1) lays down the well-known rule nemo dat quod non habet (you cannot give what you do not have). Principle 9(1) is subject to the acquisition rule of Principle 8, which functions as an exception to the consequences of the application of the nemo dat rule. The effect of Principle 8 is not that the transferor is entitled to transfer more property rights than he has, but that he has the power to do so. Thus, a bona fide acquirer is released from conflicting property rights, and no right based on a property claim can be asserted against a bona fide acquirer.

This work was financed within the framework of the Prometeo 2023 project of the Regional Ministry of Innovation, Universities, Science and Digital Society (CIPROM/2022/26) "Present and future of the regulation of cryptoassets in the EU [LegalCripto]", whose principal investigator is Carmen Pastor Sempere. The basic ideas contained herein were presented in the author's paper with the same title, given on November 13, 2024 at the IV International Congress on "UNIDROIT Principles on Digital Assets and Private Law: Context, Content, Perspectives", organized also by BAES Research Group of the University of Alicante on November 13 and 14, 2024.

The chapter has been written within the framework of the Project TED2021-129787B-I00, funded by MCIN/AEI/10.13039/501100011033 and by the European Union "NextGenerationEU"/PRTR, called KEY SELF-CONSUMPTION COMMUNITIES IN ENERGY TRANSITION (P.I. Vañó).

M. J. Vañó Vañó (✉)
Department of Commercial Law, Manuel Broseta Pont, University of Valencia, Valencia, Spain
e-mail: maria.j.vano@uv.es

C. Pastor Sempere and D. A. Morán Bovio (eds.), UNIDROIT *Principles on Digital Assets and Private Law*, Law, Governance and Technology Series 80,
https://doi.org/10.1007/978-3-032-11001-5_15

Principle 9(2): the safe harbour rule

9.2. Principle 9(2) lays down the principle of estoppel: a transferee acquires all the transferor's property rights that were transferred to him or that the transferor had the capacity to transfer. However, Principle 9(2) makes it clear that, if a transferor transfers less than all of its ownership rights in the digital asset, the transferee only acquires the rights that were transferred.

9.3. Under Principle 9(2), a transferee of a person who was a bona fide acquirer of ownership rights in a digital asset and any subsequent transferee acquires the rights of the bona fide acquirer, i.e. free from conflicting ownership rights and from bringing claims relating to those conflicting rights that may succeed. This is so even if the transferee at the time of the transfer did not meet the applicable requirements as a bona fide acquirer (for example, if it had the knowledge specified in Principle 8(5)(a), if applicable, with respect to the digital asset).

2 Reflections

Principle 9, included in section III on control and transfer of rights, reflects concepts deeply rooted in commercial law, particularly regarding the transfer of goods and rights. In the digital context, this Principle connects to the need for legal certainty in the transfer of intangible assets, such as digital assets, an increasingly relevant issue in modern commerce.

This Principle, on digital assets, addresses the transfer of ownership rights in digital assets, establishing that a transferor can only transfer the rights it has over an asset, which is known as the *nemo dat quod non habet* rule ("no one can transfer more than he has"). This rule is fundamental to ensure legitimacy in the transfer of digital assets, thus protecting bona fide acquirers. Under Principle 8, an exception to this rule is established whereby bona fide acquirers are protected against claims, even if the original transferor did not have full rights to the digital asset. This exception is particularly relevant in a digital environment, where the speed of transactions and the decentralisation of ownership complicate traditional rights verifications.

During the Preparatory Work and Exploratory Workshop, held on 17–18 September 2020, the UNIDROIT Working Group discussed the implications of this Principle, especially as it interacts with Principle 8 on good faith acquisition. The workshop highlighted the relevance of emerging technologies and how they transform the nature of custody and transfer of digital assets,[1] in particular the members discussed how this Principle applies to the transfer of digital assets, raising the challenges arising from the immutable and decentralised nature of the blockchain. It also

[1] UNIDROIT 2020 - Study LXXXII - W.G.1 - Doc. 2, November, pars. 50–56.

notes that civil law systems limit the recognition and transfer of ownership, including exceptions to the *nemo dat* principle, to tangible property.[2]

At the second session, held in March 2021, significant progress was made in the discussion of the *nemo dat* principle *and the protection of the bona fide acquirer*. Group members noted that due to the speed and complexity of digital transactions, there was a need to incorporate a clear framework to enable validation of rights acquired in decentralised environments. In addition, the concept of "control" over digital assets, rather than mere formal ownership, was discussed as a key indicator for determining the validity of the transfer of rights. It was emphasised that actual control over a digital asset should be the basis for ensuring the legal certainty of transactions, thus adjusting the *nemo dat* principle to the digital context[3].

At the third session, in June 2021, the initial drafts of the Principles were reviewed, including those related to the transfer of rights and good faith acquisition. During the discussions, experts emphasised that the speed of transactions in the digital domain required stronger mechanisms to ensure that acquired rights were effective, regardless of possible flaws in the chain of title. This led to the proposal of the "safe harbour rule," which ensures that an acquirer who has acted in good faith is not harmed by earlier errors in the chain of title. It was discussed how to apply this rule within the general framework of the UNIDROIT Principles to ensure that acquirers in good faith could rely on the legitimacy of digital asset transfers[4].

The Commentary to Principle 9 was developed in detail at the Seventh Session of the Working Group in December 2022[5], during which it was reaffirmed that a bona fide transferee should be protected in digital asset transactions, even when the original transferor does not hold all full rights to the asset. This protection is reflected in the possibility of acquiring rights free of conflict, provided that the good faith criteria set out in Principle 8 are met.

This Principle also corresponds to international standards, such as those developed by UNCITRAL. The private international law approach and interoperability with the UNIDROIT Principles ensures that vested rights are clear, transparent and properly supported globally, providing a robust legal framework for jurisdictions that adopt it.

---

[2] UNIDROIT 2020 - Study LXXXII – W.G.2 – Doc. 3, pars. 27–30, The discussion addresses the issue that civil law systems limit the recognition and transfer of ownership, including exceptions to the *nemo dat* principle, to tangible assets. This approach creates significant challenges for digital transactions, where assets are intangible and traditional rules do not provide adequate solutions.

[3] UNIDROIT 2020 - Study LXXXII - W.G.2 - Doc. 3, 16–18 March, pars. 27, 30. Par. 27: Initial discussion on the need to adjust traditional principles such as "*nemo dat*" in decentralized systems. It is mentioned that technical control could be key to validating rights. Par. 30: It discusses how digital environments require clear exceptions to the "*nemo dat*" to protect the innocent acquirer in complex contexts.

[4] UNIDROIT 2021 - Study LXXXII - W.G.3 - Doc. 4, July, pars. 30–33. Pars. 35: Introduction of the Safe Harbour Rule, linked to the application of '*nemo dat*' in digital markets, and 41: Emphasis on the legal security of digital transactions, highlighting the importance of technical control over assets as a practical substitute for title deeds, are particularly noteworthy.

[5] UNIDROIT 2023 - Study LXXXII - W.G.7 - Doc. 5, December, pars. 19–21.

At the first session of the Working Group, held in November 2020, the need to protect acquirers of digital assets was discussed, focusing on the legitimate transfer of rights. Issues of "disposition and acquisition" were identified as one of the key issues to be addressed. During the discussions, consideration was given to how to apply the principle *nemo dat quod non habet*, i.e., that no one can transfer more rights than they own. This is particularly relevant in the digital context, where the nature of assets and the speed of transactions complicate traditional ownership verifications. In addition, it was stressed that distributed registry technology, such as blockchains, posed new challenges for the transfer of rights, as the decentralised structure could make it difficult to clearly track the ownership of assets. During the session, it was highlighted that the framework should ensure legal certainty for transferees operating in good faith in these technological environments[6].

Finally, the seventh session, in December 2022, further refined Principle 9, focusing on how to ensure the protection of bona fide acquirers in a context where emerging technologies may complicate the verification of ownership. During this session, it was concluded that it was critical that the adopted Principles provide sufficient flexibility to adapt to technological advances and changes in global digital markets, while still protecting legal stability and market efficiency. Group members also emphasised the importance of an appropriate balance between legal certainty and efficiency of blockchain transactions, integrating best practices from international and European regulation. In particular, paragraph 15 discusses how private keys and technical control should be integrated into the analysis of legal ownership, and paragraphs 19 to 21 developed an in-depth discussion on how to protect the bona fide acquirer and adapt *nemo dat* to the digital context.[7]

These preparatory works cannot be understood without reference to the UNCITRAL Model Law on Electronic Commerce,[8] which also addresses such issues by stressing the importance of transparency and clarity in the assignment of digital rights, establishing a direct correlation with the principles of good faith and the legal certainty that trade in digital assets requires. This reinforces the idea that assignees should be protected against unexpected or conflicting claims on the assets they acquire.

This text is one of the most relevant frameworks in the context of digital commerce and the transfer of digital assets, providing principles that seek to ensure legal certainty and transparency in transactions of this type of assets; a framework that reinforces control, legitimacy and clarity in the transmission of these rights.

In the context of international digital trade, the UNIDROIT Principles on Digital Assets find notable parallels with the United States Uniform Commercial Code (UCC), particularly with regard to the control and protection of transferees. Through its recent Article 12, the UCC regulates controllable electronic assets,

[6] UNIDROIT 2021 - Study LXXXII - W.G.1 - Doc. 4, November, pars. 46–50.

[7] UNIDROIT 2023 - Study LXXXII - W.G.7 - Doc. 5, December, pars. 33–36.

[8] https://uncitral.un.org/sites/uncitral.un.org/files/media-documents/uncitral/en/19-04970_ebook.pdf.

including cryptocurrencies, and establishes standards to ensure safe and legitimate transactions.[9]

UCC defines "control" as the ability to prevent others from obtaining substantial benefit from an asset and the ability to transfer that control to another person (§ 12–105(a)). This concept is aligned with the principles of technical and legal control that the UNIDROIT Principles promote, reinforcing legal certainty in international transactions. In addition, § 12–104(d) UCC includes a safe harbour rule, like that in Principle 9(2), which protects transferees against conflicting claims if the asset was acquired in good faith and with value.

These parallels underscore the convergence of international and national standards, highlighting the importance of harmonising regulatory frameworks to foster trust and interoperability in global digital markets.

The Model Law establishes that, for a digital transaction to be secure, it is essential that market participants are clear about the rights they are acquiring or transferring. In this sense, UNIDROIT Principle 9 aligns perfectly with this requirement, as it stresses that a transferor cannot transfer more rights than it owns (*nemo dat quod non habet*), therefore it must be transparent and without hidden defects. Furthermore, this text emphasises the importance of effective control to legitimise a transaction. This concept is especially relevant in the regulation of digital assets, where physical possession does not exist and control is determined by cryptographic keys or other electronic means. In Principle 9, it is reaffirmed that only those with legitimate and effective control can transfer a digital asset. This ensures that the transaction is legally sound and that the transferee receives full rights. This text also advocates the protection of bona fide acquirers, a principle that is reinforced in UNIDROIT Principle 9 discussed above. According to this text, in electronic transactions it is essential that purchasers acting in good faith are protected against claims by third parties that could jeopardise the rights acquired. In the context of digital commerce, this is particularly important, given that the intangible nature of digital assets can make pre-existing rights difficult to trace.

One of the objectives of the Model Law on Electronic Commerce is to encourage harmonisation of international regulation to facilitate cross-border electronic commerce. In this regard, UNIDROIT Principle 9 is designed to be implemented in a manner consistent with the laws of various jurisdictions, allowing digital assets to be transferred securely in global markets. This text reinforces such interoperability, ensuring that digital asset transactions are recognised and respected in multiple legal systems.

International interoperability also plays a crucial role in addressing *non-domino* procurement. For example, the Uniform Commercial Code (UCC) and MiCA Regulation offer protection to the bona fide transferee in transactions where prior rights cannot be fully traced. This ensures that, in global digital markets, assignees can

---

[9] The development of Principle 9 was based, in part, on concepts adopted from the UCC (Article 12), particularly its definition of 'control' as a combination of technical power and ability to identify, tailored to the needs of digital markets.

rely on regulatory systems to protect their rights, even in jurisdictions with different approaches to digital asset ownership.

On the other hand, this text also addresses the use of technological solutions and the need to regulate digital asset custody services. The proper management of these assets by custodians is essential to ensure that their control is not compromised. This aspect takes on particular relevance in Principle 9, which recognises that digital asset transactions may involve intermediaries. In this context, transparency and accountability of such intermediaries are essential to safeguard the rights of transferees.

2.1 *Nemo Dat Quod non Habet*

Principle 1 establishing the *nemo dat quod non habet* principle is addressed in detail in the discussions of the UNIDROIT Working Group on Digital Assets and Private Law, specifically at the Seventh Session (December 2022)[10]. The discussions highlighted the complexity of applying this principle in decentralised systems, where digital assets are often controlled through private keys rather than traditional ownership documentation. The Working Group emphasised that this rule serves to ensure that only those with legitimate rights can transfer digital assets, thereby protecting the stability and transparency of transactions. However, the principle is subject to the good faith acquisition exception outlined in Principle 8, which allows bona fide transferees to take assets free of conflicting claims, even in cases where the transferor may lack full ownership. These considerations are critical for adapting *nemo dat* to the realities of blockchain technology and digital markets.

This principle is particularly relevant in the context of digital assets, as ownership of digital assets can be difficult to verify due to the decentralised nature of transactions on blockchain or distributed networks. Discussions at the seventh session of the Working Group also suggested that the Commentary to Principle 9 should make clear reference to the type of rights that a transferor may hand over to a transferee, especially where rights are limited or partially transferred.

In the digital realm, the *nemo dat quod non habet* principle becomes even more relevant due to the intangible nature of digital assets, such as cryptocurrencies, tokens or goods stored on blockchains. Unlike tangible goods, digital assets can be transferred instantaneously across global networks and can be difficult to trace, opening the door to potential fraudulent or erroneous transfers. The lack of a physical medium or traditional documentation increases the risk of a person attempting to transfer a digital asset without having legitimate rights to it.

The reinforcement of this principle in digital private law is essential to protect confidence in the market. Failure to ensure that digital asset transactions are governed by this rule could make the market unstable and unreliable. The possibility of an acquirer receiving an asset without effective legal backing creates uncertainty, which

[10] UNIDROIT 2023 - Study LXXXII - W.G.7 - Doc. 5, December, pars. 33–36.

can discourage investment and the use of digital assets in global commerce. Therefore, the clear and effective incorporation of the *nemo dat quod non habet* principle in digital asset transactions contributes to legal certainty by establishing that only those who have a valid right to the asset can transfer it.

This principle also has practical implications in digital commerce, as it makes it possible to clearly delimit the liability of the parties. If a transferor transfers a digital asset without having the legitimacy to do so, the transferee could be exposed to claims from third parties who do have legitimate rights to that asset. The application of the *nemo dat* principle mitigates this risk by providing a consistent legal framework that protects both the transferee and the integrity of the market.

This principle has been a fundamental pillar in commercial and civil law throughout legal history. In fact, in Spanish law, it is deeply rooted in the Civil Code and other regulations related to the ownership and transfer of assets. However, in the field of digital assets, the applicability of this principle requires a review from a broader perspective, integrating both European regulations and international standards.

The European Union has increasingly addressed the issue of digital assets, although it has not yet fully harmonised the rules on the ownership and transmission of these assets. However, Directive (EU) 2019/770 on contracts for the supply of digital content and services sets some parameters for regulating digital transactions. Although this directive focuses more on contractual obligations, it provides a useful framework for understanding how the *nemo dat quod non habet* principle can be applied in the context of digital rights and asset transfers.

Regulation (EU) 2022/858, which establishes a pilot framework for distributed ledger technology (DLT), is another key regulation in this area. This Regulation introduces principles related to the transfer of financial instruments through technologies such as Blockchain, highlighting the importance of ensuring that ownership and rights to digital assets are managed in a manner consistent with traditional principles, including *nemo dat quod non habet*. While the Regulation focuses on financial instruments, its focus on the secure transfer of rights is also relevant to broader digital assets such as tokens.

For its part, Regulation (EU) 2023/1114 of the European Parliament and of the Council on cryptoasset markets (MiCA) reinforces this fundamental principle by establishing a clear and rigorous framework for the issuance, offering and trading of cryptoassets in the European Union. MiCA ensures that only those who legitimately own a cryptoasset can transfer it, aligning with the *nemo dat* principle, which holds that no one can transfer more rights than they own. This regulation requires cryptoasset service providers (CASPs) to verify the legitimacy of ownership before a transaction is completed. By implementing strict verification and control rules, MiCA ensures that cryptoassets can only be transferred by their legitimate holders, which reinforces legal certainty in the digital asset market. In this way, MiCA establishes a trusted environment for transactions, minimising the risks of rights being transferred without a proper legal basis, in accordance with the *nemo dat quod non habet* principle.

The *nemo dat* principle takes on critical importance in the digital age, where digital assets and electronic identities are becoming increasingly relevant. In the context of Regulation (EU) 2024/1183, this classic principle of law is significantly strengthened in the area of digital assets under the new European digital identity framework. The Regulation establishes a secure infrastructure for electronic identification and trust services, such as qualified electronic signatures and electronic seals, which ensure that any digital transaction is backed by a rigorous identity and authenticity verification process. This is key to the application of *nemo dat quod non habet*, as it ensures that only legitimate holders of a digital asset can transfer it. In a digital environment where intangible assets are transferred quickly and across multiple jurisdictions, the implementation of the eIDAS 2 Regulation ensures that intermediaries and platforms facilitating transactions use advanced technologies to verify beneficial ownership before a transfer is completed. This not only protects transferees, but also strengthens legal certainty in the digital marketplace, aligning with the principles of control and legitimacy set out in the UNCITRAL Legal Framework on Electronic Assets.

The United Nations Commission on International Trade Law (UNCITRAL) has pioneered the development of international legal frameworks for electronic commerce and transactions. Through the Principles on Digital Assets, it has comprehensively addressed the regulation of these assets and the transfer of rights in digital environments, providing a robust and consistent approach to their management. The UNCITRAL Model Law on the Use and Cross-Border Recognition of Identity Management and Trust Services (LMIC)[11] emphasises that control and legitimacy of rights over electronic assets are essential to ensure secure and legal transactions. This approach reinforces the *nemo dat quod non habet* principle at the international level, providing a framework that can be adopted by national and regional jurisdictions to regulate the ownership and transfer of digital assets. The Model Law on Electronic Commerce also establishes standards that support the need for clarity of ownership and transfer rights, ensuring that parties acquiring electronic assets do so under conditions of legality and transparency.

The UNIDROIT Principles on Digital Assets and Private Law, built in part on UNCITRAL's previous work, create a coherent framework for regulating the transfer of rights in digital environments, such as electronic assets, cryptocurrencies and other digital property. This framework addresses an essential aspect for the secure functioning of the digital marketplace: the legitimacy of rights and effective control over electronic assets. In the digital world, where intangible assets such as digital assets can change hands almost instantaneously, legitimacy and control are key to ensuring that transactions are secure and enforceable. This reinforces the *nemo dat quod non habet* principle in the international arena, establishing that only whoever legally owns an asset can transfer it. In this way, UNCITRAL creates global standards that ensure confidence in the acquisition and transfer of these assets in international trade.

[11] https://uncitral.un.org/sites/uncitral.un.org/files/media-documents/uncitral/es/mlit_sp.pdf.

The UNCITRAL Model Law on Electronic Commerce[12] is another fundamental document that supports the need for clarity in the ownership and transfer of rights in digital assets. This document stresses that parties involved in the acquisition of electronic assets must be fully assured that the transfer of rights is carried out under conditions of legality and transparency. This is particularly relevant for transferees in the context of digital assets, who depend on the integrity of legal systems to protect their rights acquired in good faith.

UNCITRAL's proposed standards not only provide a general framework for electronic commerce as a whole, but also provide specific guidance for the regulation of electronic assets, ensuring that national and regional jurisdictions can adopt frameworks that ensure that property rights are respected and digital transactions are conducted securely and efficiently. UNCITRAL's work has laid the groundwork for many countries to implement consistent regulations that facilitate secure electronic commerce, and its focus on protecting the rights of bona fide acquirers has been vital to ensuring security in digital markets. The Court of Justice of the European Union (CJEU) has not articulated a general rule governing the protection of the bona fide acquirer comparable to the classical *nemo dat quod non habet* doctrine developed in national systems of property law. Nor has it made the subjective good faith of the acquirer a decisive element in determining the effects of transfers of assets or rights. However, its case law in the field of consumer protection under Directive 93/13/EEC provides important guidance on the structural limits of remedies once a transfer has taken place. In cases such as Banco Santander (Case C-598/15),[13] Kušionová (Case C-34/13)[14] and Banco Primus (Case C-421/14),[15] the CJEU has consistently held that the effectiveness of consumer protection must be reconciled with the principle of legal certainty and with the stability of transactions completed in accordance with national law. As a result, EU law does not necessarily require the retroactive invalidation of transfers already carried out, even where the underlying contractual relationship between the original parties is affected by unfair terms. From a dogmatic perspective, this approach does not amount to a direct recognition of the good faith of the acquirer as a substantive requirement, but it performs a functionally equivalent role. By limiting the disruptive effects of defects arising in the contractual relationship between transferor and consumer, the CJEU implicitly safeguards the reliability of subsequent transfers and the integrity of acquired positions. This functional concern closely aligns with the rationale underlying UNIDROIT Principle 9, which addresses the position of the transferee by separating defects in the transferor's entitlement from the legal position of the transferee who acquires rights through a valid transfer. In the context of digital assets—where chains of entitlement are often opaque, transfers are rapid, and ex ante verification of title is difficult—the need for such functional protection becomes particularly acute. Although articulated

[12] UNCITRAL Model Law on Electronic Commerce: https://uncitral.un.org/en/texts/electronic-commerce/modellaw/electronic_commerce.

[13] https://eur-lex.europa.eu/legal-content/ES/TXT/?uri=CELEX:62015CJ0598.

[14] https://eur-lex.europa.eu/legal-content/PT/TXT/?uri=CELEX:62013CJ0034.

[15] https://eur-lex.europa.eu/legal-content/ES/ALL/?uri=CELEX:62014CJ0421.

through different legal techniques, both the CJEU's case law and UNIDROIT Principle 9 reflect a shared objective: preserving transactional certainty by preventing defects in prior relationships from automatically undermining the position of downstream transferees.

Another relevant case is C-264/14 (Skatteverket v. David Hedqvist), where the CJEU established that cryptocurrency transactions were exempt from VAT, recognising cryptocurrencies as a means of payment in economic transactions. This judgment, although limited to tax law, confirms that transactions involving cryptocurrencies may fall within existing legal categories of economic exchange under EU law.[16]

Regarding the rights of transferees in digital assets, CJEU Judgment No. C-400/22 of May 30, 2024 (VT and UR v. Conny GmbH)[17] may serve as a useful reference for the role of transparency and informed consent in digital contracting. In this case, the CJEU addressed the need for sellers to provide a clear and explicit indication of the obligations that consumers assume when making an online purchase, which is linked to good faith purchasing in digital commerce. The C-400/22 judgment addresses a key issue in relation to electronic contracts and the obligation to pay, in particular whether an order button must clearly indicate that the consumer assumes an obligation to pay, irrespective of whether that obligation is subject to future conditions. In this case, the issue was raised by the German courts with respect to Directive 2011/83/EU on consumer rights.

The case involved a dispute over whether or not the consumer, by clicking on an online order button that did not contain clear wording ("order with obligation to pay"), was bound by the terms of the contract. The CJEU concluded that the consumer was not legally bound if the button did not comply with the explicit requirements of Directive 2011/83/EU.

This rule reinforces the importance of transparency and informed consent in digital transactions, which are also key elements for ensuring legal certainty in asset transfers. Although the CJEU case concerns an online service contract, the principles set out can be transposed to the context of digital assets. For a transaction to be valid and binding, it is crucial that the parties are properly informed about the obligations they are assuming; a principle that applies equally to the acquisition of digital assets.

In case C-400/22, it is emphasised that the acquirer, in this case a consumer, must be clearly informed of the contractual obligations. If he is not, the acquisition of rights may be affected, as the due informative process was not complied with. Applied to the context of digital assets, the ruling reinforces the importance of transparency and adequate information in the assignment of rights, as we have repeatedly stated. The judgment highlights that, in digital environments, contractual obligations cannot arise unless the acquirer is clearly informed of the commitments assumed, thereby reinforcing transparency as a prerequisite for legal certainty in electronic transactions.

The C-400/22 ruling also has broader implications for the regulation of digital asset transactions, as it highlights the importance of platforms and service providers

[16] https://eur-lex.europa.eu/legal-content/ES/TXT/?uri=CELEX:62014CJ0264.

[17] ECLI:EU:C:2024:436, https://e-justice.europa.eu/ecli/ECLI:EU:C:2024:436.

ensuring that acquirers fully understand their rights and obligations. In the case of tokens, cryptocurrencies or any other type of digital asset, this principle of clarity is crucial for transferees to be able to assert their rights in good faith, avoiding future disputes over the validity of transactions.

The ruling reinforces the idea that bona fide acquirers must be adequately informed about the legal implications of the transaction, and that if they do not receive such information clearly (for example, if a "buy" button does not explicitly state the obligation to pay), they are not bound by the contract. This ensures that the transferee's rights under Principle 9 are respected, especially in a digital environment where the transmission of assets is rapid and sometimes opaque.

In the case of digital assets, where Principle 9 protects transferees against possible irregularities in the transfer of rights over assets that were not adequately supported by the transferor, the CJEU case law provides additional support for the idea that consumers or acquirers should be protected when acting in good faith in digital transactions.

In this regard, the *nemo dat quod non habet* principle, adapted to the digital environment, remains a key instrument to protect legal certainty and confidence in the market, providing a consistent structure for both tangible and digital assets. By harmonising this principle with European rules, international standards and CJEU case law, the regulatory framework that will ensure the stability and legality of trade in digital assets worldwide is strengthened.

2.2 *Bona Fide Purchaser*

As previously noted, this subprinciple, based on the *nemo dat quod non habet* rule, ensures that a person cannot transfer more rights than he owns over a digital asset. This is especially relevant in the field of digital assets, where the intangible nature of these assets makes it more difficult to verify the ownership and legitimacy of transfers. This principle is essential in commercial law because it protects both transferors and transferees from erroneous or fraudulent transfer of rights. In digital transactions, maintaining clarity about the rights being transferred is essential to ensure legal certainty and trust between the parties.

However, there is an important exception to this rule, which is the protection of the bona fide acquirer. As stated in UNIDROIT Principle 8, the bona fide acquirer is protected, even if the transferor does not own all the rights to the digital asset. This means that, if a person acquires a digital asset without being aware of the existence of claims or disputes over its ownership, and acts honestly, he will retain the acquired rights, even if the transferor was not the legitimate owner. This mechanism reinforces trust in transactions and prevents the acquirer from being penalised for problems in the previous chain of title that were not his knowledge or responsibility.

Good faith is one of the central pillars in the protection of the rights of the parties involved in a transaction. In the digital context, where assets can change ownership very quickly and claims on them may not be easily visible, this protection becomes even more important.

Moreover, Regulation (EU) 2023/1114 also plays a crucial role in providing a framework that protects bona fide acquirers in the field of cryptoassets. MiCA establishes strict transparency and due diligence requirements for service providers, ensuring that acquirers have access to clear and accurate information about the assets they acquire. This approach allows bona fide acquirers to be confident that the rights they are acquiring are legitimate, without risk of future claims. By establishing these standards, MiCA ensures that bona fide transferees are protected even if there are defects in the chain of title of which they are unaware. This protection is essential in a digital marketplace where transactions are fast and complex. Much the same as UNIDROIT Principle 9, MiCA reinforces security and confidence in digital asset transactions, ensuring that bona fide acquirers are not harmed by hidden defects or irregularities in transactions.

Regulation (EU) 2024/1183 provides additional protection for acquirers of digital assets who act without knowledge of potential defects in the acquired rights. The regulation establishes a digital trust infrastructure to verify the identity of transferors and the legitimacy of transactions, which is essential to ensure that bona fide transferees are not harmed by subsequent claims. The use of qualified electronic seals and strong authentication services minimises the risks of fraud and increases transparency in the transmission of digital assets, ensuring that acquirers can trust the validity of the transferred rights. This reinforces the *bona fide acquisition* sub-principle in UNIDROIT Principle 9, providing a robust legal framework that protects acquirers of digital assets across the European Union by ensuring that transactions are transparent, secure and free from hidden defects, in accordance with the highest international and European standards, such as those set out in the Model Law on Electronic Commerce.

In the preparatory texts of Principle 9 on transferee's rights, the importance of the protection of the bona fide acquirer was significantly emphasised. This principle is aligned with the concept of *nemo dat quod non habet*, which states that no one can transfer more rights than he has. However, in the context of digital assets, this principle is complemented by the good faith acquisition rule set out in Principle 8, which ensures the protection of acquirers who are unaware of possible claims on the transferred rights.

The legislative process that led to the drafting of Principle 9 was addressed at meetings of the UNCITRAL Working Group[18], during which the implications of ensuring that bona fide transferees are protected against any subsequent claims when acquiring a digital asset, provided they act without knowledge of conflicting rights, were discussed in depth. The approach sought to balance legal certainty and efficiency in the digital marketplace.

It was discussed that the principle of good faith is crucial for transferees in digital asset markets, where transactions are fast and chains of title are not always clear due to the digital nature of the assets, which posed a great challenge for the protection

---

[18] UNIDROIT 2023 - Study LXXXII - W.G.7 - Doc. 5, December, pars. 33–36.

of the transferee against possible conflicts of rights so that the good faith exception had to be included in Principle 8.

During the seventh session of the Working Group in December 2022, the need to clarify the scope of the Principle was affirmed to ensure that transferees can rely on the legitimacy of transfers, provided they act in good faith. Group members highlighted the importance of integrating technological advances into the legal framework, thus enabling global digital commerce to be more secure and trustworthy.

The subprinciple of good faith acquisition in UNIDROIT Principle 9 reflects fundamental protection for transferees of digital assets who act without knowledge of conflicting rights. This subprinciple, closely linked to the concept of *nemo dat quod non habet*, can be better understood in light of European case law and UNCITRAL instruments addressing transactional certainty and the allocation of risks in digital and electronic transactions.[19]

In addition to the cases mentioned above, we consider the ruling in case C-433/20 (Austro-Mechana vs. Strato AG)[20], by the CJEU on March 24, 2022, which establishes that the term "reproductions in any medium" includes storage on third-party servers, as occurs in cloud computing, which has direct implications for digital asset transactions.

While UNIDROIT Principle 9 expressly addresses the position of transferees acting without knowledge of conflicting rights, European case law has not developed a corresponding doctrine of good faith acquisition. Nevertheless, certain CJEU judgments illustrate the structural difficulties inherent in digital environments, where rights and legal qualifications may not be immediately apparent to market participants. In Austro-Mechana v Strato AG (Case C-433/20), the Court clarified that the storage of protected works on third-party servers constitutes a reproduction within the meaning of Directive 2001/29, confirming that legal rights may subsist even where users do not exercise direct control over the technological infrastructure. Although this judgment does not concern the acquisition or transfer of rights, it highlights the opacity of digital systems and the challenges faced by participants in identifying the legal status of digital content. This context underscores the importance of rules, such as those set out in UNIDROIT Principle 9, which aim to allocate risks and protect transactional certainty where acquirers cannot reasonably detect pre-existing rights or defects in digital asset transactions.

UNCITRAL standards have also been instrumental in the composition of this subprinciple. The UNCITRAL Model Law on Electronic Commerce establishes the importance of clarity in the ownership and transfer of rights in digital transactions. This approach, which aligns with the good faith subprinciple of Principle 9, highlights that acquirers of electronic assets should be protected if they act without knowledge of possible defects in the transferred rights. UNCITRAL has insisted that the transferee's trust in the transaction is a pillar for the proper functioning of the digital market, and to this end, it is essential that platforms or intermediaries ensure the transparency and legitimacy of transfers. This international framework complements the UNIDROIT

[19] UNIDROIT 2023 - Study LXXXII - W.G.7 - Doc. 5, December, pars. 19–21, 33–36.

[20] https://eur-lex.europa.eu/legal-content/ES/ALL/?uri=CELEX:62020CJ0433.

regulation by providing clear principles that ensure that the rights of transferees are respected and that electronic transactions are secure and transparent.

Finally, the UNCITRAL Legal Framework on Identity and Control of Electronic Assets reinforces the idea that effective control over digital assets is key to legitimise their transfer. In this context, protection of the bona fide acquirer implies that the rights of the transferee must be respected, providing that the transferee acquires an asset under the appearance of legitimate control by the transferor.

2.3 *Harbour or Refuge Rule*

The safe harbour rule in Principle 9 of the UNIDROIT Principles on Digital Assets ensures that a transferee acquires all the rights that the transferor had regarding the capacity to transfer, even if the transferee does not fully meet the requirements to be considered a bona fide acquirer at the time of the transfer.[21] This means that, if an original transferee acquired the digital asset in good faith, any subsequent transferee also acquires those rights, even if he himself does not meet the bona fide requirements.

This principle is designed to provide legal protection and certainty in a digital market where exhaustive verification of transferred rights may be complex or subject to technological difficulties. This rule is key to ensuring legal certainty in the transfer of digital assets. In a decentralised digital asset environment, where it is difficult or nearly impossible to perform a complete verification of the legitimacy of the rights in each transaction, the safe harbour rule acts as a safe harbour mechanism that protects bona fide transferees against claims that may arise due to defects in the chain of title.

In addition, this rule interacts with the figure of *non-domino* acquisition in scenarios where control over a digital asset does not necessarily imply legitimacy of rights. The legal certainty offered by the "safe harbour rule" protects assignees by preventing errors in the previous chain of ownership from compromising acquired rights. This approach resolves traditional tensions of the *nemo dat* principle in technological environments, aligning legal stability with the dynamics of digital assets.

This rule ensures that bona fide transferees of digital assets are protected in transactions, even if at some prior point in the chain of title there are irregularities or defects. This principle is supported and complemented by European regulations such as the eIDAS 2 Regulation, the MiCA Regulation, and the DLT Regulation, which provide a solid framework to ensure legal certainty in digital rights transfers.

In the European context, the safe harbour rule embodied in UNIDROIT Principle 9 does not find a direct counterpart in the case law of the Court of Justice of the European Union, as the CJEU has not developed a doctrine of bona fide acquisition in relation to the transfer of rights. However, its jurisprudence in the field of consumer protection

[21] The figure of *non-domino* acquisition was discussed at the First Session of the Working Group (November 2020), where the complexity of applying this principle in blockchain-based transactions was recognized, where technical control does not always imply legal legitimacy.

illustrates the tension between the effectiveness of legal remedies and the principle of legal certainty. In Case C-154/15 (Gutiérrez Naranjo), the Court addressed the temporal effects of the nullity of unfair contractual terms, emphasising the primacy of effective consumer protection under Directive 93/13/EEC. Although this judgment does not concern third-party acquirers or the transfer of rights, it highlights the broader challenge of balancing corrective justice with transactional stability. This structural concern provides useful context for understanding the rationale of UNIDROIT Principle 9, which explicitly addresses the allocation of risks in chains of transfers by protecting transferees against defects arising at earlier stages of the transaction.[22]

In relation to electronic identification and digital transactions, the eIDAS 2 Regulation provides additional safeguards through secure electronic authentication mechanisms. Electronic verification and trust in identity certification systems are crucial to ensure that transactions are valid and that vested rights are adequately protected. In this sense, the UNIDROIT safe harbour rule is supported by the requirement that electronic transactions verified under systems such as eIDAS be secure and that parties can rely on the legitimacy of the rights transferred without the need to verify each step in the chain.

On the other hand, the MiCA Regulation reinforces this principle in the field of cryptoassets, ensuring that platforms and service providers meet high standards of transparency and diligence in verifying ownership, such that transferees should be protected if they are confident in the legitimacy of assets acquired through regulated platforms. This waterfall protection, where the rights of a bona fide transferee are passed on to successive acquirers, is at the heart of the safe harbour rule of Principle 9.

Finally, the DLT Regulation (2022/858) provides an additional security framework for distributed ledger technology (DLT) and blockchain-based transactions, ensuring that transfers meet high standards of security and transparency. Verification and recording mechanisms in blockchain, while enabling traceability of transactions, are not always clear as to the underlying ownership. In this sense, the safe harbour rule becomes more relevant, ensuring that a subsequent bona fide acquirer, who cannot exhaustively verify the entire transaction chain, is not harmed by defects in ownership at earlier stages of the transaction. In preparatory work, the importance of this principle to provide stability in the chain of digital transfers was stressed. Cascading protection of successive transferees, who inherit the rights acquired by a bona fide transferee, was one of the solutions proposed to prevent digital transactions from being called into question by subsequent claims related to lack of rights at some earlier stage of the transfer.

---

[22] https://eur-lex.europa.eu/legal-content/ES/ALL/?uri=CELEX:62015CJ0154.

2.4 *Application of the* Nemo Dat Quod Non Habet *Principle in Digital Environments, Blockchain and Decentralised Transactions*

The *nemo dat quod non habet* principle, which states that no one can transfer more rights than he or she owns, faces significant challenges in digital environments, especially in the context of *blockchain* and decentralised transactions. While this principle has been a mainstay in traditional commercial law, its application in the digital ecosystem requires deeper analysis due to the unique characteristics of digital assets.

In a traditional transaction, verification of ownership of an asset is done through centralised registries and trusted sources of documentation. However, in a public *blockchain* or decentralised network, the lack of a central entity to guarantee the validity of ownership rights to a digital asset (such as a cryptocurrency or a token) complicates this process. Instead of relying on a central registry, ownership is based on the possession of cryptographic keys, which creates a new problem: control of the key is what determines the ability to transfer the asset, not necessarily the legitimacy of the right to it.

This creates direct tension with the *nemo dat quod non habet* principle, since, in a decentralised environment, a person who controls the private keys of a digital asset can transfer it, regardless of whether he or she is the legitimate owner or not. For example, in a *blockchain* system, if a third party acquires an asset without knowing that it was transferred by someone without legitimacy over it, the underlying technology may not provide clear mechanisms to reverse or invalidate such a transaction. In this regard, questions arise as to how the bona fide acquirer should be protected and how traditional legal frameworks can be integrated into these new systems[23].

The speed of transactions on a *blockchain*, coupled with the immutable nature of the records once validated, adds a layer of complexity. The *nemo dat* rule may seem obsolete when a digital asset, such as a cryptocurrency, is instantly and irreversibly transferred once the transaction is validated. Traditional verifications, which in classic merchant trading could take days or weeks, are inapplicable in these scenarios, as *blockchain* transactions take a matter of seconds or minutes and are distributed across nodes in multiple jurisdictions.

In these cases, the figure of the bona fide acquirer, contemplated as an exception to the *nemo dat* principle, becomes more relevant. UNIDROIT Principle 8 on digital assets already recognises the need to protect acquirers who, without knowledge of the transferor's lack of legitimacy, obtain a digital asset. However, the implementation of this principle in *blockchain* environments still poses challenges. Given that transactions are immutable, how could a bona fide acquirer be retroactively protected

[23] During the first working group meeting, the complexity of applying *nemo dat* to *blockchain* transactions was highlighted, as control of the digital asset, rather than ownership, determines its transfer. This poses a particular challenge in decentralized systems, where ownership may not be documented or difficult to verify. UNIDROIT 2020 - Study LXXXII - W.G.1 - Doc. 2, September, pars. 51–53.

if the original ownership was defective? Here, smart contracts and DAOs (Decentralised Autonomous Organisations) could play a key role, enabling the creation of automated dispute resolution mechanisms in real time, although such solutions are at an early stage of development.

Another important challenge to the *nemo dat quod non habet* principle is the use of digital escrow and multisignature (multisig) solutions. In these arrangements, ownership of a digital asset does not necessarily reside with a single person, but control may be distributed among several parties who must jointly sign a transaction to transfer the asset. The implications for ownership in this model are complex: if one of the signatories attempts to transfer the asset without the consent of the others, a direct tension arises with the *nemo dat* principle.

In addition, in digital custody systems, such as wallets held by a third-party custodian, the private keys are controlled by an intermediary, which can create situations where the custodian has the technical ability to transfer the asset without the ownership or legitimate right to do so. This situation can occur, for example, in cases of insolvency of the custodian, where the digital assets under custody could become part of the assets available to creditors, leaving the customer without protection over assets that, in theory, belong to him.

Once transactions have been verified and recorded in the blockchain, they cannot be altered or reversed. This creates a problem for the *nemo dat quod non habet* principle in cases of fraud. If a person transfers a digital asset that he or she does not legitimately own, the transaction will be recorded on the blockchain as valid, and traditional dispute resolution mechanisms, such as return of ownership, are not operational. Immutability, which is one of the most valuable aspects of the *blockchain* in terms of security, also becomes a barrier to correcting errors or fraud. In this context, the application of *nemo dat* must be adapted, perhaps by developing governance systems on the *blockchain* that allow illicit transactions to be reversed in certain cases, without compromising trust in the immutability of the network.

2.5 Impact on Trade and Digital Transactions

UNIDROIT Principle 9, together with international and European regulations, such as the MiCA Regulation and the DLT Regulation, is crucial to establish a framework that promotes security and efficiency in digital markets. In an environment where digital assets, such as cryptoassets, circulate rapidly and thorough verifications of ownership can be complex, ensuring legal certainty in transactions is essential to strengthen trust among market players.

The MiCA Regulation (2023/1114), which regulates cryptoasset markets in the European Union, reinforces this principle by requiring high standards of transparency and verification from cryptoasset service providers (CASPs). These requirements ensure that cryptoasset transactions are conducted with full confidence in the legitimacy of the assets purchased, which boosts market efficiency by facilitating faster and safer exchange of these digital assets. The traceability and verification imposed by MiCA provide an additional layer of security, minimising the risks associated with a lack of clarity in the chain of title, which, in turn, incentivises greater participation in digital commerce. In addition, MiCA's approach is consistent with UNCITRAL's preparatory work, which stresses the importance of "good faith acquisition" and provides clarity on the rights transferred in digital asset transactions.

At the international level, UNCITRAL standards have been crucial to ensure reliable digital commerce. The Legislative Guide on Electronic Commerce Law establishes a clear framework that ensures that electronic transactions are conducted transparently and under conditions of adequate legal certainty, which in turn increases the efficiency of digital commerce. The UNCITRAL Legal Framework on Identity and Control of Electronic Assets reinforces this principle by requiring that digital asset transactions be conducted under effective and verifiable control, which gives acquirers greater confidence in the legitimacy of the rights they acquire. This approach contributes significantly to market security by allowing market players to operate with legal certainty, regardless of the complexity of the transaction. During the UNCITRAL Working Group sessions, the implications of the *nemo dat quod non habet* principle in the digital age were discussed at length. At the second session of the Working Group (March 2021), the discussion on the protection of bona fide acquirers in decentralised transactions was advanced, emphasising that the "acquisition of control" over a digital asset, rather than mere ownership, should be the key factor in validating the transfer of rights.

The DLT Regulation (2022/858) complements this regulatory acquis, which regulates market infrastructures based on distributed ledger technology (DLT), and also reinforces security and efficiency in digital transactions. This regulation ensures that transactions based on technologies such as blockchain meet the highest security standards, ensuring that transferred rights are legitimate and verifiable. By facilitating traceability and automatic validation of transactions through decentralised technologies, the DLT Regulation enables more efficient digital trading, while also reducing operational costs and minimising the risk of errors or fraud in transfers. This not only improves market efficiency, but also enhances transaction security, providing a more stable and reliable environment for digital market participants.

2.6 Final Reflections and Analysis of the Principle

The *nemo data quod non habet* rule has been the mainstay of traditional commercial law, and also of UNIDROIT Principle 9 on the transfer of rights in digital assets. However, its implementation in a digital environment poses unique challenges, particularly due to the intangible and decentralised nature of digital assets, such as cryptocurrencies or non-fungible tokens (*NFTs*). The focus of this Principle is to ensure the legitimacy of transactions, which is crucial in markets where speed and the lack of a centralised registry complicate traditional ownership verifications.

Principle 9 ensures that no one can transfer more rights than they legitimately own. However, in decentralised environments such as blockchains, the verification of rights is not as clear as in traditional systems. In the blockchain network, technical control over digital assets is determined by cryptographic keys, which poses a fundamental problem: control over keys may not coincide with legal ownership.

In the discussions of the UNIDROIT Working Group at its second session in March 2021, this issue was addressed, highlighting that the "technical possession" of a digital asset, based on the control of the keys, must be complemented by a clear legal framework that ensures the legitimacy of the transaction leading to the inclusion of the protection of the bona fide acquirer in Principle 8, which acts as an exception to *nemo dat* and ensures that those who acquire an asset without knowledge of prior irregularities can maintain their rights.

Let us imagine a practical example of a digital art collector buying an NFT on a decentralised platform. In this case, the NFT is transferred through a transaction validated on a blockchain, which guarantees the immutability of the record. However, if the seller was not the rightful owner of the NFT (e.g., if he hacked the cryptographic keys of the true owner), the buyer could face claims. This is where Principle 8 comes into play, which protects the bona fide buyer, who acquired the NFT without knowledge of the seller's lack of legitimacy. This protection guarantees market stability by providing confidence in the legitimacy of digital transactions, transparency and verification regarding cryptoasset service providers (CASP), thereby ensuring full trust in the legitimacy of cryptoasset transactions concerning the acquired assets and protecting bona fide acquirers[24].

In this framework, it is crucial to reflect on the key functions of Principle 9, its practical applicability in digital environments and the possible future directions that this legal concept will have to follow in order to remain relevant in the context of constant technological change.

In the digital context, the figure of acquisition *a non domino* acquires a new meaning. While the principle *nemo dat quod non habet* states that no one may transfer more rights than he or she possesses, there are important exceptions to this rule when the transferee is protected in good faith, as reflected in UNIDROIT Principle 8.

In particular, in decentralised environments, where transactions are fast and verification of ownership is not always clear, it is possible for an asset to be transferred by someone who does not have full legitimacy. However, the protection of the assignee in good faith prevents the latter from losing the acquired rights if he acted without knowledge of defects in the chain of title.

In addition, the *non-domino* exception finds support in international regulations such as the MiCA Regulation in the European Union, which requires high standards of diligence to verify the legitimacy of assets before they are transferred. This ensures

[24] MiCA 2023/1114, art. 7 regulates marketing communications to ensure that they are clear, fair and not misleading, and include information consistent with the cryptoasset "white paper", arts. 39 and 47 set out redemption requirements for asset referenced tokens and e-money tokens, which include the obligation to hold reserve assets and clear redemption policies (redeem them or convert them into the underlying security to which they are linked) and arts. 87 and 91 address the prohibition of market abuse, including price manipulation and insider trading.

that even if an asset is transferred without full rights, the transferee can be confident in the legitimacy of the verification system.

Non domino acquisition not only protects the transferee but also fosters the stability of digital markets by providing legal certainty in transactions where full tracing of prior rights is not possible. This approach is essential to harmonise international regulations with the dynamics of digital assets, such as cryptocurrencies or tokens.

One of the main functions of Principle 9 is to ensure that a person can only transfer those rights of which he or she is the legitimate owner. This principle, although simple in its formulation, contains problems when confronted with the decentralised ecosystem of the blockchain. In this environment, control over an asset is based on the possession of cryptographic keys, which means that the technical ability to transfer an asset is not always linked to legitimate ownership.

The challenge here, as has already been pointed out in the UNCITRAL Working Group discussions, lies in the dissociation between technical control and legal rights. While in traditional transactions ownership can be easily verified through centralised registries, in decentralised networks this process is complicated by the absence of a central body to certify the validity of rights.

In this sense, one of the great merits of Principle 9 is to have introduced protection mechanisms for bona fide acquirers, ensuring that the rights they acquire in a digital transaction, even in environments where ownership is complex to verify, cannot be claimed by third parties. The interconnection with Principle 8 is key here, since it extends an exception that protects bona fide acquirers against possible defects in the ownership of rights, ensuring stability in transactions.

The second function of Principle 9 is to provide a framework that combines the need for speed and efficiency in digital transactions with the assurance of legal certainty. This balance is particularly relevant in a context where the speed of transactions on the blockchain clashes with the immutable nature of the records. Once a transaction is recorded on the blockchain, it cannot be reversed or altered, thereby leading to contention in case of fraud or errors in the transfer of rights.

In the UNIDROIT Preparatory Works, the need was highlighted to develop flexible legal mechanisms that allow the rectification of situations in which the transfer of a digital asset is made without the necessary rights or in cases where the acquirer was not informed of hidden defects. One possible solution proposed is the integration of smart contracts and technologies such as DAOs (Decentralised Autonomous Organisations), which could automate dispute resolution processes in real time. This would open the door to mechanisms that guarantee the protection of the bona fide acquirer without compromising the decentralised nature of digital transactions.

The success of Principle 9 lies not only in its formulation within the UNIDROIT Principles, but in its ability to interoperate with other international and regional regulation. Notable here is the role of the MiCA Regulation and the DLT Regulation, which provide regulatory frameworks in the European Union specifically designed to address the transparency and legitimacy of transactions in cryptoassets and assets based on distributed ledger technology.

MiCA, for example, reinforces the need for CASPs to verify the legitimacy of cryptoasset ownership before permitting a transaction, thereby aligning directly with the objective of Principle 9. This regulation, by requiring high standards of diligence, ensures that cryptoasset transactions are not compromised by defects in the chain of title, thus providing a safer and more reliable environment for bona fide acquirers.

At the international level, the UNCITRAL Model Law on Electronic Commerce reinforces these concepts by stressing the importance of transparency in the transfer of rights in digital assets. During the Digital Assets Working Group sessions, emphasis was placed on the need to adapt traditional concepts of ownership to reflect the reality of global markets for intangible assets, ensuring that legal frameworks are flexible enough to effectively regulate international transactions.

A paradigmatic case in the regulatory interoperability framework is the cross-border purchase of cryptocurrencies on platforms based in different countries. While MiCA establishes clear guidelines in the EU, local regulations in other jurisdictions may not offer the same protection to bona fide acquirers. In this case, international cooperation and mutual recognition of regulations are essential to avoid disputes and ensure reliable transactions.

Principle 9 must remain flexible and adapt to digital markets as they evolve. The speed of technological innovation means that traditional legal rules will need to be revised periodically to keep pace with developments in blockchain technology and cryptocurrencies.

The integration of tools such as smart contracts and decentralised technologies poses opportunities to strengthen the *non-domino* procurement framework. These tools can ensure that bona fide transferees have clear mechanisms to defend their rights even in cases of illicit transfers. Likewise, the adoption of international standards, such as those developed by UNCITRAL and UNIDROIT, ensures that legal frameworks are robust and flexible enough to respond to the complexities of digital assets.

For example, a key proposal would be the creation of a global governance mechanism for blockchain-based transactions, where the UNIDROIT principles can be integrated as a guide for dispute resolution in cross-border transactions. This governance system could facilitate collaboration between different jurisdictions, allowing the Principles developed by UNCITRAL to be recognised and applied globally, thus avoiding conflicts in the interpretation of rights and obligations in international environments.

Additionally, it is essential to continue exploring how technological tools can be used to strengthen legal certainty without hindering market efficiency. Smart contracts and decentralised solutions, although at their inception, offer an opportunity to automate the validation of rights in real time, ensuring that transactions are smooth but secure. In technological terms, smart contracts offer an opportunity to strengthen legal certainty in digital transactions. These contracts could be programmed to automatically run title verifications before completing a transaction. For example, in the sale and purchase of an NFT, the smart contract could include a clause guaranteeing that only the rightful owner can transfer the asset, which would significantly reduce the risk of fraud and protect the bona fide acquirer.

References

Council Directive 93/13/EEC of 5 April 1993 on unfair terms in consumer contracts
https://eur-lex.europa.eu/legal-content/EN/TXT/?uri=CELEX:31993L0013 last visited 1 February 2025
Digital Assets and Private Law Working Group // First session (remote) // Rome, 17 – 19 November 2020 //// UNIDROIT 2020 // Study LXXXII – W.G.1 – Doc. 2 // English only // November 2020 https://www.unidroit.org/english/documents/2020/study82/wg01/s-82-wg01-02-e.pdf last visited 1 February 2025
Digital Assets and Private Law Working Group // First session (remote) // Rome, 17 – 19 November 2020 //// UNIDROIT 2021 // Study LXXXII – W.G.1 – Doc. 4 // English only // November 2021 https://www.unidroit.org/english/documents/2021/study82/wg03/s-82-wg03-04-e.pdf last visited 1 February 2025
Digital Assets and Private Law Working Group // Second session (remote) // Rome, 16 – 18 March 2021 //// UNIDROIT 2021 // Study LXXXII – W.G.2 – Doc. 3 (rev. 1) // English only / / March 2021 https://www.unidroit.org/english/documents/2021/study82/wg02/s-82-wg02-03-e.pdf last visited 1 February 2025
Digital Assets and Private Law Working Group // Seventh session (hybrid) // Rome & Zoom, 19 – 21 December 2022 //// UNIDROIT 2022 // Study LXXXII – W.G.7 – Doc. 5 // English only // December 2022 https://www.unidroit.org/wp-content/uploads/2023/03/W.G.7-Doc.-5-Summary-Report-of-the-7th-Session-1.pdf last visited 1 February 2025
Digital Assets and Private Law Working Group // Third session (hybrid) // Rome, 30 June – 2 July 2021 //// UNIDROIT 2021 // Study LXXXII – W.G.3 – Doc. 2 (rev. 1) // English only // July 2021 https://www.unidroit.org/english/documents/2021/study82/wg03/s-82-wg03-02-rev01-e.pdf last visited 1 February 2025
Digital Assets and Private Law Working Group // Third session (remote) // Rome, 30 June – 2 July 2021 //// UNIDROIT 2021 // Study LXXXII – W.G.3 – Doc. 4 // English only / / July 2021 https://www.unidroit.org/english/documents/2021/study82/wg03/s-82-wg03-04-e.pdf last visited 1 February 2025
Directive (EU) 2019/770 of the European Parliament and of the Council of 20 May 2019 on certain aspects concerning contracts for the supply of digital content and digital services
https://eur-lex.europa.eu/legal-content/EN/TXT/?uri=CELEX:32019L0770 last visited 1 February 2025
Directive 2011/83/EU of the European Parliament and of the Council of 25 October 2011 on consumer rights, amending Council Directive 93/13/EEC and Directive 1999/44/EC of the European Parliament and of the Council and repealing Council Directive 85/577/EEC and Directive 97/7/EC of the European Parliament and of the Council
https://eur-lex.europa.eu/legal-content/EN/TXT/?uri=CELEX:32011L0083 last visited 1 February 2025
Regulation (EU) 2022/858 of the European Parliament and of the Council of 30 May 2022 on a pilot regime for market infrastructures based on distributed ledger technology, and amending Regulations (EU) No 600/2014 and (EU) No 909/2014 and Directive 2014/65/EU
https://eur-lex.europa.eu/legal-content/EN/TXT/?uri=CELEX:32022R0858 last visited 1 February 2025
Regulation (EU) 2023/1114 of the European Parliament and of the Council of 31 May 2023 on markets in crypto-assets, and amending Regulations (EU) No 1093/2010 and (EU) No 1095/2010 and Directives 2013/36/EU and (EU) 2019/1937
https://eur-lex.europa.eu/legal-content/EN/TXT/?uri=CELEX:32023R1114 last visited 1 February 2025
Regulation (EU) 2024/1183 of the European Parliament and of the Council of 11 April 2024 amending Regulation (EU) No 910/2014 as regards establishing a framework for a European Digital Identity

https://eur-lex.europa.eu/legal-content/EN/TXT/?uri=CELEX:32024R1183 last visited 1 February 2025
Regulation (EU) No 910/2014 of the European Parliament and of the Council of 23 July 2014 on electronic identification and trust services for electronic transactions in the internal market and repealing Directive 1999/93/EC
https://eur-lex.europa.eu/legal-content/EN/TXT/?uri=CELEX:32014R0910 last visited 1 February 2025
UNCITRAL Model Law on Electronic Commerce (1996) with Guide to Enactment (1996) and additional article 5 bis as adopted in 1998
https://uncitral.un.org/sites/uncitral.un.org/files/media-documents/uncitral/en/19-04970_ebook.pdf last visited 1 February 2025

Reflections on Section IV: Custody

Principle 10
Custody

Agustín Madrid-Parra

(1) In these Principles:

(a) "custodian" means a person who provides services to a client pursuant to a custody agreement as defined in paragraphs (3) and (4), and is acting in that capacity;
(b) "sub-custodian" means a custodian who provides services to another custodian pursuant to a custody agreement as defined in paragraphs (3) and (4), and is acting in that capacity;
(c) "client" means a person to whom a custodian provides services pursuant to a custody agreement as defined in paragraphs (3) and (4).

(2) A custodian "maintains" a digital asset for a client if:

(a) that custodian has control of the digital asset; or
(b) that custodian enters into a custody agreement, as defined in paragraph (3), with a sub-custodian with respect to the digital asset in the circumstances set out in Principle 11(4).

(3) Subject to paragraph (4), an agreement for services to a client in relation to a digital asset is a "custody agreement" if:

(a) the service is provided in the ordinary course of the service provider's business;
(b) the service provider is obliged to obtain (if this is not yet the case) and to maintain the digital asset for the client; and
(c) the client does not have the exclusive ability to change the control of the digital asset within the meaning of Principle 6(2).

This work was financed within the framework of the Prometeo 2023 project of the Regional Ministry of Innovation, Universities, Science and Digital Society (CIPROM/2022/26) "Present and future of the regulation of cryptoassets in the EU [LegalCripto]", whose principal investigator is Carmen Pastor Sempere. The basic ideas contained herein were presented in the author's paper with the same title, given on November 13, 2024 at the IV International Congress on "Unidroit Principles on Digital Assets and Private Law: Context, Content, Perspectives", organized also by BAES Research Group of the University of Alicante on November 13 and 14, 2024.

A. Madrid-Parra (✉)
Pablo de Olavide University, Sevilla, Spain
e-mail: amadrid@upo.es

C. Pastor Sempere and D. A. Morán Bovio (eds.), Unidroit *Principles on Digital Assets and Private Law*, Law, Governance and Technology Series 80,
https://doi.org/10.1007/978-3-032-11001-5_16

(4) An agreement to which paragraph (3) applies is not a custody agreement if it is clear from the agreement that, if the service provider enters into an insolvency-related proceeding, the digital asset would be part of the service provider's assets available for distribution to its creditors.
(5) The relationship between the custodian and the client may exist notwithstanding that the client may be acting in any capacity on behalf of a third party in relation to the digital asset.

1 Official Commentary

Commentary

General

10.1. The purpose of Section IV is to set out private law principles relevant to custody of digital assets. Other law, including regulatory law, may also apply to the provision of custody services. Custody, broadly speaking, is where a person (usually a legal person, which may be a regulated entity), maintains a digital asset on behalf of and for the benefit of another, a client (which may be another custodian), in a manner that gives the client special protection against unauthorised dispositions of the asset and against the insolvency of the custodian who maintains the digital asset. It only applies where the person providing the custody services does so in the ordinary course of its business. The special protection for the client referred to is likely to be achieved in private law by the client having a proprietary right of some sort in the asset, although the precise technique by which this protection is achieved will vary according to the private law of the relevant jurisdiction. As mentioned in Commentary 6.5 and 6.6, custody is an example of a situation where one person may have control (as defined in Principle 6) of a digital asset while another person (the client) may have a proprietary right in that asset.

10.2. It is quite common that the same service provider carries out various activities other than custody, including trading digital assets for its clients, trading digital assets on its own account, operating a marketplace ('exchange" or "trading platform'), etc. Principle 10 only applies to the service of custody, irrespective of other activities carried out by the person providing this service and irrespective of the provider's regulatory status. Wherever the word "custodian" is used, it refers to that person insofar as it is acting the capacity of custodian. Whatever Principle 10 states about custodians only applies to custody services and not to other services provided by those persons.

10.3. Whether the services provided by a provider are custody services will depend on whether the agreement between the service provider and its client is a custody agreement. Principle 10(3) defines a custody agreement. Principle 10(1) defines the important parties in relation to custody. The person controlling the asset is either a "custodian" (in which case it controls the assets for a "client" who is not a custodian) or a "sub-custodian" (in which case it controls the asset for a client who is a custodian, and who has entered into a custody agreement with a client in relation to that asset). A sub-custodian is also a custodian within the definition in Principle 10(1).

Maintaining a digital asset

10.4. The purpose of Principle 10(2) is to introduce the concept of "maintaining" a digital asset, which is wider than the (factual) concept of "control" as defined in Principle 6. The word "maintain" is defined as encompassing two situations in which a custodian "maintains" a digital asset for a client. The first is where a custodian has control of an asset within the meaning of Principle 6. The second is where a custodian is the recipient of custody services, that is, where another custodian (a sub-custodian) is obliged to control the asset for that custodian. Where a sub-custodian is used, the sub-custodian and the custodian both "maintain" the asset. In this situation, the custodian enters into a custody agreement with the sub-custodian and becomes its client. The custodian, therefore, has rights against the subcustodian under that custody agreement. There could also than one layer of custodians. For example, if there were three layers, the sub-custodian itself "maintains" the asset for the custodian, because a third custodian is obliged to control the asset for that sub-custodian.

Custody agreement

10.5. Principles 10(3) and 10(4) provide a method to identify whether an agreement is a custody agreement or not. They perform two functions.

10.6. First, sub-paragraphs (a), (b) and (c) of Principle 10(3) serve as a definition of a custody agreement, and therefore of custody. Subparagraph (a) makes it clear that to be a custodian, a service provider must be acting in the ordinary course of its business. Sub-paragraph (b) sets out the core duty of a custodian (see also Principle 11(1)). It covers three situations. The first is where the custodian, having entered into a custody agreement with the client, does not control the digital asset which is the subject matter of the agreement, for example, (a) if the client has not yet transferred a digital asset to the custodian or the custodian has not yet received it for the client, (b) if the custodian has exercised a right of use (see Principle 11(1)), or (c) if the custodian in is breach of its obligations and fails to control the digital asset that is the subject of the custody agreement. In each of these examples, the custodian is obliged to obtain the digital asset which is the subject of the agreement. If the digital asset is treated as fungible (see Commentary 11.6), the obligation will be to obtain a digital asset of the description specified in the agreement. The second situation is where the custodian does control the digital asset, in which case the custodian is obliged to continue to control that digital asset until otherwise instructed by the client or until the custodian exercises its right of use, if it has one (see Principles 11(1)(a) and 11(1)(b)). The third situation is where a custodian does not control the digital asset itself, but is the recipient of custody services, that is, where a subcustodian controls the asset for that custodian. In the second and third situations the custodian "maintains" the digital asset as defined in Principle 10(2). Principle 10(3)(c) makes it clear that an agreement is not a custody agreement if the client has the exclusive ability to change the control of the digital asset (for the meaning of "change of control', see Principle 6(2)). This situation is discussed in Commentary 10.14 to 10.19. The exclusive ability referred to in Principle 10(3)(c) is that referred to in Principle 6(1)(a)(iii) and therefore is subject to the relaxation of the concept of "exclusivity" set out in Principle 6(3).

10.7. The second function of Principles 10(3) and 10(4) is to address the line between a custody agreement and an agreement under which any assets maintained by the service provider form part of that service provider's assets available for distribution to its creditors if it enters into an insolvency-related proceeding (such an agreement is discussed in Commentary 10.20). This latter type of agreement can look similar to a custody agreement, as both are situations in which the client does not have control of the digital asset, and the service provider maintains an account in which the client's entitlement is recorded (a record of client entitlement is also (or should be) kept under a custody agreement, see Principle 11(3)(a)). However, under this type of (noncustody) agreement the client is exposed to the insolvency risk of the account provider. A client taking on such a risk should be aware that it is doing so, whereas the risk is not present under a custody agreement (as long as the custodian fulfils its obligation to maintain the digital asset). For this reason, an agreement under which the client does not have control is presumed to be a custody agreement unless it is made clear in the agreement that assets held by the service provider form part of the service provider's assets available for distribution to its creditors if it enters into an insolvency-related proceeding (see Principle 13(2)). It is not necessary for this, or any particular, form of words to be used as long as this consequence is clear to clients. Principle 10(4) is designed to act as an incentive to service providers to make the nature of the agreement clear on its face.

10.8. A state may wish to protect a client who enters into a non-custody agreement which exposes the client to the insolvency risk of the service provider. Various examples of such regulatory protection are set out in Commentary 10.21.

Principle 10(5)

10.9. Principle 10(5) makes it clear that, without affecting the existence or operation of the custody relationship, the client could be acting on behalf of a third party in any capacity. This could cover situations such as agency or nomineeship, and could also include where the client (in the relevant jurisdiction) holds the asset on trust for someone else (e.g., the client could be an investment fund or an individual holding the asset for a family member) or that the functional equivalent could occur in other jurisdictions.

Illustrations of custody

10.10. There now follow two illustrations of situations in which the relationship between the service provider and the client is one of custody, which are to be read in comparison with the examples of non-custody in Commentary 10.13 onwards. The first illustration of custody is a general description of a custodial wallet (sometimes called a hosted wallet) and the second is a specific illustration of where such a service could be provided within a wider context. The term "wallet" in the following illustrations is used in the colloquial sense in which it is used in the market, that is, software (or hardware) that enables a person to interact with a digital asset, for example, via*the generation and management of public and/or private keys. The means by which, and by whom, this interaction is effected depends on the type of wallet. As provided in Principles 10(3) and 10(4) and Commentary 10.7, an agreement between a client and a service provider in the context set out in Commentary 10.11 and 10.12 will be a custody agreement unless it is made clear that the assets controlled by the service provider form part of the service provider's assets available for distribution to its creditors if it enters into an insolvency-related proceeding, in which case the agreement falls within the illustration discussed in Commentary 10.20.*

Custodial or hosted wallet

10.11. ***Illustration 1****. In a custodial or hosted wallet arrangement, users transfer digital assets to the wallets of a service provider. The service provider (the custodian) holds the private keys of the wallet to which the digital asset is thereafter connected. Hosted wallets often appear in the context of trading platforms, where an intermediary facilitates trades of digital assets between users. An example of the provision of hosted wallet services as part of a trading platform service is given in Commentary 10.12. Service providers often offer more than one kind of wallet service, allowing users to take advantage of both self-custody and custodial wallet solutions (for self-custody see Commentary 10.15 to 10.17) because the two different types of wallets serve different purposes.*

Trading account

10.12. ***Illustration 2****. A, a service provider, offers what it terms a "trading account', which is the functionality within a wallet that enables a user to buy and hold all digital assets purchased with fiat currency through A. The contract between A and its client expressly provides that title to the digital assets in the trading account belong to the user and does not transfer to A, and emphasises that digital assets in the trading account are not the property of A and are not loaned to A. Some transactions between A's clients initiated from a trading account occur off-chain, and are recorded only by accounting ledger entries in the records of A. A transaction between a self-custody wallet (provided by A or by another service provider) and a trading account provided by A, on the other hand, would occur on-chain.*

llustrations of non-custody arrangements

10.13. There are a number of situations where a person controls a digital asset which are not custody and where any agreement with a service provider is not a custody agreement, as defined in Principles 10(3) and 10(4). The following paragraphs describe and illustrate examples of these situations.

10.14. ***Illustration 3: Where a person, such as an investor, controls a digital asset****. A person (such as an investor) can control a digital asset by using some hardware or software. This is the case where, for example, she runs a full node (or a light node) on the blockchain on which the asset is registered or where she uses wallet software or service to access the blockchain. In all these cases, the investor keeps control of the digital asset because she stores and uses the private key and does not entrust or surrender it to a third party. The provider of the wallet used by the investor only provides the means (hardware or software) by which the investor stores and uses her private keys. The investor is exposed to the risk of the wallet malfunctioning, but her digital assets are not controlled by the provider. The insolvency of the provider would affect its ability to operate or maintain the wallet but has no legal impact on the digital assets controlled by the investor. The relationship between the investor and the person providing the hardware or software is purely contractual and is governed by the terms of the agreement between them.*

10.15. Self-custody is where a user holds private keys either using software solutions deployed directly on their own computer or mobile phone, or using cloud-based software-as-a-service non-custodial wallets. The two options are quite similar: the chief difference is in the location where the private keys are held. In both cases, the client controls the digital asset. The two options are illustrated in the following two paragraphs.

Self-custody by wallet software

10.16. ***Illustration 4.*** *"Self-custody" in this paragraph refers to the use of wallet software, of which an example is given in this paragraph. "XX" is open source software, developed by a global community of developers and designers. It is compatible with a variety of hardware wallets. The user of XX creates a wallet password and secret recovery phrase, which are stored, together with the private keys, in an encrypted format on the mobile phone or computer on which the XX software is installed. Transactions conducted through wallets using XX software are broadcast on-chain.*

Self custody by cloud-based software-as-a-service

10.17. ***Illustration 5.****Y, a service provider, provides a non-custodial wallet for users. A user creates an account, and creates a password, which gives the user access to an encrypted file kept by Y on the blockchain containing a "seed" (a secret private key recovery phrase), the users" private keys and addresses of digital assets. The password is not stored by Y and must be kept safe and confidential by the user herself. Y has no access to the user's private keys, seed, or password. When a password or seed phrase is used correctly, the file containing private keys is decrypted locally on the user's computer or mobile phone, and the user can carry out transactions, which are conducted directly on-chain. Y stores the encrypted file in the cloud, while when the XX software is used (see Commentary 10.16), the encrypted file is stored locally on the user's computer or mobile phone. Users of the software-as-a-service model, therefore, could find themselves in difficulty should Y ever decide to stop providing the wallet services.*

Safeguarding of private keys

10.18. ***Illustration 6: Where a business provides safeguarding of private keys.****Another arrangement is where a provider safeguards its client's private keys or provides software or hardware to facilitate the client's safeguarding its private keys. Depending on the features, the provider of the software or hardware may (or may not) have the ability to use the client's private keys and thus take control of the client's digital assets. However, this is not the purpose of this type of arrangement and typically the provider will be prohibited from using the client's private keys for any purpose that has not been agreed by the client. The client still has control of the digital asset, and has the ability to change the control of the asset (using the terminology in Principle 6(1)(a)(iii)). This business model is therefore not a custody service as defined in Principle 10, even though it is sometimes called "custody" by market participants. In contrast, where a service provider provides a custody service, its clients transfer their digital assets to addresses or private keys controlled by that service provider, or the service provider acquires digital assets which it controls for the client. An example of safeguarding of private keys follows in the next paragraph.*

10.19. The Z wallet generates private keys within the device, and then stores the keys there. This provides very secure cold wallet storage, by keeping the keys unconnected, and thus out of reach from online hackers and other threats, from the moment of generation until the moment of use. The software on the Z hardware is not intermediated, as no third-party intermediary has access to the keys held on the Z wallet. When a user wants to transact with the keys held in a Z wallet, they use software similar to a mobile phone app store to access services provided by other providers to send, buy, or sell digital assets.

Agreement for delivery of digital assets

10.20. ***Illustration 7: An agreement for delivery of digital assets.****A fintech firm or a financial institution, such as a dealer, an exchange, or a trading platform, may incur an obligation to deliver a certain quantity of a given digital asset to a client because it has received the asset from the client or because it has acquired the asset in the primary or secondary market for the client. The firm or institution will maintain an account (similar to a bank account, as opposed to the bailment or custody of assets belonging to the client) on which credits and debits of a particular digital asset are recorded from time to time so that the account balance evidences at any time the quantity of such digital asset the firm or institution is obliged to deliver to the client (or, as the case may be, may claim from the client). For each digital asset, such an account operates in the same way as a current account in a fiat currency. The investor does not have control of digital assets; she merely has an unsecured personal claim against the account provider. If the account provider becomes insolvent, the claim for the delivery of a digital asset is likely to be converted into a (fiat) money claim and will rank pari passu with the claims of all other unsecured creditors, although in some jurisdictions distribution of digital assets themselves may be permitted. If the digital asset is not fungible, the relevant claim is for delivery of a specific asset rather than for a generic quantity of digital assets of a certain description. This, however, should not alter the legal characterisation of the obligation as a personal right or its treatment as an unsecured claim in the insolvency of the obligee.*

10.21. A State may consider whether regulatory law should mitigate the risk for some or all types of clients who enter into the type of agreements described in Commentary 10.20. One example would be a requirement for providers of this type of account to hold a certain amount of capital. Another example would be a requirement to hold liquid assets commensurate to the value of digital assets that the provider owes to its clients, which may be accompanied by a preference over such assets for the clients on the insolvency of the account provider. Other examples are a requirement for specific disclosure of the relevant risks in the agreement, a requirement that providers of this type of account must be regulated entities conforming to standards, or a limitation on the type of people who can become clients (as in many crowd-funding regulations).

Decentralised autonomous organisations

10.22. Decentralised autonomous organisations (DAOs) use code (also called smart contracts or apps) stored and executed on a blockchain to control certain digital assets. An investor may transfer a digital asset to a particular smart contract so that its code will determine when and to whom the digital asset will be ultimately transferred. This situation is different from self-custody, custody, and a personal claim as described in Commentary 10.20 if there is no identifiable person, natural or legal, who controls the digital assets subject to the smart contract. In some jurisdictions a DAO can be a legal person, or a trust, or the smart contracts are controlled by natural or legal persons in which case there is an identifiable person. However, in other cases the DAO is just a web of smart contracts with no involvement of a natural or legal person. The operation of the smart contract may depend on some form of vote or consensus among participants in the blockchain, but a voting or consensus mechanism can hardly qualify as joint control of the assets by all persons entitled to participate. For the reasons given in this paragraph, a structure involving a DAO is unlikely to involve custody, but this will depend on the specific arrangement in each case.

2 Reflections

2.1 Introductory

Principle 10 is the first of the four that comprise Section IV of these UNIDROIT Principles on Digital Assets and Private Law. The Section is devoted to the custody of such assets. Principle 10 deals with the personal elements involved in the custody relationship and the legal configuration of the "custody agreement" as a contractual instrument on which custody is based.

This subject has been the subject matter of discussions in the preparatory work from the outset, and in the Exploratory Workshop held on 17 and 18 September 2020 by the Working Group on Digital Assets and Private Law. It sets out by highlighting the relevance of custody in the practical operation of digital assets.[1] It starts by considering custody as the need to use an intermediary for the acquisition and subsequent holding of digital assets for the acquirer. It is argued that digital assets raise many of the same legal issues traditionally raised in the custody context but also raise new ones that need to be addressed. An example might be whether a custodian service provider is obliged to provide its users with access to a new cryptocurrency created by a third party through a hard bifurcation (*forking*).[2] It was considered appropriate that the draft Principles address these types of novel issues relating to the custody of digital assets.

Accordingly, the fourth session of the Exploratory Workshop addressed the environments in which an acquirer of digital assets chooses to hold the assets through a custodian and compared "direct" holding to various custodial holding structures.[3] Five options were presented that users could use to hold cryptocurrencies (mainly using Bitcoin as an example). The first option to directly interact with the blockchain protocol might be to hold the cryptocurrency directly. This could be done by downloading the Bitcoin Core software that contains a wallet. The second option would

[1] UNIDROIT 2020 – Study LXXXII – W.G.1 – Doc. 2, November.

[2] This issue had been addressed in at least two trials in the United States, Cf. UNIDROIT 2020 – Study LXXXII – W.G.1 – Doc. 2, November, par. 66.

[3] UNIDROIT 2021 – Study LXXXII – W.G.1 – Doc. 3, March, par. 75.

be to use a Simplified Payment Verification (SPV) wallet. Using non-custodial third-party software and/or hardware, the third option for holding cryptocurrencies could be to use online wallets (non-custodial online wallets do not allow technical access to a user's private keys). However, with online wallets, the user cannot fully control their private keys, so if they forget their password and seed phrase, the assets are lost forever. Also, since the private keys were decrypted on the client side, the system is vulnerable to computer malware and attacks on software providers. The fourth option would be to use a hardware wallet. The fifth option could be holding cryptocurrencies using a custodial wallet provider exchange. This option provides a user-friendly experience and sometimes even offers offline storage options.[4]

It was noted that in the United States, some States had digital custody regulations, which limited the assets that custodians could hold and manage based on the regulator's concerns regarding the use of certain cryptocurrencies. Thus, for example, the New York Department of Financial Services (DFS) imposed the most extensive regulations, which included requiring a custodian licensee to adopt specific policies and procedures for vetting a digital asset before offering custody services, publishing a "green list" of virtual currencies approved for custody; requiring a licensee to submit information about other digital assets to the DFS for review before holding such digital assets; and requiring the identity of the individual client or counterparty (i.e. "anonymous" cryptocurrencies were excluded).[5]

It was also noted that individual and institutional custodians used either hot (online) or cold (offline) storage media, although most custodians used a combination of both. The omnibus or split wallet model was also used—most custodians also used a combination of these for different types of storage. It was also noted that US law allowed the duties of a securities intermediary to be freely modified by agreement between custodians and clients, with the ability to agree that a digital asset was a financial asset and that custodians could obtain and hold digital assets through distributed ledger technology.[6] One difference noted in the practice of the transmission of negotiable securities[7] and cryptocurrencies refers to the period existing in the case of the transmission of securities between the moment the client gives the purchase or sale order and the settlement thereof. In the case of digital assets such as cryptocurrencies, there is no such period because the user operates by sending

---

[4] UNIDROIT 2021 – Study LXXXII – W.G.1 – Doc. 3, March, par. 76–80.

[5] UNIDROIT 2021 – Study LXXXII – W.G.1 – Doc. 3, March, par. 89.

[6] UNIDROIT 2021 – Study LXXXII – W.G.1 – Doc. 3, March, par. 90 y 92.

[7] UNIDROIT has extensive experience with securities intermediaries (Geneva Securities Convention and Legislative Guide on Intermediated Securities). But the custody of digital assets presents particular challenges for private law. The range of possible legal relationships that have traditionally applied to the custody of securities (such as transfer of title, trust and/or bailment, agency and other contractual relationships) may not be suitable or need adjustment for application to digital assets, which raise particular issues. The vagueness of contractual terms governing custody arrangements is another reason to consider Principles to guide the characterisation of the rights of custodians' clients and provide legal certainty. The lack of, or only nascent, regulatory responses to offer protection to custodians' clients underscores the need to consider such Principles. Cf. UNIDROIT 2020 – Study LXXXII – W.G.1 – Doc. 2, November, par. 67.

the cryptocurrency to a smart contract for immediate settlement. Added to this is the difficulty of knowing whether a cryptocurrency that is transferred is previously encumbered by constituting a movable security.[8]

2.2 The General Concept of Custody

The concept of custodianship, in general, was discussed at the same working session. Still, it was particularly raised in response to a question from a participant regarding direct holding situations, where a holder shared his private key with another party under a multi-signature agreement for collateral purposes. In this scenario, the question arises as to whether a party participating in a multi-signature agreement that could block transactions on an asset would be treated as a custodian of the asset for private law or regulatory purposes, especially given the consequences of illiquidity seen in the insolvency of Lehman Brothers, so that custodianship had to be tested in court. It was noted that the logic behind the requirements for custodians was established (in the United States) to prevent advisors from misusing their clients' assets. In any case, a custodian would largely only act on instructions issued by the owner of an asset. It was also noted that this consideration was important in cases where multi-signature arrangements existed not for security reasons but as multiple holders of the same asset, and one of the key holders played a crucial role in the asset transaction. In such situations, imposing a statutory safekeeping obligation on that party might be useful.[9]

Also, from the outset, a recurring question arose when addressing the drafting of any international legal instrument: the "synchronisation" between Anglo-Saxon law and continental law (common law and civil law). The question was raised around a basic and fundamental institution linked to the custody relationship, which is the Trust law tradition that provides the client with protection in common law contexts. It would, therefore, be necessary to explore, in civil law, to see what the equivalent in civil law would be to provide the client with the same degree of protection in both legal systems concerning the digital assets entrusted to the custodian. In addition, the complexity presented by the traceability and recognition of a property right over a certain digital asset (Bitcoin, for example) was highlighted, if there is a custody relationship over it in an omnibus environment, in which the custodian does not distinguish between the specific assets of one or other clients. In such a case, a property right over a specific asset cannot be determined. This refers to the issue of commingling assets from different clients, which might require a set of legal rules to protect clients. Without proof of ownership, the holder was presumed to be the owner, and the client would be left with only a contractual right to the asset. It was added that this situation could be resolved by having a separate pool (from the custodians' assets) for the client's assets on a legal basis. Clients would be classified as co-owners,

[8] UNIDROIT 2021 – StudyLXXXII – W.G.1 – Doc. 3, March, par. 93.

[9] UNIDROIT 2021 – StudyLXXXII – W.G.1 – Doc. 3, March, par. 95.

who would share pro rata in the pool and not share assets with the custodian. The other solution would be SPVs (simplified payment verification wallets), created and incorporated solely to hold client assets. Concerning the United States, it was noted that while commodatums were a last resort, they could be a useful mechanism for digital assets. However, commodatums were not useful in an omnibus environment or where the custodian's assets were commingled.[10]

The "theft" of passwords, not just forgetfulness, was pointed out as a relevant issue concerning the custody of digital assets, both by the owner and a third-party custodian. Someone may gain access to a password and use it without the legitimate owner or the custodian being aware of it. The use of multi-signature wallets was pointed out as a possible solution. It was noted that cybersecurity risks for custodians are another important problem and require careful examination.[11]

Finally, the Working Group's exploratory session noted a paradoxical fact in the history of digital assets: Bitcoin was largely driven initially to reduce the role of intermediaries; however, a commercial need for intermediation has since emerged, putting custodians back at the system's centre. This does not prevent efforts to bring directly held digital assets to market more easily.[12]

It was concluded that the Principles should consider that a custodian must ensure that it securely maintains custody of its clients' (owners') digital assets. This entails obligations under private law and potential liabilities under digital asset regulatory regimes. Accordingly, the Working Group could consider what relationship with a digital asset amounts to "custody" to trigger a custodian's private law and regulatory obligations (which may differ from one another). It will also be important to consider what should be expected of a custodian for it to meet its obligations to safeguard client assets. Furthermore, in the absence of regulatory regimes for such custody, or in the face of emerging but undeveloped and untested regimes, private law rules may be essential to protecting owners.[13] The following questions were therefore formulated for the Working Group[14]:

- What relationships between an owner, the relevant digital asset, and another person amount to "custody" in order to establish a legal relationship of a particular kind?
- Would custody require the custodian to maintain its unique private key for digital assets residing in a public blockchain environment? Or would access to the owner's private key suffice?

---

[10] UNIDROIT 2021 – StudyLXXXII – W.G.1 – Doc. 3, March, par. 96.

[11] UNIDROIT 2021 – StudyLXXXII – W.G.1 – Doc. 3, March, par. 98.

[12] UNIDROIT 2021 – StudyLXXXII – W.G.1 – Doc. 3, March, par. 99.

[13] UNIDROIT 2020 – Study LXXXII – W.G.1 – Doc. 2, November, par. 68, where, among the UNIDROIT Instruments, reference is made to the UNIDROIT Convention on Substantive Rules for Intermediated Securities (2013) https://www.UNIDROIT.org/instruments/capital-markets/geneva-convention https://www.UNIDROIT.org/wp-content/uploads/2021/06/convention.pdf, a Convention of which there is a Spanish version carried out under the auspices of the Language Interpretation Office of the Ministry of Foreign Affairs and Cooperation of the Kingdom of Spain https://www.Unidroit.org/instruments/capital-markets/geneva-convention/other-languages/ https://www.Unidroit.org/wp-content/uploads/2021/06/convention-spanish.pdf.

[14] *Ibidem.*

- How would multi-signature agreements be treated?
- Can more than one person have custody of digital assets?

The relevance and connection of the legal configuration of custody with another key legal institution, namely insolvency, to which the seventh (and last) Section of the Principles is devoted, was also highlighted. Even within the fourth Section devoted to custody, its previous article (13) deals with protecting the client's digital assets from the creditors of an insolvent custodian. With this aim, the Exploratory Workshop has already examined client protection in the event of insolvency of cryptocurrency custodians, on whom most cryptocurrency investors depend, which may be exchanges or specialised custodians that offer cryptocurrency services.[15] The risk at this point is focused on the fact that there is a difference in legal protection provided under the regulation of insolvency and custody in different legal systems. It was noted that bankruptcy or insolvency entails a significant risk when holding crypto-assets through a custodian. The legal qualification and enforcement of rights and interests in insolvency differ from one jurisdiction to another and should be carefully examined. The legal issues that arose in some insolvencies of cryptocurrency custodians were examined.[16] It was noted that in Japan, a court held that digital assets should be considered from a contractual perspective rather than a property law perspective, which meant that clients had a mere contractual claim against the debtor. This was not beneficial to clients seeking to recover their assets. In another insolvency case under Italian law, clients were treated as owners of digital assets. Still, those were not separate but commingled with the custodian's assets, which did not benefit clients as it resulted in clients only having a contractual claim against the custodian. In another case, under New Zealand law, digital assets were considered to be commingled with the assets of other clients, but the courts assumed that a trust had been established. Therefore, a property right was found to exist over the assets that the custodian held for its clients. However, the ruling also noted a separate trust for each type of cryptocurrency, which meant that a shortfall in a particular type of cryptocurrency was only distributed among clients with interests in that specific type of cryptocurrency.[17]

It was made clear that a key issue in the custody of digital assets is segregation in separate accounts following the general regulation of financial institutions. In the case of insolvency, the criteria for apportionment among clients should be addressed if it has to be applied due to a deficit in the amount of available cryptocurrencies.[18]

---

[15] UNIDROIT 2021 – Study LXXXII – W.G.1 – Doc. 3, March, par. 81.

[16] UNIDROIT 2021 – Study LXXXII – W.G.1 – Doc. 3, March, par. 82.

[17] UNIDROIT 2021 – Study LXXXII – W.G.1 – Doc. 3, March, par. 83.

[18] UNIDROIT 2021 – Study LXXXII – W.G.1 – Doc. 3, March, par. 84 y 86.

2.3 Content of the Custody Relationship

The questions raised above were addressed at the first session of the Working Group held from 17 to 19 November 2020.[19] The first step was to distinguish between the purely contractual scope of the custody relationship and its issues in insolvency. The topic was approached from the first perspective, and it was decided to make a first approximation based on the different types of wallets on the market.[20]

Since a plurality of legal relationships may fall within the concept of custody, it would be necessary to determine which ones fall within the scope of the Principles. The deposit of money for purchasing digital assets is not the same as the custodian's deposit of these for custody - and management.[21] It was pointed out as a fundamental question whether it is possible to deposit an intangible asset, such as a digital asset, in the possession of a custodian while retaining ownership. In civil law jurisdictions, the deposit of fungible assets, such as money, implies the loss of ownership and its replacement by a credit right (irregular deposit of money). However, as an exception, in the case of securities, the legal regime is articulated to provide legal certainty to the market so that it is possible to deposit these with an intermediary without losing ownership. In common law systems, a similar result is achieved by establishing a trust by contractual means. It was indicated that, as a starting point, one could refer to the Legislative Guide on Intermediated Securities,[22] adopting a functional perspective by focusing on situations where an investor expects that a custodian would protect the assets belonging to the investor.[23]

The aim was to examine the similarities between intermediated securities (such as stocks and bonds) and digital assets (such as Bitcoin and Ethereum) to propose similar rules based on the similarities between them. The approach of national regulators in Europe was likely to have similarities, while in the United States, the differences were

---

[19] UNIDROIT 2021 – Study LXXXII – W.G.1 – Doc. 4, March.

[20] UNIDROIT 2021 – Study LXXXII – W.G.1 – Doc. 4, March, par. 72–76; in note 5 to this last paragraph, reference is made to the IOSCO (International Organization of Securities Commissions) document, *Issues, Risks and Regulatory Considerations Relating to Crypto-Asset Trading Platforms*, Final Report, February 2020 https://www.iosco.org/library/pubdocs/pdf/IOSCOPD649.pdf where the International Organization of Securities Commissions presents a work identifying various risks related to crypto-asset trading platforms. Here, custody is understood as controlling the private key that confers the factual (technological) power to transfer the crypto-asset. Obviously, this concept of custody differs from that traditionally used in relation to financial assets. Cf. pp. 12–13 and 42–43 of the aforementioned Report. See also UK Law Commission, *Digital assets and ETDs in private international law: which court, which law? Call for evidence*, February 2024, p. 41, https://lawcom.gov.uk/project/digital-assets-and-etds-in-private-international-law-which-court-which-law/; https://cloud-platform-e218f50a4812967ba1215eaecede923f.s3.amazonaws.com/uploads/sites/30/2024/02/Conflicts-full-document-FINAL-pdf-1.pdf

[21] UNIDROIT 2021 – Study LXXXII – W.G.1 – Doc. 4, March, par. 76–77.

[22] UNIDROIT Legislative Guide on Intermediated Securities https://www.Unidroit.org/instruments/capital-markets/legislative-guide/ https://www.Unidroit.org/wp-content/uploads/2021/06/LEGISLATIVE-GUIDE-English.pdf https://www.Unidroit.org/wp-content/uploads/2021/06/LEGISLATIVE-GUIDE-Spanish.pdf

[23] UNIDROIT 2021 – Study LXXXII – W.G.1 – Doc. 4, March, par. 78, 80-82.

more marked in custody. In any case, there is one clear difference: States have private law regulations relating to securities, while in the case of digital assets, there is no such regulation due to the lack of a clear conceptualisation and the added difficulty of cross-border projection of digital assets.[24]

Therefore, it should begin by determining the nature of digital assets and then proceed to examine the custody relationship over them. The methodology for preparing the Principles should address the question of what a digital asset is, what custody is, and whether this is considered a regular or irregular deposit. This involves determining whether custody implies that the custodian incorporates the asset into its balance sheet or whether it merely provides software as an electronic wallet. In any case, the practical reality is the existence of a wide variety of types of contracts when it comes to articulating the custody of digital assets based on the regulation to which, where applicable, the custodian intermediary adheres.[25] It seemed clear that each type of custody arrangement needed to be examined to determine what investor protection was necessary in each case.[26]

When considering the role of nodes in the distributed network system and the rights and interests of those who connect to those nodes from outside the system, the need to distinguish between different modes of participation was noted: protocol implementers, miners, simplified payment verification (SPV), and custodians. The operator at a node may or may not additionally offer custodial services to third parties. Given the plurality of technology used, the Principles approach should be technologically neutral.[27] Harmonisation of national laws could not be sought either. Rather, protective measures should be indicated for digital asset holders, leaving it up to the States to ensure that their legal systems allow this in accordance with their private law, regardless of whether "cold" or "hot" wallets are used.[28]

2.4 *The First Approach to the Formulation of the Custody Principle*

The Working Group was organised into Subgroups. Based on the above, Subgroup 1 prepared a proposal with the following basic content[29]:

[24] UNIDROIT 2021 – Study LXXXII – W.G.1 – Doc. 4, March, par. 84–86.

[25] UNIDROIT 2021 – Study LXXXII – W.G.1 – Doc. 4, March, par. 87–90.

[26] UNIDROIT 2021 – Study LXXXII – W.G.1 – Doc. 4, March, par. 98.

[27] UNIDROIT 2021 – Study LXXXII – W.G.1 – Doc. 4, March, par. 100–102. The principle of technological neutrality, that is, of normative neutrality regarding the use of technology, was already included in the Guide for the incorporation of the UNCITRAL Model Law on Electronic Signatures (2001) into domestic law, par. 5, 14, 27, 32, 34, 67, 82, 88 y 107 https://uncitral.un.org/sites/uncitral.un.org/files/media-documents/uncitral/es/ml-elecsig-s.pdf

[28] UNIDROIT 2021 – Study LXXXII – W.G.1 – Doc. 4, March, par. 104–110.

[29] UNIDROIT 2021 – Study LXXXII – W.G.2 – Doc. 2, March, par. 95.

1. The owner of a digital asset is the person who, alone or jointly with one or more other people, has control of that asset pursuant to Principle [X] Control.

Keys: Control is used as an equivalent of possession and is a matter of fact. Multisig wallets do not necessarily mean joint ownership.

2. A holder of a digital asset is held as a custodian on behalf of another person (known as the client) if:

(a) The holder is not authorised to transfer that asset or to use it for its own benefit, except to the extent permitted by law or by the client;
(b) The holder is obliged to transfer that asset following the client's instructions; and
(c) The holder has obligations to the client in relation to the safekeeping of such asset or of a set of assets that includes it.
Keys: The approach is functional and neutral (it includes both the assumption of trust and the assumption of the contractual relationship. The three conditions/obligations contained in a), b) and c) must be met for the holder of a digital asset to be a custodian.

3. The relationship between the custodian and the client may exist despite a third party having rights against the client in relation to the digital asset.

Keys: This is the case of a trust (for example, an investment fund).

4. A custodian's duties to his client may include:

(a) The duty to maintain a record of the digital assets held for each client;
(b) The duty to maintain digital assets of the types and in amounts identical to the records it maintains for its clients at all times;
(c) The obligation to acquire digital assets promptly if necessary to comply with obligation b);
(d) The duty to keep digital assets held for one's own account separate from assets;
(e) Subject to any rights granted to the custodian or other person, the duty to transfer all benefits derived from a digital asset to the client for whom it holds that asset.
Keys: Each client's assets must be kept separate from the custodian's assets. There must be a correlation between client records and the digital assets over which the custodian actually has control.[30]

5. A digital asset held for a client by a custodian

(a) may be subject to a security right granted to that custodian by the client;
(b) may be subject to a [real] [right] guarantee in favour of that custodian arising by operation of law.
Key: A custodian has a security interest in the asset it holds for a client.

---

[30] The obligations contemplated here derive from the UNIDROIT Geneva Convention. UNIDROIT 2021 – Study LXXXII – W.G.2 – Doc. 3, April, par. 11.

6. A holder is not a custodian of a digital asset merely by maintaining an account in a client's name and is obliged to transfer that asset or an equivalent asset to that client or another person.

Key: It describes the situation where a person (for example, an exchange) operates in the same way as a bank.

7. If a holder enters into insolvency proceedings, a digital asset held by the holder as custodian of a client's account does not form part of the holder's assets for distribution to its creditors.

Key: The consequences of the custodian's insolvency are presented functionally rather than using legal concepts such as ownership.

The Working Group considered the Subgroup's proposal at its second session held from 16 to 18 March 2021.[31] It was noted that the custody situation is one of the different situations in which a holder can possess a digital asset. Questions were raised about the convenience of using terms such as holder[32] or owner of digital assets and the importance of considering the possibility of different levels of shared control, where the figure of the sub-custodian should be inserted.[33]

Following a discussion on fungibility in general and intangible assets in particular, it became clear that the Sub-Working Group's proposal failed to capture this issue.[34] It was also noted that no sanction was contemplated in the event of a breach of obligations by the custodian. It was concluded that the Principle of Custody should consider the variety of ways in which records relating to digital assets are kept. Therefore, any definition should be made in functional or factual terms.[35]

2.5 *Progress in the Formulation of the Principle of Custody*

The Working Group considered the revised proposal of the Subgroup[36] at its third session, held from 30 June to 2 July 2021.[37] The following were new features in the latest version:

- Custody activity must occur in the context of the practice of a business.

[31] UNIDROIT 2021 – Study LXXXII – W.G.2 – Doc. 3, April. Summary report of the second session.

[32] It was recalled that the UNCITRAL Model Law on Electronic Transferable Records (2017) avoided using the term "holder" when introducing control as a functional equivalent of possession. UNIDROIT 2021 – Study LXXXII – W.G.2 – Doc. 3, April, par. 17.

[33] UNIDROIT 2021 – Study LXXXII – W.G.2 – Doc. 3, April, par. 10–12 y 16.

[34] UNIDROIT 2021 – Study LXXXII – W.G.2 – Doc. 3, April, par. 18–20.

[35] UNIDROIT 2021 – Study LXXXII – W.G.2 – Doc. 3, April, par. 23–24 y 27–28.

[36] UNIDROIT 2021 – Study LXXXII – W.G.3 – Doc. 2 (rev. 1), June, par. 77–78.

[37] UNIDROIT 2021 – Study LXXXII – W.G.3 – Doc. 4, July. Summary report of the third session.

- The digital asset custody regime does not apply to other situations such as direct ownership, safekeeping of private keys, the obligation to deliver a digital asset or implementations using smart contracts.
- The figure of the sub-custodian is introduced.

At the third session of the Working Group, it was noted that the submission of a digital asset to a smart contract did not entail a case of custody but rather a "suspension" of control by the owner of the asset, who, for example, could have constituted a security interest using the smart contract, which, when the time came, would be self-executed on the programmed terms.[38] The Group agreed that the difference between fungible and non-fungible tokens should not be mentioned in the custody Principle.[39] It was also noted that the custodian's duties set out in the Principle were binding because there would no longer be a custody situation if they were excluded. The duties contemplated, therefore, form part of the concept of custody, which implies obligations to the client concerning the safeguarding of assets.[40] In any case, the list is not exhaustive; a State may include more duties.[41]

The criterion is reiterated that when digital assets are integrated into the custodian's balance sheet, there is no custody situation in the terms defined in the Principles. In such a situation, the client is not protected against the custodian in the event of the custodian's insolvency.[42] Ultimately, the key element in setting up custody is the contract between the custodian and the client. It is essential that the contract clearly defines the custody relationship and the terms or conditions under which it is carried out. If the contract is ambiguous, legal uncertainty arises. Hence, the Working Group proposed that States be encouraged to consider the use of presumptions in the case of an ambiguous agreement between the parties.[43]

At the fourth session held from 2 to 4 November 2021,[44] the Working Group was presented with the revised proposal of the Subgroup, which included use cases to distinguish cases of practice that would or would not qualify as custody. The examples mentioned in the previous session that are not considered custody are thus introduced into the text of the Principles as examples.[45] The importance of using the term "hold" rather than "control" when referring to the sub-custodian's activity concerning digital assets was stressed.[46] The aim was to highlight differences in the custody characteristics carried out by the custodian and the sub-custodian. Clearly, including the sub-custodian figure in the Principles was not a smooth process.[47]

---

[38] UNIDROIT 2021 – Study LXXXII – W.G.3 – Doc. 4, July, par. 81–83.

[39] UNIDROIT 2021 – Study LXXXII – W.G.3 – Doc. 4, July, par. 86.

[40] UNIDROIT 2021 – Study LXXXII – W.G.3 – Doc. 4, July, par. 90–92.

[41] UNIDROIT 2021 – Study LXXXII – W.G.3 – Doc. 4, July, par. 107.

[42] UNIDROIT 2021 – Study LXXXII – W.G.3 – Doc. 4, July, par. 111–113.

[43] UNIDROIT 2021 – Study LXXXII – W.G.3 – Doc. 4, July, par. 118.

[44] UNIDROIT 2021 – Study LXXXII – W.G.4 – Doc. 3, December. Summary report of the fourth session.

[45] UNIDROIT 2021 – Study LXXXII – W.G.4 – Doc. 2, October, Annex III, Appendix 1.

[46] UNIDROIT 2021 – Study LXXXII – W.G.4 – Doc. 3, December, par. 47 y 52.

[47] UNIDROIT 2021 – Study LXXXII – W.G.4 – Doc. 3, December, par. 68–73.

At the fifth session held from 7 to 9 March 2022,[48] the Working Group already had a first draft of all the structured Principles.[49] Section V was devoted to custody; it included Principles 12–15. It drew on the previous work by the Working Group.[50] Custody, duties and sub-custody appeared in three separate Principles (12, 13 and 15) with corresponding commentaries. The Group agreed that the wording should be revised.[51]

For the sixth working session that took place from August 31 to September 1, 2022,[52] the Group had been provided with a revised version of the draft Principles.[53] In this latest revision, the last Principle of the Section previously labelled sub-custody was re-labelled insolvency of a custodian, distributing the regulation of sub-custody among several Principles of the Section.[54] The first Principle of the Section retained the general label of custody. In the context of custody, it is noted that the term "hold" is to be understood as equivalent to "possession".[55] The Working Group's discussions again highlighted the difficulty in this context of using the terms "maintain", "hold", and "control". In this regard, it was stated that the important issue was that the assets held by the custodian would be excluded from the assets at risk of liquidation in the event of the custodian's insolvency.[56] For this purpose, knowing whether the digital asset is included in the custodian's balance sheet is relevant. In most cases it is not, although if it is, it is not part of the custodian's assets in the event of insolvency.[57]

It was noted that Principle 12 purported to define custody but contained more of a description of a custody arrangement. It also discusses self-custody, sub-custody, and other services that resemble custody but are not.[58] It was noted that the project pointed out the differences between custodians and exchanges, which by and large were not obvious.[59] It was concluded that the drafting committee should carefully review the text of the Principle in light of the issues raised in the Working Group's discussions.[60]

---

[48] UNIDROIT 2022– Study LXXXII – W.G.5 – Doc. 4, April, Summary report of the fifth session.

[49] UNIDROIT 2022– Study LXXXII – W.G.5 – Doc. 2, February, Master copy of black letter Principles. UNIDROIT 2022– Study LXXXII – W.G.5 – Doc. 3, February, Master copy of the Principles and Comments.

[50] UNIDROIT 2022– Study LXXXII – W.G.5 – Doc. 4, April, par. 119.

[51] UNIDROIT 2022– Study LXXXII – W.G.5 – Doc. 4, April, par. 122.

[52] UNIDROIT 2022– Study LXXXII – W.G.6 – Doc. 4, November, Summary report of the sixth session.

[53] UNIDROIT 2022– Study LXXXII – W.G.6 – Doc. 2, August, Master copy of the draft principles and comments. UNIDROIT 2022– Study LXXXII – W.G.6 – Doc. 3, August, Issues paper. UNIDROIT 2022– Study LXXXII – W.G.6 – Doc. 3, Annex (Comments received by the Steering Committee).

[54] UNIDROIT 2022– Study LXXXII – W.G.6 – Doc. 3, August, par. 4.

[55] UNIDROIT 2022– Study LXXXII – W.G.6 – Doc. 3, August, par. 92.

[56] UNIDROIT 2022– Study LXXXII – W.G.6 – Doc. 4, November, par. 147–148, 154 y 155.

[57] UNIDROIT 2022– Study LXXXII – W.G.6 – Doc. 4, November, par. 156.

[58] UNIDROIT 2022– Study LXXXII – W.G.6 – Doc. 4, November, par. 146–148 y 157.

[59] UNIDROIT 2022– Study LXXXII – W.G.6 – Doc. 4, November, par. 151.

[60] UNIDROIT 2022– Study LXXXII – W.G.6 – Doc. 4, November, par. 160.

At its seventh session, held from 19 to 21 December 2022,[61] the Working Group had a more refined version of the Principles.[62] The Section on Custody is now numbered IV, comprising Principles 11 to 13. Principle 11 on custody sets out formal definitions including custodian, sub-custodian and client. In addition, it explains what a custody arrangement is. In this Principle, as throughout the text of the Principles, the term "hold" is replaced by "maintained".[63] The provided examples aim to afford the most suitable illustrations possible on transactions with digital assets related to the content of the Principle, either to highlight that they would or would not be covered by the assumption.[64] The Working Group supported the draft of Principle 11, noting that it would be relocated, and asked the Drafting Committee to develop the Commentary further.[65]

At the request of the Working Group, the UNIDROIT Secretariat launched an online public consultation on 10 January 2023, which was open until 28 February 2023.[66] The comments received are contained in a document, 17, having regard to Principle 10 on Custody.[67] The eighth meeting of the Working Group was held in a hybrid format from 8 to 10 March 2023. This session addressed the comments received through the online public consultation. The Working Group deliberated on the comments received in a Principle-by-Principle format.[68] The topics of private international law, custody and control elicited the longest discussions. It was also decided to expand the reference to the relationship between the Principles and other international instruments, notably the UNCITRAL Model Law on electronic transferable records. The Group agreed with the final structure of the Principles, and concluded that the draft instrument was nearing completion and should be submitted to a ninth *ad hoc* session for adoption. It was agreed that the Drafting Committee would implement any remaining comments and seek additional input from UNCITRAL and the Hague Conference to finalise the text.[69]

The following are some comments that were put forward on the subject of custody (Principle 10): The matter of what level of control the provider and the client must have for the service to qualify as a custody service was addressed. Logically, if the service provider controls the asset under Article 10(3)(b), then by definition, the

---

[61] UNIDROIT 2023– Study LXXXII – W.G.7 – Doc. 5, February, Summary report of the seventh session.

[62] UNIDROIT 2022– Study LXXXII – W.G.7 – Doc. 2, December, Master copy of the draft Principles and comments. UNIDROIT 2022– Study LXXXII – W.G.7 – Doc. 3, December, Issues paper.

[63] UNIDROIT 2022– Study LXXXII – W.G.7 – Doc. 3, December, par. 91. UNIDROIT 2023– Study LXXXII – W.G.7 – Doc. 5, February, par. 41.

[64] UNIDROIT 2022– Study LXXXII – W.G.7 – Doc. 3, December, par. 92. UNIDROIT 2023– Study LXXXII – W.G.7 – Doc. 5, February, par. 44.

[65] UNIDROIT 2023– Study LXXXII – W.G.7 – Doc. 5, February, par. 46.

[66] UNIDROIT 2023– Study LXXXII – W.G.8 – Doc. 4, February, par. 4. UNIDROIT 2023– C.D. (102) 6, April, par. 16.

[67] UNIDROIT 2023– Study LXXXII – W.G.8 – Doc. 4, February, par. 225–241.

[68] UNIDROIT 2023– Study LXXXII – W.G.8 – Doc. 2, February. Draft UNIDROIT Principles on digital assets and private law. Vid. Also, UNIDROIT 2023– Study LXXXII – W.G.8 – Doc. 3, February.

[69] UNIDROIT 2023– C.D. (102) 6, April, par. 18.

client cannot have the exclusive power to change control under Article 10(3)(c). In this regard, Types 2 and 3 of cryptocurrency services included in the draft are compared. In practice, applying the scenario under Type 3 may be complicated.[70]

Regarding sub-custody, it is noted that in such a case, the "client" will be understood as the custodian who is a client of the sub-custodian. In practice, the figure of the sub-custodian is not included in the ordinary course of the custodian's business (although the opposite is also stated). It is added that, in the jargon of digital communities, "maintaining" can inclusively mean procedures that go beyond the preservation of digital assets, such as, producing an additional copy for security reasons or taking special security precautions, which may go beyond the basic intention of the Principle, which seems to be the simple holding of a digital file on deposit.[71]

Regarding the link between the definition of custody and the concept of control as exclusive, it is stated that it presents uncertain contours that should be clarified. Such would be the case of staking of digital assets or when multi-party computing (MPC) mechanisms are used, which allow the division of a cryptographic key into several encrypted fragments ('secret shards'), and only the combination of all the encrypted fragments can enable the execution of transactions and movements of the assets.[72]

Another interesting comment points out the relationship of the custody with the civil institution of the depositary or with the agency contract ('hosted wallet' where the custodian facilitates the digital operations of its clients -controlled digital assets- with other people, which would be an example of custody of digital assets).[73] Another comment states that the lines appear to be blurred between a deposit account and a trading account, particularly as agreements with cryptocurrency exchanges often suggest providing custody without expressly stipulating that "title" to digital assets remains with the client. For client protection, it could be clarified that, as a rule, clients retain or obtain such ownership also in a deposit account (i.e. where there is no express clause saying that ownership remains with the client) unless expressly provided otherwise.[74]

Finally, a ninth ad hoc session of the Working Group was held online on 5 April 2023, at which the draft Principles and Commentaries submitted by the Drafting Committee were reviewed. In addition, the Working Group discussed comments from

---

[70] UNIDROIT 2023– Study LXXXII – W.G.8 – Doc. 4, February, par. 226.

[71] UNIDROIT 2023– Study LXXXII – W.G.8 – Doc. 4, February, par. 228 y 231 on the novelty of the term "maintain". In par. 235 and 237, on the contrary, it is stated that custody and sub-custody are a widespread phenomenon in practice.

[72] UNIDROIT 2023– Study LXXXII – W.G.8 – Doc. 4, February, par. 232.

[73] UNIDROIT 2023– Study LXXXII – W.G.8 – Doc. 4, February, par. 236. In this regard, it should be noted that there are many practical or legal situations that are referred to as custodians. The European Law Institute's Principles on the Use of Digital Assets as Security consider the custodian as one of the possible forms of "intermediary". See definition of "intermediary" in the European Law Institute, ELI Principles on the Use of Digital Assets as Security,Report, Vienna, 2022, p. 17, https://www.europeanlawinstitute.eu/fileadmin/user_upload/p_eli/Publications/ELI_Principles_on_the_Use_of_Digital_Assets_as_Security.pdf

[74] UNIDROIT 2023– Study LXXXII – W.G.8 – Doc. 4, February, par. 240.

observers participating on behalf of UNCITRAL and HCCH. The Group requested that the Drafting Committee implement a limited number of final comments and changes, after which the instrument could be submitted to the Governing Council for adoption at its 102nd session.[75] It was finally approved at the session held in Rome from 10 to 12 May 2023.[76]

2.6 A Gloss on the Principle and Commentaries

Having seen the elaboration process of Principle 10 (Custody) within the iteration of the Principles through to their final approval, it is now fitting to examine the structure and content of the finally approved text. Any interpretations that are made of the final text must consider the itinerary of the entire process through to the ultimately approved content and the objective sought in the final text.

As pointed out, Principle 10 is the first in Section IV of the Principles. They both share the same title: Custody. This marks a clear permanent connection between the content of the Principle itself and that of the entire Section, as well as generally with the entire instrument of the Principles and with some of them more specifically. However, the comments now made here focus fundamentally on Principle 10 without prejudice to the connections with other specific Principles to which reference may be made.

The text is structured in 5 sections, followed by Comments (from 10.1 to 10.22). Section 1 contains three basic concepts, the definition of which is not limited to Principle 10 itself, but expressly indicates that their effects extend to all the Principles. These are the three personal elements that may form part, as subjective elements, of the custody contract. The custodian and client will always be parties to the contract. The sub-custodian may or may not exist.

Section 1

Section 1. a) describes the figure of the "custodian" as a subject, natural or legal person, since the text does not distinguish between them, that provides a client with custody services by a contract or agreement between both parties for this purpose. It is not indicated that the custodian must be professionally engaged only in providing such services. It may engage in the provision of other services, related to digital assets or otherwise, but here, it is considered only in its capacity as a provider of the custody service. To speak of a custodian, the two aforementioned subjective elements (the custodian and the client) must exist, plus the objective element, the custody agreement or contract, in the terms set out in Sections 3 and 4, to which Section 1. a) makes express reference.

---

[75] UNIDROIT 2023– C.D. (102) 6, April, par. 19.

[76] UNIDROIT 2023– C.D. (102) Misc.2, May, par. 7. UNIDROIT 2023– C.D. (102) 25, August, par. 106.

Section 1. b) contemplates the figure of the "sub-custodian". Its characteristic note is that it provides custody services to another custodian based on a custody agreement, understood in the terms of Sections 3 and 4. This expressly mentions a phenomenon or modus operandi common in commercial practice: the provision of the service through the collaboration of a third party to whom the first obligor turns. This is usually common in agency agreements, especially in the financial sector. There is a concatenation of contracts (or subcontracts, agency agreements or otherwise) to provide the service agreed with the principal (client). Section b), like a), ends by referring to the fact that it "acts as such". It implicitly indicates that the provision of the custody service, whether as custodian or sub-custodian, does not necessarily imply that it is the only activity that one or the other carries out. However, it is the only relevant one as far as the Principles are concerned.

In Section 1. c), the "client" is identified as the person (natural or legal) to whom the services are provided, that derive from a custody agreement on certain digital assets. The client is the party that has the right to receive the services from the custodian. Again, reference is made to the objective element: the right to the services of which the client is a creditor arises from the custody agreement entered.

Section 2

Section 2 of the Principle delimits what custody service consists of. It is understood to consist of "managing" a digital asset for the client while maintaining control of said asset. This action can be carried out directly or through a sub-custodian, provided that the this has been decided with the client in accordance with the terms of Principle 11.4. This implies that the client authorises the conclusion of the custody contract between the custodian and the sub-custodian. The possibility of the custodian providing the service through a sub-custodian without the client's authorisation is excluded. It is not enough for the client to be aware that the custodian uses the sub-custodian route; authorisation is required.

Section 2 uses the term "maintain" to refer to the custody task. Defining exactly what custody consists of without incurring tautology or imprecision is no easy feat. In fact, in the original text, it was decided that the custodian "maintains", thus in quotation marks. It is recognised that the term may have shortcomings. It is not only about conserving, but implies a dynamic action (the possibility of transfer) without necessarily giving way to "active management". It is not about planning and executing the active management of another's assets. Therefore, the expression that a custodian "manages" an asset for a client may be excessively broad. It may manage if this has been agreed with the client, but custody does not necessarily have to imply such management. Suppose custody is understood as "keeping". In that case, this term may be too narrow, leading to the belief that the custodian cannot transfer and does not have control of the digital asset, as required by paragraph 2(a) of the Principle.

Section 2. a) suggests that the essence of custody lies in having control of the digital asset. If the asset owner does not go to a custodian, they are the only ones with custody, that is, control of the asset. If they secure the services of another person to take custody of the digital asset, the owner no longer has exclusive control. As the case may be, the custodian or sub-custodian becomes the holder with control and the obligation to take custody of the asset belonging to the client.

The Introduction (paragraph 0.15) clarifies that the concept of "control" plays a fundamental role in the Principles. Express reference is made to Principles 6 and 7 and Principle 10. Control is understood as a factual situation in which someone has the factual authority to act and dispose of the digital asset. However, this factual situation implies legal consequences. By comparison with tangible assets, a legal fiction is established so that the functional equivalence of control is recognised to determine who holds possession of an intangible asset, such as a digital asset. Therefore, the legal effects of control will have legal consequences or others depending on what national law attributes to the fact of possession for ownership, custody, guarantee, transfer or disposal of patrimonial assets.

The UNCITRAL Model Law on Electronic Transferable Records (2017: MLETR) introduced the concept of control as a key element to articulate the use of electronic documents as an instrument for the transmission of rights, whether they are obligatory (credits) or real (goods). Article 11 of said Model Law, entitled "Control", applies the principle of functional equivalence enshrined in articles 6, 7 and 8 of the UNCITRAL Model Law on Electronic Commerce (1996) to the fact of possession or transmission of an electronic transferable record.[77] Although there is some terminological diversity, the legal-economic reality referred to by the expressions "electronic transferable document" and "digital asset" is coincident. In both cases, it is information in an electronic or digital format with patrimonial content. When the MLETR was being drawn up, the adjective "electronic" was added to the classic names (in this case, "transferable document") to indicate that it was moving from the traditional paper medium to the new electronic medium (whatever the latest technology to be used: magnetic, optical, digital, quantum, that is, an alternative to the tangible medium with direct human access). The definition of "electronic transferable record" in Article 2 of the MLETR refers to Article 10, in which the principle of functional equivalence is applied to the transferable document or title in paper form. Consequently, the task of "constructing " the concept of electronic transferable records must be carried out. It is such a document that, by electronic means, achieves the functions assigned by the legal system to the electronic document on paper,[78] provided that the following requirements are met (art. 10.1 MLETR: application of the principle of functional equivalence):

---

[77] «Article 11. Control

1. Where the law requires or permits the possession of a transferable document or instrument, that requirement is met with respect to an electronic transferable record if a reliable method is used:

(a) To establish exclusive control of that electronic transferable record by a person; and
(b) To identify that person as the person in control.»

[78] «"*Transferable document or instrument*" means a document or instrument issued on paper that entitles the holder to claim the performance of the obligation indicated in the document or instrument and to transfer the right to performance of the obligation indicated in the document or instrument through the transfer of that document or instrument.» (art. 2 MLETR).

Art. 10.1 MLETR: Application of the Principle of Functional Equivalence

(a) The electronic record contains the information that would be required to be contained in a transferable document or instrument; and

(b) A reliable method is used:

(i) To identify that electronic record as the electronic transferable record;

(ii) To render that electronic record capable of being subject to control from its creation until it ceases to have any effect or validity; and

(iii) To retain the integrity of that electronic record.

As already indicated, both the Principles and, previously the MLETR, have avoided using the term "holder" because this term evokes the physical possession of a tangible physical asset. In any case, if this term is used to refer to the person who has control of an electronic transferable record or a digital asset (such as a crypto-asset). We need to bear in mind that it carries a strong dose of metaphorical component, resulting from the indicated legal fiction of functional equivalence between control and possession. In the MLETR, it was decided to refer to the holder of the right, the person entitled to demand compliance or transfer, where appropriate, the right "incorporated or represented" and not to use the traditional term "holder" but rather the expression "person exercising control". Thus, control became crucial in defining and configuring the electronic transferable record. The same is true in the case of the Principles. When the term "holder" is used in the Commentaries, it should be understood more as the owner with control and not so much as the person who owns a physical asset. Regardless of whether the term is understood metaphorically or functionally, there is no doubt that a legal equivalence is being expressed.[79]

The technological challenge lies in designing a system that is sufficiently reliable to achieve the levels of security necessary to guarantee control of the information contained in an electronic or digital medium (electronic document or digital asset) and the identification of the person who exercises control and has access to it, whether to proceed with its transmission, to the establishment of limited rights in rem, or when the time comes, to exercise the rights that the document or asset confers. Therefore, control becomes essential for establishing digital asset ownership and its custody or transmission. The transfer of the asset is realised through the transfer of control. In short, it is understood that when a physical element is delivered, the transfer of possession performs the function of transferring control over it. That is why, in the

[79] On the basis of respect for the pre-existing substantive law of each State, both the MLETR and the Principles aim to be respectful of the existing legal status quo or what each State may establish in the future. It does not seek to introduce any substantive modification in the legal system of each State. Its purpose is limited to establishing the electronic or digital functional equivalence of the new legal economic instruments that the development of technology makes available to operators of the global economic system. Cf. par. 23 of the Explanatory Note of the MLETR.

digital world, the transfer of control is equivalent to *traditio*, with the pertinent legal effects attributed to it in each legal system.

Control is conceived as exclusive. The technology used must guarantee such exclusivity.[80] Control must be exclusive, whatever the technological system used, because it cannot be exercised by third parties not entitled to do so. The question that arises as a challenge for the Law is the legal articulation of the factual possibility that control can be exercised in a shared manner. When this occurs, it must be ensured whether said exercise is carried out as the owner (owner with title to the asset), as the beneficiary of a security right (secured creditor), or as the manager, for example, as a custodian or sub-custodian who safeguards by preserving or, where appropriate, transmitting. This is where the challenge of coordination and coherence between the technological design of the system applied and the legal consequences of the implemented model lies. In each case, it will be necessary to see what using a multi-signature digital wallet (shared control) implies. Likewise, the different legal effects of using a technological system for digital assets and exercising control with said technical tools in the various legal systems in the world must be considered. Thus, for example, the Trust law option in the civil law system differs from the common law system.

The concept or description of what is to be understood as control is found in Principle 6. This key concept expands its fundamental effect throughout the Principles, in some cases having special relevance, such as Principle 10. The exercise of control becomes an essential element of the content of the custody function that the custodian must deploy directly (Section 2. a) or through a sub-custodian (Section 2. b). Principle 6 must be completed with Principle 7 to determine which person, identified or not, legitimately exercises control over a digital asset.

Section 2. b), as already stated, refers to Principle 11.4) which requires the client's authorisation or regulation that the custodian sign a custody agreement with a sub-custodian. The lack of authorisation by the client can only be remedied through a regulation by the legislator or regulator so that custody can be outsourced, precisely because this implies powers to exercise control over digital assets.

Section 3

This section sets out the fundamental objective element of the custody relationship. It is the 'custody agreement'. Custody of digital assets is not imposed by legal mandate. It is a legal relationship between a service provider and a client. It is created and configured under the terms stipulated in a contract between both parties. A custody agreement can only be considered for the Principles if the following three requirements are met:

(a) The service is provided in the ordinary course of the service provider's activity. It must, therefore, be a business or professional economic activity. The service

[80] See par. 119 of the Explanatory Note to the MLETR. Both the Model Law and the Principles adhere to the so-called principle of technological neutrality, since when referring to digital technological systems they do not opt for any in particular. Traditional centralized electronic registry systems or distributed registry systems, more or less decentralized, can be used, using technologies such as "blockchain" or others (current or future).

provider must carry out its activity of custody of digital assets regularly on the market. Otherwise, it would not be a custody agreement, in the technical legal sense of the Principles, if the one entered into by the person who owns the assets with another person (natural or legal) who only occasionally performs said service (for whatever reason), but who does not regularly perform it on the market.

(b) The service provider must obtain (if it has not already done so) and manage the digital asset for the client. The asset may have been transferred by the client (whatever the form of transfer: by tabular annotation -book-entry system- or by recording in a new token replacing the previous one) and acquired by the provider by executing an order from the latter. In any case, what is relevant is that, from then on, the provider must provide the client with the "management" service of the digital asset. The verb "maintain" is used again in the original text in English, as in Section 2. Therefore, rather than managing, it is about preserving or maintaining the asset as an element of the client's assets. However, this is dynamic maintenance in the sense that it implies the possibility of carrying out any act of administration or disposal following the instructions of the client (principal in the custody relationship).

(c) The client does not have the exclusive power to change control of the digital asset within the meaning of Principle 6(2). While exclusivity is inherent to control, the need for the client's control not to be absolute is evident here. The "change of control", which involves the transfer of actual power over the asset and may include the modification, replacement, or even elimination of the asset, results in the client not having exclusive control of the assets. If this were the case, we would not be dealing with a custody relationship, which must always confer a *de facto* power of control on the custodian provider, even though it is not absolute. Neither the custodian can appear as the asset owner, even if it were for the client's benefit, nor can the client retain exclusive power for the "change of control". However, as will be seen, in the event of the custody service provider's insolvency, the client must have the right of separation *ex iure dominii* in the bankruptcy proceedings.

Section 4

In line with Principle 13(2), paragraph 4 of Principle 10 provides an element of contrast, which becomes one more requirement (the fourth), added to the three established in paragraph 3, for a custody agreement to be considered as such. To do so, the traditional test bench of legal institutions is used, which is the legal regime that applies to it in the event of insolvency. It is formulated in rather negative terms. Even if the three requirements demanded by paragraph 3 are met, the contract will not be considered "custody", in the strict sense of the Principles, if its clauses indicate that, in the event of insolvency (bankruptcy) of the service provider, the digital assets will form part of the assets of the estate available for distribution among its creditors.

In the described factual situation, it is understood that through the contract entered into, the provider does not only assume custody of the digital assets but also their ownership or property. It does not remain in mere apparent or formal ownership, as would be the case with a trust, because the client holds the real ownership, so what is established is a trust in favour of the client. For the Principles, the differentiating and limiting criterion is the position of the assets in the event of insolvency. If creditors can liquidate the digital assets held by the bankrupt service provider, then the contract is not considered a custody contract. In such a case, it is understood that the client does not hold ownership or property of the assets, but rather a credit right against the provider, and the client must therefore participate in the bankruptcy proceedings together with the other creditors subject to the principle of par *condicio creditorum*. In such a situation, there is no custody contract, which is limited to the maintenance or, where appropriate, management of digital assets over which the service provider has control, although not absolute, but subject to the decisions of the titular owner, the client.

Section 5
However, notwithstanding what has been stated, the contracting client does not always have to be the owner of the digital assets. It may be a third party acting on behalf of or representing the owner. This is established in Section 5 of the Principle. Representation structures may vary. They range from the occasional representation of a mandate or commission to the professional management of other people's assets, such as portfolio management (in its different forms) or investment fund management. Such professional economic activity is usually provided by credit institutions, investment entities (investment services companies) or, in some forms, insurance companies.

Commentary *General (10.1. – 10.3).* The profile of custodians and sub-custodians is developed.

Management of a digital asset (10.4.). The breadth of "management" is explained, which is broader than "control". Management can be extended in a chain through successive sub-custodians.

Custody agreement (10.5.-10.-8). The different custody cases are dealt with. It should be noted that the exclusive power referred to in Principle 10.3.c) is contemplated in Principle 6.1.a)(iii) and, therefore, is subject to the relaxation of the concept of "exclusivity" established in Principle 6.3. On the other hand, it is noted that the custody agreement is incompatible with the risk of custodian insolvency.

This issue must be made clear in the custody contract. Principle 10(5) (10.9.). The possibility of the client acting on behalf of another person is discussed.

Custody examples (10.10). Two examples are given, which should be considered in comparison with the non-custodial examples in Sections 10.13 et seq. The term 'wallet' is used in the colloquial sense in which it is used in the market.

Custodial or Hosted Wallet (10.11). Example 1. Custodial or Hosted Wallet Agreement—where the custodian holds the wallet's private keys.

Trading Account (10.12). Example 2. A functionality within a wallet that a service provider offers to clients who purchase and hold digital assets purchased with fiat currency. The assets belong to the client; the custodian is neither the owner nor the borrower.

Examples of Non-Custodial Agreements (10.13). The following examples may contain a contract between the service provider and a client, but it is not a custodial agreement within the meaning of the Principles.

Example 3 (10.14–10.15).

When a person (such as an investor) controls a digital asset using some hardware or software and a private key that is not trusted or given to a third party, this is self-custody. The user keeps private keys safe through software solutions deployed directly on their computer or mobile phone or through non-custodial cloud-based software-as-a-service wallets. These are two quite similar options:

Self-custody by wallet software (10.16). Example 4. The user has open-source software. He creates a wallet password and a secret recovery phrase, which are stored with the private keys in an encrypted format on the mobile phone or computer.

Self-custody by cloud-based software-as-a-service (10.17). Example 5. The service provider provides a non-custodial wallet to the user, who creates an account and a password, which gives him access to an encrypted file held by the provider on the blockchain containing a "seed" (a secret private key recovery phrase), the users' private keys, and the addresses of the digital assets. The provider does not store the password; the user must keep it secure and confidential. The provider also cannot access the user's private keys, seed, or password. The user operates from their computer or mobile phone.

Safeguarding private keys (10.18–10.19). Example 6. When a company provides the safekeeping of private keys or software or hardware to facilitate the client's safekeeping of their private keys, the provider is typically prohibited from using the client's private keys for any purpose not agreed to by the client. The cold wallet in which the private keys are held provides highly secure storage out of the reach of hackers and other threats from their generation to the time of their use.

Digital asset delivery agreement (10.20–10.21). Example 7. A fintech company or financial institution, such as a dealer, exchange, or trading platform, may have an obligation to deliver a certain amount of a digital asset to a client because it has received the asset from the client or because it has acquired the asset on the primary or secondary market for the client. It works like a bank account. Investors do not have control over digital assets; they have an unsecured personal claim against the account provider. It will be up to each State to establish rules to mitigate risk in some or all cases of clients entering into such arrangements.

Decentralised Autonomous Organizations (10.22). Decentralised autonomous organisations (DAOs) use code (also called smart contracts or applications) stored and executed on a blockchain to control certain digital assets. An investor can transfer a digital asset to a particular smart contract so that its code determines when and to whom the digital asset will ultimately be transferred. This is different from self-custody, custody, or a credit claim. A structure involving a DAO is unlikely to involve custody but will depend on the specific arrangement in each case.

Principle 11
Duties Owed by a Custodian to Its Client

Maria del Mar Bustillo Saiz

(1) A custodian owes the following duties to its client in relation to a digital asset it maintains for that client:

(a) the custodian is not authorised to transfer the digital asset, or use it for its own benefit, except to the extent permitted by the client and by other law;

(b) the custodian is obliged to comply with an instruction given by the client to transfer the digital asset, unless:

(i) the custodian is prohibited from complying with the instruction by other law or by any agreement between the custodian and a third party to which the client is a party or has consented;

(ii) the custodian is not obliged, by other law or by an agreement with the client, under certain circumstances, to comply with the instruction;

(c) the custodian is obliged to safeguard the digital asset.

This work was financed within the framework of the Prometeo 2023 project of the Regional Ministry of Innovation, Universities, Science and Digital Society (CIPROM/2022/26) "Present and future of the regulation of cryptoassets in the EU [LegalCripto]", whose principal investigator is Carmen Pastor Sempere. The basic ideas contained herein were presented in the author's paper with the same title, given on November 13, 2024 at the IV International Congress on "UNIDROIT Principles on Digital Assets and Private Law: Context, Content, Perspectives", organized also by BAES Research Group of the University of Alicante on November 13 and 14, 2024.

Work carried out within the framework of the research project funded by the Ministry of Science and Innovation entitled "The consolidation of the digital revolution and its challenges: adaptation of the competitive strategies of economic operators and the ordering rules of the markets". PID2022- 139741OB-C2. IP C.A. HERRERO SUÁREZ.

M. Bustillo Saiz (✉)
University of Valladolid, Valladolid, Spain
e-mail: mmbustillo@uva.es

C. Pastor Sempere and D. A. Morán Bovio (eds.), UNIDROIT *Principles on Digital Assets and Private Law*, Law, Governance and Technology Series 80,
https://doi.org/10.1007/978-3-032-11001-5_17

(2) Unless prohibited by the custody agreement or by other law, a custodian may maintain digital assets of the same description for two or more of its clients as an undivided pool.

(3) The duties owed by a custodian to its client may include:

> **(a) the duty to keep a record of the digital assets it maintains for each client;**
>
> **(b) the duty at all times to securely and effectively maintain digital assets in accordance with the records it keeps for its clients;**
>
> **(c) the duty to acquire digital assets promptly if this is necessary to satisfy the duty under sub-paragraph (b);**
>
> **(d) the duty to separate the digital assets maintained for clients from the digital assets maintained for its own account;**
>
> **(e) subject to any right granted to the custodian or to another person, the duty to pass the benefits arising from digital assets to the client for whom it maintains those assets.**

(4) Where authorised by a client or by other law, a custodian may fulfil its duties to its client under this Principle by entering into a custody agreement with a sub-custodian if the sub-custodian is bound by the duties set out in this Principle.

(5) A digital asset maintained by a custodian for a client may be subject to a security right:

> **(a) granted to that custodian by the client;**
>
> **(b) in favour of that custodian arising by operation of other law; or**
>
> **(c) granted to a third party by the client.**

1 Official Commentary

Commentary

Principle 11(1)

11.1. Principle 11(1) sets out duties which are owed by a person providing custody services under an agreement with a client. These are basic duties and a State should not permit them to be excluded by the terms of the custody agreement. If the custodian is a sub custodian, the sub-custodian's client is itself a custodian.

11.2. The duty in Principle 11(1)(a) refers to the inability of the custodian to use the digital asset for its own benefit except as permitted by the client and by other law (as defined in Principle 2(4)). The client may consent to that use either by contract or by an instruction to the custodian, and may consent to a use more limited than that permitted by other law. The other law of a State may permit a custodian to have a right of use in respect of digital assets in relation to which it provides custody services: this permission may be contained in regulation and/or in private law. In the latter case, the extent of the permission may depend on the way in which a custody relationship is characterised by that private law.

11.3. The duty in Principle 11(1)(b) makes the basic point that a custodian is a person who must deal with the digital asset according to the client's instructions. However, this obligation is qualified by any prohibition on such dealing to be found in other law, including criminal or regulatory law, or any agreement made between the custodian and any third party to which the client is a party or has consented. If the client has granted the custodian a security right in the digital asset, or any such security right has arisen by operation of law, this will also qualify the custodian's obligation (see Principle 11(5)). Moreover, other law, or the agreement with the client, may specify particular circumstances in which the custodian is not obliged to comply with the client's instructions. This would further qualify the basic obligation.

11.4. Principle 11(1)(c) makes it clear that the custodian must owe to the client some duties in relation to safeguarding of the digital asset. Safeguarding includes the attainment of the result set out in Principle 13(2) (that the assets safeguarded are not to be part of the assets available for distribution to the custodian's creditors if it enters into an insolvency-related proceeding). The details of these safeguarding duties will typically be included in the custody agreement. A State can choose which private law safeguarding duties should be imposed on a custodian, and therefore cannot be excluded by agreement. Some suggestions for States are contained in Principle 11(3).

11.5. The language of Principle 11(1) is intended to be functional and neutral between legal cultures. In some jurisdictions, the relationship between custodian and client will be legally characterised as a trust while in other jurisdictions it may be characterised as a contractual or other type of legal relationship.

Principle 11(2)

11.6. Principle 11(2) addresses the common situation where a custodian maintains digital assets of the same description for several clients. The phrase 'of the same description' is used in these Principles to refer to digital assets that are treated by market participants as fungible (see also Principles 13(5) to 13(7)). Fungibility is not a technical characteristic of a digital asset, but a matter of market practice. The record of any unit (or quantity) of a digital asset in a digital ledger is individualised because it is, by definition, capable of control, see Principle 2(2). However, as a matter of market practice, many digital assets (such as cryptocurrencies) are treated as fungible so that any such unit or units will satisfy an obligation to deliver the digital asset.

11.7. Subject to other law or to the custody agreement, Principle 11(2) permits a custodian to maintain digital assets for several clients as an undivided pool. This has two consequences. First, the custodian may control an undivided pool of client assets using one or more private keys, so that no specific unit or quantity of that digital asset is specifically allocated to a particular client. If the custodian maintains digital assets for several clients with a sub-custodian, maintaining them as an undivided pool means that the custodian need not have a separate sub-account with the sub-custodian for each client. As a result, for any particular digital asset, an undivided pool includes all digital assets of that description controlled by the custodian for its clients using one or more private keys as well as all digital assets of that description maintained with one or more sub-custodians. Second, when the custodian receives an instruction of a client in respect of a digital asset maintained for its clients as an undivided pool, it may comply with that instruction using any unit or quantity of such digital asset that it controls directly or that it maintains with a sub-custodian. This is because these various units or quantities of the digital asset are all of the same description, i.e., they are treated as fungible, as explained above in Commentary 11.6. Where the custodian is not allowed to maintain an undivided pool, it must implement what is often called full segregation. The reference to 'a custodian' in Principle 11(2) also applies to a sub-custodian, whose clients are custodians.

Principle 11(3)

11.8. Principle 11(3) sets out private law duties which a State may wish to ensure are owed by a custodian to its client, although it is for a State to choose whether it wishes to do so, in which case it would have to make the chosen duties mandatory and non-excludable by agreement. Separately, a State may wish to impose these duties on custodians as a matter of regulatory law, that is, by imposing duties for which there is no private law redress but breach of which may incur sanctions imposed by the State. Again, it should be recalled that if the custodian is a sub-custodian, the client is a custodian. For the result of Principle 13(2) to be attained under some domestic laws, the duty under Principle 11(3)(d) must not be permitted to be excluded by the terms of the custody agreement. A State may choose to impose a similar duty as a matter of regulatory law.

11.9. The duty in Principle 11(3)(a) is that a custodian must keep a record of the digital assets it maintains for every client. That record may either be kept separately from the distributed ledgers which record the respective digital assets or, if technology allows, be part of the information stored in the distributed ledger.

11.10. The duty in Principle 11(3)(b) is that the custodian owes a duty to maintain assets correlating to those records. Thus, if the record shows that a custodian maintains 1 bitcoin for A, the custodian must maintain at least 1 bitcoin.

11.11. The duty in Principle 11(3)(c) is to replace any missing assets, in other words, to reconcile what the custodian actually maintains to the client records. The assets acquired must, of course, be of the same description and in the same quantity as the assets recorded in the records.

11.12. The duty in Principle 11(3)(d) relates to the custodial duty to separate client assets from house assets (i.e., the custodian's own assets). A custodian may separate its clients' digital assets from its own by controlling them using different private keys or by maintaining them on different accounts with a sub-custodian. The legal effect of this depends on the applicable law.

11.13. Principle 11(3)(d) does not address the segregation of assets of any particular client. Rather than maintaining client assets of the same description as an undivided pool, a custodian may offer to a client the possibility of the custodian maintaining the assets of that client separately from the assets of the same description of other clients (so-called full segregation). That would require the custodian to control the client's assets using a separate private key or to maintain them in a separate account with a sub-custodian so that such assets are exclusively allocated to the client. The legal effect of such arrangement will depend on the applicable other law, and may vary from jurisdiction to jurisdiction.

11.14. The duty in Principle 11(3)(e) to pass on to the client all the benefits of the digital asset is subject to any right granted to the custodian or to another person. The benefits of a digital asset may include voting rights, monetary dividends, distributions in kind (e.g., 'airdrops'), and additional digital assets that may be created as a result of a network-wide event such as a 'fork'.

Principle 11(4)

11.15. Principle 11(4) makes it clear that a sub-custody structure, can be used. Under this structure, the custodian maintains the digital asset by entering into a custody agreement with a sub-custodian with respect to that asset (see Principle 10(2) and Commentary 10.4). Such a structure can be used if the sub-custodian is bound by the duties set out in Principle 11. A custodian would, however, be in breach of its own duties to the client if the sub-custodian was not subject, in the sub-custody agreement, to the mandatory and non-excludable private law duties of a custodian under the applicable law. These duties are those set out in Principle 11(1) plus those listed in Principle 11(3) that the relevant State has chosen to make mandatory. Other law determines the extent to which, if any, a custodian is responsible to its client with regard to the non-performance by the sub-custodian of its duties under Principle 11 and the sub-custody agreement.

Principle 11(5)

11.16. Principle 11(5) recognises that a custodian may have a security right in the digital asset it maintains for a client. For example, the client may owe the custodian fees, for which the custodian wishes to be secured, or the custodian may have lent the client money to acquire the digital asset. A security right under Principle 11(5)(a) would be made effective against third parties by control under Principle 15, since the custodian either controls the digital asset itself or has entered into a custody agreement with a sub-custodian in relation to the asset. A client can also grant a security right in a digital asset maintained by a custodian to a third party (this follows from the nature of a digital asset set out in Principle 3(1) and Principle 14(1)). However, in that case either the secured creditor would need to make the security right effective against third parties by control under Principle 15 by the custodian maintaining the digital asset for the secured creditor or it would need to make the security right effective against third parties by a means (available under other law) other than control.

2 Reflections

2.1 Context

Principle 11 is the second of the four principles that make up Section IV of the UNIDROIT Principles on Digital Assets and Private Law, a section whose objective is to establish the Private Law principles relevant to the custody of digital assets (Commentary 1 to Principle 10). In this sense, it is necessary to highlight an intimate and interdependent relationship between the four principles integrated in this section and, very especially, between Principles 10, 11 and, in part, 13, when the first describes how the custody contract and the relationships are configured to which it gives rise, the second providing the framework in which the duties of the custodian towards its contractual clients must be and, where appropriate can be, configured, both circumscribed by the necessary protection of the client's digital assets against the insolvency of the custodian that imposes the third principle, by excluding them from forming part of its distributable assets among its creditors.

Indeed, if custody in general terms consists of one person (normally legal and regulated), managing a digital asset in the name and benefit of another, a client (who may be another custodian), necessarily offering special protection against unauthorized disposals (in accordance with the general perspective of these Principles according to their par. 0.1 and 02) of the asset and in the face of insolvency of the custodian that maintains the digital asset (Commentary to Principle 10.1), it is obligatory to accept that within the framework of these UNIDROIT Principles, custody and duties owed by the custodian are largely synonymous terms since, referring to the concept of custody, we simultaneously describe the imperative duties of the custodian as shown in Principle 10.(3)(b) "the service provider is obligated to obtain (if not already done so) and manage the digital asset for the client".

This result is hardly surprising in the neutral and functional perspective of the legal concepts embraced by the Principles, imposed by the need to offer useful solutions to the different jurisdictions and legal cultures, since it is only a manifestation of said aspect that, precisely, has no other purpose than to identify the rights and obligations that must arise from the custody contract in accordance with the model offered by best practices and international standards, without labelling them in divergent and variable legal categories depending on the jurisdictions.[1] This fact, the adoption of this common approach to the legal issues raised by the custody of digital assets, explains the inseparability of the concept and/or principle of custody from the obligations owed by the custodian. The situation that falls within the principle of custody is one in which the custodian owes some non-excludable duties to the client in relation to the safeguarding of assets, thereby ensuring that certain objectives are met (e.g., treatment of assets in case of insolvency of the custodian).[2]

Accordingly, non-custodial wallet software service providers, if they simply offer password escrow services for customers to keep their passwords for the various websites they access, should not be subject to custodial duties.[3] Indeed, the premise of these duties is that they presuppose control by the custodian, so that if the client can control the digital asset on his own without any contribution from the custodian, if the client has exclusive control of the asset, then it is excluded from the custodian"s ability to fulfil his or her duties and the relationship will not qualify as a custodial relationship under Principle 10(3)(c).[4] Principle 10 certainly sought to define custody, and in doing so laid the foundation for the following Principles, which describe the obligations of a custodian and explain other private law issues related to the custody situation, including insolvency.[5]

---

[1] Unidroit. (2020). – Study LXXXII – W.G.1 – Doc. 2, November 2020, par. 12. https://www.unidroit.org/prepar... Preparatory work.

[2] Unidroit. (2020). – Study LXXXII – W.G.1 – Doc. 2, November 2020, par. 18; Unidroit. (2021). – Study LXXXII – W.G.3 – Doc. 4 July 2021, par. 90 and par. 92–93; Unidroit. (2022). – Study LXXXII – W.G.6 – Doc. 3 August 2022, par. 87. https://www.unidroit.org/prepar... Preparatory work.

[3] Unidroit. (2021). – Study LXXXII – W.G.3 – Doc. 4 July 2021, par. 98 and also par. 71, 73, 89 and 102. https://www.unidroit.org/prepar... Preparatory work.

[4] Unidroit. (2021). – Study LXXXII – W.G.2 – Doc. 3 April 2021, par. 8 and par. 10. https://www.unidroit.org/prepar... Preparatory work.

[5] Unidroit. (2022). – Study LXXXII – W.G.6 – Doc. 4 November 2022, par. 146. https://www.unidroit.org/prepar... Preparatory work.

2.2 The Precedents: Preparatory Works

Based on the discussions held during the first and second joint workshops (Rome, 6 and 7 May 2019, and Vienna, 10 and 11 March 2020, respectively) by UNIDROIT and UNCITRAL, a document was presented setting out the proposal from the Secretariat on the most appropriate scope for this project, which would develop Principles related to the legal position of intermediaries involved in token markets, among other aspects, such as exchanges and custodians, in view of the frequency with which the provision of digital asset custody services are used in practice, on the one hand, and the vagueness of contracts, on the other hand, in order to provide protection for clients.

Indeed, for many market participants, the need to employ an intermediary for the acquisition and subsequent holding (custody) of digital assets for the acquirer is the most practical approach. However, digital asset custody services raise some novel legal questions regarding traditional custody contexts that the project must take into account. For example, two lawsuits in the US have grappled with the question of whether a custodian service provider is required to provide its users with access to a new cryptocurrency created by a third party (via hard fork), so it may be appropriate for the project to consider principles for such novel issues. Likewise, the series of possible legal relationships that have traditionally been applicable to the custody of securities (such as title of transfer, trust and/or bailment, agency and other contractual relationships) may not be appropriate or may need to be adapted to apply to digital assets, which pose particular problems. These circumstances and the vagueness of the contractual terms governing custody arrangements are reasons to consider these Principles as a guide to characterise the rights of custodians and clients, and to provide legal certainty. The lack of regulatory responses (or their only emergent nature) to provide protection to custodians' clients underscores the need to consider these Principles.[6]

Subsequent sessions explored practical and legal aspects of custodial holding of brokered digital assets from the perspective of an acquirer and a custodian. It was highlighted how using an EXCHANGE or custodian wallet provider involved trusting a third party with the private keys, in addition to having to trust whether the custodian had taken appropriate security measures and was trustworthy. The importance of users themselves taking appropriate security measures to ensure the security of their assets was also underscored, encouraging practices such as encryption, multi-signature wallets, the use of multiple types of wallets and other online and offline security mechanisms.

In the event of custodian insolvency (how to distribute the deficit among the clients of a crypto custodian) the necessary protection for clients could be guaranteed, among other mechanisms, by establishing a regulatory obligation for custodians to properly determine which assets belong to which clients, through an administrative/public law solution that would be aligned with the general regulation of financial entities.

---

[6] UNIDROIT. (2020). – Study LXXXII – W.G.1 – Doc. 2, November 2020, par. 11–12 and 66–67. https://www.unidroit.org/prepar... Preparatory work.

It was noted that such a solution was important, even with strong private law rules, since, without proper asset management, private law rules have no effect.[7]

Likewise, on examining the regime developed in American practice for the custody of cryptoassets it was noted that all custodians (individual and institutional) faced similar problems: the use of hot (online) or cold (offline storage), with most custodians using a combination of both. Most custodians also used a combination of the omnibus and separate wallet model; and although multi-signature wallets were a standard, they highlighted the need for adequate controls over the use of signatures.[8]

In the process of elaborating the Principles, the need was pointed out for the project to identify what type of principles it wanted to articulate with respect to how the custodian should behave and what duties it should have, pointing out that one possibility was to establish a set of minimum standards, similar to what was done in the UNIDROIT Geneva Convention on substantive law rules applicable to intermediated securities,[9] which says that there is a contract, and also the minimum rules that the contract had to respect. Complementarily, with regard to regulatory law, IOSCO (International Organization of Securities Commissions) had identified risks related to cryptoasset trading platforms, some of which overlapped with the scope of the project, as is the case of the safeguarding of digital assets, which raised the question of whether the draft should provide practical guidance to parties on how to structure their agreements, whether it should propose default rules when the established rules or omissions by the parties are considered inadequate or non-existent, or whether it should be left to the parties to decide how to structure their agreements in contracts.

It is assumed that there is a wide variety of strategies used to offer custody services for digital assets: some operate as banks, holding assets for the client under express contracts; others provide custody through a multi-signature (software) wallet; others are trust companies that provide services for regulated financial products… In this context, the final objective was the protection of consumers and investors, warning that a deficit could occur even outside the case of insolvency (case of stolen and missing assets).[10]

These debates resulted in the preparation of the Preliminary Draft of Principle Y on Custody, in which the mandatory and optional duties provided for the custodian practically coincide with those that were finally included in the Principles. Although they are structured through a single Principle, it fails to address the fulfilment of

---

[7] UNIDROIT. (2021). – Study LXXXII – W.G.1 – Doc. 3, March 2021, par. 75, 80 and 84. https://www.unidroit.org/prepar… Preparatory work.

[8] UNIDROIT. (2021). – Study LXXXII – W.G.1 – Doc. 3, March 2021, par. 97 and 90–91. https://www.unidroit.org/prepar… Preparatory work.

[9] UNIDROIT Convention on Substantive Rules for Intermediated Securities (2013) https://www.Unidroit.org/instruments/capital-markets/geneva-convention https://www.Unidroit.org/wp-content/uploads/2021/06/convention.pdf.

[10] UNIDROIT 2021 – Estudio LXXXII – W.G.1 – Doc. 4, March, 2021, par. 75–76 and 88–106, where mentions of the IOSCO document are collected (International Organization of Securities Commissions), *Issues, Risks and Regulatory Considerations Relating to Crypto-Asset Trading Platforms*, Final Report, February 2020 https://www.iosco.org/library/pubdocs/pdf/IOSCOPD649.pdf.

duties in a sub-custody structure and in relation to omnibus accounts. Principle Y is based on the fact that a holder of a digital asset holds it as custodian on behalf of another person (client) if the established duties are owed. If those duties are not owed, the holder is not a custodian. The duties that a custodian must fulfil are functionally defined and the custodian is not required to be the sole holder of the digital asset, multi-signature wallets can be used to give joint control to the custodian and their client.[11]

The next step in the discussion of the drafts is to contemplate sub-custody, going beyond the first level relationship (custodian-client) and considering a longer chain of possession. Principles C.9 and C.10 are the first drafts to address the issue of sub-custody. The purpose of the Principles is to ensure that the client is not disadvantaged by the use of a sub-custodian in the provision of custody services.[12]

In the presentation of the revised draft of the Principle on the Custody of Digital Assets, it was noted that the purpose of the Principle was to determine what responsibilities should be imposed on the custodian, which presupposed the existence of a legal entity.[13]

The latest version of the draft Principle C on custody, Annex 3, Appendix 1 provides, as a novelty in section C.2(a), that when a digital asset is considered fungible, a reference to the asset must be interpreted as a reference to a certain amount of assets of identical type to that digital asset.[14]

In the MASTER COPY OF THE PRINCIPLES, custody already appears divided into principles: 12 Custody, 13 Duties Owed by a Custodian to its Client, 14 Other Aspects of Custodianship and 15 Sub-Custody.[15] From here and having defined the duties owed by the custodian, it was observed that Principle 13 did not take into account the abilities of the parties, depriving them of the ability to agree on the terms and duties that they consider appropriate.[16]

In the subsequent process and until its final approval, the formal structure of the Principles was slightly updated to reflect the changes proposed by the Working Group, incorporating what is now the current Principle 11, the former Principle 14

[11] UNIDROIT. (2021). – Study LXXXII – W.G.2 – Doc. 2 (rev. 1) March 2021 par. 92 and 94–95; UNIDROIT. (2021). – Study LXXXII – W.G.2 – Doc. 3 April 2021, par. 9 and 15. https://www.unidroit.org/prepar… Preparatory work.

[12] UNIDROIT. (2021). – Study LXXXII – W.G.3 – Doc. 2 (rev. 1) June 2021. https://www.unidroit.org/prepar… Preparatory work.

[13] UNIDROIT. (2021). – Study LXXXII – W.G.3 – Doc. 4 July 2021, par. 71 and 80. https://www.unidroit.org/prepar… Preparatory work.

[14] UNIDROIT. (2021). – Study LXXXII – W.G.4 – Doc. 2 October 2021, p. 1, par. 54 ANNEX III DRAFT PRINCIPLES AND COMMENTARY Appendix 1 – SUB-GROUP 1 – Control and Custody PRINCIPLE C – Custody, p. 28. https://www.unidroit.org/prepar… Preparatory work.

[15] UNIDROIT. (2022). – Study LXXXII – W.G.5 – Doc. 2 February 2022; UNIDROIT. (2022). – Study LXXXII – W.G.5 – Doc. 3 February 2022, p. 26. https://www.unidroit.org/prepar… Preparatory work.

[16] UNIDROIT. (2022). – Study LXXXII – W.G.6 – Doc. 2 August 2022, par. 170. https://www.unidroit.org/prepar… Preparatory work.

(Other aspects of custody), which now appears as Principle 11(5), as well as the relevant text in the Commentary.[17]

2.3 *Relationships and the Application of the Principle to Current Reality*

The legal taxonomy related to digital assets is developed in coordination with UNCITRAL, so care has been taken to ensure precision and uniformity and coherence between the terms used by both organizations. Particular attention has been paid to the terminology used in key reference instruments, such as the UNCITRAL Model Law on Electronic Transferable Records –MLETR- (2017)[18] (e.g. "electronic transferable record" and "control"), as well as the UNIDROIT Convention on Substantive Standards for Intermediated Securities (2013)[19] and the UNIDROIT Legislative Guide on Intermediated Securities (2017).[20]

In terms of the relationship with existing UNIDROIT instruments, important aspects provided for in the Principles on Digital Assets and Private Law refer, among others, to the legal analysis of issues related to the provision of custody services for digital assets and related issues, to the insolvency of the digital asset custodian, elements that are linked to the Institute's work in the capital markets in the area of intermediated securities, thus providing connections with existing instruments such as the UNIDROIT Convention on Substantive Standards for Intermediated Securities (2013) and the UNIDROIT Legislative Guide on Intermediated Securities (2017).[21]

Although regulation is outside the scope of these Principles, given that there are a number of aspects addressed by the Principles that border on regulatory issues, it is worth taking it into account to ensure consistency between recommendations

---

[17] UNIDROIT. (2022). – Study LXXXII – W.G.7 – Doc. 2 December 2022; UNIDROIT. (2022). – Study LXXXII – W.G.7 – Doc. 3 December 2022, par. 1, 4–5 and 102; UNIDROIT. (2023). – Study LXXXII – W.G.8 – Doc. 2 February 2023 DRAFT UNIDROIT PRINCIPLES ON DIGITAL ASSETS AND PRIVATE LAW; UNIDROIT. (2023). – Study LXXXII – W.G.8 – Doc. 4 February 2023, PRESENTATIONS OF CONSULTATIONS ON DIGITAL ASSETS AND PRIVATE LAW. https://www.unidroit.org/prepar... Preparatory work.

[18] United Nations Commission On International Trade Law | https://uncitral.un.org/electronic_transferable_records.

[19] UNIDROIT Convention on Substantive Rules for Intermediated Securities (2013) https://www.Unidroit.org/instruments/capital-markets/geneva-convention https://www.Unidroit.org/wp-content/uploads/2021/06/convention.pdf.

[20] UNIDROIT Legislative Guide on Intermediated Securities, for the Implementation of the Principles and Standards of the Geneva Securities Convention https://www.Unidroit.org/instruments/capital-markets/legislative-guide/ https://www.Unidroit.org/wp-content/uploads/2021/06/LEGISLATIVE-GUIDE-English.pdf https://www.Unidroit.org/wp-content/uploads/2021/06/LEGISLATIVE-GUIDE-Spanish.pdf.

[21] UNIDROIT. (2020). – Study LXXXII – W.G.1 – Doc. 2, November 2020, par. 23 and 31; UNIDROIT. (2021). – Study LXXXII – W.G.2 – Doc. 2 (rev. 1) March 2021, par. 34. https://www.unidroit.org/prepar... Preparatory work.

for private law and any regulatory approach. The connection between both areas is more pronounced precisely in aspects such as custody, given that a large number of the assets under discussion are in the hands of custodians and intermediaries.[22] Furthermore, although the difference between private law and regulatory duties lies primarily in how one and the other are enforced, in some cases there is an overlap.[23] In this perspective, it is interesting to mention the regulation stemming from the EU contained in Regulation (EU) 2022/858 on a pilot regime for market infrastructures based on decentralized registry technology (Pilot Regulation, in particular article 7 points 5 and 6) are of interest, and Regulation (EU) 2023/1114 relating to cryptoasset markets and amending Regulations (EU) No. 1093/2010 and (EU) No. 1095/2010 and Directives 2013/36/EU and (EU) 2019/1937 (MiCA, in particular article 75 thereof). Along the same lines, we must consider the Spanish regulations provided for in Law 6/2023, of March 17, on Securities Markets and Investment Services (LMVSI, articles 6 et seq.), which are still pending regulatory development.

To the extent that custodians are normally regulated entities, the same regulatory rules serve to delimit the scope of application of Principle 11 to current reality. Banks, investment services companies, market infrastructures based on distributed ledger technology contemplated in the Pilot Regulation (article 7 point 5), are of interest for the custody of a linked asset, as is also the case of entities in charge of maintaining the distributed registry in accordance with the LMVSI (article 8 numbers 4, 5 and 6) which must be one of the entities authorized to carry out the activity provided for in letter a) of article 126 of the LMVSI, i.e., the auxiliary investment service consisting of the custody and administration of financial instruments on behalf of clients. Among others, cryptoasset service providers that provide custody and administration services for cryptoassets, contemplated in MiCA (article 75) must also be mentioned.

2.4 Gloss of Principle 11 and Comments

The purpose of this Principle is to establish principles relevant to the custody of digital assets.

Given the process of elaboration of Principle 11 within the framework of the successive drafts of the Principles until their final approval, it is time to analyse the content of Principle 11 and the accompanying comments as they have been specified in their final writing. The text is structured in 5 sections, which are followed by the Comments (from 11.1 to 11.16).

---

[22] UNIDROIT. (2020). – Study LXXXII – W.G.1 – Doc. 2, November 2020, par. 36. https://www.unidroit.org/prepar... Preparatory work.

[23] UNIDROIT. (2021). – Study LXXXII – W.G.4 – Doc. 3 December 2021, par. 54. https://www.unidroit.org/prepar... Preparatory work.

2.4.1 Comment

Principle 11 is very casuistic and clearly establishes the obligations/duties related to private law that a custodian owes to his client, as well as the elements that make up a custody agreement in this regard.[24]

The different subsections of this Principle detail different types of duties that a custodian has and their level or degree of applicability. Principle 11(1) deals with the minimum mandatory duties, Principle 11(3) describes the initially additional duties of a custodian, although States may decide to incorporate these duties among the mandatory duties specified in Principle 11(1). Principle 11(2) is related to the use of an omnibus account and the options and resulting management rules for the custodian. Principle 11(4) deals with the custodian using the services of a sub-custodian to provide the custodial service entrusted to him, and finally, Principle 11(5) (originally located in a different part of the Principles) describes the types of collateral that may exist over a digital asset held by a custodian for its client[25] given the impact this has on the fulfilment of its duties.

Although the need for this Principle 11, which stipulates the duties of custodians, has been questioned, as it refers mainly to contractual obligations of custodians, especially considering that such duties of the custodian should be a matter addressed and covered by the regulatory laws of the relevant countries, it has prevailed on considering that the obligations imposed on the custodian towards its client are reasonable, and it is appropriate that the Principle holds that the State should not allow such basic duties to be excluded. In this sense, the use of neutral and functional language allows the Principle to operate in legal systems that establish or qualify such legal relationships in different ways.[26]

Indeed, Commentary 11.5 states that the language of Principle 11(1) is intended to be functional and neutral between different legal cultures. In some jurisdictions, the relationship between custodian and client will legally qualify as a trust, while in other jurisdictions it may qualify as a contractual or other type of legal relationship. Custody (intermediation or indirect possession) in these Principles may therefore encompass different legal characterizations in national laws (including bailment, trust, etc.). Hence, the aim is to define the main characteristics and legal incidents of the custody relationship regardless of its legal classification. Accordingly, Principle 11(1) defines the duties that a custodian must perform. Thus, if the duties established in letters (a), (b) and (c) of this section are not owed, the holder is not a custodian.

Multi-signature wallets can be used to give joint control to the custodian and his client, but the client's exclusive control over the digital asset will exclude the

---

[24] UNIDROIT. (2022). – Study LXXXII – W.G.6 – Doc. 4 November 2022, par. 170; UNIDROIT. (2021). – Study LXXXII – W.G.2 – Doc. 2 (rev. 1) March 2021, par. 171; UNIDROIT. (2023). – Study LXXXII – W.G.8 – Doc. 4 February 2023, pp. 92–94, Comment 5. https://www.unidroit.org/prepar… Preparatory work.

[25] UNIDROIT. (2023). – Study LXXXII – W.G.7 – Doc. 5 February 2023, par. 47. https://www.unidroit.org/prepar… Preparatory work.

[26] UNIDROIT. (2022). – Study LXXXII – W.G.6 – Doc. 3 August 2022, par. 98. https://www.unidroit.org/prepar… Preparatory work.

possibility of the custodian fulfilling its duties and therefore prevent the relationship from qualifying as one of custody.[27]

Principle 11(1): the mandatory duties of the custodian

Principle 11(1) establishes the duties that must be fulfilled by a person who provides custody services under an agreement with a client: this concerns the lack of authorization (for) and consequent duty to refrain from transferring or using the digital asset for his or her own benefit, the obligation to comply with the instructions given by the client to transfer the digital asset and, finally, the obligation to safeguard the digital asset. As it stands, Comment 1 of Principle 11 gives rise to the sub-custody structure, stating that if the custodian is a sub-custodian, the sub-custodian's client is in turn a custodian.

While we are dealing with basic duties, a State should not allow them to be excluded by the terms of the custody agreement.

Section (1) of Principle 11 imposes mandatory duties on custodians that are not susceptible to relaxation or relief by the States, and as Comment 1 of this Principle warns, the imperative nature of these duties is justified. It is interesting to underline this because the custody services that are contemplated in these Principles are those that arise or are covered by a custody agreement between the client and his custodian. Consequently, it was deemed essential to specify that said contract or agreement cannot lawfully fail to observe compliance with any of the imperative duties provided for in this section, since that circumstance would cause the loss of the condition of a custody contract in which they are not contemplated, pursuant to the preparation process. The custodian position is defined by the duties imposed on it; duties and custody are almost synonymous. The principle of custody has also been recognised as a definition of the obligations owed by the person providing the custody service. Hence, if said obligations are not owed, the service provided will not be custodial.[28] The pursued objective is clearly to provide the client with protection that cannot be repealed by agreement.[29]

In view of the foregoing, the wording of Principle 11 brings our attention to the qualification of those initially non-excludable duties in relation to that provided for in letter a) "except to the extent permitted by the client and by other law", in relation to the provisions in letter b) "unless" "he is prohibited from complying with the instruction by another law or by any agreement…" or "he is not obligated, by virtue of another law or by an agreement…", and as provided in letter c), defining par excellence of custody (obligation to safeguard the digital asset) refers, in the specific configuration of the sub-duties that would comprise it, to the decision made in this

[27] Vid., in relation to the Draft Principle Y on Custody UNIDROIT. (2021). – Study LXXXII – W.G.2 – Doc. 2 (rev. 1) March 2021, par. 95 and 92; UNIDROIT. (2021). – Study LXXXII – W.G.2 – Doc. 2 (rev. 1) March 2021, ANNEX II Appendix 1, pp. 43–44. https://www.unidroit.org/prepar… Preparatory work.

[28] UNIDROIT. (2021). – Study LXXXII – W.G.3 – Doc. 2 (rev. 1) June 2021, par. 77 and p. 24. https://www.unidroit.org/prepar… Preparatory work.

[29] UNIDROIT. (2023). – Study LXXXII – W.G.8 – Doc. 4 February 2023, pp. 92–94, Comment 6. https://www.unidroit.org/prepar… Preparatory work.

regard by the parties to the custody agreement and, also and previously, by the States themselves when opting for the nature, binding or not, of the additional duties of the custodian as stated, with some important nuances, in section (3) of Principle 11 read in conjunction with Commentary 11.4.

These qualifications are justified not only by the existence of normative provisions that the content of the custody contract must or can respect, as is natural, but also, and perhaps most decisively, because of what it implies as a limitation or graduation of the imperativeness of the duties, the qualifications are justified simply because it was desired to take into account the different demands that the provision of the custody service may require in each case, sending the specification and scope of the duties owed by every custodian to the parties. This was pointed out in the process of developing the Principles[30] and in the public consultation to which they were submitted, especially in view of the broad concept of digital assets that these Principles deal with, since the obligations derived from the custody of digital assets that resemble money or securities cannot be the same as those derived from the custody of an NFT of art, they both certainly give rise to the essential nature of the custodian's obligation to support any loss of digital assets.[31]

Principle 11(1)(a): Prohibition of using the digital asset for the custodian's own benefit

Principle 11(1)(a) provides for the prohibition by the custodian to use the digital asset for its own benefit, except to the extent consented by the client or other law as defined in Principle 2(4), i.e. the Law of a State other than the Law of Principles.

To this end, the client may consent to such use by the custodian, either by contract or by means of an instruction given to the custodian, and has the option of consenting to a more limited use than that permitted by other law.[32]

The other law of a State may allow a custodian to have a right of use in respect of digital assets in relation to which it provides custody services (it may cover situations where digital assets are transferred by operation of law[33]) by specifically providing for this in regulation and/or in private law. In the latter case, the scope of the authorization may depend on the way in which the custody relationship is configured in that private law.

An important element of Principle 11 is therefore the prohibition on custodians from using the digital asset for their own benefit, except to the extent permitted by

---

[30] UNIDROIT. (2022). – Study LXXXII – W.G.6 – Doc. 4 November 2022, par. 170. For example, the Draft Principle Y on Custody. 2 (b) contemplates that the holder is obliged to [alienate] [transfer] that asset following instructions from the client, without any qualification (UNIDROIT. (2021). – Study LXXXII – W.G.2 – Doc. 2 (rev. 1) March 2021, par. 171). https://www.unidroit.org/prepar... Preparatory work.

[31] UNIDROIT. (2023). – Study LXXXII – W.G.8 – Doc. 4 February 2023, pp. 92–94, Comments 4, 6 and 10. https://www.unidroit.org/prepar... Preparatory work.

[32] UNIDROIT. (2021). – Study LXXXII – W.G.2 – Doc. 2 (rev. 1) March 2021, ANNEX II, Appendix 1, pp. 43–44. https://www.unidroit.org/prepar... Preparatory work.

[33] UNIDROIT. (2023). – Study LXXXII – W.G.8 – Doc. 4 February 2023, pp. 92–94, Comment 2. https://www.unidroit.org/prepar... Preparatory work.

the client and other law. However, it is very pertinent to clarify the limitations or uses that the custodian may have by virtue of the law and the express referral of the client, or if, on the contrary, he has absolute capacity in terms of use and enjoyment[34] since, in the latter case, equated to a case of total transfer of the assets to the "custodian", the thresholds of the custody relationship may be crossed, as contemplated in the Principles.[35] In particular, because said digital assets will have been integrated into the assets of the "custodian" and will form part of its estate in bankruptcy, while the aim of the Principles was to protect the client from the consequences of custodian insolvency.

However, for the benefit of the client, it is presumed in Principle 10 (4), in the absence of a clear expression in the contract of said circumstance ("it is not a custody agreement if it is clearly apparent from the agreement"), that the relationship is custodial in accordance with the requirements of Principle 10 (3), that is, when the service is provided in the ordinary course of the service provider's business, the service provider is obliged to obtain (if it has not already done so) and manage the digital asset for the client, and the client does not have the exclusive power to change control of the digital asset within the meaning of Principle 6(2).

To this end, it seems appropriate to note that the last sentence contained in previous versions was removed from the final wording of comment 11.2, which literally read "It is unlikely that another law would allow a custodian to have a completely unlimited right of use in relation to said assets" and that the Steering Committee warned could not be true, as the experience in the bankruptcies of cryptocurrency exchanges in the US has shown. It seems that said exchanges have used clients' digital assets without restrictions, and it is not clear whether the customer had agreed to allow the custodian to use or dispose of the digital asset, and the custodian has a duty to obtain the digital asset for the customer when the customer wants the Exchange to deliver it. Such a duty exists and it must be non-waivable because it is essential in a custodial relationship, or, if waived, the waiver must require disclosure to the client that it simply has a general unsecured contractual right against the custodian, without obligation to maintain the digital asset for the client, an aspect that leads to the question of knowing to what extent the client can waive the obligations of the custodian.[36] The client cannot waive the duty of custodian to maintain the digital asset for the client because resignation entails an exit from the custodial relationship provided for in these UNIDROIT Principles.

As has already been anticipated, the Principles have taken a firm position in this regard for the benefit of the client, by presuming, in the absence of a clear expression in the contract of said circumstance ("it is not a custody agreement if

---

[34] UNIDROIT. (2023). – Study LXXXII – W.G.8 – Doc. 4 February 2023, pp. 92–94, Comment 9; UNIDROIT. (2021). – Study LXXXII – W.G.3 – Doc. 2 (rev. 1) June 2021, p. 24. https://www.unidroit.org/prepar… Preparatory work.

[35] UNIDROIT. (2022). – Study LXXXII – W.G.6 – Doc. 4 November 2022, par. 171–172. https://www.unidroit.org/prepar… Preparatory work.

[36] UNIDROIT. (2022). – Study LXXXII – W.G.7 – Doc. 3 December 2022, par. 106–107; UNIDROIT. (2023). – Study LXXXII – W.G.8 – Doc. 4 February 2023, pp. 92–94, Comment 3. https://www.unidroit.org/prepar… Preparatory work.

the agreement clearly shows that, in the event that a procedure related to insolvency affects the service provider, the digital asset would form part of the assets of the service provider available for distribution among its creditors"), that the relationship is one of custody, meeting the requirements of Principle 10(3), without this problem being reduced to a mere question of contractual interpretation and, consequently, the custodian's obligation to maintain the digital asset for the client, according to principle 10(4). The solution contained in the Principles reflects the reaction of its drafters to the concern of several experts that many contracts had a vague scope of duties and terms of use, and regarding the nature of the relationship between the client and his counterparty, suggesting that, in case of ambiguity, the agreement be presumed to be a custody agreement.[37]

This solution is of particular importance furthermore, in a context where it is quite common for the same company to carry out various activities other than custody, including the maintenance of trust accounts for its clients, the marketing of digital assets in the accounts of its clients, marketing of digital assets on its own account, operating a market ("exchange" or "trading platform"), etc. This Principle only applies to the custody service, regardless of other activities carried out by the person providing this service and independently of the regulatory status of the company.[38] This perspective from which the limits of use or transmission in their own name of digital assets imposed on the custodian, as such custodian, are highlighted and make greater sense, and that, perhaps, without this explanation and differentiation of functions that the same subject can perform, it is not easy to understand the restriction that the concept of custody represents for them.

In the scenario under analysis, one of those situations referred to in Commentary 10.6 of these Principles materializes, in which there is a custody agreement whereby the custodian does not hold the digital asset that is the subject of the agreement on behalf of a client, assuming that section (b) of Principle 10.3 establishes the fundamental obligation of a custodian, which is to obtain (if it has not already done so) and manage the digital asset for the client, with Comment 10.6 expressly referring to Principle 11(1) that we are currently analysing. The custodian does not control the digital asset that is the subject of the agreement when the custodian has exercised a right of use, with Comment 10.6 expressly referring again to Principle 11(1) that we analysed, remembering that in previous versions express reference was made to a limited right of use.[39] That limited nature of the use of the digital asset by the custodian was removed from the final version. Despite this, the situation has not changed substantially because in these cases the custodian is obliged, if the

---

[37] UNIDROIT. (2021). – Study LXXXII – W.G.3 – Doc. 4 July 2021, par. 105 and ss and par. 112; UNIDROIT. (2021). – Study LXXXII – W.G.2 – Doc. 3 April 2021, par. 11. https://www.unidroit.org/prepar… Preparatory work.

[38] UNIDROIT. (2021). – Study LXXXII – W.G.4 – Doc. 2 October 2021, par. 54. And see Comment 10.2 of the Principles. https://www.unidroit.org/prepar… Preparatory work.

[39] UNIDROIT. (2021). – Study LXXXII – W.G.4 – Doc. 2 October 2021, Annex 3, Appendix 1, p. 28; UNIDROIT. (2022). – Study LXXXII – W.G.7 – Doc. 2 December 2022, MASTER COPY OF THE DRAFT PRINCIPLES AND COMMENTS 2, 4 and 5 of Principle 11. https://www.unidroit.org/prepar… Preparatory work.

conditions just stated are met, to obtain the digital asset that is the subject of the agreement for the client. If the digital asset is considered fungible (see Comment 11.6), the obligation will be to obtain a digital asset of the description specified in the agreement.

Principle 11(1)(b): Obligation to comply with instructions given by the client
Principle 11 (1) (b) establishes the key idea in this type of contracts that a custodian is a person who has the duty to manage and treat digital assets in accordance with the instructions given by the client, limiting its action in relation to transactions, unlike the comment that starts by considering the instructions as the general line of action of the custodian in any of his functions.

Indeed, the duty of Principle 11(1)(b) specifies that the custodian must operate with the digital asset in accordance with the client's instructions, but this duty is immediately qualified and, moreover, it draws attention to the casuistry regarding the source of the nuances that may force the lawful limitation or paralysis of following-up on the instructions given by the client.

As could not be otherwise, this duty of the custodian is limited firstly by any legal prohibition provided for in another law, including criminal law or regulatory law, as clarified in Commentary 11.3. The same prohibition on following instructions may arise from any agreement entered into between the custodian and any third party to which the client is a party or has consented, as may happen when a guarantee is constituted over the digital asset managed by the custodian in favour of a third party by the client, and the secured creditor enforces said security interest against third parties through control by the custodian that manages the digital asset for said secured creditor, pursuant to Principle 15.

Other law, or the agreement with the client, may additionally specify particular circumstances in which the custodian is not required to comply with the client's instructions, further qualifying the basic obligation. For example (although in Comment 11.3. these are mentioned as independent assumptions), if the client has granted the custodian a right of use over the digital asset, or if the client has granted a security over the digital asset, or if said right of use guarantee has arisen by legal imperative, this will also qualify the custodian's obligation (see Principle 11(5)).

In short, there are multiple and varied causes that may lawfully limit or paralyze the following of the instructions given by the client, which may have their origin in legal or agreed prohibitions from following the instructions, or in legal or agreed circumstances that justify the non-obligation of executing them in specific cases, noting for each reason the need and reasonableness of verifying the validity of the instructions by the custodian.

It is obvious that when a client's account is frozen or blocked, the client can no longer have control, hence in the process of developing these principles, and in the absence of express formulation of limitations on following the instructions, including "except to the extent prohibited by law" was recommended in the then-corresponding

Principle 13(b).[40] "Fraud, evasion of existing obligations or responsibilities, rules on agency law, restrictions on transfers to minors…" are all reasons that must validly restrict compliance with any instructions given by a client. As jurisprudence has sanctioned, "no rule prohibits a custodian from questioning the authenticity of his clients' instructions and, if he fails to do so, he acts at his own risk. He must act reasonably, no more and no less." A custodian who transfers assets pursuant to an instruction cannot be required to do so "immediately" if there is reasonable doubt as to the validity of the instruction. This can place him in the dilemma described in The Houda: "If they do not follow the instructions, they are potentially liable given the duty imposed by law to follow them, if they follow them, there is a risk that the instruction was incorrect (fraud), being liable to the original owner for an unlawful transfer by failing to safeguard the digital asset in (1)(c)" (The Houda [1994] 2 Lloyd's Rep 541, 554 and 558).[41]

Principle 11(1)(c): Obligation to safeguard digital assets

Principle 11(1)(c) obliges the custodian to safeguard the digital asset, and to that extent implies or clarifies that there must be some duties that the custodian owes to the client in relation to such safeguarding of the digital asset. The specific duties in which this safeguard is specified will normally be included in the custody agreement, but the States are given the option to compulsorily demand private law safeguard duties from the custodian that are not excludable by the will of the parties, with Principle 11 (3) providing some suggestions to that effect, as indicated in Commentary 11.4.

The only thing that this Commentary imperatively warns about is Principle 11.4, in accordance with that established in Principle 10.4 of the UNIDROIT principles (it is not a custody agreement if it is clear from the agreement that, in the event that it affects the service provider, a procedure related to the insolvency, the digital asset would form part of the assets of the service provider available for distribution among its creditors), is that the safeguard includes the achievement of the result established in Principle 13(2), that is, the guarantee that the safeguarded assets are not part of the assets available for distribution among the custodian's creditors if the custodian is affected by insolvency-related proceedings.

Principle 11(2): Management of digital assets as an undivided common fund

Principle 11(2) addresses the common circumstance where a custodian manages digital assets of equal characteristics for multiple clients, and provides that, unless prohibited by the custody agreement or other law, the custodian may manage such digital assets of equal characteristics for two or more of its clients as an undivided common fund.

---

[40] UNIDROIT. (2022). – Study LXXXII – W.G.6 – Doc. 3 August 2022, par. 99; UNIDROIT. (2021). – Study LXXXII – W.G.3 – Doc. 4 July 2021, par. 93. https://www.unidroit.org/prepar… Preparatory work.

[41] UNIDROIT. (2023). – Study LXXXII – W.G.8 – Doc. 4 February 2023, pp. 92–94, Comment 2; UNIDROIT. (2022). – Study LXXXII – W.G.6 – Doc. 2 August 2022, p. 33. https://www.unidroit.org/prepar… Preparatory work.

Commentary 11.6 clarifies that the term "with the same characteristics" is used in these Principles to refer to digital assets that market participants treat as fungible (see also Principles 13(5) to 13(7)). Given the doubts about the compatibility of the consequences that such a characterization normally implies with cryptoassets, in particular, the substitutability of one for another, since the idea of decentralized ledgers is that all asset flows can be tracked and followed, and therefore, all the individual cryptoassets identified in those transactions, which is why an asset can be fungible, but not substitutable.[42] It is immediately noted in the Comment that fungibility, far from being a technical characteristic of a digital asset, actually translates into a (simple) matter of market practice. In fact, it was observed that banknotes had serial numbers, but for most users they were purely fungible, implying that fungibility was not necessarily an intrinsic characteristic of the asset itself, but rather a subjective evaluation by users. Clients may have custodians who hold assets treated as fungible, as well as specific assets identified for specific clients (fully segregated accounts).[43]

The recording of any unit (or quantity) of a digital asset in a digital ledger is necessarily individualized since, by definition, it is susceptible to control, as Principle 2(2) expressly establishes when defining a "digital asset" as an electronic document that can be controlled. However, as a matter of market practice, many digital assets (such as cryptocurrencies) are treated as fungible, so that such unit or units will satisfy an obligation to deliver the digital asset.

Section 11.6 of the Commentary is therefore limited to clarifying that the fungibility of digital assets does not affect or hinder the possibility of identifying them individually, because by definition they are susceptible to control. However, the fact that they have the same characteristics means that when responding to an instruction, the custodian can use any of them to execute the instruction (such unit or units will satisfy an obligation to deliver the digital asset) because it is assumed that through their fungibility, these digital assets are interchangeable (since their characteristics are the same, especially when it is noted that fungibility is only a market practice, which does not affect their technical configuration).

In accordance with these Principles, once the fungibility or equal characteristics of digital assets have been verified, subject to another Law or the custody agreement, custodians are authorized to manage digital assets for several clients as an undivided common fund (Principle 11(2).

Commentary 11.7 of the UNIDROIT Principles explains that this has two consequences. First, the custodian may control an undivided pool of client assets using one or more private keys, so that no specific unit or quantity of that digital asset is specifically allocated to a particular client. If the custodian maintains digital assets for several clients with a sub-custodian, maintaining them as an undivided pool means

---

[42] UNIDROIT. (2022). – Study LXXXII – W.G.6 – Doc. 3 August 2022 – ANNEX, p. 38; UNIDROIT (2023). – Study LXXXII – W.G.8 – Doc. 4 February 2023, pp. 92–94, Comment 7. https://www.unidroit.org/prepar... Preparatory work.

[43] UNIDROIT. (2021). – Study LXXXII – W.G.2 – Doc. 3 April 2021, par. 19. https://www.unidroit.org/prepar... Preparatory work.

that the custodian need not have a separate sub-account with the sub-custodian for each client (as indicated in Comment 13.7 in this last situation, their rights against the sub-custodian will be undivided). As a result, the undivided pool includes all such digital assets controlled by the custodian for its clients using one or more private keys, as well as all such digital assets managed with one or more sub-custodians. On the other hand, the reference to "a custodian" in Principle 11(2) also applies to a sub-custodian whose clients are custodians.

Secondly, when the custodian receives an instruction from a client regarding a digital asset managed for its clients as an undivided pool, it may comply with such instruction using any unit or quantity of such digital asset that it directly controls or manages with a sub-custodian, since those different units or quantities of the digital asset all have the same characteristics and are treated as fungible.

When the custodian is not permitted to manage an undivided pool, complete segregation must be implemented. The meaning of segregating digital assets, taking into account their intangible nature, consists of holding digital assets in separate wallets, segregated vaults, or through separate entries in a balance sheet…, different technological mechanisms could make assets fungible or non-fungible.[44] The Principles therefore allow for different methods to structure custody. In fact, the terms and conditions of the largest crypto exchanges include two forms of custody: (1) segregated custody where custodians manage cryptoassets per client, that is, individually; and (2) an omnibus account model where the custodian manages a pool of crypto assets held collectively for clients.[45]

In the process of developing these Principles, it was noted that the meaning of an undivided fund was not clear. It was clarified that this referred to an omnibus (general) account and that this would be expressly indicated in the comment.[46] Later, Commentary 6 of Principle 11 of the UNIDROIT DRAFT PRINCIPLES ON DIGITAL ASSETS AND PRIVATE LAW clarifies that when the custodian holds an undivided pool of assets for its clients, it controls a number of fungible digital assets, but they are not specifically identified in the chain of assets or private keys related to a specific client. Instead, the number of assets that the custodian holds for each client is recorded on the custodian's books (similar to the records maintained in a common or general account—omnibus—in relation to brokered securities). It is also highlighted that there could be many reasons for this situation, and one possibility

[44] UNIDROIT. (2021). – Study LXXXII – W.G.2 – Doc. 3 April 2021, par. 19. https://www.unidroit.org/prepar… Preparatory work.

[45] UNIDROIT. (2021). Study LXXXII – W.G.1 – Doc. 3 March 2021, par. 81. https://www.unidroit.org/prepar… Preparatory work.

[46] UNIDROIT. (2023). – Study LXXXII – W.G.7 – Doc. 5 February 2023, par. 50; UNIDROIT. (2023). – Study LXXXII – W.G.8 – Doc. 4 February 2023, pp. 92–94, Comment 5. https://www.unidroit.org/prepar… Preparatory work.

is that a custodian executes book-entry transfers of digital assets between its clients rather than changing control of the digital assets.[47]

It is difficult to represent this type of transmission in a way that is reconciled with the operation of a distributed registry, and this is only normal because the transmission operates outside of it. Transmission of ownership is not reflected in the blockchain, it is only recognized in the internal records of the custodian, and therefore all the efficiencies potentially linked to DLT and the use of smart contracts, cryptographic processes, registration of transactions in an automated, immutable, transparent, almost immediate way are lost in this type of transmissions.[48]

Comment 6.5 advises that a change in control from one person to another, defined in Principle 6(2), must be distinguished from a transfer of a digital asset or an interest therein, that is, from a transfer of real rights (as contemplated in Principle 2(5)(a) "transmission" of a digital asset means the change of a real right in the digital asset from one person to another). The question of whether there is a valid transfer of rights in rem over a digital asset is a matter for other standards and is not addressed in these Principles (Principle 3(3) and Commentary 2.26). While in many situations the transfer of real rights will be accompanied by a change in control, in others this appears not to be the case when there are omnibus accounts managed by a custodian. Control is relevant in the context of digital asset custody. Under a custody agreement, a service provider is obliged to manage the digital assets of its clients, either by controlling the digital assets itself or by entering into a custody agreement with a sub-custodian under which the sub-custodian controls the digital assets for the service provider (Principle 10). This is an example of one person (the custodian) having control, while the real rights are passed onto or remain with the client (Comment 6.6).

Conversely, where there is a segregated account or one in which a custodian manages a set of assets (and the corresponding private key) for that particular client, any transfer to another client would have to take place through a change of control. If digital assets are not fungible, they can only be held in a segregated account.[49]

Principle 11(3): Duties that a custodian may owe to his client

Principle 11(3) establishes some private law duties owed by the custodian to its client—with respect to the custody of the digital asset—which, from the perspective of the Principles, and in general, are not considered mandatory nor therefore an

[47] UNIDROIT. (2023). – Study LXXXII – W.G.8 – Doc. 2 February 2023; UNIDROIT. (2022). – Study LXXXII – W.G.6 – Doc. 3 August 2022, par. 98; UNIDROIT. (2021). – Study LXXXII – W.G.4 – Doc. 2 October 2021, pp. 30–31, par. 54 in relation to the latest version of the draft Principle C on custody. https://www.unidroit.org/prepar… Preparatory work.

[48] OECD (2021), Regulatory Approaches to the Tokenisation of Assets, OECD Blockchain Policy Series, www.oecd.org/finance/Regulatory-Approaches-to-the-Tokenisation-of-Assets.htm, p. 23; UNIDROIT. (2022). – Study LXXXII – W.G.6 – Doc. 3 August 2022 – ANNEX, p. 49. https://www.unidroit.org/prepar… Preparatory work.

[49] UNIDROIT. (2021). – Study LXXXII – W.G.4 – Doc. 2 October 2021, p. 30; UNIDROIT. (2022). – Study LXXXII – W.G.7 – Doc. 2 December 2022, MASTER COPY OF DRAFT PRINCIPLES AND COMMENTS. https://www.unidroit.org/prepar… Preparatory work.

integral part of the condition of custodian,[50] but that a State may wish to regulate and choose to have it guaranteed by a custodian to its client. In that case, the State must establish these duties as imperative and not excludable by agreement (Commentary 11.8). These obligations have been derived from the UNIDROIT Geneva Convention. This is a non-exhaustive list. Yet again, let us recall that if the custodian is a sub-custodian, the client is a custodian.

On the other hand (separately), a State may wish to impose these duties on custodians as a matter of regulatory law, that is, by imposing duties for which there is no compensation or remedy under private law, but that any breach thereof could result in sanctions being imposed by the State. From this perspective, the Pilot Regulation, the LMVSI and MiCA contemplate parallel regimes of duties and the consequent responsibility towards the injured parties, which produces overlaps or superposition with the UNIDROIT Principles.

The initially dispositive nature of these duties has a limit, since to achieve the result of Principle 13(2) in some national laws (that is, that a digital asset that a custodian involved in an insolvency-related procedure manages for the client is not part of that custodian's assets available for distribution to its creditors) the Principle 11(3)(d) duty should not be allowed to be excluded by the provisions of the custody agreement.[51] This is the duty to separate the digital assets managed for clients from the digital assets managed by the custodian for itself. However, the State may choose to impose a similar obligation as a matter of regulatory law.

Principle 11(3)(a): Duty to keep a record of the digital assets managed for each client

The duty to maintain accurate records of digital assets for each client (what assets it holds for each client) can be flexibly fulfilled by the custodian, either separately from the distributed ledgers that record the respective digital assets (on computers or a DLT), or if technology allows, it can be part of the information stored in the distributed ledger.[52] It is therefore a duty for which there is no prescribed how, it is left to the industry to determine the best way to fulfil it, the record could be anywhere within the technology, but the record should be a separate piece of information from the actual record of the holder of the digital asset,[53] which could be used in the insolvency of the custodian, as it is a way to preserve the client's priority in the event of insolvency. Without proper record keeping, there would be no way to identify the client's assets in the event of insolvency of the custodian, thereby reducing the client's status to that of an unsecured creditor.

---

[50] UNIDROIT. (2021). – Study LXXXII – W.G.2 – Doc. 3 April 2021, par. 11 and 24. https://www.unidroit.org/prepar… Preparatory work.

[51] UNIDROIT. (2022). – Study LXXXII – W.G.6 – Doc. 2 August 2022; UNIDROIT. (2023). – Study LXXXII – W.G.8 – Doc. 2 February 2023, DRAFT UNIDROIT PRINCIPLES ON DIGITAL ASSETS AND PRIVATE LAW, Commentary 7. https://www.unidroit.org/prepar… Preparatory work.

[52] UNIDROIT. (2021). – Study LXXXII – W.G.1 – Doc. 4 March 2021, par. 108 and 110. https://www.unidroit.org/prepar… Preparatory work.

[53] UNIDROIT. (2021). – Study LXXXII – W.G.2 – Doc. 3 April 2021, par. 22. https://www.unidroit.org/prepar… Preparatory work.

In the preparatory work, both its regulatory nature (punishable in the administrative sphere if violated) and private law duty have been discussed, and regarding the latter, it has been questioned whether, being a fundamental duty of the custodian, it could be considered included or not in the definition of custodian itself, generally rejecting that record keeping is an essential duty for the definition of custodian. In any event, it would be a duty applicable to anyone who falls within the definition of custodian. However, some US court decisions under Article 8 of the UCC (Uniform Commercial Code) have concluded that recordkeeping was only a public duty enforceable by regulators, rather than a duty enforceable through public and private avenues. UNCITRAL apparently encountered similar problems in drafting the MLETR regarding obligations to maintain records of contracts entered into electronically, ultimately rejecting this proposal due to its regulatory nature and because such an obligation for digital contracts would be a discriminatory requirement with regards to classical contracting methods, which do not entail the obligation of recordkeeping.

On the other hand, providing these custody services in practice shows that the offer is very varied, from some custody services that update each transaction on side chains instead of zeroing the ledger, to service offers that only use the general ledger and no other separate record other than that of the holding itself.

The key to the solution adopted in this regard by these UNIDROIT principles is provided by the reflections of Mr. Jeremy Bacharach, pointing out that in Switzerland the question is whether the assets can be kept off the balance sheet, considering that they could be kept that way if there were the possibility of segregating them into an insolvency case. Consequently, the incentive to comply with private law was the accounting benefit of not having these assets on the balance sheet,[54] which is almost equivalent to the unavoidable obligation in some jurisdictions provided for in letter (d) to separate the custodian's own assets from those of their clients.

The bottom line is that the situation with digital assets, compared to traditionally brokered securities, is more flexible and presents more variety in terms of record keeping, holding, control and custody.[55]

Principle 11(3)(b): Duty to securely and effectively manage equivalent digital assets at all times with the records it maintains for its clients

The custodian is obliged to manage, safely and effectively, assets correlative to the records it maintains for its clients, in such a way that if the record shows that a custodian manages 1 Bitcoin for A, the custodian must manage at least 1 Bitcoin. Comment 11.10 warns that this is an essential obligation of every custodian in general, and that it should be independent of the imposition of additional records to the one that takes place in the distributed registry on which its exploitation is based. Effective and secure compliance with this obligation is guaranteed by imposing the obligation to constantly maintain a volume of digital assets correlative to the records it maintains for its clients on the custodian, as provided for in Principle 11(3)(c).

---

[54] UNIDROIT. (2021). – Study LXXXII – W.G.2 – Doc. 3 April 2021, par. 22–25. https://www.unidroit.org/prepar... Preparatory work.

[55] UNIDROIT. (2021). – Study LXXXII – W.G.2 – Doc. 3 April 2021, par. 27 and 28. https://www.unidroit.org/prepar... Preparatory work.

Principle 11(3)(c): Duty to promptly acquire or replace lost digital assets of the client

This duty consists of replacing any lost assets, that is, acquiring digital assets without delay by the custodian that reconciles what the custodian actually manages with the client's records, so that they are equivalent. Only then can he ensure that he safely and effectively manages his clients' digital assets at all times, as required by Principle 11(3)(b). The assets acquired must be, naturally, of identical characteristics, not the same ones that were specifically delivered, and have the quantity as the assets recorded in the records.[56]

This duty of the custodian clearly translates into a norm of responsibility for him regarding lost digital assets. Custody of digital assets gives rise to increased risks that a custodian may commit fraud or theft, lose a private key necessary to transfer a client's digital asset values, or could even transfer a client's digital assets to an unknown or unwanted address, without the ability to reverse a fraudulent or erroneous transaction.[57] Hence, custody is defined by its technological specialization aimed at guaranteeing the security of the asset and controlling the risk of cybersecurity or theft.

If this responsibility comes into play or is limited to custody as exclusive control, it will never be fulfilled in practice, since the very existence of cryptoassets is conditional on many nodes cooperating and recognizing the code itself as an asset. Therefore, literally no participant has "exclusive control" and no custodian has the factual ability to enforce that other nodes respect the very existence of cryptoassets, emphasizing the need to restrict the Principles to the core of private law and leave aside the financial regulation with which custodians must comply. It is doubtful that a custodian-centric liability rule makes sense in fully decentralized environments.

But a complete DeFi setup doesn't happen that often if we look at who has control of the code. If, on the other hand, the custodian relationship specifies which individual assets belong to each owner/client, who prevails if the custodian transfers the owner/client's digital assets to a bona fide third-party transferee? The rule of protection of the acquirer in good faith leads de facto to the responsibility of the custodian. In theory, the solution would be to claim against all nodes that jointly execute the DLT. In practice though, that would entail significant costs.

Therefore, any commercially viable ledger will require a certain degree of centralization to function properly. This is particularly true to ensure compliance with financial regulations on custody matters,[58] which also cover civil liability (see for example article 7.6 of the Pilot Regulation or article 8.6 of the LMVSI or article 75 of MiCA). Moreover, in relation to financial instruments, the loss or theft of the keys should not lead to the theft or loss of the values, since smart contract issuance must incorporate

---

[56] UNIDROIT. (2021). – Study LXXXII – W.G.2 – Doc. 3 April 2021, par. 21. https://www.unidroit.org/prepar… Preparatory work.

[57] OECD (2021), Regulatory Approaches to the Tokenisation of Assets, OECD Blockchain Policy Series, www.oecd.org/finance/Regulatory-Approaches-to-the-Tokenisation-of-Assets.htm, p. 24.

[58] UNIDROIT. (2022). – Study LXXXII – W.G.6 – Doc. 3 August 2022 – ANNEX, pp. 35 and ss; UNIDROIT. (2021). – Study LXXXII – W.G.1 – Doc. 4 March 2021, par. 107. https://www.unidroit.org/prepar… Preparatory work.

limitations on the transmission of those financial instruments and allow the custodian to return them to their owner.[59] On the other hand, the use of multi-signature wallets, whose use can be structured in different ways, avoids those problems.[60]

If, in the absence of regulatory regimes for custody, or in the face of emerging and untested regimes, private law rules can be essential for the protection of clients,[61] conversely, existing regulatory regimes will also contribute to their protection, and to a large extent will overlap.

Principle 11(3)(d): Duty to separate clients' digital assets from the custodian's own assets

The custodian's obligation to separate or segregate the client's digital assets from the custodian's own or domestic digital assets to which this Principle refers is also contemplated as a regulatory obligation of administrative/public law of financial entities. This is an important solution, and one that is useful in that it reinforces effective compliance with the rules of private law and thereby guarantees the observance of this duty also provided for in private law, and it is especially relevant for the protection of the client in the event of the custodian's insolvency.[62]

The assumptions made in the preparatory work of these Principles regarding the insolvencies of cryptocurrency custodians leave clear evidence of this. The segregation of assets held by custodians on behalf of clients can generate risks for proprietary assets when such segregation is inadequate or non-existent, which has especially been projected in relation to assets in omnibus accounts, since they are held in the name of the intermediary instead of in named accounts of the beneficial owners. The investor consequently bears the risks of the custodian, which would materialize in the event of the insolvency of the custodian.[63] In this sense, it has been observed that if Bitcoin, for example, presents better traceability than other cryptocurrencies, in the case of a traceable transaction a property law interest in a certain asset could be demonstrated, while in an omnibus configuration a proprietary interest in a specific asset cannot be determined. In the absence of proof of ownership, the holder is considered the owner, and the client would only have a contractual right over the asset, a purely personal claim (see the cases Mt. Gox, Bitgrail and Cryptopia for comparison purposes). This situation could be resolved by having a common fund for clients' assets, legally separated from the custodians' assets. Clients would be classified as co-owners, who

[59] NSMC. (2024). Frequently Asked Questions and Answers about Financial Instruments based on Distributed Ledger Technologies (DLT), May 29 2024, p. 13. https://www.cnmv.es/FAQ_IFbasadosTRD PDF.

[60] UNIDROIT. (2021). – Study LXXXII – W.G.1 – Doc. 3 March 2021, par. 98. https://www.unidroit.org/prepar... Preparatory work.

[61] UNIDROIT. (2020). – Study LXXXII – W.G.1 – Doc. 2 November 2020, par. 68. https://www.unidroit.org/prepar... Preparatory work.

[62] UNIDROIT. (2021). – Study LXXXII – W.G.1 – Doc. 4, March 2021, par 98; UNIDROIT. (2021). Study LXXXII – W.G.1 – Doc. 3 March 2021, par. 82 and ss. https://www.unidroit.org/prepar... Preparatory work.

[63] OECD (2021), Regulatory Approaches to the Tokenisation of Assets, OECD Blockchain Policy Series, www.oecd.org/finance/Regulatory-Approaches-to-the-Tokenisation-of-Assets.htm, p. 26.

have a pro rata share in the pool and do not share (or commingle) assets with the custodian.[64]

Consequently, the relationship between asset safeguarding and asset segregation by a custodian seems quite clear.

Commentary 11.12 clarifies how the custodian can fulfil this obligation of separating its clients' digital assets from its own, either by controlling them using different private keys or by managing them in different accounts with a sub-custodian,[65] therefore the legal effects will differ depending on the applicable law. Indeed, operationally, separation often gives rise to legal segregation, depending on the applicable law. Segregation, particularly in common law countries, could be achieved through trusts, while in civil law countries, a law may be necessary to ensure segregation,[66] see article 15 LMVSI for example.

Comment 11.13 advises that Principle 11(3)(d) does not address the segregation of assets of any particular client. In this latter perspective, a custodian, rather than managing assets of clients with the same characteristics as an undivided whole, can offer a client the possibility of managing that client's assets separately from the assets of other clients with similar characteristics. This is the so-called total segregation, already mentioned when commenting on section (2) of Principle 11, which is materialized through the same means that make it possible to segregate the clients' assets with respect to the custodian's own. It will require the custodian to control the client's assets using a separate private key or manage them in a separate account with a sub-custodian, so that those assets are exclusively linked to the client. Again, please note that the legal effect of such a segregation agreement will depend on the other applicable law and may vary from one jurisdiction to another.[67]

Regarding the duty to segregate the digital assets of a particular client from those of another client, the possibility of transferring it to the current equivalent of Principle 11(1) was considered. There was agreement to consider that, given the different ways in which this problem is addressed in different jurisdictions, the duty should be retained in the equivalent of the current Principle 11(3), with additional clarity and guidance provided in the Commentary regarding its importance as best practice.[68]

---

[64] UNIDROIT. (2021). – Study LXXXII – W.G.1 – Doc. 3 March 2021, par. 96 and 81 and ss;UNIDROIT. (2021). – Study LXXXII – W.G.2 – Doc. 3 April 2021, par. 8 and par. 10. https://www.unidroit.org/prepar... Preparatory work.

[65] See, e.g. UNIDROIT. (2022) – Study LXXXII – W.G.6 – Doc. 2 August 2022, p. 36, Blockchain.com Trading Account. https://www.unidroit.org/prepar... Preparatory work.

[66] UNIDROIT. (2021). – Study LXXXII – W.G.1 – Doc. 3 March 2021, par. 86. The consequences of the custodian's insolvency are established in a functional way and not using legal concepts such as ownership or possession (UNIDROIT. (2021). – Study LXXXII – W.G.4 – Doc. 2 October 2021, p. 30, in relation to draft Principle C on custody). https://www.unidroit.org/prepar... Preparatory work.

[67] Paragraphs 90 and 92 of the UNIDROIT Legislative Guide on Intermediate Securities (2017) illustrate the situation in detail. https://www.Unidroit.org/instruments/capital-markets/geneva-convention. https://www.Unidroit.org/wp-content/uploads/2021/06/convention.pdf.

[68] UNIDROIT. (2023). – Study LXXXII – W.G.7 – Doc. 5 February 2023, par. 53. https://www.unidroit.org/prepar... Preparatory work.

Principle 11(3)(e): Duty to transfer benefits derived from digital assets to the client

This duty to transfer all the benefits of the digital asset to the client is recognized without prejudice to any rights granted to the custodian or another person, as would be the case, for example, if these subjects (the custodian or a third party) were to have a security interest in digital assets.

Commentary 11.14 deals with breaking down the possible content of the benefits derived from a digital asset, which may include voting rights, monetary dividends, distributions in kind (e.g., "airdrops", i.e. a free distribution of tokens sent to active users' wallets) and additional digital assets that may be created as a result of a network-wide event, such as a "fork".

Hard forks are possible in permissionless networks. Forks create a chain split, and when the old chain is abandoned they are known as network upgrades. When a hard fork occurs in a DLT, clients are entitled to the benefit of the fork, i.e. assets on both branches of the chain. Due to a lack of regulation in certain jurisdictions, certain custodians refuse to deliver a branch's assets to clients, causing unfair treatment and harm to the owners of the asset.[69] The Principles address this risk through regulation of letter (e) of Principle 11(3), in response to the demands regarding this issue.[70]

Principle 11(4): Fulfilment of duties using a sub-custody structure

Principle 11(4) authorizes the use of a sub-custody structure, that is, the custodian may fulfil its duties to its client to manage the digital asset through a custody agreement with a sub-custodian in respect of such asset. Accordingly, a custodian can fulfil its custodial duties not by controlling the digital asset, but by being a client of another custodian[71] (see Principle 10(2) and Commentary 10.4). Such custodian authorization for sub-custody may come either from the client or from another law that, for example, allows licensed custodians to offer sub-custody services; By one means of authorization or another, there is the necessary certainty, among other things, to address and bring an end to the bad practices frequently used by custodians.[72]

This type of structure can only be used if the sub-custodian is subject to the mandatory and non-excusable private law duties of a custodian under the applicable law, which are the duties set out in Principle 11(1) plus those listed in Principle 11 (3) that the relevant State has decided to make imperative. Otherwise, if the sub-custodian were not subject in the sub-custody agreement to these private law duties, the custodian would be in breach of its own duties to the client. As recognized in the first draft that addresses the issue of sub-custody, in view of the convenience of considering these chains of tenure longer than the first level relationship (custodian-client) it is

---

[69] OECD (2021), Regulatory Approaches to the Tokenisation of Assets, OECD Blockchain Policy Series, www.oecd.org/finance/Regulatory-Approaches-to-the-Tokenisation-of-Assets.htm, p. 25.

[70] UNIDROIT. (2022). – Study LXXXII – W.G.6 – Doc. 2 August 2022, par. 171. https://www.unidroit.org/prepar… Preparatory work.

[71] UNIDROIT. (2021). – Study LXXXII – W.G.4 – Doc. 3 December 2021, par. 69. https://www.unidroit.org/prepar… Preparatory work.

[72] UNIDROIT. (2022). – Study LXXXII – W.G.6 – Doc. 4 November 2022, par. 172–173. https://www.unidroit.org/prepar… Preparatory work.

not obvious how this legal relationship works in practice and, as Commentary 11.15 itself reproduces, the Principles are designed to ensure that A's client is not disadvantaged or weakened by the use of B as a sub-custodian, compared to the position in which A himself provided the custody service.[73] Consequently, the sub-custodian is bound by the obligations established in Principle 11, as a means of offering the client the same protection and guarantees that a custodian would offer.

The Principles do not contemplate the possible liability of the client-custodian to its client with respect to the performance or non-performance by the sub-custodian of its duties under Principle 11 and the sub-custody agreement. That eventuality will be determined, where appropriate, by another law (Commentary 11.15). The only thing that is done is to condition the possibility of hosting a sub-custody structure to those situations in which the sub-custodian is subject to the duties that arise from Principle 11.

Principle 11(5): Digital asset managed by a custodian subject to a security right

Principle 11(5) recognizes that a custodian may have a security right in the digital asset it manages for a client. The client may owe fees to the custodian, for which the latter wishes to be guaranteed, or the custodian may have lent money to the client to acquire the digital asset. A security right under Principle 11(5)(a) would be made effective and enforceable against third parties through control of the digital asset under Principle 15, since the custodian either controls the digital asset itself or has entered into a custody agreement with a sub-custodian in relation to the asset (Commentary 11.16).[74]

A client may also grant a security right in a digital asset managed by a custodian to a third party, as is apparent from the nature of a digital asset set forth in Principle 3(1) and in Principle 14(1), as it may be the object of real rights. This is the latest assumption incorporated into Principle 11(5)[75] probably because "some lenders use securities intermediaries to enhance their security interests through the acquisition of control, which also confers superpriority, even over a previous registration"[76] (see current UNIDROIT Principle 16). Indeed, in that case the secured creditor needs to enforce the security right against third parties through control by the custodian that manages the digital asset for said secured creditor, pursuant to Principle 15 (and see

---

[73] UNIDROIT. (2021). – Study LXXXII – W.G.3 – Doc. 2 (rev. 1) June 2021, Principle C.9 and its explanation; UNIDROIT. (2022). – Study LXXXII – W.G.6 – Doc. 4 November 2022, par. 173. https://www.unidroit.org/prepar... Preparatory work.

[74] UNIDROIT. (2021). – Study LXXXII – W.G.4 – Doc. 2 October 2021 p. 30, collateral is probably automatically perfected in this situation (US position), although this is inconsistent with the Financial Collateral Directive in the EU and relevant regulations in the UK. https://www.unidroit.org/prepar... Preparatory work.

[75] UNIDROIT. (2022). – Study LXXXII – W.G.7 – Doc. 2 December 2022, MASTER COPY OF DRAFT PRINCIPLES AND COMMENTS, Commentary 13; UNIDROIT. (2020). – Study LXXXII – W.G.1 – Doc. 2 November 2020, par. 72. https://www.unidroit.org/prepar... Preparatory work.

[76] UNIDROIT. (2021). – Study LXXXII – W.G.1 – Doc. 3 March 2021, par. 30. https://www.unidroit.org/prepar... Preparatory work.

Comment 15.8), but also could enforce the security right against third parties by a means available under another law, other than control, for example, registration (see Principle 17.2 and Commentaries 17.8 and 17.9 to assess the greatest difficulties faced in the execution of the guarantee in these cases).

As the Commentary on Principle 15.1 clarifies, a State should recognize that a security right in a digital asset can be made effective against third parties through control, which would apply precisely to a situation in which the secured creditor (the custodian itself in this case) controls the digital asset, but also when a custodian holds the digital asset for the secured creditor, including through a sub-custodian. Control represents the functional equivalent in cases where security rights are created and made effective against third parties through the possession of a document or title issued on paper.[77]

Be that as it may, the right of guarantee enforceable against third parties by the corresponding means recognized in the corresponding State, interferes with the fulfilment of the custodian's duties, as has been seen throughout these reflections.

2.5 *Critical Observations*

As general observations, the structure or formal ordering, if you prefer, of the duties imposed on the custodian are somewhat surprising. In principle, it is not generally understood that the duties included in Principle 11(1) are obligatory, and those contemplated in Principle 11(3) are mandatory only if the States decide so. Except in relation to the duty identified in letter (a) of Principle 11(3) (i.e. duty to keep a record of the digital assets it manages for each client), it appears that the rest of the duties, both those mentioned in point (1) as well as point (3) of Principle 11 should be imperative because the work of custody of digital assets cannot be understood without them and neither can the responsibility that is presumptively drawn from the writing of any of them if they are not observed (in cases of loss of digital assets and in cases of insolvency).[78]

On the other hand, it seems that the first duty to mention should be the one contemplated in letter (c) of Principle 11(1), as this is the foundation and basis of the rest of the duties and the demands that diligent compliance entails. This is because the obligation to safeguard the digital asset contemplated in letter (c) of point (1) largely identifies the legal configuration of the content of the custodian's position, which itself includes the content of letters (a) and (b) of point (1) and also explains the limitations or exclusions it includes. In particular, Commentary 11.4 expressly states that this duty includes those included and suggested in Principle 11(3).

---

[77] UNCITRAL Model Law on Electronic Transmissible Documents (2017), para. 108, in relation to its article 11.

[78] In a similar sense UNIDROIT. (2022). – Study LXXXII – W.G.7 – Doc. 3 December 2022, par. 109. https://www.unidroit.org/prepar… Preparatory work.

References

NSMC. (2024). Frequently Asked Questions and Answers about Financial Instruments based on Distributed Ledger Technologies (DLT), May 29 2024. https://www.cnmv.es/FAQ_IFbasadosTRD last visited 15 January 2025.

OECD. (2021). Regulatory Approaches to the Tokenisation of Assets, OECD Blockchain Policy Series. www.oecd.org/finance/Regulatory-Approaches-to-the-Tokenisation-of-Assets.htm last visited 15 January 2025.

UNIDROIT. (2017). Legislative Guide on Intermediated Securities, for the Implementation of the Principles and Standards of the Geneva Securities Convention. https://www.Unidroit.org/instruments/capital-markets/legislative-guide/.

UNCITRAL. (2017). Model Law on Electronic Transmissible Documents. https://uncitral.un.org/electronic_transferable_records.

Digital Assets and Private Law Working Group // First session (remote) // Rome, 17–19 November 2020 //// UNIDROIT 2020 // Study LXXXII – W.G.1 – Doc. 2 // English only // November 2020. https://www.unidroit.org›2020›s-82-wg01-02-e PDF last visited 15 January 2025.

Exploratory Workshop on Digital Assets and Private Law // Rome and Zoom (17–18 September 2020) [13:00–17:00 (CEST)] //// UNIDROIT 2021 // Study LXXXII – W.G.1 – Doc. 3 // Original: English // March 2021. https://www.unidroit.org/2021/s-82-wg01-03-e PDF last visited 15 January 2025.

Digital Assets and Private Law Working Group // First session (remote) Rome, 17–19 November 2020 //// UNIDROIT 2021 // Study LXXXII – W.G.1 – Doc. 4 // English only // March 2021. https://www.unidroit.org/prepar… Study LXXXII – W.G.1 – Doc. 4: Summary Report of the 1st session. 2nd Working Group Meeting. last visited 15 January 2025

Digital Assets and Private Law Working Group // Second session (remote) Rome, 16–18 March 2021 //// UNIDROIT 2021 // Study LXXXII – W.G.2 – Doc. 2 (rev. 1) // English only // March 2021. https://www.unidroit.org/s-82-wg02-02rev-01-e PDF last visited 15 January 2025

Digital Assets and Private Law Working Group // Second session (remote) Rome, 16–18 March 2021 //// UNIDROIT 2021 // Study LXXXII – W.G. 2 – Doc. 3 // English only // April 2021. https://www.unidroit.org/2021/s-82-wg02-03-e PDF last visited 15 January 2025.

Digital Assets and Private Law Working Group // Third session (remote) Rome, 30 June–2 July 2021 //// UNIDROIT 2021 // Study LXXXII – W.G.3 – Doc. 2 (rev. 1) // English only // June 2021. https://www.unidroit.org/s-82-wg03-02-rev01-e PDF last visited 15 January 2025.

Digital Assets and Private Law Working Group // Third session (remote) Rome, 30 June–2 July 2021 //// UNIDROIT 2021 // Study LXXXII – W.G.3 – Doc. 4 // English only // July 2021. https://www.unidroit.org/2021/s-82-wg03-04-e PDF last visited 15 January 2025.

Digital Assets and Private Law Working Group // Fourth session (hybrid) Rome, 2–4 November 2021 //// UNIDROIT 2021 // Study LXXXII – W.G.4 – Doc. 2 // English only // October 2021. https://www.unidroit.org/prepar… Preparatory work last visited 15 January 2025.

Digital Assets and Private Law Working Group // Fourth session (remote) Rome, 2–4 November 2021 //// UNIDROIT 2021 // Study LXXXII – W.G.4 – Doc. 3 // English only // December 2021. https://www.unidroit.org/uploads/2022/03/St PDF last visited 15 January 2025.

Digital Assets and Private Law Working Group // Fifth session (hybrid) Rome, 7–9 March 2022 //// UNIDROIT 2022 // Study LXXXII – W.G.5 – Doc. 2 // English only // February 2022. https://www.unidroit.org/uploads/2022/03 PDF last visited 15 January 2025.

Digital Assets and Private Law Working Group // Fifth session (hybrid) Rome, 7–9 March 2022 //// UNIDROIT 2022 // Study LXXXII – W.G.5 – Doc. 3 // English only // February 2022. https://www.unidroit.org/uploads/2022/03 PDF last visited 15 January 2025.

Digital Assets and Private Law Working Group // Sixth session (hybrid) Rome, 31 August–2 September 2022 //// UNIDROIT 2022 // Study LXXXII – W.G.6 – Doc. 2 // English only // August 2022. https://www.unidroit.org/uploads/2022/08 PDF last visited 15 January 2025.

Digital Assets and Private Law Working Group // Sixth session (hybrid) Rome, 31 August–2 September 2022 //// UNIDROIT 2022 // Study LXXXII – W.G.6 – Doc. 3 // English only // August 2022. https://www.unidroit.org/uploads/2022/08 PDF last visited 15 January 2025.
Digital Assets and Private Law Working Group // Sixth session (hybrid) Rome & Zoom 31 August–2 September 2022 //// UNIDROIT 2022 //Study LXXXII – W.G.6 – Doc. 4 // English only // November 2022. https://www.unidroit.org/uploads/2022/12 PDF last visited 15 January 2025.
Digital Assets and Private Law Working Group // Seventh session (hybrid) Rome, 19–21 December 2022 //// UNIDROIT 2022 // Study LXXXII – W.G.7 – Doc. 2 // English only // December 2022. https://www.unidroit.org/uploads/2022/12 PDF last visited 15 January 2025.
Digital Assets and Private Law Working Group // Seventh session (hybrid) Rome, 19–21 December 2022 //// UNIDROIT 2022 // Study LXXXII – W.G.7 – Doc. 3 // English only // December 2022. https://www.unidroit.org/uploads/2022/12 PDF last visited 15 January 2025.
Digital Assets and Private Law Working Group // Seventh session (hybrid) Rome & Zoom 19–21 December 2022 //// UNIDROIT 2023 // Study LXXXII – W.G.7 – Doc. 5 // English only // February 2023. https://www.unidroit.org/uploads/2023/03 PDF last visited 15 January 2025.
Digital Assets and Private Law Working Group // Eighth session (hybrid) Rome, 8–10 March 2023 //// UNIDROIT 2023 // Study LXXXII - W.G.8 – Doc. 2 // English only // February 2023. https://www.unidroit.org/uploads/2023/03 PDF last visited 15 January 2025.
Digital Assets and Private Law Working Group // Eighth session (hybrid) Rome, 8–10 March 2023 //// UNIDROIT 2023 // Study LXXXII – W.G.8 – Doc. 4 // English only // February 2023. https://www.unidroit.org/uploads/2023/03 PDF last visited 15 January 2025.

Principle 12
Innocent Client

Ester Becerril Fernández

(1) **Subject to paragraph (2), where a custodian maintains a digital asset pursuant to a custody agreement as defined in Principles 10(3) and 10(4), no rights based on a proprietary claim to that asset may be successfully asserted against the client.**

(2) **Paragraph (1) does not apply if the client, at the time from which the custodian maintains the digital asset for that client, actually knows or ought to know that another person has an interest in the digital asset and that the acquisition violates the rights of that other person in relation to its interest.**

(3) **If digital assets are maintained by a custodian for two or more clients as an undivided pool, paragraphs (1) and (2) apply to each client for whom the digital assets are maintained.**

1 Official Commentary

Commentary

12.1. Principle 12 addresses the situation where a custodian or sub- custodian obtains control of a digital asset and maintains that asset for a client, or, if the asset is maintained as an undivided pool, for a group of clients (the latter situation is addressed in Commentary 11.6 and 11.7 and in Principle 11(2)). Principle 12 provides that the client cannot be subject to a successful claim to that asset brought by a person whose rights are violated by the change of control to the custodian, unless the client

This work was financed within the framework of the Prometeo 2023 project of the Regional Ministry of Innovation, Universities, Science and Digital Society (CIPROM/2022/26) "Present and future of the regulation of cryptoassets in the EU [LegalCripto]", whose principal investigator is Carmen Pastor Sempere. The basic ideas contained herein were presented in the author's paper with the same title, given on November 13, 2024 at the IV International Congress on "UNIDROIT Principles on Digital Assets and Private Law: Context, Content, Perspectives", organized also by BAES Research Group of the University of Alicante on November 13 and 14, 2024.

E. Becerril Fernández (✉)
University of Valladolid, Valladolid, Spain
e-mail: esterbf94@hotmail.com

C. Pastor Sempere and D. A. Morán Bovio (eds.), UNIDROIT *Principles on Digital Assets and Private Law*, Law, Governance and Technology Series 80,
https://doi.org/10.1007/978-3-032-11001-5_18

knows or ought to have known of that violation of rights. It is, therefore, an adaptation of the innocent acquisition rule tailored for the circumstances of custody. The standard of 'innocence' is that set out in Principle 8(5)(a), although, in accordance with Principle 8(1)(b), a State has flexibility to adapt this standard to be consistent with its own good faith purchase and take free rules. Principle 12 does not address the situation where the client itself has granted a right in the digital asset to a third party.

12.2. Principle 12 applies at each level of custody, if there is more than one level. Thus, if a sub-custodian maintains a digital asset for a custodian (who then maintains that digital asset for a client, see Principle 10(2)), Principle 12(1) applies to that custodian as client (vis-à-vis the sub-custodian). Principle 12(1) also then applies to the client of the custodian because the custodian maintains that digital asset for that client.

12.3. There are a number of ways in which a custodian could come to obtain control of a digital asset for a client. Depending on the factual situation and the manner in which the applicable law analyses that situation, the position of the client is governed either by Principle 8 or Principle 12. Some illustrations of possible situations are set out in the next paragraphs.

12.4. Illustration 1. A custodian obtains control of a digital asset in the course of a transfer of that asset to it for its own account and the custodian is an innocent acquirer under Principle 8, since the relevant requirements are satisfied. Later, as part of a subsequent sale transaction, the custodian transfers the digital asset to a client, and maintains it for that client. In this situation, there would be no need for Principle 12 to apply. This is because, under Principle 9(2) no successful claims in respect of the asset could be made against the custodian, and therefore no successful claims could be made against the client for whom the custodian maintained that digital asset. Principle 9(2) provides that a transferee acquires all the proprietary rights that its transferor had.

12.5. Illustration 2. If a client instructed its custodian to obtain a digital asset on its behalf, in circumstances where the custodian acted purely as an agent or representative of the client, it is likely that the client would also qualify as an innocent acquirer under Principle 8 if the control by the custodian was treated as that of the client and the client otherwise satisfied the requirement for innocent acquirer status.

12.6. Illustration 3. If a custodian obtained control of a digital asset in circumstances other than those in Illustration 2 in order to maintain it for a client (or a number of clients in the case of digital assets to be held as an undivided pool (see Principle 11(2)) Principle 12 would apply.

12.7. Principle 12 applies equally whether or not the digital asset is part of an undivided pool maintained for several clients. As stated in Principle 12(3), where digital assets are maintained as an undivided pool, Principle 12 applies to each client in the same way. Thus, unless a client knows or ought to know of another person's violated right to a digital asset which forms part of the pool, no claims can be asserted against that client in respect of that digital asset or any others in the pool. Principle 12 does not affect the position of the clients in the pool with respect to each other, which is that all clients share rateably and proportionately in the pool, including in the case of insolvency of the custodian (see Principles 13(5) and 13(7)).

2 Reflection

2.1 Introduction

A more thorough analysis of the content and structure of the final text that configures Principle 12 (Innocent client) is necessary after having carried out a brief review of the process of its constitution.

Principle 12 is the third principle in Section IV of the Principles, which is entirely devoted to custody. Therefore, the principle to be analysed must be understood within the legal-regulatory and doctrinal framework contemplated in the previous pages in relation to the pure definition of custody of digital assets. Consequently, there are numerous references to Principle 10: Custody in the text relating to Principle 12.

The Principles define custody as a relationship whereby the custodian is a person who holds and keeps the digital asset, but on behalf of and for the benefit of another person: the client. In this way, the custodian gives special protection in relation to unauthorized dispositions of the asset, as well as in the event of insolvency of the custodian itself. In short, the entire content of Section IV refers to the person who carries out custodial activities during the regular development of his or her activity and it must therefore be analysed from this perspective.

The concept of "innocent" was first considered during the preparatory work at the Exploratory Workshop held on 17 and 18 September 2020 by the Working Group on Private Law and Digital Assets. Right from the outset, it was noted that it was very difficult to specify the concept of negotiability until it was known what types of digital assets were to be covered. For example, the UNCITRAL Model Law on Electronic Transferable Records (MLETR) only contemplated that an asset could be negotiable, without going into details, although it did recognise a real situation that was already occurring in the market. The aim of the draft was to determine whether an asset should be considered transferable or not. The main question concerned the necessary protection that innocent acquirers should have, including through novation. All of this related to issues such as invalidity or reversal of transfers. It was noted that the Legislative Guide on Intermediate Securities could be useful.

It was then agreed that the presence of a new set of digital assets brought with it the need to consider possible transfer arrangements. It was concluded that a set of questions relating to purpose and innocent acquisition needed to be addressed. These questions were similar to those seen in respect of intermediary securities. They were considered not to be technologically neutral, and therefore reference would need to be made to certain regulatory issues which were outside the scope of the project. On the issue of negotiability and bona fide acquisition, it was determined that two sets of rules needed to be considered. Distinguishing between the applicable rules if the acquisition was innocent or the applicable rules if a non-innocent acquisition was envisaged. The latter scenario linked to legal rules such as the MLETR, where innocent acquisition is not envisaged.[1] In relation to innocent acquisition, it was also indicated at that meeting that there might not be a need to distinguish between an acquirer who obtains outright legal title and the acquirer who only has a limited interest in the asset, such as a security interest. For example, the Geneva Convention stipulated that in certain circumstances the assumptions could be simplified because the nature of the transferred right did not matter.

It is necessary to start from the idea that Principle 12 entitled "Innocent Client" is a crystallization of the principle of innocent acquisition contemplated in Principle 8, but adapted to the specific circumstances that arise in custody. The rule must be applied to each level of custody. For example, if there is a relationship formed by a sub-custodian that holds the digital asset and a custodian, the innocent client principle would apply to the latter.[2] In this way, depending on the factual situation raised, the protection of the innocent client will be achieved by Principle 8 or by Principle 12.

Specifically, to make the Principle more concrete, the proposed text on the twelfth principle is structured in just three sections, which are followed by their corresponding "Comments" (12.1–12.7). The clear objective of the Principle is to avoid ownership claims against the client.

2.2 *Section 1*

The first section makes direct reference to the meaning that "good faith" should have in digital asset custody relationships: avoiding claims regarding the ownership of said assets.

As previously stated, the essence of custody lies in having control of an asset and under this premise, it is easy to determine who holds ownership in each specific case. Custody allows the digital asset to be managed on behalf of the client, while maintaining control over it.

There may be different situations. On the one hand, if there is no custodian and the owner of the asset is the sole custodian, he has ownership of the asset and, consequently, absolute control over it. On the other hand, if the owner of the asset

[1] UNIDROIT 2020 – Study LXXXII – WG1 – Doc. 4, November.

[2] Castillo Iborra, F. UNIDROIT PRINCIPLES ON DIGITAL ASSETS AND PRIVATE LAW. Journal of Financial System Law 6. September 2023 Pages 365–380. https://doi.org/10.32029/2695-9569.02.11.2023.

does not exercise custody, but enters into a contract with a person who is responsible for safeguarding the asset, said owner does not have control over it. Therefore, it will be the custodian or sub-custodian who will be the holder of control and is obliged to safeguard its custody by contract. The crux of the matter lies in the concept of control. Thus, the person who has control (be it the owner or a custodian or sub-custodian) will have the power to dispose of the asset, together with the legal consequences that derive from their de facto powers.

It is interesting to note that digital assets are considered intangible assets, but it is also possible to draw an analogy with respect to the concept of control over tangible assets. Consequently, the powers and legal consequences of being the owner of an intangible asset will depend on what is contemplated in national law in relation to possession in terms of custody, guarantees, dispositions and transfers of patrimonial assets.

Based on this content, the first section of Principle 12 indicates that claims against the client based on existing real rights over a digital asset should not prosper, since it is the custodian who manages it, not the client. The third party involved who may have seen their rights violated, after a change of control of the digital asset, does not have the power to file a claim against the client of the asset.

Despite the above, the text recognises two circumstances in which the third party can act and assert its right against the client. Firstly, when it is the client who recognises the existence of its better right; and secondly, when the client should have known that an infringement of the right of a third party was taking place, when control to the custodian was transferred.

However, despite the precision of this first section, Principle 12 does not refer at any point to the case whereby the client itself grants a right in rem to a third party over its digital asset. In this case, two problematic issues would arise. On the one hand, whether the client has the capacity to act or a sufficient degree of control over the asset to be able to encumber the digital asset with a right in rem. To the extent that the client has no responsibility over the existing rights in rem over the asset, he may also lack the capacity to dispose of it, in order to charge a right in rem over it. Perhaps in this case, express knowledge of the custodian or sub-custodian would be necessary, as the person who manages it and assumes responsibility, not the client. On the other hand, if the above were possible, with or without the custodian's knowledge, the degree of responsibility assumed by the custodian or sub-custodian would have to be defined. If the digital asset was encumbered with his knowledge, he must be fully liable for any damages caused to the third party, and the customer is fully released. Conversely, if the right in rem was established without his knowledge, we could face a third exception in which the third party can act and enforce its right against the customer.

2.3 Section 2

This second section points out that Principle 12 should be applied by custody levels.

To be precise, in the event that there is a chain of custody involving a client, a custodian and also a sub-custodian of the digital asset, in accordance with the first paragraph Principle 12 will apply to the custodian linked to the relationship between it and the sub-custodian. Therefore, a third party may not make claims on real rights over the digital asset against the custodian, if the one managing the asset is a sub-custodian. However, at the same time, Principle 12 continues to apply to the relationship established between the client and the main custodian. The original text does not provide examples, but in this case, it is seen as a fundamental element to correctly interpret the meaning of this second section. Let us imagine, for example, the figure of a bank custodian. That is, an entity that safeguards its clients' financial assets. They could be assets such as stocks, bonds, or cash. The bank custodian must maintain the assets while being responsible for protecting them. It keeps them from the moment the investor-clients purchase them until they subsequently sell them. The bank custodian routinely charges a custody fee to its clients in exchange for the clients being able to assert their rights against it in the event of non-compliance or mismanagement of their obligations. It is common in the securities market for the bank custodian to switch custody to another entity. This is what has commonly been called the chain of custody for securities. The new custodian is legally similar to our sub-custodians. Banking tradition has been based on stating that changing custodians does not affect clients, neither during the process nor once the change has occurred. Changing custodians is usually due to economic, legal, or service provision reasons. In those circumstances, for example, in the event of insolvency of the sub-custodian, the initial custodian would be liable to the client. The insolvency of the sub-custodian, in the case of banking, could cause delays in the execution of orders that entail mobilisation of deposited assets, or a partial loss of the deposited securities. But in all these cases, the client-investor must act against the initial custodian, not the sub-custodian, as that is against whom the initial custodian will act. This assumption is related to the Principle dedicated to insolvency in the case of digital assets.

2.4 Section 3

Finally, the third section of the Principle refers to the possible scenarios that may occur in practice, where it will be necessary to distinguish whether Principle 8 (acquisition in good faith) or Principle 12 (Innocent Client) will be applied to the existing custody relationship.

Three enlightening examples are provided. The first two refer to two types of contractual relationships for which the application of Principle 12 is not necessary: the rights and duties between the assignor and the assignee and the rights and duties arising from an agency contract. These are cases to which Principle 9 and Principle 8 should respectively be applied.

In the first example, the custodian obtains control of a digital asset in the course of a transfer of that asset for its own account, and the custodian is a bona fide transferee under Principle 8. The relevant requirements are met. Later, as part of a subsequent sale transaction, the custodian transfers the digital asset to a client and manages it on behalf of the client. In this circumstance, there would be no need to apply Principle 12. This is because, under Principle 9(2), no claims can be made against the custodian in relation to the asset and therefore no claims can be made against the client for whom the custodian holds the digital asset. Principle 9(2) provides that a transferee acquires all the property rights that its transferor had.

The key element in the proposed example is that the transfer of the asset is a sale transaction carried out on one's own account and not on someone else's account. Therefore, the custodian is unclaimable.

In light of this practical case, the unnecessary application of Principle 12 is clearly evident, as Principle 8, the bona fide acquirer, applies to the custodian, and Principle 9, to the agent who subsequently assigns its rights to the client by virtue of the transfer of the digital asset. Since Principle 9 already establishes that claims made against the custodian will not be successful, consequently, after the transfer, such claims against the client will not prosper either. Therefore, this case falls outside the scope of application of Principle 12, and falls within the scope of Principle 9, to which we refer, regarding the relationship between transferor and assignee.

The second example contemplates that if a client instructed its custodian to obtain a digital asset on its behalf, in circumstances where the custodian is acting purely as an agent or representative of the client, the client would likely also qualify as a bona fide acquirer under Principle 8. This would be the case provided that the custodian's control would be deemed to be that of the client and the client otherwise satisfied the requirements to be considered a bona fide acquirer.

In this case, the legal transaction carried out is the purchase of an asset and, as was the case in the first example, in this second practical case, Principle 12 is not applicable, but rather Principle 8 on the acquisition in good faith. In this case, when an agency or representation relationship with the client occurs, the client also implicitly meets the requirements to be considered a bona fide purchaser.

Consequently, all other cases that may occur in real life when digital asset transfers occur, provided that there is no agency or assignment relationship, should be subject to the scope of Principle 12. This conclusion is the third example contemplated in the analysed text: if a custodian were to obtain control of a digital asset in circumstances other than those in Example 2 in order to manage it for a client (or several clients in the case of digital assets held as a common and undivided fund (see Principle 11(2)), Principle 12 would apply. In other words, the fundamental characteristic of an agency or assignment contract is the existence of a representation function. Specifically, the custodian represents the client in the purchase or sale of the asset. In these two cases, Principle 8 applies. However, where the custodian does not exercise any power of representation vis-à-vis the client, Principle 12 applies. In this case, the custodian is not acting on behalf of anyone. The custodian has custody of the asset and may transfer or encumber it as it sees fit, provided it ensures its proper safeguarding. For this reason, an external third party does not have the right to demand liability from the client (who is not responsible), but rather from the custodian, who acts in the client's best interest, not on behalf of anyone else.

In conclusion, Principle 12 is a closing or protection clause for the client, which is intended to protect him from any type of liability that could be claimed, except in those cases where the client was aware of acting in bad faith.

This hypothesis is very reminiscent of the so-called title theory and the way it is contemplated in traditional doctrine of continental European codes.

In historical European continental law, the methods of acquiring property and other real or patrimonial rights are regulated, and among them the legal value of possession and occupation is also recognized.

Thus, for example, the Spanish Civil Code establishes the different methods for acquiring property and other rights in-rem.[3] Specifically, it indicates that property is acquired by occupation. Both property and other rights over assets can be acquired and transferred by law, by donation, by testate and intestate succession, and as a result of certain contracts, through tradition. In other words, this article establishes that the transfer of property or other rights in-rem requires the existence of two elements: certain contracts or tradition. Therefore, the acquirer will only become the owner of the property right, or any other right over the asset, when the transfer has taken place and is based on a valid contract for the transfer of ownership or a property right.

The theory of title and mode refers to the conceptual formalisation of the requirements established in Roman *tradition.* Consequently, States with a Latin tradition of law, such as Spain and Italy, must take into account this unanimous doctrine on the derivative transfer of property or other rights in-rem provided that there is a causal title (*justa causa*) and, in addition, a mode or tradition, in order for the asset to be considered transferred. However, other European countries do not follow the same doctrine and choose to spiritualise tradition, accepting that transfer occurs by the mere consent of the parties or by the mere delivery of the asset, with the causal title being irrelevant. This is the case in French and German law, respectively. For example, in the French Civil Code, it establishes that ownership is transferred by the effect of the contract, without the need for physical delivery or mode, except in specific cases, such as movable property that requires tradition for its enforceability against third parties. Furthermore, in the area of sale, it provides that the sale is perfected between the parties and the property is acquired by fee simple by the buyer from the seller, as soon as there is an agreement on the item and the price, even if the item has not been delivered or the price paid.[4]

It is worth noting the tendency of many States to equate control with possession and, consequently, custody with powers of control with possession.

Principle 12 of this document is in line with law in many other States where control is equated to possession, for example, to Chapter One of Title V of the Spanish Civil Code, on possession. It is true that neither the document under analysis nor any of the experts who participated in the preparatory discussions made a distinction between the concepts of possession and ownership, limiting themselves to discussing the

[3] Bercovitz Rodriguez-Cano, R. Commentaries on the Civil Code (Duo). Aranzadi Publishing House. 2021.

Edition number: 5th ed.

[4] *Légifrance* website. *Le service public de la diffusion du droit.*

concept of custody. However, the wording of the Principle 12 (Innocent Client) resembles the concept of good faith contemplated in several articles of the Spanish Civil Code and the civil codes of other Western countries.

Firstly, possession of goods and rights can be held in one of two ways: either as the owner, or as the holder of the thing or right to keep or enjoy them, with the ownership belonging to another person. This statement can be accurately identified with the concepts of custody, client, custodian, and sub-custodian studied in the principles outlined above. That is, possession, which various States and international documents such as UNCITRAL frequently equate with control, can be understood in the concept or capacity of owner-proprietor or as holder of another property right (possession, limited property right, trustee, lienholder, etc.), and this allows for the equating of the functions of custodian and sub-custodian.

Secondly, a person who is unaware that his title or method of acquisition contains any defect that invalidates it is considered a possessor in good faith. There are various codes or statutory laws that consider a person who possesses the item (has control or custodial control capabilities) to be a good-faith possessor, even though they are unaware of the existence of an invalidating defect in the client's ownership or in the transfer. The traditional response of Spanish national statutory law to this situation has been the non-recovery by the innocent acquirer, and this solution is now being extended to the context of custody of digital assets.

For this reason, a distinction is made between situations of ignorance of the defect and situations in which one knew or should have known, through ordinary diligence, that another person had a legitimate preferential interest and that the acquisition was violating that third party's rights. Similarly, a person in the opposite situation is considered a possessor in bad faith.

These statements are undoubtedly analogous to the content of the second section of Principle 12, which states that the client's virtual asset is recoverable if they knew or should have known that another person had a legitimate interest overriding their own, and that their acquisition violated that third party's rights. That is, if at the time the custodian is managing the digital asset for the client, the client actually acquired it in bad faith. This is the only case in which the document under analysis holds the client accountable: if they suspect or are aware of irregularities.

Furthermore, in Western law, there is a general presumption of good faith in transactions, from which it follows that the third party claiming bad faith is the one who must prove its existence or gross negligence (a factual question requiring an express declaration). We must emphasise that in the Principles we are analysing, this issue is not expressly addressed, meaning it is left to the statutory law of each State. This is undoubtedly a very important question from a procedural perspective. However, although it could be understood as implicit in the document, the experts decided not to clarify who should bear the burden of proof in order to hold the client of the digital asset liable.

Likewise, this second section of Principle 12 is closely related to the legal idea that establishes that possession acquired in good faith does not lose this character except in the case, and from the moment, in which there are acts that prove that the possessor was unaware that he or she possessed the thing improperly. Applied to the case of digital assets, the possessor would be the client, who is presumed to have initially acquired in good faith (Principle 8) until proven otherwise. Finally, if possession was acquired in good faith, it is presumed that possession continues to exist in good faith until proven otherwise. This precept is closely related to Example 2 of Principle 12 previously analysed. Since the same presumption was established. That is, it is likely that in an agency relationship, the client also met the requirements to be considered a bona fide acquirer. Only after proving that the client was aware that he or she improperly possessed the asset is the status of innocent acquirer lost. The text points out that, according to the above, this is an issue in which the burden of proof will be determined by the State and the consequences will be those derived from the Principle.

In conclusion, the discussed Principle states the same thing idea in 12.1, which establishes when there are reasonable presumptions and what consequences arise from the breach of that reasonable presumption.

The content of Principle 12 also requires a careful consideration of its similarity to the content of several European civil codes regarding the prescription of ownership and other property rights. In particular, it emphasizes the idea that the possessor's good faith consists of the belief that the person from whom they received the thing was its owner and was entitled to transfer its ownership. This presumption is similar to the previously examined second section of Principle 12, in which the transfer of custody of the digital asset occurs.

Another reference that can be used to develop the application of Principle 12 is the irrevocability of securities contemplated in Commercial Law. The irrevocability of securities is applied and found in countries that follow the model of the Geneva Uniform Exchange Law on securities, which has been the reference for the regulation of securities in most Western and Asian countries. The international unification of the law of bills of exchange, promissory notes, and cheques came to fruition in Geneva in 1930, where the Geneva Uniform Law was drafted. This was the result of the Conventions signed in June 1930 and March 1931. The principle of irrevocability was already contemplated in this law.

A security refers to any document containing an economic right to payment and collection, which allows it to be transferred. In Spanish law, the common characteristic is that the right to collection or payment is incorporated into the security and facilitates the circulation of rights, thereby guaranteeing greater legal security and business agility.

For example, under German and Swiss law, possession of the document is essential for the acquisition, use, or transfer of the right it embodies. It may also include corporate shares. Italian law, on the other hand, is more restrictive and advocates the opposite position.

Returning to the subject of commercial law, it is important to highlight the legal principle that bearer securities are transferable by means of delivery of the document. A security acquired by a third party in good faith and without gross negligence will not be subject to claim. The rights and actions of the legitimate owner against those responsible for acts that have deprived them of ownership will be safeguarded. Once again, this content is reminiscent of the content in Principles 8 and 12 of the document analysed in this book in particular, the concept of irrecoverability based on possession of the security in good faith and without gross negligence. It does not provide for any exceptions. It even defends irrecoverability in cases of theft or robbery. Therefore, traditional doctrine on securities is the inspiration for the regulation of Principles 8 and 12, in which we transfer the equivalence of the concept of possession to the concept of control and custody—in other words, custody with control powers.

The following are some examples of national regulations that include this principle of irrevocability. In Spain,[5] it was necessary to wait until the approval of Law 19/1985, of July 16, on Bills of Exchange and Cheques, which also includes this principle in article 19. This indicates that the holder of the bill of exchange will be considered the legitimate holder of the bill of exchange when he justifies his right by an uninterrupted series of endorsements, even if the last endorsement is blank. For this purpose, crossed-out endorsements are considered unwritten. When a blank endorsement is followed by another endorsement, the signer of the latter shall be deemed to have acquired the bill by means of the blank endorsement. When a person is dispossessed of a bill of exchange, for whatever reason, the new holder who justifies his right in the manner indicated in the preceding paragraph shall not be obliged to return the bill if he acquired it in good faith. Regarding Principle 12, the holder of a bill of exchange could be a legal entity, similar to the custodian of the digital asset, and similarly, transfer by endorsement resembles the traceability of the transfer of the digital asset, which can change hands from custodian to sub-custodian without limit. In this case, the client, or the custodian who transferred the digital asset to another sub-custodian, could not be held liable if the acquisition was made in good faith. Exchange regulations also establish that the defendant in an exchange action may not raise objections against the holder based on his or her personal relationships with the drawer or with previous holders, unless the holder, when acquiring the bill, knowingly acted to the detriment of the debtor. That is, the so-called inapplicability of causal objections. When the first holder of the instrument endorses it, the causal objections that the signatory could exercise against him or her are extinguished (objections based on personal relationships). If an endorsement were to occur again, the causal exceptions between the first and second holders would likewise be lost. This is fully applicable to the digital asset market with respect to the custodian and subsequent sub-custodians.

In French law, cheques are regulated in the French Civil Code (Articles 1621 and 1622), and the principle of irrevocability is reflected in the idea that once a check has been delivered to the beneficiary or a legitimate person, it cannot be claimed by either the issuer or the financial institution, except in certain cases such as fraud or material error. Again, the French system offers additional protection to third parties acting in good faith. Similarly, the Italian Civil Code establishes the principle of irrevocability in Article 1478: "*Vendita irrevocable.*" In the German Civil Code (BGD), this principle is reflected in Article 929. There, the principle of irrevocability is implicitly linked to the fact that, once ownership has been transferred

[5] MENÉNDEZ MENÉNDEZ, A. Exchange Law: Studies on Exchange Law and Checks, Civitas, Madrid, 1986.

to the buyer through delivery, the seller cannot claim back the sold item, except in the case of transactional defect or fraud. Finally, in Common Law, the principle is addressed in the context of the sale of goods through the *Sale of Goods Act* of 1979, Section 17, and in the Bills of Exchange Act of 1882. Although irrevocability is not expressed in the same way as in other legal systems, the provisions regarding transfer of ownership and the buyer's rights are equivalent. Its treatment is similar in American law, contemplated in Sections 2-401 and 2-403 of the *Uniform Commercial Code.*

Irrevocability of claims even appears in the Chinese Civil Code, in article 173, along with the implicit reference to it that is developed in Chinese Contract Law.

In short, within the regulation of traditional exchange rights, it is understood or presumed that a purchaser acts in good faith when they demonstrate a formal chain of transmissions. Principle 12 seeks a similar effect on the formal chain or traceability of custody. This provides legal certainty in commercial transactions and adapts to the need for digital asset transfers in the digital market, where digital asset transfers can be carried out in milliseconds and by artificial intelligence machines in the context of crypto-asset portfolio management, which is common on digital asset trading platforms.

For all these reasons, the drafters of the Principles have sought a functional equivalence adapted to the digital context to achieve uniform and similar effects regardless of the specific regulations each State has on this matter.

Therefore, Principle 8 and Principle 12 (Innocent Customer) could be drafted to ensure treatment similar to that provided for the innocent acquisition of securities in commercial law.

A similar situation exists in Spanish legislation governing mortgage institutions. In short, the drafting of Principle 12 draws from different national laws regarding the treatment of bona fide purchasers of real estate. Specifically, the Principle is inspired by this specific treatment in States that follow a registry system, because in States that do not follow a comparable registry system, a judgment is made on the preference of the titles presented by the parties.

For example, article 34 of the Mortgage Law in Spain refers to third party mortgage holders acting in good faith, and states that a third party who acquires any right for valuable consideration from a person recorded in the Registry as having the power to transfer it, will be protected once his right is registered, even if the grantor's right is subsequently annulled or terminated due to causes that are not recorded in the same Registry. The good faith of the third party is always presumed until it is proven that he knew of the inaccuracy of the Registry. Gratuitous purchasers will not enjoy any more registry protection than that enjoyed by their predecessor or transferor. Although at first glance, the purpose of this article seems to be to protect the third-party mortgagee, the purpose of the article is actually to protect the true owner (a person with full powers to transfer). The ultimate objective pursued by Principle 12 is to protect the customer of the digital asset.

In France, this principle is enshrined in the French Civil Code and is related to the protection of bona fide third parties in a real estate transaction (Article 2279). Similarly, it is reflected in Article 1153 of the Italian Civil Code, which establishes that a bona fide purchaser of real estate may acquire ownership of the property, even if the seller is not the legitimate owner, provided that the property is duly registered in his or her name in the corresponding Registry. In Germany, the similarity is duly established in Article 892 of the BGD (Border Registry of Real Estate). In the United Kingdom, it is enshrined in Article 28 of the Land Registration Act of 2002. In the United States, the bona fide purchaser principle for real estate is regulated under the property registration system, which varies from State to State, although the fundamental legal concept is registration priority and protection of bona fide purchasers. There, the registration system for this type of property is based on the principles of *notice* and *race-notice.* In states governed by the *notice system*, a bona fide purchaser has priority if he or she has no knowledge of any other claims to the property, regardless of the time of registration. Only the purchaser's good faith and lack of knowledge of other prior claims matter. In States that apply the *race-notice system*, a bona fide purchaser has priority over other claimants provided that he or she registers his or her title before anyone else, unless he or she has knowledge of prior claims. Although the Uniform Commercial Code does not directly apply to real estate, it does influence property transactions in general, and this code offers protection to bona fide purchasers without distinction. The Recording Act also requires that real estate transactions be recorded in the Land Registry of the corresponding county or city. Finally, in China, Article 160 of the Civil Code and Article 12 of the Real Estate Registration Law stand out as provisions that also contemplate this principle.

In addition, it is important to refer to the so-called Anglo-Saxon *trusts.* This figure is a private contract (*trust deed*) by which a person decides to transfer assets or rights to another person, in trust, so that they can carry out loyal administration of the asset, for the benefit of third parties. It is a contractual relationship involving three different parties: the original owner of the asset or right (*settlor*), the natural or legal person designated as administrator (*trustee*) and a third party beneficiary of the transaction. Actors have similar positions to those of the client, custodian or sub-custodian and third parties interested in the digital asset.

The "trust" figure is a typical substitution mechanism in Common Law. However, the multiple benefits it creates in relation to the management of assets and rights, has caused many other countries to adapt this type of business in their national regulations. It is an investment vehicle that guarantees a high level of asset protection. It is important to note that the trust model is the contract model used in many digital asset management arrangements, in many digital asset portfolio management agreements, and is one of the reasons why control of the asset is held, or held in custody.

However, there may be variations in the concept of trust between States that would have different consequences.

For example, the Spanish Civil Code contemplates what is known as fideicommissary substitution. In other words, a type of hereditary substitution regulated in Article 781 et seq. It states that fideicommissary substitutions, by virtue of which the heir is entrusted with preserving and transferring all or part of the inheritance to a third party, will be valid and effective as long as they do not exceed the second degree, or are made in favour of persons living at the time of the testator's death. Likewise, it comprises a triple relationship involving the settlor (testator), the fiduciary heir, and the trustee. Unlike the Anglo-Saxon model, which only recognises trusts in the area of inheritance, the potential usefulness of this mechanism for the future regulation of digital assets is greater in the Anglo-Saxon configuration.

Finally, is worth mentioning other sources of inspiration for Principle 12, which may allow for possession of control or custody. For example, the regulation of various types of contracts, such as loans, the establishment of guarantees, or pledges, among others. There is a direct relationship with the underlying contracts that determines the legitimacy of the transferor of the asset. In the interest of ensuring legal certainty, the same principle applies.

Lastly, the seventh section of the analysed Principle indicates that regardless of whether the digital asset is part of a common and undivided fund managed by several clients or is not integrated into said fund, the twelfth Principle must be applied. Principle 12 must be taken into account for all clients, since it does not influence the positions they have in the common fund. Consequently, no client can be required to take responsibility for claims filed against the digital asset itself, or any other asset that is part of the common fund. All of this will be applicable except in the event that one of the clients was aware of the violation of the right of a third party with respect to the same digital asset, as analysed in the second section of the principle.

Therefore, since clients participate in the common fund in an equitable and proportional manner, in the event of any type of insolvency of the custodian itself, the provisions of Principle 13, sections five and seven, would have to be observed.

In conclusion, Principle 12 entitled "Innocent Customer" is a materialization of the principle of innocent acquisition contemplated in Principle 8, but adapted to the specific circumstances that arise in custody. Consequently, both principles are closely linked. On the one hand, Principle 8 deals with acquisition in good faith if the requirements of control and legitimacy of the digital asset are met. Principle 12, on the other hand, focuses on safeguarding the client's liability vis-à-vis third parties, since it is the custodian or sub-custodian who can truly know if there is legitimacy or specific control. Clients who need and require the help of a custodian for management do not have control over it and therefore have no liability. Liability must be assumed by the custodian or sub-custodian in the case of claims. The innocent client, due to legal guarantees and promotion of the circulation of assets, is unclaimable.

Principle 12 is a closure principle that seeks to provide greater legal certainty and agility to the transmission of digital assets, while facilitating the development of traceability monitoring protocols.

Principle 13
Insolvency of a Custodian and Creditor Claims

Nicolás Augoustatos Zarco

(1) A digital asset that a custodian maintains for a client under a custody agreement is not available for the satisfaction of claims of creditors of the custodian.

(2) If a custodian enters into an insolvency-related proceeding, a digital asset that it maintains for a client under a custody agreement does not form part of that custodian's assets available for distribution to its creditors.

(3) If a custodian maintains a digital asset for a client with a sub-custodian, and the custodian enters into an insolvency-related proceeding, the rights it has against the sub-custodian in respect of that digital asset do not form part of the custodian's assets available for distribution to its creditors.

(4) If a custodian enters into an insolvency-related proceeding, the insolvency representative must take reasonable steps:

> **(a) for the control of a digital asset maintained for the custodian's client to be changed to the control of that client or of a custodian nominated by that client;**
>
> **(b) for any rights, the custodian has against any sub-custodian regarding a digital asset maintained for the custodian's client to be transferred or otherwise made accessible to that client, including through transfer to another custodian nominated by that client.**

This work was financed within the framework of the Prometeo 2023 project of the Regional Ministry of Innovation, Universities, Science and Digital Society (CIPROM/2022/26) "Present and future of the regulation of cryptoassets in the EU [LegalCripto]", whose principal investigator is Carmen Pastor Sempere. The basic ideas contained herein were presented in the author's paper with the same title, given on November 13, 2024 at the IV International Congress on "UNIDROIT Principles on Digital Assets and Private Law: Context, Content, Perspectives", organized also by BAES Research Group of the University of Alicante on November 13 and 14, 2024.

N. Augoustatos Zarco (✉)
Pablo de Olavide University, Seville, Spain
e-mail: naugzar@upo.es

C. Pastor Sempere and D. A. Morán Bovio (eds.), UNIDROIT *Principles on Digital Assets and Private Law*, Law, Governance and Technology Series 80,
https://doi.org/10.1007/978-3-032-11001-5_19

(5) Paragraphs (6) and (7) apply if all of the following requirements are fulfilled:

(a) a custodian enters into an insolvency-related proceeding;

(b) digital assets of the same description are maintained by the custodian for two or more clients as an undivided pool and

(c) the quantity of digital assets maintained by the insolvent custodian for those clients is less than the aggregate quantity of digital assets of the same description that it is obliged to maintain for those clients ('shortfall').

[(6) The shortfall is met first by any digital assets of the same description maintained by the custodian for itself][1]

(7) Any [remaining] shortfall shall be borne by the clients for whom the custodian maintains the digital assets as an undivided pool, in proportion to the respective quantity of digital assets of the same description that the custodian must maintain for those clients.

(8) If a custodian maintains a digital asset for a client with a sub-custodian, and the sub-custodian enters into an insolvency-related proceeding, the custodian must seek to obtain control of that digital asset from the insolvency representative or to maintain the digital asset with another sub-custodian.

1 Official Commentary

Commentary

Principle 13(1)

13.1. Principle 13(1) applies where the custodian has not entered into an insolvency-related proceeding. It makes it clear that digital assets maintained by a custodian for a client are not available to satisfy the claims of the custodian's creditors. This result parallels the substance of paragraph (2), which provides that digital assets maintained for clients are not part of the assets available for distribution to the custodian's creditors if it enters into an insolvency-related proceeding. These provisions reflect the baseline concept that such digital assets belong to clients, not custodians.

Insolvency-related proceeding

13.2. Principles 13(2) to 13(8) apply if a custodian enters into an insolvency-related proceeding. 'Insolvency-related proceeding' is defined in Principle 2(6), but it should be borne in mind that a State might specify a special type of insolvency regime for

[1] Principle 13(6) is an optional provision which a State may choose to adopt. If it does so, the word 'remaining' in Principle 13(7) would need to be retained. Note: This footnote appears in the text of the Principles.

certain types of financial institutions, which could include some custodians of digital assets. Suppose this is the case, and the special regime does not fall within the definition in Principle 2(6). In that case, a State will need to modify the definition of insolvency-related proceedings in relation to those custodians accordingly. Similarly, if the consequences set out in Principle 13 were not possible under the special regime, Principle 13 would need to be modified accordingly.

Principle 13(2)

13.3. Principle 13(2) sets out the consequences of the insolvency of the custodian in a functional way rather than using legal concepts such as property or ownership. On the custodian's insolvency, the digital assets it maintains for clients as a custodian are not part of the assets available for distribution to its creditors. If, on the other hand, a service provider is not a custodian because its agreement with the client is an agreement for the delivery of digital assets (see Illustration 7 in Commentary 10.20), any assets it controls will usually be part of its assets for distribution to its creditors. A service provider could be a custodian in relation to some clients ('act in that capacity' within the meaning of Principle 10(1)) and not a custodian in relation to other clients (because the agreement is of the type mentioned in the previous sentence). The effect of Principles 10(3) and 10(4) is that any agreement which has the three characteristics of a custody agreement set out in Principle 10(3) will attract the consequences in Principle 13(2) unless the agreement makes it clear that this is not the case. In Principle 13(2), the 'custodian' could be a sub-custodian and the 'client' could be a custodian.

Principle 13(3)

13.4. Principle 13(3) sets out the consequences when a digital asset is held through a sub-custodian (see Principle 11(4)). As explained in Commentary 10.4, when a custodian maintains a digital asset through a sub-custodian, the custodian (who will be the client of the sub-custodian under a custody agreement) has rights against that sub-custodian under the custody agreement. If the custodian is insolvent, its rights against the sub-custodian are not part of the custodian's assets available for distribution to its creditors.

Principles 13(4) to 13(7)

13.5. Principles 13(4) to 13(7) give guidance as to suitable rules which should (or, in the case of Principle 13(6), could) apply in relation to digital assets (or if a sub-custodian is used, rights against the sub-custodian) if a custodian enters into an insolvency-related proceeding. These rules are not comprehensive; the applicable insolvency law governs all other issues that could arise in these circumstances. It should be noted that a custodian or sub-custodian could have a security right over, or another type of right to, digital assets maintained for its clients (see Principle

11(5)). The effect of this on the actions taken by an insolvency representative would be a matter of other law.

13.6. Principle 13(4) imposes a duty on the insolvency representative to take reasonable steps so that the client can obtain the digital assets maintained for it by the custodian. If the digital assets are maintained by the custodian by entering into a custody agreement with a sub-custodian (Principle 10(2)(b)), the duty on the insolvency representative relates to the custodian's rights against the sub-custodian. The client may want to obtain control of the digital assets (or obtain the rights against the sub-custodian) itself or may want another custodian to maintain them on its behalf. The insolvency representative may need to take certain steps to achieve this result, such as obtaining the private key(s) relating to those digital assets.

13.7. Principles 13(5) to 13(7) apply where digital assets of the same description are maintained by a custodian for its clients as an undivided pool (see Principle 11(2) and Commentary 11.6). Undivided pools of digital assets of the same description are explained in Commentary 11.6 and 11.7. A custodian can maintain digital assets as an undivided pool by controlling the assets itself or form of words, entering into a custody agreement with a sub-custodian regarding an undivided amount of digital assets. In this latter situation, its rights against the sub-custodian will be undivided. Principles 13(5) to 13(7) deal with the situation where there is a shortfall of digital assets, or rights against the sub-custodian, of a particular description. Principle 13(5) explains the situation of shortfall. In the insolvency-related proceeding of a custodian, there may be potentially as many shortfalls as there are undivided pools.

13.8. If there is a shortfall, a State may wish to provide that the loss is first met by any digital assets of the same description maintained by the custodian on its own account, whether by controlling those assets itself or by use of a sub-custodian. This approach follows that of Article 25 of the Geneva Securities Convention. However, under that Convention, a State can make a declaration that this rule is not to apply in that State. In a similar way, it is a policy decision for a State whether or not to adopt the rule set out in Principle 13(6). For this reason, Principle 13(6) is in square brackets.

13.9. Under Principle 13(7) the loss of digital assets (or rights against a sub-custodian) caused by the shortfall should be borne pari passu by all the clients for whom the custodian is obliged to maintain the assets of which there is a shortfall. In other words, if there is a shortfall of digital asset A and/or rights against any sub-custodian that relate to digital asset A, and none in respect of digital asset B, the shortfall in respect of A is shared rateably among all clients for whom the custodian is maintaining an undivided pool of A. The approach follows that of Article 26(2) of the Geneva Securities Convention. If a State chooses to adopt the rule in Principle 13(6), then the word 'remaining', which is in square brackets in Principle 13(7), applies. Otherwise, that word is not required.

Principle 13(8)

13.10. Principle 13(8) sets out the consequences of the insolvency of a sub-custodian when a digital asset is maintained through that sub-custodian (see Principle 11(4)). In these circumstances, the custodian must seek to change control of the digital asset from the insolvent sub-custodian, either to itself or to another sub-custodian. If the custodian is insolvent, its rights against the sub-custodian under the custody agreement do not form part of its assets available for distribution to its creditors.

2 General Reflections

2.1 Introduction—Systematic Placement of Principle 13

Before we begin to analyse the content of Principle 13, a brief introduction is necessary to explain why this Principle appears where it does and not elsewhere in the Principles.

Principle 13, entitled 'Insolvency of a custodian and creditor claims', is located in Section IV of the Principles, which, in turn, is entitled 'Custody'. This section aims to regulate the situation (very common in practice, on the other hand) in which digital assets are not held by their owner directly, but through the intervention of a third party (an intermediary) referred to as the custodian by the Principles.

It should be noted that Principle 13 is not the only principle that addresses insolvency situations. Without prejudice to Principle 6(2), which defines insolvency-related proceedings, insolvency is also addressed by Principle 19, practically sharing the same title.

Principle 13 deals with the custodian's insolvency; more specifically, it addresses the situation when the custodian of digital assets is affected by insolvency proceedings. Hence, the location of this principle has been moved to Section IV of the Principles, where various aspects related to the custodian are regulated within the Principles, including the consequences that occur when the custodian is affected by insolvency proceedings.

In other words, Principle 19 considers the insolvency of the owner of the digital asset. In contrast, Principle 13 deals with the insolvency of custodians when they are not actually the owner of the digital asset. This is why the regulation of the custodian's insolvency is placed in Section IV of the Principles, which is intended to provide a reference framework for various aspects related to the custody of digital assets.

2.2 *Some Terminological Details*

Before proceeding to the study of Principle 13, it is interesting to briefly analyse some terminological issues, which, although other Principles may deal with them, are useful for a better understanding of the content of Principle 13.

2.2.1 The Custodian

The definition of the figure of the custodian (i.e., what is understood by the term custodian) is provided in Principle 10; therefore, we refer to the Commentary on that Principle. However, a few lines should be devoted to this matter since Principle 13 deals with the custodian's insolvency.

From the first meetings of the UNIDROIT Work Group (henceforth Working Group), the need to regulate the figure of the custodian became apparent, as practice showed that intermediaries held a large number of digital assets.[2] This prompted the need to devote a specific part of the Principles to the figure of the custodian and related issues. The final result was Section IV of the Principles.

In accordance with the Principles, a custodian is a person who meets all the requirements outlined in Principle 10. Although a custodian could be any person, the Principles are more than likely referring to a financial market professional. Several data and facts could lead us to reach this conclusion. Thus, Principle 10(1) speaks about a person providing services to a client, which necessarily leads one to think of a professional. Principle 10(3)(a) requires that the custody service be provided in the ordinary course of the service provider's business[3]; or the reference to "exchange" or "trading platform" in Commentary 10.2. Therefore, the custodian must be a professional.[4]

2.2.2 Insolvency-Related Proceeding

This is another term that should be explained, given that the insolvency of a custodian of digital assets is precisely the subject matter of Principle 13.

The term 'insolvency-related proceedings' is defined in Principle 2(6), within Principle 2, which contains the general definitions used throughout the Principles. Principle 2(6) reads as follows:

---

[2] Digital Assets and Private Law Working Group // First session (remote) // Rome, 17 – 19 November 2020 //// UNIDROIT 2020 // Study LXXXII – W.G.1 – Doc. 1 // English only // November 2020, p. 9, marg. 36.

[3] A circumstance that is corroborated in Commentary 10.6.

[4] The conclusion is consistent with those reached by the Working Group. Thus, for example, at the March 16–18, 2021 session, the following examples of custodian were noted: crypto-fiat exchange service providers; crypto-exchange service providers; crypto-asset stock exchange (Digital Assets and Private Law Working Group // Second session (remote) // Rome, 16 – 18 March 2021 //// UNIDROIT 2021 // Study LXXXII – W.G.2 – Doc. 2 // English only // March 2021, p. 36, marg. 117).

'Insolvency-related proceeding' means a collective judicial or administrative proceeding, including an interim proceeding, in which, for the purpose of reorganisation or liquidation, at least one of the following applies to the assets and affairs of the debtor: (a) they are subject to control or supervision by a court or other competent authority; (b) the debtor's ability to administer or dispose of them is limited by law; (c) the debtor's creditors' ability to enforce on them is limited by law.

This definition is completed, or complemented, by Commentary 2.28.

The Principles use a broad concept of insolvency proceedings. As noted in Commentary 2.28, the definition '*seeks to include all forms of collective, insolvency-related procedures.*' The characteristics of this insolvency proceeding appear to be as follows:

It is a collective proceeding, i.e., a proceeding involving several creditors of the same debtor. So, they cannot individually lay claim to the debtor's assets or rights.

In principle, it is a procedure that a judicial or administrative authority must oversee. The latter opens up the possibility of including special intervention by States to solve situations of corporate crises affecting certain strategic sectors.[5] However, this requirement of judicial or administrative supervision of the proceedings is not definitive, as Commentary 2.28 recognises the possibility of insolvency proceedings even where the debtor's assets '*are not subject to the control or supervision of the court or an administrative authority*'. Consequently, the term 'Insolvency-related proceeding' also includes out-of-court collective bargaining proceedings to resolve the debtor's financial or economic difficulties.

In conclusion, for the Principles, an insolvency-related proceeding may be a judicial proceeding, an administrative proceeding or an out-of-court proceeding, provided that it produces some legal effect and is aimed at resolving the debtor's financial difficulties. It is a procedure that requires limiting the debtor's capacity to administer or dispose of its assets or rights (i.e., the debtor cannot freely administer or dispose of them) nor freely manage its affairs.

Finally, it is a procedure in which the creditors' ability to execute the debtor´s assets or rights is limited by law.

The requirements or situations outlined in Principle 2(6), relating to judicial or administrative supervision, limitation of the debtor's ability to control its assets and affairs, and limitation of the creditors' ability to lay claim to the debtor's assets and rights, need not occur at the same time for the proceeding to be considered an insolvency-related proceeding. As the cited Principle 2(6) states, it is sufficient for any one of them to be present for the procedure to be considered as such.

As indicated above, the concept of insolvency proceedings used in the Principles is broad and includes any collective proceeding intended to solve a debtor´s economic crisis. In this sense, the notion of insolvency proceedings used in the Principles differs

[5] In the European Union, e.g., Regulation (EU) nº 806/2014, of The European Parliament and The Council, of 15 July 2014, establishing uniform rules and a uniform procedure for the resolution of credit institutions and certain investment firms in the framework of a Single Resolution Mechanism and a Single Resolution Fund and amending Regulation (EU) nº 1093/2010.

somewhat from that used in other UNCITRAL legislative texts. Thus, for example, the idea of insolvency proceedings used by the Principles is not equivalent to that followed by the 2004 UNCITRAL Legislative Guide on Insolvency Law,[6] where insolvency proceedings necessarily require court supervision, or that contained in the 2009 UNIDROIT Convention on Substantive Rules for Intermediated Securities[7] ('Geneva Securities Convention'), which requires supervision by a court or other competent authority. In the Principles, on the contrary, the insolvency proceeding may be subject to supervision by a judicial authority, but also by an administrative authority, or, in cases of pre-bankruptcy restructuring proceedings, neither of them may be required.

2.2.3 The Insolvency Representative

This is another interesting term to analyse since it is expressly referred to in Principle 13(4). In addition, there is another, even more important issue, which is that the term 'Insolvency Representative' seems to be foreign to the insolvency literature in many States.[8] On the other hand, unlike the term Insolvency Proceeding, analysed above, the term Insolvency Representative is not expressly defined in Principle 6, yet it is used recurrently throughout the text of the Principles. The Principles assume an understanding of this concept; however, clarifying what is intended would enhance overall understanding.

The early sessions held by the Working Group employed the term 'Insolvency Administrator'.[9] In future sessions, the term 'Insolvency Representative' started to be used recurrently, with no explanation for this change. This explanation does not appear until the session held between 31 August and 2 September 2022, when the Secretary-General pointed out that it would be appropriate to replace the term

[6] UNCITRAL Legislative Guide on Insolvency Law (2004); B. Glossary; 2. Terms and definitions; (u): *"Insolvency proceedings": collective proceedings, subject to court supervision, either for reorganization or liquidation.*

[7] UNIDROIT Convention on Substantive Rules for Intermediated Securities, 2009, article 1, (h): *"insolvency proceeding" means a collective judicial or administrative proceeding, including an interim proceeding, in which the assets and affairs of the debtor are subject to control or supervision by a court or other competent authority for the purpose of reorganisation or liquidation.*

[8] For example, in Spanish insolvency law, there are the figures of 'Insolvency Administrator', 'Restructuring Expert' and, to a lesser extent, 'Insolvency Mediator' —. In European Law, Regulation nº 2015/848 of The European Parliament and The Council, of 20 May 2015, on insolvency proceedings, use the term 'Administrator'.

[9] At the session of the Working Group held in Rome from 17 to 19 November 2020, it can be read: '*73. Private-law property rules provide an incomplete picture of the legal treatment of digital assets unless the treatment of those rights in insolvency proceedings also are considered. Categorisation of digital assets as some form of property or other rights enables their return to the holder or realisation by the insolvency administrator for the benefit of the estate. Further, the realisation of value is not only affected by legal categorisation but also the factual nature of digital assets*' (Digital Assets and Private Law Working Group // First session (remote) // Rome, 17 – 19 November 2020 //// UNIDROIT 2020 // Study LXXXII – W.G.1 – Doc. 2 // English only // November 2020, p. 18, marg. 73).

'Insolvency Administrator' with 'Insolvency Representative' to maintain a certain terminological consistency with UNCITRAL legal texts.[10]

Without a specific definition of the term 'Insolvency Representative' in the Principles, the UNCITRAL legal texts arguably represent a valid source to determine its meaning. UNCITRAL Legislative Guide on Insolvency Law defines insolvency representative as '*a person or body, including one appointed on an interim basis, authorised in insolvency proceedings to administer the reorganization or the liquidation of the insolvency estate*'.[11] This concept of an insolvency representative should apply in the context of the Principles; indeed, it is the one that appears to be followed in the Principles.

2.3 *Law Applicable to the Custodian´s Insolvency*

This is an issue worthy of reflection, since the Principles only provide a rather vague definition that falls short of a more categorical definition. This is due to the fact that the answer is not actually found in Principle 5, but rather in its Commentary.

Principle 5(3) states:

The law applicable to the issues addressed in Principles 10 to 13, including whether an agreement is a custody agreement, is the domestic law of the State expressly specified in that agreement as the law that governs the agreement, or if the agreement expressly provides that another law is applicable to all such issues, that other law.

According to the literal wording of the above Principle, the law applicable to the issues addressed in Principles 10 to 13 is indicated in the custody agreement. Among the topics addressed in these Principles is the problem of the custodian's insolvency, specifically in Principle 13. This raises the question of which law applies to the custodian's insolvency because, according to the literal wording of Principle 5(3), it could initially be concluded that regulation of the custodian's insolvency is in the hands of the parties to the custody agreement; i.e., it is the custodian and the

---

[10] '*The Secretary-General noted that several other Principles included provisions relating to insolvency, and in particular the Principle on custody. As such, additional consideration should be given to keeping Principle 21 separate. Additionally, if it were decided to have it as a separate Principle, proper cross-references would need to be added to the Commentary. It was added that terminological consistency with other internal texts was important. As such, the term 'insolvency administrator' should be replaced with 'insolvency representative'. Furthermore, the section presently mostly only related to secured transactions and not other insolvency-related matters, which was something that needed to be explained in the Commentary. Finally, it was also noted that issues related to enforcement in the context of insolvency were also important to consider and mention in the Commentary*' (Digital Assets and Private Law Working Group // Sixth session (hybrid) // Rome & Zoom, 31 August – 2 September 2022 //// UNIDROIT 2022 // Study LXXXII – W.G.6 – Doc. 4 // English only // November 2022, p. 14, marg. 79).

[11] UNCITRAL Legislative Guide on Insolvency Law (2004); Glossary; 2. Terms and definitions; (v).

client who can voluntarily decide under which law —*lex concursus*— the custodian's insolvency would be regulated. This could lead to regulatory dumping because the custodian always seeks the most favourable insolvency law.

On the contrary, it would seem more logical to understand that the rule contained in Principle 5(3) refers exclusively to private law issues related to the substantive or contractual aspects of the custody agreement but not to public or regulatory law issues, such as the law applicable to the custodian´s insolvency, whose regulation should be left out of this Principle. There are several passages in the text of the Principles that support this conclusion.

Principle 5(6) states that Principle 5 governs all property issues relating to digital assets concerning any event that occurred before the insolvency proceedings began, from which it follows that when insolvency proceedings take place, the State's insolvency law should apply and not that of the Principles. This conclusion could be corroborated by Principle 5(7), which proclaims the supremacy of substantive or procedural rules governing insolvency.

Comment 0.9 implies that the Principles only cover private law issues relating to digital assets, but not regulatory or public law,[12] and insolvency law is one of them. This idea is repeated in Commentary 1.1.[13]

The specific conflict of laws rule provided in Principle 5(3) determines the applicable law in the relationship between a custodian and its client, but it is limited in scope. This rule only concerns the issues addressed in Principles 10 to 13, including whether the agreement is a custody agreement. Principle 13 addresses issues arising if a custodian enters into an insolvency-related proceeding. As shown in Principles 5(6) and 5(7), the conflict of laws rule in Principle 5(3) applies to contractual and proprietary issues addressed in Principles 10 to 13. Still, the applicable insolvency law will govern insolvency law issues.

In any case, Commentary 5.19 seems to settle the matter, proclaiming the preeminence of the national law of the States to regulate insolvency matters concerning the law of Principles. This Commentary states:

---

[12] The first part of Commentary 0.9 states: '*The organisational neutrality of these Principles also does not mean that they are intended to be implemented outside of private law. These Principles cover only private law issues relating to digital assets and, in particular, proprietary rights. Thus, they specifically address digital assets where these are the object of dispositions and acquisitions, and where interests in those assets are to be asserted against third parties. As a matter of principle, they do not cover rules that are to be enforced by public authorities which in many jurisdictions would be called 'regulation' or 'regulatory law (...)*'.

[13] Commentary 1.1 reads: '*These Principles are meant to serve as guidelines for States to enable their private laws to be consistent with best practice and international standards in relation to the holding, transfer and use as collateral of digital assets, as defined in Principle 2(2). The Principles cover only private law issues relating to digital assets and, in particular, proprietary rights. Thus, they specifically address digital assets where these are the object of dispositions and acquisitions, and where interests in those assets are to be asserted against third parties. As a matter of principle, they do not cover rules that are to be enforced by public authorities (which in many jurisdictions would be called 'regulation' or 'regulatory law') (...)*'.

The specific conflict of laws rule provided in Principle 5(3) determines the applicable law in the relationship between a custodian and its client, but it is limited in scope. This rule only concerns the issues addressed in Principles 10 to 13, including whether the agreement is a custody agreement. Principle 13 addresses issues arising if a custodian enters into an insolvency-related proceeding. As is shown by Principles 5(6) and 5(7), the conflict of laws rule in Principle 5(3) applies to contractual and proprietary issues addressed in Principles 10 to 13, but insolvency law issues will be governed by the applicable insolvency law.

In conclusion, the custody agreement law will govern the contractual or private law aspects of the relationship between the custodian and the customer. In contrast, regulation of the custodian's insolvency proceedings is left to the national laws of the States under their applicable conflict of laws rules.

3 Reflections on Each Principle

3.1 Principle 13(1)

The Principles are based on an essential, basic, or core idea (one might say) that two different people cannot control the same digital asset. Control over a digital asset can only be exercised by one person. This means that one person cannot control a digital asset through another. There is only one exception: when an intermediary under a custody agreement manages the digital asset. In this case, the ownership of the asset is vested in its owner (the investor) while effective control rests with the custodian. In this case, the intermediary controls the asset of course, but does so on behalf of or in the interest of its client. Therefore, except in cases where there is a custody agreement, control and ownership of the digital asset are vested in the same person. In contrast, where there is a custody agreement, there is a dissociation between ownership of the digital asset and control of the digital asset.

The idea expressed in the previous paragraph is essential to understanding the rules in Principle 13(1) and Principle 13(2). This is because these rules can only be conceived if it is understood that, only in the case of a custody agreement, there can be a separation between ownership and effective control over the digital asset.

On closer reading, Principles 13(1) and 13(2) are similar, as they do not provide two different solutions. Rather, they contain the same solution for two different situations. Still, the solution is, after all, the same: the digital assets that a custodian manages for a client under a prior custody agreement cannot be laid claim to by the custodian's creditors. This occurs whether the custodian is insolvent or not. The only difference is the following scenario: Principle 13(1) provides the solution in a situation where the custodian is financially sound, and Principle 13(2) provides the solution in a scenario where the custodian is insolvent.

The central idea set out in the previous paragraph is clearly stated in Commentary 13.1, which points out that the solution provided in paragraph (1) of Principle 13 (that digital assets managed by the custodian for a client are immune from the claims of the custodian's creditors when the custodian is not in insolvency) is aligned with that provided for in paragraph (2), which provides that the digital assets managed by the custodian do not form part of the assets of the custodian's insolvency estate.

Comment 13.1 concludes with the following sentence: '*These provisions reflect the baseline concept that such digital assets belong to the clients, not the custodian*'. This sentence confirms the basic idea of the Principles that the same digital asset cannot be controlled by two different people, unless there is a custody agreement. This explains that a custodian's creditors cannot lay claim to the digital assets maintained by a custodian because they belong to its client. This is the solution set out in Principle 13(1) and Principle 13(2) in case of the custodian's insolvency. Both solutions directly result from the idea that digital assets are the client's property.

3.2 *Principle 13(2)*

The rule contained in this paragraph (2) is the essence of the whole of Principle 13, which, as is well known, is intended to regulate the effects of a custodian's insolvency. This paragraph begins the substantive exploration of the impact of the custodian's insolvency on the digital assets it controls for its clients. Indeed, except paragraph (1), paragraphs (2) to (8) (which are the remaining paragraphs of Principle 13) deal with the insolvency of the custodian, as Commentary 13.2 well indicates.

Principle 13(2) contains a rule that undoubtedly represents one of the most important concerns raised since the Working Group's sessions began. Indeed, at the second session of the Working Group, attention was already drawn to the empirical fact that many investors used intermediaries to manage their digital assets and that a large number of these assets were in the hands of intermediaries.[14] It was noted that, for many participants in digital asset markets, it was necessary to have an intermediary for the acquisition and subsequent holding of digital assets.[15] Even at that early stage in the initial sessions, the need to address the consequences of the intermediary's insolvency was raised, as an issue that the Principles should resolve.[16]

The issue of custodian insolvency was raised more specifically at the Working Group session held on 17–18 September 2020. This session warned of the serious risk

[14] Digital Assets and Private Law Working Group // First session (remote) // Rome, 17 – 19 November 2020 //// UNIDROIT 2020 // Study LXXXII – W.G.1 – Doc. 2 // English only // November 2020, p. 9, marg. 36.

[15] Digital Assets and Private Law Working Group // First session (remote) // Rome, 17 – 19 November 2020 //// UNIDROIT 2020 // Study LXXXII – W.G.1 – Doc. 2 // English only // November 2020, p. 16, marg. 66.

[16] Digital Assets and Private Law Working Group // First session (remote) // Rome, 17 – 19 November 2020 //// UNIDROIT 2020 // Study LXXXII – W.G.1 – Doc. 2 // English only // November 2020, p. 8, marg. 31.

that the bankruptcy of an intermediary could pose to its clients.[17] In fact, examples of real cases were provided (beyond the famous bankruptcy of Lehman Brothers), and it was noted that not all of them were resolved in the same way by national courts, thereby representing a legal certainty problem that the Principles should resolve. Hence:

i) The example of the MtGox[18] bankruptcy was given, and how, in this case, the Japanese courts ruled that the clients did not have ownership rights over the digital assets held by the intermediary, but only a mere credit or contractual right against the bankruptcy estate, which prevented the clients from recovering their assets as they were merely creditors of the estate, in competition with the other creditors of the intermediary.[19]
ii) The example of BITGRAIL[20] was discussed. In this case, unlike MtGOX, the Italian courts did recognise the client's rights over the digital assets held by the intermediary. Still, since the custodian had not kept its client's digital assets in separate accounts, there was no choice but to recognise the client's claim on the intermediary's assets.[21]
iii) The example of CRYPTOFIA[22] was also examined. In this case, the New Zealand courts recognised client ownership of digital assets, but with a peculiarity: they established separate funds or departments for each class of digital assets (e.g. Bitcoin; Ethereum) so that in the event of a shortfall in a particular cryptocurrency, the risk would be assumed by the clients of that specific asset, with all the assets of that same class held by the custodian being distributed among all of them.[23]

The working sessions continued, and at the one held on 16 and 18 March 2021, the Working Group set out the objectives of what would become the Principles themselves, including addressing the problems that could arise in the event of the custodian's insolvency.[24] The Working Group believed it would be more appropriate

[17] Exploratory Workshop on Digital Assets and Private Law // Rome & Zoom, 17 – 18 September 2020 //// UNIDROIT 2021 // Study LXXXII – W.G.1 – Doc. 3 // Original English // March 2021, p. 18, marg. 81.

[18] Japanese Bitcoin trading platform bankrupted in 2014.

[19] Exploratory Workshop on Digital Assets and Private Law // Rome & Zoom, 17 – 18 September 2020 //// UNIDROIT 2021 // Study LXXXII – W.G.1 – Doc. 3 // Original English // March 2021, p. 18, marg. 82.

[20] Italian trading platform brankrupted in 2018.

[21] Exploratory Workshop on Digital Assets and Private Law // Rome & Zoom, 17 – 18 September 2020 //// 2021 // Study LXXXII – W.G.1 – Doc. 3 // Original English // March 2021, p. 18, marg. 82.

[22] New Zealand platform broken in 2019.

[23] Exploratory Workshop on Digital Assets and Private Law // Rome & Zoom, 17 – 18 September 2020 //// UNIDROIT 2021 // Study LXXXII – W.G.1 – Doc. 3 // Original English // March 2021, p. 18, marg. 82.

[24] Digital Assets and Private Law Working Group // Second session (remote) // Rome, 16 – 18 March 2021 //// UNIDROIT 2021 // Study LXXXII – W.G.2 – Doc. 2 (rev. 1) // English only // March 2021, p. 4, marg. 13.

to solve practical problems, the solutions which should be the same for all States, rather than to address deeper issues such as the legal nature of digital assets. Each State would then resolve this issue under its domestic law but adopt the practical solutions set out in the Principles.[25] At this session, a draft of what would eventually become Principle 13(2) was formulated,[26] which takes up the essential idea that digital assets held by a custodian on behalf of its clients do not form part of the insolvency estate in the event of insolvency proceedings.[27] The Principle almost took on its final wording, being formulated as Principle 13(1), at the session held on 19–21 December 2021, under the following terms:

If a custodian enters into any insolvency proceeding, a digital asset that it maintains on behalf of a client under a custody agreement does not form part of that custodian's assets for distribution to its creditors.[28]

Having conducted this brief analysis of the genesis of Principle 13(2) as it stands today, it is now time to look at its content. In essence, the Principle states that if a custodian falls into insolvency proceedings, the digital assets it manages for its clients under a custody agreement do not form part of the assets distributable to its creditors. In simpler terms, they do not form part of the assets of its insolvency estate. This solution is not, moreover, unknown in insolvency law of many States. It is what is known under the Latin expression '*separatio ex iure dominii*', which means that the owner of an asset has the right to separate it from the assets of the insolvency estate of the person who possesses it by any legally valid title but is not its true owner. Nor is it an unknown solution for other UNCITRAL legal texts. In this regard, for example, the UNCITRAL Legislative Guide on Insolvency Law provides for the possibility of excluding assets owned by other persons but in the possession of the

---

[25] Digital Assets and Private Law Working Group // Second session (remote) // Rome, 16 – 18 March 2021 //// UNIDROIT 2021 // Study LXXXII – W.G.2 – Doc. 2 (rev. 1) // English only // March 2021, p. 9, marg. 39.

[26] Principle Y, Custody, paragraph 7: '*If a holder enters insolvency proceedings, a digital asset that it holds as a custodian for the account of a client does not form part of the holder's assets for distribution to its creditors*' (Digital Assets and Private Law Working Group // Second session (remote) // Rome, 16 – 18 March 2021 //// UNIDROIT 2021 // Study LXXXII – W.G.2 – Doc. 2 (rev. 1) // English only // March 2021, p. 24).

[27] The idea is clearly stated in the explanation to the Principle: '*This paragraph sets out the consequences of the insolvency of the custodian in a functional way rather than using legal concepts such as property or ownership. On the custodian's insolvency, assets it holds for clients are not part of the distributed estate. If a holder is not a custodian, any assets it holds will be part of its assets for distribution to its creditors. That will be the case where the holder falls within the situation described in paragraph 6 as well as all situations covered in paragraph 2 other than that of a holder*' (Digital Assets and Private Law Working Group // Second session (remote) // Rome, 16 – 18 March 2021 //// UNIDROIT 2021 // Study LXXXII – W.G.2 – Doc. 2 (rev. 1) // English only // March 2021, p. 24).

[28] Digital Assets and Private Law Working Group // Seventh session (hybrid) // Rome, 19–21 December 2022 //// UNIDROIT 2022 // Study LXXXII – W.G.7 – Doc. 2 // English only // December 2022, p. 43.

debtor on the date of the opening of the insolvency proceedings from the insolvency estate.[29]

Let us now proceed to the analysis of the main elements of Principle 13(2).

For the solution under Principle 13(2) to occur, the relationship between the service provider or intermediary and the client must be a custody arrangement within the meaning of the Principles, i.e. an arrangement that meets the requirements of Principle 10(3). In this sense, a custody arrangement exists when: (1) the service is provided in the ordinary course of the intermediary's business; (2) the provider or intermediary is obliged to obtain and maintain the digital asset for the client; and (3) the customer does not have the exclusive ability to change control of the digital asset within the meaning of Principle 6(2). In these circumstances, the digital assets held for its clients do not form part of its insolvency estate.

Conversely, it can be concluded that if there is no custody arrangement as defined in the Principles, the rule in Principle 13(2) does not apply. In this case, the digital assets held by the custodian on behalf of its clients would be part of the assets of its insolvency estate. The question then arises as to when an agreement between an intermediary or a service provider is not considered a custody agreement within the meaning of the Principles.

They would not be considered custody agreements, according to the Principles:

a) When the client has the exclusive ability to change control of the digital asset, as this is a situation contrary to that prescribed by Principle 10(3)(c).[30] The client controls the digital asset because he controls the private key, which is not provided to the service provider or intermediary. Several examples of this situation are set out in the text of the Principles:

   i) Where a person, such as an investor, controls the digital asset through some form of hardware or software that allows it to hold the private key without providing it to the intermediary. The intermediary merely provides the client with the software or hardware to operate the assets (wallet). The provider´s insolvency could affect the operation of the wallet, but the digital assets are not controlled by the provider (see Comment 10.14).
   ii) Self-custody, either directly by the client, using freely available software not provided by any service provider, referred to as 'Self-custody by wallet software' (see Commentary 10.16), or through software provided by a provider,

[29] UNCITRAL Legislative Guide on Insolvency Law (2004); Part. 2; II.A.3: '*Assets excluded from the insolvency estate (a) General exclusions: The insolvency law may exclude certain assets from the estate. Insolvency laws adopt different approaches to this issue. Assets excluded from the estate may include, for example, certain assets owned by a third party that are in the possession of the debtor when the proceedings commence, such as trust assets and assets subject to an arrangement (whether contractual or otherwise) that does not involve a transfer of title, but rather use of the assets and return to the owner once the purpose for which they were in the possession of the debtor has been fulfilled*'. Examples of contractual arrangements that allow the obligor to have possession of the property owned by a third party include, in a footnote, bailment or deposit agreements (see p. 80).

[30] The Principle 10(3)(c) reads as follows: '*The client does not have the exclusive ability to change the control of the digital asset within the meaning of Principle 6(2)*'.

referred to as 'Self-custody by software-as-a-service in the cloud' (see Commentary 10.17).

b) When the intermediary provides the client with a safeguarding of private keys service. In this case, it is technically possible that the provider may have control over the customer's private keys, since he provides the software or hardware to store them, but he does not have the client´s authorisation to do so. Control over the private keys is only instrumental, because the purpose of the agreement with the client is to protect the keys of its digital assets (see Commentary 10.18).
c) Where the relationship between the client and the supplier is merely an agreement to deliver digital assets. Here, there is no custody arrangement because the purpose of the agreement with the provider is for the provider to acquire digital assets for the client; that is, the intermediary has received the order from the customer to acquire digital assets in the market. The intermediary obviously controls the asset, which he does not lose until he delivers it to the customer, but the relationship is not one of custody because the provider does not control the customer's assets, but controls assets that he has acquired for the customer. In this sense, the customer only has the right to claim the delivery of an amount of assets from the intermediary, equivalent to that which he has instructed the intermediary to acquire. For the sake of comparison, in this case, the relationship between the customer and the intermediary is similar to that which arises with the purchase of securities on regulated markets (see Commentary 10.20).
d) Finally, the holding of digital assets through Decentralised Autonomous Organisations (DAO) does not represent a custody arrangement either because, generally, there is no person, natural or legal, who can be identified as responsible for the DAO, and because DAOs operate through a mechanism of consensus or voting between nodes (participants in the DAO) that can hardly be compatible with the idea of control of the digital asset in the hands of one person (see Commentary 10.22).
e) An agreement from whose wording or content it can be clearly construed that the client's digital assets managed by the custodian would be included in the latter's estate in the event of insolvency proceedings cannot be considered a custody agreement, even if the requirements set forth in Principle 10(3) are met (which according to the Principle, would be qualified as a custody agreement). This is clear from the text of Principle 10(4),[31] and is confirmed by Commentary 10.7, which states that *'(…) an agreement under which the client does not have control is presumed to be a custody agreement unless it is made clear in the agreement that assets held by the service provider form part of the service provider's assets available for distribution to its creditors if it enters into an insolvency-related proceeding. It is not necessary for this, or any particular, form of words to be used as long as this consequence is clear to clients. Principle 10(4) is designed*

[31] Principle 10(4) read as follows: '*An agreement to which paragraph (3) applies is not a custody agreement if it is clear from the agreement that, if the service provider enters into an insolvency-related proceeding, the digital asset would be part of the service provider's assets available for distribution to its creditors*'.

to act as an incentive to service providers to make the nature of the agreement clear on its face'.

None of the above situations qualify as custody arrangements. Therefore, Principle 13(2) does not apply to them. On the contrary, the clients' assets would be distributed among the intermediary's creditors, i.e. they would be part of the assets of the intermediary's insolvency estate. This is reflected in Commentary 13.3, in the following terms:

On the custodian's insolvency, digital assets it maintains for clients as custodian are not part of the assets available for distribution to its creditors. If, on the other hand, a service provider is not a custodian because its agreement with the client is an agreement for the delivery of digital assets (see Illustration 7 in Commentary 10.20), any assets it controls will usually be part of its assets for distribution to its creditors...

However, in some of the examples mentioned above and included in the Commentaries to Principle 10, reference is made to situations where this conclusion may seem surprising. Indeed, what happens in situations such as self-custody, where the intermediary does not control the asset? Should the client's assets be part of the intermediary's assets for distribution to its creditors? This is not a logical solution or response, not only because the assets belong to the client but also because the intermediary does not have control over the assets.

Ultimately, the application or not of Principle 13(2) depends not only on whether or not there is a custody agreement within the meaning of the Principles, but also on whether or not the intermediary has control over the digital assets. The following summary may explain our conclusions on this matter:

1) The intermediary controls the digital asset owned by the client under a custody agreement: Principle 13(2) applies. Therefore, the custodian's creditors cannot lay claim to the customer's digital assets, even if the custodian were to enter into insolvency proceedings.
2) The intermediary controls the digital asset owned by the client, but there is no custody agreement between them: Principle 13(2) does not apply. Therefore, the client's digital assets can be laid claim to by the custodian's creditors, even in the event of the custodian's bankruptcy. In this case, the client would only have a claim against the custodian, which would be asserted in the custodian's insolvency.
3) The intermediary does not control the digital asset owned by the client (e.g., self-custody): Principle 13(2) does not apply, but the client's digital assets also cannot be laid claim to by the intermediary´s creditors, even if he enters in insolvency proceedings, not only because the intermediary does not own the assets, but also because the intermediary does not have control over them.

Some final remarks to conclude the reflections on Principle 13(2). The first relates to the actions to be taken by the Insolvency Representative concerning the digital assets of the insolvent custodian's client. Principle 13(4)(a) requires the Insolvency Representative to take appropriate steps to bring the digital asset into the effective control of the client or another custodian appointed by him, for example, by providing the private keys previously obtained from the insolvent custodian to the client, as indicated at the end of Commentary 13.6.

The second is that the same intermediary may act as custodian for some clients and non-custodians for others. In this case, the consequences of Principle 13(2) would only apply to clients with whom there is a custody agreement (see Commentary 13.3).

The third has already been commented on in previous pages, but is worth recalling. Principle 13(2) should be read in conjunction with Principle 13(1) since, after all, it leads us to the same solution: that the digital assets that a custodian maintains for its client cannot be laid claim to or subject to enforcement by the custodian's creditors. The solution (we repeat) is the same; only the scenario in which it applies is different: Principle 13(1) when the custodian is in a financially healthy situation and Principle 13(2) when it is insolvent. In more colloquial language, Principles 13(1) and 13(2) represent two sides of the same coin. This solution is the direct consequence of the underlying principle that digital assets belong to the client, not the custodian (see Commentary 13.1). It is clear, then, that the rule contained in Principle 13(2) is a confirmation of this idea but, at the same time, an exception to another core idea of the Principles, according to which a digital asset cannot be maintained through another person, except in cases of custody (see Commentary 0.6).

The last assessment is procedural in nature. Principle 13(2) (as, in general, Principle 13 itself) deals with the consequences of the custodian´s insolvency but not the situation when the client becomes insolvent. In this case, it will be necessary to look at the guidelines in other Principles, especially in Principle 19 (see, in particular, Commentary 19.4).

3.3 *Principles 13(3) and 13(8)*

Reflections on Principles 13(3) and 13(8) should be carried out together since they have a common denominator: the presence of a sub-custodian.

Principle 13(3) addresses the consequences of a custodian's insolvency if he holds his client´s digital assets through another custodian, i.e. a sub-custodian. The possibility that the custodian may use a third party to conduct its business is permitted by the Principles. Principle 11(4)[32] expressly allows it, as do Commentaries 10.4[33]

---

[32] Principle 11(4) states: '*An agreement to which paragraph (3) applies is not a custody agreement if it is clear from the agreement that, if the service provider enters into an insolvency-related proceeding, the digital asset would be part of the service provider's assets available for distribution to its creditors*'.

[33] Commentary 10.4 reads: '*The purpose of Principle 10(2) is to introduce the concept of 'maintaining' a digital asset, which is wider than the (factual) concept of 'control' as defined in Principle 6. The word 'maintain' is defined as encompassing two situations in which a custodian 'maintains'*

and 11.15.[34] Under this sub-custody agreement, the custodian loses control over the digital asset, which is passed over to the sub-custodian but not the management of it (see Commentary 10.4), which continues to be retained by the custodian for its client. Based on the central idea of the Principles that a digital asset cannot be controlled through another person (see again Commentary 0.6), what occurs here is an arrangement of legal situations: the sub-custodian has effective control of the digital asset, the custodian manages the digital asset and the client is the owner or holder of the digital asset.

If observed, the solution contained in Principle 13(3), where the insolvent custodian acts through a sub-custodian, is no different from the solution contained in Principle 13(2), where there is no such custodian: in neither case can the digital assets owned by the client be laid claim to by the custodian's creditors. Therefore, the solution provided for in Principle 13(3) is a continuation of that provided for in Principle 13(2). It could not be otherwise because both Principles deal with the custodian´s insolvency. The only difference is how the custodian acts and how the clients' digital assets are controlled. Principle 13(2) assumes that the custodian effectively manages and controls the client's digital assets. In contrast, Principle 13(3) assumes a situation where the custodian manages but does not effectively control the client's digital assets.

However, because the custodian does not effectively control the client's digital assets, in the event of the custodian's insolvency, the protection of the client's digital assets must be articulated differently than if the custodian were acting without a sub-custodian. In this situation, the client's immunity cannot rest directly on the digital assets because the custodian does not control them; it rests on the custodian's rights over the sub-custodian regarding those assets. As Commentary 13.4 indicates in its final part: '*If the custodian is insolvent,* ***its rights against the sub-custodian are not part of the custodian's assets available for distribution to its creditors***[35]'. This conclusion is reiterated in Commentary 13.10,[36] at the end.

Since the insolvent custodian does not have control over its client's assets, which are controlled by the sub-custodian, protection of the custodian's client will require

---

a digital asset for a client. The first is where a custodian has control of an asset within the meaning of Principle 6. The second is where a custodian is the recipient of custody services, that is, where another custodian (a sub-custodian) is obliged to control the asset for that custodian. Where a sub-custodian is used, the sub-custodian and the custodian both 'maintain' the asset. In this situation, the custodian enters into a custody agreement with the sub-custodian and becomes its client. The custodian, therefore, has rights against the subcustodian under that custody agreement...'.

[34] Commentary 11.15 states: '*Principle 11(4) makes it clear that a sub-custody structure, can be used. Under this structure, the custodian maintains the digital asset by entering into a custody agreement with a sub-custodian with respect to that asset…*'.

[35] Author´s underlining.

[36] Commentary 13.10 reads as follow: "*Principle 13(8) sets out the consequences of the insolvency of a sub-custodian when a digital asset is maintained through that subcustodian (see Principle 11(4)). In these circumstances, the custodian must seek to change control of the digital asset from the insolvent sub-custodian, either to itself or to another sub-custodian. If the custodian is insolvent, its rights against the sub-custodian under the custody agreement do not form part of its assets available for distribution to its creditors*'.

the Insolvency Administrator to take steps to exclude those assets from distribution to the insolvent custodian's creditors, as required by Principle 13(4)(b). As such, the Insolvency Representative should obtain the private keys to those assets from the sub-custodian and either give them to the custodian's client so that the client can acquire direct control over the digital assets or have them transferred to another custodian of its choice, as noted in the final part of Commentary 13.6.

Principle 13(8), for its part, addresses the consequences for the client's digital assets when the sub-custodian becomes insolvent. The first of these is included in the text of the same Principle. The custodian must try to obtain control of the digital assets controlled by the sub-custodian, either to control them itself or to control them through another sub-custodian, as Commentary 13.10 indicates. This change of control over the digital asset will require the custodian to reclaim the private keys of the digital assets from the sub-custodian's Insolvency Representative or require him to transfer them to another sub-custodian (see Commentary 13.6).

The second consequence stemming from the sub-custodian´s insolvency certainly does not appear in the text of Principle 13(8), but it is aligned with the structure of the Principles. If, under the sub-custody agreement, the custodian becomes a client of the sub-custodian (see, in this regard, Commentaries 10.4[37] and 13.4[38]), and, under Principle 13(2), the client´s digital assets do not form part of the estate to be distributed to the custodian's creditors; it seems clear that the rights that the custodian (client) has against the sub-custodian (custodian) under the second custody agreement cannot form part of the estate of the sub-custodian's insolvency proceeding either. The distinction is, as explained above, that the custodian, who is not the owner of the digital asset, does not control it, so immunity cannot be predicated in respect of the digital assets, but rather in respect of the custodian's rights over the sub-custodian to claim delivery of the digital assets it controls for the custodian's clients.

3.4 *Principle 13(4)*

This principle has been discussed in the reflections on Principles 13(2) and 13(3), so we refer to them.

[37] Where it reads: '*(…) the custodian enters into a custody agreement with the sub-custodian and becomes its client…*'.

[38] Where it says: '*(…) As explained in Commentary 10.4, when a custodian maintains a digital asset through a sub-custodian, the custodian (who will be the client of the subcustodian under a custody agreement) has rights against that subcustodian under the custody agreement…*'.

3.5 Principles 13(5), 13(6) and 13(7)

Given the obvious connection between these three principles, it seems appropriate to analyse them together.

Principles 13(5), 13(6) and 13(7) also deal with custodian insolvency, as does Principle 13(2), although under different circumstances. In this sense, and as a matter of principle, it could be thought that these three Principles contain a solution that displaces that provided for, as a general rule, in Principle 13(2), provided that the circumstances indicated therein are present: in particular, in Principle 13(5). In this way, it could be construed (and, we repeat, only as a matter of principle) that when the circumstances stated in Principle 13(5) occur, the solution in Principle 13(2) does not apply, but rather the other one contemplated in these other Principles. In other words, the rules of Principles 13(5), 13(6) and 13(7) would override the rule in Principle 13(2), which would not apply in the circumstances set out in Principle 13(5). Nothing could be further from the truth, as will be discussed below.

Principles 13(5), 13(6) and 13(7) deal with a peculiar situation that may occur during the insolvency of the custodian, which the Principles refer to as a 'shortfall'.[39] The shortfall problem occurs when the custodian manages its clients' digital assets as a common fund or as an undivided pool, and this is the case when those digital assets are fungible or, as the Principles indicate, are 'digital assets of the same description'.

Let us now analyse these special circumstances under Principle 13(5) that justify the remedies provided for in Principles 13(6) and 13(7).

a) The first is that the custodian is involved in insolvency proceedings. At this point, little more can be added regarding the custodian's insolvency, which has already been analysed in the preceding pages.
b) Second. The custodian manages digital assets with the same description for two or more clients as a common and undivided pool. Some clarifications are needed on this requirement.

 'Digital assets of the same description' is a term the Principles use to refer to digital assets that clients consider fungible with each other, i.e., that have the same characteristics (e.g., Bitcoins, Ethereum, etc.). When the custodian manages digital assets of the same description for its clients, following a client's orders, the custodian may comply by delivering the same amount of digital assets of the same description as those of the client, regardless of whether the digital assets it delivers are controlled by the custodian directly or by a sub-custodian, or whether they are digital assets that the custodian manages for itself or digital assets that it manages for other clients. The only important thing is that the custodian delivers an amount of digital assets equivalent to what the client is asking for to the client, and, of course, that they are of the same description.

[39] The issue of the shortfall is another concern that became apparent very early on in the Working Group's sessions (Digital Assets and Private Law Working Group // Second session (remote) // Rome, 16 – 18 March 2021 //// UNIDROIT 2021 // Study LXXXII – W.G.2 – Doc. 2 (rev. 1) // English only // March 2021, p. 44).

The Principles not only allow a custodian to manage a client's digital assets jointly with those of other clients, as long as they are digital assets of the same characteristics, but rather, on the contrary, assume that this will be the general rule. Indeed, Principle 11(2) states that, unless prohibited by the custody agreement or other rules, a custodian may manage digital assets of the same description for two or more of its clients as an undivided pool. In other words, the general rule is the possibility to manage the digital assets as an undivided pool; only where this is prohibited by law or by the custody agreement itself, the management of the client's digital assets should be segregated from the other digital assets of different clients (see Commentary 11.7[40]). Moreover, asset management on a segregated basis is envisaged only as a possibility that the custodian can offer to the customer (see Commentary 11.13[41]).

c) Third. There is a shortfall in a particular category of digital assets of the same description that the custodian manages for its clients.[42]

The Principles do not expressly define the shortfall (see Principle 2). In fact, Principle 2(7) refers its conceptualisation to Principle 13(5). The latter principle defines the shortfall as 'the quantity of digital assets maintained by the insolvent custodian for those clients is less than the aggregate quantity of digital assets of the same description that it is obliged to maintain for those clients. A shortfall is, therefore, the difference between the total amount of digital assets that the custodian manages for its clients and the amount it has available if it has to return them to those clients. In other words, there is a shortfall if, faced with an obligation to make restitution, the custodian does not have sufficient digital assets, provided, of course, that they are digital assets of the same characteristics ('digital assets of the same description' in the terminology of the Principles).

Given these three circumstances specified in Principle 13(5), the consequences or solutions provided in Principles 13(6) and 13(7) are applicable. However, the solutions contemplated in Principles 13(6) and 13(7) do not have the same binding force.

Principle 13(6) is presented as an eminently dispositive or voluntary rule, i.e. States may adopt it or not, as they see fit. This is precisely why Principle 13(6) appears in square brackets (see Commentary 13.8, at the end). In contrast, the rule contained in Principle 13(7) is mandatory, and States must implement it in their

---

[40] Commentary 11.7, in its final part, reads: '*Where the custodian is not allowed to maintain an undivided pool, it must implement what is often called full segregation*'.

[41] Commentary 11.13 reads: '*Principle 11(3)(d) does not address the segregation of assets of any particular client. Rather than maintaining client assets of the same description as an undivided pool, a custodian may offer to a client the possibility of the custodian maintaining the assets of that client separately from the assets of the same description of other clients (so-called full segregation). That would require the custodian to control the client's assets using a separate private key or to maintain them in a separate account with a sub-custodian so that such assets are exclusively allocated to the client...*'.

[42] In a given category of digital assets of the same description or in several or, even, all of them. As Commentary 13.7 indicates at the end, in the insolvency-related proceeding of a custodian, there may be potentially as many shortfalls as there are undivided pools.

domestic law. In short, to address the shortfall situation that may arise in the event of a custodian´s insolvency, in respect of digital assets controlled under the technique of common or undivided funds of digital assets of the same description, States may adopt the solutions provided for in Principles 13(6) and 13(7), or only the solution contemplated in Principle 13(7), if they choose to dispense with that of Principle 13(6). There are, therefore, two different scenarios, depending on whether the two solutions provided in Principles 13(6) and 13(7) are adopted or only that of Principle 13(7).

Scenario 1 *Successive or staggered implementation of the solutions provided for in Principle 13(6) and Principle 13(7).*

In the event of a shortfall, this should initially be covered by all digital assets of the same characteristics managed by the custodian for itself (Principle 13(6) and Commentary 13.8). The fact that a custodian manages digital assets for its clients does not preclude it from holding digital assets for itself. If it has its own digital assets, provided that they are of the same characteristics (of the same description) as the digital assets of the customers affected by the shortfall, the shortfall must first be covered by the digital assets of the same characteristics owned by the custodian. One caveat: shortfall coverage must occur with digital assets of the same characteristics owned by the custodian, not with digital assets of another description owned by other clients, e.g. with Bitcoins held by the custodian for itself, but not with Ethereum (see illustration in Comment 13.9).

If observed, the solution contained in Principle 13(6) involves recognising, within the custodian's insolvency, a privilege in favour of the clients of those digital assets that suffer the shortfall. Indeed, the digital assets that the custodian controls for itself, since they are presumed to be its property, must form part of the assets of its insolvency proceeding and are intended to satisfy all its creditors. Establishing, as Principle 13(6) does, that the custodian's digital assets, which are of the same description as those affected by the shortfall, must be used first to cover it, satisfying the clients who own those digital assets affected by the shortfall, implies recognising them a privilege within the insolvency, to the detriment of the rest of the custodian's creditors, since these digital assets of the custodian, even though they form part of its assets, will not be used to pay the rest of the creditors. The custodian's other creditors would only be paid when the digital asset owner affected by the shortfall is paid, provided that there are sufficient custodian-owned digital assets to cover the remaining shortfall after the shortfall was covered. For this reason, Principle 13(6) has probably been designed as a voluntary provision because not all States may wish to implement it, recognising this privilege to favour certain custodian clients.

If, despite recourse to the digital assets held by the custodian for itself, there is still a shortfall in favour of clients because those assets are not sufficient to cover it, the remedy provided for in Principle 13(7) should be implemented. In this first scenario, recourse to the remedy under Principle 13(7) is subsidiary to Principle 13(6). In other words, only when the digital assets that the custodian holds for itself are not sufficient to cover the shortfall should the rule in Principle 13(7) be used (see Commentary 13.8).

In summary, for this first scenario: initially, the solution provided in Principle 13(6) is adopted, covering the shortfall with the custodian's digital assets, and only if this is not sufficient, and there is still a shortfall, is it covered by resorting to the Principle 13(7) remedy.

Scenario 2 *Application of the Principle 13(7) solution alone.*

Given that application of Principle 13(6) and its solution is voluntary, some mandatory measures should be provided to alleviate the shortfall that the custodian may incur regarding certain digital assets held in custody for its clients should a shortfall occur. While Principle 13(6) is voluntary, and States are free to apply it as they deem fit, Principle 13(7) is presented as mandatory, and States may not dispense with it. Principle 13(7), therefore, always applies whether the custodian's digital assets are used to cover the shortfall first or not.

If States have provided for the implementation of Principle 13(6), Principle 13(7) applies in a subsidiary manner (scenario 1). If, on the other hand, States do not incorporate Principle 13(6) into their domestic law, Principle 13(7) applies directly (scenario 2).

Principle 13(7) provides that, in the event of a shortfall on certain digital assets of the same description managed by the custodian for its clients, the risk of such shortfall should be borne or assumed by the clients who own these digital assets. In other words, if, at the time of the opening of insolvency proceedings, the custodian does not have sufficient digital assets of the same description (either assets controlled directly by the custodian or its clients or controlled by a sub-custodian for the custodian), then the clients should suffer the shortfall. In this situation, the custodian's clients will not receive the digital assets they should receive.

The solution in Principle 13(7) involves applying the *pari passu* rule to all the custodians' clients affected by the shortfall (see Commentary 13.9). however, it also consists of subjecting those clients to the risk of the custodian's insolvency, which represents a relaxation of one of the core ideas of the Principles, whereby digital assets belong to the clients and not to the custodian (see Commentary 13.1, at the end), because even if they do belong to customers, they will not be able to receive or recover them in full.

Some final remarks to conclude the reflections on Principles 13(5), 13(6) and 13(7). At the beginning of the reflections on these Principles, we raised the question of whether the solutions they contain displace or derogate from that generally provided for in Principle 13(2), which, as is well known, is the general core of Principle 13, devoted to regulating the custodian´s insolvency. At the time, we held that this was not the case. We now proceed to argue our conclusion.

The rule contained in Principle 13(2) represents the essence of Principle 13 as a whole. This central idea has existed since the first sessions of the Working Group. It does not seem logical to understand the rules contained in Principles 13(5), 13(6) and 13(7) as an exception to this central idea, but it could be.

Principle 13(2) is presented as a principle of general application whenever digital assets are held through a custodian. In this sense, no distinction is made according to the type of digital assets managed by the custodian: whether they are digital assets that, because they are fungible, are managed as an undivided pool or whether they are managed in a segregated manner. Principle 13(2) tends to be applied in any case, even when digital assets are managed as an undivided pool. Moreover, Principle 13(2) would apply if, even where digital assets are managed as an undivided pool, and therefore a shortfall situation would not arise.

Even if there is a shortfall, the Principle 13(2) rule would not necessarily be rendered ineffective, and would still apply. Indeed, if the solution of Principle 13(6) is chosen, providing that the custodian's digital assets cover the shortfall, those assets are excluded from payment to the custodian's other creditors, but those creditors are not recognised as being entitled to lay claim to the digital assets that the custodian manages for its clients, which, in any case, would be immune from payment. In other words, the digital assets the custodian manages for its clients would not be available for distribution to its creditors, as Principle 13(2) states. If, on the other hand, the rule of Principle 13(7) is adopted, providing that the shortfall is covered by the clients holding the digital assets affected by the shortfall, they may bear the risk of their custodian's insolvency, not receiving the amount of digital assets they should, but those digital assets affected by the shortfall are not intended for the payment of the custodian's other creditors. Therefore, the digital assets that the custodian manages for its clients would not be available for distribution to its creditors, as proclaimed by Principle 13(2).

In conclusion, the rules contained in Principles 13(6) and 13(7) do not displace or derogate from, but rather complement, the general rule of Principle 13(2), albeit only in the circumstances contemplated in Principle 13(5).

3.6 Principle 13(8)

This principle has been discussed in the reflections on Principle 13(3), so we refer to them.

References

Digital Assets and Private Law Working Group // First session (remote) // Rome, 17 – 19 November 2020 //// UNIDROIT 2020 // Study LXXXII – W.G.1 – Doc. 2 // English only // November 2020. chrome-extension://efaidnbmnnnibpcajpcglclefindmkaj/https://www.unidroit.org/english/documents/2020/study82/wg01/s-82-wg01-02-e.pdf (last visited 16 January 2025)

Exploratory Workshop on Digital Assets and Private Law // Rome & Zoom, 17 – 18 September 2020 //// UNIDROIT 2021 // Study LXXXII – W.G.1 – Doc. 3 // Original English // March 2021. chrome-extension://efaidnbmnnnibpcajpcglclefindmkaj/https://www.unidroit.org/english/documents/2021/study82/wg01/s-82-wg01-03-e.pdf (last visited 16 January 2025)

Digital Assets and Private Law Working Group // Second session (remote) // Rome, 16 – 18 March 2021 //// UNIDROIT 2021 // Study LXXXII – W.G.2 – Doc. 2 (rev. 1) // English only // March 2021.
chrome-extension://efaidnbmnnnibpcajpcglclefindmkaj/https://www.unidroit.org/english/documents/2021/study82/wg02/s-82-wg02-02rev-01-e.pdf (last visited 16 January 2025)
Digital Assets and Private Law Working Group // Sixth session (hybrid) // Rome & Zoom, 31 August – 2 September 2022 //// UNIDROIT 2022 // Study LXXXII – W.G.6 – Doc. 4 // English only // November 2022.
chrome-extension://efaidnbmnnnibpcajpcglclefindmkaj/https://www.unidroit.org/wp-content/uploads/2022/12/W.G.6-Doc.-4-Summary-Report-of-the-6th-Session.pdf (last visited 16 January 2025)
Digital Assets and Private Law Working Group // Seventh session (hybrid) // Rome, 19–21 December 2022 //// UNIDROIT 2022 // Study LXXXII – W.G.7 – Doc. 2 // English only // December 2022.
chrome-extension://efaidnbmnnnibpcajpcglclefindmkaj/https://www.unidroit.org/wp-content/uploads/2022/12/W.G.7-Doc.-2-Draft-Principles-and-Commentary.pdf (last visited 16 January 2025)

Reflections on Section V: Secured Transactions

Principle 14
Secured Transactions: General

Miguel Ángel Pendón Meléndez

(1) Digital assets can be the subject of security rights.

(2) If a digital asset is linked to another asset, other law applies to determine the legal effect on that other asset of the creation of a security right in that digital asset.

(3) If a digital asset is linked to another asset, other law applies to determine the legal effect on that other asset of a security right in that digital asset being made effective against third parties.

1 Official Commentary

Commentary

Principle 14(1)

14.1. Principle 14(1) builds on Principle 3(1) which states that digital assets (as defined in Principle 2(2)) can be the subject of proprietary rights. Security rights are proprietary rights, and, therefore, digital assets can be the subject of security rights. Principle 14 reflects the general principle that secured transactions regimes should enable the use of any type of movable asset as collateral. This approach allows prospective secured creditors to decide for themselves which of the digital assets have any collateral value.

This work was financed within the framework of the Prometeo 2023 project of the Regional Ministry of Innovation, Universities, Science and Digital Society (CIPROM/2022/26) "Present and future of the regulation of cryptoassets in the EU [LegalCripto]", whose principal investigator is Carmen Pastor Sempere. The basic ideas contained herein were presented in the author's paper with the same title, given on November 13, 2024 at the IV International Congress on "UNIDROIT Principles on Digital Assets and Private Law: Context, Content, Perspectives", organized also by BAES Research Group of the University of Alicante on November 13 and 14, 2024.

M. Á. Pendón Meléndez (✉)
Departamento de Derecho Mercantil, Facultad de Derecho, University of Cádiz, Jerez de la Frontera (Cádiz), Spain
e-mail: miguel.pendon@uca.es

C. Pastor Sempere and D. A. Morán Bovio (eds.), UNIDROIT *Principles on Digital Assets and Private Law*, Law, Governance and Technology Series 80,
https://doi.org/10.1007/978-3-032-11001-5_20

14.2. Section V applies to transactions under which a security right in a digital asset is granted to a secured creditor to secure the performance of any existing, future, or contingent obligations of the grantor or another person. These transactions, covered by Section V, are called 'secured transactions' in the Commentary to Section V. The Principles in Section V are not intended to interfere with domestic law conceptions of security right or domestic security law, except to the extent that such law should be changed to deal specifically with security over digital assets. Many proprietary aspects concerning security rights are governed by other law (see Principles 3(3)(c), 3(3)(e) and 3(3)(g)). The Principles presuppose the existence of some rules (such as the existence of methods other than control of making a security right effective against third parties (which is presupposed by Principle 16) or the requirement to notify the grantor and third parties prior to disposal of a digital asset in enforcement of a security right) and explain how those rules would operate in the context of enforcing security rights in digital assets.

14.3. The Principles are not only for those States that have implemented the UNCITRAL Model Law on Secured Transactions or a law based on approaches similar to the UNCITRAL model. Therefore, the type of transactions which fall within the category of 'secured transactions' and the types of rights which fall within the term 'security right' will depend on the applicable domestic law. For example, the term 'secured transactions' will typically include transactions creating various types of 'security rights', such as pledges, charges, or security assignments. It may also cover outright transfers: whether 'secured transactions' include such transfers will depend on domestic secured transactions law. For example, the UNCITRAL Model Law on Secured Transactions and some domestic secured transactions laws apply to outright transfers of receivables. The Geneva Securities Convention covers collateral transactions that are created by the grant of an interest in intermediated securities in the form of security interests and title transfer collateral agreements. Some domestic laws provide for fiduciary transfers of ownership that transfer 'ownership' of the asset to the creditor with the sole purpose of securing an obligation. Outright transfers of digital assets may be used in various contexts. It is therefore important that secured transactions law should be coordinated with a State's generally applicable rules governing outright transfers of digital assets. Another example of where domestic laws may differ relates to whether making a security right effective against third parties is seen as separate from creating a security right. In jurisdictions where some security rights are effective against third parties from the moment they are created, references in these Principles to making a security right effective against third parties should be read as references to the creation of a security right (see also Commentary 14.8).

14.4. In adopting these Principles, a State may need to amend existing secured transactions legislation by including special rules for digital assets as set out in Section V. In doing so, the digital asset to which these special rules apply will have to be defined, using the definition in Principle 2(2). For example, under the UNCITRAL Model Law on Secured Transactions (or any similar domestic secured transactions law) this would have the effect of carving out digital assets from the broader body of 'intangible assets' to which the generally applicable rules already apply (e.g., third-party effectiveness by registration only). This would complement any existing definitions of special types of assets (e.g., deposit accounts) for which asset specific rules might have been provided (e.g., third-party effectiveness may be achieved by control). Where a digital asset is linked to another asset ('the other asset'), that other asset may well fall within a specific category in the domestic law of a State, such as a category of 'securities' (bearing in mind that the existence and legal effect of the link is a matter for other law, see Principle 4). The nature of the link itself may, as a matter of other law, result in the linked digital asset falling within a specific category, such as that of negotiable documents or instruments (see Commentary 4.22). In these situations, the secured transactions rules specific to that category of asset will apply to the other asset or to the digital asset itself as appropriate.

14.5. States should consider providing for rules specific to digital assets. These rules may be made applicable to digital assets as a type of collateral or further distinctive rules could apply to various categories of linked digital assets. States should not attempt to provide for secured transactions rules specific to each of many categories of linked digital assets that would result in a complicated system. The concept of control set out in Principle 6 should apply equally to the third-party effectiveness of security rights in all types of digital assets (linked and non-linked) (see Principle 15).

14.6. The Principles in Section V address certain aspects of third party effectiveness, priority and enforcement relating to security rights over digital assets. There will be many aspects of secured transactions that are governed by other law (as defined in Principle 2(4)). The rules determining the law applicable to proprietary aspects of secured transactions are set out in Principle 5(1) (subject to Principle 5(5)).

14.7. ***Illustration 1.****The secured transactions law of State X does not carve out digital assets from the broader category of intangible assets. Control is a recognised mechanism for making a security right effective against third parties but is available only for bank accounts and intermediated securities. A secured creditor who has control of a digital asset may thus need to register to make its security right effective against third parties. Upon implementation of these Principles, the registration would be a redundant step in terms of providing public notice to third parties as, in the situation described, the secured creditor would be in control of the digital asset (as defined in Principle 6) which would make the security right effective against third parties by control under Principle 15.*

Principles 14(2) and 14(3)

14.8. Principles 14(2) and 14(3) reflect Principle 4 which provides that the existence of, requirements for, and legal consequences of any link between a digital asset and another asset (either a real-world asset or a digital asset) are a matter for other law. If, for instance, a link between a digital and a real-world asset is recognised under other law as operating as a negotiable document, the creation and third-party effectiveness of a security right in the digital asset would extend to the real-world asset. If it were not so recognised, a security right would extend to the digital asset only. This approach is consistent with, for instance, Article 16 of the UNCITRAL Model Law on Secured Transactions that provides for the creation of a security right in a negotiable document that may extend to goods. However, it does not define a negotiable document, as this is not a matter of secured transactions law. Furthermore, Principles 14(2) and 14(3) follow the approach of Article 17 of the UNCITRAL Model Law on Secured Transactions under which a security right in an asset does not extend to an 'associated asset', so that, for example, a security right in intellectual property does not extend to a tangible asset with respect to which that intellectual property is used. Accordingly, if some other law does not establish a link between the two assets, the creation of a security right in one of the two assets would not affect the other asset. The opposite situation, where a security right is taken in a real-world asset that is purported to be linked to a digital asset, is not covered by the Principles, because these Principles deal with digital assets only. As explained in Commentary 14.2, these Principles do not interfere with domestic conceptions of security rights. In some jurisdictions, creation and third-party effectiveness are indistinguishable (see Commentary 14.3), in which case that State may not need to implement Principle 14(3).

14.9. ***Illustration 2****. In State X, an invoice is not seen as an embodiment of the underlying right to payment. Factor A regularly takes control of digital invoices for due diligence purposes. This would not create a security right in the receivable nor make it effective against third parties. Factor B regularly takes a security right over receivables owed under invoices which are issued in the form of digital assets. The security right is made effective against third parties. This would not create a security right in the digital assets, i.e., digital invoices, nor make it effective against third parties. Thus, in practice, because there is no effective link between the receivable and invoice, a security right over the digital invoice would not have any value in a similar way to a security right in a paper-invoice that does not embody a right to payment.*

2 Reflections

2.1 Preliminary

The modern economy is largely predicated on the availability of access to international sources of finance. Accordingly, credit constitutes one of the foundational pillars of national economic and productive systems. For this reason, States seek to guarantee both agility and legal certainty in the access to, circulation of, and availability of credit—much of which originates from international financial markets. A legal system that ensures predictability and provides efficient mechanisms for the creation, recognition, protection, and enforcement of security interests facilitates access to credit by entrepreneurs under optimal conditions of legal certainty.

In short, it is particularly advantageous for States to have an effective system of credit collateral, which will be felt in the economic and financial system (including economic growth), by contributing to the security in the circulation of the means of business financing that, in general, is found in worldwide markets[1]; a system of collateral that must be aligned with international models and practices. Indeed, in various international fora it is insisted that the modernisation of the secured credit regime, approached from the point of view of the best international uniformity, would contribute to reduce inequalities between developed and developing countries, as all of them would compete under similar rules for access to low-cost credit. A secured transactions regime model would particularly benefit the parties to the agreement: the debtor, insofar as it has access to sources of financing that would otherwise be "forbidden" (or would be difficult to access and under more burdensome conditions); the secured creditor, because it enjoys greater security in the recovery (repayment) of its investment (loan) if it has the guarantee provided by an asset that can be quickly and safely executed.

Broadly speaking, every jurisdiction maintains its own secured transactions framework—more or less modernised and comprehensive—governing both the types of security devices and the assets over which they may be created. Frequently, however, these frameworks have developed incrementally over time, through legislative amendments responding to new commercial realities, or through the tacit or express recognition by regulatory authorities of practices devised by professional stakeholders. The outcome is often a fragmented and inconsistent body of provisions, not always harmonised, integrated, or updated.

This scenario, as briefly outlined above, has motivated numerous national initiatives in recent years to reform secured transactions law. These reform efforts have

[1] *Vid. Introduction*, Model Law on Secured Transactions, European Bank for Reconstruction and Development: "There is a direct relationship between the legal framework and the attitude of the investor. If there is a law on secured transactions which is seen to give practical protection and remedies in the case of non-payment of a debt then security can become a major part of the investment decision, both for local and international investors. If the investor is not persuaded that the law gives real protection and remedies then it becomes irrelevant" (https://www.ebrd.com/news/publications/guides/model-law-on-secured-transactions.html).

largely been driven by the growing diversity of assets that may serve as collateral, particularly assets recognised as having market value. Whereas traditional collateral frameworks were historically predicated on two categories—movable property (e.g., pledges) and immovable property (e.g., mortgages)—the emergence of diverse asset classes in the marketplace, including the distinction between "tangible assets" (e.g., goods and equipment) and "intangible assets" (e.g., intellectual property and dematerialised securities), challenged the compatibility of existing frameworks with contemporary commercial realities. The consolidation of new business (and goods) models brought about by the so-called "information society" (the application of technology to the conduct of all human, social or economic activity) shakes the foundations of legal systems, which are gradually being forced to replace paper (the basis of all commercial activity, as it documents relationships and allows for their proof) with computerised (electronic, digital) records (or files).

Technology also facilitates universal access to international markets, previously reserved for only a few. The replacement of paper by electronic communications has led to the growth of international trade. The relevant markets today are neither national markets nor those defined by geographically proximate areas (even grouped into more or less complex political and economic units); the perspective is now global. Many States are, under these considerations, reforming their legal systems, facing either partial reforms (updating their legal systems) or a thorough revision of all their regulations to bring them into line with the most recent trends and practices.[2] For this reform process, whether more specific or more ambitious, there are numerous initiatives by international organisations and institutions, including the work started in 2002 by UNCITRAL (United Nations Commission on International Trade Law), which has crystallised in several Uniform Law instruments, including the *UNCITRAL Legislative Guide on Secured Transactions* (2007) and the *UNCITRAL Model Law on Secured Transactions* (2016). Some of these texts will be discussed below.

The principal advantage of legal harmonisation instruments developed within international organisations lies in their inclusive and representative drafting processes. Working groups typically include States from diverse legal traditions and levels of economic development, alongside legal professionals, economists, relevant international bodies, and commercial stakeholders. The resulting texts thus reflect globally vetted best practices and function as balanced models for contractual and regulatory design.

In this context, UNIDROIT undertook the task of developing *Principles* on Digital Assets, with the objectives expressly stated (see comments on the *Introduction* above). And since the aim is to seek basic rules to cover and facilitate commercial transactions with these new asset models, the prospect of secured transactions is an essential element. There have been considerable challenges in this regard. In pursuit of legal certainty in international transactions involving digital assets, it has been necessary to address: the variability of national legal terminology and conceptual frameworks; the availability (or absence) of legal constructs across jurisdictions; the need for internal coherence (within the instrument itself) and external consistency

---

[2] *See* the information available at https://securedtransactionslawreformproject.org/.

(with other international instruments taken as reference); and, above all, the technological novelty of digital assets themselves. A central debate has concerned the recognition of proprietary rights in digital assets—a matter of fundamental importance in the context of secured credit. These and other issues will be examined in greater detail in the subsequent pages.

2.2 Presentation and Generalities

Principle 14 (Secured transactions: general) is the first of Section V (Secured transactions) of the *Principles.* The purpose of the section is to define the regime proposed by UNIDROIT for transactions involving agreements or contracts to create "*securities*" (or "*collateral*"; we will return briefly to the question of the distinction between the two terms below) involving digital assets. The first thing that strikes one when reading the *Principle* is the substantial overlap between the heading of the *Section* and that of the *Principle* itself. As will be discussed below in the course of these comments, *secured transactions* are not finally regulated in the *blackletters* of the *Principles*, but, taking the concept of the extremes of these kinds of agreements and contracts for granted (or considering it unnecessary to attempt an account of these transactions), their meaning and relevance are reflected upon in the *Commentaries.*

Principle 14 is composed of two distinct parts: *Principle 14(1)*, which appears to set out a general (perhaps even unnecessary) consideration that serves as an introduction to the whole section (and justifies it); and the *rules* in *Principles 14(2)* and *14(3)*, with a specific *mandate* in relation to linked assets. The two parts listed above are probably not sufficiently close in regulatory concept to be presented together in a single *principle.* There is also no justification for treating significantly different issues under the rubric of the *Principle*, which appeals to its "general" (cross-cutting, text-wide) character. *Principle 14(1)* can be seen as setting out an issue that transcends the section in which it is located and is intended to impact on the whole text of the *Principles*; however, *Principles 14(2)* and *14(3)* address very specific issues and a special regime for certain digital assets (linked digital assets). However, this content was essentially retained throughout the text, without, for example, opting for a separation of the mandates, a reordering that would perhaps have been more in line with the subject matter. Probably, because of its particular nature and regime, the issue of security over linked digital assets would have merited an ad hoc*principle* in the UNIDROIT text, just as it was considered to require a separate mandate in *Section I (Scope and definitions)* of the *Principles* (*Principle 4 Linked assets*).

Finally, and for the purpose of drawing attention to a purely formal aspect of the text, *Principle 14* is one of those which, together with *Principles* 2, 4, 6, 10, 12, 16 and 17, completes the *Commentaries* with sections called "Illustration". Although the purpose of these sections is obvious (as their name indicates, to illustrate the mandates of the *Principle* with examples), their real value (in relation to the rest of the *Commentaries*) is not specified anywhere (although, as they are included in the *Commentaries*, they would be considered as such).

2.3 Some Notes on the **Iter** *of the* **Principle 14**

In the first versions of the draft *Principles* available to the Working Group, both the heading of Section V and the name of the *Principle* under discussion (at that time *Principle 16*) referred to "collateral transactions".[3] The term was eventually corrected to "security transactions". Regardless of the fact that, in very specific areas, the terms "*security*" and "*collateral*" may offer nuances that differentiate them and produce different results (particularly in view of the rules of some States, which mainly opt for one of them in their own legal regime), the use (and thus the change) of either term in the *Principles* has no relevance and no practical consequences. Legally, both terms are meant to produce the same effect, neither altering the ends of the *Principle 14* mandate nor its scope of application. As an example of the two terms being "interchangeable", one can cite, for example, European law (in the context of the contracts and transactions to be defined in each case).[4]

However, the choice of the term "*security*" (which would not only imply a preference, or a random decision, for one of them, but also implies a reflection on the opportunity to exclude the other) is evidence of the Working Group's choice to adopt a common terminology (agreed by consensus among the members of the Working Group). It is a matter of choosing the term that is probably the most established in the most recent international instruments (which are expressly cited in the *Commentaries*, as will be explained below). It is therefore a term that is more easily understood by States familiar with the texts promoting international uniformity, largely because these uniform texts were drafted taking into account the diversity of legal systems and agreeing on a common terminology.

Reaching consensus on legal terms in international instruments requires a complex process, as the concepts are based on well-defined legal traditions and institutions in the laws of States. This national terminology is, in turn, often conditioned by various branches of the legal systems (not only the private and public perspectives in general, but also often the regulatory, registry, insolvency...). The work of the UNIDROIT Working Group was particularly complicated when dealing with legal institutions deeply rooted in the world's two "predominant" systems, *civil law* and *common law*. When it comes to guarantees, the two systems present discrepancies that are not easy to overcome: the former, preserving the traditional formulae of the institutions, resisting novelties that do not fit into its firmly established principles; the latter, more attentive to novelties and to the role they play in new relationships and transactions. Thus, the choice of a term (or the apparent claim to institutions) is

---

[3] *Vid.* https://www.unidroit.org/wp-content/uploads/2022/03/W.G.5.-Doc.-2-Master-Copy-of-the-Black-Letter-Principles-Comparison.pdf.

[4] An example is Directive 2002/47/EC of the European Parliament and of the Council of 6 June 2002 *on financial collateral arrangements*, which in its French version is called Directive 2002/47/EC du Parlement européen et du Conseil du 6 juin 2002 *concernant les contrats de garantie financière* (similar to other countries: Italy, Germany, etc.); while in the English version the name is Directive 2002/47/EC of the European Parliament and of the Council of 6 June 2002 *on financial collateral arrangements*.

not intended to respond (or be conditioned) to the provisions of any particular legal system; it is a terminology specific to the instrument.

The mere formal coincidence of the text with figures of a legal system does not imply the projection (the "international promotion") of that regime of a domestic law; the choice is based on the purpose of facilitating a viable approximation of the systems. It is a requirement of the "jurisdictional neutrality" demanded by the *Principles* in their *Introduction* (see above the commentary on this *rule* which, however, is not included in the text in the form of a *blackletter*, but as a *Commentary* or reflection that would be projected on all the *Principles*).

The most recent uniform texts are bringing the two perspectives closer together. Thus, in many States, as a result of the work carried out by UNCITRAL[5], greater flexibility can be observed in the reinterpretation of national rules on guarantees. Thus,

---

[5] The reference text on uniform law on secured transactions, which was the formal conclusion of the work undertaken by UNCITRAL, is the *UNCITRAL Model Law on Secured Transactions* (2016) (available at https://uncitral.un.org/en/texts/securityinterests/modellaw/secured_transactions); however, the following year it would be supplemented with an ad hoc guide: *UNCITRAL Model Law on Secured Transactions: Guide to Enactment* (2017) (available at https://uncitral.un.org/en/texts/securityinterests/modellaw/secured_transactions/guide_to_enactment). The Model Law does not use the term "collateral" at all in its normative proposal, while in the Guide to Enactment its use is residual (only once, *see* number 378). For the definition of "securities" *see* Article 2 *(hh)*, for "security agreement" *(jj)* and for "security right" *(kk)*. Naturally, there is no need for a specific definition of the term "transaction" in these texts, since the aim is to include within its scope any transaction of a commercial nature or purpose that calls for a security regime, regardless of its name: this is one of the requirements, and the consequences, of the adoption of a "functional" criterion in the design of the security regime designed by UNCITRAL, which means including within its scope of application any contract or agreement whose purpose (and effect) is to secure an obligation.

In uniform texts, it can often be decided to adapt the common (majority) terminology to the terminological specialities required by some states, when it is a question of facilitating the implementation of the uniform text in legislations that offer certain "resistance" or conceptual difficulties in adapting to the new terminology. Generally, these inconveniences would not be insurmountable if the common terminology (a clear commitment to uniformity, its meaning and its results) were to take precedence over the (often limited) perspective imposed by the tradition of national law. In any case, when such a conflict exists and the possibility of overcoming it is seen, the terms or the perspective of the legal figures in the uniform law instruments can be modified (to a limited extent). And in this sense it is noted in footnote 1 (note to the title) of the UNCITRAL Model Law on Secured Transactions that "1 "Secured transaction" means a transaction that creates a security right in a movable asset. Thus, there is no substantive difference between the title of the Model Law in the language versions that do not use the term "secured transaction" and the title of the UNCITRAL Legislative Guide on Secured Transactions". This explains why, for example, in French, the standard is identified as *Loi type de la CNUDCI sur les sûretés mobilières*, and in Spanish, *Ley Modelo de la CNUDMI sobre Garantías Mobiliarias*. The option followed, however, implies a departure from the terminology already decided in previous sessions, as expressed in the "basic" Guide, published in 2007; although it should also be recalled that, since its inception, UNICTRAL Working Group VI was called in Spanish, precisely "Garantías reales" (*see* A/CN.9/WG.VI/WP.1 of 7 February 2002, at https://docs.un.org/es/A/CN.9/WG.VI/WP.1).

Moreover, reference to the work of UNCITRAL is necessary not only because of the texts themselves, but also because of the wealth of studies and analyses on which they are based, which contribute to the dissemination of the Commission's documents but, at the same time, create a new scenario of reflections and contributions, which will inform national rules.

the reference to *security transactions* is a "familiar" expression in the legal sphere and may therefore be more appropriate and feasible to facilitate the incorporation of the mandates and meaning of the *Principles* in one's own national law. The UNCITRAL "system" of "secured transactions" (security interests) provides a rigorous analysis of state-of-the-art security transaction techniques in domestic and international markets. Building on this earlier work, notably the *UNCITRAL Legislative Guide on Secured Transactions* (2007)[6], which would serve as the basis for subsequent work, other guides have been drafted to form an extensive and harmonised body of law. These works are expressly called for by the *Principles* (see, for example, *Commentary 14.3*); sometimes to establish a comparison with the different criteria (or extensions) followed by one and the other institution. In any case, the minutes of the Working Group's sessions, and the very list of its members and guests (who often participated in UNCITRAL's working sessions), show the relevance of the set of texts that make up the "system of guarantees" developed by UNCITRAL for the discussions and the completion of the UNIDROIT *Principles* in that common area.[7]

In its initial versions, the *Principle* (numbered 16)[8] had 5 paragraphs and an extension of number 1. Thus, after the general wording (which has remained essentially unchanged in the different versions, with minimal modifications, due to the "collateral - security" terminology; we will return to this point briefly below), a further sub-paragraph (in number 1) and two more paragraphs were envisaged. This is a modification that is worth noting, at least basically, as these are options on which the Working Group reflected, assessing whether they should be included or maintained in the final text of the *Principles*. In this way, these deletions represent a standpoint. Moreover, it is relevant to determine whether they were excluded either because it was considered that these paragraphs were not necessary (insofar as they would simply develop ideas that were already included in other sections of the UNIDROIT instrument), and would imply a reiteration that could make the *Principles* difficult to understand and harmonise; or because it would involve including "new" provisions or mandates in a general *principle* and presentation of the special security regime, considering that such an extension of the mandate in *Principle 14* was not appropriate or relevant (although, where appropriate, its content could be incorporated in other *principles*). In any case, the Working Group's decision is relevant to delimit ("negatively") the mandate of the *Principle* (and, by extension, also the scope of the *Principles* in relation to guarantees).

---

[6] *Vid*. https://uncitral.un.org/en/texts/securityinterests/legislativeguides/secured_transactions.

[7] *Vid*. https://www.unidroit.org/wp-content/uploads/2022/03/W.G.5.-Doc.-2-Master-Copy-of-the-Black-Letter-Principles-Comparison.pdf.

[8] *Vid*. https://www.unidroit.org/wp-content/uploads/2022/03/W.G.5.-Doc.-3-Master-Copy-Principles-plus-Comments-with-Questions.pdf.

The first of the above options would include the deletion of the text that "developed" or completed number 1 of the *Principle*[9], which called for a broad concept of "digital asset" in the framework of an equally broad interpretation of the idea of "property" (more correctly, "property rights" or "economic rights").[10] At the time, the paragraph was merely a reiteration (in principle, unnecessary) of an idea that is constant throughout the text of the *Principles*, to the extent that it constitutes one of their foundations (the location of digital assets within property law) and whose formal expression is found in *Principle 3.* Its purpose, then, was merely to clarify the very mandate that it would develop, and to promote an interpretation of concepts that, in any event, derived from the correct interpretation of other *Principles* and *Commentaries* of the text.[11]

Although it is not recorded in the debate on this issue that it was stated in these terms, the deleted provision was in fact an expression, not sufficiently refined (although useful, because of its simplicity and descriptive character) of the so-called "principle of functional equivalence". This principle, one of those that make up the set of "principles of electronic commerce - or electronic contracting" was formulated in terms generally accepted throughout the world in the *UNCITRAL Model Law on Electronic Commerce with the Guide to Enactment 1996 with the new article 5 bis adopted in 1998* (New York, 1999)[12]; see articles 5 and 5.bis and 9 of the aforementioned Model Law. Essentially, an adequate application of this principle takes into account the *ratio* and the foundations of the rules, protecting the possibility that the mandate of the precepts, whose formulation was made under the technical and technological imperatives of the moment of their drafting, can be raised above their literal meaning, applying also to new realities if an identity of reason (sufficient functional equivalence) can be appreciated between the old and the new ones. The principle is satisfactorily developed with the concurrence of other previous principles (in particular, the "principle of technological neutrality", which implies drafting and interpreting the rules in terms that are impartial with respect to the technology of each moment (and with the will to apply equally to future technical advances). In the comments to the *Introduction, supra,* I have already had the opportunity to refer to these principles, with regard to the principle of technological neutrality that the

---

[9] The deleted paragraph stated: "(a) References in secured transactions laws to movable assets, personal property or any similar notion should be understood to include digital assets".

[10] It is not appropriate to bring to these reflections the debate within the Working Group (and reflected in the *Principles* and their *commentaries)* regarding the use of the term "property" or "property rights". Both concepts, although different, can produce similar effects; but the latter is more flexible (and therefore preferable) than the former, and would therefore be more easily adopted by states. This is reflected in the *Principles.*

[11] Therefore, in reality, rather than being part of *principle 16* (at that time that was its numbering) it should have been conceived either as a separate principle, or as part of a qualified *commentary* in *the Introduction to* the *Principles,* or, if necessary, by including it in *principle 3* in any of these ways. In sum, what the finally deleted paragraph called for was no more than a consistent interpretation of the *Principles.*

[12] Available at https://uncitral.un.org/en/texts/ecommerce/modellaw/electronic_commerce.

Principles call for; concluding that its absence in the text of UNIDROIT is a lacuna that should be filled in future revisions.

The second option would probably include the two paragraphs, also deleted, which were drafted as separate mandates from number 1, and which developed the *Principle* with particular aspects[13]. The wording was not yet refined because, for example, it simply called for "the law", in general, without specifying that it was in fact calling for the application of "the law of the State" or, in terms of the Principles, "the other law". This was evident from a reading of the *Commentary* accompanying the two paragraphs, which clarified that national secured transactions laws may provide for specific rules for certain types of assets, even if the assets were issued in digital form. Unless amended, the *Principles* would recognise such State law, as it would be embedded in a system of its own, which could not be modified or replaced in the light of the *Principles*: this has never been the objective, but only to limit the scope of application of the *Principles* to digital assets in some respects (incidentally and partially, to linked assets, *Principle 4* and *Principle 14*). Again, these are issues that could be resolved with proper interpretation of the *Principles* (albeit in their most refined version), as they necessarily project onto a prior national safeguards regime, which does not provide for a specific regime for digital assets or which is not aligned with the *Principles.*

2.4 *Analysis and Reflections on* Principle 14

Principle 14(1) is a consequence (an effect) of the choices made in the *Principles*; the content of the *rule* it expresses is necessary, insofar as it derives from other "parts" (*Principles* and *Commentaries*) of the document, with which it must be consistent. Strictly speaking, therefore, there was no need for this *Principle.* Its main usefulness (and this was probably appreciated by the drafters in the Working Group) is to reiterate the idea that digital assets can be the subject of rights (assimilated or in the strict sense) of ownership. The debate on this issue, which involves important differences between legal systems and jurisdictions, is a constant in the text of the *Principles,* both in relation to *blackletters* and in their consideration and application (the *Commentaries*). Notwithstanding the fact that the issue has been resolved in a general way for the whole UNIDROIT instrument (*Principle 3(1): "A digital asset can be the subject of proprietary rights*"), the *Commentaries* frequently return to the issue in an attempt to explain its consequences for different issues addressed by the *Principles.*

---

[13] "(2) The law should provide distinct rules in relation to creation of a security right and effectiveness against third parties for digital assets where their individual features and characteristics are such that the application of specific rules, distinct from those applying to intangible assets generally, would be necessary.

(3) Separation of digital assets from the general category of intangible assets would enable the State to consider specific approaches, such as third party effectiveness by control.

Indeed, notwithstanding these reflections on the necessity in the strict sense of *Principle 14(1)*, the Working Group considered it important to start *Section V* by highlighting again this idea, which implies the consideration of digital assets as a new "form" of property (insofar as they can be the subject of property rights or, in *civil law* terminology, rights of a proprietary nature). Any doubts or assessments about the traditional property regime and its projection onto digital assets can therefore be reproduced in relation to their use as collateral in a transaction. However, a new and different perspective is now added: while the question of ownership in the strict sense obliges, in many legal systems, to rethink the very foundations of the institution (which was not conceived under the parameters sought by digitisation), the use of the digital asset within secured transactions is more concerned with its "value" (that which the parties consider; that is, the capacity or utility so that the asset, its value, can be used to guarantee the performance of an obligation) in the market, than with its nature. Thus, the conceptual effort of revising a legal system is less for the use of a digital asset as collateral (for example, of NFTs representing collectibles); whereas the prospect of recognising the typical attributes of ownership (also of legal standing, if rights are involved) to a digital asset generally requires a greater effort of revision for the rights of States.[14]

The reference to the question of ownership in the *Principles* ultimately involves a call to national law ("other law" in the terminology of the *Principles*) to shape the regime of digital assets as "special" property. Then, as a necessary consequence of this first choice, there is also a call to national law to determine the regime of security interests (at least in the scope of application of the *Principles*) in digital assets. In both cases, State law establishes the intensity of these specialities; which is a limit (at least formally and conceptually) to uniformity. Although this call for the application of national rights is expressed in *Principles 14(2)* and *14(3)*, for the cases envisaged therein (in relation to linked assets), there is no precise statement in this respect in *Principle 14(1)* or in the part of the *Commentary* that refers to it, which is analysed below in these pages.

---

[14] One of the general objectives of the *Principles* is to provide sufficient protection to holders of digital assets, to creditors with security interests in digital assets or, in general, to those who deal in any way with this special type of assets. The most appropriate protection would seem to be to revert to the perspective of property (in the *civil law* systems, probably to the sphere of "economic rights"). This view explains and justifies *principle 3(1)* (under which digital assets can be the subject of property rights). For *civil law* countries the range of possibilities offered would basically be along one of the following lines: that a new rule would recognise that digital assets, not fitting into the usual forms of property (over things or rights, tangible or intangible), would constitute a third category, new and in line with current technical reality; that, by applying the principles of functional equivalence, states would find a way to project previous legislation on digital assets (thus falling into one of the known and regulated categories); or, finally, recourse to an "axiom", such as the mandate of *Principle 3(1)*. States can provide the required protection for digital assets in any of these ways, although the one that promotes the *principles* is, logically, the one proposed, because it ensures (seemingly at least) more easily the uniformity sought, by not involving substantial changes to national laws that legislators might be reluctant to make.

Note that, formally, *Principle 14(1)* does not address the question of ownership of the digital asset, although this is the focus of the (brief) argumentation of the *Commentary*. Its very simple mandate merely provides that "Digital assets can be the subject of security rights". It is in the *Commentary* that the question of ownership as a basis (or for the purpose of equating) for the possibility of security over digital assets is raised (recalled). As indicated above, the issue has already been resolved in *Principle 3*; the perspective taken throughout the text in relation to property rights in digital assets defines an essential (structural) element in the configuration of the *Principles* and in the coherence of their precepts. As a consequence, the *Commentary* concludes: "Security rights are proprietary rights, and, therefore, digital assets can be the subject of security rights".

Such formulation is accurate and, within the conceptual framework established by the Principles, appears to be the only viable one, insofar as it adheres to the functional approach underpinning the entire UNIDROIT instrument. This, however, does not preclude potential interpretative concerns in certain jurisdictions, particularly where the underlying asset giving rise to the digital asset is subject to a special legal regime (e.g. certain rights or entitlements), which may affect both ownership and the legal standing of the purported holder.

Assuming this as the point of departure, the *Commentary* immediately qualifies the initial assertion, doing so in terms consistent with both the objective of *Principle 14* (to address general considerations concerning digital assets in the context of secured transactions) and its systematic placement at the outset of the relevant section. Accordingly, the relevant criterion for considering a digital asset as capable of constituting collateral is not its classification as a proprietary asset per se, but rather its recognition and market value—its valuation or perceived suitability by the parties as a transactional element. More broadly, this rests on the economic interest the digital asset may present for specific transactions.

The *Commentary* further notes that "Principle 14 reflects the general principle that secured transactions regimes should facilitate the use of any type of movable asset as collateral. This approach enables prospective secured creditors to assess for themselves which digital assets may hold collateral value." The recourse to the *Commentary*—given the abstract and open-ended nature of the Principle—might initially suggest the necessity of an ad hoc rule for a matter that, arguably, does not warrant special treatment.

Strictly speaking, the *Commentary* on *Principle 14(1)* is rather limited, consisting solely of a single paragraph—paragraph 14.1—which merely reiterates the aforementioned conceptual reflections. Paragraphs 14.2 through 14.7 shift focus to the broader content of the section, outlining the rationale and orientation of the subsequent *Principles* (14 to 17), which elaborate and adapt, in light of secured transactions involving digital assets, issues already addressed more generally elsewhere in the instrument.

This relatively brief treatment of *Principle 14(1)* contrasts with the extensive deliberations that took place within the Working Group—deliberations that were not so much centred on its wording (which was generally well received), but rather on the implications of referring to proprietary rights in the context of digital asset collateralisation. This again highlights the need to reconsider the necessity and framing of this *Principle.*

Two observations may be offered regarding the normative formulation of *Principle 14*: the first, of a minor—perhaps merely stylistic—nature, concerns its literal phrasing; the second pertains to its material scope of application—namely, the category of transactions to which it is intended to apply. Firstly, the *Principle* states that digital assets may constitute the "subject" of security rights. In some jurisdictions—particularly those rooted in civil law traditions—this reference to "subject" may evoke the notion of the right-holder (i.e. the person to whom proprietary rights pertain), whereas the asset itself would more properly be regarded as the "object" of the security right. Naturally, legal systems (and languages, in both their colloquial usage and technical-legal terminology) have their own conventions and nuances. In this case, the use of "subject" is consistent with the idiom of the Anglo-American legal tradition, under which the *Principle* was drafted. In contrast, in other jurisdictions, the *Principle* might be rephrased either to explicitly state that digital assets are the "object" of the secured transaction, or to clarify that they may be "subject to" (i.e., fall within the scope of) security arrangements.

The second question requires further reflection on the "transactions" that constitute the *raison d'être* of the *Principle* and of the *Section.* Moreover, the *Principles* do not define what is to be understood by "transactions" or, more precisely, what kind of transactions, or in what circumstances, would, by their nature (strictly speaking), be subject to the *Principles.* In fact, although *Principle 14* is called "Secured transactions: general" (as is Section V, in which the *Principle* is located: "Secured transactions"; a heading that would be extended to the rest of the *Principles* that comprise it), its *blackletter* makes mention of the transactions on which, if any, it is intended to apply.

One of the challenges facing the *Principles* is the number and diversity of "assets" that can be represented in digital form.[15] A similar consideration can be made in relation to contracts (or, more broadly, agreements) whose purpose is to constitute forms of security for the performance of obligations: there will be as many contractual models as practice and the needs of entrepreneurs will determine. To a large extent, this difficulty in delimiting the number or typology of transactions derives from the nature of the asset over which the security is provided; in the case of digital assets, moreover, from the regime attributed by national legislation to both the asset and the digital assets themselves. The combination of both aspects implies that, provided that there is a common interest between the parties, attributing value (essentially commercial) to a digital asset, they may enter into agreements that allow the value of the asset to be pledged to the performance of (current or future) obligations. The contractual possibilities would amount to an open and flexible (and probably contested in each jurisdiction) list of transactions that each State may consider appropriate to the scope of application of the *Principles*; some of which will be expressly regulated, with a specific regime, in its domestic law, while others will be allowed within the scope of contractual freedom. It was therefore considered that there was no need either to define or list the "model guarantees" (in the sense of agreements) known

[15] It does not seem possible to draw up a closed or "definitive" list of types of digital assets, as they are constantly being revised, as is the case with the technology that can support them. Certainly, the technology seems stable for the time being, around the so-called "decentralised ledgers (DLT) and blockchain technology (in both cases, on the basis of encryption or digital certificates and electronic signatures). The UNIDROIT *Principles* expressly declare themselves to be "technology neutral". This declaration entails several consequences. Some, as a direct application of the principle: for example, that the wording of the *Principles* does not take into account any particular technology, being applicable to any of them, including (possibly) those to be developed in the future. It thus affects the scope of application of the rule, which considers the past (prior law) and the future (the reality yet to come). Some of the consequences of technological neutrality are indirect: for example, in terms of its consequences, it means that under the scope of application of the rule there is no a priori discrimination of one technology in favour of another. On these issues see some reflections above, in the comments to the *Introduction to* the *Principles*. But if the technology is momentarily "stabilised", its application to goods and rights ("assets") is not exhausted. As new "traditional" assets are incorporated into their digital (electronic) format, new digital assets will be created. The law applicable to these new formats may vary, depending on their nature: from prior law (to the extent that it can be interpreted to accommodate the new reality) to a new ad hoc law, and somewhere in between. And the fact is that, in general, neither the rules nor the legislators nor those who are called upon to apply the precepts (and only partially, society) are familiar with the opportunities and challenges posed by digital technology; and doubts will always arise as to the legal qualification required by such disparate novelties as digital files or digital records, the wide variety of tokens that are emerging (gaming, access, legitimisation, crypto-art, crypto-collectibles, and crypto-gaming tokens…) and the relationship between the figures that are contained in the new rules, and the relationship between the figures that are being created and those that are being created in the digital world.) and what relationship do the classic asset figures have with the regime of domain names, digital financial assets, NFTs, crypto-assets, non-fungible tokens, etc. (which, on the other hand, are sometimes used as a means of payment). (which, on the other hand, are sometimes fungible, such as the so-called crypto-currencies, and in other cases are non-fungible, i.e. digital assets that represent a unique asset that cannot readily be interchanged with other digital assets - visual rights, serial numbers, etc.). In this complex world, moreover, the digitisation of certain assets, which give rise to linked assets, is a further complication.

(or recognised) by the legal systems or markets, always adapted (in their very name or in certain aspects of their regime: creation, effectiveness against third parties, registration, etc.) to the terms of national laws.

Although on the surface, the *Commentary* to *Principle 14* does not provide a useful concept of a "transaction"[16], two ideas stand out from the rest of the reflections and examples in the *Commentary*. The first is the influence of the UNCITRAL texts on secured transactions on the regulation of security over digital assets in the UNIDROIT *Principles*. The mere reading of the *Commentary* shows how the studies and comparisons take the *UNCITRAL Model Law on Secured Transactions* (2016)[17] as their primary basis. Second, the proposal or "guidance" sought by the *Principles* on secured transactions is based on the prior national secured transactions legislation of any State. Thus, to the extent that a State has specific rules for a particular type of asset, including a digital asset (which would be compatible in its design with the *Principles*), those rules should preferably be applied as they stand, without the *Principles* having to assess whether they should be modified. This is a consequence of the line of work followed by UNIDROIT, which (rightly) considers that the essential purpose of the *Principles* is to coexist with national rules and to ensure their adaptation to a uniform regime (the *Principles* can neither replace nor supplant national laws, because they do not offer a viable system, on their own, of secured transactions that would exhaust the regime of digital assets).

2.5 *Specialities of Linked Digital Assets*

The basic regime for linked assets is contained in *Principle 4*[18]. This is a complex matter, not only because of the need to take into account the link between the two

[16] *Commentary 14.2* does provide a definition, although it is formulated not as such in the strict sense, but to delimit the scope of application of the section: "Section V applies to transactions under which a security right in a digital asset is granted to a secured creditor to secure the performance of any existing, future, or contingent obligations of the grantor or another person. These transactions, covered by Section V, are called 'secured transactions' in the Commentary to Section V".

[17] The *UNCITRAL Legislative Guide on Secured Transactions. Terminology and recommendations* (https://uncitral.un.org/sites/uncitral.un.org/files/media-documents/uncitral/en/terminology-and-recs.18-1-10.pdf) did provide a definition ("Secured transaction means a transaction that creates a security right. Although an outright transfer of a receivable does not secure the performance of an obligation, for convenience of reference the term also includes an outright transfer of a receivable"); although the concept would evolve fromalmemte (not so in the guidance) in the *UNCITRAL Model Law on Secured Transactions*, article 2: "(jj) "Security agreement" means: (i) An agreement, regardless of whether the parties have denominated it as a security agreement, between a grantor and a secured creditor that provides for the creation of a security right; and (ii) An agreement that provides for the outright transfer of a receivable".

[18] In the following terms: "The digital assets to which these Principles apply include a digital asset linked to another asset. The other asset may be tangible or intangible (including another digital asset). Other law applies to determine the existence of, requirements for, and legal effect of any link between the digital asset and the other asset, including the effect of a transfer of the digital asset on the other asset.

assets, but also because each asset may have a different nature and legal regime.[19] Thus, in the case of a digital asset linked to a digital image, the two share the same digital nature: However, if the link relates to a negotiable document in digital format (e.g. a bill of lading, document of title), the relevant connection is to the underlying goods—typically governed by the legal regime of constructive possession. The *Principle* addresses the creation and perfection of a security interest; however, in the context of linked assets, the respective assets may be subject to distinct rules governing their circulation and may in fact be transferred independently. This possibility may compromise the legal certainty that a secured transactions framework is intended to provide.

Principle 4 states that the legal effect and existence of the link between a digital asset and some other asset was determined by "other law". *Principle 14(2)* and *14(3)* adopt the same approach, stating that the law of the State determines the legal effect on the other asset of the creation of the security and, likewise, the law of the State determines the effect on the linked asset of the creation of a security interest in the digital asset that is effective against third parties.[20]

---

[19] "Issues which the Working Group may wish to address include, for example: [...] Whether digital assets should be recognised as a specific type or types of collateral to allow the application of rules (e.g., on control) specific to that type only? [...] For instance, for creation of a security interest,

(a) What kinds of property rights the holder has in a digital asset (coordinated with the discussion on proprietary interests)? (b) How does a holder create a security interest where the digital asset is held by a custodian, including where the digital assets are held in a fungible bulk? To what extent should the rules on third-party effectiveness through registration apply and alternative approaches (e.g., some form of control) considered? Assuming "control" would be a method of third-party effectiveness, the actions necessary to acquire control for this purpose will need to be defined, and the following issues considered:

(a) Should "control" perfection have a super-priority over earlier registered interests? (b) Should it be possible to create subordinate security interests in digital assets? (c) Should it be possible for more than one creditor to have control over a digital asset? (d) Should creditors holding security interests in digital assets have the benefit of good faith purchase or other take-free rules? [...] What, if any, special rules should apply to the enforcement of security interests in digital assets? In addition, should certain rules that, for instance, require notification of third parties prior to disposal unless the collateral is sold on a recognised market continue to apply? The application of the existing rules may preclude automated enforcement and liquidation of the collateral triggered by oracles. [...] What are the duties of issuers and third parties (e.g., custodians; explored in detail in a separate section above) vis-à-vis secured creditors who made their security interests effective against third parties by registration? [...]"; cf. Unidroit 2021 - Study LXXXII - W.G.1 - Doc. 3, https://www.unidroit.org/english/documents/2021/study82/wg01/s-82-wg01-03-e.pdf, num. 72; and Unidroit 2020 - Study LXXXII - W.G.1 - Doc. 2, pp. 17 and 18. https://www.unidroit.org/english/documents/2020/study82/wg01/s-82-wg01-02-e.pdf.

[20] The third-party effectiveness of these assets raises a wide range of questions. Thus, the determination of the methods to make them enforceable. For example, the *UNCITRAL Model Law on Electronic Transferable Records* (2017) opts for registration and possession (for tangible assets) as the main methods; although it provides specific rules for assets that allow other methods to be considered: control agreements, designation as holders of bank accounts, (legitimate) possession of negotiable documents, book entries in the case of non-intermediated securities, etc. It also raises questions of priority, which in the aforementioned UNCITRAL text includes, for example, the date of registration.

The formulation of this *Principle* is challenging, as there is a lack of precise terminology to identify each of the assets, to define the nature of the link between them, and to clarify the legal basis of the relationship—whether contractual, statutory, or both—depending on whether the asset in question is tangible or intangible. To facilitate the articulation of the *Principle*, the *Commentary* introduces a distinction between the original asset (referred to as a "real-world asset") and the digital asset (its digital representation). The relationship between the original asset and the underlying goods to which it is linked—e.g., goods being transported (in the case of a bill of lading) or goods held in storage (in the case of a warehouse receipt)—is governed by the law of the relevant State. In both examples, the underlying asset is a tangible good, which simplifies the analysis.

The most illustrative example, in terms of exposition, is that of "documents of title"—instruments that represent the goods and permit their negotiation, and, in some cases, the transfer of ownership (if explicitly provided for in a sale contract), or the creation of security interests. The bill of lading is the most widely known and utilised document of title—including in the context of secured transactions—particularly in international trade. The complex legal relationships surrounding the bill of lading—such as the entrustment of goods to a third party for custody and transport, where the holder lacks direct possession but retains economic interest—have conferred upon it distinctive legal attributes (e.g., negotiability of the document and negotiability of the cargo). This complexity precludes its treatment as merely an ancillary instrument (i.e., the security interest) subordinate to the principal contract (i.e., the contract of carriage) under which the main asset (the document) is issued, representing the underlying marketable goods.

The question of the interaction of all these relationships has been satisfactorily resolved in the field of trade proper to the title. Regardless of the formula imposed by each legal system, the legal and commercial bases of the bill of lading enjoy substantial international uniformity as a consequence of the Brussels Convention of 1924 [International Convention for the Unification of Certain Rules of Law relating to Bills of Lading, signed in Brussels on 25 August 1924 ("the Hague Rules")] and generally accepted international practices.[21]

[21] The so-called "Hamburg Rules" [*United Nations Convention on the Carriage of Goods by Sea* (Hamburg, 1978)], although also in force (https://uncitral.un.org/en/texts/transportgoods/conventions/hamburg_rules), have not been sufficiently well received in the international sphere. For their part, the "Rotterdam Rules" [*United Nations Convention on Contracts for the International Carriage of Goods Wholly or Partly by Sea* (New York, 2008)] have not entered into force (https://uncitral.un.org/en/texts/transportgoods/conventions/rotterdam_rules). But all these texts, each with the prestige of the good work of their drafters and of the body that approved them (UNCTAD and UNCITRAL, respectively) coincide in these aspects in the regulation of the bill of lading. The work of some international associations (e.g. the Baltic International Maritime Council, BIMCO; https://www.bimco.org/) consolidate this international uniformity with their model forms.

Within this internationally defined legal context, supplemented by national laws (i.e., "other law"), the harmonisation of the legal treatment of the bill of lading has proven more achievable. This was reflected in the *UNCITRAL Model Law on Electronic Commerce with Guide to Enactment 1996, with the addition of Article 5 bis adopted in 1998.* Articles 16 and 17 of that Model Law introduced specific provisions for transport documents, aimed solely at enabling their digital processing, while the remainder of the regime remained subject to the legal rules applicable to the carriage of goods. Similar developments can be observed in the *Rotterdam Rules*, which provide for the digital issuance of transport documents and establish rules for verifying control over such documents; in the *UNCITRAL Model Law on Electronic Transferable Records*, which addresses the digitisation of commercial documents based on the principle of functional equivalence; and in the *UNCITRAL Model Law on Secured Transactions*, particularly in Article 16.[22]

By virtue of this, the circulation of the transport document (in general, the endorsement), whether issued in paper or digital format, implies the transmission of the rights incorporated in the title (in *civil law* doctrine, the idea of "incorporation" explains the inseparable link established between the title and the right -to obtain delivery of the goods at destination-, which is the basis of the representative -translative- effectiveness of the title). Thus, the digitisation of the transport document preserves both the contractual and possessory relationship between the document and the goods. It does not, however, affect the underlying contractual obligations, nor does it alter the legal regime governing the circulation or disposition of either the document or the goods, as provided in the relevant contract. The reference in *Principles 14(2)* and *14(3)* UNIDROIT to "other law" accordingly signals the continued application of the pre-existing legal framework governing the document prior to its digitisation, as well as the associated contractual arrangements.

This approach is, in fact, the only viable option in the context of linked digital assets, since digitisation does not—and cannot—alter the applicable substantive or contractual legal rules.

---

[22] "*Negotiable documents and tangible assets covered by negotiable documents.* A security right in a negotiable document extends to the tangible asset covered by the document, provided that the issuer of the document is in possession of the asset at the time the security right in the document is created".

Principle 15
Control as a Method of Achieving Third-Party Effectiveness

María Teresa Touriñán Morandeira and Luis Arnáez Fernández

A security right in a digital asset can be made effective against third parties by control of the digital asset if one of the following requirements is fulfilled:

(a) the secured creditor has control of the digital asset as defined in Principle 6; or

(b) a custodian maintains the digital asset for the secured creditor as set out in Principle 10(2).

1 Office Commentary

Commentary

Reasons for control as a method of third-party effectiveness

15.1. Principle 15 provides that, in addition to any other methods of third-party effectiveness that apply to a security right in a digital asset under other law, a State should recognise that a security right in a digital asset may be made effective against third parties by control. This would apply in a situation where the secured creditor controls the digital asset, but also where a custodian maintains the digital asset for the secured creditor, including through a sub-custodian. Third-party effectiveness

This work was financed within the framework of the Prometeo 2023 project of the Regional Ministry of Innovation, Universities, Science and Digital Society (CIPROM/2022/26) "Present and future of the regulation of cryptoassets in the EU [LegalCripto]", whose principal investigator is Carmen Pastor Sempere. The basic ideas contained herein were presented in the author"s paper with the same title, given on November 13, 2024 at the IV International Congress on "UNIDROIT Principles on Digital Assets and Private Law: Context, Content, Perspectives", organized also by BAES Research Group of the University of Alicante on November 13 and 14, 2024.

M. T. Touriñán Morandeira (✉)
Vilalba, Galicia, Spain
e-mail: mttourinan@registradores.org

L. Arnáez Fernández
Tamarite de Litera, Aragon, Spain
e-mail: larnaez@registradores.org

C. Pastor Sempere and D. A. Morán Bovio (eds.), UNIDROIT *Principles on Digital Assets and Private Law*, Law, Governance and Technology Series 80,
https://doi.org/10.1007/978-3-032-11001-5_21

generally requires a secured creditor to take a step to publicise its security right, which may, for example, include delivery of possession, notification of the obligor, registration, and control. Some of these methods are not applicable to digital assets (e.g., delivery of possession of a tangible object).

15.2. While in many States registration would generally render a security right in most (or all) types of assets effective against third parties (e.g. in all movable assets covered by the UNCITRAL Model Law on Secured Transactions), registrations are not commonly effectuated in the crypto-lending market, leaving some credit risk in the transaction. Furthermore, in States that do not have a registration system for security rights, market participants may not be aware of the digital asset as defined in Principle 6; or Secured Transactions 101 existing requirements for third-party effectiveness or such requirements may be an obstacle to market practices.

15.3. Market participants generally take some steps to preclude the borrower from accessing the encumbered digital asset, typically by transferring it from the wallet of a borrower to a wallet of the secured creditor, or by placing it under the control of the secured creditor (e.g., in a multi-signature arrangement). Under some laws those steps may already be recognised as a method to make the security right in the digital asset effective against third parties. A transfer to a wallet held by the secured creditor or its agent would then be sufficient to protect the security right against third-party claims, including in the case of the insolvency of the borrower. Since these Principles do not interfere with the domestic conception of security rights, the protection in insolvency may be conferred by recognising the third-party effectiveness and priority, or excluding the digital asset from the estate of the debtor because it has been transferred to the secured creditor outright. Under laws that do not recognise such steps, the failure to register may be fatal for the secured creditor. In any case, the existing requirements for third-party effectiveness may create uncertainty for those who take digital assets as collateral.

15.4. Secured transactions and related laws may already provide for change of control over an asset to be sufficient to transfer it, whether outright or by way of security. Where laws already recognise some form of control over specified types of movable assets, security rights in digital assets that would fall under that type of a movable asset could be made effective against third parties by that form of control. For example, this might be the case of digital assets linked to securities held with securities intermediaries, depending on the effect of the link under other law. However, there are likely to be many other types of digital assets for which control mechanisms have not been provided in secured transactions laws.

15.5. In the past, regimes governing security rights in certain types of assets have been amended to reflect the emerging industry practice (e.g. book entries to securities accounts in which financial collateral is held). As mentioned in commentary 15.3, the prevailing practices in 'crypto-lending' do not rely on registration and other traditional methods of achieving third-party effectiveness.

Control as a method of third-party effectiveness

15.6. A State should refer to the definition of control in Principle 6 elsewhere in its law relating to digital assets and, if not, include the definition of control in Principle 6 in its secured transactions law as a means to achieve third-party effectiveness of a security right in a digital asset. Control within this definition exists when a secured creditor acquires a set of abilities with respect to the digital asset. Principle 15 (in conjunction with Principle 6(3) and Principle 10(2)) provides that the secured creditor may exercise the requisite abilities directly, through a third-party custodian or in cooperation with other parties, such as in a multi-sig arrangement (see commentary 6.13). Incorporation of control in the law of a State as a means of third-party effectiveness of a security right will affect the structure of its priority rules, which is explored below in Principle 16 on priority, and facilitate enforcement, which is explored in Principle 17.

15.7. Recognition of control in a secured transactions law consistent with Principle 15 could result in a situation where the applicable law provides for multiple methods of third-party effectiveness. If a digital asset falls under a type of asset for which the secured transactions law has provided one or more methods to achieve third-party effectiveness, a security right may be made effective against third parties by any one of those methods. Principle 15 does not preclude a State from designating control as the sole method of third-party effectiveness with respect to security rights in digital assets, consistently with its general secured transactions law (e.g. the law of a State may provide for control as the sole method of third-party effectiveness with respect to security rights in deposit accounts).

15.8. There are three situations in which control under these Principles may be used to make the security right effective against third parties. First, the secured creditor may acquire the requisite abilities prescribed in Principle 6. Second, the secured creditor may share these abilities with other parties, which would also constitute control under Principle 6 (see further commentary 6.11). Third, a party that is currently in control (e.g. a custodian) may agree to exercise the relevant abilities on behalf of the secured creditor. A version of this third situation is where a custodian maintains a digital for a client by entering into a custody agreement with a subcustodian (see Principle 10(2)).

Control shared by secured creditor and debtor

15.9. Commentary 15.9 to 15.13 addresses the situation where the secured creditor and the debtor share the abilities in Principle 6(1)(a) (this falls within the second situation referred to in commentary 15.8). Principle 6(3) allows these abilities to be shared by multiple parties without compromising the existence of control. However, a person may have these factual abilities but, as a result of an agreement, that person's right to exercise one or more of those abilities may be legally restricted.

15.10. For some (non-digital) assets, other law may already recognise a degree of sharing of the right to dispose of the asset between the secured creditor and grantor without compromising the security right's effectiveness against third parties by control. This may vary from State to State. For instance, a security right in a bank account may be effective against third parties but the control agreement may enable the grantor to dispose of the asset until the secured creditor instructs the depository institution not to honour instructions from the grantor.

15.11. Principle 15 recommends that States design their rule on third-party effectiveness based on the sharing of factual abilities to align with Principle 6. Restrictions on the secured creditor's right to exercise the factual abilities will prevent the secured creditor's control being sufficient for effectiveness against third parties. Examples of such restrictions are where the secured creditor cannot, as a matter of fact, dispose of the digital asset and where the secured creditor is not permitted, by agreement, to dispose of the digital asset without the debtor's consent.

15.12. A State may wish to apply the approach to the third-party effectiveness of security rights with respect to other assets (see commentary 15.10) to digital assets as well. If so, it may be sufficient in some States for the secured creditor to be in a position to exercise control when the debtor defaults, with the debtor retaining the right to exercise the factual abilities until that point. However, other States may require, for third-party effectiveness, that the debtor has no right to exercise the factual abilities. This is a policy choice of the State.

Illustrations of control

15.13. Illustration 1. In State A, which has not adopted the Principles, a secured creditor takes a non-possessory pledge over a portfolio of digital assets. The applicable law does not provide a specific mechanism to make a security right effective against third parties with respect to digital assets but provides that registration is the sole mechanism to achieve third-party effectiveness over any intangible assets provided as collateral. The secured creditor has required its borrower to transfer the relevant digital asset to a third-party wallet controlled by the secured creditor through a multisignature arrangement but does not make a registration. Later, the borrower enters into an insolvency-related proceeding. The secured creditor could lose its security right as it was not made effective against third parties in accordance with the law of State A. On the other hand, in State B which has adopted the Principles into its law, the secured creditor could have made its security right effective on the borrower's insolvency by control.

15.14. Illustration 2. Digital assets are maintained by a custodian for a client. The custodian undertakes to exercise the control abilities for the secured creditor. If the State has incorporated 'control' as a method of third-party effectiveness in its secured transactions regime, the security right will be effective against third parties.

2 General Considerations

2.1 Preparatory Work

In the elaboration of Principle 15, which sets out the standards for action on third-party effectiveness of security rights in movable assets, two fundamental moments can be distinguished. Firstly, the work carried out in March 2021, which establishes four fundamental principles that should govern the subsequent drafting of the Principles discussed herein (Study LXXXII – W.G.2 – Doc. 2 (rev. 1), pp. 32–35; Study LXXXII – W.G.2 – Doc. 3, pp. 15–22), and secondly, the subsequent meetings in which these principles of effectiveness against third parties, which are now included in the final document, were finalised (Study LXXXII – W.G.3 – Doc. 2 (rev. 1), pp. 44–49; Study LXXXII – W.G.4 – Doc. 2, pp. 49–55).[1]

About the principles listed with the letters A, B, C and D, three basic lines have served to structure the security right:

Digital assets may serve as collateral for obligations
The asset may be collateralised and this power should be recognised as a basic principle of the digital law on collateral.

> *Principle B: Digital assets are eligible as collateral*
>
> The law should permit the use of any digital asset as collateral. References in law to chattel, personal property or any similar notion for collateral purposes should be construed as including digital assets, regardless of whether the digital assets are characterised as property or are liable to a proprietary right in that jurisdiction (Study LXXXII – W.G.2 – Doc. 2 (rev. 1), p. 33).

Parties are free to create mechanisms of security rights in digital assets
In this context, several mechanisms of security rights may be created, and these may range from a mere transfer of possession to a fiduciary ownership of the thing given as collateral, provided that this is allowed by the law of each State.

> In this Principle, (*Principle A* ***Secured transactions law applies to digital assets***) the reference to "secured transactions" shall typically include transactions creating various types of **security rights**, such as **pledges**, **encumbrances** or **security assignments**, but also **outright transfers** where these may apply to certain types of digital assets, such as those that are functional equivalents of **securities** or **receivables**. The **Geneva Securities Convention** regulates collateral transactions created by the granting of an interest in intermediated securities, in the form of **security interests** and **title transfer collateral agreements**. The **UNCITRAL Model Law** applies to outright transfers of receivables. Some domestic laws provide for **fiduciary transfers of ownership** transferring ownership of the asset to the creditor with the sole purpose of securing an obligation. It is therefore important that secured transactions law should be coordinated with a State's generally applicable rules governing outright transfers of digital assets.

[1] More information at: https://www.unidroit.org/work-in-progress/digital-assets-and-private-law/#1622753957479-e442fd67-036d.

In this sense, the security interest set out primarily involves a transfer of possession or control of the asset, giving rise to the final enunciation of the principle under discussion.

> A secured transactions regime may define a security right as a **right in rem over a movable asset**, without defining "movable asset". On the one hand, individuals may grant interests in any of their assets, whether tangible or intangible, present or future. This contrasts with more restrictive laws, and lists specific types of assets that can be encumbered. Such an approach may require amending the law permitting to use digital assets as collateral. On the other hand, the notions of **chattel, personal property, assets,** or **objects** that may be liable to a security right are generally left undefined in secured transaction regimes, leading to uncertainty as to whether these notions cover digital assets.
>
> A security right may not be defined by law, but rather understood in **case law** and **doctrine** as a right in property. Under these regimes, a security right may be created in any type of property, tangible or intangible, present or future; anything that is transferable and identifiable.
>
> Some laws permit the creation of an interest in anything that can be traded, including intangible assets. Although **stock, claims** or **rights** may be listed as examples of intangible property in the relevant statutory provision, it is typically unclear whether digital assets would be covered. In principle, under these regimes, an interest can be created in any intangible property, including digital assets. However, an explicit treatment in the legislation would provide greater **legal certainty**.

Security rights may be given irrespective of the extent of the asset holder's right in the asset

To collateralise an asset, it is not necessary that the collateral holder is also the owner of the proprietary right in rem over the asset, but collateral over more limited rights in rem is also admissible.

> *Principle C: Security rights may be created over the rights and powers of the grantor concerning digital assets.*
>
> The law should facilitate the creation of a security right in the digital asset through an agreement between the parties [Note: depending on the structure of these principles, general statements of this nature may or may not be necessary for the individual principles]. The law should allow any person to create a security right in a digital asset to secure any type of obligation, even if the person does not have a right in the digital asset that qualifies as a proprietary right under the generally applicable law, but has the power to transfer control of the digital asset. The law should not require a detailed or technical description of the digital asset in a security agreement, and should automatically extend the security right to any income from the digital asset. (Study LXXXII – W.G.2 – Doc. 2 (rev. 1), p. 34).

On the other hand, in the discussions after this principle, the considerations made at the sixth meeting are remarkable. At that meeting it was established:

– The need for a system for the return of collateral to the creditor if the asset is held by a custodian as a mediate possessor of the asset.

  One Member of the Working Group noted that two issues could be considered in addition to the substantive rules on the insolvency of a custodian. The first would be to have a substantive rule stating the insolvency representative should cooperate to have the digital asset distributed or returned to clients in the event of insolvency. The second issue would be what would happen if there was a shortfall and how to manage it.

- Establishing a differentiation between the custodian and sub-custodian on the basis that the latter executes on behalf of the custodian and not the principal client.

  One Member of the Working Group added that the duties of a custodian and sub-custodian were not the same. The client would not have a general right to enforce in the insolvency of a sub-custodian, but rather that would be a right that the custodian would enforce on behalf of the client.

3 Reflections

The Principle at hand regulates the effect the right created based on that act or agreement may generate against non-parties in the agreement on digital assets. The purpose of the following reflection is to answer the following questions:

1. To what type of digital assets could this Principle refer, or if it could apply to all types of digital assets (relationship between Principle 15 and Principle 2).
2. How does this Principle fit in with the principles governing the applicable substantive law (relationship between Principle 15 and Principle 5).
3. The effect the original term "effectiveness", literally "*efectividad*" but translated as "*oponibilidad*" in Spanish, has.
4. How the term custody or deposit is construed concerning Principle 6.
5. To what alternative means of producing "effectiveness" the article (concerning Principle 16) could refer.
6. What the practical purpose of this article is.

An attempt to provide a possible answer to these questions shall be made, from the perspective of Spanish law, following, to a certain extent, the same thread as the original Commentaries on the text.

About the type or concept of digital asset to which this Principle would apply, it is obvious that these Principles repeatedly state and affirm that although the digital asset defined in Principle 2 brings together pure and non-pure assets, and may therefore have a physical or immaterial underlying, the Principles only regulate the transfer of the digital asset as it results from Principle 5. According to the latter, the transfer of the real asset is left to "the other law",[2] i.e. it is up to domestic law to regulate the

[2] This conclusion in an international arena is consistent with The Uniform Fiduciary Access to Digital Assets Act, adopted by the UNIFORM LAW COMMISSION (hereinafter ULC), defines in its Sect. 2–10 the Digital asset as.

"an electronic record in which an individual has a right or interest. The term does not include an underlying asset or liability unless the asset or liability is itself an electronic record"

That expressly excludes underlying assets.

conditions under which the "link" is made and the transfer of the digital asset, which in turn, implies the transfer of the underlying real-world asset.[3]

Thus, the possible issuance of one or more digital assets representing all or part of an asset does not interfere with the collateralisation rules, contractual rules and rules relating to the transfer of ownership of such assets. It is also consistent with the operation of the registrations of non-fungible assets (whether movable or real estate, tangible or intangible assets, provided that they are liable to registration), since even if it is held that digital assets can represent all or part of an underlying asset (tangible or intangible), the agreements and situations liable to registration shall not relate to the digital asset but to the underlying asset. Therefore, the token itself does not alter the content and scope of the existing registrations and entries in the registers that reflect the publicity of the traditional legal system.

> *(a) the law applicable to the third-party effectiveness of a security right in a digital asset that has been made enforceable against third parties by a method other than control; (b) the law applicable to determine the priority between conflicting security interests that have been enforceable against third parties by a method other than control.*

This is explained and developed in the original UNIDROIT Commentaries when it is explained that 5(5) by expressly mentioning in 5.22 and 23 that:

> *it would be inappropriate to determine the law governing a registration system for security rights, which must be based on objective indicia (...) that could be recognised by a third party searcher of the registry (...) and provides the other law to determine the law applicable to determine the priority between such conflicting security rights.*

This aspect is reiterated when addressing Principle 16, with which Principle 15 must reconcile since the UNIDROIT Commentaries 16.(5) lay down that:

"such as funds held in an online bank account. Because records may exist in both electronic and non-electronic formats, this definition clarifies the scope of the act and the limitation on the type of records to which it applies. The term includes types of electronic records currently in existence and yet to be invented. It includes any type of electronically-stored information, such as (1) information stored on a user's computer and other digital devices; (2) content uploaded onto websites; and (3) rights in digital property. It also includes records that are either the catalogue or the content of an electronic communication. This text does not contain any conflict of law provisions".

At the European level, it is consistent with the NIZA classification.

Also at the national level with the General Directorate of Taxes in a binding consultation of 2022:

"the NFT or non-fungible 'tokens' are digital certificates of authenticity that, through blockchain technology (the same that is used in cryptocurrencies) is associated with a single digital file. Therefore, the NFTs act as unique digital assets that cannot be exchanged with each other, since no two are alike and whose underlying asset can be anything that can be digitally represented such as an image, a graphic, a video, music or any other digital content, including works of art as may be, where appropriate, those that are liable to consultation".

[3] See, in this volume, Reflections to Principle 5 ant Principle 2.

Principle 5(1) determines the Law applicable to a conflict between a security right that has been enforceable against third parties by control and a competing security right that has been enforceable against third parties by means other than control, such as registration. As specified in Principle 5(5)(b), other rules determine the law applicable to a conflict between security rights enforceable against third parties by a method other than control.

In other words, it is the domestic and substantive law that shall make such a decision protected from the claimed effectiveness against third parties.

However, what is the practical reason for this decision of breakdown and necessary normative coexistence? The question is logical insofar as the full applicability of the Principles is only possible in pure digital assets, whose disposition for trade is global and transnational, and which are not determined or guided to intimately relate to the legislation of a specific State. The applicability of the DALP though, creates a legal vacuum that voluntarily refers to it being covered by the conflicting rule at stake when talking about non-pure digital assets (representative of a tangible or intangible asset in the real world), given that the DALP voluntarily leaves the underlying asset out of its regulation by not establishing rules on the link or connection between the real asset and the digital asset.

Therefore, what is the logic of establishing a system of third-party effects if, on the one hand, third-party effects are regulated by "the other law" and the priority between collateral is also left to "the other law"? Indeed, for pure digital assets, establishing a means of third-party effectiveness to determine who is protected in the event of multiple secured creditors or cases of fraud and double selling may make sense. Furthermore, unlike non-pure digital assets (linked to an underlying asset), where other means of publicity may take place, custody seems to be the chosen one as it gives control over the asset.

However, the actual applicability of the Principle is limited. On the one hand, because if custody according to Principle 6 is equivalent to control, and control is equivalent to possession,[4] the very example put forward by UNIDROIT in its Commentaries is blurred, since referring to the non-possessory pledge, Principle 15 takes us back to an ordinary pledge which is legally an older contract and less benign for the debtor. This is so because according to the DALP, control is equivalent to possession and, therefore, the collateral is not without displacement (without transfer of possession if it is assumed that control is equivalent to possession). On the other hand, if the concept of control is relevant for deposit or custody, cases of concurrence of creditors with control over the same thing shall be hardly found since the current state of technology leads to the sole use of the keys associated with that digital asset which are not shared. Consequently, in legal terms, that would rather be a case of creditor subrogation and not exactly a case of a collision of creditors and priority of collateral.

[4] In this context, having possession of a digital asset is equivalent to having control over that asset. When control is held by a custodian, it is similar to the role of a mediator in possession. This gives rise to the classic distinction between mediate possession and immediate possession, or that of the possessor as owner and possessor other than owner.

Lastly, it is to be explained to what type of means of control Principles 15 and 16 may refer. It is not expressly mentioned in the Principle itself but in its explanatory Commentaries, UNIDROIT apparently understands it as referring to the information registers that may exist concerning the digital asset. In this sense, it shall in practice be construed as the wrongly named records or book entries that may have been made within its network or through the custodian concerning the digital assets. Given that the other means of control are left to "the other law", the possibility of collision with legal registers is implicitly excluded, as they are alien to this aspect of the legal system since their purpose is to collect publicity against third parties of the security rights over the underlying asset. However, this underlying asset, whether material or immaterial, has never been a digital asset, and if it were, registration would not relate directly to the token and would not encumber it in itself, but to the act or contract generated. Moreover, in this last, and for the time being, still improbable case, the priority is determined by the *Lex registrationis*, which, according to the DALP, would be "the other law" and which, in the case of legal registers of mere effectiveness or material and substantive effect against third parties (such as the Spanish one), legislation undoubtedly gives it prevalence over any other means of control or possession, physical or virtual, concerning the creation of security interests enforceable against third parties to legally regulated domestic registers, as it shall be seen later on.

It would therefore seem that for DALPs to be enforceable in a broader sphere than the uniquely digital, the only thing left to do is to urge lawmakers to establish, where appropriate, a system for accessing this token, either entirely uniquely virtual or linked to a tangible or intangible real-world asset, to legally register non-fungible movable assets, if it has not already been done.[5] In the unlikely event that the pure digital asset were to access the corresponding legal registration it would be governed by the rules of the latter to be fully operational against third parties in the real world, with control or custody as means of effectiveness, therefore, disappearing in this new reality.

[5] According to Spanish law regarding chattel mortgages and non-possessory pledges, security rights tied to digital assets may be registered in the property register as per Articles 45 and following.

Following these initial considerations, the doctrinal question of control as a means of third-party effectiveness of the security right, and whether this is the most effective way of protecting the balance between the interests of the debtor and the creditor, shall be analysed.

To this end, let us begin with some conceptual problems.

3.1 Conceptual Problems

Firstly, the question from the point of view of the law of things and the traditional doctrine on rights in rem must be analysed.

When dealing with the characteristics of all rights in rem, the Roman doctrine transferred to our civil law fundamentally distinguishes between immediacy, creditor's right of pursuit and third-party effectiveness.

Immediacy refers to the direct and immediate power that the holder has over the thing liable to our right.

A creditor's right of pursuit relates to the capacity of the holder to pursue the thing to the place where it is located, under the Roman principle: *ubi rem mea invenio, ibe vindico.*

Third-party effectiveness refers to the holder's power to enforce it against all third parties.

These characteristics are capable of being all rights in rem, so they are drafted as a flexible scheme that allows rights in rem to be configured in different ways, providing them with different content, but respecting the basic scheme of action.

In this sense, Professor Diez Picazo (1978, Vol. II, p. 41) states:

> "The concept of a right in rem is defined by the coordinates forming the immediate and absolute character of this special type of legal power".

Immediacy and possession must not be confused in any way.

As pointed out, immediacy is the power to enjoy the right, directly over the thing, without the need for intermediaries, although this immediacy does not necessarily imply possession, a quality that is only predicable of rights in rem involving possession as one of their intrinsic powers.

In this sense, rights in rem entailing possession, such as ownership or usufruct, and rights in rem not entailing possession, such as mortgages, can be distinguished. In both cases, the holder shall have immediate power over the thing, even if it does not entail possession of the right.

Effectiveness and possession should not be confused either. Effectiveness is capable of being asserted over all rights in rem, regardless of whether they incorporate possession within the list of their powers.

Thus, José María Miquel González (Vol. II, p. 2367) states:

> "The right in rem is characterised by the absolute enforcement of the actions protecting it, which means that the holder can bring actions against anyone unaware of or who harms their right (...) the absolute exercise of the power is manifested in various effects, firstly, in the all-encompassing nature of the actions in rem against any third party".

The right in rem is by nature enforceable, since, as pointed out, effectiveness is one of the essential characteristics of all rights in rem. Any system of defence of rights in rem must guarantee the capacity of any holder to make their right enforceable against all. This effectiveness has historically been guaranteed by two main means:

3.2 *Publicity of the Right in Rem and the Factual Element of Possession*

Concerning publicity, which is articulated through the Land Registry, Pau Pedrón (2004, pp. 28–29) states:

> "There is no doubt, therefore, that rights in rem are enforceable in themselves, without the need for publicity (...) Consequently, the Land Registry does not attribute effectiveness to rights in rem, because these rights are already endowed with these effects before accessing publicity. The only thing that the registry does is hinder this effectiveness and place restrictions on it. Hence, from a strictly civil perspective, we should not speak of the effectiveness of the Registry, but only of ineffectiveness".

The same author, namely Pau Pedrón (2004, pp. 28–29) continues by stating that some data of a different nature needs to be taken into account:

1. One of a sociological nature. The effectiveness derived from the contract could be justified in societies other than today's, with reduced population centres, in which the creation of rights could be known through the contract (...) but today businesses do not have, in themselves, a solemnity and publicity that transcend. The mode or tradition, still preserved in Spanish law, is probably a residue - atrophied, minimised - of that solemnity and publicity, but today it does not fulfil that function at all. The maximum degree of uselessness of the publicity of the negotiation is in the instrumental transfer of the possession, which is hidden in a secret protocol.
2. Another of a strictly legal nature. As Diez Picazo has written, "Law is not an abstract and general formalisation with a universal value, which aims to shape human conduct so that the future conforms to pre-established models. In law, what is primary and immediate are conflicts of interest to which a solution must be found, the most correct or the most acceptable one." In this matter, there is a conflict of interests between the holder of the right and the third party, between the transferor and the transferee. The effectiveness derived from the contract resolves this conflict in an unbalanced way, protecting only one of the interested parties. I believe it is in this sense that Miquel writes: "The claim to absolute effectiveness of rights in rem implies a need for publicity, which is manifested in a very special way through the Land Registry and to some extent also through

possession, although the publicity function of possession is usually exaggerated and not always correctly understood".

As this author points out, possession is the classic element which has served as the basis for the publicity of rights in rem and allows for achieving effectiveness against all.

However, this publicity system, based on the immediate control of the thing, is less effective than that provided by the security system through a public register.

In this sense, possession fulfils a function more related to immediacy or direct power over the thing, provided that this possession is integrated into the list of powers of the related right in rem.

It should be borne in mind that there is an amalgam of rights in rem that are not characterised by possession and whose effectiveness cannot be publicised in this way.

In this group, security rights in rem are of vital importance, whose main function of serving as a basis for future enforcement cannot, and must not, result in a loss by the holder of the real right of ownership of the enjoyment of the products that the thing may bear while it is fulfilling the function of security.

3.3 *Terminological Clarification*

In the context of the Principles at hand, a digital asset is defined as any electronic document, in the sense of information stored on an electronic medium and capable of being retrieved, which can be liable to control. This definition is in line with the spirit of the Principles, expressed in Principle One, which are intended to serve as international standards concerning the regulation of rights in rem over digital assets. Therefore, their function is to serve as a framework and guideline so that all laws relating to digital assets can be covered by them.

However, this broadness in the definition is the root of certain problems when it comes to specifying the basic structural elements of the law of things, such as cases of transfer or encumbrance. When working with such a broad concept of digital assets, the classification of digital assets must be subject to further analysis in order to establish how each of these categories behaves in the security interest referred to in this Principle.

Three fundamental types of digital assets can be considered, where:

1. The digital asset, in the token sense, is a mere representation of an underlying asset that is also a digital asset. In this sense, the asset works as a token representing a digital file and has value on its own.

   This type of asset only serves an on-chain digital reality, as they only exist and develop in a digital ecosystem.
2. The digital asset, in the token sense, is a representation of an underlying asset that exists in the off-chain world. In this case, the asset fulfils the function of a

digital document representing the ownership of the physical asset, but without integrating this right in rem.

In this case, the digital document is drafted as a private right with the disposition of a right in rem, but it does not imply immediate acquisition of this right in rem.

3. The digital asset, in the token sense, represents the underlying asset that has a correlation in the off-chain world and also incorporates the right in rem on the underlying asset.

   In this case, depending on the nature of the underlying asset, movable tokens, if the underlying property is movable, and real estate tokens, if the underlying property is real estate, can be distinguished.

Characteristically, these assets incorporate the right in rem to the digital asset only if the material law of each State (the other law) recognizes this connection or link between the digital asset and the underlying asset, by incorporating the former, the right in rem, on the latter, as analysed in the section on reflections.

When analysing the use of digital assets as collateral, the need to analyse each of these categories is obvious, to see how this collateral works in each case and whether the concept of control envisaged for them can produce the same effects and whether or not it is the most appropriate mechanism for these purposes.

Before moving on to analyse this, it is necessary to expose the existing models of security rights for the objects of the physical world in order to know the consequences and effects that a similar deployment would have in the digital world.

Security rights are classified in accordance with their origins, according to a double criterion:

1. The existence or not of displacement of possession to the creditor.
2. If the asset over which the security right is created, is movable or real estate.

Regarding displacement of possession, mortgage and pledge are distinguished.

The mortgage has been drafted, ever since Roman law, as a security right in rem which does not entail possessory displacement, which had undoubted advantages for the holder of the security right in rem, but above all, for the holder of the possession of the mortgaged thing.

For the former, a security right is created, enforceable against all, but which does not generate any expense in the conservation of the thing, since they do not have direct possession of the thing, but a right of preferential enforcement.

The latter allows them to continue owning the thing, which entails its full control, allowing the receipt of results and the defence of their right. In addition, the collateral value is preserved as a promotion of the territorial credit, insofar as the property already mortgaged can be remortgaged. This establishes a priority and preference system that, depending on the systems, have come to be dominant in the Roman system, in which each mortgage has the mortgage rank of the date on which it is created, or of the plots of value, typical of the Germanic system, in which the objective value of the mortgaged property is parcelled, allowing the creation of as many mortgages as there are plots of value. On this basis, the principle of freedom of ownership is respected, since the subsequent alienation of the mortgaged thing is allowed regardless of whether or not it is mortgaged.

This security system has worked best in private law, due to the advantages described above, even if it requires the establishment of a strong system of publicity, through property registration, making these security rights enforceable against all, regardless of the possessor or owner of the mortgaged property at any given time.

On this matter, García García (2019, Vol. I, p. 1140) argues:

> "Registration is a legal requirement of the existence of the right since the lack of registration prevents the enforcement of the foreclosure action, and just the personal claim derived from the loan would be possible".

Even so, what are the features the mortgage presents, compared to the other rights in rem, of which the registration cannot be claimed?

1. The mortgage is a right constituted by registration. It is invisible and can only be known by the Register.
2. There is no possessory displacement when acquiring the mortgage title.

Regarding this second requirement, Sanz (1945, p.36) states:

> "For the mortgage right in rem there is no transfer of the possession since possession is alien to it. That is why our Civil Code replaces it with the registration in the land registry, which is necessary for the mortgage right in rem to become enforceable".

This strengthening of the registry function in mortgage matters is established to end the situation of hidden encumbrances on real estate before the Land Registry, which the acquirers did not have the opportunity to know at the time of acquisition.

On this point, the Mortgage Law of 1861 pursues the publicity of the Mortgages through the establishment of the fundamental principle of publicity as one of its fundamental principles, which implied the disappearance of the hidden and general mortgages, to establish the territorial credit, based on the security of the mortgage and the payment of what was offered.

In contrast to the mortgage, security rights in rem are developed, requiring the displacement of possession of the thing from the holder of the collateralized thing to the secured creditor. The most important case of this type of collateral is the pledge.

A pledge arises as an alternative to the mortgage right in rem based on the difficult identification of the pledged object, which, due to its movable nature, is difficult to pursue in the event of a breach of the obligation. Possession is thus constituted as the legitimizing element of the creditor's power. Therefore, this right becomes immediate and direct for the creditor, and in some way enforceable against third parties, preventing a transfer of possession not held by a person other than the creditor or their representative in possession.

The legislation on collateral developed after the Civil Code demonstrates that the transfer of possession is a lesser evil. This last choice is available to the creditor if immediacy and effectiveness cannot be achieved in any other way. In this sense, the doctrine construes that the requirement of the transfer of possession has no other purpose than to produce a state of fact that hinders the possibility of material disposition of the thing by the pledgor.

On this matter, Castán (2015), Vol. II, pp. 737–738) criticizes the pledge right in rem when stating:

> "The pledge has had an importance in history. The concept of this contract or right in rem - indicates Covián - has a character of permanence from the most ancient times to the present, which reveals that its origin obeyed a need commonly felt by mankind. But despite this, it must be recognized that the pledge offers great practical disadvantages, motivated by the harm caused to the owner by the loss of possession of the pledged thing. The mortgage is a much more perfect form of collateral, which, if it has not completely replaced the pledge, is because of the difficulty it presents, in the case of certain types of property, to secure the rights of the creditor without putting them in possession of the thing. The mortgage - Planiol says in this respect - offers perfect security, whenever there is no reason to have the material disappearance or concealment of the thing; thus it works marvellously for real estate and ships. But for tangible movable assets that the creditor can easily hide or pass into other hands, the mortgage does not fulfil any function".

He is therefore pacific in the scientific doctrine that, if there is a possibility of collateral not entailing loss of possession, preference must be given to the one entailing this transfer of possession. Similarly, the Spanish law on chattel mortgages and non-possessory pledges meets this need for more efficient forms of collateral, embracing the new dimension adopted by chattel in the current social context.

In this sense, the preliminary recitals of this law state:

Law of 16th December 1954, on Compulsory Expropriation

The traditional pledge and mortgage rights in rem, with their respective limitation to chattel and real estate, and with their characteristics of displacement and non-displacement of possession, is undoubtedly insufficient to meet all the needs of the security right. Scientific doctrine emphasized the serious disadvantages of depriving the debtor of possession of the pledge, especially in the case of valuable chattel for agricultural or industrial purposes. The displacement of possession is detrimental to the debtor, by depriving them of adequate assets; to the national economy by paralyzing elements of work and production and, with them, sources of wealth; and even to the creditor by reducing the debtor's economic capacity and the possibility of meeting their obligations in a normal manner. The experience demonstrated that the pledge was being reduced to merely sumptuous things, for being ineffective concerning things necessary for the work of man; and when necessity made it necessary to pledge the latter, the disastrous practical results of the collateral made clear the need for another legal entity to overcome its disadvantages.

On the other hand, the newly acquired importance of movable things at the momentum of modern industrial development and the appearance of new property in the legal sense, difficult to classify among movable assets or real estate, led to think of the so-called pledge without non-possessory pledge and chattel mortgage, making the security right viable for this property, difficult to adapt to the classic models due to their value or their nature.

In general, legislation has partially solved the problem taking into account the different objects liable to collateral. The non-possessory pledge and chattel mortgage was accepted in many countries under the mechanism of agricultural, rural or farming, livestock, hotel, automobile or business or commercial establishment pledges.

Security rights can also be classified according to the nature of the asset given as collateral, thus distinguishing between chattel and real estate.

In the case of real estate, identification is clear, so that, once the security right in the property is created, the disappearance or concealment of the collateralized object does not entail any risk for the creditor. That is why real estate is not collateralized by delivering the thing, and only the mortgage right in rem on it is admitted.

Having said that, chattel historically has required the transfer of the thing to the creditor to secure its collateral. Therefore, the pledge has been identified with the chattel, and the mortgage with the real estate.

However, modern doctrine on collateral replaces this Roman classification and emphasizes the identifiability of the chattel. Therefore, collateral which does not require the transfer of possession may be created when the chattel is liable to identification and registration in a registry. This registry shall enable publicity similar to real estate publicity on collateral created in it.

Regarding this concept of identifiability, Article 1: "Scope of application" of the Law on Instalment Sale of Chattels refers to:

Article 1. Scope of Application

1. This Law's purpose is to regulate instalment sale contracts of non-consumable and identifiable tangible chattel, loan contracts intended to facilitate their acquisition, and the collateral constituted to ensure the fulfilment of the obligations arising therefrom.

2. For this Law, identifiable property shall be considered to be all those in which the trademark and serial or production number are indelibly or inseparably marked on one or more of their fundamental parts, or which have some distinctive characteristic that reasonably excludes their confusion with other property (Law 29/1998, of 1th July, regulating Contentious-Administrative Matters)

These considerations about the identification of property have allowed the application of concepts proper to the mortgage right in rem to chattel, giving rise to the chattel mortgage or the pledge of incorporeal rights.

Three important conclusions can be drawn from these considerations:

1. The possessory displacement, in the sense of the factual and legal control of the collateralized thing is detrimental, in general, to the holder of the thing and the promotion of the credit, since it blocks the economic content of the collateralized thing.

   In this sense, Diez Picazo (2008, p. 158) states:

"We believe that the idea of *causa servitutis* is a very useful factor for solving the problem of the limits of atypical rights in rem in those legal systems admitting the *numerus apertus*. To constitute an atypical right in rem, the pure and simple will of the owner or the will of the owner in agreement with another person is not enough. It is necessary that the social economic function, with the conveyance of the right in rem to be obtained, demand the special form of affectation of the property that the right in rem carries with it and that the legitimate utility to be obtained and the nature of this utility, about the property forming it, impose it".

2. Modern legislative trends focus on effectiveness through a publicity system based on a legal property registry, in which the priority between security rights conveyed concerning the same thing is defined.
3. The residual value of possessory displacement as a collateral measure is relegated to the category of fungible chattels that are not susceptible to identification.

3.4 How Is This Classic Doctrine Coordinated With Security Systems for Digital Assets?

Given the foregoing, the issue of security over digital assets can be addressed to determine the most logical interpretation of Principle 15, which imposes the control of assets as a means of collateral.

At the outset, it must be noted that in the on-chain world the concept of control fulfils the purpose that is given to the possessory displacement of the collateralized thing in the off-chain world.

What this Principle entails, therefore, is the admissibility, as a precedent form of collateral, of the pledge over any other form, such as the mortgage. This statement is apparently contradictory to the trend followed by the doctrine and modern legislators described above since the exception becomes a general rule.

As pointed out above, the very broad concept of digital assets expressed in these Principles requires that any analysis intended to address any issue relating to them must take into account the classification given on these assets. Thus, the given question shall be addressed by attending to the three types of assets listed above:

3.4.1 Digital Assets That Do Not Have a Correspondence to an Underlying Asset of the Off-Chain World and That Only Have Virtuality and Existence in a Digital Ecosystem

In this case, purely digital cryptoassets may be found, such as cryptocurrencies, or NFTs not referenced to analogue realities.

The list of assets found in this category is not homogeneous either, since, as it has been exemplified, assets can have different characteristics, which shall now be examined:

Consumability: A property in general, and an asset in particular, is considered fungible when it is substitutable for another within the same type to which it belongs. Among fungible assets, cryptocurrencies can be highlighted, as they represent an asset substitutable by another asset of the same nature.

Identifiability:[6] It deals with the feature of individualization, so that, despite being characterised by its belonging to a certain type, this type can be delimited, making identification of the asset or group of them possible within the type of belonging.

The doctrine has named this group of assets "assets limited as to use".[7]

Utility: According to this categorisation, assets representing a utility outside the chain and those only serving as a means of payment in the digital ecosystem can be distinguished. As a categorisation of the latter, cryptocurrencies, or tokens serving as a means of payment can be considered. As an example of tokens that generate utility, tokens representing membership rights can be referred.

Based on this classification, the classic concept of collateral with transfer of possession in the case of control assets shall necessarily apply to assets that are fungible, non-identifiable, and that do not provide a utility to the holder, beyond that of serving as an element of transfer or exchange within the chain of ownership, and that are not fungible. This interpretation shall be more uncertain when the asset is non-fungible, identifiable and also provides a utility to the holder.

In that event, the cases in which the non-possessory pledge causes prejudice to the debtor or holder of the pledged thing, which is not entirely justified considering that this system could be satisfactorily replaced by another of publicity, and the advantages that this provides as exposed above, shall be approached.

In this sense, modern legislation, and Spanish legislation in particular, answers this question by registering non-fungible, identifiable and non-consumable digital assets in the Property Registry. The collateral issued on these assets is publicized in the Property Registry which additionally allows to endow them with priority, conserving the economic value of the thing and channelling the principle of freedom of ownership.

It should be noted that digital assets, as a movable element existing in a distributed registry environment, are susceptible to programming by the issuer of the asset, it being possible to draft this publicity regime in the asset's code itself, so that ignorance of publication of the collateral in the Registry cannot be opposed by any third party who is aware of the content of the asset.

---

[6] The law on the chattel mortgage and non-possessory pledge uses this concept to classify the property which can be or cannot be liable to this collateral.

[7] In the digital world, this limitation of types can be done through different means such as assets' negotiation in different platforms or marking tokens drafted to create a certain effect.

3.4.2 Assets Representing a Private Right Associated with a Property Outside the Digital Ecosystem

Within this category, the following assets can be found: digital assets representing a collection right within the category of what are traditionally called transferable securities, securities representing aliquots of the capital of a company, contractual securities relating to chattel, or the misnamed real estate tokenization, which incorporates partner rights in vehicle companies owning the real estate, or debt issuance contracts made by these same entities.

As previously seen, this category also has a heterogeneous composition, but the assets are characterised by the fact that they refer to an element outside the digital network of which they are part.

In this context, the collateral mechanisms over them can be classified into three models of pledge, recognized by scientific doctrine and most modern laws:

- Pledge of securities: Negotiable securities are drafted as a movable object, endowed with economic content, which can be liable to the pledge. In this sense, negotiable securities attribute a certain utility to their holder, so a case of collateral in which it would be preferable to opt for the effectiveness derived from publicity and not for that derived from possession or control is faced.

  On this matter, the Pilot Regime applicable to the Spanish stock market, introduced the establishment of encumbrances on securities represented by means of distributed registration technologies in its Article 12, providing:

  2. The establishment of the encumbrance shall be enforceable against third parties from the moment when the corresponding registration has been made (Law 6/2023, of 17th March, on Securities Markets and Investment Services).

- Pledge of Rights: The Pledge of Rights is an issue liable to debate in the doctrine, due to their characteristic incorporeal nature.

  On this matter, Felipe Clemente de Diego y Gutiérrez points out:

  > "When a right is pledged, it is clear that a pledge right in rem as the one studied cannot be conveyed since the right in rem requires a tangible thing; but a right is formed by the model or type of the right in rem, which can give satisfaction to the creditor if their debt is not yet paid".

  More specifically, the pledge on credits poses certain problems, since it is considered in the event of a transfer of the credit title, a conditional assignment of the credit, made for collateral purposes.
- Securities: legislation on securities, such as bills of exchange, cheques and promissory notes, allows that such rights represented in the form of securities are also liable to collateral, through the delivery of the title, called an endorsement.

  In this sense, the transferability of the title is blocked by the creditor, who keeps their own title while waiting for the satisfaction of their right. It is referred to by the law under the denomination collateral value or pledge value.

From these examples, the fundamental criterion to be extracted is that, in those cases in which the collateral so requires, the digital asset must be transferred to the creditor, operating analogously to the securities seen, as the creditor has no other mechanism to enforce its security.

However, there are cases such as negotiable securities, in which possession is replaced by registration.

3.4.3 Digital Assets Embodying a Right in Rem Over the Object Represented in the Off-Chain World

Digital assets embodying a right in rem over the thing represented are liable to the collateral regime of the underlying asset, which has a great influence not only on the type of security right in rem admitted but also on the law applicable to them, which shall be the law of the place where the asset is located, in general, as analysed.

Logically, the collateral shall only apply to tokens referenced to movable assets, but not to the so-called real estate tokens, which are outside the scope of the pledge, being only liable to the collateral mortgage.

For chattel, the collateral is admitted in the case of specific and determined property, or property limited as to use, since the former can be identified, and the latter is limited concerning a place where they can be deposited.

As previously mentioned, in the case of the former, it would be more appropriate to resort to forms of collateral that do not diminish the utility of the ownership's holder, such as the chattel mortgage or non-possessory pledge.

Regarding the latter, the pledge regime is similar to the so-called warrants.[8]

This mechanism refers to the case in which certain merchandises are placed with a depository agent, being represented through deposit receipts.

In this sense, the transfer of this receipt implies the transfer of the merchandise within the indicated place, allowing the creditor to enforce the collateral in case of non-payment of the secured obligation.

At this point the need for the property to be stored in a specific place must be taken into account, understanding that this is the only way that the fiction of the possessory transfer required by the pledge is fulfilled.

This regime would be analogically applicable to digital assets that refer to property of this nature, also taking into account the need to identify them by means of a physical deposit of the assets in a specific place.

---

[8] In Spanish law, this figure is regulated in Articles 193 and subsequent of the Commercial Code, being highlightable to this purpose, Article 194:

"The receipts general deposit warehouses issue for the products and merchandise that they accept for custody will be negotiable, will be transferred by endorsement, assignment or any other transferable title of ownership, depending on whether they are nominative or to the bearer, and will have the strength and value of commercial knowledge. These receipts will necessarily express the type of merchandise, with the number or quantity they represent" (Royal Decree of 22nd August 1885, in which the Code of Commerce is published).

3.5 Conclusions

From the above, we can derive three conclusions regarding Principle 15:

1. Application of the Principle concerning the effectiveness of security interests in digital assets against third parties may present significant conflicts in Private International Law when the asset is connected to off-chain physical or real property, in which the security system is governed by "the other law." This conflict does not arise, or at least not with the same intensity, in the case of purely digital assets that exist solely within the digital ecosystem.
2. The concept of effectiveness does not fully align when referring to control of the digital asset, as it implies confusion between the concepts of enforceability and immediacy. Enforceability through possession has been generally rejected by domestic doctrine in favour of enforceability derived from public registration in a rights registry.
3. It is necessary to categorise assets into three classes, according to the presence or absence of an off-chain reality with which they are associated, and to apply the criterion of control transfer, or possessory transfer, to those assets that exhibit characteristics of fungibility, easy concealment, and absence of rights beyond utility within the chain of transmissions. When these requirements are not met, security systems that do not entail possessory transfer, such as chattel mortgages or pledges without dispossession, should be employed.

References

Castán Tobeñas J (2015) Derecho civil español, común y floral. Tomo VI, Derecho de sucesiones. Volumen 2, Los particulares regímenes sucesorios. La sucesión testamentaria, forzosa, intestada, contractual y excepcional. Reus Editorial, Madrid

Diez Picazo, L. (2008). *Fundamentos del Derecho civil patrimonial* (Vol. III). Thomson Civitas.

Diez Picazo y Ponce de León L (1978) Fundamentos del Derecho civil patrimonial. Vol. II. Las relaciones obligatorias (Estudios y comentarios de legislación). Thomson Civitas, Madrid

Digital Assets and Private Law Working Group // Second session (remote) // Rome, 16 – 18 March 2021 //// UNIDROIT 2021 // Study LXXXII – W.G.2 – Doc. 2 (rev. 1) // English only // March 2021. https://www.unidroit.org/english/documents/2021/study82/wg02/s-82-wg02-02rev-01-e.pdf Last visited 28th January 2025

Digital Assets and Private Law Working Group // Second session (remote) // Rome, 16 – 18 March 2021 //// UNIDROIT 2021 // Study LXXXII – W.G.2 – Doc. 3 // English only // April 2021. https://www.unidroit.org/english/documents/2021/study82/wg02/s-82-wg02-03-e.pdf Last visited 28th January 2025

Digital Assets and Private Law Working Group // Third session (remote) // Rome, 30 June – 2 July 2021 //// UNIDROIT 2021 // LXXXII – W.G.3 – Doc. 2 (rev. 1) // English only // June 2021. https://www.unidroit.org/english/documents/2021/study82/wg03/s-82-wg03-02-rev01-e.pdf Last visited 28th January 2025

Digital Assets and Private Law Working Group // Fourth session (hybrid) // Rome, 2 – 4 November 2021 //// UNIDROIT 2021 // LXXXII – W.G.4 – Doc. 2// English only // October

2021. https://www.unidroit.org/wp-content/uploads/2021/11/Study-82-WG4-Doc.-2-Revised-Issues-Paper-1.pdf Last visited 28th January 2025

García García J M (2019) Legislación hipotecaria y del crédito inmobiliario (1ª ed.), Vol. I. Aranzadi, Navarra

Ley de 16 de diciembre de 1954 de expropiación forzosa https://www.boe.es/eli/es/l/1954/12/16/(1)/con Last visited 28th January 2025

Ley 29/1998, de 13 de julio, reguladora de la Jurisdicción Contencioso-administrativa https://www.boe.es/eli/es/l/1998/07/13/29/con Last visited 28th January 2025

Ley 6/2023, de 17 de marzo, de los Mercados de Valores y de los Servicios de Inversión https://www.boe.es/eli/es/l/2023/03/17/6/con Last visited 28th January 2025

Miquel González J M (1994) Derecho real. In: EJB, Madrid, vol. II, p. 2367

Pau, A. (2004). *La prioridad registral: Un nuevo enfoque*. Fundación Beneficientia et Peritia Iuris.

Real Decreto de 22 de agosto de 1885 por el que se publica el Código de Comercio https://www.boe.es/eli/es/rd/1885/08/22/(1)/con Last visited 28th January 2025

San Hernández A (1945) Comentarios a la nueva Ley Hipotecario. Viuda de M. Navarro, Madrid

UNIDROIT (2023) UNIDROIT Principles on Digital Assets and Private Law. Rome (Italy): International Institute for the Unification of Private Law (UNIDROIT). ISBN 978–88–86449–49–6 https://www.unidroit.org/wp-content/uploads/2024/01/Principles-on-Digital-Assets-and-Private-Law-linked-1.pdf Last visited 28th January 2025

UNIDROIT (2023) Principle 15 Control as a method of achieving third-party effectiveness. UNIDROIT Principles on Digital Assets and Private Law. Rome (Italy): International Institute for the Unification of Private Law (UNIDROIT), pp. 100–104. ISBN 978–88–86449–49–6 https://www.unidroit.org/wp-content/uploads/2024/01/Principles-on-Digital-Assets-and-Private-Law-linked-1.pdf Last visited 28th January 2025

Principle 16
Priority of Security Rights

Pablo Sanz Bayón and Rafael del Castillo Ionov

A security right in a digital asset that is made effective against third parties by control in accordance with Principle 15 has priority over a security right in the digital asset that is made effective against third parties only by a method other than control.

1 Official Commentary

Commentary
Priority of secured creditor with control

16.1. Principle 16 addresses the situation where one secured creditor has made its security right in a digital asset effective against third parties by registration or another method recognised by the applicable law, but has not obtained control of the digital asset, and another secured creditor has made its security right in the same digital asset effective by control (pursuant to Principle 15). In this situation, Principle 16 provides that the latter would have priority even if it took the steps to obtain control after the former made its registration or otherwise made its security right effective against third parties. This is in contrast to the general rule (under the UNCITRAL Model Law on Secured Transactions and in many States), which is that the priority among competing security rights in the same asset is determined based on the temporal order of when the security right was made effective against third parties

This work was financed within the framework of the Prometeo 2023 project of the Regional Ministry of Innovation, Universities, Science and Digital Society (CIPROM/2022/26) "Present and future of the regulation of cryptoassets in the EU [LegalCripto]", whose principal investigator is Carmen Pastor Sempere. The basic ideas contained herein were presented in the author's paper with the same title, given on November 13, 2024 at the IV International Congress on "UNIDROIT Principles on Digital Assets and Private Law: Context, Content, Perspectives", organized also by BAES Research Group of the University of Alicante on November 13 and 14, 2024.

P. Sanz Bayón (✉)
UNED National University of Distance Education, Madrid, Spain
e-mail: psanz@der.uned.es

R. del Castillo Ionov
CEU San Pablo University, Madrid, Spain

C. Pastor Sempere and D. A. Morán Bovio (eds.), UNIDROIT *Principles on Digital Assets and Private Law*, Law, Governance and Technology Series 80,
https://doi.org/10.1007/978-3-032-11001-5_22

(typically, the order of registration). However, the law may grant priority to security rights in certain encumbered assets that are made effective against third parties by using a specific method for obtaining third-party effectiveness. For example, a security right in a negotiable instrument that has been made effective against third parties by possession typically has priority over other security rights made effective against third parties by other means. Similarly, the law of a State may recognise asset-specific priority rules for bank accounts, intermediated and non-intermediated securities, money, negotiable documents, and other types of assets.

16.2. This approach, applied to digital assets by Principle 16, may be justified in a number of ways. First, providing for the non-temporal priority recognises that the secured creditor that took the additional steps was relying to a greater extent on the encumbered asset. This is similar to a situation where a secured creditor takes possession of a negotiable document, which would give it priority over a security right made effective against third parties by registration, under some domestic regimes. Second, the secured creditor who made its security right effective against third parties by control would not need to search the registry. Again, this is similar to the position in relation to other assets, such as negotiable instruments, in that a party taking possession is not expected to search a registry, which reduces the cost of dealing with the asset and enhances its negotiability. Moreover, it is often not practical for a secured creditor taking security over a digital asset to search the registry. For transactions with digital assets, the prospective secured creditor might not even know which registry to search as the transferor, or its identity or its location, might be unknown. Third, this priority approach also reflects the lending practice ('margin lending') where creditors may extend credit to their clients to enable them to acquire a digital asset with respect to which they expect to have priority over an earlier-in-time registration. Fourth, it aligns the priority position with the position on default, when the secured creditor in control is best placed to enforce the security right, and provides an incentive for secured creditors to place themselves in this favourable position. By giving a secured creditor the ability to obtain priority, the rule contributes to market certainty. Moreover, the approach in Principle 16 is consistent with the secured transactions rules in international instruments, including the UNCITRAL Model Law on Secured Transactions and the relevant provisions of the Geneva Securities Convention, that give priority to secured creditors that acquired some form of control over the collateral.

16.3. In most States, other law has conferred some degree of transferability, typically negotiability, on some assets that allows transferees to cut off security rights made effective against third parties by registration or other means. For instance, a transferee of money takes free of a security right if it takes possession of money without knowledge that it violates the rights of a secured creditor. A transferee is defined in these Principles to include a secured creditor (see Principle 2(5)). Since these Principles confer a high degree of negotiability on digital assets, their transferees (including secured creditors, see Principle 2(5)) will be able to benefit from the same approach, set out in Principle 8. Most secured creditors would be expected to satisfy the requirements of the innocent acquisition principle, including acting in good faith, without any disqualifying knowledge and extending value that a State may impose in accordance with Principle 8(1)(b). This is particularly true because, as described above, a secured creditor that makes its security right effective against third parties by control will not be expected to search any secured transactions registry. While under Principle 8 a secured creditor may qualify as an innocent acquirer only if it acts without knowledge of a competing interest, the effect of Principle 16 is that the secured creditor that takes control would have priority over one that registers irrespective of knowledge. The same result would be achieved under many secured transactions laws, including the UNCITRAL Model Law on Secured Transactions (see Article 45) which provides that knowledge of a competing security right does not affect the priority of a security right.

Control by more than one secured creditor

16.4. More than one secured creditor can obtain control (or share the relevant abilities) over the digital assets, which includes making their security right effective against third parties. This situation may arise where the digital asset is held by a custodian who agrees to maintain the digital asset for multiple secured creditors. Generally, the two creditors would be expected to regulate their respective priority in a subordination or inter-creditor agreement. In the absence of an agreement, the priority conflict may be determined based on the general priority rule contained in the applicable secured transactions law, which would typically reflect the first-in-time principle, i.e., the secured creditor who was the first to obtain an acknowledgment of the custodian would have priority.

Applicable law

16.5. Principle 5(1) determines the law applicable to a conflict between a security right made effective against third parties by control and a competing security right made effective against third parties by means other than control, such as registration. As specified in Principle 5(5)(b), other law determines the law applicable to a conflict between security rights made effective against third parties by a method other than control. For instance, under the UNCITRAL Model Law on Secured Transactions the law applicable to the priority of a security right in an intangible asset is the law of the grantor's location. This priority conflict is not addressed in this Principle, and is a matter of general secured transactions law. 16.6. Illustration. A security right in all the assets of the borrower is made effective against third parties by registration. Upon disposal of encumbered inventory by exchanging it for digital assets, those digital assets are collected by the borrower and deposited with a custodian that has control over the digital assets. The custodian extends a loan to the borrower that is secured with all digital assets under its control. The security right of the custodian has priority over the security right in the digital assets claimed as proceeds of the inventory, assuming that the secured transactions law recognises control as a method of obtaining effectiveness against third parties (see Principle 15), and gives priority to a security right made effective against third parties by control (see Principle 16).

2 Reflections

2.1 Context and Background

Principle 16 is part of a global legal landscape in full transformation, indelibly marked by the emergence and proliferation of digital assets—a category that ranges from the well-known cryptocurrencies and non-fungible tokens (NFTs), to *stablecoins* and other emerging digital financial instruments.[1] This new technological and economic reality has created an urgent need to adapt the traditional rules governing secured transactions, originally designed for a world of predominantly tangible goods, to the particularities of this new digital environment.

Principle 16, in particular, establishes a priority rule that gives preference to the secured creditor that obtains "control" over a digital asset, over other creditors who have made their rights effective in different ways, such as registration. This provision represents a significant innovation in the field of guarantee law and, to some extent, a break with the classical paradigms that have dominated this area of law for decades.

In order to fully understand the scope and significance of Principle 16, it is crucial to analyse the historical and normative context in which it is framed in detail. Traditionally, the right of secured transactions—also known in the Anglo-Saxon sphere as "secured transactions law"—has been based on two fundamental pillars to determine the priority between several creditors competing in the same asset: the publicity of the lien and the temporal priority in its creation.

Publicity, which is generally achieved through the registration of the security right in public registers—whether of movable property, commercial or other specialised registers—or, in some cases, through the physical possession of the asset subject to the guarantee, has the primary objective of making the existence of said lien known to third parties, thus protecting potential purchasers or other creditors. On the other hand, temporal priority, which is summarised in the general principle *prior tempore, potior iure,* establishes an apparently simple rule: the creditor who first registers his security right, or who makes it enforceable by other legally recognised means, has preference over creditors who do so subsequently.

However, the emergence and rise of digital assets, as defined in Principle 2(1) of the UNIDROIT Principles as *controllable electronic records* and further characterised in Principle 6, have posed a real challenge to these traditional pillars of security law.

Digital assets, in their diversity, share a number of characteristics that distinguish them from tangible goods and make it difficult to directly apply the classic rules. They

[1] Principle 16 was initially raised as Principle 17 or 18, during the shaping of the development of secured transactions.

lack physical corporeality, exist and are transferred through technological networks that are often decentralised and based on *blockchain* technology, and their market value can experience significant fluctuations in short periods of time. These inherent peculiarities of digital assets complicate, and in some cases make the application of traditional mechanisms of publicity and priority impossible.

Dematerialisation resulting in the absence of a specific physical location prevents the existence of a single, centralised, and universally recognised "place" where a lien on a digital asset can be registered in a way that is enforceable *erga omnes*. A token, NFT, or cryptocurrency "exists" in distributed networks, on *blockchains*, or on centralised platforms, but without a precise geographic location that allows for the application of traditional rules on registration.

Added to this difficulty is the inherent speed and cross-border nature of transactions with digital assets. These operations can be executed in a matter of seconds and across multiple jurisdictions, making the exhaustive verification of possible prior taxes registered in registries—which are usually national or, at most, regional—an extremely complex, costly and, in practice, unfeasible task in many cases.

Last but not least, the "possession" of a digital asset does not materialise in the physical possession of it, as is the case with a traditional movable property, but is manifested in the "control" of the private keys or the technological mechanisms that allow the asset to be disposed of. This concept of "digital control" differs radically from the classical notion of possession and therefore requires a new legal approach.

Against this backdrop of technological and conceptual disruption, the normative response prior to the adoption of the UNIDROIT Principles was characterised, at the global level, by its fragmentation and, in many cases, by its manifest insufficiency. The vast majority of national secured transactions laws lacked specific rules designed for digital assets, anchored as they were in concepts and categories designed for a world of predominantly tangible goods.

At international level, while providing a valuable general framework for the modernisation of this area of law, the UNCITRAL Model Law on Secured Transactions did not address the crucial issue of priority in the specific context of digital assets in detail, leaving an important regulatory gap. At the European Union level, sectoral regulations, such as Regulation (EU) 2023/1113 (TFR) on transfers of funds and certain crypto-assets, and Regulation (EU) 2023/1114 on Markets in Crypto-Assets (MiCA), focused mainly on the regulation and supervision of crypto-asset service providers, establishing rules on authorisation, transparency and investor protection, but leaving–the issue of priority of rights in the field of private law in the background, or directly failing to address it, which is precisely the fundamental aspect for the efficient functioning of secured transactions.

Within this context of regulatory fragmentation, the Uniform Commercial Code (UCC) of the United States represented a notable exception and, ultimately had a decisive influence. The amendments to Article 9 of the UCC, which governs secured transactions, incorporated the concept of "control" as a mechanism for perfecting (i.e., making effective against third parties) a security right in certain types of intangible assets, including, first, "negotiable electronic records" and, more recently, "digital assets" themselves.

This innovative approach, which gives priority to the creditor exercising effective control over the asset, beyond mere registration, had a significant and direct influence on the drafting of Principle 16 of the UNIDROIT Principles. In fact, Principle 6 of the UNIDROIT Principles, which precisely defines the concept of "control" in the context of digital assets, is directly inspired by the conception and regulation of the UCC.

The adoption of this control-focused approach however, was not without intense debate and controversy. In order to understand the depth of the normative change that Principle 16 entails, it is essential to highlight the internal discussions that took place within the UNIDROIT *Steering Committee* during the process of developing the Principles.

In the initial phases of the discussion, there was strong resistance to the idea of giving priority to the creditor who had control of the digital asset regardless of whether or not it had knowledge of the existence of prior security rights registered in a registry. Several members of the Committee expressed concern that this rule might undermine the fundamental principle of good faith, which has traditionally been a pillar of contract law and the law of guarantees, as well as the legal certainty that, at least in theory, public records provide. However, after intense deliberations, the argument prevailed that the particular nature and intrinsic characteristics of digital assets—their high negotiability, ease of transfer, and the inherent difficulty, if not impossibility, of carrying out thorough and reliable registry verification in a digital and cross-border environment—justified this departure from the traditional rule of temporal priority and the adoption of a new paradigm based on effective control.

2.2 Functional Approach to Security Rights in Secured Transactions

2.2.1 Terminological Note

The term *secured transactions* refers to credit-granting transactions carried out by financial institutions with commercial companies to finance their activity. Such transactions are characterised by the fact that repayment or amortization of the credit is guaranteed by the creation of a security right (almost always movable) over the debtor's assets (the company receiving the credit).

The problem arises from the fact that in the law of the Roman civil tradition (Civil Law) this concept of secured operations or transactions does not exist. This type of transaction is regulated in different legislative bodies, without there being any specific regulation for them. In turn, in the tradition of Civil Law, the guarantees provided in these transactions are also widely varied and are governed by different regulatory texts.

However, it is well known that Common Law dominates the world of business and international financing. This is why we are increasingly encountering the concept of "secured transactions" in international financing transactions. Although the term secured transactions may not be the most correct outside of English, it can be assumed for the purposes of this analysis. The concept of secured transaction encompasses what in continental civil law is usually conceived as two different transactions, but which in common law are intimately linked. On the one hand, there is: (i) the granting of secured credit; (ii) and on the other hand, the constitution of the guarantee (security interest) that ensures repayment of the credit.

Both transactions are usually carried out simultaneously. The concept of secured transaction therefore refers both to the operation of granting the secured credit and to the guarantee itself granted by the debtor and which, is almost always a movable guarantee. The two transactions can be carried out through two independent contracts—a credit agreement and a security agreement—or in a single contract that includes all the agreements of the parties. Since this legal concept did not exist in many non-English-speaking countries, it was decided to refer to the second part of the transaction considering that this name was more correct, and for Spanish speaking readers, for example, it would be easier to understand.

The Model Law refers: *"Secured transaction" means a transaction that creates a security right in a movable asset. Thus, there is no substantive difference between the title of the Model Law in the language versions that do not use the term "secured transaction" and the title of the UNCITRAL Legislative Guide on Secured Transactions.*

The purpose of a secured transaction is to provide credit to businesses in a simple, fast and affordable way, while the lender obtains guarantees of repayment of the credit. The parties involved are: (i) the credit institution, which acts as lender (also called debtholder and secured creditor); (ii) and the company that receives it, which is the debtor or borrower. The credit transaction usually takes the form of a loan or a credit facility.

2.2.2 Scope of the Categories Used: Collateral, Registration, Asset and Control

A debtor's security is not a guarantee, but a security interest by which the lender acquires a right in rem over one or more of the borrower's goods or assets. A pledge is therefore constituted on the assets given in guarantee, which are usually referred to as collateral. Transactions secured by real property guarantees such as mortgages, which are regulated differently in the field of real-property law, do not usually fall into the category of secured transactions.

There are a considerable number of advantages for the lender in this type of transaction, since repayment of the credit does not depend on the mere promise of the debtor, but the lender receives a special security right, that is, a security right over certain assets. This allows the lender to exercise control after default, in order to recover the credit without litigation and to have priority in case of bankruptcy.

In the event that the debtor does not repay the credit that has been granted within the agreed terms, the lender may enforce the guarantee in order to obtain the amount owed. Many forms of movable assets or personal property can be created: such as the borrower's inventory; their receivables; and on equipment or machinery—but also on digital assets. To this end, Principle 16 provides a priority criterion based on the concept of control. It is worth mentioning in this regard that Sect. 2 of the Uniform Fiduciary Access to Digital Assets Act, adopted by the Uniform Law Commission (ULC) defines the Digital Asset as "an electronic record in which an individual has a right or interest. The term does not include an underlying asset or liability unless the asset or liability is itself an electronic record".

2.2.3 Scope of the Object of Secured Transactions with Digital Assets

The conceptual definition of "digital asset" expressly excludes underlying assets, such as funds held in an online bank account. Since records can exist in both electronic (book-entry) and non-electronic (analogue) formats, this definition clarifies the scope of the law and the limitation of the type of records to which it applies. The term includes the types of electronic records that currently exist and others that have not yet been invented.

2.3 Significance of Principle 16

2.3.1 Critical Analysis of the Fundamentals of Priority by Control According to UNIDROIT

The wording of Principle 16 introduces a substantial modification to the traditional priority regime in secured transactions, by providing that a security right is created through the "control" of the digital asset.

As defined in Principle 15, control prevails over any other security that has been made effective only through alternative mechanisms, such as registration in a public registry or any other method of publicity other than control. This rule represents a significant break with the classic principle of temporal priority, allowing a later creditor in time to displace an earlier creditor in priority, as long as the former manages to gain effective control over the digital asset in question. This regulatory innovation is not arbitrary, but is based on a series of practical and theoretical considerations that reflect the particular nature of digital assets and the dynamics of the market in which they are traded.

The Official UNIDROIT Commentaries, which accompany and explain the text of the Principles, provide several justifications for this innovative control-based priority rule. First, it is argued that the creditor who goes to the trouble and bears the cost of gaining control over the digital asset is demonstrating a greater degree of trust and commitment to said asset as collateral for the underlying obligation. This greater degree of implication, which bears some analogy to the taking of physical possession of movable property in traditional security rights, justifies, from this perspective, the granting of a position of higher priority.

Second, it is argued that the option of control as a mechanism for the creation and perfection of the guarantee reduces the need to resort to registration and, therefore, reduces transaction costs. Given that the digital nature of these assets facilitates their direct and immediate control by the creditor, it is considered that verification of the existence of previous encumbrances registered in registers—which can be multiple, geographically dispersed and difficult to access—is considered to be less relevant and efficient than simple takeover. This justification is similar to that underlying the priority by possession rule in the case of negotiable instruments, where possession of the physical title gives preference, regardless of any registration.

Thirdly, the Official Commentaries refer to the practice of "*margin lending*" in the crypto-asset environment. In this type of financing, it is common for the creditor to finance the acquisition of a cryptoasset by the debtor, with the expectation of obtaining direct control over said cryptoasset as collateral for the loan. This practice, which has spread rapidly in the industry, is based on the premise that control gives the creditor a secure priority position and relieves it of the need to carry out complex and costly searches in multiple records, whose reliability and integrity can also be questionable.

Finally, it is argued that control-based priority is aligned with effectiveness in the enforcement of the security. The creditor that has effective control over the digital asset is in the best position to enforce the collateral and liquidate the asset in the event of default by the debtor, without the need to resort to complex and potentially time-consuming judicial or administrative proceedings.

The consequences of this control-based priority rule are profound and significantly alter the security rights landscape. First, and as already mentioned, there is a break with the rule of merely temporary priority. Even if creditor "A" has registered its security right in a public registry beforehand, and creditor "B" then subsequently acquires "control" over the same digital asset, creditor "B" will displace creditor "A" in priority.

Second, and even more remarkably, Principle 16 does not require that the creditor obtaining control do so in good faith, i.e., without knowledge of the existence of prior security rights registered in favour of other creditors. Even if creditor "B" is aware of the existence of the security right registered by creditor "A", the rule of priority by control prevails, giving "B" preference. This provision departs from the traditional doctrine of acquisition in good faith and has generated heated debates.

It is also important to analyse the interaction between Principle 16 and the innocent acquisition rule set out in Principle 8. The latter principle states that a creditor or acquirer acting without knowledge of the existence of conflicting rights over the digital asset can benefit from special protection. However, even in the event that the controlling creditor becomes aware of the existence of a previously registered security right in favour of another creditor, Principle 16, consistent with the position taken by the UNCITRAL Model Law on Secured Transactions in articles 45 et seq., confers priority on control, reaffirming the primacy of this mechanism over registry publicity in the context of digital assets.

While it is true that the UNCITRAL Model Law on Secured Transactions provides a general and internationally harmonised framework for secured transactions, it does not, however, specifically address the issue of priority in the context of controllable digital assets. Despite this omission, it is possible to identify significant points of contact and divergences between the UNCITRAL Model Law on Secured Transactions and Principle 16 of the UNIDROIT Principles.

On the one hand, there are notable convergences. The UNCITRAL Model Law on Secured Transactions, like Principle 16, recognises that, in certain circumstances, possession or control of an asset may confer priority over registration. This rule applies, for example, to negotiable securities and intermediated securities. Principle 16, in this sense, extends this logic, already present in the UNCITRAL Model Law on Secured Transactions, to the new category of digital assets.

Similarly, Article 45 of the UNCITRAL Model Law on Secured Transactions provides that a creditor's knowledge of the existence of a competing security right does not affect the determination of priority, a rule that is in line with the approach of Principle 16, which gives priority to the controlling creditor, even if the creditor has knowledge of the existence of a prior registered security right.

On the other hand, there are important divergences. The UNCITRAL Model Law on Secured Transactions, as a whole, continues to place greater emphasis on registration as the primary and preferred method of perfecting a security right. Principle 16, on the other hand, establishes a significant exception to this general rule, by prioritising control over registration for digital assets. This is a fundamental difference. Moreover, the UNCITRAL Model Law on Secured Transactions does not define the concept of "control" in the specific context of digital assets in the very detailed and precise manner that Principle 6 of the UNIDROIT Principles does. This lack of specific definition leaves a normative gap that Principle 16, with its innovative approach, seeks to fill.

2.3.2 Control-Based Priority: Configuration, Features and Effects

The configuration of the Principle is based on the definition of "control" set out in Principle 6. This concept, which is fundamental to the application of the rule, encompasses both direct control—exercised by the creditor himself through the possession of the private keys or technological mechanisms that make it possible to dispose of the asset—and indirect control—exercised through an intermediary, such as a custodian, acting on behalf of the creditor, and that it contractually undertakes not to carry out any transaction without its consent.

It is crucial to note that Principle 16 applies exclusively to controllable digital assets, which excludes those assets that, by their very nature or the way they are designed, cannot be subject to exclusive or shared control by a creditor. The priority by control rule, while displacing registration or other methods of publicity as a determining factor of priority, does not completely eliminate them from the legal landscape. These mechanisms may still be relevant for other purposes, such as third-party effectiveness of the security against third parties in general, or for the creation of security rights in non-controllable digital assets.

There are various defining characteristics of control-based priority, and they mark a substantial difference from the traditional regime. Firstly, it is an absolute priority. The creditor that obtains control over the digital asset displaces any other creditor that does not have control, regardless of the temporal order in which the competing guarantees have been created or made effective. The date of registration, or any other form of publicity, becomes irrelevant for the purposes of determining priority.

Second, and even more remarkably, priority by control operates, in principle, irrespective of the controlling creditor's knowledge of the existence of prior security rights created in favour of other creditors. The good or bad faith of the controlling creditor, in this context, is not a determining factor, which represents a significant departure from the traditional doctrine of acquisition in good faith. This feature has been the subject of debate and criticism, as will be discussed below.

Third, priority by control has a marked possessory character, even if it is a digital "possession" or one mediated by a custodian. Control, in this sense, is assimilated to the physical possession of a movable asset in terms of its effects of publicity and opposability against third parties. Fourth, the possession of control greatly facilitates the enforcement of the guarantee in the event of default by the debtor.

The legal effects of priority by control are therefore far-reaching. The main effect is the *erga omnes effectiveness* of the right of the controlling secured creditor. This creditor can assert its preferential right against any third party, including other creditors—with or without prior registration-, acquirers of the digital asset, or even against the bankruptcy estate in the event of the debtor's insolvency.

As a direct consequence of the above, the creditor with control *displaces,* in the order of priority, the previous creditors that do not have control, relegating them to a subordinate position. This displacement operates *ex lege*, by the mere fact of obtaining control, without the need for any additional act. The creditor with control also acquires the right to enforce the guarantee directly and efficiently, without the need to resort to complex judicial or administrative procedures. It may, for example, proceed with the sale of the digital asset or its appropriation—if so agreed—always respecting the applicable rules on consumer protection and the duties of diligence and good faith. In addition, once the secured claim is satisfied, the creditor's control is extinguished. Likewise, the possible liability of the creditor with control should not be ignored in cases where there is an abusive exercise of control.

2.3.3 Practical Examples of the Application of Principle 16

To fully understand the scope and effectiveness of Principle 16 in practice, it is illustrative to examine a number of factual scenarios that would demonstrate how the control-based priority rule operates in different contexts and with different types of digital assets.

Pledge on cryptocurrencies in Multi-Sig Wallet

Let us consider a scenario where a debtor (D) owns a certain amount of cryptocurrency, stored in a personal digital wallet. Initially, D grants a security interest in those cryptocurrencies in favour of a first creditor (A1). This guarantee is duly registered in a movable property registry, if there is a registry applicable to this type of digital assets in the corresponding jurisdiction.

Subsequently, D needs to obtain additional financing and agrees with a second creditor (A2) to create a new guarantee on the same cryptocurrencies. However, A2, aware of the risks associated with mere registration and seeking to secure its priority position, requires as a *sine qua non* that cryptocurrencies be transferred to a *multi-sig* wallet. This digital wallet is characterised by requiring authorisation, i.e. the digital signature, of multiple parties—in this case, both D and A2—in order to carry out any transfer of funds.

In this scenario, A2 obtains "control" over the cryptocurrencies within the meaning of Principle 6, since, while it does not have exclusive control (it needs D's concurrence), it does have effective control that allows it to prevent D from unilaterally disposing of the cryptocurrencies. The multisig wallet, by its very nature, prevents any movement of funds without A2's approval. In accordance with the priority rule set out in Principle 16, A2, as the controlling creditor, displaces A1 in priority, notwithstanding the fact that A1 had previously registered its security right in the registry. Registration, in this case, is ineffective in granting the highest priority.

Guarantee on NFTs on a centralized custody platform

Let us now imagine a debtor (D) who owns several NFTs (non-fungible tokens) that represent ownership or rights over digital artworks. Initially, D grants a security right in favour of a creditor (A1), and this guarantee is registered in a public registry, if one is applicable to NFTs in the relevant jurisdiction. However, D retains the private key that allows him to control and transfer the NFTs.

Subsequently, D seeks additional financing and agrees with a second creditor (A2) to constitute a guarantee over the same NFTs. A2, seeking greater security and, above all, priority, requires that the NFTs be deposited with a specialised custody platform that offers digital asset blocking or escrow services. This platform, acting as custodian (C), contractually agrees with A2 not to allow any transfer or disposal of the NFTs without the express written authorization of A2.

In this scenario, A2, through the custodian (C) acting as its agent, gains "control" over the NFTs, as defined by Principle 6. The fact that the NFTs are "locked" on the platform and that C is contractually obligated not to allow their transfer without A2's consent, implies that D has lost the ability to freely dispose of the assets.

As a result, and in accordance with Principle 16, A2, as a controlling creditor, acquires priority over A1, notwithstanding the prior registration of A1's security.

Stablecoin collateral

Suppose that a company (E) issuing stablecoins—cryptocurrencies designed to maintain a stable value relative to a fiat currency, such as the dollar or euro—has its reserves deposited in a bank account. A creditor (A1) registers a generic security right in E's "all present and future digital assets" in a traditional registry.

Subsequently, E needs to obtain additional financing and agrees with a second creditor (A2) to create a guarantee on a specific amount of stablecoins. In order to secure its priority position, A2 requires that those stablecoins be transferred to a digital wallet whose sole control resides in A2.

In this case, by gaining direct and exclusive control of the stablecoins transferred to its wallet, A2 displaces A1 in priority, even *if* A1's collateral was broader in scope ("all digital assets") and had been previously registered. The fact that stablecoins can theoretically be backed by underlying assets (euros in a bank account) does not alter the application of the control-based priority rule of Principle 16, which focuses on direct control of the digital asset itself.

2.3.4 Custodians as Critical Infrastructure in Transactions Secured with Digital Assets

In necessary conjunction with Principle 10, which regulates the custody of digital assets, Principle 16 gives custody service providers a central, and potentially very powerful, role in the ecosystem of transactions secured with these assets.

By holding private keys or technological mechanisms that allow them to control and dispose of digital assets, custodians become, de facto, facilitators—and to some extent, arbiters—of the constitution and effectiveness of control-based guarantees. Their function, therefore, transcends mere passive custody, to become a key element in the dynamics of priority.

The figure of the custodian can take various forms, one of the most relevant being that of the custodian as agent of the secured creditor. In this case, the custodian acts on behalf of the creditor, exercising control over the digital asset in their name and on their behalf, following their instructions. For this agency relationship to be effective and enforceable against third parties, the existence of a tripartite agreement between the debtor (original owner of the asset), the secured creditor and the custodian is essential. This agreement must clearly and unambiguously state that the custodian contractually agrees not to permit any transfer, disposition, or encumbrance on the digital asset without the prior, express, written consent of the secured creditor. Such an arrangement drastically limits the debtor's ability to dispose of the asset, giving the creditor indirect, but very effective, control over the asset.

The reality of the digital asset market, however, is often more complex than this ideal three-way model. It is not uncommon for chains of custody to be intricate, involving multiple intermediaries and sub-custodians, where a digital asset can pass through several layers of custody before reaching its final destination. Principle 16 continues to apply in these complex scenarios, provided that the secured creditor can demonstrate, through contractual documentation and transaction traceability, that it maintains effective control over the asset throughout the chain. The key, therefore, lies in the possibility of tracing the "thread" of control, from the creditor to the asset, regardless of the number of intermediaries involved.

In return, this central position of custodians in the framework of Principle 16 entails a series of significant responsibilities and obligations. As depositories of the trust of both debtors and creditors, custodians are obliged to act with the utmost diligence, professionalism and transparency. One of their main duties is to inform creditors and customers in a timely, complete and truthful manner about any relevant change in the disposal rights over the digital assets held in custody, including the receipt of seizure notices or the existence of claims from third parties.

They must also implement rigorous procedures to verify the identity and legitimacy of the instructions they receive, adopting robust security measures, such as two-factor authentication and verification of digital signatures, and compliance protocols to prevent fraud and money laundering. In addition, they are obliged to act impartially, avoiding granting control over the same asset to multiple creditors, unless there is a clear and express subordination agreement between them. Failure to comply with these duties can have serious consequences for custodians, both contractually and non-contractually, and they may be liable for damages caused to debtors or creditors due to their negligence, wilful misconduct or bad faith.

Precisely because of this concentration of power that Principle 16 grants to custodians, making them true "guardians" of priority in the digital realm, the need for adequate regulatory oversight and the possible imposition of fiduciary duties on these actors is becoming increasingly evident. The ultimate goal is to ensure that custodians do not abuse their privileged position or unduly favour one creditor to the detriment of another, thus ensuring fairness and transparency in this emerging market.

2.3.5 Registration and Control: Two Conflicting Priority Models

While not completely eliminating the relevance of secured transactions registries, Principle 16 clearly subordinates their effectiveness to that of control in the specific case of digital assets that can be controlled. This subordination creates tension, a potential conflict, between two systems of tax publicity, which, although they have historically coexisted, are now in a different hierarchical relationship.

On the one hand, we have the traditional system of public registry, which has been the main, and often the only, mechanism for making the existence of encumbrances in assets known to third parties and establishing the order of priority among creditors. The register offers, at least in theory, a high degree of legal certainty, based on the *erga omnes publicity* of registered rights and on the application of the principle of temporal priority.

On the other hand, Principle 16 introduces control as an alternative, and for digital assets, superior mechanism of advertising and priority. This new system is based on effective possession—even if it is digital possession mediated by a custodian—and on the real and current capacity to dispose of the asset. Control, in the context of digital assets, prevails over mere registration.

This tension between registration and control, this paradigm shift, poses a series of practical and theoretical challenges that must be rigorously addressed. One of the main ones is the asymmetry of information and the risk that this generates for creditors. A creditor who relies exclusively on the information contained in a public registry may be surprised by the existence of a subsequent creditor who has gained control over the digital asset, and of whom he had no prior knowledge, nor could he have had prior knowledge through the registry. This situation is particularly problematic if the registry does not reflect, or does not have the technical capacity to reflect, the existence of control agreements, which is common in current practice. Control, and the identification of the party exercising control, is not always transparent, even to the most sophisticated market participants.

This new reality imposes the obligation to carry out much more thorough and proactive due diligence on creditors who wish to secure their claims with digital assets than simply consulting a public registry. Creditors should go further and actively investigate whether there are any other creditors who may have gained effective control over the asset. This investigation may involve contacting the debtor directly, the potential custodians that they use and, in certain cases, conducting searches and analyses on the blockchain itself, if the asset in question is public and traceable.

Secured transactions registries, on the other hand, face the challenge of adapting to this new reality if they intend to maintain their relevance in the context of digital assets. Its adaptation could involve, for example, incorporating, as far as technically possible, information on the existence of control agreements on digital assets. Another option would be to issue clear and explicit warnings to registry users about the possibility of unregistered creditors with control and about the primacy of control over registration in the case of digital assets. A third way of adaptation could be the development of interoperability mechanisms and cooperation with digital asset custody platforms, with the aim of obtaining up-to-date and reliable information on asset control, although this poses complex technical and legal challenges.

2.4 Guidelines for a Legislative Policy and Final Reflections

The underlying issue of the paradigm shift introduced by Principle 16 invites us to reflect on a review of legislative policy. Some authors understand that it would be a matter that should be left to domestic law. Others identify the problems that transposing these Principles into legal systems would pose because of the conflicts that might arise. This question raises the subject of whether legal systems should develop hybrid frameworks that preserve some traditional elements of good faith protection, while recognising the practical realities of digital asset transactions and business.

Principle 16 basically implies a splitting of the effectiveness of security rights (between those that include control and those that do not), and this can be a practical source of problems between a central public registry, analogue and not fully digitised, and a cybernetic, decentralised and programmable ecosystem. In this regard, it might be appropriate to clarify and assess the meaning of the expression: "for a method other than control".

The *travaux préparatoira* of the Principles recalls that the third-party effectiveness of a security right generally requires a secured creditor to take steps to provide publicity of the security right, which may include delivery of possession (pledge), notice to the debtor (of the assignment of the security right), and registration or control (of the security right). The reality is that, as we have discussed in this analysis, some of these (traditional) mechanisms are not applicable to digital assets.

In fact, registrations are not commonly made in the crypto asset lending market. Cryptographic assets (tokens) supported by distributed ledger technologies, DLT (Blockchain)—which are not the only digital assets which UNIDROIT DAPLs aims to address—are not recorded in the ledger in the way that an entry is made in a central and public registry. Operators or market participants typically transfer digital assets from a borrower's wallet to a wallet under the control of the secured creditor (P2P). The UNIDROIT DAPLs could establish some qualification for the case of movable guarantees on digital assets and those specifically determined by a distributed ledger technology ("cryptographic" digital assets, cryptoassets).

On the other hand, the original wording of Principle 16 itself did not imply the possibility of multiple creditor control or control. However, during Working Group 6 some experts suggested that several creditors could have shared control over digital assets. In this sense, paragraph 4 of the Commentary to Principle 16 addresses the possibility that multiple creditors may have shared control over digital assets, which is increasingly common in complex financial transactions.

Principle 16 recognises that, in such cases, the priority conflict may be resolved by an agreement between creditors or, in the absence of such an agreement, by applying the temporal priority rule based on the time at which each creditor gained control. This situation highlights the increasing complexity of custody relationships in the digital asset ecosystem.

Unlike tangible assets, digital assets can be managed and controlled by private cryptographic key custody or asset exchange and transaction management service providers (CASP in the European MICA environment, for example). These custodians can extend their services to multiple creditors, raising critical questions about how shared control is defined and regulated.

The reliance on agreements between creditors reflects a pragmatic approach where creditors must regulate their respective priorities through private contracts. These arrangements can certainly offer flexibility and allow creditors to structure their relationships in a way that reflects their risk tolerance and financial strategies. However, the lack of a clear regulatory framework governing shared control could lead to controversies and disputes, especially in situations where the interests of one creditor are subordinated to those of another without adequate contractual safeguards.

In the absence of an agreement, Principle 16 suggests recourse to the general law of secured transactions, particularly the first-in-time rule. This can create tensions, especially when digital assets are held in custody by entities that recognise multiple creditors at different times. The possibility of such conflicts underscores the need for more robust legal mechanisms to address priority between creditors in shared control scenarios, particularly given the global and decentralised nature of digital asset transactions.

To address these concerns, lawmakers could consider developing guidelines or best practices for custodians operating in the digital asset space, addressing issues such as transparency, conflict of interest management, and the obligation to act in the best interests of creditors. In addition, the use of smart contracts can provide a more automated and transparent approach to determining priority among creditors. Smart contracts can be programmed to enforce pre-agreed terms, reducing the potential for disputes and ensuring that priority is objectively determined based on the terms of the agreement.

On the other hand, paragraph 6 of the Commentary to Principle 16 provides a practical illustration of how priority conflicts arise when traditional assets are converted into digital assets. In the example, an inventory encumbered by a registered security interest is converted into a portfolio of digital assets through its disposal, and these digital assets are deposited with a custodian who extends a loan secured by the assets under its control.

The secured creditor that has control over the digital assets has priority over the creditor that had a registered interest in the original inventory. This example highlights a critical issue at the intersection of traditional and digital assets, namely how rights to physical or traditional assets should be treated once they are transformed into digital assets.

Under traditional security rights law, a creditor is permitted to maintain a security right in proceeds arising from the sale or transformation of encumbered property. However, in the realm of digital assets according to DAPL UNIDROIT, control (Principle 5) over the new (already digital) asset takes precedence or preference, potentially subordinating or nullifying the interest of the previous creditor.

This situation creates a potentially problematic loophole for creditors who rely on traditional or analogue record mechanisms, as they may find themselves losing priority to a new creditor that has gained control over an asset's digital products. This poses a serious challenge in terms of the balance between legal certainty and efficiency in secured transactions (chattel guarantees), particularly in insolvency scenarios, where several creditors may claim competing interests in the same assets.

Moreover, the role of the custodian in this example cannot be underestimated. Custodians, by virtue of their control over digital assets (Principle 5), effectively and de facto become guardians of priority in the world of digital assets. This involves attributing significant and perhaps excessive power to digital asset custodians, who can determine which creditors have effective security interests in the digital realm, based on their control over digital assets. In the light of this situation, it might be advisable to better define custody practices at the domestic level and the possible imposition of a more comprehensive framework of fiduciary duties on custodians, thereby ensuring that custodial service providers do not unduly favour one creditor over another.

Finally, Principle 16 invites us to reflect on legislative policy with regard to the decentralised finance (DeFi) sector, a reality that, as we have mentioned, poses numerous legal challenges in terms of priority between creditors, since control over digital assets in DeFi differs substantially from traditional systems of registration and custody.

On DeFi platforms, assets are frequently locked in smart contracts or liquidity pools, making it difficult to accurately determine who holds effective control or custody, and therefore, priority over those assets. The decentralised nature of DeFi, without an intermediary to regulate and oversee these transactions, increases uncertainty and makes it difficult to resolve conflicts over the ownership and control of digital assets.

In this sense, the rise of decentralised finance adds an additional layer of complexity to this tension between record and control. In the DeFi ecosystem, control over digital assets often moves away from traditional custody and record models. Assets are often locked in smart contracts or deposited in liquidity pools, making it extremely difficult to determine precisely who has effective control, and consequently priority.

The very decentralised and, in many cases, pseudo-anonymous nature of DeFi, without a central authority or intermediary to regulate and oversee transactions, increases legal uncertainty and complicates the resolution of potential conflicts between creditors. While smart contracts could, in theory, offer a more automated and transparent approach to prioritisation, their practical implementation and interaction with traditional security law pose a considerable challenge today.

Therefore, obtaining certainty will not always be possible when invoking Principle 16 in certain contexts or casuistry. Principle 16, while a necessary step forward in adapting secured transactions law to the digital age, is not without criticism and concerns. Its significant departure from traditional principles, particularly with regard to the erosion of the role of good faith and the primacy of control over registration, has generated intense debate in the literature and among legal practitioners.

One of the most recurrent criticisms focuses on the erosion of the principle of good faith. The traditional doctrine of acquisition in good faith, a fundamental pillar of contract law and property law, establishes that a purchaser who acts in good faith, that is, without knowledge of the existence of claims or prior rights of third parties over the acquired asset, must be protected in its acquisition. Principle 16, however, alters this doctrine by prioritising control over the digital asset even if the creditor gaining control has knowledge of the existence of previously registered interests in favour of other creditors. This rule raises fundamental questions about the role that good faith should play in digital transactions and whether its erosion, for the sake of the efficiency and negotiability of digital assets, undermines the basic protections afforded to creditors who have relied on traditional publicity mechanisms, such as registration.

The internal discussions that took place within the UNIDROIT Steering Committee when developing the Principles reflect the intensity of this controversy. As noted above, there was considerable initial resistance to the idea of prioritising control regardless of the creditor's knowledge of the existence of prior registered rights. This resistance was based on deep concerns that such a rule might undermine fundamental principles of fairness and legal certainty, the pillars on which the secured transaction system rests. This highlights the tension between the need to adapt to the unique characteristics and rapid evolution of digital assets, and the importance of preserving established legal principles that protect creditors who act in good faith and rely on information contained in public records.

In the face of this tension, exploring the possibility of developing "hybrid frameworks" was put forward. Such frameworks would seek a balance between protecting good faith, at least to some extent, and recognising the practical realities and efficiency demands of digital asset transactions. Legal systems that choose to implement the UNIDROIT Principles may wish to consider adopting normative approaches that, without completely relinquishing the primacy of control, introduce safeguards or exceptions to protect creditors who have relied on the registry information in good faith.

Another area of concern deals with the possibility of multiple creditors having shared control over the same digital asset. This situation, which is addressed in paragraph 4 of the Commentary to Principle 16, poses significant practical challenges. While Principle 16 provides that, in the absence of an agreement between creditors, the rule of temporal priority will apply, this solution may not be satisfactory in all cases, especially if the chain of custody is complex or if the agreements between creditors and custodians are not sufficiently clear.

The suggestion that legislative guidelines or best practices for custodians should be developed, addressing aspects such as transparency, management of conflicts of interest and the imposition of fiduciary duties, is a sensible response to this concern. In addition, exploring the use of smart contracts to automate the determination of priority between creditors in situations of shared control represents a promising, albeit technologically complex, way to increase legal certainty and reduce the risk of disputes.

Finally, the application of Principle 16 poses specific challenges in relation to tokenised assets and the treatment of traditional assets. The example in paragraph 6 of the Commentary, which describes the situation in which a property is tokenised and the tokens are transferred to a custodian exercising control, highlights a potential conflict with traditional concepts of security rights. The question of how assets derived from the transformation or sale of an original encumbered asset should be treated in the context of digital assets is a grey area that requires further regulatory analysis and development.

Traditional secured transactions law generally allows a creditor to maintain its security right in the proceeds of the original asset. However, Principle 16, by prioritising control over the new asset—the digital asset resulting from the tokenisation or sale of the original asset—could have the effect of extinguishing the interest of the previous creditor who relied on traditional registration mechanisms. This situation creates a "potentially problematic loophole" and can constitute a source of uncertainty for creditors dealing with traditional assets that may be susceptible to transformation into digital assets.

Principle 17
Enforcement of Security Rights

José Caro Catalán

(1) **Enforcement of a security right in a digital asset is subject to other law, including any requirement to proceed in good faith or in a commercially reasonable manner, or both.**

(2) **If a security right in a digital asset maintained by a custodian is made effective against third parties other than by control, the secured creditor is entitled to enforce its security right only pursuant to an order of a court or other public authority, unless the custodian agrees otherwise.**

1 Official Commentary

Commentary

General

17.1. Principle 17 concerns legal rules governing enforcement of security rights rather than technologies that may facilitate the enforcement of security rights in general (e.g., locating and remotely disabling the collateral). These and other aspects regarding effective enforcement are explored in another project of UNIDROIT on 'Best Practices for Effective Enforcement'.

17.2. Principle 17 does not prescribe particular enforcement methods for security rights in digital assets. Generally available methods provided under other law would apply, including judicial enforcement. This Commentary provides guidance to States

This work was financed within the framework of the Prometeo 2023 project of the Regional Ministry of Innovation, Universities, Science and Digital Society (CIPROM/2022/26) "Present and future of the regulation of cryptoassets in the EU [LegalCripto]", whose principal investigator is Carmen Pastor Sempere. The basic ideas contained herein were presented in the author's paper with the same title, given on November 13, 2024 at the IV International Congress on "UNIDROIT Principles on Digital Assets and Private Law: Context, Content, Perspectives", organized also by BAES Research Group of the University of Alicante on November 13 and 14, 2024.

J. Caro Catalán (✉)
University of Cádiz, Cádiz, Spain
e-mail: jose.caro@uca.es

C. Pastor Sempere and D. A. Morán Bovio (eds.), UNIDROIT *Principles on Digital Assets and Private Law*, Law, Governance and Technology Series 80,
https://doi.org/10.1007/978-3-032-11001-5_23

as to how existing enforcement rules, such as those included in Chapter VII of the UNCITRAL Model Law on Secured Transactions, should apply in relation to such security rights. The law of a State should not preclude secured creditors from exercising remedies that may exist under other laws or have been provided for in the security agreement. When digital assets become widely used in securities transactions, derivatives, and similar financial structures, States should ensure that close-out netting is available to parties to such transactions. As explained above in the Commentary to Principle 14, these Principles do not recommend changes to the characterisation of secured transactions under the applicable law. In some cases in the enforcement of rights, thus, the applicable other law may impose no, or lower, requirements on secured creditors that have acquired a digital asset outright.

17.3. All enforcement actions, including disposal, collection of payment (if the right to payment of a monetary obligation is the asset to which a digital asset is effectively linked) and acceptance of the collateral, in full or partial satisfaction of the secured obligation, should be available in relation to security rights in digital assets. In enforcing their rights, secured creditors must proceed in accordance with the applicable enforcement rules contained in a general secured transactions law, including, for example, requirements to proceed in a commercially reasonable manner, provide notifications, distribute any proceeds in accordance with the priority rules, etc. *In some cases, the inherent design of the digital asset may prevent the exercise of certain enforcement rights. General rules governing enforcement of security rights included in international standards on secured transactions appear to be flexible enough to accommodate the expectation of digital assets lenders and other relevant parties. However, States should take into account a number of considerations, which are set out in Commentary 17.4 to 17.7.*

17.4. The method used to make the security right effective against third parties can have an impact on the ability to enforce security rights. Control is a facilitator of enforcement upon default, so that if a security right is made effective against third parties by control, enforcement by the secured creditor is likely to be reasonably straightforward. However, if a security right in a digital asset is made effective against third parties by registration rather than by control, it is likely to be difficult in practice for the secured creditor to enforce against that asset without the cooperation of the grantor, since the grantor retains control of the asset. Thus, the secured creditor might need to obtain a court order, after default, to obtain control if the grantor refuses to transfer it. This situation would be analogous to the grantor refusing to surrender possession of a tangible asset. Furthermore, control might have been transferred to another secured creditor who would have priority (see Principle 16). The general enforcement rules of the secured transactions law then determine whether and how a senior secured creditor may take over the enforcement process.

17.5. Secured transactions laws typically balance the interests of affected parties by imposing certain requirements on secured creditors when enforcing a security right, such as to provide notifications to affected parties. However, secured transaction laws may also provide that these requirements will not apply in certain situations. For instance, Article 78(8) of the UNCITRAL Model Law on Secured Transactions provides for exceptions from the requirement to provide a notification when the asset may speedily decline in value or is sold on a recognised market. These kinds of exceptions would, arguably, apply to many, though not all, digital assets (e.g., bitcoin may speedily decline in value while stable coins may not, and some NFTs may already trade on recognised markets while others do not). Enforcement provisions in secured transactions laws may not need to be changed to accommodate digital assets if these exceptions are crafted broadly to accommodate future developments. Some States also have bespoke enforcement procedures for specific types of assets which do not include any notification requirements (for example, in relation to intermediated securities, Article 33 of the Geneva Securities Convention provides for enforcement by sale or appropriation of securities without notice). It would be consistent with Principle 17 for a State to provide for an analogous enforcement procedure in relation to security rights over digital assets, particularly those which are similar to the types of assets for which such enforcement procedures already exist.

17.6. The recognition of exceptions from the generally applicable enforcement provisions facilitates automated enforcement. An example of automatic enforcement is where liquidation of a digital asset occurs automatically when the collateral-to-loan ratio falls under a specified threshold. This would be an enforcement of a security right if the fall in the ratio is a default under the terms of the security agreement. Many system designers are not aware of how the secured transactions enforcement rules apply. Even if systems have been designed to fit within any exceptions from the general enforcement provisions, the secured creditor would still need to proceed in a commercially reasonable manner or in conformity with some other applicable standard, such as good faith.

17.7. Courts may need some guidance on the interpretation of any exceptions to the enforcement requirement when it comes to digital assets. For instance, in relation to one of the exceptions mentioned in Commentary 17.5, a 'recognised market' is one in which the items sold are fungible and prices are not subject to individual negotiation, such as stock or commodity exchanges. The intended goals of the recognised market exceptions is to facilitate the efficiencies and cost savings that the special treatment may provide without disadvantaging affected parties. Although a recognised market need not be subject to regulation or supervision, the existence of regulatory requirements or guidelines may provide useful guidance for applying this exception. The test of whether or not the market would qualify for the exception is a functional one. It is not based on the 'type' of market. These are some of the parameters that would determine whether an exchange for digital assets actually qualifies as a recognised market.

Principle 17(2)

17.8. If a custodian maintains the digital asset for the grantor, extra-judicial enforcement will entail action by that custodian on the instructions of the secured creditor. An intermediary will be unwilling to follow those instructions if the secured creditor is unknown, and many secured transactions laws include provisions protecting intermediaries in this situation. For example, Article 82(4) of the UNCITRAL Model Law on Secured Transactions provides that, in relation to a security right over a bank account, extra-judicial enforcement is only available when the bank has agreed to act on the instructions of the secured creditor. Principle 17(2) provides for the protection of custodians of digital assets in the enforcement of a security right. If the security right has been made effective against third parties by control under Principle 15, the custodian would maintain the digital asset for the secured creditor, and would typically owe some duties to that secured creditor, including to change the control of the digital assets if instructed by the secured creditor (see Principle 11(1)(b)). In contrast, if the security right has been made effective by a method other than control, such as by registration, the custodian would not owe any duties to that secured creditor. In those situations, the secured creditor will need to obtain an order from a court or other public authority, if the custodian does not agree to act on the instructions of the secured creditor.

17.9. ***Illustration.****A security right was made effective against third parties by control where the secured creditor is one of the three parties to a multi-signature arrangement. While the grantor is also a party to this arrangement, the third person acts on behalf of the secured creditor. An action of two parties is required to cause a change of control. Upon default, the multi-signature arrangement is triggered, and the encumbered digital asset is transferred under the 'sole' control of the secured creditor resulting in the acceptance of the collateral in satisfaction of the secured obligation or enabling a foreclosure sale. However, any requirements under the applicable other law as to acceptance of the collateral in satisfaction of the obligation would continue to apply.*

2 Reflections

2.1 Context

Principle 17 ("Enforcement of Security Rights") is placed at the end of Section V ("Secured Transactions"). Section V contains four Principles which address the main elements of transactions under which a security right in a digital asset is granted to a secured creditor to secure the performance of any existing, future, or contingent obligations of the grantor or another person (see Commentary 14.1). Under the general objective of the Principles, Section V is not intended to provide a comprehensive regulation of secured transactions in digital assets. Rather, it provides clear rules that apply to the key aspects of these transactions (see Introduction 0.2). In particular, the topics selected for their relevance during the preparatory work were: (i) scope, (ii) creation, (iii) perfection, (iv) priority, (v) obligor's rights and obligations, (vi) custodians and issuers, (vii) enforcement, and (viii) conflict of laws.[1] Each of these topics roughly corresponds to a Principle. Thus, in addition to addressing the basic issues of secured transactions from a private law perspective, Section V takes a comprehensive approach to the subject, including extrajudicial and judicial enforcement.

Devoting a Principle to the enforcement of security rights is a provident decision. After all, the effectiveness of a security right depends on its enforceability in the event of default. The particularities of digital asset transactions make it appropriate to address certain enforcement issues, notwithstanding the applicability of general secured transactions laws. The Working Group was aware of this from the beginning of the preparatory works. In its second session, it was noted that: "a Principle should consider what rules are necessary to enable enforcement of security rights in DAs [digital assets] that also provide adequate protection to affected parties, such as competing claimants."[2] As subsequently discussed, this initial purpose was expanded during the preparatory works.

2.2 *Precedents*

2.2.1 Second Session of the Working Group (March 2021)

Section V originally included four principles, as does the final version. However, although the final content of the section has changed significantly since the earlier versions. The first Principle of the initial draft (Principle A) stated that "secured transaction law applies to digital assets."[3] The second principle (Principle B) provided that secured transaction regimes should enable digital assets to be used as collateral. The third principle (Principle C) noted that security rights may be created in the grantor´s rights and powers concerning digital assets. Finally, the fourth principle (Principle D) recognised the possibility that distinct rules for different categories of digital assets may apply to some aspects of creating a security right and effectiveness against third parties. As can be observed, this initial version did not address enforcing security rights.

---

[1] UNIDROIT 2021—Study LXXXII—W.G.2—Doc. 2 (rev. 1), par. 115.

[2] UNIDROIT 2021—Study LXXXII—W.G.2—Doc. 2, (rev. 1), par. 115.

[3] The text of the principle provided that "The law should establish simple and sound rules in relation to collateral transactions involving digital assets". UNIDROIT 2021—Study LXXXII—W.G.2—Doc. 2 (rev. 1), p. 31. UNIDROIT 2021 – Study LXXXII—W.G.2—Doc. 2, (rev. 1), par. 115, Fig. 4: Principle A: Secured transaction law applies to digital assets.

2.2.2 Third Session of the Working Group (June 2021)

The second draft of Section V presented at the third session of the Working Group was virtually identical to the previous one.[4] The only exception was Principle C, where relevant modifications were introduced. In contrast to the first draft, this version referred to the effectiveness of security rights in digital assets against third parties, not the creation of security rights. It was established that security rights may be made effective against third parties through control.[5] To this end, after ordering that the "law should recognise control as a mechanism to achieve third-party effectiveness of a security right", it recommended recognising different forms of control "that reflect how the digital asset is held and the type of creditor that extends credit on the security of the digital asset."[6]

Despite this amendment, the previous discussion of sub-group 3 -secured transactions- focused on "issues concerning digital twins, particularly the legal aspects of digital twins where a State has recognised that an asset might embody rights to another asset and how that recognition occurred.",[7] as well as the need for specific regulation of DeFi transactions and insolvency proceedings. Again, enforcement issues of security rights in digital assets were left out of the discussion.

2.2.3 Fourth Session of the Working Group (November 2021)

Regarding enforcing security rights in digital assets, the most significant progress can be found in the third draft of Section V, which was presented at the fourth session of the Working Group. The third draft introduced modifications to most Principles of Section V. In this sense, Principle B was amended by deleting the final sentence.[8] Principles C and D remain with slight amendments -especially relevant in the Commentary- and altered order. In contrast, Principle E was subject to significant changes. Whereas the second draft established priority rules in insolvency cases, the third draft established priority rules in general.[9]

[4] A second draft of Section V can be found in UNIDROIT 2021 – Study LXXXII—W.G.3—Doc. 2, (rev. 1), pp. 44–50.

[5] UNIDROIT 2021—Study LXXXII—W.G.3—Doc. 2, p. 47. UNIDROIT 2021 – Study LXXXII—W.G.3—Doc. 2, (rev. 1), p. 47, Figure: Principle C: Security rights may be made effective against third parties by control.

[6] UNIDROIT 2021—Study LXXXII—W.G.3—Doc. 2, p. 47. UNIDROIT 2021 – Study LXXXII—W.G.3—Doc. 2, (rev. 1), p. 47, Figure: Principle C: Security rights may be made effective against third parties by control.

[7] UNIDROIT 2021—Study LXXXII—W.G.3—Doc. 4, par. 119.

[8] The deleted sentence was "Regardless of whether digital assets are characterised as property or subject to a property right in that jurisdiction". See UNIDROIT 2021—Study LXXXII—W.G.4—Doc. 2, p. 51. Figure: Principle B: Digital assets are eligible to be collateral.

[9] UNIDROIT 2021—Study LXXXII—W.G.4—Doc. 2, p. 55, Figure: Principle E: Priority of security rights in digital assets made effective against third parties by control. According to the third draft, "the law should provide that where a security right in a digital asset has obtained third-party

The main novelty in the third draft however, is the inclusion of a new Principle dealing with the enforcement of security rights in digital assets. The drafting of Principle F—the first direct antecedent of Principle 17—was entitled: "Effective Enforcement of Security Rights in Digital Assets". As clarified in the Commentary, despite the broad ambit of the title, the scope of application of this Principle—at least in this version—does not include technologies that may facilitate the enforcement of security rights in digital assets or judicial enforcement.

The first paragraph stated, "The law should allow secured creditors to enforce their security rights in digital assets in a simple and quick manner. To that end, the law should not impose undue formalities or requirements that would make the enforcement process cumbersome". This statement—which was not included in the definitive version—perfectly summed up the Working Group's intention when designing this Principle: the law should provide flexible, efficient and effective remedies for enforcing security rights in digital assets. In this sense, considering that secured transactions law usually sets some requirements for secured creditors to exercise their rights, the draft comments stated that "under certain situations, these requirements may not apply" to many digital assets[10]—Bitcoin is used as an example because its value may speedily decline—.[11]

The second paragraph stated, "The interest of third parties, particularly custodians, should be protected".[12] This provision was justified by the concern of Sub-Group-3 to protect third parties in certain scenarios. As warned in the summary report, "there may be challenges in relation to third-party protection (e.g. custodians)".[13] Some key ideas were set out in the Commentary to properly protect third parties: (i) When enforcing their rights, secured creditors must act in a commercially reasonable manner and fulfil specific conditions that balance the interests of affected third parties; (ii) States should be mindful of some limitations related to the mechanism used to make the security right effective against third parties, which can have an impact on the ability to enforce security rights.[14] Extrajudicial enforcement is only possible if the third-party intermediary voluntarily agrees to comply with the creditor's instructions. Otherwise, enforcement is only possible with a judicial order.

Finally, the third paragraph further developed the previous ones by stating that: "Given the nature of digital assets, the law should recognise that enforcement actions

---

effectiveness through control, the security right should have priority over a security right in the digital asset of a person who does not have control".

[10] UNIDROIT 2021—Study LXXXII—W.G.4—Doc. 2, p. 57, Figure: Principle F: Effective Enforcement of Security Rights in Digital Assets.

[11] In the summary report (UNIDROIT 2021—Study LXXXII—W.G.4—Doc. 3, par. 93) it was highlighted that exemptions from the procedural requirement "may be disposed of". As stated in the summary, "it was asserted that digital assets would, for the most part, qualify for exemption on this point due to certain characteristics of digital assets, such as the risk of rapidly deciding value".

[12] UNIDROIT 2021—Study LXXXII—W.G.4—Doc. 2, Figure: Principle F: Effective Enforcement of Security Rights in Digital Assets.

[13] UNIDROIT 2021—Study LXXXII—W.G.4—Doc. 3, par. 91.

[14] UNIDROIT 2021—Study LXXXII—W.G.4—Doc. 2, p. 57, Figure: Principle F: Effective Enforcement of Security Rights in Digital Assets.

may be taken automatically and that some requirements for enforcement, such as to provide a notification of disposal, should not apply."[15] Therefore, despite the qualms related to pre-programmed actions,[16] Sub-Group-3 defended its viability. The Commentary states, for example, that the rules "should not render a pre-programmed action that occurs automatically, such as causing liquidation of the digital asset when the collateral-to-loan ratio falls under a specified threshold ineffective."[17]

At the end of this version, two questions were addressed to the Working Group that influenced the course of the following session: (i) Does the draft Principle adequately cover the aspects relevant to enforcing security rights in digital assets? (ii) Should additional aspects be covered?

2.2.4 Fifth Session of the Working Group (March 2022)

The draft presented at the fifth session of the Working Group is identical to the previous one, both in the text and the Commentary. Only a few formal changes were made: it was provisionally numbered 19—in this version, the letters used to identify the Principles were eliminated—and the two final questions were deleted.[18] However, the summary report of the fifth session pointed out some relevant issues related to enforcing security rights in digital assets.[19]

It was noted that the Digital Assets Project was coordinating with the Enforcement Project on this matter.[20] Up to that point, there were initial discussions to clarify the enforcement areas each project intended to address, aiming to prevent any overlap and identifying areas where the projects could complement each other effectively. It was pointed out that the draft covered two aspects of enforcement; one referred to the insolvency law of the forum concerning the enforcement of any remedies, and the other one was Principle 19—current Principle 17—which dealt with the enforcement of security rights. Regarding the latter, it was clarified that Principle 19 "concerned the enforcement of security rights only, which did not concern enforcement of rights of holders or persons in digital assets, which was potentially the subject matter for a new Principle to be drafted in coordination with the Enforcement Working Group".[21]

---

[15] UNIDROIT 2021—Study LXXXII—W.G.4—Doc. 2, p. 57, Figure: Principle F: Effective Enforcement of Security Rights in Digital Assets.

[16] In the summary report (UNIDROIT 2021—Study LXXXII—W.G.4—Doc. 3, par. 91) it was highlighted that "Enforcement in general required balancing the rights of creditors and some third parties, and it may be that these pre-programmed actions did not actually comply with the applicable enforcement provisions".

[17] UNIDROIT 2021—Study LXXXII—W.G.4—Doc. 2, p. 56, Figure: Principle F: Effective Enforcement of Security Rights in Digital Assets.

[18] UNIDROIT 2022—Study LXXXII—W.G. 5—Doc. 3, p. 38–40.

[19] UNIDROIT 2022—Study LXXXII—W.G. 5—Doc. 4, p. 14.

[20] "Enforcement: Best Practices", Study LXXVI B: Best Practices For Effective Enforcement" (https://www.unidroit.org/work-in-progress/enforcement-best-practices/#1644493658763-89df3b2e-4a80, last visit: 05/02/2025).

[21] UNIDROIT 2022—Study LXXXII—W.G. 5—Doc. 4, p. 14.

2.2.5 Sixth Session of the Working Group (August 2022)

In contrast to the previous draft, the one presented at the sixth session of the Working Group incorporated relevant changes to this Principle.[22] The first noticeable item is the new wording. The three paragraphs were modified for stylistic reasons.[23]While the first two are slightly modified, the third was completely rewritten.

In this version, Principle 19 (1) was more concise. It stated, "A secured creditor should be able to enforce its security rights in a digital asset simply and quickly, without the imposition of undue formalities or requirements that would make the enforcement process cumbersome."[24]This wording consolidated the idea that Principle 19 (1) was drafted to improve the entire Principle's cohesion and explain how enforcement works in the context of a security right in a digital asset.[25]

Principle 19 (2) maintained the essence of the previous versions, although it is perceived to be a little more concrete. This greater accuracy is due to the replacement of "third parties" with "other intermediaries" and the inclusion of the last sentence specifying that protection will be provided "on the enforcement of security rights in the digital asset."[26] Despite these changes, members of the Working Group pointed out that Principle 19 (2) "was still too broad and should be reconsidered."[27]

Following the same pro-automatic enforcement approach, Principle 19 (3) stated that "there should not be any requirements [as a matter of Principles law] inconsistent with the automatic enforcement of a security right in a digital asset".[28] Thus, in contrast to the previous draft, the feasibility of automatic enforcement was tacitly recognised.[29] Along with this statement, a single general exception was incorporated: "except to the extent that it is necessary to ensure that the enforcement is carried out in a commercially reasonable manner".[30] As acknowledged in the preparatory work, the reference to the concept of "commercially reasonable manner" in Para. 3 was added because of Art. 79 of the UNCITRAL Model Law on Secured Transactions, which will be noted below, as the reference text for the Working Group.[31]

This version made important amendments to the Commentary. Beyond the formal issues, it introduced interesting ideas. First, it clarified that the Principle "does not prescribe particular enforcement methods for security rights in digital assets: it merely provides guidance to States as to how existing enforcement rules should

---

[22] UNIDROIT 2022—Study LXXXII—W.G. 6—Doc. 2, p. 48–50.

[23] UNIDROIT 2022—Study LXXXII—W.G.6—Doc. 4, p. 20.

[24] UNIDROIT 2022—Study LXXXII—W.G.6—Doc. 3, p. 84.

[25] UNIDROIT 2022—Study LXXXII—W.G.6—Doc. 4, p. 21.

[26] 19 (2) The interests of custodians and other intermediaries should be protected on the enforcement of a security right in a digital asset.

[27] UNIDROIT 2022—Study LXXXII—W.G.6—Doc. 4, p. 20.

[28] UNIDROIT 2022—Study LXXXII—W.G. 6—Doc. 2, p. 48.

[29] The previous version stated that: "the law should recognize that enforcement actions may be taken automatically". UNIDROIT 2022—Study LXXXII—W.G. 5—Doc. 3, p. 38.

[30] UNIDROIT 2022—Study LXXXII—W.G. 6—Doc. 2, p. 48.

[31] UNIDROIT 2022—Study LXXXII—W.G. 6—Doc. 3, p. 87.

apply concerning such security rights."[32] Second, a new paragraph was introduced to describe the different scenarios depending on the method used to make the security right effective against third parties.[33] Finally, the amendment of paragraphs 7 and 8, which shed some light on automatic enforcement and the interpretation of Principle 19 (3), is worth noting.

Despite the draft changes, many doubts and objections were raised at the end of the sixth session—particularly about the Commentary, which can be appreciated in the summary report.[34] Among many others, the following points should be highlighted:

- It was noted that Commentary 19.1 should provide additional clarity on the issue of debtor protection where a secured creditor did not comply with the extrajudicial provisions on enforcement provided by the relevant law.[35]
- It was suggested that a reference to other international instruments in this area should be included in Commentary 19.3.[36]
- Regarding Commentary 19.5, it was noted that its links with Commentary 19.4 and art. 78 of the UNCITRAL Model Law on Secured Transactions should be emphasised.[37]
- Additionally, it was noted that a reference to "automatic enforcement" should not be made, as this may confuse readers, and it was related to notions of public policy.[38]
- It was suggested that consistency and cross-referencing between Principles 19 and 20 should improve.[39]
- It was pointed out that Principle 19 (3) was "vague and might not be acceptable to policymakers."[40] It was suggested that the Drafting Committee consider the input collected at the joint workshop with the UNIDROIT working group on Effective Enforcement and improve the draft.
- Finally, several doubts and objections were raised about the provision for automatic enforcement in Principle 19 (3).

2.2.6 Seventh Session of the Working Group (December 2022)

Considering the doubts and questions raised, it is unsurprising that significant modifications to this Principle were presented at the next session.[41] The first noteworthy aspect was the change of number and title. In the draft presented at the seventh

[32] UNIDROIT 2022—Study LXXXII—W.G. 6—Doc. 3, p. 84.
[33] See par. 4 UNIDROIT 2022—Study LXXXII—W.G. 6—Doc. 3, p. 85.
[34] UNIDROIT 2022—Study LXXXII—W.G. 6—Doc. 4, p. 20–23.
[35] UNIDROIT 2022—Study LXXXII—W.G. 6—Doc. 4, p. 20.
[36] UNIDROIT 2022—Study LXXXII—W.G. 6—Doc. 4, p. 20.
[37] UNIDROIT 2022—Study LXXXII—W.G. 6—Doc. 4, p. 20.
[38] UNIDROIT 2022—Study LXXXII—W.G. 6—Doc. 4, p. 20.
[39] UNIDROIT 2022—Study LXXXII—W.G. 6—Doc. 4, p. 21.
[40] UNIDROIT 2022—Study LXXXII—W.G. 6—Doc. 4, p. 21.
[41] UNIDROIT 2022—Study LXXXII—W.G. 7—Doc. 2, p. 53.

Working Group Meeting, this Principle was finally assigned number 17, and the word "enforcement" was deleted from the title.[42] In addition, the wording of the Principle was subject to significant changes affecting its external formation and content. Notable improvements were also made to the Commentary.

As in the definitive version, Principle 17 only had two paragraphs in this draft. The first paragraph already adopted a content similar to the final version, merely pointing out that "enforcement of a security right in a digital asset is subject to other law, including any requirement to proceed in a commercially reasonable manner". It can be held that Principle 17 (1) took over the content of the former Principle 19 (1) and (3). However, it did so by considering some of the objections raised at the 6th Working Group Meeting, fostering the idea that enforcement of security rights over digital assets should be governed by the general rules on secured transactions and removing the reference to automatic enforcement.[43]

Principle 17 (2) is a concretisation of the former Principle 19 (2), which stated the need to protect the interests of third-party intermediaries in the enforcement of security interests in digital assets. In this sense, Principle 17 (2) states that "If a security right in a digital asset held by a custodian is made effective against third parties other than by control, the secured creditor is entitled to enforce its security right only pursuant to a court order, unless the custodian agrees otherwise". This amendment was also suggested at the 6th Working Group Meeting, where the scope of Principle 19 (2) was criticised as being too broad.[44] This wording of principle 17 (2) is included in the definitive version.

The Commentary was also amended in this version. Some of the most notable changes are briefly outlined below:

- Internal[45] and external references[46] were added.
- It was specified that the Principles do not recommend "changes to the characterisation of secured transactions under the applicable law."[47]
- Regarding automated enforcement, it was specified that recognising exceptions from the generally applicable enforcement provisions facilitates it. It was also clarified that "even if systems have been designed to fit within any exceptions

[42] This was one of the suggestions in the 6th Working Group Meeting. Notably, a working group member suggested that this word "could be deleted as it did not make much of a difference as to the substance". UNIDROIT 2022—Study LXXXII—W.G. 6—Doc. 4, p. 21.

[43] As it is stated in the Summary Report of 7th Working Group Meeting, "references to automatic enforcement had been removed from the text and only mentioned in the Commentary" (UNIDROIT 2023—Study LXXXII—W.G.7—Doc. 5, p. 14).

[44] UNIDROIT 2023—Study LXXXII—W.G. 6—Doc. 4, p. 21.

[45] It includes new references to the principles 12, 14, 15 and 16. UNIDROIT 2023—Study LXXXII—W.G. 7—Doc. 2, p. 53–54.

[46] It includes new references to UNCITRAL Model Law on Secured Transactions. UNIDROIT 2023—Study LXXXII—W.G. 7—Doc. 2, p. 53–54.

[47] UNIDROIT 2023—Study LXXXII—W.G. 7—Doc. 2, p. 53.

from the general enforcement provision, the secured creditor must still proceed in a commercially reasonable manner."[48]

- When interpreting the aforementioned exceptions it was added that the courts may need some guidance to apply them properly. In particular, the Commentary refers to art. 78(8) of the UNCITRAL Model Law on Secured Transaction's exception, which concerns the disposal of the encumbered asset on a recognised market.[49]

Beyond these changes, the summary report of this session reflects some of the issues discussed in this Principle. The discussion on the relation between Principles 17 and 18 should be highlighted. In this sense, the different scope of application of the two Principles was emphasised—"Principle 17 related only to situations where a party had a security right in a digital asset, whereas Principle 18 was more general"[50]—. Based on this idea, it was noted that implementing these Principles in State law would normally be carried out through different rules, which, in the opinion of the Working Group, justifies the autonomy of both principles.[51] Second, it was observed that there was an overlap between Principles 17 and 18: if a security right cannot be enforced extrajudicially, the only option available will be judicial enforcement. In such a scenario, Principle 18 becomes relevant. In response, the drafting committee proposed various alternatives to "ensure that Principle 17 addressed judicial and extrajudicial enforcement of security rights in digital assets, with adequate references to other law where necessary."[52]

2.2.7 Eighth Session of the Working Group (March 2023)

Despite these suggestions, the amendments in the draft presented in the eight Working Group Meetings were minor.[53] In this last draft, Principle 17 (1) remains almost unchanged. Only one nuance was introduced: the concept of "good faith" was included as equivalent to "proceed in a commercially reasonable manner". Thus, Principle 17 (1) states: "Enforcement of a security right in a digital asset is subject

[48] UNIDROIT 2023—Study LXXXII—W.G. 7—Doc. 2, p. 54.

[49] It is explained in the commentary that a recognized market "in one in which the items sold are fungible and prices are not subject to individual negotiation, such as stock or commodity exchanges. The intended goals of the recognized market exceptions is to facilitate the efficiencies and cost savings that the special treatment may provide without disadvantaging affected parties". Furthermore, it adds that "although a recognized market need not be subject to regulation or supervision, the existence of regulatory requirements or guidelines may provide useful guidance for applying this exception. The test whether or not the market would qualify for the exception is a functional one". UNIDROIT 2023—Study LXXXII—W.G. 7—Doc. 2, p. 54.

[50] UNIDROIT 2023—Study LXXXII—W.G. 7—Doc. 5, p. 14.

[51] UNIDROIT 2023—Study LXXXII—W.G. 7—Doc. 5, p. 15.

[52] UNIDROIT 2023—Study LXXXII—W.G. 7—Doc. 5, p. 15.

[53] UNIDROIT 2023—Study LXXXII—W.G. 8—Doc. 2, p. 57.

to other law, including any requirement to proceed in good faith and/or in a commercially reasonable manner."[54] It seems clear that this amendment was intended to make the Principle easy to apply both in common and in civil law.[55]

Changes to Principle 17 (2) were also minor. In this version, the word 'held' was replaced by 'maintained'—in line with the rest of the text—and the possibility of "enforcement by a public authority other than a court" was recognised. This latter change allows application of Principle 17 (2) in countries where enforcement is administrative.

The changes made in the Commentary were also very slight. Undoubtedly, what is most relevant is the final inclusion of judicial enforcement in the scope of the Principle. To this end, the following sentence was deleted from the first paragraph of the Commentary: "This Principle does not concern judicial enforcement that may need to be resorted to when extra-judicial remedies are unavailable/unenforceable". In addition, the second paragraph stated that "generally available methods provided under other law would apply, *including judicial enforcement*"[56]—the sentence in italics is added in this version—.

At the end of its seventh session, the Working Group decided that the draft should be subject to public consultation, with the idea of receiving feedback from the industry.[57] Following this decision, the UNIDROIT Secretariat launched a public consultation on 10 January 2023. At the end of the consultation period, 44 different sets of comments were received, including 341 individual comments. However, the input received was only useful for modifying Principle 13 (Insolvency of custodians) and its Commentary, and Commentaries 10.4 and 11.14. Neither the text of Principle 17 nor its Commentary were modified, so it is not worth devoting any further attention to the public consultation in this Section.[58]

2.3 *Relations with Other Instruments*

Principle 17 must be interpreted in context, so analysing its relations with other instruments at the internal and external levels is important. This issue is particularly relevant in the case of the Principles because they do not aim to address all contractual and proprietary matters relating to digital assets (see Introduction 0.10). Instead, the Principles are based on the premise that general rules are applicable with appropriate adaptations. For this reason, references to other laws are made throughout the text.

---

[54] UNIDROIT 2023—Study LXXXII—W.G. 8—Doc. 2, p. 57.

[55] This idea can be deduced from the Summary Report of the 7th session, where it was noted that "that this requirement [referring to the obligation to act in a commercially reasonable manner] would be particularly difficult to apply in civil law countries". UNIDROIT 2023—Study LXXXII—W.G. 8—Doc. 2, p. 57.

[56] UNIDROIT 2023—Study LXXXII—W.G. 8—Doc. 2, p. 57.

[57] UNIDROIT 2023—Study LXXXII—W.G. 8—Doc. 4, p. 1.

[58] UNIDROIT 2023—Study LXXXII—W.G. 8—Doc. 4, p. 5.

In the interest of bringing some order to this section, it is worthwhile distinguishing between internal and external relations. Internal relations refer to the connection with other Principles and other UNIDROIT instruments. External relations, on the contrary, refer to the connection of Principle 17 with other international instruments—that UNIDROIT has not created. Theoretically, the latter category also includes the relations of Principle 17 with State laws. However, that subject is beyond the scope of this paper.

2.3.1 Internal Relations

Principle 18

In terms of internal relations, beyond its obvious connection with the rest of the Section it falls under, Principle 17 is closely related to Principle 18. After several amendments, the definitive version of Principle 17 refers to both extrajudicial and judicial enforcement.[59] Thus, if a security right in a digital asset cannot be enforced extrajudicially, the creditor can only take judicial action. In this case, Procedural Law—and Principle 18—become relevant. As discussed in the following chapter, Principle 18 merely declares the applicability of States' procedural rules to litigation involving digital assets, indicating the need to make the necessary adaptations in the Commentary. Principle 18 thus complements the content of Principle 17 by providing the general framework for procedural issues relating to digital assets.

Best Practices for Effective Enforcement

Considering the above, Principle 17 directly relates to UNIDROIT on "Best Practices for Effective Enforcement."[60] As the PADPL website notes, "there is a natural fit with the Best Practices of Effective Enforcement, which will analyse the impact of new technologies on enforcement as one of its main objectives." This necessary connection between the two projects was considered when the Principles were elaborated.[61] In this sense, UNIDROIT has made a major effort to coordinate the two projects. A clear demonstration is the two workshops that UNIDROIT organised on the subject: (1) Internal Consultation Workshop: Best Practices of Effective Enforcement (2020)[62] and (2) Workshop on Issues Related to Enforcement in Digital Assets. The first was of a more general purpose, although a panel on the impact of new technologies on enforcement was already in place, where issues related to digital assets were

[59] This must be deduced from the text of the principle itself when it states that: "the secured creditor is entitles to enforce its security right only pursuant to an order of a court or other public authority, unless the custodian agrees otherwise". Judicial enforcement is also mentioned in the commentary.

[60] This project is expressly mentioned in the Commentary on Principle 17 (para. 1).

[61] At the 1st Working Group Meeting it was already pointed out that: "A variety of legal issues arise in practice. Some of them, especially on enforcement of security interests, would benefit from coordination with the UNIDROIT project on Enforcement". UNIDROIT 2020—Study LXXXII—W.G.1—Doc. 2, p. 17.

[62] (https://www.unidroit.org/effective-enforcement-project-discussed-in-exploratory-workshop/; last visit: 05/09/2024).

discussed.[63] The second, however, was rather more concrete and devoted considerable attention to coordinating Principle 17 with the Best Practices of Effective Enforcement project.[64]

At this stage, assessing how the two texts complement each other is impossible, as the Best Practices of Effective Enforcement project has not yet been completed. However, it is clear from Principle 17, and its Commentary, that there will be a complementary relation. As the Commentary states (see Commentary 17.1), the scope of Principle 17 is limited to the rules governing the enforcement of security rights, paying special attention to extrajudicial enforcement. References to judicial enforcement are scarce, and they align with the Principles' general approach to procedure matters.[65] For this reason, in the case of judicial enforcement of a security right in a digital asset, the future instrument of Best Practices of Effective Enforcement may be more useful.

Geneva Convention

The Geneva Convention (UNIDROIT Convention on substantive rules for intermediated securities) was adopted at a diplomatic conference in Geneva on 9 October 2009. The main purpose of the Convention is to offer harmonised transnational rules to reduce the legal risk associated with holding securities through intermediaries. However, the Geneva Convention's scope of application is limited to only core aspects of intermediated securities holding transfer.[66] In this sense, the Geneva Convention deals with several matters related to intermediated securities. For instance, it deals with account holders' rights regarding intermediated securities and their effects on third parties, as well as the priority among competing interests and interests granted by an intermediary or rules intended to ensure the integrity of the intermediated holding system.[67]

Regarding Principle 17, the most relevant provision of the Geneva Convention is art. 33. In the first place, this article states that collateral enforcement may be affected by way of sale or, if agreed, appropriation or close-out netting (art. 33.1 and 33.2). In the second place, it provides that it should be possible to enforce collateral relatively easily and quickly (i.e. without prior notice, approval by a court, or a public

---

[63] (https://www.unidroit.org/work-in-progress/digital-assets-and-private-law/#1488897069871-af7a84cf-bd9a; last visit: 05/09/2024).

[64] The full workshop can be viewed at the following link: (https://www.youtube.com/watch?v=4u5VWv6ahLI&t=9200s; last visit: 05/09/2024). In particular, it is specially relevant to this matter the Roundtable 2 that focused on the enforcement of security rights in the context of secured transactions involving digital assets.

[65] "Other laws to address procedural matters, including the enforcement of rights relating to digital assets" (see Introduction 0.18).

[66] UNIDROIT Legislative Guide on Intermediated Securities: Implementing the Principle and Rules of the Geneva Securities Convention, May 2017, p. 34 (https://www.unidroit.org/wp-content/uploads/2021/06/LEGISLATIVE-GUIDE-English.pdf; last visit: 05/02/2025).

[67] See UNCITRAL—Third International Colloquium on Secured Transactions. Presentation by José Angelo Estrella Faria (https://uncitral.un.org/sites/uncitral.un.org/files/media-documents/uncitral/en/jose_angelo_estrella_faria_edited.pdf; last visit: 12/10/2024).

auction), as well as in the case of insolvency.[68] Commentary 17.5 states that it would be consistent with Principle 17 to provide analogous enforcement rules for security rights over digital assets. In particular, it would be appropriate in cases where the digital assets are similar to those for which these enforcement rules are designed. It should be noted that the Comments refer to the Convention as an example so that the same logic could be applied to other instruments.

2.3.2 External Relations

UNCITRAL Model Law on Secured Transactions

The UNCITRAL Model Law on Secured Transactions applies to security rights in movable assets, that is, property rights in movable assets, created by an agreement to secure payment or other performance of an obligation, regardless of whether the parties have denominated them. The Model Law provides an integral and comprehensive set of rules for this type of transaction, including rules for enforcing collateral. In this sense, The Model Law offers several ways to enforce a security right. The most common ways to enforce a security right under the Model Law are[69]:

(i) Selling the encumbered asset and recovering what is owed from the proceeds.
(ii) Leasing or licensing the encumbered asset and recovering what is owed from the rent or royalty payments.
(iii) Acquiring the encumbered asset in total or partial satisfaction of the amount due.

These rules are relevant because, as stated in Commentary 17.3, secured creditors must proceed by the applicable rules to enforce their digital asset security rights. Therefore, all these possibilities must be available to them.

European Law Institute Principles on the Use of Digital Assets as Security

Finally, and although not mentioned in the Commentary, the relation of Principle 17 with the European Law Institute (ELI) Principles on the Use of Digital Assets as Security is worth noting.[70] This principle was approved by the ELI in 2022 to address the use by private parties, whether a natural or legal person, of digital assets as security for credit. Principle 5 regulates the enforcement of security rights in digital assets in a quite different orientation, as these Principles do not give the same relevance to the notion of "control". For this reason, it was noted at the 5th Working Group

---

[68] UNIDROIT Legislative Guide on Intermediated Securities: Implementing the Principles and Rules of the Geneva Securities Convention, p. 104 (https://www.unidroit.org/wp-content/uploads/2021/06/LEGISLATIVE-GUIDE-English.pdf; last visit: 12/10/2024).

[69] UNCITRAL Practice Guide to the Model Law on Secured Transactions, p. 78 (https://uncitral.un.org/sites/uncitral.un.org/files/media-documents/uncitral/en/19-10910_e.pdf; last visit: 12/10/2024).

[70] ELI Principles on the Use of Digital Assets as Security: Report of the European Law Institute, 2022. (https://www.europeanlawinstitute.eu/fileadmin/user_upload/p_eli/Publications/ELI_Principles_on_the_Use_of_Digital_Assets_as_Security.pdf, last visit: 10/09/2024).

Meeting that "it would be more helpful to draw comparisons between the UNIDROIT Project and international instruments such as the Geneva Securities Convention and the UNCITRAL Model Law on Secured Transactions."[71]

2.3.3 Two Key Issues: Requirements Imposed on Secured Creditors to Enforce a Security Right and Special Protection Rules for Custodians

A special mention should be made of Principle 17's relation with the UNCITRAL Model Law on Secured Transactions and the Geneva Convention concerning two key issues of security rights in digital assets: the requirements—and its exceptions—imposed on secured creditors to enforce a security right and the special protection rules for custodians.

In the first place, the requirements imposed on secured creditors to enforce a security right are discussed. Commentary 17.3. states that certain requirements are often imposed by secured transactions law, such as to provide notifications to affected parties. However, such rules usually have exceptions. In this sense, Commentary 17.5. uses art. 78.8 of the UNCITRAL Model Law on Secured Transactions and Art. 33 of the Geneva Securities Convention as examples. The first provides exceptions to the notification requirement where the asset may speedily decline in value or is sold on a recognised market.[72] The second one allows enforcement by selling or appropriating securities without notice. According to the Commentary, such rules may also apply to digital assets. These exceptions are relevant because they facilitate automated enforcement (see Commentary 17.6.).

In the second place, on the protection rules for custodians while enforcing a security right over a digital asset, Commentary 17.8 links Principle 17.2 with art. 82.4 of the UNCITRAL Model Law on Secured Transactions. The latter states that a security right over a bank account can only be enforced extrajudicially if the bank has agreed to act on the instructions of the secured creditor (Commentary 17.8).[73] Principle 17.2 provides a similar rule to protect custodians when a security right over a digital asset has been made effective by a method other than control. In these situations, the secured creditor "is entitled to enforce its security right only pursuant to an order of a court or other public authority unless the custodian agrees otherwise."

---

[71] UNIDROIT 2022—Study LXXXII—W.G.6—Doc. 4, p. 19.

[72] Art. 78 (8) of the UNCITRAL Model Law on Secured Transactions: "The notice referred to in paragraph 4 need not be given if the encumbered asset is perishable, may decline in value speedily or is of a kind sold on a recognized market".

[73] Art. 82 (4) of the UNCITRAL Model Law on Secured Transactions: "If a security right in a right to payment of funds credited to a bank account has been made effective against third parties by registration of a notice, the secured creditor is entitled to collect or otherwise enforce its security right only pursuant to an order of a court, unless the deposit-taking institution agrees otherwise".

2.4 Applying Principle 17 in Practice

The scenarios involving enforcing security rights in digital assets do not differ significantly from enforcing security rights in other types of assets. The World Bank Group has elaborated a Guidance Paper that provides insight into distributed ledger technology (DLT) and highlights the junctures at which this new technology impacts secured transaction frameworks.[74] In particular, the document "Distributed Ledger Technology & Secured Transactions: Legal, Regulatory and Technological Perspectives—Guidance Notes Series. Note 1: Collateral Registry, Secured Transactions Law and Practice" provides valuable illustrations where Principle 17 may be relevant.[75]

As it is described in this document, the usual scheme for this type of enforcement is quite simple, but in practice, it can be reproduced in several ways:

Scenario 1. *A borrower, through a lending platform, sends its digital assets to the collateral wallet of a secured creditor to secure the repayment of a loan. The secured creditor can be either the lending platform itself or a third party, in which case the platform may act as a custodian of the collateral. The collateral wallet may also have the capability to satisfy the secured obligation through a smart contract automatically. For example, in the event that the loan-to-collateral value ratio dips below a certain threshold, the collateral is automatically liquidated.*[76]

Scenario 2. *A secured transaction will entail a different enforcement mechanism when no custodian is involved, such as when the digital asset is deposited directly into a wallet of the secured creditor. However, the process for automatically liquidating the digital assets upon the occurrence of certain conditions may apply.*[77]

According to Principle 17, in the previous two scenarios, enforcement should not be problematic because the secured creditor has control of the digital asset, either directly or through a custodian. Therefore, in the event of default, the security right may be enforced out of court, subject to the requirement to proceed in good faith or a commercially reasonable manner.

---

[74] World Bank Group. Distributed Ledger Technology & Secured Transactions: Legal, Regulatory and Technological Perspectives—Guidance Notes Series. Note 3: Distributed Ledger Technology and Secured Transactions Frameworks: A primer, 2020.

[75] World Bank Group. Distributed Ledger Technology & Secured Transactions: Legal, Regulatory and Technological Perspectives—Guidance Notes Series. Note 1: Collateral Registry, Secured Transactions Law and Practice, 2020. In 3rd and 4th Working Group meetings, reference to this document is included in "additional resources".

[76] World Bank Group. Distributed Ledger Technology & Secured Transactions: Legal, Regulatory and Technological Perspectives—Guidance Notes Series. Note 1: Collateral Registry, Secured Transactions Law and Practice, 2020. p. 29.

[77] World Bank Group. Distributed Ledger Technology & Secured Transactions: Legal, Regulatory and Technological Perspectives—Guidance Notes Series. Note 1: Collateral Registry, Secured Transactions Law and Practice, 2020, p. 29.

Scenario 3. *A third possibility is when the secured creditor perfected by registering a notice without taking any other action to facilitate enforcement. In this case, it will need to identify the relevant collateral and demand its surrender, relying on cooperation by the grantor. Surrender of the collateral in custody of a third party may require a court order, similar to enforcing a security right in a bank account perfected by registration.*[78]

In this case, Principle 17.2 would apply. As a result, the secured creditor is only entitled to enforce its security right through judicial means unless the custodian agrees to cooperate. The analogy with the enforcement of collateral in a bank account is appropriate. The conclusion that can be reached from *Scenario 3* is that it is more efficient to transfer control to secured creditors. Control ensures that the enforcement can be carried out quickly and easily. However, as explained in this document, the transfer of control may not be an option in certain cases. For example, when the grantor's business is trading with digital assets.[79]

The forms in which these transactions are articulated vary widely. Contractual freedom allows for very different models of secured transactions in digital assets. The most interesting ones are those that enable extrajudicial enforcement. The multi-signature agreement is one of the most widely used models. For this reason, an example of this kind of contract is included in Commentary 17.9.:

Scenario 4. *In the case described in Commentary 17.9., a contract is concluded between three parties: the debtor, the secured creditor and a third party acting on behalf of the latter. The contract stipulates that control of the digital asset is shared by the three parties but that in the event of default, control may be transferred exclusively to the secured creditor. In practice, this type of multisig agreement is called 2–3 wallets. A 2–3 wallet requires two copayers to sign a transaction. Copayer A creates the transaction proposal. Either of the remaining copayers (copayer B or copayer C) can approve the transaction proposal. A 2–3 wallet has three copayers but requires only two signatures.*[80]

In this technological environment, another common use case is smart contracts. Smart contracts are innovative technology based on blockchain and digital signatures that allow the automation of contract enforcement in a secure, transparent, and efficient manner. This kind of technology is suitable for secured transactions. There are

---

[78] World Bank Group. Distributed Ledger Technology & Secured Transactions: Legal, Regulatory and Technological Perspectives—Guidance Notes Series. Note 1: Collateral Registry, Secured Transactions Law and Practice, 2020, p. 29.

[79] World Bank Group. Distributed Ledger Technology & Secured Transactions: Legal, Regulatory and Technological Perspectives—Guidance Notes Series. Note 1: Collateral Registry, Secured Transactions Law and Practice, 2020, p. 30.

[80] "What is a Multisignature (Multisig) or Shared Wallet?", Bitpay, October 2024 (https://support.bitpay.com/hc/en-us/articles/360032618692-What-is-a-Multisignature-Multisig-or-Shared-Wallet#:~:text=For%20example%2C%20a%203%2D3,the%20number%20of%20copayers%20needed.; last visit: 24/09/2024).

different types of smart contracts, some simple and others more complex. However, their main feature is that the software automatically executes a preprogrammed action if a condition is met.

A simple scheme is one in which a custodian holds a digital asset—security right—until the debtor completes the loan payment to the secured creditor. In the event of default on one of the payments, the smart contract transfers control of the digital asset directly to the secured creditor. Another possibility is that the digital asset liquidation occurs automatically if the collateral-to-loan ratio falls below a certain threshold (17.6). An interesting illustration was described in the second session of the Working Group:

Scenario 5. *The MakerDao system is an online service provider using smart contracts deployed on the Ethereum blockchain, which allows users to create structures that function like collateral transactions. Users surrender control of digital assets that are used as "collateral" by the system. Users then receive access to an amount of a system-generated stablecoin (i.e., a cryptocurrency designed to minimise the volatility of the price of the stablecoin, relative to some other asset). The newly created stablecoins are, by design, always over-collateralized and resemble property loans. If the ratio of the value of the withdrawn stablecoin to the value of the collateral hits a limit, the collateral can be liquidated using a semi-automated process. A user can also provide an amount of the stablecoin back to the system to reclaim their "collateral". The smart contracts automate all functionality required to use the system, which does not require an identifiable counterparty to function, and allows the user to obtain a liquid asset while maintaining market exposure.*[81]

In these cases, the feasibility of automatic enforcement will depend on the requirements set out in the general enforcement rules. In any case, the secured creditor must always act in a commercially reasonable manner or must conform with some other applicable standard, such as good faith (see Commentary 17.6). Grantor and debtor may waive their rights, but only after default.[82]

Sometimes, though, these mechanisms will be insufficient or unavailable for enforcement. This may occur, for example, where the grantor has control of the digital asset and decides not to cooperate with the secured creditor. In this scenario, the secured creditor might need a court order to obtain control. For this reason, Principle 17.2 references judicial enforcement, and the Commentary notes that "generally available methods provided under other law would apply, including judicial enforcement" (17.2). However, the possibility of judicial enforcement seems more theoretical than practical. As will be discussed in the considerations on Principle 18, judicial enforcement over digital assets presents several challenges that need to be addressed to ensure its effectiveness. Some of these challenges are the difficulty in identifying the person in control of the digital asset, preservation of the digital asset, or the

[81] UNIDROIT 2021—Study LXXXII—W.G.2—Doc. 2, p. 26.

[82] World Bank Group. Distributed Ledger Technology & Secured Transactions: Legal, Regulatory and Technological Perspectives—Guidance Notes Series. Note 1: Collateral Registry, Secured Transactions Law and Practice, 2020, p. 30.

need to involve several jurisdictions in enforcement. Although the Principles refer to judicial enforcement, they do not address these challenges directly. They recognise the relevance of adapting procedural regulation to develop digital assets. However, they merely identify the key issues that need to be addressed without elaborating on possible solutions.

Depending on the applicable national law, diverse scenarios may arise concerning judicial enforcement of security rights. The procedural law may recognise the possibility of directly enforcing the security right. In other words, it is possible that the secured creditor does not have to litigate in court to acknowledge the existence of its right. State law will require that the security rights contract meets certain requirements in these cases. If this possibility is not recognised by law, the judicial enforcement of the security right will be slower and more costly. Furthermore, the success of enforcement will be more uncertain, as the creditor will have to prove his claim in the process.

Finally, it should be noted that, depending on the judicial enforcement system in each State, enforcement may be carried out directly by a court or other public or private bodies to which the law assigns this function.

2.5 *Purpose of Principle 17*

The purpose of Principle 17 was made clear at the second session of the Working Group. At that time, it was noted that there was a need to create a Principle for each of the key issues of the secured transactions regime. Enforcement was among those key aspects. As stated above, the initial idea of the Working Group was to draft a Principle that set out the rules to enable the enforcement of security rights in digital assets, with the condition that these rules would provide adequate protection for all parties concerned. However, the aim of the Working Group was never to regulate the enforcement of security rights in digital assets. In line with the general approach of the Principles, a more modest objective was adopted from the beginning: to clarify the applicability of the general remedies provided for in the laws of the States, with the necessary adaptations required by the special nature of digital assets.[83] In this regard, Principle 17.1 clarifies that "enforcement of a security right in a digital asset is subject to other law, including any requirement to proceed in good faith or in a commercially reasonable manner, or both".

From this point of view, the main objective of Principle 17.1 seems to be to ensure that the level of protection of the security right over digital assets is the same as that of the security right over other types of assets. To this end, the best approach was to declare—as Commentary 17.3 does—that: "all enforcement actions, including disposal, collection of payment (...) and acceptance of the collateral, in full or partial satisfaction of the secured obligation, should be available in relation to security rights in digital assets". The Commentary clarifies the applicability of these remedies and

[83] UNIDROIT 2021—Study LXXXII—W.G.2—Doc. 2, p. 30.

notes that the exceptions generally provided for in the general secured transaction rules are equally applicable to digital assets (17.5). This is also an essential measure to ensure the same level of protection.

A different—and more concrete—purpose can be discerned in Principle 17.2. The best way to identify the purpose of this Principle is to examine its antecedents. In this sense, Principle F of the draft presented at the Working Group's fourth session—the direct antecedent of Principle 17.2—stated that "the interest of third parties, particularly custodians, should be protected."[84] This first draft was later redrafted and expanded in subsequent Working Group sessions. Still, it is interesting for its clarity on the Principle's purpose: to protect custodians. As noted in the Commentary to this draft, "this approach mirrors the rules that protect intermediaries, such as banks, against unknown third-party creditors."[85]

However, while the initial drafts opted to recognise such general protection for custodians, in subsequent sessions, the scope of such protection became more specific. As can be deduced from Commentary 17.8—and from the text of Principle 17.2 itself-, the aim is to safeguard the position of custodians when the secured creditor seeks to enforce a security right without having control of the digital asset. This issue merits further consideration.

As discussed in the Workshop on Issues Related to Enforcement in Digital Assets,[86] two scenarios must be distinguished when analysing the enforcement of security rights in digital assets: (1) the creditor has control over the digital asset; (2) the creditor does not control the digital asset. In the first scenario, extrajudicial enforcement is usually straightforward. In such cases, the digital asset may be held by a custodian on behalf of the secured creditor. However, in such a situation, the custodian does not need special protection; it simply has to comply with the secured creditor's instructions.

The second scenario, in contrast, covers all those situations in which the secured creditor, despite claiming ownership of security rights, does not have control over the digital asset. In these cases, the secured creditor can make effective its right by registration. However, it also covers situations where registration has not been properly done, or there is no registration. The right may exist irrespective of how it is made effective against third parties. The law must provide mechanisms for secured creditors to protect their rights. In these cases, the debtor or a custodian will hold control. Therefore, if a default occurs, the creditor should be able to obtain control of the digital asset or directly enforce its right without acquiring control of it. A more complicated situation arises when a custodian holds control of the digital asset (without an agreement between the custodian and the creditor). In such cases, the

[84] UNIDROIT 2021—Study LXXXII—W.G.4—Doc. 2, p. 56.

[85] UNIDROIT 2021—Study LXXXII—W.G.4—Doc. 2, p. 57.

[86] The full workshop is available at the following link: (https://www.youtube.com/watch?v=4u5VWv6ahLI&t=9200s; last visit: 27/09/2024). In particular, it is specially relevant to this matter the Roundtable 2 that focused on the enforcement of security rights in the context of secured transactions involving digital assets.

custodian may refuse to transfer control to the secured creditor because the secured creditor is, to all intents and purposes, a third party.

In light of the above, the purpose of Principle 17.2 is better understood. The purpose of this Principle is to clarify that the custodian has no duty to cooperate with the secured creditor in this second scenario. The rule has little merit since applying general secured transactions law could have reached the same conclusion. However, in a new and complex reality such as digital asset trading, a Principle that excises doubts and provides legal certainty to market operators is not superfluous. However, the purpose of Principle 17.2 is not only to protect custodians in these scenarios. A secondary objective can be inferred: to clarify that the secured creditor has the right to apply to a court for enforcement of the security right.

Principle 17.2 *in fine* states that "a secured creditor is entitled to enforce its security right only pursuant to a court or other public authority order, unless the custodian agrees otherwise". Again, this rule merely recognises something already clear before adopting the Principles: secured creditors also have the right to effective judicial protection, regardless of whether the security right is over a digital asset. This fundamental right is recognised in virtually all States under some international treaties such as the International Covenant on Civil and Political Rights (1966),[87] European Convention on Human Rights (1950)[88] or Charter of Fundamental Rights of the European Union (2012).[89]

References

Digital Assets and Private Law Working Group. (2021). Second session (remote). Rome, 16–18 March 2021. UNIDROIT 2021—Study LXXXII—W.G.2 – Doc. 2. English only. March 2021. https://www.unidroit.org/english/documents/2021/study82/wg02/s-82-wg02-02rev-01-e.pdf. Last visit January 29, 2025.

Digital Assets and Private Law Working Group. (2021). Third session (remote). Rome, 30 June–2 July 2021. UNIDROIT 2021—Study LXXXII—W.G.3—Doc. 2. English only. June 2021. https://www.unidroit.org/english/documents/2021/study82/wg03/s-82-wg03-02-rev01-e.pdf. Last visit January 29, 2025.

Digital Assets and Private Law Working Group. (2021). Third session (remote). Rome, 30 June–2 July 2021. UNIDROIT 2021—Study LXXXII—W.G.3—Doc. 4. English only. July 2021. https://www.unidroit.org/english/documents/2021/study82/wg03/s-82-wg03-02-rev01-e.pdf. Last visit January 29, 2025.

[87] Art. 14.1: "All persons shall be equal before the courts and tribunals. In the determination of any criminal charge against him, or of his rights and obligations in a suit at law, everyone shall be entitled to a fair and public hearing by a competent, independent and impartial tribunal established by law (…)".

[88] Art. 6.1.: "In the determination of his civil rights and obligations or of any criminal charge against him, everyone is entitled to a fair and public hearing within a reasonable time by an independent and impartial tribunal established by law.

[89] Art. 47.1.:" Everyone whose rights and freedoms guaranteed by the law of the Union are violated has the right to an effective remedy before a tribunal in compliance with the conditions laid down in this Article".

Digital Assets and Private Law Working Group. (2021). Fourth session (remote). Rome, 2–4 November 2021. UNIDROIT 2021—Study LXXXII—W.G.4—Doc. 2. English only. October 2021. https://www.unidroit.org/wp-content/uploads/2021/11/Study-82-WG4-Doc.-2-Revised-Issues-Paper-1.pdf. Last visit January 29, 2025.

Digital Assets and Private Law Working Group. (2021). Fourth session (remote). Rome, 2–4 November 2021. UNIDROIT 2021—Study LXXXII—W.G.4—Doc. 3. English only. December 2021. https://www.unidroit.org/wp-content/uploads/2022/12/Study-82-WG4-Doc.-3-Summary-Report.pdf. Last visit January 29, 2025.

Digital Assets and Private Law Working Group. (2021). Fifth session (hybrid). Rome, 7–9 March 2022. UNIDROIT 2022—Study LXXXII—W.G.5—Doc. 3. English only. February 2022. https://www.unidroit.org/wp-content/uploads/2022/03/W.G.5.-Doc.-3-Master-Copy-Principles-plus-Comments-with-Questions.pdf. Last visit February 05, 2025.

Digital Assets and Private Law Working Group. (2022). Fifth session (hybrid). Rome, 7–9 March 2022. UNIDROIT 2022—Study LXXXII—W.G.5—Doc. 4. English only. April 2022. https://www.unidroit.org/wp-content/uploads/2022/12/Study-82-WG5-Doc.-4-Summary-Report-of-the-5th-session-Final.pdf. Last visit February 05, 2025.

Digital Assets and Private Law Working Group. (2022). Sixth session (hybrid). Rome, 31 August–2 September 2022. UNIDROIT 2022—Study LXXXII—W.G.6—Doc. 2. English only. August 2022. https://www.unidroit.org/wp-content/uploads/2022/08/W.G.6-Doc.-2-Master-Copy-of-the-Draft-Principles-and-Comments-clean.pdf. Last visit February 05, 2025.

Digital Assets and Private Law Working Group. (2022). Sixth session (hybrid). Rome, 31 August–2 September 2022. UNIDROIT 2022—Study LXXXII—W.G.6—Doc. 3. English only. August 2022. https://www.unidroit.org/wp-content/uploads/2022/08/W.G.6-Doc.-3-Tracked-Principles-and-Issues-Paper.pdf. Last visit February 05, 2025.

Digital Assets and Private Law Working Group. (2022). Sixth session (hybrid). Rome, 31 August–2 September 2022. UNIDROIT 2022—Study LXXXII—W.G.6—Doc. 4. English only. August 2022. https://www.unidroit.org/wp-content/uploads/2022/12/W.G.6-Doc.-4-Summary-Report-of-the-6th-Session.pdf; Last visit February 05, 2025.

Digital Assets and Private Law Working Group. (2022). Seventh session (hybrid). Rome, 19–21 December 2022. UNIDROIT 2022—Study LXXXII—W.G.7—Doc. 2. English only. August 2022. https://www.unidroit.org/wp-content/uploads/2022/12/W.G.7-Doc.-2-Draft-Principles-and-Commentary.pdf. Last visit February 05, 2025.

Digital Assets and Private Law Working Group. (2022). Seventh session (hybrid). Rome, 19–21 December 2022. UNIDROIT 2022—Study LXXXII—W.G.7—Doc. 5. English only. February 2022. https://www.unidroit.org/wp-content/uploads/2023/03/W.G.7-Doc.-5-Summary-Report-of-the-7th-Session-1.pdf. Last visit February 05, 2025.

Digital Assets and Private Law Working Group. (2025). Eighth session (hybrid). Rome, 8–10 March 2023. UNIDROIT 2023—Study LXXXII—W.G.8—Doc. 2. English only. February 2023. https://www.unidroit.org/wp-content/uploads/2023/03/W.G.8-Doc.-2-Draft-Principles-and-Commentary-Clean.pdf. Last visit February 05, 2025.

Digital Assets and Private Law Working Group. (2023). Eighth session (hybrid). Rome, 8–10 March 2023. UNIDROIT 2023—Study LXXXII—W.G.8—Doc. 4. English only. February 2023. https://www.unidroit.org/wp-content/uploads/2023/03/W.G.8-Doc.-4-Public-Consultation-Comments-with-Annexes-1.pdf. Last visit February 05, 2025.

ELI Principles on the Use of Digital Assets as Security: Report of the European Law Institute. (2022). https://www.europeanlawinstitute.eu/fileadmin/user_upload/p_eli/Publications/ELI_Principles_on_the_Use_of_Digital_Assets_as_Security.pdf. Last visit February 05, 2025.

UNICITRAL Third International Colloquium on Secured Transactions. *Presentation by José Angelo Estrella Faria.* https://uncitral.un.org/sites/uncitral.un.org/files/media-documents/uncitral/en/jose_angelo_estrella_faria_edited.pdf. Last visit October 12, 2024.

UNICITRAL Practice Guide to the Model Law on Secured Transactions (p. 78). https://uncitral.un.org/sites/uncitral.un.org/files/media-documents/uncitral/en/19-10910_e.pdf. Last visit October 12, 2024.

UNIDROIT Legislative Guide on Intermediated Securities: Implementing the Principle and Rules of the Geneva Securities Convention, May 2017. https://www.unidroit.org/wp-content/uploads/2021/06/LEGISLATIVE-GUIDE-English.pdf. Last visit February 05, 2025.

World Bank Group. (2020). Distributed Ledger Technology & Secured Transactions: Legal, Regulatory and Technological Perspectives—Guidance Notes Series. Note 3: Distributed LedgerTechnology and Secured Transactions Frameworks: A primer. https://documentos.bancomundial.org/es/publication/documents-reports/documentdetail/541741588053800973/distributed-ledger-technology-and-secured-transactions-framework. Last visit February 05, 2025.

World Bank Group. (2020). Distributed Ledger Technology & Secured Transactions: Legal, Regulatory and Technological Perspectives—Guidance Notes Series. Note 1: Collateral Registry, Secured Transactions Law and Practice. https://documents1.worldbank.org/curated/en/288371588055212339/pdf/Collateral-Registry-Secured-Transactions-Law-and-Practice.pdf. Last visit September 24, 2024.

Reflections on Section VI: Procedural Law Including Enforcement

Principle 18
Procedural Law
Including Enforcement

Isabel Villar Fuentes

Unless otherwise provided for in these Principles, other law applies in respect of procedural matters, including enforcement, relating to digital assets.

1 Official Commentary

Commentary

18.1. Principle 18 makes it clear that the ordinary procedural law of a State, will apply to (i) any court proceedings concerning non-enforcement matters involving digital assets, (ii) any procedures for the enforcement of court orders involving digital assets, or (iii). Execution by way of authority with respect to digital assets. The first category includes proceedings which are not enforcement proceedings: such proceedings would include priority contests and proceedings in which it was necessary for a person to prove that they had control of a digital asset (see Principle 7). Category (ii) is self-explanatory. What is meant by category (iii) is explained in the rest of this paragraph. Execution is the process through which a creditor can obtain satisfaction of its claim against an obligor, by reaching and applying the value of an asset of the obligor or by a public authority obtaining rights in, or control over, such an asset. Depending on the jurisdiction (and the situation), this process can be triggered by various means including a court judgment or court order, an enforceable arbitral award, an out-of-court settlement which is given effect by law other than the law of contract or by an authentic document such as a document issued by a notary or other

This work was financed within the framework of the Prometeo 2023 project of the Regional Ministry of Innovation, Universities, Science and Digital Society (CIPROM/2022/26) "Present and future of the regulation of cryptoassets in the EU [LegalCripto]", whose principal investigator is Carmen Pastor Sempere. The basic ideas contained herein were presented in the author's paper with the same title, given on November 13, 2024 at the IV International Congress on "UNIDROIT Principles on Digital Assets and Private Law: Context, Content, Perspectives", organized also by BAES Research Group of the University of Alicante on November 13 and 14, 2024.

I. Villar Fuentes (✉)
University of Cádiz, Cádiz, Spain
e-mail: isabel.villar@uca.es

C. Pastor Sempere and D. A. Morán Bovio (eds.), UNIDROIT *Principles on Digital Assets and Private Law*, Law, Governance and Technology Series 80,
https://doi.org/10.1007/978-3-032-11001-5_24

public authority, or another enforceable instrument as defined by law. The process is carried out by a public authority or a private actor under the supervision of a public authority.

18.2. However, depending on the content of the procedural law of a particular State, some adaptations either to the law or the way the law operates in practice may be advisable in order to take account of the distinctive features of digital assets. Commentary 18.3 to 18.7 set out some examples of features, or combinations of features, which might make adaptations advisable.

18.3. In order to enforce a court order involving digital assets, or execution by way of authority with respect to digital assets, it will often be necessary for a public authority or a person authorised by a public authority to take control of one or more digital assets. This, however, may not be straightforward, compared to taking control (or taking possession) of other types of assets. For example, in a situation where the person who controls the digital asset is identified, that person might refuse to reveal the password which gives access to the wallet and/or the private key. It will therefore be necessary for a court (or other authority) to order that person to make a change of control or to otherwise enable access to the asset. It would be advisable for procedural law, and its operation, to facilitate this.

18.4. Where the identified person in control of the digital asset is a custodian, the public authority or person authorised by the public authority will want to instruct the custodian to make a change of control or to otherwise enable access to the asset. Again, unless the custodian agrees to do this, it would be necessary for a court (or other authority) to order the custodian to make a change of control or to otherwise enable access to the asset. It would be advisable for procedural law, and its operation, to facilitate this.

18.5. Another possible difficulty arising from the distinctive features of digital assets is that it will not always be straightforward to identify the person in control of the relevant digital asset. In this situation, the public authority, or person authorised by the public authority, may wish to obtain information from a third party, such as a custodian. For example, the information could be the information mentioned in Principle 6(1)(b). In other situations, information from a third party could be required more generally to enable proceedings or any process (such as an execution process) to be commenced or otherwise to be effective. In relation to all these situations, it would be advisable for procedural law, and its operation, to facilitate the necessary information to be obtained, although a balance will need to be struck between this facilitation, on one hand, and confidentiality and privacy requirements, on the other.

18.6. One feature of digital assets is that they can be transferred easily and quickly. In some situations, even though a tracing claim against substitute assets may remain (depending on the applicable other law), the value represented can be lost. Therefore, asset preservation could be important in court or other proceedings or in an execution process. It would be advisable for procedural law to facilitate this, for example, by providing for interim relief such as a freezing order or an order that control of digital assets be transferred to the court or other public authority.

18.7. A further feature of digital assets and the systems on which they are recorded is that they have no physical situs and the people who control them from time to time may be in many different jurisdictions. As a result, proceedings or execution processes are likely to be cross-border and involve courts or public authorities in many different jurisdictions. It would therefore be advisable for procedural law to take this into account.

18.8. Detailed work on the subject of execution by way of authority in respect of digital assets is being carried out by the UNIDROIT *project on 'Best Practices for Effective Enforcement' and for specific guidance, reference is made to the future work of this project.*

2 Reflections

2.1 Introduction

Principle 18 is an exclusive component of Section VI, Procedural Law, including the enforcement of the UNIDROIT Principles on Digital Assets and Private Law. Section VI, therefore, it has procedural treatment of digital assets as its sole objective. Principle 18 proclaims the application of the ordinary procedural law of each State, including enforcement with respect to digital assets.

Principle 18 identifies three scenarios in which procedural law may be involved: on the one hand, judicial proceedings unrelated to enforcement, proceedings to comply with a court order and, finally, judicial proceedings for the enforcement of judicial assets.

These procedural issues were not specifically addressed in a individualised manner until the eighth working session, although it is true that references to them, even if tangential, did arise at the first working sessions.

In the First Working Session, held from 17 to 19 November 2020, two distinct lines of work were identified: the legal treatment of digital assets in relation to insolvency proceedings and the enforcement of property rights over digital assets outside of insolvency proceedings. The latter, among those mentioned above, are addressed by Principle 18.

At the First Working Session, the question arises as to whether it is appropriate to include issues relating to the enforcement of judgments on digital assets in the Principles.[1]

---

[1] UNIDROIT 2020 – Study LXXXII – W.G.1 – Doc. 2, November, p. 18 - 20.

With regard to enforcement, the need to coordinate the development of the Principles on Digital Assets with the UNIDROIT Project on Enforcement was stressed at the outset of the Working Sessions. Along the same lines, account is taken of the application of emerging international standards that have arisen in the field of secured transactions, such as the UNCITRAL Model Law on Secured Transactions. To the extent possible, the project will also consider the application of other frameworks on the law of secured transactions, in particular those that have developed specific standards for digital assets.[2]

In this regard, in order to clarify and facilitate both the tracing and recovery of assets in general, and the specific cases of digital assets hosted in decentralized processes, the second working session focuses on issues related to the enforcement of judgments on digital assets which represent a bridge between the study and UNIDROIT Study LXXVI on Principles of Effective Enforcement. The project can also benefit from the emerging work of UNCITRAL on the tracing and recovery of civil assets. The decentralized, anonymous, autonomous and irrevocable processes involved in distributed ledger technology (DLT) have posed unique challenges for the tracing and recovery of certain digital assets (for example, cryptocurrencies), in particular in insolvency cases for the purpose of enforcing creditors' rights.[3]

Work on the drafting of Principles 17 and 18, as such, began at the seventh working session in 2022, and distinguishing between the objectives of both of them is important. Principle 17 Enforcement of security interests in digital assets, in Commentary 17.1 specifies that it does not refer to judicial enforcement that may be necessary when extrajudicial remedies are not available or cannot be enforced. These and other aspects relating to effective enforcement are studied in another UNIDROIT project on Good Practices for Effective Enforcement Procedures.[4]

Principle 18 had a first and initial draft, also at the seventh Working Session, but it was not fully developed until the eighth Working Session.

The final draft of Principle 18 states "Except as otherwise provided in these Principles, other rules shall apply in procedural matters, including enforcement, in relation to digital assets." The delimitation, referred to above, regarding the scope of this Principle is clear, referring to judicial proceedings, both non-enforcement (such as priority), and those related to enforcement, as well as those intended to execute a court order on digital assets.[5]

In the specific case of enforcement, it is taken into account that the satisfaction of the debt by the creditor with the obtaining and application of an asset of the debtor can be carried out by means of a court judgment, a court order, an arbitration award, an out-of-court agreement, an authentic document or any document that the law recognizes as an enforceable title. However, it is noted that the obtaining and application of a digital asset has some peculiarities caused by the technologies used that require adaptations to the Law of the States.

---

[2] UNIDROIT 2020 – Study LXXXII – W.G.1 – Doc. 2, November, p. 17.

[3] UNIDROIT 2020 – Study LXXXII – W.G.2 – Doc. 2, March, p. 37.

[4] This drafting of Principle 17 was developed in the seventh Working Session.

[5] Commentary 18.1.

One of these peculiarities, motivated by the technologies, was highlighted at the second working session: an important subset of questions within the framework of this section is related to the tracking and tracing of digital assets through transaction channels that may be novel, since they are based on new technologies and business models.[6]

The special nature of DLT reveals adaptations as essential, not only in the tracking and tracing of the digital asset, but also in access to it (taking control or taking possession).[7] Blockchains, whether there is a third party (custodian) or whether it is completely private, can pose problems of access to the private key, therefore, it will be necessary for a court (or other authority) to order that person to make a change of control or otherwise allow access to the asset. It would be advisable for procedural law, and its operation, to facilitate this.[8]

However, in some cases it is unknown who actually controls the digital asset, which is an added difficulty to the assumptions in Commentaries 18.3 and 18.4. In these cases, reference is made to the consideration of custodian established in principle 6.1. b): "A person has "control" of a digital asset if: the digital asset, or the relevant protocols or system, allow that person to identify itself as having the abilities established in sub-paragraph (a)".[9] In those cases where it is not possible to identify the person who controls the digital asset, it is necessary to resort to other means of Procedural Law that allow identification, while respecting confidentiality and privacy.[10]

Commentary 18.6 raises the need to preserve assets in a judicial procedure, given the easy transfer of the same. In this case, the convenience of adopting precautionary measures arises, such as preventive seizure or transfer of control of the litigious asset to the court or public authority.

As a consequence of the easy transfer of assets, cited, and the relocation of the records that contain them, the various transactions change temporally and geographically. Consequently, the procedures acquire a cross-border character, involving various jurisdictions that require a solution by Procedural Law to identify jurisdiction and judicial competence.[11]

---

[6] UNIDROIT 2021 – Study LXXXII – W. G. 2 – Doc. 2 (rev. 1), March, p. 36.

[7] Commentary 18.4.

[8] Commentary 18.3.

[9] The capabilities detailed in Principle 6.1.a) are: "(i) the exclusive ability to prevent others from obtaining substantially all of the benefit from the digital asset; (ii) the ability to obtain substantially all of the benefit from the digital asset; and (iii) the exclusive ability to transfer the abilities in sub-paragraphs (a)(i), (a)(ii) and (a)(iii) to another person."

[10] Commentary 18.5.

[11] Commentary 18.7.

2.2 Background

The work on Principle 18 was framed under the heading Remedies and Enforcement within Working Subgroup 3 "Secure Transactions".

In heading 8. "Remedies and Enforcement", Working Subgroup 3 addresses issues that would give rise to Principles 17 and 18.

At the first working session, Subgroup 3 ventured into potential difficulties in relation to "following and tracing digital assets through transaction pathways that may be novel, as they are based on new technologies and business models".[12] These issues are made clear in Principle 18.4 and Procedural Law still needs to address them.

Likewise, it is important to mention the convenience of supporting work in the field of enforcement with the work of UNCITRAL on the tracing and recovery of civil assets, taking into account the special characteristics of digital asset registries. "Decentralized, anonymous, autonomous, and irrevocable processes involved in distributed ledger technology (DLT) has raised unique challenges for the tracing and recovery of certain digital assets (e.g., cryptocurrency), particularly in insolvency for the purpose of enforcing the rights of creditors. An UNCITRAL Colloquium discussed various challenges that arise from tracing and recovering digital assets such as cryptocurrencies, air miles, and virtual online game itmes".[13]

At that session, Ms. Rodríguez de las Heras Ballell warned that there are some loopholes regarding digital assets in the UNCITRAL Principles. To this end, she distinguishes three possible positions in order to remedy this issue: treating digital assets as a new modality with new rules; identifying categories of digital assets with real assets (both tangible and intangible) or not making new specific rules and applying the existing ones, but with a series of adjustments "for the creation, perfection, custody, delivery and transferability of digital assets, legally or technologically.[14] Along the same lines, she warns that the UNCITRAL MLST in the judicial or extrajudicial claim provides for a notice to competing plaintiffs that is not operative in the digital assets market since it is a market for instantaneous transactions.[15] Finally, with regard to how to resolve the conflict of laws, the UNCITRAL MLST addresses the law of the location of the asset, in the case of tangible assets, and the location of the grantor, in the case of intangible assets. Such location criteria are difficult to transpose into digital assets. As possible references for the location of

[12] UNIDROIT 2020 – Study LXXXII – W.G.1 – Doc. 2, November 2020, p. 19.

[13] UNIDROIT 2020 – Study LXXXII – W.G.1 – Doc. 2, November 2020, p. 20.

[14] UNIDROIT 2020 – Study LXXXII – W.G.1 – Doc. 3, November 2020, p. 10.

[15] UNIDROIT 2020 – Study LXXXII – W.G.1 – Doc. 2, November 2020, p. 10. Ms. Rodriguez de las Heras Ballell comments that e irreversibility of certain actions in DLT systems, as well as the lack of traceability, led to several additional issues in execution. It was also noted that private key transfers were not recorded in the ledger, which added complexity and allowed for untraceable actions within the DLT system. She also highlighted the issues posed by smart contracts for pre-programmed execution, which were not aligned with the mechanisms found in the UNCITRAL MLST and might not meet applicable requirements.

digital assets it proposes: that of the holder of the keys, that of the nodes or even that of a wallet provider as a receiver of deposits.

At the second working session, under section 8. "Resources and enforcement", the difficulties posed by decentralized registries to change a registry, by virtue of a court order, are again highlighted.[16]

At this working session, the questions that arise and possible coordination with UNCITRAL and the UNIDROIT Compliance Project must continue to be assessed at the following working meetings.

At the following working sessions, the Enforcement Section is not addressed; only in the fifth working session is the germ of what would become Principle 17 developed, included as Principle 19: "Effective Enforcement of Security Rights in Digital Assets". However, the issue of Procedural Law is not developed, including the execution of Principle 18 analysed here.

The truth of the matter is that the first results of drafting Principle 18 did not arrive until the seventh working session, where it was only mentioned and a comment was made limiting its scope: ordinary procedural law will apply in general to any judicial procedure involving digital assets or to any procedure for the enforcement of judicial decisions involving digital assets.[17]

Principle 18 was fully drafted at the eighth working session, in which the wording of the Principle statement was modified and the eight final Commentaries were developed.

At that session, Section VI, which had been called "Enforcement" throughout the process of drafting the Principles, was renamed as "Procedural Law, including Enforcement". In the same vein, Principle 18 "Compliance", as of this last working session, saw its title changed, replicating that of Section VI Procedural Law, including Enforcement.[18]

The change in designation is justified by the delimitation of categories included in the first Commentary of Principle 18 "(i) any judicial proceedings relating to matters other than enforcement affecting digital assets, (ii) any proceedings for the enforcement of court orders affecting digital assets, or (iii) enforcement by the judicial authority with respect to digital assets."

The scope of the Principle is not limited to enforcement, the wording of the seventh working session was clearer: "it will apply generally to any procedure involving digital assets or any procedure for the enforcement of judicial decisions involving digital assets."

This eighth working session compiles the issues raised by the members of the working groups in all the Principles.

In relation to Principle 18, it is worth highlighting, first of all, the comment by Dr. Benjamin Hayward (Monash University), who states that Principle 18 establishes, in non-exhaustive terms, that, in respect of procedural matters relating to digital assets, another law applies. The concept of other law is defined as "the law of a State to

---

[16] UNIDROIT 2020 – Study LXXXII – W.G.2 – Doc. 2, March 2021, p. 37.

[17] UNIDROIT 2020 – Study LXXXII – W.G.7 – Doc. 2, December 2022, p. 56.

[18] UNIDROIT 2020 – Study LXXXII – W.G.8 – Doc. 3, February 2022, p. 69.

the extent that it is not the law of the Principles" (Principle 2(4)), while the law of the Principles "means any part of the law of a State that falls within the scope of application of these Principles" (Principle 2(3)). He suggests that the statement of this principle needs a qualification, otherwise it would conflict with the provisions of Principle 5 Applicable Law.[19]

On this issue, there are positions in favour of the approach of Principle 18, where the applicable procedural law corresponds to that of each State, without warning of doubts in its application, as is the case brought forward by Mr. Purin.[20]

The potential problem at this point lies in the clear distinction between what are "procedural matters" and "substantive law", an essential starting point for determining whether the applicable law is determined by Principle 5 or by the law of the State. The differentiation between procedural matters and substantive matters may vary in the different systems, which is why the Commercial Law Centre of the University of Aberdeen suggests the inclusion of a clear reference to what is procedure and what is substance.[21]

Underlying this whole issue is the fear of distorting the purpose of the Principles, insofar as the reference to the procedural legislation of each of the States could hinder the desired harmonization.

Ms. Harkin, in order to preserve the benefits desired by the Principles, proposes the inclusion of some "standards or minimums" of a procedural nature to avoid the disparity of procedural criteria in the corresponding States.[22] This position is defended with two examples that have been previously presented in this work and that are indeed likely to raise certain issues.

This is the case of "control of the digital asset", presented by Ms. Harkin, which, according to Principle 15, is sufficient to achieve effectiveness among third parties. The doubt that would arise would be the case in which a State adds the procedural requirement "such as notice and/or registering the guarantee".

Another challenge raised by Ms. Harkin is the one referred to in Commentary 7 of Principle 18: a characteristic of digital assets and the systems or platforms in which they are registered is that the persons who control them may be located in different jurisdictions, which makes the international enforcement of judgments difficult, compared to the enforcement of arbitral awards. The New York Convention on the Recognition and Enforcement of Foreign Arbitral Awards, of June 10,

---

[19] UNIDROIT 2020 – Study LXXXII – W.G.8 – Doc. 4, February 2023, p.108, Paragraph 304.

[20] UNIDROIT 2020 – Study LXXXII – W.G.8 – Doc. 4, February 2023, p.108, Paragraph 306.

[21] UNIDROIT 2020 – Study LXXXII – W.G.8 – Doc. 4, February 2023, p.108, Paragraph 307. The Commercial Law Centre of the University of Aberdeen gives as an example Article 5 of the Proposal for a Regulation of the European Parliament and of the Council on the law applicable to the effects vis-à-vis third parties of assignments of receivables, where a "non-exhaustive list of procedural issues" is agreed. This issue, however, is not subject to debate, but is highlighted for its clarity by Mr Purin (Deputy General Counsel, OKX ME) in commentary 5 to Principle 18 or by Mr Mendoza (UNIDROIT Correspondent in Guatemala) in commentary 7.

[22] UNIDROIT 2020 – Study LXXXII – W.G.8 – Doc. 4, February 2023, p.109, Paragraph 309.

1958, facilitates international enforcement in more than 160 States,[23] and supports arbitration to achieve efficient execution.

2.3 Challenges

Principle 18 is unlike the rest of the Principles, since it detracts from the issues covered by the rest of the Principles, and instead refers them to State law.

The spirit of the UNIDROIT Principles on Digital Assets and Private Law is an original attempt to create - and not just to identify - an international standard on the patrimonial aspects of digital assets.[24] New and different technological realities require an international framework that facilitates legislators and users to address the "patrimonial use of digital assets." This framework is delimited in the Foreword of the Principles to the areas in which the nature and characteristics of digital assets required a legal qualification or in which ad hoc solutions were demanded.[25] The aim is to fill gaps and provide legal certainty in pre-existing private law, referring the rest of the issues to domestic private law.

In the specific case of Procedural Law and Enforcement, Principle 18 transfers everything related to it to "other rules", meaning by such "ordinary Procedural Law of a State", as indicated in Comment 18.1 of the Principle.

The Procedural Law of each State will be sovereign in judicial proceedings, whether or not they are for enforcement, and in the execution of a court order that falls on digital assets.

While it is true that Commentary 18.2 of the Principle warns, in a general way, of necessary adaptations or facilities that Procedural Law must contemplate, it also specifically raises concrete examples in Commentaries 18.3 to 18.7.

In the problems that are evident in Commentaries 18.3 to 18.7, three categories are identified:

a. Identification of the person who controls the digital asset and change of control:
    i. Assumption of control of the digital asset by a public authority or authorized person (18.3).
    ii. Change of control of the asset by the custodian (18.4).
    iii. Identification of the person controlling the digital asset (18.5).
b. Adoption of precautionary measures (18.6).
c. Diversity of jurisdictions and cross-border enforcement based on this classification, some reflections are raised for each of the cases.

---

[23] UNIDROIT 2020 – Study LXXXII – W.G.8 – Doc. 4, February 2023, p.109, Paragraph 309.

[24] UNIDROIT PRINCIPLES ON DIGITAL ASSETS AND PRIVATE LAW, Foreword, p. i.

[25] UNIDROIT PRINCIPLES ON DIGITAL ASSETS AND PRIVATE LAW, Foreword, p. i.

2.3.1 Identification of the Person Controlling the Digital Asset and Change of Control

Taking control (possession) and identifying the person who holds it in the digital asset is revealed to be more complex for the public authority, compared to other assets, due to decentralized registry technologies.

At the second working session, a general question is raised about how property rights over digital assets can be enforced given the nature of the technical system in which digital assets are created, maintained and managed. For example, when a distributed registry system does not depend on a central counterparty with authorization to change the registry in response to a court order, questions will arise about how property rights are enforced in the corresponding ledger. For this reason, a reflection on the technology that supports most of these assets is appropriate.[26]

It is worth starting from the concept coined by the EU in the Decentralized Registry Technologies Regulation, which defines DLT as a technology that allows the operation and use of decentralized registries and the decentralized registry as a repository of information that keeps records of transactions and is shared through a set of DLT network nodes and is synchronized between said nodes, using a consensus mechanism.[27]

Among the purposes of the The DLT Regulation, it highlights guaranteeing "the continuity and continued transparency, availability, reliability and security of the services provided, including the reliability of any smart contracts that are used, regardless of whether those smart contracts are created by the DLT market infrastructure itself or by a third party following outsourcing procedures".[28]

In this regard, in 2018 the Commission cooperated in the establishment of a European Blockchain Services Infrastructure (EBSI)[29] and recognises the importance of legal certainty and a clear regulatory regime in areas related to blockchain-based

---

[26] UNIDROIT 2020 – Study LXXXII – W.G.2 – Doc. 2, March 2021, pp. 36–37.

[27] Art. 2, Paragraphs 1) and 2) of the Decentralized Ledger Technologies Regulation 2022/858. This art. 2, in its paragraphs 3), 4) and 5) raises other definitions of interest regarding these blockchain-based technologies: "3) 'consensus mechanism': the rules and procedures by which an agreement is reached to validate a transaction between the TRD network nodes; 4) 'TRD network node': a device or process that is part of a network and that possesses a complete or partial copy of the records of all transactions in a decentralized registry; 5) 'TRD-based market infrastructure': a TRD-based multilateral trading system, a TRD-based settlement system or a TRD-based trading and settlement system."

[28] REGULATION (EU) 2022/858 OF THE EUROPEAN PARLIAMENT AND OF THE COUNCIL of 30 May 2022.

on a pilot regime for market infrastructures based on distributed ledger technology, and amending Regulations (EU) No 600/2014 and (EU) No 909/2014 and Directive 2014/65/EU Regulation on Market Infrastructures based on Distributed Ledger Technology 2022/858, p. 8.

[29] https://ec.europa.eu/digital-building-blocks/wikis/display/EBSI/Home. The Commission within the framework of the EU Blockchain Observatory and Forum establishes the European Blockchain Partnership (EBP), and cooperates in establishing a European Blockchain Services Infrastructure (EBSI) On 10 April 2018 the EU and Norway, with 8 more countries subsequently joining. The European Blockchain Services Infrastructure (EBSI) consists of a peer-to-peer network of interconnected nodes running a blockchain-based service infrastructure. Each member of the European Blockchain

applications. It is currently developing a legal framework favourable to innovation in the areas of digital assets (tokenisation) and smart contracts that protects consumers and provides legal certainty to businesses. The Commission strongly supports a pan-European framework that hopes to avoid legal and regulatory fragmentation.

It could be said that blockchain is not a simple isolated record, as it does not only record and save an agreement or transaction, but rather it records a complete sequence of several agreements or transactions. That is why it is also recognised as a ledger "digital ledger technology".

It is decentralised technology, as there is no authority (third party) that hosts and manages the transactions, since the transactions themselves are located in the chain itself, to which all its nodes (terminals that have access to the chain) have access. Verification controls are carried out by authorizing nodes, using peer-to-peer (P2P) technology. The decentralized nature of the technology is also supported by the fact that all nodes have access to all the information in the blockchain. Consequently, blockchain is also known as a "record book", since without a third party storing and certifying the contents, the chain itself houses them in each of its blocks. It is also immutable, since each of the transactions recorded by the authorized nodes generates an unalterable hash. Immutability is supported by the procedure that provides security for the authorizing or verifier nodes. The hash is verified by the authorizing nodes that, using cryptographic encryption, verify that the hash has not been modified and only then is the block closed, allowing the opening of the next one. Since each of the blocks is connected by a link that causes the next one to open when the previous one is closed after verification, it is self-executing, without the possibility of interfering in the execution thereof.

In relation to the problems raised in this first section of identification of the person who controls the digital asset and change of control, it is important to distinguish the types of blockchains:

Public Blockchains

Public blockchains are characterized by free access, so that none of the transactions can be hidden and they are authorized or free, each node is authorized to carry out the relevant transactions.

Within public blockchains, however, there are some unauthorized ones, as is the case of those used in cryptocurrencies. For example, Bitcoin or Ethereum, in these chains the work of the authorizing nodes (miners) is considerable and remunerated.

Private Blockchains

There are also private blockchains, where access is restricted to authorized nodes that are the only ones that can carry out transactions. These chains are the ones that are usually used by supply chains and data storage. One example of this is the Morpheus Network, which is a supply chain with blockchain technology supported by smart contracts. Morpheus Network combines private chains that are also integrated into

---

Partnership (EBPS) – the 27 EU countries, Norway, Liechtenstein and the Commission – will run at least one node.

a global public and authorized chain. It is part of the private blockchain system, so that users must be authorized by the blockchain network and can only enter if they receive an invitation.

Users interact with the chain through nodes, using a private key to sign their transaction, which upon completion is redirected to the network with their public key. When entering the network with the public key, the transaction signed with the private key connects with its peer. The certainty of the origin, authentication and integrity of the content signed with the private key is guaranteed with cryptography, which is closed and generates a seal in time.

Mixed Blockchains

Finally, the mixed version consists of public chains (permissioned blockchain), which only give access to certain nodes to carry out transactions, while not hiding them.

Furthermore, the European Market in Crypto-Assets Regulation (MiCA) within the European framework, offers measures that could be useful for States in the procedural treatment of identification of the person who exercises control of the digital asset and change of control of it.

The European Market in Crypto-Assets Regulation (MiCA) defines crypto-assets as a digital representation of value or rights that can be transferred and stored electronically, using decentralized registry technology or similar technology (art. 3.1.6).[30]

The concept of cryptocurrency was further defined by Directive 2015/849, which defined it as a digital representation of value not issued or guaranteed by a central bank or public authority, not necessarily associated with legal tender, not considered to be currency, but accepted by natural or legal persons as a means of payment and which can be transferred, stored or negotiated via electronic means.

The new European Market in Crypto-Assets Regulation (MiCA) imposes certain requirements on both crypto-asset issuers and crypto-asset service providers. Crypto-asset issuers are required to provide complete and transparent information on the crypto-assets they issue, as well as to comply with disclosure and transparency conditions. Regarding service providers, it determines the obligation to be registered as such and to comply with money laundering regulations.

These transparency and information measures would be key for States to apply Procedural Law in the issues at hand. In order to shed some light on the section under consideration, Identification of the person who controls the digital asset and change of control, it should be noted that the first equation that must be resolved is the identification of the person who controls the digital asset (18.5). The complexity of this task will vary, depending on the public, private or semi-private nature of the chain, as explained above.

The Best Practices for Effective Enforcement Working Group also warns of the obstacles in this identification: "Experts then discussed the problem of tracing of,

---

[30] Regulation (EU) 2023/1114 of the European Parliament and of the Council of 31 May 2023 on markets in crypto-assets, and amending Regulations (EU) No 1093/2010 and (EU) No 1095/2010 and Directives 2013/36/EU and (EU) 2019/1937 (Text with EEA relevance).

and access to, digital assets for the purpose of enforcement. It was suggested that in many legal systems enforcement agents lacked the means to trace digital assets without the debtor's cooperation, especially when they were kept in a personal wallet with no intermediary, and that other means of putting the non-compliant debtor under pressure should be considered".[31]

Concerns about tracking and recovering assets are seen as more complex, as they will have to be located and the person who controls them identified. This is stated in the second working session: "The decentralized, anonymous, autonomous and irrevocable processes involved in distributed ledger technology (DLT) have posed unique challenges for the tracking and recovery of certain digital assets (for example, cryptocurrencies), particularly in cases of insolvency in order to enforce creditors' rights".[32]

Cryptocurrencies, in particular, have two implementation modes: legal platforms-centralized cryptocurrency services and decentralized service platforms.

Legal platforms with centralized cryptocurrency services highlight the role of "specialized intermediaries" thereof. Wallet providers are companies that provide users with electronic wallets, i.e. mechanisms for storing, saving and transferring Bitcoin or other cryptocurrencies. Specifically, in addition to providing the electronic wallet, the wallet provider stores the private keys of the account, facilitates the transactions of users and exchangers and, ultimately, acts as an intermediary.

The operation of these cryptocurrency wallets is based on the know your customer maxim, which is why the amounts, frequency of transactions and the clients using wallets must be identifiable. In accordance with Directive 2018/843, providers of electronic wallets are obliged to provide this information and to store it, always while preserving the data of their clients in accordance with the General Data Protection Regulation. Likewise, they must report suspicious transactions to the competent authority of the Member State and to the FIU (Financial Intelligence Unit), with a provision for strong administrative and criminal sanctions as a deterrent.

On the contrary, decentralized service platforms imply greater difficulty in identifying the subjects (natural or legal person) and the transactions carried out. In these cases, there is no intermediary figure, which is why the electronic wallet provider disappears. The situation is aggravated if one takes into account that, both in Spain and in the Eurozone, decentralized cryptocurrency services monopolize more than 50% of the trading activity of these services.

The "Liechtenstein Blockchain Law" presented by Mr. Nägele at the first working session is paradigmatic here, where the decentralized system itself provides reliable technology: "TT" (trustworthy technology) systems were used in legislation to reflect technological neutrality and referred to systems that functioned without intermediaries and in which users could trust. The main functions of tokens were legitimation (for the benefit of the beneficiary), release (for the benefit of the debtor) and transport (the transfer of the underlying rights).[33]

---

[31] UNIDROIT 2022 – LXXVIB – W.G.3 – Doc. 6, January 2022, p.9.

[32] UNIDROIT 2020 – Study LXXXII – W.G.2 – Doc. 2, March 2021, p. 37, section 122.

[33] UNIDROIT 2020 – Study LXXXII – W.G.1 – Doc. 1, November 2020, pp. 13–14.

In short, Mr. Nägele specifies that the combination of a system of trusted technologies as well as a legal framework for transactions within them enabled effective execution of digital transactions with respect to their real-world assets in Liechtenstein. To bridge the gap between the physical and digital world, ensure execution, avoid rights conflicts and enable identification and storage of real-world assets, the Act created physical validators, who were persons who ensured the execution of rights in accordance with the agreement, in terms of property rights, represented by tokens in TT systems.

The absence of intermediaries would undoubtedly make it difficult to identify the person exercising control, since each user acts within the system independently. However, the "physical validators" mentioned by Mr. Nägele in the Liechtenstein Blockchain Act can be of great value as guarantors of the execution of rights in accordance with the agreement.

Nonetheless, identification of the person controlling the digital asset, as well as the tracking and recovery of assets in these technologies is complex from the perspective of civil procedural law. Procedural law in the criminal field has technological investigative procedures, such as the case of Chainalysis Reactor,[34] used by police forces around the world. In this line, GAFILAT has developed the Guide on Relevant Aspects and Appropriate Steps for the Investigation, Identification, Seizure and Confiscation of Virtual Assets.[35]

On the contrary, asset tracing and recovery in private law does not meet the conditions of criminal investigation and therefore its requirements, so that fundamental rights are not violated.

The necessary balance between asset tracing and recovery without clashing with fundamental rights is referred to at the first UNIDROIT working meeting on Best Practices for effective implementation: The President noted that there was general agreement that the instrument would have to address the interaction with constitutional principles and, in particular, with fundamental rights and principles related to legal protection, although it was considered premature to decide on its content and whether such principles should be included in an introductory part or elsewhere. The reference role of the protection of fundamental rights had been highlighted: when proposing best practices that facilitate the application of the law, their compatibility with existing constitutional frameworks should be checked.[36]

This UNIDROIT Project on Best Practices for Effective Enforcement, which is the recommended reference document for the Project on Digital Assets and Private

[34] https://www.chainalysis.com/. Chainalysis has classified more than 29 types of danger that are distributed in 4 alert levels: low, intermediate, high and severe. In the intermediate level you can find suspicious transactions between individuals; in the high level you can find purchases on the darknet, fraudulent stores and transactions linked to scams. The platform also detects if the cryptocurrencies exchanged come from a high-risk jurisdiction, such as countries like Russia, Venezuela or Iran.

[35] "Guía sobre Aspectos Relevantes y Pasos Apropiados para la Investigación, Identificación, Incautación y Decomiso de Activos Virtuales" December/2021.

[36] UNIDROIT 2020 – Study LXXVIB – W. G. 1. – Doc. 4, November 2020, p. 3.

Law,[37] as noted in the background, also highlights the unique nature[38] of access to information and transparency, and tracking of the debtor's assets, the latter being a very important element for which the impact of technology would be particularly relevant (for example, electronic records would facilitate the tracking of assets).[39]

The judicial work of tracking and recovering digital assets, therefore, has a narrow scope of action in the sphere of private law and is conditioned by the different types of technologies adopted in each jurisdiction.

The specific impact of the different technologies that are used raises a general question on how property rights over digital assets can be enforced given the nature of the technical system in which digital assets are created, maintained and managed. For example, where a distributed ledger system does not rely on a central counterparty with the authority to change the ledger in response to a court order, questions will arise as to how ownership rights are enforced in the relevant ledger. However, the general question of how to enforce ownership rights in the case of unknown holders is not new per se, and it is possible that existing concepts can be adapted to address the enforcement of ownership rights over digital assets.[40]

On the other hand, the existence of a custodian, for the purposes of effecting the change of control, is also somewhat difficult. This was noted in the March 2021 session, where Mr. Luc Thévenoz clarified that paragraph 6 referred to a situation where a party owed DA to different persons and the fact that the party maintained accounts was not indicative of it being a custodian (for example, the party could be a seller, a brokerage firm operating or acting as a bank). There could be a personal claim against the party (but not a property claim that would provide protection in the event of insolvency), and the party needed to keep records; however, this did not imply that it was a custodian.[41]

This position on wallet providers, cited above on centralized platforms, interprets that they cannot be considered as custodians in the strict sense.

However, according to Principle 10 this exclusion is not determinative:

(a) 'custodian' means a person who provides services to a client pursuant to a custody agreement as defined in paragraphs (3) and (4), and is acting in that capacity; (2) A custodian 'maintains' a digital asset for a client if: (a) that custodian has control of the digital asset; or (b) that custodian enters into a custody agreement, as defined in paragraph (3), with a sub-custodian with respect to the digital asset in the circumstances set out in Principle 11(4). (3) Subject to paragraph (4), an agreement for services to a client in relation to a digital asset is a 'custody agreement' if: (a) the service is provided in the ordinary course of the service provider's business; (b)

[37] UNIDROIT 2021– Study LXXXII – W. G. 2. – Doc. 2, March 2021, p. 37.

[38] UNIDROIT 2020 – Study LXXVIB – W. G. 1. – Doc. 4, November 2020, p. 6, they confirmed that, in principle, digital assets would not need an alternative framework, while the question would be how to best integrate technology into existing procedures, which may influence the nature of the proceedings.

[39] UNIDROIT 2020 – Study LXXVIB, GT1, Doc. 4, p.5.

[40] UNIDROIT 2021 Study LXXXII – W. G. 2. – Doc. 2, March 2021, pp. 36–37.

[41] UNIDROIT 2021 – Study LXXXII – W. G. 2. – Doc. 3, March 2021, p. 5.

the service provider is obliged to obtain (if this is not yet the case) and to maintain the digital asset for the client; and (c) the client does not have the exclusive ability to change the control of the digital asset within the meaning of Principle 6(2).

More specifically, Principle 10 provides an example of custody (10.10):

The term 'wallet' in the following illustrations is used in the colloquial sense in which it is used in the market, that is, software (or hardware) that enables a person to interact with a digital asset, for example, via the generation and management of public and/or private keys. The means by which, and by whom, this interaction is effected depends on the type of wallet. As provided in Principles 10(3) and 10(4) and Commentary 10.7, an agreement between a client and a service provider in the context set out in Commentary 10.11 and 10.12 will be a custody agreement unless it is made clear that the assets controlled by the service provider form part of the service provider's assets available for distribution to its creditors if it enters into an insolvency-related proceeding [...].

In that case, the service provider using the "wallet" must be interpreted as a custodian and therefore obliged to provide the private key of the digital asset, in order to carry out the change of control.

In this case, as in any other case of change and assumption of control, coercion is required, which will be determined by the different legal systems, in principle by the competent judicial body or public authority.

2.3.2 Adoption of Precautionary Measures

The sixth Commentary on Principle 18 states that a characteristic of digital assets is that they can be transferred easily and quickly. It is worth noting that the risk of volatility of digital assets is greater than that of other assets, which is why the need to adopt some type of precautionary measures would be a priority. Commentary 18.6 itself suggests a precautionary seizure order or an order to transfer control of the digital assets to the court or other public authority as a means of preserving the asset, both in declaratory and executive judicial proceedings.

Precautionary protection in judicial proceedings is a pillar of effective judicial protection, since it guarantees the execution of the judgment. This protection is revealed to be essential in both judicial and arbitration proceedings, since the condition of *periculum in mora* is inherent to judicial assets due to the speed of transfers in them. However, the possibility of adopting precautionary measures again encounters the same obstacle as in the previous section on Identification of the person who controls the digital asset and change of control.

In order to be able to make a precautionary measure of any nature effective, it will be necessary, first of all, to identify the person who controls the digital asset in order to be able to carry it out.

The possible scenarios of precautionary protection condition its operation. If it is about cryptocurrencies, the difference between legal platforms-centralized cryptocurrency services and decentralized service platforms was previously referred to.

In the first case of centralized services, if the platform in question has been identified, by court order, and after fulfilling the requirements of each jurisdiction, it may be subject to seizure of the cryptocurrency. This seizure requires the control of the cryptocurrency for its materialization, in favour of the court or public authority. For this, the private key necessary to carry out the transactions must be in the possession of the corresponding authority.

However, cryptocurrencies developed on decentralized service platforms imply an obstacle in the application of precautionary measures and consequently of the execution itself, which may be necessary.

Another scenario arises with NFTs. Despite being hosted on a DLT, the platform on which they are located is identifiable and allows them to be made available to the competent judicial or public authority to be kept in a wallet. NFTs have various uses, including proof of the authenticity of an artistic work or collateral for obtaining a loan.

If we refer to smart contracts formalised on blockchain, we start from a principle of mutual trust between the parties. In this case, that means the possibility of including a condition that would allow a judicial body to access it, read it, modify it or take control of it. If the courts or competent public authorities had access to the "ecosystem" of DLTs in smart contracts from their management system, precautionary measures, specifically, control of the ecosystem, would be feasible.

Commentary 18.6 again transfers to procedural law and the implementation necessary to update it to the new legal realities caused by technologies.

2.3.3 Diversity of Jurisdictions and Cross-Border Enforcement

Commentary 18.7 of the Principles poses another challenge for State procedural law, by highlighting another characteristic of digital assets and the systems in which they are recorded, in that they do not have a physical location and the persons who control them at any given time may be located in many different jurisdictions.

Firstly, the technologies themselves, on which digital assets are based, of a decentralized nature, may have different nodes in different States, as well as verification terminals.

Similarly, the transactions that can be carried out on DLTs are not affected by borders and therefore allow rapid international transactions. As a consequence, legal systems and therefore jurisdictions are often diverse.

The Principles highlight in the FOREWORD that "it is essentially a transactional instrument, which seeks to assist legislators and users in solving the complexities that concern the proprietary use of digital assets".[42] In this sense, it is "an original attempt

[42] UNIDROIT PRINCIPLES ON DIGITAL ASSETS AND PRIVATE LAW, Roma 2023, p. i.

at creating – not merely identifying – an international standard on the proprietary aspects of digital assets".

These aspirations make clear that "the prudent approach adopted by the Principles, which only cover those areas where the nature and characteristics of digital assets required legal clarification or where ad hoc solutions were demanded. The rest – the majority – of private law matters are left to domestic law, although, even where reference is made to "other law" (as it is called), helpful guidance and legal analysis is provided in the Commentary…".[43]

In relation to procedural law, section 0.18 of CORE CONCEPTS AND RULES states: "the Principles generally provide for the application of other law to address procedural matters, including the enforcement of rights relating to digital assets. See Principle 18.".[44]

The third working session delimits the scope of the Principles in terms of applicable law: "The scope of this Project is limited to the issues of applicable law, while other issues are likely to be explored by the Hague Conference on Private International Law or other organisations. On this note, the WG agreed at its first session that close collaboration and coordination with the HCCH regarding PIL matters (applicable law) was highly desirable."[45]

The coordinated work between these organizations is also included in the HCCH: "the HCCH participated as an observer in the first session of UNIDROIT's Working Group on Digital Assets and Private Law, held online from 17 to 19 November 2020. UNCITRAL and UNIDROIT are also working on the development of a legal taxonomy in relation to the different DLT-related applications. This taxonomy may have an impact on future PIL work at the HCCH. At workshops jointly organised by UNCITRAL and UNIDROIT in May 2019 and in March 2020, these organisations hosted experts' groups to develop a legal taxonomy to apply to emerging technologies and their applications. The PB is in regular dialogue with UNCITRAL and UNIDROIT".[46]

The objectives of the HCCH in its preliminary document of November 2020 are:

- Jurisdiction and choice of court (e.g., how to determine the competent court to resolve a dispute in relation to a crypto asset).
- Applicable law and choice of law (e.g., what is the most appropriate connecting factor defining the law applicable to a transaction via blockchain).

---

[43] UNIDROIT PRINCIPLES ON DIGITAL ASSETS AND PRIVATE LAW, Roma 2023, p. i.

[44] UNIDROIT PRINCIPLES ON DIGITAL ASSETS AND PRIVATE LAW, Roma 2023, p. 7.

[45] UNIDROIT 2021 – Study LXXXII – W.G.3 – Doc. 2, June 2021, p. 54. Refers to "the HCCH is looking at the possibility of a new normative project in this area which would look at applicable law, jurisdiction, recognition and enforcement, choice of law, and choice of forum. The Permanent Bureau of the HCCH has published a preliminary document regarding "Developments with respect to PIL implication of the digital economy, including DLT" (Prel. Doc. No 4 of November 2020), and the HCCH's Council on General Affairs and Policy recently confirmed the mandate for the PB to continue to follow private international law implications relating to developments in the field of DLT."

[46] "Developments with respect to PIL implication of the digital economy, including DLT" (Prel. Doc. No 4 of November 2020), II. Coordination with UNCITRAL and UNIDROIT, paragraphs 5–6.

- Recognition and enforcement (e.g., how to enforce a foreign judicial decision in relation to a service regulated by a smart contract).[47]

The digital economy has an inextricably cross-border nature and requires regulations by States that offer a framework of legal certainty.[48] In some jurisdictions, this framework has been fragmented and has distinguished between the control of cryptocurrencies and the rest of DLT.

The HCCH warns that "PIL challenges in relation to connecting factors relate to the fact that traditional geographical locations ("situs") may not be of relevance to the functioning of a DLT network. The allocation of jurisdiction among national courts is one of the issues that arise in relation to digital assets based on DLT."[49]

Some of the EU regulatory initiatives in these matters have been referred to above, however, the question of the choice of connection to determine the competent national jurisdiction does not have a unified answer as yet.

Annexe I – Overview of Connecting Factors of "Developments with respect to PIL implication of the digital economy, including DLT"[50] presents a list of connection factors with advantages and limitations of each one, which is a starting point for a complex topic.

- Lex situs: this traditional rule of determining the location of the asset could be applied in the case of exogenous tokens that represent tangible assets. However, in decentralized DLT systems, the very nature of the technology means that it is embedded in different territories, therefore, different jurisdictions. Therefore, geographic connection is not possible in DLTs.
- Elective Situs: the law chosen by the participants in the transaction, apparently easy to apply and based on the autonomy of the parties' will. However, problems are evident in non-permissioned systems where the parties will not be able to make this choice.
- Modified elective situs: the choice of law made by the parties may be limited by the regulation and technology of the DLT. The will of the parties may not be implemented due to the limitations imposed by the company's regulators. This limitation may be posed by evasive ends or be contrary to public order. Another obstacle is the absence of a single central authority, but rather different regulators.

---

[47] "Developments with respect to PIL implication of the digital economy, including DLT" (Prel. Doc. No 4 of November 2020), II. Coordination with UNCITRAL and UNIDROIT, paragraph 7.

[48] GBBC Global Standard Mapping Initiative - GSMI (2020), p. 2–25. "The Global Blockchain Business Council, the Global Standard Mapping Initiative (GSMI) 2020, emphasised the need for uniform global standards to facilitate impactful and responsible cross-border innovation.23 The Report, which represented an "unprecedented effort to map and analyse the current blockchain landscape", noted the fragmentation of regulatory approaches across the world, and that "existing efforts to coordinate across jurisdictions have been piecemeal at best and chaotic at worst".

[49] "Developments with respect to PIL implication of the digital economy, including DLT" (Prel. Doc. No 4 of November 2020), II. Coordination with UNCITRAL and UNIDROIT, paragraph 16.

[50] "Developments with respect to PIL implications of the digital economy, including DLT" (Prel. Doc. No 4 of November 2020), II. Coordination with UNCITRAL and UNIDROIT, pp. 9–10.

- Deemed election: another variation of the lex situs in which it is the regulatory authority that sets the "situs". In this case, there is a risk that a single jurisdiction is the one that hears all the transactions. In turn, there is a need for all parties to be aware of this determination of the law, to which they would have to adhere compulsorily.
- Chosen law of the transaction/transfer/assignment: the parties are subject to the applicable law of the assignment, however, the speed of DLT systems can cause different transfers to give rise to different laws of application.
- Place of Relevant Operating Authority/Administrator (PROPA): the applicable law is that of the place of the relevant authority/administrator. Potential problems arise in cases of changing relevant authorities or in DLTs where there are no relevant authorities/administrators.
- Primary Residence of the Encryption Private Master keyholder (PREMA): in this case the applicable law is determined by the location of the private master key. The existence of an entity that holds a master key relevant to the system, with the help of which coercive transactions can be carried out, for example, based on a court order (main residence of the holder of the Private Encryption master key). It can also cause problems if several authorities hold a master key and it is worth noting the increase in keys to serve court orders.
- Location of issuer master account: the law is located at the location of the issuer master account. If the claims are directed to the issuer, it is an effective system, but if the action is directed against the administrator, the chosen law would not coincide.
- Location of participant: applies law of the place where the system participant is resident, has centre of main interest, or is domiciled. In DLT systems it is not operative.
- Law of private user key: the determination of applicable law is made by the location of the user's private key, however, determining where the main holder's residence is located can be challenging.
- Codex Law: the law of the code used for the distributed ledger is chosen.

References

UNIDROIT Digital Assets and Private Law Principle 2(2) https://www.unidroit.org/wp-content/uploads/2024/01/Principles-on-Digital-Assets-and-Private-Law-linked-1.pdf last visited 24 October 2024

Digital Assets and Private Law Working Group // Eight session (hybrid) // Rome, 8 – 10 March 2023 1. //// UNIDROIT 2023 // Study LXXXII – W.G.8 – Doc. 4// English only / / February 2023 https://www.unidroit.org/wp-content/uploads/2023/03/W.G.8-Doc.-4-Public-Consultation-Comments-with-Annexes-1.pdf last visited 24 October 2024

Digital Assets and Private Law Working Group // Eight session (hybrid) // Rome, 8 – 10 March 2023 1. //// UNIDROIT 2023 // Study LXXXII – W.G.8 – Doc. 3 // English only // February 2023 https://www.unidroit.org/wp-content/uploads/2023/03/W.G.8-Doc.-3-Draft-Principles-and-Commentary-Compared.pdf last visited 24 October 2024

Digital Assets and Private Law Working Group // Seventh session (hybrid) // Rome, 19 – 21 March 2022 1. //// UNIDROIT 2021 // Study LXXXII – W.G.7 – Doc. 2 // English only / / December 2022 https://www.unidroit.org/wp-content/uploads/2022/12/W.G.7-Doc.-2-Draft-Principles-and-Commentary.pdf last visited 23 October 2024
Digital Assets and Private Law Working Group // Second session (remote) // Rome, 30 June – 2 July 2021 1. //// UNIDROIT 2021 // Study LXXXII – W.G.3 – Doc. 2 // English only // June 2021 https://www.unidroit.org/english/documents/2021/study82/wg03/s-82-wg03-02-rev01-e.pdf last visited 23 October 2025
Digital Assets and Private Law Working Group // Second session (remote) // Rome, 16 – 18 March 2021 1. //// UNIDROIT 2021 // Study LXXXII – W.G.2 – Doc. 1 // English only // March 2021 https://www.unidroit.org/english/documents/2021/study82/wg02/s-82-wg02-02rev-01-e.pdf last visited 20 October 2024
Digital Assets and Private Law Working Group // First session (remote) // Rome, 17 – 19 November 2020 1. //// UNIDROIT 2020 // Study LXXXII – W.G.1 – Doc. 1 // English only / / November 2020 https://www.unidroit.org/english/documents/2020/study82/wg01/s-82-wg01-01-e.pdf last visited 13 0ctober 2024
Regulation (EU) 2022/858 of the European Parliament and of the Council of 30 May 2022 on a pilot regime for market infrastructures based on distributed ledger technology, and amending Regulations (EU) No 600/2014 and (EU) No 909/2014 and Directive 2014/65/EU (Text with EEA relevance) https://eur-lex.europa.eu/eli/reg/2022/858/oj/eng last visited 22 October 2024
EU Blockchain Observatory and Forum https://ec.europa.eu/digital-building-blocks/wikis/display/EBSI/Home last visited 23 October 2024
Regulation (EU) 2023/1114 of the European Parliament and of the Council of 31 May 2023 on markets in crypto-assets, and amending Regulations (EU) No 1093/2010 and (EU) No 1095/2010 and Directives 2013/36/EU and (EU) 2019/1937 https://eur-lex.europa.eu/eli/reg/2023/1114/oj/eng last visited 23 October 2024
Developments with respect to PIL Implications of the Digital Economy// March 2022// Document Prel. Doc. No 4 REV of January 2022 // CGAP2022 https://assets.hcch.net/docs/b06c28c5-d183-4d81-a663-f7bdb8f32dac.pdf last visited 22 October 2024
GBBC Global Standard Mapping Initiative - GSMI (2020) https://gbbcouncil.org/wp-content/uploads/2020/10/GSMI-Legal-Regulatory-Report.pdf last visited 19 October 2025

Reflections on Section VII: Insolvency

Principle 19
Effect of Insolvency on Proprietary Rights in Digital Assets

Jorge Feliu Rey

(1) A proprietary right in a digital asset that has become effective against third parties under Principles law or other law is effective against the insolvency representative, creditors, and any other third party in an insolvency-related proceeding.

(2) Paragraph (1) does not affect the application of any substantive or procedural rule of law applicable by virtue of an insolvency-related proceeding, such as any rule relating to:

> **(a) the ranking of categories of claims;**
>
> **(b) the avoidance of a transaction as a preference or a transfer in fraud of creditors; or**
>
> **(c) the enforcement of rights to an asset that is under the control or supervision of the insolvency representative.**

This chapter expands and updates the text of a lecture delivered at the IV International Congress entitled "UNIDROIT Principles on Digital Assets and Private Law: context, content, perspectives ", organized by the Legalcripto by BAES Research Group, held at the University of Alicante (Spain) on 13 and 14 November 2024.This work is a result and funded within the framework of: Proyecto "Presente y futuro de la regulación de los Criptoactivos en la UE [Legalcripto]". Proyecto Prometeo 2023, CIPROM/2022/26, grupos de investigación de excelencia, de la Generalitat Valenciana (P.I. Carmen Pastor). Likewise, the Ministry of Science and Innovation's research project PDI2023-149583-C21, "Adaptación del Derecho Español para la adquisición, transmisión, gravamen y ejecución de los activos digitales en los negocios" (P.I. Teresa Rodriguez de las Heras Ballell / Manuel Alba Fernández).

J. Feliu Rey (✉)
Universidad Carlos III de Madrid, Madrid, Spain
e-mail: jorge.feliu@uc3m.es

C. Pastor Sempere and D. A. Morán Bovio (eds.), UNIDROIT *Principles on Digital Assets and Private Law*, Law, Governance and Technology Series 80,
https://doi.org/10.1007/978-3-032-11001-5_25

1 Official Commentary

Commentary

General

19.1. Principle 19 deals with the effect of insolvency on a proprietary right in a digital asset. Principle 3(1) says that 'Digital assets can be the subject of proprietary rights', which means that a person who has a proprietary right in a digital asset can assert that right against third parties, if it has been made effective against third parties. Principle 19 confirms that a proprietary right in a digital asset which is effective against third parties is effective against relevant parties in an insolvency-related proceeding. As explained below, the subject of the insolvency-related proceeding ('the debtor') may be the person who has the proprietary right or it may be another person.

19.2. Apart from situations falling within the innocent acquisition rule in Principle 8 and the rule in Principle 15 whereby a security right can be made effective against third parties by control, Principle 3(3) establishes that whether a person has a proprietary right in a digital asset and whether a proprietary right in a digital asset has been made effective against third parties is a matter of 'other law' (that is, any part of the law of a State that is not Principles law (Principle 2(4))). Principle 19(1) provides for the pre-insolvency effectiveness to continue in an insolvency-related proceeding: the precise result of that effectiveness will also depend on the circumstances and on the applicable other law. In general, however, as recommended in part two of the UNCITRAL Legislative Guide on Insolvency Law (2004) (see recommendation 35), the debtor's estate will comprise assets of the debtor, which are those in which the debtor has a proprietary right, to the extent of that proprietary right.

Typical situations

19.3. The consequences of the operation of Principle 19 can be illustrated by considering three typical situations. (1) The insolvency of a person who 'owns' a digital asset, or who, as a secured creditor, has acquired a security right in a digital asset, (2) the insolvency of a person, who, as a debtor, has granted to its creditor a security right in a digital asset as collateral, and (3) the insolvency of a custodian, who controls a digital asset for a client. The client will wish to retrieve its digital asset. Principle 19 primarily concerns situations (1) and (2), which are considered in Commentary 19.4 to 19.8, which, by way of example, illustrate the operation of Principle 19 in the context of an insolvency-related proceeding resulting in a distribution to creditors. Situation (3) (insolvency of a custodian) is considered specifically in Principle 13 and the Commentary to that Principle. Insolvency of a sub-custodian is covered by Principle 13(8).

Situation (1)

19.4. Situation (1) can arise in a number of variations. In the first variation of situation (1) a person owns and controls a digital asset, for example, by using wallet software as a form of 'self-custody' (see Commentary 10.15 to 10.17). When this person becomes insolvent, the digital asset forms part of that person's estate, since the person's proprietary right remains effective on insolvency (Principle 19(1)). Under typical insolvency law, the insolvency representative can infringe upon an insolvent person's proprietary rights in that they can exercise an insolvent person's proprietary rights for the benefit of that insolvent person's creditors. Thus, the insolvency representative may assume control over the insolvent person's digital assets, sell those assets and distribute the proceeds amongst the creditors. Notably, 'control' here is used in a broad sense, and not as defined in Principle 6. Therefore, in situation (1), the insolvency representative is likely to want to retrieve the digital asset, and sell it for the benefit of the insolvent person's creditors. Taking control of the digital asset, however, may not be straightforward, compared to taking control of other types of assets. Access to the wallet and/or the private key is likely to be passworded, and the insolvent person might refuse to reveal the password. Whether (and how) the insolvency representative can obtain a court order against the insolvent person ordering him to reveal the password will depend on the applicable insolvency law.

19.5. The second variation of situation (1) is where the insolvent person has a proprietary right in the digital asset but the asset is maintained for him by a custodian. The insolvent person's proprietary right is effective despite the insolvency-related proceeding, and the insolvency representative, as above, will want to retrieve and sell the digital asset. This time, it is easier for the insolvency representative, since if the applicable insolvency law allows her to take control of the insolvent person's assets, she will be able to instruct the custodian to transfer the asset to her control or to a third party to whom she has agreed to sell the asset.

19.6. The third variation of situation (1) concerns the situation where a person becomes insolvent who, as a secured creditor, has acquired a security right in a digital asset. To make her security right effective, this person may have obtained control of the relevant digital asset, or may have made her security right effective by other methods available under the applicable law (see also Principle 16 and the Commentary to that Principle). Both instances are similar to the first variation, in that both in the first and in this third variation, the insolvent person has a proprietary right (as 'owner' or as secured creditor, respectively) in the digital asset. When the secured creditor becomes insolvent, the security right in the digital asset forms part of that person's estate, since the person's proprietary right remains effective on insolvency. See further Commentary 19.4.

19.7. The fourth variation of situation (1) is where the insolvent person acquired, as a secured creditor, a security right in the digital asset but the asset is maintained for her by a custodian. This variation is similar to the second variation. The insolvent creditor's security right remains effective despite the insolvency-related proceeding. See further Commentary 19.5.

Situation (2)

19.8. There are also a number of variations of situation (2). In the first variation, a person owns and controls a digital asset in some sort of self-custody arrangement (see Commentary 10.15 to 10.17) and that person has granted a security right in the digital asset to his creditor. On that person's insolvency, the creditor may wish to enforce the security right in the digital asset during the debtor's insolvency. Under Principle 19(1) the creditor's security right is not affected by the insolvency. This means that (depending on the applicable insolvency law and concrete situation) the security right can be enforced by the creditor or the insolvency representative can realise the value of the asset and pay the creditor out of this value. In any event, the creditor's security right will have the same effect as a security right in any other asset (which will depend on the applicable insolvency law, see, for example, Commentary 19.12), but the same possible difficulties about obtaining control of the asset mentioned above will occur. The same analysis applies if the digital asset is maintained by a custodian for the insolvent person, except that unless the custodian has agreed to act on the instructions of the secured creditor, an order from a court or other authority will be required (see Principle 17(2)). If the secured creditor has taken control of the digital asset, it is much easier for it to enforce the security right extra- judicially (see Commentary 17.4), but whether it can do so will depend on the applicable insolvency law.

Principle 19(2)

19.9. While Principle 19 is meant to leave a person's proprietary rights in a digital asset unaffected by insolvency, this protection is not absolute (see also Principles 5(6) and 5(7)). For example, the application of the other law of a State may result in the preference of another person's rights over the relevant digital asset. Principle 19(1) does not affect the operation of such a rule, whether it is substantive or procedural, providing that it applies by virtue of the insolvency- related proceeding. These rules may be found in any part of the law of a State that is not Principles law (i.e., that is 'other law' as defined in Principle 2(4)), including its tax law, insolvency law, general private law, and its procedural law. Principle 19(2) lists three examples of instances where the relevant rules of the other law of a State may affect the rights of creditors, which are not affected by Principle 19(1).

19.10. The first example, set out in Principle 19(2)(a), concerns the ranking of categories of claims. An applicable State's law governing the priority order in which claims on the insolvent estate or on specific assets forming part of the estate are to be ranked, will typically dictate that certain categories of creditors have preference over other creditors (including secured creditors). For example, the law of a State may prescribe that fiscal authorities have priority over secured and unsecured creditors in relation to certain assets of the insolvent person, or that the costs of the insolvency-related proceeding have preferential status over other secured and unsecured creditors' claims on the insolvent estate.

19.11. The second example, set out in Principle 19(2)(b), concerns the fraudulent transfer of assets. Under the applicable State's insolvency or private law, a transfer of ownership of digital assets may typically be rescinded by the transferor's insolvency representative, if the transfer was made in a prescribed period prior to the insolvency and if the transferor transferred the digital assets to defraud its (other) creditors. Thus, a State's insolvency or private law may infringe upon the proprietary right in a digital asset of a person who has acquired that digital asset. Similarly, the applicable insolvency or private law may enable a transfer of digital assets amounting to a 'preference' to be rescinded by the insolvency representative of the transferor, if certain conditions are fulfilled.

19.12. The third example, set out in Principle 19(2)(c), clarifies that, if the insolvency representative has taken 'control' of the digital asset as described in Commentary 19.4, Principle 19(1) does not affect the operation of any rule of the applicable law relating to the enforcement of rights to that asset whether by the insolvency representative or anyone else. For example, a rule providing for a stay on enforcement by a secured creditor would not be affected by Principle 19(1). Principle 19(2)(c), read in conjunction with Principle 19(1), therefore also implies that third parties, including the system that operates the (record of the) digital assets in question, must acknowledge and accommodate the insolvency representative's exercise of the insolvent person's rights in these digital assets. For custody situations, see Principle 13.

2 Reflections

2.1 Introduction: Background

2.1.1 The Location of the Principle

The current Principle 19 is located in Section VII on Insolvency and is the only Principle comprising this section. However, in the first drafts, it was initially known as Principle 20[1] and was later changed to 21,[2] with the original title "Effect of

[1] Study LXXXII - W.G.5 - Doc.2.

[2] Study LXXXII - W.G.6 - Doc. 2.

Insolvency on Proprietary [and Security] Rights in Digital Assets". On the other hand, the original versions of the Principle were located in Section VIII, not VII. It was not until the 7th meeting of the Working Group (hereinafter WG) that the numeral and the section coincided with the current version, which is the definitive one.[3]

2.1.2 The Background to the Content of the Principle

Logically, one of the legal issues that received attention from the outset by the WG was how to deal with Digital Assets in insolvency[4], and we believe this is due to two main reasons: because of what was happening in reality and because without a Principle devoted to insolvency, the system would be incomplete.

Indeed, at the first meetings that took place between 17 and 19 November 2020, the need for the project to reflect the practical and jurisprudential reality of digital assets was already apparent. In this regard, the words of Professor Charles Money Jr. are very exemplary, who noted that "people were continuing to use these digital assets; they were being stolen, were the object of insolvency proceedings, or the object of litigation, and private law was not able to address these issues in a way that provided satisfactory solutions, hence the need for this project to reflect on these questions"[5]. Furthermore, Mr. Philipp remarked, "(…) he observed that the need for legal certainty only became important when there was a concrete problem such as a legal dispute or an insolvency proceeding"[6].

On the other hand, and as a consequence of the above, if these Principles did not reflect today's reality, the system would be incomplete. As the first papers submitted to the WG forewarned, "private-law property rules provide an incomplete picture of the legal treatment of digital assets unless the treatment of those rights in insolvency proceedings also are considered".[7]

Based on these observations, and in order to respond to these realities, the first documents already mentioned the need for the legal treatment of digital assets in relation to insolvency, while not ignoring the complexity of dealing with digital assets in insolvency. The question had therefore become not whether it was appropriate to include this issue in the principles, but how to accommodate insolvency rules for digital assets.

Of course, the first issue was the categorisation of digital assets, since their consideration as an object of property or other rights would allow them to either be returned

[3] Study LXXXII - W.G.7 - Doc. 2.

[4] Study LXXXII - W.G.1 - Doc. 2, paragraphs 73–76.

[5] Study LXXXII - W.G.1 - Doc. 4, paragraph 24.

[6] Study LXXXII - W.G.1 - Doc. 4, paragraph 27.

[7] Study LXXXII - W.G.1 - Doc.2, Issuer Paper, para. 73. Also in Study LXXXII - W.G.2 - Doc. 2 (rev.1), para. 116.

to their owner, or for them to be realised in benefit of the estate in the event of insolvency. In relation to the latter situation, the realisation of the digital asset was not only affected by the legal categorisation but also by its factual nature.

Even as early as the first meeting at which insolvency issues were discussed, a clear division was made between the insolvency of the custodian and other insolvency cases. This distinction responded to what was proposed in the issues paper[8], which suggested to the WG that insolvency should be approached from different points of view according to each party: the owner of the digital assets, custodians and intermediaries, and the holders of a security interest in the assets.

The paper raised a number of issues with respect to digital assets in insolvency for the WG's consideration: the categorisation of assets and their integration in the estate; their valuation and value realisation; the different actors to be taken into account (owners, custodians, intermediaries and secured creditors); the possible suitability of insolvency law for digital assets; and the possibility that digital assets may be treated differently, depending on their nature, similar to cash or other intangibles.

During the following sessions of the WG, insolvency was dealt with and discussed under the work on "Control and Custody", mainly in relation to the insolvency of the custodian, to which a separate Principle would be drafted.

It was at the 5th session of the WG when the first draft of the Principles was produced.[9] In the aforementioned version, and as mentioned above, the current Principle 19 was originally Principle 20 under the title "Effect of Insolvency on Proprietary [and Security] Rights in Digital Assets", located in Section VIII (instead of Section VII, where it is now). As can be noted from a simple reading of the title, the word "Security" was included in square brackets, a term that was removed from the current version, as we shall see later.

Beyond its formal evolution and final drafting, there is a deeper substantive background that marked the course of the debate. From this material perspective, a somewhat revealing evolution can be traced. What is interesting about this first draft is that it proposed two different versions of the Principle. One which followed the guidelines of the UNIDROIT Convention on Substantive Rules for Intermediated Securities (2009) (hereinafter, Geneva Securities Convention),[10] in relation to effectiveness in the event of insolvency, and the other which focussed more on the logic of security rights in secured transactions. Both versions are set out below.

First version

The first version of principle 20 was worded as follows:

SECTION VIII: INSOLVENCY

Principle 20: Effect of Insolvency on Proprietary [and Security].

---

[8] Study LXXXII - W.G.1 - Doc.2. "The purpose of the document is to provide a starting point for the Working Group's deliberations and structure for discussions at the first meeting" (paragraph 2 in fine).

[9] Study LXXXII - W.G.5 - Doc. 2. Master Copy of Black Letter Principles.

[10] UNIDROIT Convention on Substantive Rules for Intermediated Securities (2009).

Rights in Digital Assets

(1) The law should provide that rights and interests that have become effective against third parties under Principle 9 (innocent acquirer rule) or Principle 17 (control as a method of third party effectiveness of security rights) are effective against the insolvency administrator and creditors in any insolvency proceeding.

(2) Paragraph (1) does not affect the application of any substantive or procedural rule of law applicable by virtue of an insolvency proceeding, such as any rule relating to:

(a) the ranking of categories of claims;

(b) the avoidance of a transaction as a preference or a transfer in fraud of creditors; or

(c) the enforcement of rights to property that is under the control or supervision of the insolvency administrator].[11]

As can be appreciated, the first version is very similar to the current version of the Principle, which starts from the same substantive basis as the current Principle: the effectiveness of rights and interests in digital assets against third parties in insolvency proceedings. It continues in paragraph 2 with an exception rule, whereby paragraph 1 does not affect the substantive or procedural rules applicable under insolvency proceedings, setting out specific exemplary cases.

As we have already noted, this version follows the wording of Article 14 [paragraphs 1 and 2] of the Geneva Securities Convention devoted to the legal effects of insolvency. Thus, the aforementioned article states as follows.

Article 14
Effectiveness in insolvency

1. Rights and interests that have become effective against third parties under Article 11 or Article 12 are effective against the insolvency administrator and creditors in any insolvency proceeding.

2. Paragraph 1 does not affect the application of any substantive or procedural rule of law applicable by virtue of an insolvency proceeding, such as any rule relating to:

(a) the ranking of categories of claims;

(b) the avoidance of a transaction as a preference or a transfer in fraud of creditors; or

[11] Study LXXXII - W.G.5 - Doc. 2, p. 42.

(c) the enforcement of rights to property that is under the control or supervision of the insolvency administrator.

However, if we take a closer look at the wording of this article, and specifically at paragraph 1, we can see that its scope of application, unlike the current Principle, was very limited, as it expressly mentioned two Principles, 9 (innocent acquirer rule) and 17 (control as a method of third party effectiveness of security rights) providing for the only effectiveness situations where digital assets are enforceable against the insolvency administrator and creditors in any insolvency proceedings.

If we make a comparison with the current version, we can observe that this one is much broader in two respects: with respect to how it has been made effective against third parties, and against whom. With regard to the first, instead of referring to two Principles, 9 and 17, the current version refers to effectiveness having occurred by virtue of the Principles law or "other law", defined in the Principles as *a State´s law to the extent that it is not Principles law.*[12] The reference is therefore broader. With regard to the subjects, it is no longer only vis-à-vis the insolvency representative and the creditors, but also vis-à-vis any other third party.

In paragraph 2, differences can also be identified. The wordings are almost identical except for the following terms: "insolvency proceeding" is replaced by "insolvency-related proceeding"; "enforcement of rights to property" by "enforcement of rights to an asset"; and "insolvency administrator" by "insolvency representative". These changes, some of which are not trivial, will be discussed later.

Second version

The second version of the text is more restrictive than the first version, moving away from the current wording and focusing on security interests in assets.

SECTION VIII: INSOLVENCY

Principle 20: Effect of Insolvency on Proprietary [and Security].

Rights in Digital Assets

(1) The law should specify that where a security right in a digital asset is effective against third parties under the applicable secured transactions law, it will be recognised as effective against the insolvency administrator and competing claimants in any insolvency proceeding.

(2) The priority of a security right in digital assets established under the applicable law should be the same, except if, pursuant to insolvency law, another claim is given priority.

---

[12] Principle 2 (4).

(3) Secured creditors should be entitled to claim the value of encumbered digital assets].[13]

In this version, the effectiveness against the insolvency representative and competing claimants in insolvency proceedings will depend on whether the security right in a digital asset is effective against third parties under the applicable law on secured transactions.

The Commentary accompanying this principle followed the basic principle that insolvency law should recognise the third-party effectiveness and priority of a security right and should not impair it solely because the collateral is a digital asset. Similarly, the law governing priority of claims, avoidance actions and limitations on enforcement of security rights in assets that are under the control or supervision of the insolvency representative should not be affected by the fact that it is a digital asset.

In the logic of security rights, the realisation of the value of the asset is an essential element protecting the rights of secured creditors. In principle, and as a starting point, the recognition of digital assets as collateral and their effectiveness in insolvency proceedings should be unquestioned. If we take a closer look at the phenomenon though, one of the issues that the WG had to address was the problem of the valuation of digital assets, as many of them are highly volatile and fluctuate greatly in value. Similarly, the valuation date and the method of calculation had to be considered. This in turn depends on the categorisation of the digital asset and its intended purpose.

The Commentary ended with illustrations that attempt to reflect the content of the Commentary and two questions to the WG. The illustrations are as follows,

Illustrations

A security right in a digital asset is granted to a lender, and later the borrower becomes subject to an insolvency proceeding. The insolvency administrator claims that the digital asset is not property, and thus a security right has not been created, or otherwise challenges the third-party effectiveness of a security right beyond the parameters set out in the applicable secured transactions law.

The insolvency law requires the valuation to refer to the effective date of commencement of insolvency proceedings. The insolvency representative administering the insolvency proceedings values the secured creditor's claim based upon the market price of the digital asset at the time of the commencement of the proceedings, which is substantially lower than the value at the time of a distribution.

The questions were as follows:

Questions

[13] Study LXXXII - W.G.5 - Doc. 2, p. 42.

Q.27. What, in the opinion of the Working Group, should be the content and scope of the insolvency principle?

Q.28. Which of the two alternatives presented in the draft principle does the Working Group consider to be preferable?

It was at the 6th session that the insolvency section of the Principles began to be discussed in more depth, and the content and wording was refined in line with the current version.[14]

At this meeting, several changes were made to the insolvency section. Firstly, the Principle was renumbered as number 21 and not 20, as was previously the case. Secondly, and more importantly, the first version of the Principle was adopted, as that was the version favoured by most of the members of the Steering Committee,[15] and the second version was eliminated.

On the other hand, it was questioned whether the scope of the Principle should be extended. In other words, should it apply to all property and security rights, or only to those derived from Principle 9 (innocent acquirer rule) and 17 (control as a method of third party effectiveness of security rights). On the other hand, it was also discussed whether the analysis on valuation, that had already been drafted, should be maintained. These two questions were left open for discussion at the next meeting of the WG.[16]

Other issues discussed in the WG included the modification of the word "insolvency administrator" to "insolvency representative" to ensure consistency of terminology with other texts (e.g. UNCITRAL secured transactions texts). The need for cross-references in the Commentaries to the Principles, as there were others that also dealt with insolvency aspects was also addressed. In this regard, the Principle dealing with insolvency of the custodian should be retained, but separately from this Principle which deals with insolvency in a wider manner.

The version read as follows:

SECTION VIII: INSOLVENCY

*Principle **21**: Effect of Insolvency on Proprietary [and Security].*

Rights in Digital Assets

*(1) The law should provide that rights and interests that have become effective against third parties under Principle 9 (innocent **acquisition** rule) or Principle 17 (control as a method of third party effectiveness of security rights) are effective against the insolvency administrator and creditors in any insolvency proceeding.*

[14] Study LXXXII - W.G. 6 - Doc.1.

[15] Study LXXXII - W.G.6 - Doc. 4.

[16] Study LXXXII - W.G.6 - Doc. 4, paragraph 77.

(2) Paragraph (1) does not affect the application of any substantive or procedural rule of law applicable by virtue of an insolvency proceeding, such as any rule relating to:

(a) the ranking of categories of claims;

(b) the avoidance of a transaction as a preference or a transfer in fraud of creditors; or

(c) the enforcement of rights to property that is under the control or supervision of the insolvency administrator.[17]

At the 7th session, reforms to the Principle were made based on the comments received in the 6th session. The number of the Principle was changed to the current 19, entitled "Effect of Insolvency on Proprietary Rights in Digital Assets". This new version of Principle 19 is now practically identical to the current version.

SECTION VII: INSOLVENCY
Principle ***19****: Effect of Insolvency on Proprietary Rights in Digital Assets*

(1) ***A proprietary right [or interest] in a digital asset*** *that* ***has*** *become effective against third parties under* ***Principles law or other law is*** *effective against the insolvency* ***representative*** *and creditors* ***and any other third party*** *in any insolvency proceeding.*

(2) Paragraph (1) does not affect the application of any substantive or procedural rule of law applicable by virtue of an insolvency proceeding, such as any rule relating to:

(a) the ranking of categories of claims;

(b) the avoidance of a transaction as a preference or a transfer in fraud of creditors; or

(c) the enforcement of rights to ***an asset****that* ***is part of the insolvency estate or*** *under the supervision of the insolvency* **representative.**[18]

This Principle is adapted to the Geneva Securities Convention, although it is of a more general nature, since it refers to all proprietary rights over a digital asset. On the other hand, this session of the WG proceeded to harmonise the terminology used

---

[17] Study LXXXII - W.G.6 - Doc. 3, p. 90. Changes are highlighted in bold.

[18] Study LXXXII - W.G.7 - Doc. 2, p. 57. The changes are highlighted in bold. For the document reflecting all changes, vid. Study LXXXII - W.G.7 - Doc. 3, p. 95 ff.

in the draft with the rest of the text, as well as with other international instruments in this field.[19]

One may also note that paragraph 19.1 begins with the phrase *A proprietary right [or interest] in a digital asset.* At this session of the WG it was agreed to delete the word *interest*, which had been used previously, in order to make the text consistent with the rest of the wording in the Principles, since in the rest of the instrument no reference had been made to this term, with the term *proprietary right* being used. Similarly, the beginning of the sentence was deleted, specifically the expression "should", since, as one WG observer pointed out, the inclusion of this word made the Principle appear to be a legislative recommendation.[20]

On the other hand, the WG discussed whether or not the reference to creditors and the *insolvency representative* was appropriate, as it was questioned whether it was possible for some creditors not to be represented by the *insolvency representative*. Similarly, and in connection with this, the term *under the supervision of the insolvency representative* was also questioned. In this respect, it was mentioned that the Geneva Securities Convention had followed a similar path, although the Convention also included the term control. Indeed, Art. 14.2.(c) of the Convention provides that *the enforcement of rights to property that is under the control or supervision of the insolvency administrator.* The word *control* was deleted because it was deemed not appropriate for the Digital Assets Principles, as it is a multi-faceted term with a strong semantic burden in relation to digital assets and other electronic negotiable documents in accordance with international harmonisation instruments.[21]The Drafting Committee was entrusted to further consider both matters above.

However, the most relevant change is the broadening of the scope of application in this new version. Indeed, if until now the scope of application was limited to those digital assets that were effective in accordance with Principle 9 and Principle 17, the new version broadens the scope of application by adding: *under **Principles law or other law,*** thereby recognising and allowing other ways under which the right becomes effective against third parties.

With regard to the Commentaries on the Principle, they have been completely reworked with respect to the previous version. The new wording presented by the Drafting Committee attempts to present a broader view of proprietary rights, as well as to provide guidance on what is part of the insolvency estate.[22] The previous comments in relation to the valuation of digital assets are deleted, leaving the possibility of reconsideration open so that a short section in relation to valuation would be included in the comments.

At the 8th session of the WG, the changes and suggestions proposed at the previous session were taken up, and the new version is as follows:

---

[19] Study LXXXII - W.G.7 - Doc. 5, paragraph 93.

[20] Study LXXXII - W.G.6 - Doc. 4, p. 82.

[21] Study LXXXII - W.G.7 - Doc. 5, para. 95.

[22] Study LXXXII - W.G.7 - Doc. 3, paragraph 127.

SECTION VII: INSOLVENCY

*Principle **19**: Effect of Insolvency on Proprietary*

Rights in Digital Assets

*(1) A proprietary right in a digital asset that has become effective against third parties under Principles law or other law is effective against the insolvency representative, creditors and any other third party in **an** insolvency proceeding.*

(2) Paragraph (1) does not affect the application of any substantive or procedural rule of law applicable by virtue of an insolvency proceeding, such as any rule relating to:

(a) the ranking of categories of claims;

(b) the avoidance of a transaction as a preference or a transfer in fraud of creditors; or

*(c) the enforcement of rights to **an asset** that **is** under the **control or** supervision of the insolvency* representative.[23]

This version differs from the current version by replacing the words "insolvency proceeding" with "insolvency-related proceeding", a change which, as we will see below, articulates the option of broadening the scope of application of the Principle.

2.2 Commentary to the Current Version

Having described the evolution of Principle 19 in its wording and substance, we now turn to the content of the current version.

We must begin by stating that the structure and content of this Principle almost identically follow the UNIDROIT *Convention on Substantive Rules for Intermediated Securities*, with the nuances that we have explained in the previous section. In other words, and as we have already mentioned, of the options that were considered, the WG chose to follow the line already set out in the Geneva Securities Convention.

The Principle is divided into two sections, which in turn establishes two general rules. The first one anchors the Principle on the general rule that a proprietary right in a digital asset is effective against different persons in insolvency proceedings. The second one however, adds a limitation to the first paragraph by a declaration of the non-absolute character of paragraph 1, i.e. of the general rule of effectiveness contained therein. Thus, the general rule contained in the first paragraph does not

[23] Study LXXXII - W.G.8 - Doc. 3, p. 71.

affect the application of other rules applicable to insolvency proceedings, in particular, and by way of example, rules relating to the ranking of categories of claims; the avoidance of a transaction as a preference or a transfer in fraud by creditors; the enforcement of rights to an asset that is under the control or supervision of the insolvency representative. In these cases, the Principle, on the one hand, refers to the provisions of another applicable rule and, on the other hand, subjects the general rule of its first paragraph to limits or conditions beyond the Principles themselves.

Before addressing both sections, by diving into both the content of the Principle and its Commentary, we can note that the WG has decided not to go into the substance of insolvency with respect to digital assets, but rather into less substantive issues, namely and primarily, to highlight the problems of gaining control of the Digital Asset in relation to its return to the holder or its realisation by the insolvency representative.

We understand that one of the reasons for this rather superficial approach is because insolvency is mainly a matter of national law, which makes it difficult to propose and agree on substantive insolvency rules. In this perspective, and just as we have avoided going into the determination of the legal nature of Digital Assets, which the Principles do not prejudge, we have chosen not to address substantive issues on which national positions may significantly diverge.

Thus, neither in the text of the Principles nor in their Commentaries do we find considerations on the possible problems related to insolvency and Digital Assets that had already been forewarned about in other fora, some of which UNIDROIT was, however, addressing in another of its projects (*Best Practices on Effective Enforcement*).[24] There are multiple issues, diverse in nature having to do with practical complexities, but also legal uncertainty generated by the digital nature of digital assets or by some of their more singular characteristics (delocalisation, volatility or illiquidity, global character, anonymity or use of pseudonyms, etc.). For example, the possibility of invalidating specific transactions within distributed ledger technology; the problems that may arise with automation in relation to the possibility of interrupting payments; or issues relating to the valuation of Digital Assets in view of their volatility.[25]

In the latest version on the other hand, it should be recalled that the scope of application in relation to insolvency proceedings acquires a particular perimeter, as Principle 19 refers to "insolvency-related proceedings", which has its own definition for the purposes of the Principles.

Thus, Principle 2 (6) defines an "insolvency-related proceeding" as

A collective judicial or administrative proceeding, including an interim proceeding, in which, for the purpose of reorganisation or liquidation, at least one of the following applies to the assets and affairs of the debtor: (a) they are subject to control or supervision by a court or other competent authority; (b) the debtor's ability to administer

[24] Project still ongoing when the Principles are adopted, https://www.unidroit.org/work-in-progress/enforcement-best-practices/.

[25] On this issue Lehmann (2025), p. 143 and following.

or dispose of them is limited by law; (c) the debtor's creditors' ability to enforce on them is limited by law.

The aim is to clarify the scope and intent of the definition of "insolvency-related proceedings" set out in the Principles, differentiating it from other more general definitions and covering the diversity of existing proceedings. Therefore, as the Commentary[26] makes clear, it is not intended to replace the general definition in the UNCITRAL Legislative Guide on Insolvency Law, but to provide a definition of its own for the purposes of the Principles and, in particular, Principle 19.

Hence, the definition is both limited in nature, as it is confined to the scope of application of the Principles, and does not seek to go beyond them, and inclusive in nature, as it encompasses a wide range of procedures, both judicial and extrajudicial, that seek to address a debtor's financial difficulties.[27]

In this sense, it departs from the Geneva Securities Convention,[28] which however, as we have previously indicated, inspires the content of this Principle, as UNIDROIT DAPL have a broader scope of application given that the debtor is subject to these Principles.

even when its assets are not subject to control or supervision of the court or an administrative authority.[29]

2.2.1 Paragraph (1)

The first paragraph starts from the logical premise already established in Principle 3 (1) that if the digital asset can be the subject of proprietary rights, then, by application of the law of such rights, it can be effective against third parties, and if it is effective against third parties, then it is effective against the relevant parties in insolvency proceedings.

The form or method by which effectiveness is achieved may be either through the provisions of the Principles, such as control (Principle 15); or through the provisions

---

[26] Comment 2.28.

[27] As Commentary 2.28 makes clear, "this definition captures the new generation of insolvency proceedings whose legal design, often labelled as "hybrid", features characteristics of both formal, in court proceedings and out of court contractual, collective workouts. The term 'insolvency related proceedings', as defined in Principle 2(6), would include full in court proceedings; proceedings the opening of which entails a limitation in the debtor's ability to manage and/or dispose of its assets outside the ordinary course of its business; or proceedings which merely trigger a temporary stay of enforcement against the debtor's assets necessary for the continuation of the business activity".

[28] The definition of "insolvency proceedings" in Art. 1 (h) of the Geneva Securities Convention is as follows: "insolvency *proceedings" means collective judicial or administrative proceeding, including an interim proceeding, in which the assets and affairs of the debtor are subject to control or supervision by a court or other competent authority for the purpose of reorganisation or liquidation.*

[29] Comment 2.28.

of other laws,[30] meaning "a State´s law to the extent that it is not Principles law".[31] If other laws determine methods of effectiveness other than control, they are equally applicable and relevant for the purposes of the Principle.

It therefore follows, in part, the same logic that underpinned the question of whether or not a person has a proprietary right in a digital asset, where we must take into account "other laws".[32] In this respect and in relation to third-party effectiveness, Principle 3(3) should be taken into account,

except as displaced by these Principles, other laws applies to all issues, including: (...) *(f) the legal consequences of third-party effectiveness of a transfer of the digital asset* and *(g) the requirements for, and legal consequences of, third-party effectiveness of a security right in a digital asset.*

Therefore, as a general rule, the question of whether a transfer and a security right, respectively, can be made effective against third parties remains, as a matter of principle, a matter for other rules[33], except where the Principles lay down other rules.[34]

These statements are brought into insolvency, hence "pre-insolvency proprietary rights on the assets that are rendered effective against third parties under applicable law generally continue to be effective against the insolvency representative, creditors, and any other third party in an insolvency-related proceeding, though this may be further nuanced depending on the circumstances and the specific rules of the applicable law"[35].

This is in line with the UNCITRAL Legislative Guide on Insolvency Law (2007), which clarifies that the estate shall consist of all the debtor's assets,[36] as well as the UNCITRAL harmonisation instrument on secured transactions. Specifically, with Recommendation 238 of the UNCITRAL Legislative Guide on Secured Transactions

[30] As we have already mentioned in the background of this Principle, this change has been an improvement on the first version of the Principle, since it did not mention effectiveness gained through other rules, and only expressly mentioned effectiveness achieved through the principles of acquisition in good faith (Principle 8) and control (Principle 15).

[31] Principle 2 (4). "Principles law" *means any part of a State´s law which implements or is consistent with these Principles* (Principle 2 (3)).

[32] Principle 3 (3).

[33] Comment 3.12.

[34] As Commentary 3.10 makes clear, the Principles set out some specific rules relating to the transfer and third-party effectiveness of a security right in a Digital Asset. For example, Principle 15, which establishes control as a method of achieving third-party effectiveness.

[35] This is stated by Anna Veneziano in Veneziano and Rodriguez de las Heras (2025), p. 31.

[36] UNCITRAL Legislative Guide on Insolvency Law (2004), Recommendation 35. *The insolvency law should specify that the estate should include: (a) Assets of the debtor, including the debtor´s interest in encumbered assets and in third-party-owned assets; (b) assets acquired after commencement of insolvency proceedings; and (c) assets recovered through avoidance and other actions.*

(2007)[37] and, partially, with Article 35 of the UNCITRAL Model Law on Secured Transactions (2016).[38]

Similarly, it is a Principle that is also reflected to some extent in other subsequent uniform texts, such as Article 15 of the UNIDROIT Model Law on Factoring (2023).[39]

Having established this general rule, and taking into account the Commentaries of the Principle, an array of different situations opens up, with assorted variants, whose resolution requires a separate analysis.

As Digital Assets can be held under different holding models - *hot wallets, cold wallets,* custodian or self-custody - their identification, traceability and recovery in insolvency proceedings will face various challenges. An effective recovery or realisation of value of the Digital Asset may require the cooperation of the holder and/or third parties with varying intensity and scope depending on the holding model.

Thus, three situations are initially differentiated based on who the insolvent person is: the holder of the right in rem in the Digital Asset (owner or secured creditor); the debtor who has granted a right in a Digital Asset; the third party who controls the Digital Asset, the custodian.

Of these three situations, only the first two are covered by this Principle. The third situation, the insolvency of the custodian or sub-custodian, is the subject matter of Principle 13 and is therefore excluded from Principle 19 and is dealt with accordingly under Principle 13.

In the first two situations, the insolvency of the holder of the proprietary right or insolvency of the debtor of the proprietary right granted on the Digital Asset, there are several variants, which could be summarised by establishing who the custodian of the Digital Asset is as a common denominator. There are several possibilities or models of custody (holding models): self-custody; custody by a third party under the directives or instructions of the insolvent person; or custody by a third party under the directives or instructions of a secured creditor who is not insolvent.

In fact, of the situations and their variants contemplated in the Principle's Commentaries, they can be grouped into three scenarios.

---

[37] Recommendation 238, under the heading "Third-party effectiveness of a security interest in insolvency proceedings", provides that *insolvency law should provide that, if a security right is effective against third parties at the time of the commencement of insolvency proceedings, action may be taken after the commencement of the insolvency proceedings to continue, preserve or maintain the effectiveness against third parties of the security right to the extent and in the manner permitted under secured transactions law.*

[38] Article 35 provides that *a security right that is effective against third parties under this Law at the time of the commencement of insolvency proceedings in respect of the grantor remains effective against third parties and retains the priority it had before the commencement of the insolvency proceedings, unless another claim has priority pursuant to [the insolvency law specified by the enacting State].*

[39] *Article 15 - Impact of the transferor's insolvency on the priority of a transfer. A transfer that is effective against third parties at the time of the commencement of insolvency proceedings in respect of the transferor remains effective against third parties and retains the priority it had before the commencement of the insolvency proceedings, unless another claim has priority pursuant to the applicable insolvency law.*

The first is when the insolvent person has self-custody of the Digital Asset. He can have control of the Digital Asset by holding the private key on a device (USB or any other digital device) called a "cold wallet" if it has no connection or remote access as it is not connected to a network. In this sense, on the one hand, the digital asset is part of the estate of the insolvent person, but, on the other, taking control or recovering the digital asset requires the cooperation of the debtor as, in principle, access to the device is normally subject to password or verification of some kind, it is not easily located or simply requires possession or physical recovery and access to the content. In addition, the debtor may employ so-called "hot wallets", which are also forms of self-custody but involve the use of a third party application or service (such as *web-based wallets*). In these cases, the debtor's cooperation is also desirable and would facilitate access, but the level of security of self-custody is lower, since remote access is possible and requires the cooperation of a third party.

The second is when the insolvent person does not have self-custody of the Digital Asset, but rather it is entrusted to a custodian. The intervention of a third party opens up other formulae that may be more efficient for the insolvency representative to take control or proceed with the transfer or realisation of value. Cooperation by the custodian will be essential to the effectiveness in recovery and transfer. If the insolvency representative can instruct the custodian in the insolvency proceedings, and for the purposes of the insolvency related proceedings permit the taking of control, or otherwise transfer or sale of the assets, the cooperation of the custodian facilitates enforcement without the need for the debtor's cooperation.

The third scenario would be a sub-variant of the second scenario, and concerns the performance of the custodian, i.e. under whose instructions it acts. If the insolvent person is not the debtor, as we explained in the first scenario, but the secured creditor with a right in a digital asset held by a third party (custodian), then unless the custodian has agreed to act on the secured creditor's instructions, the secured creditor will have to resort to a court order for enforcement. In this case, the secured creditor wants to enforce its security interest in the digital asset in the event of the debtor's insolvency as recognised by Principle 19(1). Because the custodian has control however, the custodian may be acting improperly if it has not agreed to follow such instructions or, failing that, a court order is obtained against the custodian. Alternatively, the creditor could have created its security interest by direct taking of control and, in such a case, enforcement of the security interest could, if permitted by the applicable insolvency law, be extrajudicial.

2.2.2 Paragraph (2)

As a general rule, and according to Principle 3 (2), "Principles law takes precedence over other law to the extent that they conflict". However, the Principles themselves can establish exceptions or attenuate this rule of precedence. This is exactly what Paragraph 2 aims to achieve by toning down the absolute character of Principle 19 (1).

Thus, the general rule laid down in Principle 19(1) does not affect the application of another rule applicable to insolvency proceedings.

In terms of content, paragraph 2 is a literal copy of Art. 14 (2) of the Geneva Securities Convention, and serves the same purpose: "This exception recognises that virtually all systems of insolvency law impose at least some exceptions or limitations on the effectiveness of transfers of property and the granting of limited security. Certain exceptions and limitations are generally viewed as necessary in order to preserve the integrity of insolvency proceedings and to protect and preserve important public policies of a Contracting State".[40]

This section lists three examples of cases, the most common ones, where the relevant rules of a State's other rules may affect the rights of creditors, which are not affected by Principle 19 (1):

- the ranking of categories of claims;
- the avoidance of a transaction as a preference or a transfer in fraud by creditors;
- the enforcement of rights to an asset that is under the control or supervision of the insolvency representative.

This is merely exemplary, as it would be impossible to codify a complete list of exceptions in the text of the Principle that could fit in the legal systems of all States wishing to adapt their law. This was also emphasised in the drafting of the Geneva Securities Convention, where the references were also merely exemplary in order to be acceptable to all Contracting States. "No doubt any such listing would be both over-and-under-inclusive when taking into account the varying approaches and policies of Contracting States".[41]

This exception recognises that virtually all insolvency laws impose at least some exceptions or limitations to the effectiveness of asset transfers and the granting of limited security. Certain exceptions and limitations are generally considered necessary to preserve the integrity of the insolvency proceedings and to protect and preserve important public policies of a Contracting State.

Similarly, we believe that what was stated in the commentaries to the Geneva Securities Convention, in relation to paragraph 2, would also apply here. Paragraph 2 very carefully exempts only those rules of law that are "applicable by virtue of an insolvency-related proceeding". As stated in the commentaries on the Geneva Securities Convention, "this exception is intended to capture only those rules of law that are necessarily triggered by an insolvency proceeding. It does not cover generally applicable rules of law that happen to be applicable in an insolvency proceeding, but may also apply outside the insolvency context".[42]

[40] Hideki et al. (2012), p. 89.

[41] Hideki et al. (2012), p. 89.

[42] Hideki et al. (2012), p. 89.

References

Kanda H et al (2012), Official Commentary on the UNIDROIT Convention on Substantive Rules for Intermediated Securities, Oxford University Press, Oxford.

Lehmann M (2025) Digital Assets in Insolvency Law's Maze: Key Issues and Possible Solutions. In Koller C, Lehmann M (eds) Digital Assets in Enforcement and Insolvency. Hart Publishing, p. 163–176.

Veneziano A, Rodriguez de las Heras Ballell T (2025) Digital Assets in Insolvency and Enforcement Proceedings: Some Insights from UNIDROIT's Work. In Koller C, Lehmann M (eds) Digital Assets in Enforcement and Insolvency. Hart Publishing, p. 27–44.

Digital Assets and Private Law Working Group // First session (remote) // Rome, 17 – 19 November 2020 //// UNIDROIT 2020 // Study LXXXII – W.G.1 – Doc. 1 //English only // November 2020 https://www.unidroit.org/english/documents/2020/study82/wg01/s-82-wg01-01-e.pdflast visited 15 January 2025

Digital Assets and Private Law Working Group // First session (remote) // Rome, 17 – 19 November 2020 //// UNIDROIT 2020 // Study LXXXII – W.G.1 – Doc. 2 //English only // November 2020 https://www.unidroit.org/english/documents/2020/study82/wg01/s-82-wg01-02-e.pdf last visited 16 January 2025

Digital Assets and Private Law Working Group // First session (remote) // Rome, 17 – 19 November 2020 //// UNIDROIT 2020 // Study LXXXII – W.G.1 – Doc. 4 //English only // March 2021 https://www.unidroit.org/english/documents/2021/study82/wg01/s-82-wg01-04-e.pdf last visited 16 January 2025

Digital Assets and Private Law Working Group // Fifth session (hybrid) // Rome, 7 – 9 March 2022 //// UNIDROIT 2022 // Study LXXXII – W.G.5 – Doc. 2 //English only / / March 2022 https://www.unidroit.org/wp-content/uploads/2022/03/W.G.5.-Doc.-2-Master-Copy-of-the-Black-Letter-Principles-Comparison.pdf last visited 16 January 2025

Digital Assets and Private Law Working Group // Sixth session (hybrid) // Rome, 31 August – 2 September 2022 //// UNIDROIT 2022 // Study LXXXII – W.G.5 – Doc. 2 //English only / / March 2022 https://www.unidroit.org/wp-content/uploads/2022/03/W.G.5.-Doc.-2-Master-Copy-of-the-Black-Letter-Principles-Comparison.pdf last visited 16 January 2025

Digital Assets and Private Law Working Group // Sixth session (hybrid) // Rome, 31 August – 2 September 2022 //// UNIDROIT 2022 // Study LXXXII – W.G.6 – Doc. 1 //English only // August 2022https://www.unidroit.org/wp-content/uploads/2022/08/W.G.6.-Doc.-1-Annotated-Agenda-Website-1.pdf last visited 16 January 2025

Digital Assets and Private Law Working Group // Sixth session (hybrid) // Rome, 31 August – 2 September 2022//// UNIDROIT 2022 // Study LXXXII – W.G.6 – Doc. 3 //English only // August 2022https://www.unidroit.org/wp-content/uploads/2022/08/W.G.6-Doc.-3-Tracked-Principles-and-Issues-Paper.pdf last visited 16 January 2025

Digital Assets and Private Law Working Group // Sixth session (hybrid) // Rome, 31 August – 2 September 2022 //// UNIDROIT 2022 // Study LXXXII – W.G.6 – Doc. 4 //English only / / November 2022 https://www.unidroit.org/wp-content/uploads/2022/12/W.G.6-Doc.-4-Summary-Report-of-the-6th-Session.pdf last visited 16 January 2025

Digital Assets and Private Law Working Group // Seventh session (hybrid) // Rome, 19 – 21 December 2022 //// UNIDROIT 2022 // Study LXXXII – W.G.7 – Doc. 2 //English only / / December 2022 https://www.unidroit.org/wp-content/uploads/2022/12/W.G.7-Doc.-2-Draft-Principles-and-Commentary.pdf last visited 16 January 2025

Digital Assets and Private Law Working Group // Seventh session (hybrid) // Rome, 19 – 21 December 2022 //// UNIDROIT 2022 // Study LXXXII – W.G.7 – Doc. 3 //English only / / December 2022 https://www.unidroit.org/wp-content/uploads/2022/12/W.G.7-Doc.-3-Issues-Paper.pdf last visited 16 January 2025

Digital Assets and Private Law Working Group // Seventh session (hybrid) // Rome, 19 – 21 December 2022 //// UNIDROIT 2022 // Study LXXXII – W.G.7 – Doc. 5 //English only // February 2023 https://www.unidroit.org/wp-content/uploads/2023/03/W.G.7-Doc.-5-Summary-Report-of-the-7th-Session-1.pdf last visited 16 January 2025

Digital Assets and Private Law Working Group // Eighth session (hybrid) // Rome, 8 – 10 March 2023 //// UNIDROIT 2023 // Study LXXXII – W.G.8 – Doc. 3 //English only // February 2023 https://www.unidroit.org/wp-content/uploads/2023/03/W.G.8-Doc.-3-Draft-Principles-and-Commentary-Compared.pdf last visited 16 January 2025

MIX
Papier aus verantwortungsvollen Quellen
Paper from responsible sources
FSC® C105338
FSC
www.fsc.org

If you have any concerns about our products,
you can contact us on
ProductSafety@springernature.com

In case Publisher is established outside the EU,
the EU authorized representative is:
Springer Nature Customer Service Center GmbH
Europaplatz 3, 69115 Heidelberg, Germany

Printed by Libri Plureos GmbH
in Hamburg, Germany